THE END TO END TRAIL

About the author

Andy Robinson has been walking the hills of Britain all his life, as did his father and grandfather before him. His first love is and has always been the Lake District, but since exploring the route for the End to End Trail, the Shropshire hills and the Caithness coast both keep drawing him back. He has a habit of setting off on unreasonably optimistic expeditions and usually gets away with it. But not always. His family is very supportive and puts up with a lot.

THE END TO END TRAIL

FROM LAND'S END TO JOHN O' GROATS ON FOOT

by Andy Robinson

JUNIPER HOUSE, MURLEY MOSS,
OXENHOLME ROAD, KENDAL, CUMBRIA LA9 7RL
www.cicerone.co.uk

Second edition 2019
ISBN: 978 1 85284 933 7
First edition 2007

Printed by KHL Printing, Singapore
A catalogue record for this book is available from the British Library.
All photographs are by the author.

This route and this book have been inspired by the books of John Hillaby, Alfred Wainwright and many others. It is dedicated to the memory of Elihu Burritt and of Robert and John Naylor, who seem to have been the first End to End walkers.

Updates to this guide

While every effort is made by our authors to ensure the accuracy of guidebooks as they go to print, changes can occur during the lifetime of an edition. Any updates that we know of for this guide will be on the author's website (**www.longwalks.org.uk**) or the Cicerone website (**www.cicerone.co.uk/933/updates**), so please check both sites before planning your trip. We also advise that you check information about such things as transport, accommodation and shops locally. Even rights of way can be altered over time. We are always grateful for information about any discrepancies between a guidebook and the facts on the ground, sent by email to updates@cicerone.co.uk or by post to Cicerone, Juniper House, Murley Moss, Oxenholme Road, Kendal, LA9 7RL.

Register your book: To sign up to receive free updates, special offers and GPX files where available, register your book at **www.cicerone.co.uk**.

Front cover: Duncansby Stacks, near John o' Groats (top); Land's End (bottom)

CONTENTS

Pendeen Watch lighthouse, Cornwall (Day 1)

Mountain safety

Every mountain walk has its dangers, and those described in this guidebook are no exception. All who walk or climb in the mountains should recognise this and take responsibility for themselves and their companions along the way. The author and publisher have made every effort to ensure that the information contained in this guide was correct when it went to press, but, except for any liability that cannot be excluded by law, they cannot accept responsibility for any loss, injury or inconvenience sustained by any person using this book.

International distress signal *(emergency only)*
Six blasts on a whistle (and flashes with a torch after dark) spaced evenly for one minute, followed by a minute's pause. Repeat until an answer is received. The response is three signals per minute followed by a minute's pause.

Helicopter rescue
The following signals are used to communicate with a helicopter:

Help needed: raise both arms above head to form a 'Y'

Help not needed: raise one arm above head, extend other arm downward

Emergency telephone numbers
To call out the Mountain Rescue, ring 999 or the European emergency number 112: this will connect you via any available network. Once you are connected to the emergency operator, ask for the police.

Weather reports
The Mountain Weather Information Service (MWIS) provides forecasts for Scotland's mountain areas: www.mwis.org.uk. Other useful websites include www.xcweather.co.uk and www.metoffice.gov.uk.

Key to the symbols used in the strip maps

	End to End Trail on tarmac road, arrow indicating direction
	End to End Trail on untarred road or enclosed track
	End to End Trail on clear unenclosed path or track
	End to End Trail on intermittent path: not always clear
	End to End Trail following no visible path
	Other road or enclosed track
	Other clear unenclosed path or track
	Other intermittent path
	Stream or river, arrow showing direction of flow
Br37	Canal, with lock and a numbered bridge over it
	Sea, loch or lake
	Pond or pool
	Railway
Lairg	Town or village (named in bold)
□ +	Building or group of buildings, and a church or chapel
	Other visible feature (explained by accompanying text)
	Conifer or conifers, broad-leaved tree or trees
	Summit of hill or mountain, often marked with height in metres
A	Connector to elsewhere on the same map page
d5 m2	Connector to another map page (in this case Day 5 Map 2)
sw cp	Connector to another guidebook (eg South West Coast Path)
2	Links the map to the start of a route description paragraph

The following abbreviations have sometimes been used where space was tight:
fp = footpath, fb = footbridge, PO = post office, LH & RH = lefthand & righthand

Overview map of the End to End Trail
John o' Groats
SCOTLAND
Fort William
Jedburgh
NORTH SEA
NORTHERN IRELAND
IRISH SEA
Hebden Bridge
PUBLIC OF IRELAND
Knighton
ENGLAND
WALES
N
Barnstaple
0 40km
0 20 miles
Land's End
ENGLISH CHANNEL

Acknowledgements

I owe thanks to Ben MacGregor for his assistance with the route in Caithness, and to Ian Smith for his encouragement and his advice on photography. The End to End Trail borrows parts of its route from various sources, and in particular I am grateful to the late James Roberts, author of *Walking in Somerset* (Cicerone, 1997) for showing me the way out of Bridgwater, to Denis Brook and Phil Hinchliffe for the Alternative Pennine Way, to David Paterson for the Cape Wrath Trail, and of course to all the people involved in the development of the more official routes the Trail uses.

This second edition of the guide has benefited from the feedback of many End to End walkers, who have made it possible for me to improve the route, correct some errors, and add some additional details. There have been too many to list them by name, but my thanks go to them all.

Lastly and most importantly, I'd never have got away with so much walking, or completing this book, without an unreasonable amount of tolerance, encouragement and material support from my family. The biggest share of thanks therefore has to go to Nicola, Esther and Flossie.

PREFACE TO THE SECOND EDITION

The whole route has been reviewed for the new edition of *The End to End Trail*. Every stage end has been revisited, and every detailed map has been rewalked and revised to bring it up to date. I took the opportunity to revise the route in places to take advantage of new walking routes, particularly in Scotland, and to find alternatives where people had reported the going difficult, mainly due to overgrown paths and boggy ground.

I was interested to find out how things had changed over time. The main things turned out to be:

- Lots of stiles replaced by gates. Good news for those of us whose knees are past their best, but on the other hand I do like a traditional stile.
- Many pubs, banks and village shops have closed.
- The disappearance of phone boxes. There are still a few around, particularly in remote locations with no mobile signal, but these days it's best to carry a mobile phone and charger with you if you want to stay in touch with the rest of the world.
- There are now many more waymarked walking routes in Scotland. I've taken advantage of these where I could. Additionally, one of these new routes, the John o' Groats Trail, gives a great alternative route up the east coast from Inverness.
- Cycle tracks and towpaths have been surfaced with tarmac, particularly in Scotland. Good for cyclists, but not so good for those walkers like myself who dislike walking on tarmac wherever it is.
- Many forestry plantations have been felled, particularly in Scotland. Some have been replaced by native species, and in many others it's not clear what's going to happen next. Not much has been replanted with conifers.
- The Scottish Highlands are undergoing a rash of small hydroelectric schemes that seem destined to fill every quiet valley in Scotland if they continue to multiply at the present rate. They make an awful mess, but given a few years the land seems to recover OK, often leaving useful tracks for us walkers.

Keiss Castle (Day 61)

INTRODUCTION

Where am I going? I don't quite know
What does it matter where people go?
Down to the wood where the blue-bells grow –
Anywhere, anywhere. I don't know.
AA Milne, 'Spring Morning'

Land's End and John o' Groats are the two ends of the island of Great Britain – the two points that are the furthest apart from each other. As the crow flies they are 968km (602 miles) apart. Linking the two in a single, long off-road walk gives a magnificent expedition almost exactly twice that distance, and takes you through the very best that the British countryside can offer.

Such a walk is also a great challenge, one of the greatest that many walkers have the time to attempt, and unlike many great challenges, this one is also a great experience. As well as enjoying doing it, you will also enjoy looking back on it afterwards and thinking 'I walked all the way from Land's End to John o' Groats'. What more is there to say? Make your plans and go for it!

A lot of books have been written about getting from Land's End to John o' Groats, but good reading, inspirational and useful as many of them are, this is the first to describe a route with the level of detail that walkers expect from a guide to a long-distance path. This book sets out to solve that perennial walker's problem: when walking in unfamiliar areas without a guide, you are dependent on maps that can't always tell you whether the way you are thinking of going is practical or pleasant. Is it boggy? Is that path visible on the ground? Is the path blocked by barbed wire? Is that stream fordable? Is there an insurmountable deer fence in the way? In practice, what often happens is that you end up making too many mistakes and doing too much road walking. When you are walking a long-distance route, you don't want to waste time trying to find the right way to go – it gets very frustrating. I've written this book because it's what I needed to walk from Land's End to John o' Groats the way I wanted to. I hope it will be of similar help to you.

The recommended 1956km (1215-mile) route is described using two resources. About 60% of the route is described in detail in this book, with accompanying strip maps at the end of each of the six sections. For the remainder you will be following established national trails, and will need guidebooks for the South West Coast Path, the Offa's Dyke Path, the Pennine Way and the West Highland Way. A number of variations on the recommended route of the Trail are described at the beginning of each section, and details of other guides you will need if you choose to follow them are given at the appropriate points.

The six sections of the route are divided into 61 daily stages, averaging 32km (20 miles) per day, allowing a fit walker to complete the journey in two months. The days are generally rather longer than those described in the average long-distance walk guidebook, and it will of course be up to you, the walker, to decide where to stop each night and how far to walk each day – the daily stage breaks are just suggestions.

A three-month alternative schedule can be found in Appendix A. This is for those who prefer shorter days and can afford to take longer over the journey.

The route described is mainly a high-level one, avoiding roads and keeping to the hills where practical, and **is intended for experienced hill walkers**. If you can navigate safely in poor weather in the mountains of the Lake District, Snowdonia or the Scottish Highlands, then you should be able to follow this Trail. But a word of warning – don't assume that this means you will be safe whatever happens. The route takes you into some wild and remote areas, particularly in northern Scotland, and should not be undertaken lightly. In particular the section north of Fort William should not be attempted unless you know how to navigate and survive in remote mountain areas in rough conditions (see introduction to Section 6).

Romany hint for hikers

A few years ago anyone walking long distances by choice – excepting the professional tramp – would have been considered insane.

Scattered through the book are quotations from *Romany Hints for Hikers* by Gipsy Petulengro, first published in 1936. This must have been one of the first books written about lightweight backpacking. The author knew what he was talking about, although I'm not sure I share his views on the essential nature of pyjamas or the dangers of wearing plus-fours.

There are also quotations from some of the early books written about Land's End to John o' Groats journeys. Some of these are classics, and many are more amateur affairs, but they nearly all provide insight into the challenge of an End to End journey, and make fascinating reading when you are planning your own trip. Details of all of them, and some more recent accounts, are found in the bibliography in Appendix B, and on the website www.longwalks.org.uk.

Finally, although the route is described from Land's End to John o' Groats, this book can also be used for a north to south walk, although the route-finding information has not been written with that in mind.

USING THIS GUIDE

The guidebook is divided into an introduction, six Trail sections, each of which is further divided into day stages, and three appendices.

At the beginning of each section there is a map of the area covered by the section, and an information box describing distance in kilometres and miles, the proportion of route requiring road walking, and the number of days (for both two-month and three-month schedules). The road walking has been calculated by adding up the distances on public roads and pavements next to them. It doesn't include tarmac towpaths and private roads where you are unlikely to meet traffic.

A short summary of the general nature of each of the six sections is followed by details of recommended published maps and guidebooks, then information about accommodation and equipment shops, and alternative routes where relevant.

For each day stage of the walk, the distance and amount of ascent involved are given (for more details of each day stage see Appendix A), and there is a description, including facilities and points of interest along the way. Where the day is covered by a published guidebook (eg the South West Coast Path), the description is usually brief, as all the information you need will be in your guidebook,

The head of Langsett Reservoir (Day 27)

and there is not much point in covering the same ground twice.

For the days not covered by published guidebooks, detailed annotated strip maps are included at the end of the section to make the route as easy as possible to follow. There are 163 of these maps altogether.

Appendix A provides two route summary tables, one for the two-month main schedule, and a three-month alternative schedule. Distance, metres of ascent and percentage of road walking are given for each day, with a summary of the facilities available at the end of the day.

Appendix B is a bibliography listing some of the best books about Land's End to John o' Groats, as well as other titles that are not essential but could be useful.

Appendix C has details of organisations that are useful sources of information.

Other guidebooks

In addition to this guidebook and a suitable set of Ordnance Survey maps (see 'Maps' at the beginning of each section), guidebooks to four long-distance paths will be needed:

- The South West Coast Path
- The Offa's Dyke Path
- The Pennine Way
- The West Highland Way.

I have made recommendations under 'Guidebooks' at the beginning of each section, and these are also listed in Appendix B.

Where alternative routes are suggested for parts of the Trail (eg Section 2, where the Limestone Link, Cotswold Way and Heart of England Way can be followed instead of the Offa's Dyke Path), the guidebooks you will need are described under 'Alternative routes' at the beginning of that section.

In most cases there are several alternative guidebooks, but if one is published by Cicerone, that's the one I've recommended. (I wouldn't be recommending them if they weren't good guides, although of course many of the alternatives are worth looking at.)

For Section 6 it is worth reading *The Cape Wrath Trail* by Iain Harper (Cicerone, 2013), as this includes details of some additional alternative routes that are useful in the Highlands during bad weather.

Finally, check www.cicerone.co.uk/933/updates and www.longwalks.org.uk, where updates and corrections to this guidebook will be published.

Strip maps

When some or all of the day's walking is not covered by another guidebook, my own strip maps are provided (grouped together at the end of each section), annotated with useful information to help you to follow the route without going astray.

The strip maps are not intended to be a substitute for Ordnance Survey maps, however. There are no contours marked, so they do not show the lie of the land, and they only show the recommended route and a narrow strip on either side. The strip maps should be used *alongside* OS maps, and one way of doing this is to transfer the route onto your OS maps with a soft pencil (2B or 3B), which can easily be erased later.

Many walkers will be relieved to hear that all the maps are oriented with north at the top of the page. This makes navigation easier, and since the Trail is overall south to north, for quite a lot of the time you will be holding the book the right way up as you follow the route.

Each map page has a named start and end point, and these are intended to let you know approximately where the walking starts and ends on the page. Not every page actually starts and ends exactly in a spot named on a map, so the name given reflects the nearest significant place with a name – this place could be just before or just after the actual page end point, or slightly off to the left or right. The named location is usually shown on one or other of the map pages (before or after the page break), but not always.

The text on the maps is usually in a series of numbered paragraphs on each page, and each paragraph is as close as it can be to the part of the map it relates to. This means that when looking at the map pages, expect to start reading paragraph number 1 near the bottom. If there are a number of strips of the map on one page, where practical the first is lowest down, and the higher ones follow on.

Scale: The strip maps are on a scale of 1:25,000 as far as the point where the Trail joins the Pennine Way, then at 1:50,000 from the Scottish border onwards. The reason for using two different scales is that on a 1:50,000 map it is almost impossible to show the detailed route-finding information needed to navigate intensive farming areas, such as you will meet in Somerset and Staffordshire. On the other hand, in the Highlands of Scotland there are generally far fewer features to show on a map, and using a 1:25,000 scale would have resulted in many map sections showing nothing but a dotted line across a featureless page, which would be of little use for navigation.

Key: A key to the symbols on the strip maps is provided at the beginning of the book, following the Contents list, but it includes nothing revolutionary and should be easy to use.

We decided to reduce our equipment to the lowest possible limit... even maps were voted off as encumbrances.

Robert and John Naylor, From John o' Groat's to Land's End, 1916

Distances and daily stage lengths

Distances given in the text have been measured from digital Ordnance Survey maps, so may differ slightly

Blaise Castle folly, Bristol (Day 15)

from the distances given in other guidebooks. Other people's estimates were not taken on trust, and one or two daily stage distances given in other guides turned out to be surprisingly inaccurate when remeasured. Distances for each daily stage are given to the nearest kilometre and nearest mile. Estimates from maps can't reproduce all the wiggles you really walk, so the distances quoted are more likely to be underestimates than overestimates. If you measure the same route with a GPS, that will generally give a slightly longer distance. (See Appendix A for route summary tables.)

Daily stage lengths are a matter of personal choice and ability on long-distance walks, depending on how much of the time you want to walk each day, how fast you walk, how fit you are, and how flexible you are in your accommodation requirements. On the two-month main schedule, the daily stages are usually between 25 and 40km long (15 to 25 miles), and the end points usually have some sort of accommodation either on or near the route (for most of the Trail there are plenty of alternative overnight staging points). The three-month alternative schedule keeps to an average of 23km (14 miles) a day. (See Appendix A.)

Where there is a particularly short or long daily stage there is always a reason, and the guide makes it clear what that reason is (usually a shortage of accommodation options at what would be the ideal stage end).

Where the End to End Trail follows an existing long-distance footpath, the route doesn't keep to the stages described in the recommended guidebooks, since many of the stages are too short to meet the Trail's 25 to 40km yardstick. So although you will be following the route as described in the recommended guidebook, refer to this book for daily stage lengths.

The Trail is described in six roughly equal sections. If you want to split it into a number of separate holidays, two sections can be completed in three weeks following the main schedule, so three such holidays should see you at John o' Groats. Alternatively, each of the six sections can be walked in about a fortnight using the three-month alternative schedule. Each of the section ends is easily accessible by public transport.

Distances in the route description are given in kilometres, usually to the nearest kilometre or half kilometre. I know kilometres may not be everyone's preference, but as OS maps use a 1km grid, perhaps it's time we started to get used to it. Heights are all given in metres.

THE ROUTE

The End to End Trail aims to join up as much of Britain's high ground as possible, while still keeping to a reasonably direct route from Cornwall to Caithness, and it follows existing, published long-distance paths where they fit the bill.

The South West Coast Path (SWCP) is followed, for the most part, from Land's End to Barnstaple in Devon. This is one of the national trails, so right-of-way problems have been solved, and the path follows the coast closely and usually avoids roads. This part of the route includes a lot of spectacular cliff scenery, and is definitely the most enjoyable way to start a Land's End to John o' Groats walk.

At Barnstaple the End to End Trail leaves the SWCP (which continues along the coast on a long detour to reach Minehead). Instead, the Trail heads inland to the hills – across Exmoor, over the Quantocks, on past Bristol and across the Severn, to Chepstow in South Wales.

From Chepstow the Trail follows the first half of the Offa's Dyke Path, along the River Wye and the England–Wales border.

At Knighton, halfway up the border, the Trail cuts across northeast, along Wenlock Edge and south of Telford, to join the Staffordshire Way near Penkridge, about 10km south of Stafford. The Staffordshire Way and the Limestone Way follow the River Dove north into the heart of the Peak District.

Then, rather than follow the Pennine Way on its initial purgatory over the Dark Peak peat bogs, the route of the Alternative Pennine Way is taken instead. This follows deep limestone valleys, then the gritstone

Pen-y-ghent, just before you start climbing it (Day 30)

edges and moors to the east of the Pennine Way.

Near Hebden Bridge in West Yorkshire, the Trail joins the Pennine Way and follows it up the Pennines to the Cheviots and the Scottish borders.

The Trail now turns northwest. St Cuthbert's Way is followed to Melrose, then the Southern Upland Way to Traquair. The Cross Borders Drove Road then follows paths and tracks to Peebles and across the Pentland Hills to canal towpaths and a disused railway line to get you through to the hills again, northwest of Glasgow, avoiding most of the urban sprawl around Edinburgh and Glasgow. From Loch Lomond you follow the West Highland Way to Fort William. After Fort William the Trail heads north into more remote areas of the Highlands: Glen Garry, Glen Affric, Kinlochewe, Oykel Bridge. Eventually the Highlands are left behind, and the route heads northeast to the upper waters of the River Thurso, and then up the east coast to Duncansby Head and John o' Groats.

Why this way?

Since my first holidays in the Lake District, when I was little, I've loved the hills and wilder areas of Great Britain, so that's where the End to End Trail goes. It passes through much of the best hill country (although for geographical reasons misses out Snowdonia and the Lake District), and generally follows hills and dales rather than flat plains and other vertically challenged areas. On the other hand, it is not a 'peak-bagging' exercise. Passes and valleys are usually preferred to peaks and ridges, but of course there are plenty of opportunities to visit the tops on the way if you want.

The End to End Trail is not the quickest or shortest way of getting from Land's End to John o' Groats, but it's as close as I could get to being what I consider to be the best way. It does keep to a reasonably direct route – most people will only have a limited amount of time, so extending the walk to pick off Snowdon or tick all the Munros is out – and if a route is not direct it removes some of the focus of the whole expedition – every day, every mile should take you closer to your objective.

Romany hint for hikers

Keep away from the dust and smells of cars and lorries.

The route does go past the foot of Ben Nevis, however. The symmetry of walking the length of Britain via the top of Britain's highest mountain is appealing, and although Ben Nevis is not 'officially' part of the route, it seems a shame not to climb it on the way (particularly if the weather is unusually good and you can actually see the damned thing).

Intensive agriculture tends to be avoided along the Trail, since ploughed fields and crops can be difficult and frustrating walking country, and often turn into unpleasant navigation and bushwhacking exercises. In one or two areas they are unavoidable (Somerset and Staffordshire, for example), and I have done my best to find a reasonable route through.

Most backpackers dislike walking on tarmac roads, and the route avoids them as far as is practical. Where they are unavoidable, as when crossing the Somerset Levels, the lanes followed are quiet ones. There is hardly any walking on busy roads, and large towns and cities are also avoided – this is a walk in the country, not in the suburbs. There is quite a bit of traffic-free tarmac along the canals and disused railways around Edinburgh and Glasgow, as there are few alternatives in this area that give a reasonably direct route to the Highlands. The route is intended to be entirely on either rights of way, established walking routes, or land with established open access. (Access law is different in England and Wales from in Scotland – for the Countryside Code and maps of Open Access land in England and Wales, see www.gov.uk/right-of-way-open-access-land; for Scotland's Outdoor Access Code, see www.outdooraccess-scotland.scot.)

A guiding principle is that the route is a *walking* route, and that every inch from Land's End to John o' Groats must be walked under your own steam. This means that every river and estuary is crossed *on foot,* ie by bridge or by wading (in the Highlands, for example).

So ferries are out (otherwise someone could claim to have walked from End to End by hitching a lift on a boat round the bits they didn't want to walk), and this has implications in southwest England and the Scottish

Highlands. The South West Coast Path takes ferries (eg between Rock and Padstow in Cornwall), and some of the possible routes up the west coast of the Highlands involve crossing arms of the sea. But by following alternative routes in the southwest and keeping a bit further east in the Highlands, the need for such assistance is removed.

Bridges are of course perfectly OK, since the only alternatives would be: (1) to follow the watershed all the way, which would probably be a good route but is not this one; or (2) to try to swim countless rivers and probably drown in the attempt. (Many of the routes through the Highlands described in other books feature boat trips, including John Hillaby's *Journey Through Britain* and Iain Harper's *The Cape Wrath Trail.*)

Designing your own route

If you want to devise your own route, for part or even all of the way, here are a few tips on how to do it. I would be surprised if many of the walkers using this guidebook were to follow the route described here in its entirety. Use it to help you with the bits where you don't already have a route in mind, rather than to dictate your whole journey.

In England and Wales it is not worth considering routes that don't follow rights of way marked on Ordnance Survey maps (unless you already know there's easy walking

Looking back across Porthcothan Bay to Will's Rock and Park Head (Day 5)

without obstacles). Pathless ground is usually slow to walk on, right to roam or no right to roam.

In Scotland the same applies, but of course the rights of way are largely undefined and so are not marked on maps. This means you need more local knowledge, although things have started improving, with the creation of a new Core Paths network.

In parts of the country where there is a lot of walking (eg the Peak District), you can usually follow all rights of way with little or no obstruction. In other parts of the country, don't assume that a right of way marked on an OS map can be walked along unless you have a good reason to believe it is in regular use. Crops may block it, it may be overgrown with nettles or brambles, or it may simply be untraceable. This is considerably worse in summer than spring. Waymarked routes are usually clear enough to walk, but there are exceptions.

As far as you can, rely on other walkers' knowledge about where the best walking is to be found. Local walking guidebooks are a very good source of information.

Study OS maps. For planning routes, 1:25,000 Explorer maps are much better than 1:50,000 maps, as they have a lot more detail. Most importantly, they include fences, walls and hedges, meaning that you can distinguish between unenclosed land and small fields. This is invaluable for planning routes in Scotland. You can buy a complete set of digital 1:25,000 or 1:50,000 maps for Great Britain to use on your PC/GPS at a far lower price than the paper versions.

Don't assume any route is either possible or impossible unless you or somebody else has tried it to see. It was very tempting to assume that the only way to get through Caithness to John o' Groats was on roads, just because all the previously published Land's End to John o' Groats accounts followed roads. When I went to have a look, it turned out not to be the case at all.

Avoid cities and large towns, however much you may like the centre of them. Suburbs are no fun to walk through. Plan your route through villages to give you plenty of opportunities to resupply and get a few home comforts.

GEOGRAPHY AND HISTORY

Land's End is not the most southerly point in England, and John o' Groats is not the most northerly point in Scotland – these honours belong to the Lizard and Dunnet Head respectively. The reason Land's End and John o' Groats are regarded as the end points of Great Britain is that they are the two points on the mainland of Britain that are the furthest apart from each other. To be more precise, it is actually Duncansby Head, rather than John o' Groats, that is the true furthest point – the pier and the rest of the village are about 2.5km west of Duncansby Head, where there is a lighthouse but no other habitation.

The most *direct* route from Land's End to John o' Groats is not a practical proposition for anyone. It is 967km (601 miles) long, and at its halfway point is about 18km underground below the northwest coast of the Isle of Man.

The most direct *above-ground* route is only 1km further, and by contrast is entirely practical – although it's mostly a sea journey. Until you reach Scotland the only bits of dry land you cross are the tip of Pembrokeshire and the Isle of Man. Anyone interested in following such a beeline route across country is recommended to read *Two Degrees West* by Nicholas Crane, in which he describes walking within a 2km-wide corridor from Berwick-upon-Tweed to Swanage on the south coast.

The less direct route recommended in this guidebook sticks to the British mainland. It crosses the main watershed a number of times, and when this happens it is pointed out in the book. There is a watershed between any two points on the shore of an island: it is the line that divides the water flowing to one side of the island from that flowing to the other side. The watershed between Land's End and John o' Groats is essentially the line between the streams and rivers flowing west into the Atlantic and the Irish Sea, and those flowing south and east into the English Channel and the North Sea.

I haven't been able to find out definitively when Land's End and John o' Groats first became associated with the idea of being the two extremes of Great Britain. It was certainly in the mind of the American Elihu Burritt, in 1846, when he first arrived in Britain, having been appointed US Consul

Loch Poulary, starting the climb out of Glen G[illegible] (Day 51)

to Birmingham by Abraham Lincoln. Burritt eventually walked from London to John o' Groats in 1863, and in the following year from London to Land's End and back. He believed he may have been the first person to connect the two places on foot (or at all).

Elihu Burritt was an interesting character. Born in New Britain, Connecticut, he started his working life as a blacksmith's apprentice. Subsequently he learned 50 languages, and campaigned on many humanitarian issues, including the abolition of slavery, relief from the Irish potato famine, and cheap international postage rates, and when he walked to John o' Groats and Land's End he was in his 50s. He wrote accounts of both walks, and these are listed in the bibliography in Appendix B.

Probably the first people to walk a continuous journey between Land's End and John o' Groats were Robert and John Naylor, well-to-do brothers from near Warrington, Cheshire, who set off in September 1871. It took them eight days to get to John o' Groats just to start the walk. On their arrival they read an entry in the visitors' book at the Huna Inn, near John o' Groats, as follows: 'Elihu Burrit [*sic*] of New Britain, Connecticut, U.S. America, on a walk from Land's End to John o'Groat's, arrived at Huna Inn, upon Monday Sep 28th 1863'. The visitors' book contained entries dating back to 1839. The Huna Inn that the Naylors stayed in no longer survives, but a Victorian replacement, built in 1878, still stands, although it has been a burnt-out shell since about 1980.

The Naylors walked the whole journey in one push, taking no ferries or other transport. They covered 1372 miles (2208km) and completed the walk in nine weeks. They didn't walk on Sundays, so in 54 walking days they averaged 25 miles, or 41km, a day. Much of their route was on what are now main roads, but at that time roads were of course not surfaced with tarmac, and as there were no cars or lorries, the walking environment was very different from a road walk these days.

The brothers sought out the best countryside to walk through, including the Great Glen, the summit of Ben Nevis, the Lake District, the Yorkshire Dales and the Peak District. To a large degree their approach to their walk was similar to today's long-distance walkers. John Naylor wrote up the walk 45 years later, from the notes they had made at the time, and the result, *From John o' Groat's to Land's End*, makes fascinating reading.

The End to End journey has been a popular endurance route for cyclists since the late 19th century, the first recorded ride, in July 1880, taking H Blackwell and CA Harman 13 days. The Vegetarian Cycling and Athletic Club records one of its members breaking the cycling record in 1907 and again in 1908, and another member, George Allen, walked from Land's End to John o' Groats in 1904 and again in 1908 (he published an account of his record-breaking 1904 walk). Early in the same year a certain Dr Deighton also walked south to north, getting a fair amount of local publicity as he went. EW Fox wrote an account of his walks from his home in Harrogate – to Land's End in 1905, and to John o' Groats four years later. Arnold Binns, a champion roller-skater from Hebden Bridge in West Yorkshire, skated from End to End in July 1930.

The next accounts are post-World War II. Theo Lang, then a young journalist, walked from Land's End to John o' Groats in 1946 to provide a running story for the newspaper he worked for, and he subsequently published an entertaining book (*Cross Country* – see Appendix B) based on his articles. In the First and Last Inn near Land's End he was told about someone who had arrived from John o' Groats pushing a wheelbarrow – stunt trips are nothing new! This was possibly a memory of Robert Carlyle, a Cornishman who pushed a wheelbarrow End to End three times, the first being in 1879.

Interest in walking between Land's End and John o' Groats was revitalised in 1960. At the start of the year, Dr Barbara Moore walked a road route from John o' Groats to Land's End in 22 days, to promote her belief in subsisting on a diet of juice, raw tomatoes, grass, oranges and herbs. She gained a good deal of national publicity, and this inspired Billy Butlin, the holiday camp entrepreneur, to organise a challenge walk shortly afterwards, to give his business some publicity too. In February, in bad weather, 715 optimistic competitors set off from John o' Groats, of whom 138 managed to reach Land's End.

Since then the End to End business has never looked back, with

Jedburgh Abbey (Day 39/40)

many novelty approaches, often undertaken for charity-fundraising purposes. Most of them have been along the roads, however, aiming at a fast time, fundraising or publicity, rather than enjoying the journey for its own sake. This is far from the relaxed, adventure approach of the Naylor brothers, or of most modern-day walkers on long-distance paths.

The inspiration for regarding Land's End and John o' Groats as two ends of a modern, long-distance footpath, and working out the best cross-country footpath between the two, must be attributed largely to John Hillaby. His book *Journey Through Britain*, published in 1968, is an extremely entertaining account of his walk in the mid 1960s (see Appendix B). The rest of us are walking in his footsteps, sometimes literally.

SAFETY

Survival tactics

The main safety considerations relate to walking in remote areas, and as is made clear at the beginning of this introduction, you should not even consider following certain parts of this route if you are not competent at navigating in bad weather in the mountains, so this section doesn't spell out all the obvious basics. In the Scottish Highlands in particular you must not rely on there being anyone nearby to help if you get into trouble, and neither must you assume that if something goes wrong you will be close to shelter. Solo walking is an increased risk, as there will be nobody on hand to help if something goes wrong. This doesn't mean you shouldn't walk alone, but it does mean that you should take greater precautions if you do, to reduce the risk.

Always make sure that someone knows where you are going, and that they will know you are missing if you don't arrive where and when you expect to. As with just about every safety issue, this point is most important when going into remote areas and when walking alone. Be realistic about how likely you are to be delayed, and about any difficulty you may have in contacting them to let them know you are OK. Don't risk false alarms. Phoning or texting someone who has a copy of your route every day or so is a simple way of doing this. Make sure they know what to do if you don't report in.

Take suitable equipment. A tent or a Gore-Tex bivvy bag and a sleeping bag are not only useful for overnight accommodation, but will also keep you alive with a broken leg in bad weather. (Plastic survival bags are of limited value, as once inside you get wet through in no time from condensation.) Trekking poles will help you get out of a remote place with a sprained ankle. They will also help with river crossings, and take some of the strain off your knees when things are going well. Get good equipment and clothes, and be sure you will be warm enough even if you are soaked to the skin.

Take suitable companions. At least half your party should have a map and compass, and be capable of navigation on their own in bad weather.

In remote areas take enough food to last significantly longer than you expect to be away – say, a couple of days extra. This emergency food should not need a stove in order to be eaten, since your stove going wrong may be the problem you hit. Also, if your emergency food is too nice, it won't be there when you have an emergency. If you don't like Kendal Mint Cake, for example, it makes a perfect emergency food supply – high energy for its weight, easy to eat, and unlikely to be eaten before everything else has gone.

Don't rely on anything complicated or anything with a battery in it. For example, your mobile phone probably won't work in large areas of the Highlands, and if you drop your GPS on a rock it may stop working, so if you don't know where you are without it, and can't use a compass, you could be in trouble.

Don't rely on isolated accommodation or shelters being open, or an isolated phone box being in working order. Don't assume that any phone mentioned in this (or any other) guidebook will still be there when you want it.

Be careful crossing rivers. In the Scottish Highlands beyond Fort William, the Trail crosses a number of streams and rivers that can be dangerous in flood. The danger is not the depth, but the current. If you can't stand up you will be washed downstream, possibly to a bad end, as many people have died trying to cross streams and rivers in the Highlands in spate conditions. If you are in any doubt, don't try to cross. There is usually an alternative 'long way round', although in very wet weather even a usually insignificant

River Ling, at the crossing point (Day 52)

stream can become impossible to negotiate safely. I have given warnings for those that seemed to me to pose the greatest risk, and included alternatives where practical.

Crossing is safer if you keep your boots on (you can take your socks off though!). Crossing is safer with trekking poles or a stick, but make sure your poles are not going to telescope on you halfway across. Crossing is safer in company – hold hands facing each other to give a broad base and better stability.

All the crossings on the End to End Trail are easy enough in normal conditions, but you are likely to get wet feet from time to time.

Be careful when drinking water from streams. It is still relatively safe to drink from streams in the British hills and moors, provided you are sure there is no human habitation or farming activity in the gathering grounds of the stream. Never drink from streams below significant cattle populations. You could still be unlucky and pick up a stomach bug, but it's never happened to me, and whenever I can I drink from streams rather than carry water.

Hazardous wildlife

The wildlife in Britain is not really very dangerous.

You may see snakes, particularly adders, from the first day onwards, but although they are poisonous, the chances of serious injury or death are very small. The other serious danger is from Lyme disease, which can be carried by ticks in country areas, particularly where there is bracken. This can be a very unpleasant long-term illness, and there are a few thousand cases a year in the UK.

Ticks are present in many wild areas, and are a particular nuisance in the Scottish Highlands. It is a good idea to keep your legs covered while you are walking here, particularly through bracken. If you don't, you will probably end up with a number of little black ticks firmly attached to your legs, digging in for a good meal. They are difficult to remove, and the old remedy of burning them off with a cigarette is now reckoned to be a bad idea, as it leaves the tick's mouthparts under your skin, which can lead to infection (also, few walkers smoke these days). Ticks are reputed to be easier to get off if you unscrew them anticlockwise (but don't take that as gospel). It's a good idea to carry tweezers or a tick remover.

Romany hints for hikers

To ward off gnats and mosquitoes, boil a handful of elder leaves...add a few drops of oil of lavender and rub a drop on the arms, legs and face.
Watch for weasels and stoats.

So much for the dangerous stuff. Now for the really annoying ones: mosquitoes, clegs and the dreaded midge.

Midges and mosquitoes are worst at dawn and dusk, can occur anywhere in the summer months, and although Keld on the Pennine Way is notorious for midges, they are principally a problem in the Scottish Highlands. Clegs (horseflies) can turn up at any time of day. DEET-based repellents such as Jungle Formula discourage most insects, and although DEET is not particularly good for humans either, you do need to carry it with you in the Highlands. Nothing will really keep off the midges completely though, so try to avoid the Highlands in July and August, and be equipped to cover up, even in hot weather.

WHEN TO GO

Apart from whatever personal constraints there are on when you can set out, some objective considerations that will affect your decision are as follows.

- There are restrictions on access to the Scottish hills in the deer-stalking and grouse-shooting seasons. In practice this means it is difficult to plan walking in many areas between 12 August and the end of October, and the best advice is to avoid the Scottish part of the route during this period. If you do go then, you are likely to find yourself chasing round for permission to cross land and being diverted from your route. **Do not assume that any of the route in the Scottish hills is possible between 12 August and the end of October unless you have checked first.**
- The midges and clegs in the hills, particularly in Scotland, are much worse in July and August than the rest of the year, and are likely to make your life a misery during

Hartland Quay (Day 8)

that period. For this reason, **avoid the Scottish uplands during July and August**.

- The Scottish Highlands in winter constitute a hostile environment requiring suitable experience and equipment, and this is outside the scope of anything normally described as a long-distance walk. Winter in this context stretches from October to April – extreme weather and ground conditions can occur throughout these months (and sometimes outside them). **Avoid the Highlands from October to April unless you are absolutely sure you know what you are doing.**
- To walk a long way each day you need long days. The longest days are in June, but from April to September the days are long enough for most walkers to get tired before the daylight runs out.

Taking all this into account, the recommended time of year for this walk is to start in April and finish before the end of June.

Romany hint for hikers

Do not start camping too early in the year. The middle of April is quite soon enough to begin sleeping out, and even then you are likely to experience some cold nights.

If you have to walk in the summer, then consider starting at the beginning of June at John o' Groats and walking north to south. If you do this, however, this guidebook will of course be describing the walk in the wrong direction, and be prepared for warm weather, crowds, and paths blocked by crops towards the end of the walk in the southwest.

If you intend to do the walk in separate chunks rather than all at once (see 'Distances and daily stage lengths' above), your scheduling will be more flexible. This guidebook doesn't include any information on how to get to intermediate staging points, but this should not be difficult to arrange, as all the section ends are easily accessible by public transport.

PLANNING YOUR SCHEDULE

When walking day after day, you are capable of less per day than for a big, one-off effort. Remember that a lot of the walk involves climbing and descending, and difficult terrain, and that includes the first section along the Cornish coast (although for the first week the daily stage lengths have been kept to below 32km (20 miles) a day, to give a fairly steady start to the journey), so don't start a walk like the End to End Trail unless your basic physical fitness is good. If you can get in a few days' walking before you start, that will help, particularly by hardening up your feet, but you will mainly get walking fit by starting the walk.

Romany hints for hikers

If you really want to enjoy the sport of hiking, you must first get yourself into good condition.

Do not be tempted to rush out and buy a nice-looking pair of brogues with which to start your hike...Do not wear new boots or shoes of any description.

There should be no reason why anyone capable of walking, say, the Pennine Way cannot complete this walk, although you need to be confident you can maintain the daily mileage of your planned schedule, so don't set off at an unrealistic pace. If you haven't done any training beforehand, you are unlikely to be able to follow the main schedule given in this guide until you have been walking for a couple of weeks at least. Keep to a lower daily distance until your fitness has improved.

Walking long days

The day stages suggested in the two-month main schedule are significantly longer than those normally proposed in walking guides – an average of 32km (20 miles) a day. This is in order to get the walk finished in a reasonable length of time (if you can consider two months to be a reasonable length of time).

Romany hint for hikers

Hikers are usually early risers.
Do not try to exceed twenty miles in a day, especially for the first few hikes.

Moy Bridge, built in 1822, the sole remaining original bridge on the Caledonian Canal (Day 50)

Following the three-month alternative schedule, summarised in Appendix A, or one of your own devising, you can of course make the daily stages shorter, and stretch the walk to 12 weeks or more, but it is difficult enough for most people to get more than three weeks' holiday at a time, never mind three months. A three-month trip will also cost a lot more than a two-month trip.

For all would-be walkers I've only three pieces of advice. Make sure you're in good condition, have a good pair of feet, and know how to take care of them.

Jim Musgrave, winner of the 1960 Billy Butlin race, from the foreword to The Big Walk by A Walker, 1961

You need to do three things to be able to walk long days: the first is to get reasonably fit, the second is to look after your feet, and the third is to set out early each morning.

Fitness: If you can confidently set off for a day walk of 50km (30 miles) on footpaths in reasonably hilly country, then you are probably fit enough to follow the main schedule in this book from Day 1. To get to this state of fitness (assuming you are not already there) you will need to practise. Make up your own routes, or follow published routes, and go on your own or in company. There are many organised walking events that can help, usually with refreshments provided at checkpoints around the route. If you want to find out more about these, join the Long Distance Walkers Association (LDWA) – see Appendix C for details. The LDWA organises many events and publishes details in its newsletters.

Feet and boots: It is more important to have comfortable, broken-in boots or walking shoes than to be at your absolute best at the start of the walk (you will soon either be fit or have given up). Your feet are likely to need more looking after if you are walking longer days than usual. Boots that give no trouble on 25km walks can give serious blisters over 40km, so before you set out, be sure that you have proven the capabilities of your boots and socks on a number of long days.

Setting out early each morning: Do this to maximise the amount of time available for walking. If you are camping, get up and set off straight away, eating your breakfast on the move. If you are staying in bed and breakfast, ask for an early breakfast, or pay the previous night and skip a sit-down breakfast altogether, if necessary. Try to avoid running out of daylight before you run out of walking.

Allowing for contingencies

Allow some extra days for contingency – some things will inevitably go wrong. Your feet may need a day or two to rest; you may get lost and lose a day; you may encounter weather so bad that you lose several days; your equipment may fail – boots disintegrate, tents rip. Try not to run out of time to complete the walk.

To put this into perspective, many of the authors of accounts of End to End walks (see Appendix B) were stopped temporarily due to stress injuries to their feet or legs (as was I on my walk). One of the Naylor brothers (*From John o' Groat's to Land's End*) was unable to walk properly for many days due to a swollen ankle; John Hillaby (*Journey Through Britain*) was laid up in Bristol with swollen and painful calves for a while; Chris Townsend (*The Great Backpacking Adventure*) had to stop for four days in Stafford with a badly bruised ankle; John Merrill (*Turn Right at Land's End*) suffered a stress fracture to his foot that put him out of action for weeks. They also all experienced equipment failure of one sort or another, and all were delayed by the need to wait for shops to open, or to collect a parcel from a post office – this should be enough evidence to persuade you to factor into your plans at least a week's contingency.

Mental strain

Something that is not always acknowledged is that undertaking a walk of this length can be a mental strain as well as a physical one. Many authors of accounts of End to End walks describe episodes during which they were on the point of giving up – it is difficult for most people to stay positive and single-minded for such a long time. This is one of the reasons for reading some of these accounts before you go, as they give a good picture of the mental challenge as well as the physical one.

Romany hint for hikers

It is better to stop an hour before fatigue than an hour after.

Companions

Whether you go on your own or with companions is of course up to you. Most people walking Land's End to John o' Groats seem to go on their own (presumably this is due to an inability to find anyone else daft enough to want to), and if you do so, don't forget to take extra safety precautions in case you get lost or injured in the hills (see 'Safety' above).

Please don't use this guide to take large numbers along all or part of the route. Much of it is on land that will be damaged by too much of that sort of treatment, so no mass sponsored relays, please!

EQUIPMENT

There should be no need to spell out what equipment you need for a long-distance walk, as it is assumed that if you are contemplating this route, you will be experienced enough to know already (and the other guidebooks you will need for parts of the route also include this kind of information), so again here are just a few tips.

Romany hints for hikers

You should carry a pair of pyjamas, stockings, mackintosh and one spare shirt.

Do not wear collars and ties when you are hiking.

Never wear plus-fours. Not only are they insanitary through lack of ventilation, but the straps round the leg hinder the free flow of blood and cause varicose veins.

Travel light. Nearly every guidebook says this, but the number of walkers with huge packs on long-distance paths makes it clear that a lot of people really find it difficult to separate what is necessary from what is 'nice to have'. What is not nice to have is a great weight on your shoulders, and as long as you are (1) warm enough during the day, (2) warm and dry at night, (3) able to find food and drink, and (4) prepared for emergencies, then everything else should be regarded as optional. Weigh everything you're thinking of taking, think over whether you really need it at all, then if you do need it, try to find the lightest possible version. (See 'Packing list' at the end of this section.)

Remember that things you can expect to last out a two-week walk won't necessarily last a two- or three-month one. This doesn't matter so much for things that are easy to replace on the way (a list of equipment shops is given at the start of each section), but it is a good idea to have spare funds available just in case, and

Newquay beach, unusually deserted (Day 4)

a replacement pair of boots, already broken in, ready to be sent to you if needed.

Plan what you are going to do if your tent disintegrates – have someone ready to post you a new one or lend you theirs.

John Merrill (author of *Turn Right at Land's End*) found that leather boots lasted about 2500 miles, and socks about three weeks. Hamish Brown (author of *Hamish's Groat's End Walk*) reckoned on 1000 miles for a pair of socks.

If you are keeping things in lightweight plastic bags, expect the bags to disintegrate within a couple of weeks at most.

Don't take too many spare clothes. As long as you've got something dry to wear in the evening, and enough for the worst weather you can expect, then any more is luxury.

'Three socks – two to wear and one to wash' may sound a bit extreme, but wash clothes whenever you can, and dry them overnight if you are in hostels or bed and breakfasts, or hang them from your rucksack when it's not raining.

John Merrill wore the same shorts for eight months on his coastal walk, and the same shirt for longer. They were each washed only once. I've done a week's walking in the Highlands with only one pair of socks – it was so wet they got washed continuously all day every day, and I kept them on in the evening since it was the best way to dry them out.

Don't take anything for your feet apart from your boots and your walking socks. Search the shops for the

The Hay Inclined Plane, which carried boats down to the Severn from 1792 to 1894 (Day 22)

lightest flip-flops you can find, then leave them out of your pack at the last moment (there speaks experience). Leave your boots at the door of pubs and bed and breakfasts and you are unlikely to be turned away. (Some hotels may have a different attitude, so avoid those that do.)

Take big drybags to keep things dry in your rucksack. You could consider a waterproof rucksack cover instead, but when I tried this I found it a real nuisance, as it's so hard to get into your bag when you need to.

Don't carry things from Land's End to John o' Groats that you only need for a fraction of the journey. Post maps ahead and post them home again when finished with (see 'Posting ahead' below). If you are planning to eat in pubs and cafés whenever practical, you can manage without cooking equipment until you get to Fort William, so either buy equipment in Fort William, or post it on.

Cut up your maps and guidebooks (including this one) and carry the parts you need for the trip, leaving behind what you only need for planning. If you have PC mapping software such as Memory-Map, you can just print what you need, but take care to keep the pages dry, as most PC printer ink is not waterproof.

Camping does not necessarily mean carrying a huge amount of extra weight, as long as you can afford good-quality, lightweight equipment. Consider carrying a Gore-Tex bivvy bag rather than a tent, and if you are sure you want a tent then get a very lightweight one. Until you get to Fort William, if you are going to use bed and breakfasts and hostels for most nights, a tent is not really needed. From Fort William you should equip yourself for camping and cooking anyway, even if you think you have solved all your accommodation requirements without needing to sleep out. You will often be a long way from help, and may not reach your objective every night, so one option is to buy a tent in Fort William and post your bivvy bag home if you have one. A tent rather than a bivvy bag enables you to shelter from the weather and the midges while you cook. You may also need a bigger rucksack from Fort William onwards.

If you regard taking reading matter as essential (some of us do and some of us don't), then go for maximum words per ounce – books are heavy. The best value I've found is an old Oxford World's Classic edition of Herman Melville's *Moby Dick* – nearly 600 pages for only 250g, once the hard cover was cut off.

It is possible you may encounter driving sleet or snow, even in June, when crossing the higher passes in the Scottish Highlands. **Be prepared for all conditions.**

Packing list

Below is a list of things I set off with on an unsupported walk from Land's End some years ago. I have included it as a practical example of how to keep the weight of your pack down.

Item	weight in grams
Rucksack (35 litre)	870
Rucksack liner (strong plastic bag)	60
Sleeping bag in compression sack	790
Sleeping mat (cut down)	180
Bivvy bag	560
Anorak	490
Gaiters (light but leaky)	150
One pair of trousers	330
One spare pair of underpants	60
One spare T-shirt	115
One spare pair of liner socks	30
One spare handkerchief (silk)	10
Silk headscarf (to protect bald head)	10
Toilet bag	10
Soap	35
Toothbrush (disposable hotel freebie)	5
Toothpaste	20
Disposable razor	10
Towel (small, lightweight)	50
Blister patches in box	25
Vaseline (small tin) – for feet	30
Toilet paper	20
Maps (Days 1–18, cut down)	340
Reference notes, including draft maps for this book	80
Extra writing materials (to make notes for this book)	55
Wallet, bank cards, stamps & YHA card	25
Pocket knife (lightweight)	15
Water container (flexible, 1 litre)	30

Item	weight in grams
Plastic bags and ties	60
Camera and accessories	235
Films (professional quality, not easy to restock en route)	310
Book to read (*Moby Dick*)	250
Total pack weight	**5.3kg**

To this needs to be added the weight of whatever cash, food and drink I happened to be carrying each day. I didn't generally carry much food, but since the pack was so light I found I could afford to carry a full water bottle if need be, as even with this the pack was so light I didn't really notice it. The only things I needed to add on the way were sun-screen and Ibuprofen tablets. I also carried a map case (with a compass in it) and a pair of trekking poles, and set off in shorts and a fleece. I wore the lightest waterproof walking boots I could find (1200g the pair).

At Fort William I switched to a larger rucksack, swapped the bivvy bag for an ultra-lightweight tent (1570g), and added a lightweight gas stove, a pan, a Lexan spoon and some insect repellent. This put the weight without food and drink up to 7.7kg. I also had to add a lot of dried food, so for the first time I was feeling the weight. It was still a pretty light pack under the circumstances though. Everything turned out to be needed except the blister patches!

If I were to repeat the trip, I'd have to add a mobile phone and charger, as there are no longer many public

Looking back at Padstow and the Camel estuary (Day 5)

phones around. I'd use lightweight drybags rather than plastic bags to keep my things dry. I'd take a lightweight trowel for digging toilet holes. And I'd take a tick-removing tool: they weigh virtually nothing and can be bought online or from your local vet or pet shop.

Romany hints for hikers

Cut your tent pegs from the hedges. If you do not wish to go to the trouble of making a pack, you can purchase a rucksack very cheaply nowadays.

Written information

Access to a computer scanner/printer is useful, as it allows you to copy parts of books rather than carrying the whole thing (including this one), and to photo-reduce both printed and handwritten information to get it to weigh less (use both sides of the paper!). Don't go overboard on the copying, though – please do buy the guidebooks you need (the usual guidance is that it is acceptable to make a single copy of something 'for research or private study').

Posting ahead

The main reason for having parcels posted on to you is that the maps and guidebooks you will need for the whole journey are too heavy to consider carrying all at the same time (although the fewer parcels you have, the less you will be delayed by waiting for post offices to open, or worse, by the failure of a parcel to arrive). Getting a supply of clean clothes by post is more of a luxury, but you might as well take advantage of the opportunity for this. (Include spare wrapping paper and sticky tape in each parcel to make it easy to send back the stuff you no longer need.)

A package at the end of each of the first five sections is not a bad approach: Barnstaple, Knighton, Hebden Bridge, Jedburgh and Fort William. But don't forget that parcels sometimes get lost or delayed in the post, so have a contingency plan for this.

Details of how to collect post from main post offices and the addresses of individual post offices can be found online at www.postoffice.co.uk. Alternatively, you can make arrangements with the places you are planning to stay at, such as youth hostels.

MAPS

With the possible exception of the South West Coast Path, **neither this guidebook nor any other should be relied on without having relevant Ordnance Survey or equivalent maps with you as well**. Guidebooks are fine while you are on the right path, but rarely give you the information you need to find it again when you have lost it. At least when you have a map and get lost, you are probably still on the map.

Cannock Chase heathland, Day 23

Romany hint for hikers
If you are hiking through strange places do not forget the map.

The relevant OS maps are listed under 'Maps' at the beginning of each section, while at 'Recommendations' you'll find my suggestions for what to actually take.

CARRYING FOOD

As far as Fort William, you should be able to manage carrying food for just a day or two at most – there are shops on most days, and pubs where food is available.

Romany hints for hikers
Keep to wholesome plain food and an abundance of it.
Keep a supply of potatoes on hand.

From Fort William onwards, the situation changes, as there are far fewer opportunities to restock and eat out, so stock up at Fort William with what you need for the rest of the trip (you don't generally need to carry water, as there is no shortage of it in the Highlands). Fort William has plenty of outdoor shops, so you should be able to buy anything you need here. Since you are likely to need to carry enough food to last

The Royal Oak, Boscobel House – descendants of the tree in which King Charles I hid in 1651 (Day 22)

a few days, the best option is dried food, which is light for its nutritional value. It is also a good idea to carry food that needs little or no cooking, so that you don't need to carry so much fuel. If you already have experience of backpacking on long-distance paths, you will know what you like to take, and it is of course up to you and your personal tastes.

Some suggestions are as follows.

- **Pre-prepared dried meals:** There are plenty of these around, and the quality is generally a lot better than it used to be. Most outdoor shops stock some.
- **Instant mashed potato:** Just add to boiling water and it's done (it even includes salt, so you don't need to add any).
- **Couscous:** Again you only need to mix with boiling water and leave for a few minutes – no need to cook (although you will need to add salt).
- **Polenta:** Instant polenta takes one minute to cook. Again, add salt, and preferably some fat – cheese, butter or oil.
- **Pasta:** Get the sort that cooks quickly so that you use less fuel. Quick-cook macaroni is usually easy to find, although it does need boiling for a few minutes, so uses more fuel than other carbohydrates.
- **Dried vegetables:** These are not so readily available these days, although dried onions are still relatively easy to find. Anything that needs only a few minutes to cook will do (so avoid dried peas, for example). Add the dried vegetables to the water you are heating for your potato, couscous or polenta, and by the time the stodge is ready, the veg will be ready as well.
- **Dried herbs and spices:** Take some mixed herbs or oregano to

add flavour to whatever you're cooking. Chilli powder is good value too.

- **Instant soup:** This already includes dried veg and herbs (and often other less natural ingredients as well). You can use it to flavour your stodge, not just as soup.
- **Cheese:** Some strong hard cheese, stored in a plastic bag, will keep for a long time provided the weather isn't too hot. Strong cheese means you need to carry less to get the flavour, and the fat will improve whatever you're cooking. Parmesan or strong Cheddar works well.
- **Biscuits, chocolate, etc:** These keep you going through the day, but always run out sooner than you expect!
- **Dried fruit and nuts:** These are good food value for the weight, and easy to eat on the march.
- **Fresh food:** Whatever you fancy for the first day or two after restocking – bread, fruit, etc (keep the dried stuff for when you really need it).

MONEY

Plan your finances well in advance – it is likely to cost a lot of money to complete the trip. Two months on holiday costs four times as much as a two-week holiday, and if you have to take unpaid time off work, make sure you have worked out the financial implications. (Also, don't forget the cost of getting to Land's End and getting home from John o' Groats.)

Having made sure you've got the money to finance the walk, you need to make sure you can spend it. In some areas, banks and cash machines (ATMs) are few and far between, and carrying enough cash for the

The Crask Inn – the most remote pub on the Trail (Day 57/58)

whole trip is too risky in my opinion, although it is an option. If you have a credit card, use this to pay whenever you can (but don't forget to pay it off as you go along, if you haven't got a direct debit to do this automatically). If your bank card won't work in a cash machine, then your credit card may; you will pay a charge, but at least you will get your cash. Another option to consider is opening an account that allows you to withdraw cash at any post office. As the Royal Mail adapts to the commercial world, these arrangements keep changing – ask at your local post office well before you set off to find out what services are available.

When there is a bank and/or cash machine at the end of a daily stage, I have included this information, but bank branches continue to close, so the guide will become out of date quickly in this respect. Where there is an ATM but no bank, the machine is sometimes inside a shop (often a Co-op), in which case it will only be accessible when the shop is open.

ACCOMMODATION AND SERVICES

This guide doesn't include a complete list of accommodation, as such lists quickly become out of date. Instead it includes the information you will need to collect together your own up-to-date lists. At the beginning of each section there is advice on how to get hold of accommodation information, and some general background about the accommodation situation along that section. The only times specific addresses are given are where the options are particularly limited.

Although local tourist information centres (TICs) are listed along with accommodation, it is worth pointing out that the Welsh TICs are listed on www.visitwales.com and the Scottish TICs are listed on www.visitscotland.com (rebranded 'iCentres'). Unfortunately at the time of writing it is not easy to find a list of English TICs online at www.visitengland.com, but with luck that will be resolved at some point, so it's worth checking.

Bed and breakfast

Bed and breakfast can be found on or close to the route just about everywhere, apart from the Scottish Highlands beyond Fort William. Bed and breakfast in a pub has the obvious advantage of being close to an evening meal and a drink, but on the other hand there is often noise from the bar when you are trying to get to sleep. Also, an early breakfast is less likely to be an option in a pub, as people running pubs tend not to get early nights, so can't be expected to be up too early in the morning.

It is not a good idea to book your accommodation too far ahead, since on a journey of this length there are too many things that could happen to force a change of plan. It is at least four times as likely that something will go wrong on a two-month walk than on a two-week walk. Boots disintegrate, feet and legs may need first aid and a rest, the weather may slow you down, a parcel of maps may not arrive when you expect it. Take accommodation information, and if you want to book ahead do it no more than a week in advance. A day in advance is usually enough, particularly if you have the option of camping if you need to.

If you are walking alone, bed and breakfast can be easier to find at the last minute anyway, since many bed and breakfasts are reluctant to let a double room out to a single person until they have given up on getting a booking for two.

Having said all this, accommodation on the West Highland Way and the last day or two approaching John o' Groats is often insufficient to meet demand, so booking in advance is advisable on these two sections if you can.

Youth hostels

Youth hostels provide cheap accommodation for walkers, usually in shared dormitories. There are some on the route along the South West Coast Path, some along the Pennine Way, and a few at other places on the route, all referred to in the daily stage summaries. Unfortunately the YHA and the SYHA (Hostelling Scotland) have closed down many rural hostels over the past 25 years.

Youth hostels can be busy with noisy school parties at times, but provide a good alternative to bed and breakfast, particularly for solo walkers. Facilities for cooking your own food and drying clothes are usually pretty good. You can join at the first hostel you use on the route. The YHA

Back Tor, Derwent Edge (Day 27)

Maol-bhuidhe bothy, Loch Cruoshie (Day 52)

operates those in England and Wales, while those in Scotland are run by Hostelling Scotland (see Appendix C).

Campsites

Camping is cheap, but campsites tend to be mainly in areas that holidaymakers frequent, which means, for example, that there are plenty on the South West Coast Path and in the Pennines, but not around Bristol and Glasgow. If you want to camp where there are no campsites, ask at any of the farms you pass.

If the weather is too wet, camping gets miserable, since everything you have gradually gets wetter, with little chance to dry out (apart from possibly a couple of hours in a pub in the evening). Unless you are particularly hardy and your budget is tight, combining camping with bed and breakfast or youth hostels is probably the best approach. It gives you the flexibility of always having a shelter for the night, plus the chance to dry out and get clean when you need it.

Romany hint for hikers

Generally permission to camp is given free of charge, but if a charge is made it is usually only a shilling or one and sixpence per week. If more than one and sixpence is asked, refuse to pay.

Wild camping

You don't have to find a campsite to camp. In England and Wales you can usually camp anywhere provided you have the permission of the landowner, but gaining that permission can be difficult, as locating the landowner is often not easy. Farmers are the obvious people to approach, but in some national parks they are not permitted to let you camp on their land. There is a lot of good information about how to camp wild in England and Wales at www.campsites.co.uk – go to the 'Resources' tab.

In Scotland you can camp pretty much anywhere you want to, apart from enclosed fields, as long as you're allowed to walk there. You don't need to get anyone's permission. In practice, this means that in wild country you can camp just about anywhere. It's still a good idea to avoid camping near buildings though; and there is a restriction on some areas around Loch Lomond: see end of Day 45. You can download leaflets about wild camping in Scotland from www.outdooraccess-scotland.scot – from the homepage, follow links to 'Camping'. The Loch Lomond restrictions are explained at www.lochlomond-trossachs.org.

Wherever you are wild camping, the most important thing is to leave behind you no trace that you were ever there. It goes without saying that there will be nobody to collect your rubbish. The leaflet 'Camping in Scotland' (available from the Scottish Outdoor Access website above) provides the following advice: 'If you need to urinate or defecate, do so more than 30 metres away from open water, rivers and streams. Keep well away from buildings and farm animals. Dig a hole approximately 15–20cm deep and 10–15cm in diameter to bury faeces and replace the turf.' Lightweight trowels suitable for this don't cost much: please carry one and use it. I got mine (weighing just 52g) from www.ultralightoutdoorgear.co.uk.

Bunkhouses and camping barns

There are a number of bunkhouses and camping barns on or close to the route, varying from basic to fully equipped. You generally need to take your own sleeping bag, and typically there will be a bunk, mattress or sleeping platform in a communal room. There may or may not be cooking and drying facilities. Check out https://independenthostels.co.uk and join the YHA (Appendix C), as they manage a number of camping barns.

Bothies

A bothy is a building in a remote location, suitable and available for an overnight stay. Facilities are basic – there are usually bare boards to sleep on, a table to eat off, and a fireplace to burn any fuel you can find legitimately. They are mostly in the Scottish hills, and a number are potentially useful places to stay on this walk.

They are free to stay in, and usually maintained by generous estate owners, or the Mountain Bothies Association (MBA), a voluntary organisation dedicated to the maintenance of bothies. When this guide was first published, the MBA had a policy of avoiding publicity about the location of bothies, to discourage too many people from using them. The logic behind this was that a proportion of users are vandals, so the more users the more vandalism (and they are, unfortunately, frequently vandalised). Happily, the MBA has changed its policy, and all the MBA bothies are listed on their website www.mountainbothies.org.uk. *The Scottish Bothy Bible* by Geoff Allan is an excellent book listing most Scottish bothies (see Appendix B). I would encourage you to join the MBA if you are planning to use any of their bothies. Even if you can't find the time to help on maintenance working parties, at least your subscription will go into the pot to help pay for the work.

Equipment shops

There is a good chance you will need to replace equipment as you go along, since the walk is such a long one. A list of shops that sell walking equipment is given at the start of each section, but shops come and go of course. For the latest information, the website www.yell.com is a good place to start.

Food shops

In Section 6, beyond Fort William, there are few opportunities to buy food. For this reason there is a list of food shops included in that section. (See also 'Carrying food' above.)

USING BOTHIES

If you use bothies, whether MBA bothies or not, then please observe the MBA Bothy Code:

Bothy Code

- The bothies maintained by the MBA are available by courtesy of the owners. Please respect this privilege.
- Please record your visit in the Bothy Log-Book.
- Note that bothies are used entirely at your own risk.

Respect other users

- Please leave the bothy clean and tidy with dry kindling for the next visitors.
- Make other visitors welcome and be considerate to other users.

Respect the bothy

- Tell us about any accidental damage. Don't leave graffiti or vandalise the bothy.
- Please take out **all** rubbish which you can't burn. Avoid burying rubbish; this pollutes the environment.
- Please don't leave perishable food as this attracts vermin.

- Guard against fire risk and ensure the fire is out before you leave.
- Make sure the doors and windows are properly closed when you leave.

Respect the surroundings
- If there is no toilet at the bothy, please bury human waste out of sight. Use the spade provided, keep well away from the water supply and never use the vicinity of the bothy as a toilet.
- Never cut live wood or damage estate property. Use fuel sparingly.

Respect agreement with the estate
- Please observe any restrictions on use of the bothy, for example during stag stalking or at lambing time.
- Please remember bothies are available for short stays only. The owner's permission must be obtained if you intend an extended stay.

Respect the restriction on numbers
- Because of overcrowding and lack of facilities, large groups (6 or more) should not use a bothy.
- Bothies are not available for commercial groups.

Falkirk Wheel (Day 44)

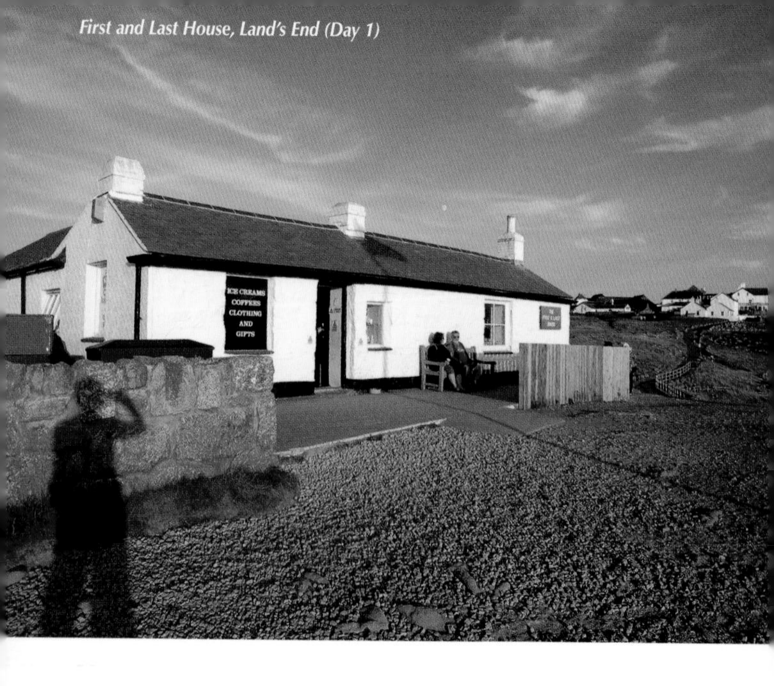

First and Last House, Land's End (Day 1)

Pubs

For many walkers, pubs are of great importance, and I have pointed out many of those that are on or near the route. Pubs are often the only places where there is any chance of finding food and drink out in the country – there is much more chance of finding a pub than a village shop, for instance. If you are camping, they are often the only places you can spend a warm and dry evening in bad weather (and of course they also serve beer, which is an essential part of the diet of many walkers, including mine).

Romany hint for hikers

If you are tramping through a village, make a meal off a nice piece of new bread and cheese washed down with a tankard of foaming ale.

Most, but not all, of the pubs mentioned serve food, and some have accommodation as well. Real ale enthusiasts will find they are well provided for as far as the Scottish border, after which prospects become patchy, although you will still be able to find some excellent beer.

SECTION 1

The South West Coast Path: Land's End to Barnstaple

Start	Land's End
Finish	Barnstaple
Distance	268km (167 miles)
Road walking	12%. This is mainly through coastal towns such as St Ives, Hayle and Newquay, plus the private Hobby Drive through the woods near Clovelly.
Days	9 (main schedule), or 13 (alternative schedule)
Maps and guides	*Land's End to Constantine Bay:* South West Coast Path guide; *Constantine Bay to Port Isaac:* this guide, strip maps Day 5 Map 1 to Day 6 Map 2; *Port Isaac to Kipling Tors:* South West Coast Path guide; *Kipling Tors to Bideford:* this guide, strip map Day 9 Map 1; *Bideford to Barnstaple:* South West Coast Path guide

From Land's End in Cornwall to Barnstaple in Devon, the Trail follows the South West Coast Path (SWCP). This is a national trail, so rights of way have been created where they were previously missing, and the route follows the coast closely.

The coastal scenery along the north coast of southwest England is so good that it seems a bit perverse to try to go any other way, although by its very nature a coastal path is rarely the most direct possible route between A and B, and this one is no exception, following the coast round headlands and bays.

Inland routes are possible, but footpaths going in the right direction are few, and you would end up walking many miles on tarmac. The south coast of Cornwall has considerably more deep estuaries and indentations to get round, meaning either taking ferries (which is not allowed on this End to End walk!) or long detours inland, often on roads. Also, the south coast doesn't really point in the right direction anyway.

The north-coast route includes so much spectacular cliff scenery that it is unquestionably the best way to start the walk (despite missing out Bodmin Moor and Dartmoor). While there are many tourist resorts in this popular holiday area, it is still very attractive, with many small seaside communities and plenty of remote coastal walking.

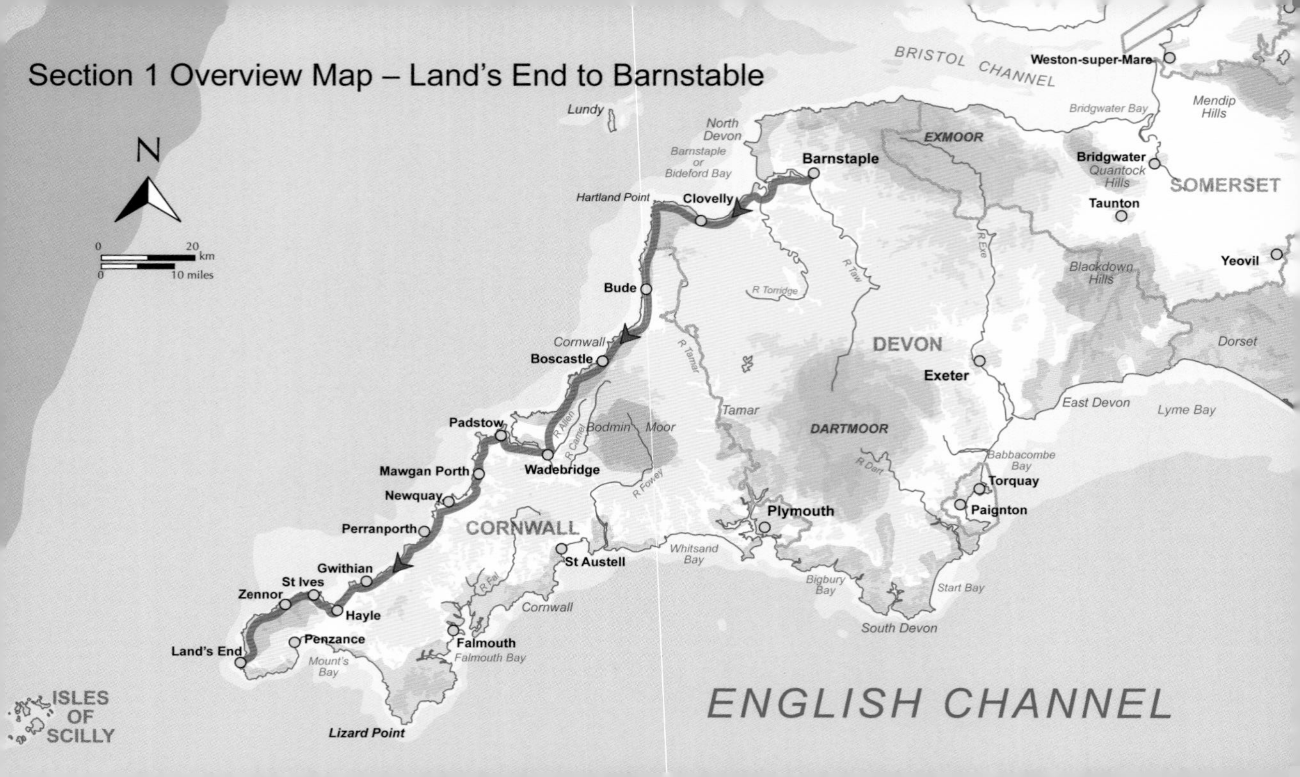
Section 1 Overview Map – Land's End to Barnstable
N
0
20
km
0
10 miles
BRISTOL CHANNEL
Weston-super-Mare
Lundy
North Devon
Barnstaple or Bideford Bay
Bridgwater Bay
Mendip Hills
EXMOOR
Barnstaple
Bridgwater
Quantock Hills
SOMERSET
Hartland Point
Clovelly
Taunton
R Exe
R Taw
Yeovil
Blackdown Hills
Bude
R Torridge
Cornwall
DEVON
Dorset
Boscastle
R Tamar
Exeter
Tamar
East Devon
Lyme Bay
Padstow
R Allen
R Camel
Bodmin Moor
DARTMOOR
Wadebridge
Mawgan Porth
R Fowey
R Dart
Babbacombe Bay
Torquay
Newquay
Plymouth
Paignton
Perranporth
CORNWALL
Whitsand Bay
St Austell
Gwithian
St Ives
Zennor
R Fal
Bigbury Bay
Start Bay
Hayle
Cornwall
South Devon
Penzance
Falmouth
Land's End
Mount's Bay
Falmouth Bay
ISLES OF SCILLY
Lizard Point
ENGLISH CHANNEL

The north coast is rocky for much of the way, and there is rarely a road along it, apart from where the path passes through coastal towns such as Newquay and St Ives. This makes for mostly excellent walking on good paths, except for occasional areas of sand dunes (often avoidable by walking on the beach). In common with many coastal walks there are plenty of steep climbs, but none are very long.

There are opportunities for shortcuts and variations, but only four places where it seemed worth recommending an alternative to the official national trail, which is after all an excellent route. Between Padstow and Rock the SWCP takes a ferry, so the alternative via Wadebridge is necessary to avoid cheating if you want to be able to claim you walked all the way.

Maps

1:25,000 Explorer maps

- 102 Land's End
- 104 Redruth & St Agnes
- 106 Newquay & Padstow
- 111 Bude, Boscastle & Tintagel
- 126 Clovelly & Hartland
- 139 Bideford, Ilfracombe & Barnstaple

1:50,000 Landranger maps

- 203 Land's End & Isles of Scilly
- 200 Newquay & Bodmin
- 190 Bude & Clovelly
- 180 Barnstaple & Ilfracombe

Guidebooks

- *The South West Coast Path* by Paddy Dillon (Cicerone, 2nd edition, 2016; reprinted 2019). This guide includes 1:50,000 OS strip maps. Unfortunately it describes the route in the wrong direction for the End to End Trail, but then so do most of the alternative guides.
- *The Complete Guide to the South West Coast Path*, South West Coast Path Association (revised annually), plus their *Reverse Guide*. The annual publication includes details of the latest changes to the route and has a comprehensive accommodation guide, although it too describes the route in the wrong direction for the Trail. Available from the SWCPA (see Appendix C), and free to SWCPA members. The *Reverse Guide* is designed to supplement the annual guide, and gives notes for walkers going in our direction.

Recommendations

For this part of the Trail you are not really in any danger of getting seriously lost, even if you rely only on the guidebook maps – the trick is to keep the sea on your left. The detailed route-finding can be surprisingly tricky at times, though, so hints from guidebooks are significant timesavers. The guidebooks are both well written and researched, and give plenty of information about the route, and points of interest along the way.

My suggestion is to get the Cicerone guide (or an alternative that also includes OS strip maps) and the South West Coast Path Association guide, to save you time in getting accommodation lists and for the other useful information it contains. Get Explorer 106 to cover the Trevone to Port Isaac shortcuts (Days 5 and 6), unless you already have Landranger 200. Get Explorer 139 to cover the shortcut from Westward Ho! to Bideford (Day 9), unless you already have Landranger 180. You should be able to manage without other maps.

Accommodation

Because this area is so popular for seaside holidays, accommodation is plentiful, although it can fill up in the summer and the Easter holidays. Apart from the most remote section, between Bude and Clovelly, there are plenty of alternative places to halt, with many bed and breakfasts and campsites. Not all campsites provide for backpackers though – some will charge the same rate as for a frame tent and a car. The annual South West Coast Path Association guide (see above) includes a comprehensive accommodation list, so is recommended, as is their website www.southwestcoastpath.org.uk and the list at www.nationaltrail.co.uk. The only additional information you may need, apart from that in your YHA handbook, is a bit more about accommodation near Land's End and around Wadebridge. The local tourist information centres for Land's End and Wadebridge are:

- **Land's End:** National Trust Visitor Centre, Station Approach, Penzance TR18 2NF, tel 01736 335530 www.visitcornwall.com. There is also a good accommodation list at www.landsendcornwall.co.uk.
- **Wadebridge:** The Red Brick Building, North Quay, Padstow PL28 8AF, tel 01841 533449 www.padstowlive.com

Accommodation is limited at a few stage end points, so you may want to consider booking ahead for these (Note: 'A' in stage numbers indicates a stage end on the alternative schedule – see Appendix A):

- **Zennor** (Day 1)
- **Gwithian** (Day 2)

- **Trevone** (Day 5, Day A6)
- **Hartland Quay** and **Stoke** (Day 8, Day A10)

Equipment shops

- Day 1: Millets, 1–2 Market Jew Street, **Penzance** TR18 2HN, tel 01736 800173
- Day 1: Mountain Warehouse, 99 Market Jew Street, **Penzance** TR18 2LE, tel 01736 367701
- Day 2: Mountain Warehouse, 35–37 Fore St, **St Ives** TR26 1HE, tel 01736 793884
- Day 3: Aztec Leisure, Old Garage, Trevellas, **St Agnes** TR5 0XY, tel 01872 552372
- Day 4: There are three outdoor shops in **Newquay**
- Day 5: Mountain Warehouse, 17 North Quay, **Padstow** PL28 8AF, tel 01841 532115
- Day 5: Countrywise, 5 Eddystone Rd, **Wadebridge** PL27 7AL, tel 01208 812423
- Day 6: Camping Sport & Leisure, Fore Street, **Tintagel** PL34 0DA, tel 01840 770060
- Day 6: Cornish Rambler, The Bridge, **Boscastle**, tel 01840 250330
- Day 7: Mountain Warehouse, 12 Belle Vue, **Bude** EX23 8JL, tel 01288 352494
- Day 7: Wroes Outdoors, 13 Belle Vue, **Bude** EX23 8JN, tel 01288 353789
- Day 9: Mountain Warehouse, Atlantic Village, Clovelly Rd, **Bideford** EX39 3QU, tel 01237 422877
- Day 9: There are four outdoor shops in **Barnstaple**

Land's End

THE START: LAND'S END

It would be difficult to conceive of any battle-ground on the face of earth or ocean, where the clutch and conflict of the elements could be more terribly grand than at Land's End.

Elihu Burritt, A Walk from London to Land's End and Back, 1865

Land's End can be found at the end of the A30, 12km beyond Penzance. Penzance can be reached by train, and from there you can either walk or hitchhike to Land's End, or catch a bus – go to www.firstgroup.com for times.

The first sight of Land's End Hotel, a low, drab-coloured building standing on the bleak headland, is apt to beget in the wayfarer who approaches it at sunset a feeling of regret that he passed through Penzance without stopping for the night.

Thos D Murphy, On Old-World Highways, 1914

There has been a hotel at Land's End for a long time – Elihu Burritt stayed there in 1864 after walking from London. More recently it has expanded into a small theme park, which is a good place to take children for a day out, but not a hiker's natural habitat. The Land's End complex usually gets a bad press from walkers, with the national press, outdoor magazines and walkers' guidebooks referring to it as an awful eyesore despoiling the whole area.

If you're there on a sunny weekend in summer you are likely to get that impression as well, but it's different when it's quieter. There are still big car parks and some ugly buildings, but the buildings are mainly together in a compact group, with the garish bits facing inwards rather than outwards. It's the number of visitors that makes it unpleasant, not the facilities. I'd much rather visit Land's End than Newquay, for example, provided it's out of season, or in the evening when it's quiet.

At Sennen the inhabitants are most primitive, and there are those amongst them who believe in witchcraft, sorcery, snake-charming and other fables of bygone generations.

Evelyn Burnaby, A Ride from Land's End to John o' Groats, 1893

Sennen, a forlorn collection of stone huts…
Thos D Murphy again

Sennen, which is the last village on the A30, 1.5km before Land's End, is a bit more respectable these days, and the place to stay the night before you set off, rather than Land's End itself, which is only a short walk along the A30. At Sennen there's a campsite (Seaview Holiday Park), bed and breakfasts, a shop and a pub. (Land's End youth hostel is actually 8km north of Land's End.) There is also a bunkhouse/B&B in Trevescan, between Sennen and Land's End (www.landsendholidays.co.uk).

Walkers are permitted through the grounds of the Land's End complex without charge. If you plan to collect evidence of your walk, don't forget to start collecting it here (see 'Recognition of your feat' at the end of this guide). Five minutes from Land's End and the theme park is forgotten – you're on your way.

DAY 1

Land's End to Zennor
The game's afoot

Distance	26km (16 miles)
Ascent	960m

For most of Section 1 you will be following the route description in your chosen guidebook, so it is not repeated here. The recommended variations from the national trail are described in full, however, on the accompanying strip maps (see end of Section 1).

On the main schedule, daily stage lengths for the first week have been kept down to below 32km (20 miles) a day (32km is the average for the whole Trail). This is to give a reasonably gentle start to the walk, although it has to be said that coastal cliff walking is often steep and rough, so it won't feel that gentle.

You may want to perform some kind of ceremony to mark the start of your expedition, and for most of the year there should be no shortage of people to take photos of you. (This will probably have to be with your camera, however, as your trip is unlikely to be taken very seriously when you haven't even started.)

I see you stand like greyhounds in the slips,
Straining upon the start. The game's afoot:
Follow your spirit; and upon this charge
Cry 'God for Harry! England and Saint George!'
William Shakespeare, Henry V

Head for the cliff top and turn right, in the direction of Sennen Cove, following your South West Coast Path guidebook. On the way round to **Sennen Cove** the cliff-top path gives superb walking from the very start. From Sennen Cove, as long as the tide isn't in too far, the sands of **Whitesand Bay** give much easier walking than the official SWCP route through the dunes. At the far side of Whitesand Bay, it's back to the cliff tops all the way to **Cape Cornwall**.

Wild flowers are everywhere in spring: violets, squills, primroses, thrift, celandines, kidney vetch, campions, white bluebells, and even an area of escaped Hottentot fig. There is also golden gorse in abundance.

Levant Tin Mine, Trewellard

Cape Cornwall is a small peninsula with a hill on top and an old tin mine chimney. From here all the way to Zennor there is evidence of the old **tin mining industry**, with many ruined buildings, tracks and spoil heaps. The Geevor mine was the last operational tin mine in Cornwall, closing in 1990, and is a scene of absolute devastation, but it is soon passed, and for the rest of the day it is back to spectacular cliff scenery. (It makes one wonder what a coastal walk would have been like when the mining was in full production – probably a lot less pleasant than it is now.)

From Cape Cornwall, continue along the SWCP to Pendeen Watch and Zennor. If you are breaking overnight at **Pendeen Watch**, 15km from Land's End, you will have to head inland to find accommodation. The road from the Pendeen Watch car park leads to Pendeen village, which has bed and breakfasts, and camping at the North Inn.

To reach Zennor itself, continue on the coastal path, crossing the footbridge in Pendour Cove (before Zennor Head), then going steeply up (steps) past a house on the right to a T-junction of paths and a National Trust signpost for Zennor Head. The SWCP continues by turning left here, but turn right and the track reaches **Zennor** in about 10 minutes.

Zennor has a very good pub, the Tinner's Arms, with a coal fire, and excellent food and beer. It's a tiny hamlet, but there are a handful of bed and breakfasts in and around the village. There is no campsite as such, but if you follow the right-hand (one-way) road out of Zennor and along the main road to the third farm on the right, you may be able to pitch camp at Higher Trewey Farmhouse. There is no longer a bunkhouse in Zennor.

DAY 2

Zennor to Gwithian

St Ives Bay

Distance 24km (15 miles)
Ascent 610m

Today the Trail follows the South West Coast Path through St Ives and round the Hayle estuary. It's 2km further if you go right round the Island – also known as St Ives Head – in St Ives, without cutting the corner.

Gurnard's Head, looking back from Zennor Head

Return to the point where you left the SWCP yesterday. The high point of the day is a tour of **Zennor Head**, glorious and remote. The Trail continues to be wild and adventurous until the descent to **St Ives**, and the first seaside resort of the walk. St Ives isn't a bad place, considering it's so dependent on income from tourism, but it marks the start of a pretty poor section of walking through to **Carbis Bay** – stick to the beach in Carbis Bay if the tide permits. For art lovers, the Tate St Ives, 2018 Museum of the Year, is a must.

Soon after this, a frustrating trudge round the **Hayle estuary** starts. It gets progressively grimmer – through a golf course, along busy roads, and through abandoned industrial wasteland on the way out of **Hayle**.

At last you reach **Hayle Towans** and the open coastline again. Walk on the beach from here if you can – it's much easier than the path through the dunes. Eventually you reach the bay by Gwithian. There are two cafés here at **Gwithian Towans**.

If you are heading for **Gwithian** itself, turn right when you reach the bay and follow the path to the village, which is a pretty place with thatched cottages. There is no shop, but there are two campsites and a pub (the Red River Inn) in the village centre, and two bed and breakfasts just outside the village.

If you are not stopping overnight at Gwithian, you can cross the silted-up bay, then go over a footbridge over the stream to reach the car park and café at **Godrevy** (SW 585 422).

DAY 3

Gwithian to Perranporth
More tin mining

Distance 30km (19 miles)
Ascent 1130m

Continuing along the South West Coast Path, the cliff-top path round Godrevy Point and along to Portreath gives another very good stretch of walking. There is a lot more evidence of the tin mining industry beyond Portreath.

Portreath itself is a good place to stop, with a surfers' beach, cafés, pubs, shops, bed and breakfasts, a youth hostel and a post office. The pasties from Portreath Bakery (by the post office) are particularly good.

From Portreath to **St Agnes Head** the path follows the cliffs again, with brief and steep descents into **Porthtowan** and then **Chapel Porth**, followed by the inevitable climbs back out of the valleys.

You don't see much of St Agnes village from the coastal path, apart from a few houses at Trevaunance Cove, and the Driftwood Spars Hotel. The hotel is a recommended halt – they brew their own beer on the premises, and the cosy bar has an open fire and a collection of fascinating photographs of local shipwrecks.

There is much evidence of **tin and tungsten mining** on the final stretch along the cliffs and round Cligga Head to Perranporth. The cliff faces show the vivid colours characteristic of metal ores, including green streaks of copper sulphate.

Droskyn Point, near Perranporth

Perranporth has plenty of facilities, including bed and breakfasts, a youth hostel, shops and pubs.

DAY 4

Perranporth to Mawgan Porth
The Gannel and Watergate Bay

Distance	28km (18 miles)
Ascent	910m

Day 4 follows the South West Coast Path through dunes, across the River Gannel and through Newquay. Don't be tempted to take a ferry across the Gannel estuary – the recommended guidebooks give full details of the four tidal and non-tidal bridges. The distance of 28km assumes you can take the shortest route across the Gannel (the longest alternative is 4km further).

There is a long stretch of dunes north of Perranporth, and as long as the tide isn't right in, the easiest walking by far is on the beach rather than in the dunes themselves (look out for the dancing shrimps though). At the end of the beach, climb up to round the cliffs on **Ligger Point** and **Penhale Point**, and descend again to **Holywell Bay**. You can avoid Holywell village altogether by crossing the stream by a footbridge in the dunes (a SWCP alternative route).

In **Crantock**, just off-route before the Gannel crossing, there is a café (which closes when it rains) and also a very good pub, the Old Albion. If the tide isn't yet low enough to use the tidal footbridge across the Gannel, this is all the excuse you need to visit Crantock.

New Quay is pretty, and is not yet overbuilt
EW Fox, 2000 Miles On Foot, 1911

Next comes **Newquay**, a big holiday resort stretching along the coast, and certainly not a rambler's paradise – things have moved on a bit since 1911. If the tide is out, the best thing to do is avoid most of Newquay – get onto the beach at the first opportunity and follow that instead of the road through the town. Newquay stretches a long way, but eventually you reach the far end, and it's back to quiet cliff tops above **Watergate Beach** until the descent into the cove at **Mawgan Porth**.

At Mawgan Porth there is accommodation, including a campsite, and by the bridge is the Merrymoor Inn (bed and breakfast).

DAY 5

Mawgan Porth to Wadebridge
The Camel estuary

Distance	28km (17 miles)
Ascent	680m

For the first part of the day, until Treyarnon Bay, the Trail continues northwards along the South West Coast Path. Between Treyarnon Bay and Padstow you can shortcut two headlands if you want (see below) to save some distance (the SWCP takes the long way round). At Padstow the Coast Path meets its first major obstacle since Land's End – the estuary of the River Camel. The SWCP takes a ferry across the estuary to Rock, so the End to End Trail follows an alternative route via Wadebridge, rejoining the Coast Path at Port Isaac on Day 6.

The cliffs from Mawgan Porth north to **Porthcothan** and beyond to Treyarnon Bay are particularly spectacular, and worth taking your time over. There are narrow headlands and inlets, and offshore stacks and islands, and it's surprising the walking itself isn't more strenuous.

The beach at Constantine Bay

There's a youth hostel at **Treyarnon Bay**, and shortly after this you pass the end of the road up to the village of Constantine Bay. Don't go up the road, but follow the coastal path in the dunes, and turn right in about 200 metres, beyond a lifeguard hut on the beach. This is the start of a shortcut along the golf course to **Harlyn Bridge** (which has a campsite nearby) – strip map Day 5 Map 1 shows the way. If you want to stay with the SWCP instead, and go the long way round via Trevose Head, this will add another 4km to the day.

About 1km after Harlyn Bridge, on the SWCP again, you reach the village of **Trevone** (if you are staying here overnight there are bed and breakfasts, a shop and a pub: the Well Parc). Leave the Coast Path here and head up the road through the village, where another End to End Trail shortcut takes you eastward directly to Padstow – see strip map Day 5 Map 2. Again, you can stick to the Coast Path via Stepper Point if you wish – it is about 5km further.

The shortcut makes a beeline for Padstow across the fields, and is pleasant enough, descending to Padstow Harbour along Church Street and its continuation, Duke Street. **Padstow** has all services, including a tourist information centre, and Rick Stein's fish restaurant (for which you will need to book well in advance).

Turn right at Padstow Harbour, and across a car park pick up the start of the Camel Trail, which the End to End Trail follows all the way to **Wadebridge** (Day 5 Map 3).

The **Camel Trail** is a popular waymarked Cornwall County Council route for cyclists and walkers. It follows a disused railway line along the River Camel from Padstow to Wadebridge, and then goes on to Bodmin. The cycle track can be unpleasantly busy during peak holiday times (another good reason for doing this walk in the spring), and the walking to Wadebridge is monotonous underfoot, but fast, with the estuary full of birdlife.

Wadebridge has shops, banks and plenty of accommodation, and there is a walker-friendly campsite at Little Bodieve Holiday Park (SW 990 735 – see Day 6 Map 1).

After a walk of about thirty miles, reached Wadebridge for tea
Elihu Burritt, A Walk from London to Land's End and Back, 1865

DAY 6

Wadebridge to Boscastle
Port Isaac Bay

Distance	32km (20 miles)
Ascent	1300m

The Trail leaves the Camel Trail in Wadebridge to cross the River Camel, then goes northwards, following the River Amble. It climbs up to cross the hills that line the north coast and descends again to rejoin the South West Coast Path at Port Isaac.

Jacket's Point switchback

The route is a good one (Day 6 Map 1). It enters meadows almost as soon as it has crossed the River Camel in Wadebridge, which is not yet entirely surrounded by suburbs. Once the busy B3314 has been left behind, more pleasant fields and meadows above the River Amble lead to the pretty village of **Chapel Amble**, which has an excellent pub, the Maltsters Arms, serving very good meals.

From Chapel Amble the dwindling stream is followed north, along wooded paths and through meadows, until the hills come close (Day 6 Map 2). These are tamed and cultivated hills, and the Trail climbs up through fields to cross the B3314 again at the old church of **St Endellion**, before descending gradually towards the coast, now laid out before you. The last kilometre to the coast is along a minor road that becomes steeper and steeper as it drops down into the quaint and typically Cornish fishing village of **Port Isaac**. There is a grocery shop with a cash machine at the top of the hill at the eastern end of the village, if you need it.

From Port Isaac, follow your SWCP guidebook again, eastward round **Port Isaac Bay** then north to Tintagel Head. This is not such a wild stretch – rather than rough moorland cliff tops, the path follows field edges for part of the time. The first bit is still hard work though, with a number of steep descents to cross streams, the last one by **Jacket's Point** being the biggest.

Trebarwith Strand is a pretty cove to pause at for lunch, and the inn here, the Port William, has tables right by the shore.

Continuing towards Tintagel Head, the path passes Tintagel youth hostel, and then you'll probably start meeting tourists visiting the ruins on the Island at **Tintagel Head**. Pay to go in and look round if you wish: a major Dark Ages site has been excavated here, but don't expect to see convincing evidence that King Arthur was ever here, or even that he existed at all. Tintagel village is inland from here. It's very touristy, and in my opinion not worth going out of your way for.

As for the story of King Arthur being both born and killed there, 'tis a piece of tradition, only on oral history, and not any authority to be produced for it

Daniel Defoe, A Tour Through the Whole Island of Great Britain, 1724–26

The cliff path soon loses most of the tourists as it bends east again past two headlands, both called **Willapark**, with the chasm of **Grower Gut** in between. The day finishes by following the narrow, winding rock channel into Boscastle Harbour.

Boscastle is a lovely spot, with a small youth hostel by the harbour, and shops and pubs nearby. It suffered a devastating flash flood in storms in August 2004, but has not lost its character as a result.

Squeezed into this gorge, there was one of the neatest, most romantic little harbours in the world

Elihu Burritt on Boscastle

DAY 7

Boscastle to Bude
Bude Bay

Distance 26km (16 miles)
Ascent 1350m

Today, follow the South West Coast Path around the gradual curve of Bude Bay. There is quite a bit more walking along field edges, and a lot of up and down. From Boscastle to Bude (and on to Hartland Point – Day 8) is one of the most strenuous stretches of the whole End to End Trail, so don't underestimate it.

To cross the valley at **Millook**, 7km beyond **Crackington Haven**, the SWCP follows the road for the descent, and after this the road remains close by for most of the way to Bude. The approach to Bude is along a pretty dreary stretch of coastline, without the high cliffs that have, up till now, been bringing a lot of the drama to the views. Even the sand is dark brown. Eventually the path rounds **Compass Point** and takes you east into **Bude**, which has all services and plenty of accommodation.

They tell me that Bude is a place that grows on you the more you see it. Well, I have seen it four times, now, and if I found it growing on me I should have it amputated.

Colin Howard, From Land's End to John o' Groats, 1939

Bude is not that bad, but it's a full-time holiday resort, and admittedly a bit short on 'olde worlde' elements. The pasties from Pengenna Pasties are highly recommended, though, and this is your last chance of a genuine Cornish pasty, because tomorrow you'll be in Devon, so stock up here.

DAY 8

Bude to Clovelly
Hartland Point

Distance	38km (23 miles)
Ascent	2090m

It's the South West Coast Path all day again today, but not for much longer, so make the most of it. This is a very strenuous day, with a lot more climbing than any other day on the entire Trail (2090m), so you should only attempt to complete it in a day if you have found the preceding days well within your abilities, and can get an early start. The alternative is to split this stage into two days, with a break near Hartland Quay (see below).

There is superb scenery again on the remote stretch north to Hartland Point, where a taxing series of switchbacks leads down one flight of steps then back up another, then good, fairly level walking east to Clovelly.

Heading north from Bude, the coast follows a pretty straight line. There are steep descents to **Northcott Mouth** and **Duckpool**, then comes **Lower Sharpnose Point**, where the path passes **Cleave Camp signalling station**, with its high fences and military warning notices.

At Higher Sharpnose Point, a stream, the **Tidna**, runs out almost to the end of the point rather than into a bay – a curious geographical feature.

At **Morwenstow**, a short distance inland from here, the eccentric poet Robert Hawker was vicar for 40 years in the mid 19th century. The path passes his cliff-top hut, built from driftwood, and the beautiful Norman parish church is well worth visiting.

Continuing north, as you cross the stream at **Marsland Mouth**, you finally leave Cornwall and enter Devon. This is after more than a week of hard walking, and no other county on the Trail takes anything like this long to traverse, until the huge Highlands and Islands region at the end of the journey.

This part of the coastline is remote, with few amenities. There is a youth hostel and a bed and breakfast at **Elmscott**, a pub/hotel at **Hartland Quay**, a bed and breakfast and an excellent simple campsite just inland at **Stoke**, and that's about it until you get to Clovelly. Stoke Barton Farm campsite has its own private footpath from the coastal path that starts south of the Hartland Quay car park and the stream: look up right to spot a gate.

The path from Hartland Quay to Hartland Point is dramatic, with wild cliff scenery and strenuous walking. Flat-topped **Lundy Island** is usually clearly in view out in the Bristol Channel. Lundy is a great place to visit if you want birdwatching, rock climbing or peace and quiet. The boat to Lundy sails from Bideford or Ilfracombe, depending on how high the tide is at Bideford.

Hartland Point is a headland of savage cliffs with a lighthouse perched precariously on the end. The walking from Hartland Point to Clovelly is good, and mostly reasonably level. There is a delightful bluebell wood at **Brownsham**, near the end of the day.

Clovelly itself is the classic 'chocolate box' fishing village, with a main street too steep for cars. It is a magnet for day-trippers, but in the evening they're nearly all gone, and it's a lot more pleasant. There is an admission charge (£7.50 in 2019) to enter the village, which is on a private estate. If you're staying in Clovelly, try to get accommodation in Clovelly itself, rather than in Higher Clovelly, so that you see the ridiculously picturesque old fishing village properly.

Clovelly village

> Talking to an old sea-dog at the inn, he tells me Clovelly is his native place, where all the inhabitants are related, so great was the custom of intermarriage
>
> *EW Fox, 2000 Miles On Foot, 1911*

DAY 9

Clovelly to Barnstaple
Barnstaple Bay

Distance	37km (23 miles)
Ascent	990m

This is the Trail's last day on the South West Coast Path, and only the first part, as far as Westward Ho!, is really coastal. The scenery is good, but not as good as much of what has gone before. The cliffs are lower, the farmland tamer, and the coves fewer.

The day starts with a very easy stretch along the Hobby Drive, a private road through the woods above the cliffs. The route continues along quiet cliff tops, often wooded, until you approach the next coastal town, Westward Ho!, named after Charles Kingsley's 1855 novel, which is set near here.

At **Kipling Tors**, just before **Westward Ho!**, you need to make a decision. The route crosses the River Torridge today. One of the two official alternatives – the ferry from Appledore to Instow at the mouth of the river – is out of bounds, so you have to reach the Long Bridge at Bideford. To do this you can either follow the SWCP all along the coast and the estuary, via Northam Burrows and Appledore, or take the End to End Trail shortcut from Kipling Tors, saving about 8km – see Day 9 Map 1.

For the shortcut, follow the SWCP until you see Westward Ho! ahead, then cut off right up the slope of Kipling Tors, an attractive hillside that overlooks the sea and gives a good start to this stretch. The rest of the shortcut is less inspiring, but it does pass a pub, the Pig on the Hill, at **Pusehill**. (If you are planning to stop overnight hereabouts, there is accommodation in Westward Ho! and in Bideford, but not currently at Pusehill.)

The shortcut rejoins the SWCP at the quay in **Bideford**. Cross the Long Bridge over the River Torridge and follow the SWCP to Barnstaple, mainly along a disused railway track that makes for easy and fast walking. For part of the way there is an alternative route across the marshes, which is slower but more interesting.

There is plenty of accommodation in **Barnstaple**, and on the way out of the town the Trail passes a pub, the Reform Inn at Pilton, which brews its own beer in a brewery behind the pub (recommended, but doesn't serve meals). There is an excellent simple campsite at Brightlycott Barton, 2km off-route (see Day 10 Map 1).

Day 5 Map 1: Constantine Bay to Trevone

3. Turn left off the road after crossing Harlyn Bridge & follow the Coast Path again round St Cadoc's Point until you reach the next village (Trevone).

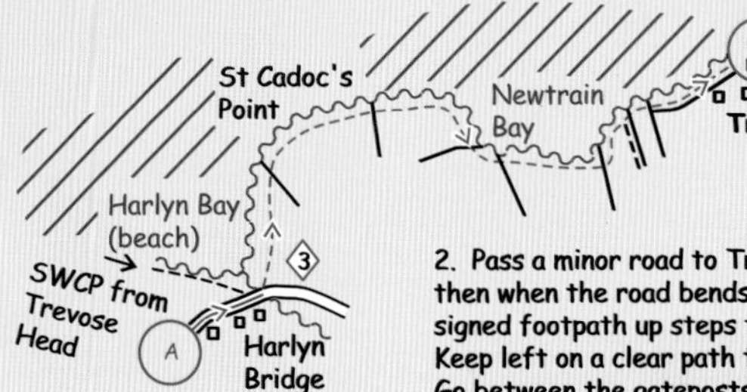

2. Pass a minor road to Trevose Head, then when the road bends left take a signed footpath up steps to the right. Keep left on a clear path to join a drive. Go between the gateposts ahead, then after a few metres turn left off the drive to cross the road & follow the signed footpath across the field opposite. This leads to a residential road. Turn right along this, then left at a T-junction & follow this road down to cross Harlyn Bridge & rejoin the Coast Path.

1. From the road end at the south end of Constantine Bay take the SWCP path in the dunes behind the beach past a lifeguard hut (on the beach). A short way after this a clear path strikes inland over the dunes: follow it & it becomes a hedged path along the edge of Trevose Golf Club. It ends at a road junction: turn sharp left on the road towards Harlyn.

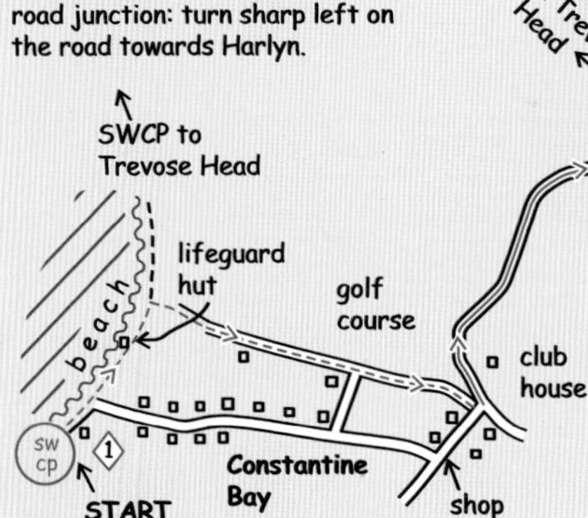

This is the first of the detailed maps in this guide: the key to the symbols used is in the front of the book. Reminder: all the maps have north at the top, & the scale of all the English & Welsh maps is 1:25,000.

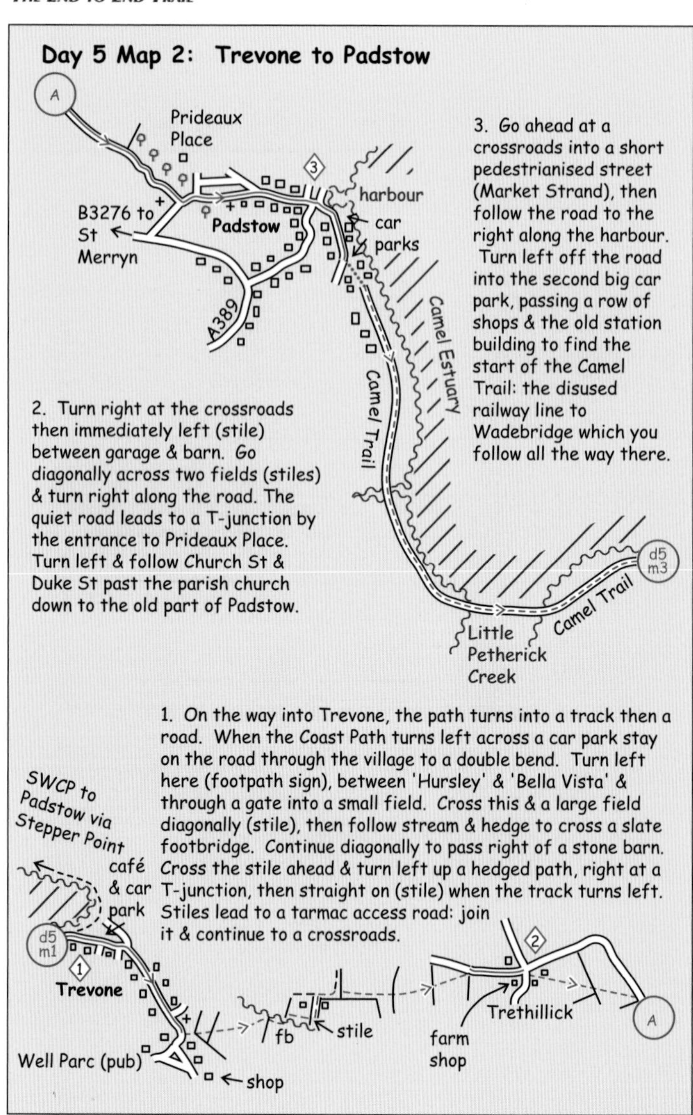

Day 5 Map 2: Trevone to Padstow
A
Prideaux Place
3
harbour
car parks
B3276 to St Merryn
Padstow
A389
Camel Estuary
Camel Trail
3. Go ahead at a crossroads into a short pedestrianised street (Market Strand), then follow the road to the right along the harbour. Turn left off the road into the second big car park, passing a row of shops & the old station building to find the start of the Camel Trail: the disused railway line to Wadebridge which you follow all the way there.
2. Turn right at the crossroads then immediately left (stile) between garage & barn. Go diagonally across two fields (stiles) & turn right along the road. The quiet road leads to a T-junction by the entrance to Prideaux Place. Turn left & follow Church St & Duke St past the parish church down to the old part of Padstow.
d5 m3
Camel Trail
Little Petherick Creek
1. On the way into Trevone, the path turns into a track then a road. When the Coast Path turns left across a car park stay on the road through the village to a double bend. Turn left here (footpath sign), between 'Hursley' & 'Bella Vista' & through a gate into a small field. Cross this & a large field diagonally (stile), then follow stream & hedge to cross a slate footbridge. Continue diagonally to pass right of a stone barn. Cross the stile ahead & turn left up a hedged path, right at a T-junction, then straight on (stile) when the track turns left. Stiles lead to a tarmac access road: join it & continue to a crossroads.
SWCP to Padstow via Stepper Point
café & car park
d5 m1
1
Trevone
Well Parc (pub)
shop
fb
stile
2
Trethillick
farm shop
A

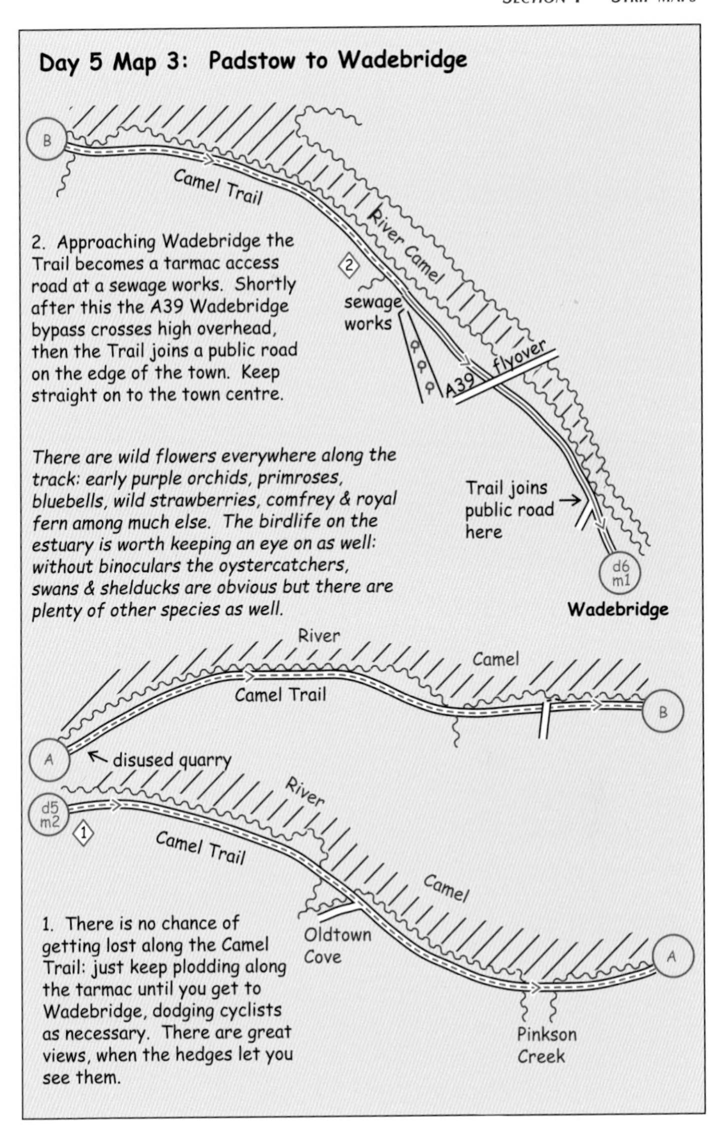
Day 5 Map 3: Padstow to Wadebridge
B
Camel Trail
River Camel
2. Approaching Wadebridge the Trail becomes a tarmac access road at a sewage works. Shortly after this the A39 Wadebridge bypass crosses high overhead, then the Trail joins a public road on the edge of the town. Keep straight on to the town centre.
2
sewage works
A39
flyover
There are wild flowers everywhere along the track: early purple orchids, primroses, bluebells, wild strawberries, comfrey & royal fern among much else. The birdlife on the estuary is worth keeping an eye on as well: without binoculars the oystercatchers, swans & shelducks are obvious but there are plenty of other species as well.
Trail joins public road here
d6 m1
Wadebridge
River
Camel
Camel Trail
B
A
disused quarry
d5 m2
1
River
Camel Trail
Camel
1. There is no chance of getting lost along the Camel Trail: just keep plodding along the tarmac until you get to Wadebridge, dodging cyclists as necessary. There are great views, when the hedges let you see them.
Oldtown Cove
A
Pinkson Creek

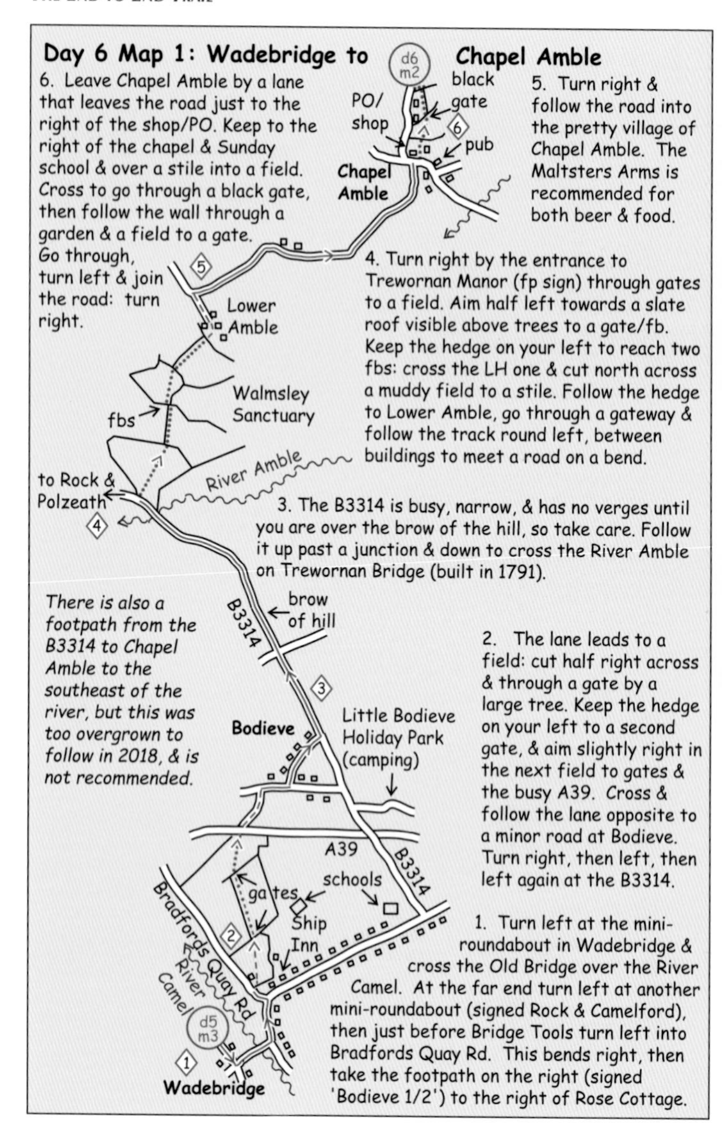

Day 6 Map 1: Wadebridge to Chapel Amble
d6
m2
6. Leave Chapel Amble by a lane that leaves the road just to the right of the shop/PO. Keep to the right of the chapel & Sunday school & over a stile into a field. Cross to go through a black gate, then follow the wall through a garden & a field to a gate. Go through, turn left & join the road: turn right.
PO/
shop
black
gate
6
pub
Chapel
Amble
5. Turn right & follow the road into the pretty village of Chapel Amble. The Maltsters Arms is recommended for both beer & food.
5
Lower
Amble
4. Turn right by the entrance to Trewornan Manor (fp sign) through gates to a field. Aim half left towards a slate roof visible above trees to a gate/fb. Keep the hedge on your left to reach two fbs: cross the LH one & cut north across a muddy field to a stile. Follow the hedge to Lower Amble, go through a gateway & follow the track round left, between buildings to meet a road on a bend.
Walmsley
Sanctuary
fbs
River Amble
to Rock &
Polzeath
4
3. The B3314 is busy, narrow, & has no verges until you are over the brow of the hill, so take care. Follow it up past a junction & down to cross the River Amble on Trewornan Bridge (built in 1791).
There is also a footpath from the B3314 to Chapel Amble to the southeast of the river, but this was too overgrown to follow in 2018, & is not recommended.
B3314
brow
of hill
3
Bodieve
Little Bodieve
Holiday Park
(camping)
2. The lane leads to a field: cut half right across & through a gate by a large tree. Keep the hedge on your left to a second gate, & aim slightly right in the next field to gates & the busy A39. Cross & follow the lane opposite to a minor road at Bodieve. Turn right, then left, then left again at the B3314.
A39
B3314
schools
gates
Ship
Inn
2
Bradfords Quay Rd
River
Camel
d5
m3
1
Wadebridge
1. Turn left at the mini-roundabout in Wadebridge & cross the Old Bridge over the River Camel. At the far end turn left at another mini-roundabout (signed Rock & Camelford), then just before Bridge Tools turn left into Bradfords Quay Rd. This bends right, then take the footpath on the right (signed 'Bodieve 1/2') to the right of Rose Cottage.

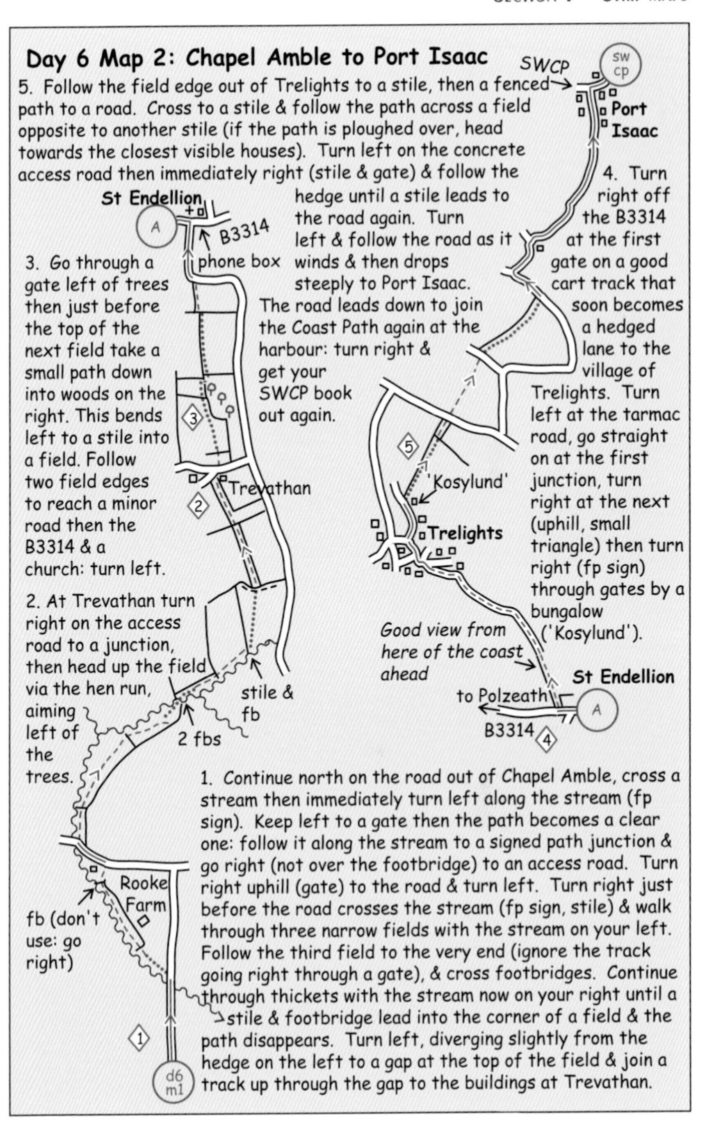
Day 6 Map 2: Chapel Amble to Port Isaac
5. Follow the field edge out of Trelights to a stile, then a fenced path to a road. Cross to a stile & follow the path across a field opposite to another stile (if the path is ploughed over, head towards the closest visible houses). Turn left on the concrete access road then immediately right (stile & gate) & follow the hedge until a stile leads to the road again. Turn left & follow the road as it winds & then drops steeply to Port Isaac. The road leads down to join the Coast Path again at the harbour: turn right & get your SWCP book out again.
SWCP
sw cp
Port Isaac
St Endellion
A
B3314
phone box
3. Go through a gate left of trees then just before the top of the next field take a small path down into woods on the right. This bends left to a stile into a field. Follow two field edges to reach a minor road then the B3314 & a church: turn left.
4. Turn right off the B3314 at the first gate on a good cart track that soon becomes a hedged lane to the village of Trelights. Turn left at the tarmac road, go straight on at the first junction, turn right at the next (uphill, small triangle) then turn right (fp sign) through gates by a bungalow ('Kosylund').
3
5
'Kosylund'
Trevathan
2
Trelights
2. At Trevathan turn right on the access road to a junction, then head up the field via the hen run, aiming left of the trees.
stile & fb
2 fbs
Good view from here of the coast ahead
St Endellion
to Polzeath
A
B3314
4
1. Continue north on the road out of Chapel Amble, cross a stream then immediately turn left along the stream (fp sign). Keep left to a gate then the path becomes a clear one: follow it along the stream to a signed path junction & go right (not over the footbridge) to an access road. Turn right uphill (gate) to the road & turn left. Turn right just before the road crosses the stream (fp sign, stile) & walk through three narrow fields with the stream on your left. Follow the third field to the very end (ignore the track going right through a gate), & cross footbridges. Continue through thickets with the stream now on your right until a stile & footbridge lead into the corner of a field & the path disappears. Turn left, diverging slightly from the hedge on the left to a gap at the top of the field & join a track up through the gap to the buildings at Trevathan.
Rooke Farm
fb (don't use: go right)
1
d6 m1

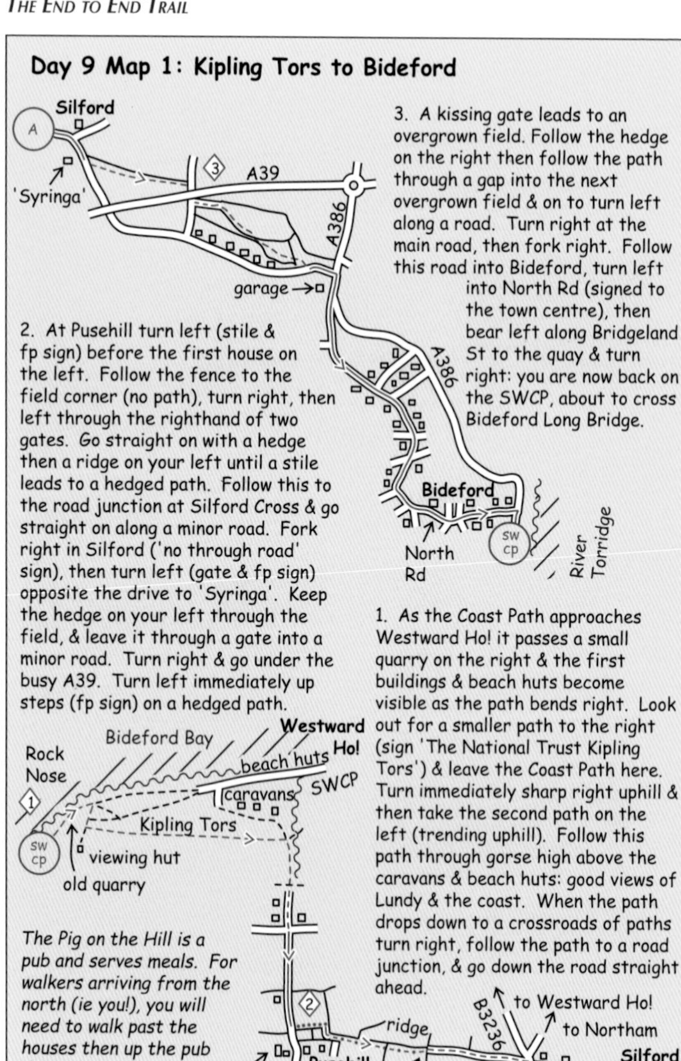
Day 9 Map 1: Kipling Tors to Bideford
Silford
A
'Syringa'
3
A39
A386
garage
3. A kissing gate leads to an overgrown field. Follow the hedge on the right then follow the path through a gap into the next overgrown field & on to turn left along a road. Turn right at the main road, then fork right. Follow this road into Bideford, turn left into North Rd (signed to the town centre), then bear left along Bridgeland St to the quay & turn right: you are now back on the SWCP, about to cross Bideford Long Bridge.
2. At Pusehill turn left (stile & fp sign) before the first house on the left. Follow the fence to the field corner (no path), turn right, then left through the righthand of two gates. Go straight on with a hedge then a ridge on your left until a stile leads to a hedged path. Follow this to the road junction at Silford Cross & go straight on along a minor road. Fork right in Silford ('no through road' sign), then turn left (gate & fp sign) opposite the drive to 'Syringa'. Keep the hedge on your left through the field, & leave it through a gate into a minor road. Turn right & go under the busy A39. Turn left immediately up steps (fp sign) on a hedged path.
A386
Bideford
North Rd
SW cp
River Torridge
1. As the Coast Path approaches Westward Ho! it passes a small quarry on the right & the first buildings & beach huts become visible as the path bends right. Look out for a smaller path to the right (sign 'The National Trust Kipling Tors') & leave the Coast Path here. Turn immediately sharp right uphill & then take the second path on the left (trending uphill). Follow this path through gorse high above the caravans & beach huts: good views of Lundy & the coast. When the path drops down to a crossroads of paths turn right, follow the path to a road junction, & go down the road straight ahead.
Bideford Bay
Westward Ho!
Rock Nose
beach huts
caravans
SWCP
1
Kipling Tors
SW cp
viewing hut
old quarry
The Pig on the Hill is a pub and serves meals. For walkers arriving from the north (ie you!), you will need to walk past the houses then up the pub drive to get in.
2
ridge
B3236
to Westward Ho!
to Northam
Silford
Pusehill
Pig on the Hill
stile
Silford Cross
to A39
A

SECTION 2

The Bristol Channel and the Welsh border: Barnstaple to Knighton

Start	Barnstaple
Finish	Knighton
Distance	330km (205 miles)
Road walking	23%. This section has the highest proportion of road walking, mainly due to a shortage of footpaths in the low-lying farmland and Levels of Somerset, and the crossing of two long motorway bridges.
Days	10 (main schedule), or 14 (alternative schedule)
Maps and guides	*Barnstaple to Chepstow:* this guide, strip maps Day 10 Map 1 to Day 15 Map 7; *Chepstow to Knighton:* Offa's Dyke Path guide

A number of published routes fill the gap between the South West Coast Path (SWCP) and Offa's Dyke Path (or the Cotswold Way, if you plan to follow this alternative: see below), but none quite fit the Trail bill, being either too indirect or missing some obvious walking opportunities, so we leave the SWCP at Barnstaple (rather than following it all the way to Minehead, which involves a much longer route round the north coast of Devon). Instead, the Trail goes inland and heads for the ranges of hills that overlook the Bristol Channel, taking in the highest points of Exmoor, the Brendon Hills and the Quantocks, before descending to cross the River Parrett in Bridgwater. The flat Somerset Levels are crossed to Cheddar and the Mendips, which again are crossed at their highest point. Once back on the plain, we follow disused railways and little-used footpaths before taking to a series of low ridges to avoid, as far as practical, the urban sprawl around Bristol. The River Avon is crossed on the M5 bridge, which has a footpath/cycleway alongside it, and more low ridges take you past Bristol and back to the coastal plain. More quiet paths lead to the original motorway bridge (now the M48) across the Severn and Wye estuaries to Chepstow in Wales on Day 15. From Chepstow the route follows the excellent Offa's Dyke Path national trail northwards to Knighton (which is nearly halfway to its end at Prestatyn on the North Wales coast).

Exmoor and the Quantocks are popular places. The walking is generally easy, and in good weather the views can be wonderful, with the paths and tracks along the ridges well used and easy to follow. After the Quantocks, the rights of

Section 2 Overview Map – Barnstaple to Knighton

way are often little used and not obvious on the ground. Invisible paths lead into Bridgwater, where the Trail has to go right through the town to cross the River Parrett. From Bridgwater the flat, former salt marshes of the Somerset Levels have to be crossed, and with few footpaths to follow, minor roads must be walked for sections of the way to Cheddar.

From Cheddar the Trail climbs to cross the Mendips, then drops back down to the plain, following footpaths and disused railway lines to the M5 crossing over the Avon. There is a foot and cycle path across this bridge, which avoids the need to walk into the centre of Bristol. (A route round to the east of Bristol would be too circuitous, and walking through the middle of the city would mean walking through miles of suburbia as well, so the route squeezes between the city and the Bristol Channel.) Rather than follow the rather industrialised coast of the Bristol Channel, the Trail goes back inland along the ridges of Kings Weston Hill, Coombe Hill and Spaniorum Hill, before crossing the flat farmland north to Aust, and the old Severn Bridge carrying the M48. This bridge also has a path for bikes and walkers, and leads to Chepstow and the start of the Offa's Dyke Path.

All the paths in the section preceding the Offa's Dyke Path can be followed in reasonable comfort, although there may be a few nettles occasionally, and not all the stiles are up to Lake District standard. Gates may be rickety and fences are sometimes electric, but paths that can't be followed while also enjoying yourself are not included in the route. (Detailed route-finding information from Barnstaple to Chepstow is on the End to End Trail strip map pages at the end of Section 2.)

From Chepstow the route along the Offa's Dyke Path roughly follows the Welsh border. The first day follows the River Wye through a lovely pastoral valley, with steep sides and limestone cliffs in places – the river has carved an impressive home for itself. Sometimes the path follows woods along the valley's edge, sometimes the riverbank, and this is a delightful stretch.

At Monmouth there is an abrupt change of direction, to follow the much smaller River Trothy west and then northwest through quiet farmland to the foot of the Black Mountains at Pandy. The mountains loom ahead alarmingly, but once the initial steep climb up from Pandy is over, the walking is easy, on good tracks along the whaleback Hatterrall ridge. When the ridge comes to an abrupt end, the path drops steeply down and into Hay-on-Wye. This is a very attractive old border town that is well worth pottering round, particularly if you like second-hand bookshops, of which the town is famously full.

From Hay the path follows the bank of the Wye again for a while, until the river meanders off east towards Hereford. The path continues north to Hergest Ridge, a smaller whaleback hill, and descends to Kington. From Kington to Knighton the path follows the old dyke itself, usually visible as a ridge through the fields.

Maps

1:25,000 Explorer maps

- 9 Exmoor
- 140 Quantock Hills & Bridgwater
- 141 Cheddar Gorge & Mendip Hills West
- 154 Bristol West and Portishead
- 14 Wye Valley & Forest of Dean
- 13 Brecon Beacons National Park (Eastern Area)
- 201 Knighton & Presteigne

1:50,000 Landranger maps

- 180 Barnstaple & Ilfracombe
- 181 Minehead & Brendon Hills
- 182 Weston-super-Mare
- 172 Bristol & Bath
- 162 Gloucester & Forest of Dean
- 161 The Black Mountains
- 148 Presteigne & Hay-on-Wye

Guidebooks

There are no suitable guidebooks covering the route in Section 2 preceding Offa's Dyke, although local walking guides are available covering most of the areas walked through. The strip maps at the end of this section, used in conjunction with OS maps, should be enough to keep you on the Trail.

- *Walking Offa's Dyke Path* by Mike Dunn (Cicerone, 2016). This guide includes a 1:25,000 OS map booklet, and this time the route is described in the right direction for us.

Recommendations

Get Mike Dunn's *Walking Offa's Dyke Path*. The map booklet is good enough to use without additional OS maps, provided you intend to stick to the official Offa's Dyke route. You should then buy Explorers 9, 140, 141 and 154, unless you already have some of the 1:50,000 alternatives.

If you intend to vary the route or use a guidebook without a wide strip of map coverage, then buy all the 1:25,000 Explorer maps listed, except for Explorer 201, unless you already have some of the 1:50,000 alternatives. Buy Landranger 148 rather than Explorer 201 to avoid buying an additional 1:25,000 map for Section 3. The number of maps in both series is the same, and the additional detail on the Explorer maps is useful in areas where the route-finding is complex. Don't rely only on a guidebook with narrow strip maps when walking Offa's Dyke – you do need OS maps as well.

Accommodation
Information is available from the following tourist information centres (TICs) and websites:

- **Barnstaple** TIC, The Square, Barnstaple, Devon, tel 01271 375000 www.staynorthdevon.co.uk
- **Exmoor** Coast and Country Ltd, tel 01984 634 565 www.exmoorholidayguide.co.uk
- www.visitsomerset.co.uk
- https://visitbristol.co.uk
- For accommodation in and near the **Quantocks** (including Bicknoller): www.quantockonline.co.uk
- For **Cheddar** and its surroundings: www.cheddarvillage.org.uk
- For **Offa's Dyke** go to www.nationaltrail.co.uk and the Offa's Dyke Association's website https://offasdyke.org.uk, which have comprehensive accommodation guides

Accommodation on Exmoor and around the Quantocks is sometimes limited, as in places the route is quite remote. You may want to consider booking ahead for some stage ends (Note: 'A' in stage numbers indicates a stage end on the alternative schedule – see Appendix A):

- **Challacombe** (Day 10, Day A14)
- **Warren Farm** and **Simonsbath** (Day 10)
- **Luxborough** (Day 11, Day A16)
- **Roadwater** (Day 11)
- **Bicknoller** (Day 12, Day A17): you will need to go off-route for accommodation
- **Sandford** (Day 14, Day A20)
- **Easton-in-Gordano** (Day 14)
- **Monmouth** (Day 16): if you want to camp at Monmouth Caravan Park, it is advisable to book in advance (tel 01600 714745)

Equipment shops

- Day 12: Millets, 42 Fore St, **Bridgwater** TA6 3NG, tel 01271 446339
- Day 13: The Gorge Outdoors, Hanlith House, The Cliffs, **Cheddar** BS27 3QA, tel 01934 742688

- Day 13: Mountain Warehouse, Draycott Rd, **Cheddar** BS27 3RU, tel 01934 740330
- Day 14: Country Innovation, 1 Broad St, **Congresbury** BS49 5DG, tel 01934 877333
- Days 14/15: There are a couple of shops off-route in **Weston-super-Mare**, and plenty in **Bristol**
- Day 16: Millets, 21 Monnow Street, **Monmouth** NP25 3EF, tel 01600 719187
- Day 18: Rohan, 23 Castle St, **Hay-on-Wye** HR3 5DF, tel 01497 822540

Alternative routes

There are many possible alternative routes for parts of this section. I have picked out a few that are particularly worth considering.

If you follow the main route of the End to End Trail from Barnstaple onto Exmoor, and the weather turns too bad for comfort, the Two Moors Way also gives you the option of heading north from Exe Head to the coast.

Alternatives from Barnstaple to the Quantocks

1. The Minehead Alternative: Follow the South West Coast Path (SWCP) all the way to its end at Minehead, then take a waymarked Macmillan Way West link to meet the main Macmillan Way West at SS 960 439 on Knowle Hill, which will take you via Withycombe and Williton to rejoin the Trail at Bicknoller, at the foot of the Quantocks. The link is described in the Macmillan Way West guidebook, but you will be following it in reverse. This route is not very direct, and misses out the Exmoor hills, so it is not the recommended way.
2. From Barnstaple, cut off the 'corner' (ie avoiding a detour to Braunton and Ilfracombe) and rejoin the SWCP further along the north coast. You can then continue to Minehead and follow the Minehead Alternative (see above). One way to cut the corner would be via Bratton Fleming (which is on the Trail) and Parracombe, to rejoin the SWCP at Woody Bay, before Lynmouth. This route doesn't appear in a guidebook, so you would need to follow maps alone.
3. From Barnstaple, follow the waymarked Macmillan Way West to the crest of Exmoor at Chains Barrow. You can then either continue on the End to End Trail across Exmoor, or descend from Exe Head on the Two Moors Way to rejoin the SWCP at Lynmouth, and then follow the Minehead Alternative (see above). Again, this route is rather indirect.

Guidebooks

- *Macmillan Way West*, Macmillan Way Association (2001); available from the Macmillan Way Association at www.macmillanway.org. This guide describes the route of the Macmillan Way West from Castle Cary in Somerset to Barnstaple.

The Cotswold Way and the Heart of England Way

This is an alternative to the End to End Trail's route via Bristol, Offa's Dyke and Shropshire. It involves leaving the main route in the Mendips, north of Cheddar (Day 14), and rejoining it on Cannock Chase in Staffordshire. The entire alternative route is on waymarked paths covered by guidebooks. The Limestone Link leads to Cold Ashton, north of Bath, then the Cotswold Way follows the Cotswolds to Chipping Campden. Alternatively, you can follow the Limestone Link for just a few kilometres then take the Monarch's Way through the middle of Bristol and join the Cotswold Way further north at Little Sodbury, which is about 4km further in total. From Chipping Campden, the Heart of England Way takes you between Birmingham and Coventry, then round north of Birmingham to Cannock Chase, where you join the Staffordshire Way and the main End to End Trail route.

Despite the quality of the Cotswold Way, this is not the recommended route for two main reasons. First, it means missing out the Welsh mountains (and indeed missing out Wales entirely). Second, it involves a lot of lowland farmland – the Heart of England Way doesn't climb over a 250m contour for its whole length.

Guidebooks

- *The Limestone Link*, Yatton Ramblers (revised 2007); available from Bath Ramblers at www.bathramblers.org.uk
- *The Monarch's Way, Book 2: Stratford-upon-Avon to Charmouth* by Trevor Antill (Monarch's Way Association, revised 2016); available from the Association at www.monarchsway.50megs.com
- *The Cotswold Way* by Kev Reynolds (Cicerone, 4th edition, 2016)
- *The Heart of England Way* by Stephen J Cross (Sigma Press, 2nd edition, 2018)

The Severn Way

The Severn Way follows the river north from Bristol. It's flat, of course, and there are a lot of meanders, so it's not very direct. You can pick it up either at the north end of the Avon Bridge over the M5, or, preferably, at Aust, rejoining the main End to End route at Ironbridge.

Guidebook

- *The Severn Way* by Terry Marsh (Cicerone, 2nd edition, 2019)

Alternative routes along the Welsh border

For anyone who has walked the Offa's Dyke path before, there are alternative routes for the first three of the four days. From Chepstow to Monmouth you can follow the Wye Valley Walk, which is waymarked and takes a parallel route up the Wye Valley. From Monmouth to Hay-on-Wye, the Offa's Dyke Castles Alternative provides a route somewhat east of the national trail, although it is not waymarked.

Guidebooks

- *The Wye Valley Walk* by the Wye Valley Walk Partnership (Cicerone, 2011; reprinted 2018)
- *Offa's Dyke Castles Alternative Route*, Offa's Dyke Association. This was formerly available from the Offa's Dyke Association, but is no longer in print. An updated version is, however, available to download from www.longwalks.org.uk (courtesy of the Offa's Dyke Association).

Pathside stream, Dunkery Beacon (Day 11)

DAY 10

Barnstaple to Warren Farm, Exmoor
The River Yeo and western Exmoor

Distance	34km (21 miles)
Ascent	1090m

From Barnstaple to Chepstow, detailed route-finding information is on the End to End Trail strip map pages at the end of this section, so you can now post your South West Coast Path guidebook home.

Today the Trail leaves the coast and heads for the hills for the first time. Pleasant wooded tracks lead inland from Barnstaple, following the River Yeo, then a gradual climb up to Bratton Fleming and a stretch of road walking bring you to the edge of Exmoor National Park. From the village of Challacombe, bridleways lead into the hills and true Exmoor moorland.

The way out of Barnstaple is a pleasant one (Day 10 Map 1), climbing up through the old village of **Pilton**, now a suburb of Barnstaple, and once the town has been left behind, so is the tarmac. An old lane, Smoky House Lane, runs east above the River Yeo. It is bounded by trees for much of the way and gives good walking, although it can be muddy in places. When it enters **Raleigh Wood**, an old wood of oaks and chestnuts, it gets even better.

When a minor road drops down into the valley from the west (Day 10 Map 2), you follow it briefly, then take to valley tracks through forestry and woodland, to cross the river and join the valley road at **Chelfham**.

Chelfham's most noticeable feature is its **railway viaduct**, which was restored in 2000, despite the fact that the railway, a narrow gauge line from Barnstaple to Lynton, has been closed since 1935.

After 1km of road northwards along the Yeo valley, you turn left at **Loxhore Cross**, then at **Loxhore Bridge** the Trail leaves the Yeo for a side valley. A track leads into woods, then you cross fields into forestry, and from **Loxhore Mill** take a short stretch of minor road, until the ascent to Exmoor starts with a stiff climb out of the valley (Day 10 Map 3) into the large village of **Bratton Fleming**.

Although Bratton Fleming is not very picturesque, it does have a shop and a bed and breakfast.

An uncle of **PG Wodehouse** was rector in Bratton Fleming for nearly 40 years, and the author used to spend his school holidays here.

From Bratton Fleming onwards, for the first time on the Trail it feels as if you are on the hills rather than in valleys, with higher hills usually visible ahead. A shortage of footpaths means that you can't avoid 3km of road walking, mostly uphill. Then an old bridleway crosses the Bray valley, and when it meets the road on the opposite side of the valley the route enters Exmoor National Park. A short stretch of road leads to **Challacombe**, the last village with a shop before Roadwater at the end of Day 11.

Challacombe is a pretty little village, with an old packhorse bridge, a ford, a shop/post office/café and a pub, the Black Venus Inn, which is a recommended halt and serves meals. There is bed and breakfast at Shoulsbarrow Farm 1km to the south, and at Home Place Farm in the village. Fill your water bottle before leaving Challacombe, especially if you're considering an overnight camp in the hills – see accommodation options suggested at Prayway Head below. There are few obvious sources of clean water on Exmoor, largely due to cattle churning up the streams.

On Exmoor itself the hills are huge, rolling expanses, the higher parts still moorland, although much of the lower land has been 'improved' in terms of farming (ie made into richer pasture and poorer walking). Walking is not too difficult, as the gradients are mainly gentle, apart from where streams such as the Exe have carved a channel, and you also have to dodge the wetter parts. A track leads east from Challacombe, south of and parallel to the B3358, up to the moorland of **South Regis Common**.

As you climb, cultivation gradually gives way to moorland, with characteristic mounded **field boundaries** that often have a fence or hedge on top. Also to be seen along here are remnants of beech tree windbreaks, planted by Frederic Knight all over his Exmoor estate in the second half of the 19th century.

At the eastern end of South Regis Common, the Trail turns north and crosses the B3358, now accompanied by the Devon/Somerset border. The Trail climbs (Day 10 Map 5) to the crest of the main Exmoor ridge at **Woodbarrow Gate** (476m), then turns east to enter Somerset properly and follow the ridge past Chains Barrow (487m) to the muddy source of the River Exe at **Exe Head**. (This is where you are glad you brought water with you – it may be moorland, but the

The River Exe and Warren Farm, from the top of the Postman's Path

cattle make the Exe too risky to drink from, even at its source.) At Exe Head the Trail crosses the Two Moors Way, which heads north from here to Lynmouth, on the coast.

On the climb up from the B3358 to Woodbarrow Gate, the route follows the main **watershed**. Water to the west flows into the Bray, then into the Taw and to Barnstaple and the Bristol Channel. Water to the east flows into the Barle, which heads southeast and joins the Exe flowing south to Exmouth, on the south coast. From Woodbarrow Gate, despite being less than 8km from the Bristol Channel, the Trail's route is in the gathering grounds of the Exe.

From Exe Head, the best route traverses the hillside above the infant River Exe, and once you're on the B3223 at **Prayway Head** a decision needs to be made about where you are going to spend the night (unless you plan to camp out discreetly in the hills, in which case you will need to have carried water from Challacombe).

The first option is to go off-route to stay in the hamlet of **Simonsbath**, where hotel accommodation is available at the Simonsbath House Hotel and the Exmoor Forest Inn. If you want to head for Simonsbath, stay on the B3223 and descend for about 1.5km. (Tomorrow you can climb back up to Warren Farm and rejoin the Trail by going via the B3223 to the east, and the bridleway north from Clovenrocks Bridge (SS 786 398), signed to Alderman's Barrow via Warren Bridge. The Postman's Path then takes you down to Warren Farm – see Day 10 Map 6.)

The second option is to head for **Warren Farm**, which is on the route and does bed and breakfast (tel 01643 831283). To reach Warren Farm more directly than the Simonsbath route, the Trail leaves the road at the crest of the ridge, at Prayway Head, and heads east across pathless, rough grazing land, parallel to the Exe but high above it to the south. When a gate on the right indicates a bridleway coming up from the B3223, and Warren Farm is visible on the opposite side of the valley, the Postman's Path drops down steeply to join the farm access road, which crosses the Exe and climbs up to the farm. Warren Farm is in a particularly isolated location, at an altitude of nearly 400m in the middle of the hills.

Your third option is to push on to the campsite at **Westermill Farm**, 6km beyond Warren Farm, and 2km off-route. The best approach is to stay on the Trail to Larkbarrow Corner, then turn right down the road to the campsite (see Day 11 Map 1).

DAY 11

Warren Farm, Exmoor, to Roadwater
High Exmoor and the Brendon Hills

Distance	29km (18 miles)
Ascent	660m

Today the route crosses the highest of the Exmoor hills, Dunkery Beacon (519m), then descends to Wheddon Cross and continues east through the farmland of the less wild Brendon Hills. The entire day is within the Exmoor National Park, and the farmland tends to be grazing land rather than crop cultivation, so the walking is generally good. There is no contest between Exmoor and the Brendons, though – after the ridge from Great Rowbarrow to Dunkery Beacon, the remainder of the day is an anticlimax. On the Rowbarrow to Dunkery ridge the views are extensive, the walking easy, and Dunkery Beacon is the highest point on the Trail before the Black Mountains in Wales.

From Warren Farm a good track crosses **Elsworthy Moor** to meet a minor road near **Larkbarrow Corner** (Day 11 Map 1). The road is lined with beech hedges, presumably another relic of Frederic Knight's estate management in the 19th century.

The route continues east across the high moors, over **Almsworthy Common**, where it meets the main watershed again (Day 11 Map 2). The watershed is followed, approximately, over **Exford Common**, then up to the highest of the Exmoor hills – **Great Rowbarrow** (510m) and, along the ridge, **Dunkery Beacon** (519m) (Day 11 Map 3).

There is an alternative bad weather route to the south of the main Great Rowbarrow–Dunkery Beacon ridge (Day 11 Maps 2 and 3), which is probably a better idea if the hills are in cloud; but if there are any views to be had at all, the panorama from the tops is a must, particularly to the north across the Bristol Channel to South Wales.

Dunkery Beacon is at the eastern end of the remaining true moors. The Trail now heads southeast, briefly on the northwest side of the watershed (River Avill), which is odd, since the Trail is going southeast from the watershed. The route quickly loses height, falling below 400m for the first time since shortly after leaving Warren Farm.

A gallop over the wild moorlands of Exmoor, with sea breezes charged with ozone, will do more to recruit the health of the jaded and blanched Londoner, than quarts of the Elizabethan Brunnen at Homburg, or the waters of German Spas

Evelyn Burnaby, A Ride from Land's End to John o' Groats, 1893

The descent by the River Avill is pleasant, rough pasture, followed by a riverside woodland path through **Blagdon Wood**. A steep climb up through **Little Quarme Wood** leads to the village of **Wheddon Cross**, the highest village on Exmoor at 300m (Day 11 Map 4).

At Wheddon Cross there is a pub, the Rest and Be Thankful, there are a number of bed and breakfasts in and around the village, and there is also a camping barn at Blagdon Farm (tel 01643 841393, see Day 11 Map 3).

From near Wheddon Cross a bridleway runs south then east up to **White Moor** and then **Lype Hill**, at 423m the highest point in the Brendon Hills. While the views are good, there is no moorland here, just improved pasture with little character.

The Trail follows the main watershed again over White Moor and Lype Hill, and from there you are back on its northwest side (and will remain so until you cross the Shropshire–Staffordshire border on Day 22).

Paths lead down to **Luxborough**, a parish split between two villages – **Churchtown** has the church, **Kingsbridge** has the pub (Day 11 Map 5).

Descent towards Roadwater

Luxborough used to provide accommodation for the iron-ore miners of the Brendon Hills (the mines were at their peak in the mid 19th century). The pub at Kingsbridge is the Royal Oak of Luxborough, although it tends to be more of a restaurant at weekends, so booking is advisable if you want a meal (tel 01984 640319). The Royal Oak has the only accommodation in the area. It is not of the budget variety, but it is certainly very comfortable. Wild camping would be possible before dropping down to Kingsbridge, or after climbing back out again, but you would need to be discreet about it unless you sought permission from one of the farms. Alternatively, consider taking an additional day over it, stopping overnight at Wheddon Cross and Roadwater.

From Kingsbridge the walking improves again. A track climbs out of the Washford valley and along a ridge (Day 11 Map 6). The views are good and the immediate environment is quiet and pastoral. A path through **Langridge Wood** then descends back to the Washford River, and the quiet valley road leads to the village of **Roadwater** in about 1.5km.

Roadwater has a pub (the Valiant Soldier, recommended), a shop/post office, and bed and breakfast at the pub and at Wood Advent Farm (just outside the village – see Day 12 Map 1).

DAY 12

Roadwater to Bridgwater
The Quantocks

Distance	36km (22 miles)
Ascent	930m

Today the Trail leaves the Exmoor National Park to climb steeply up to the main Quantocks ridge. The Quantocks are a compact group of moorland hills running northwest to southeast for about 20km (12 miles) from the coast near Watchet. The highest point is Wills Neck, and the Trail follows the ridge and crosses the top of Wills Neck, before dropping down to cross the farmland between the hills and the large town of Bridgwater. The Trail goes through the middle of Bridgwater (reluctantly), as this is the lowest place the River Parrett can be crossed.

From Roadwater a minor road then field paths climb steeply up then down the other side of a hill to cross the B3190 (Day 12 Map 1). The descent from here is through parkland to **Nettlecombe Court**. (Nettlecombe Court, in a beautiful location and with its own church, used to be the seat of the Raleighs, and is now a field centre.) The main drive from Nettlecombe Court leads to a field path above a stream, leading southeast to the village of **Monksilver**, where the route leaves the national park.

Monksilver is not particularly pretty, but does have a pub, the Notley Arms. There is no shop.

From Monksilver to Bicknoller, at the foot of the Quantocks, the Trail follows an intricate course along field edges, often on invisible paths (Day 12 Map 2). Thankfully it's only about 5km, and it does have two features of interest. The first is the view ahead of the Quantocks, and the second is the West Somerset Railway, a preserved steam railway running between Minehead and Taunton. The Trail crosses the railway at stiles just before Bicknoller, but you are likely to hear train whistles long before you get there, and if you are lucky you will see a train steam past in front of you, with the Quantocks for a backdrop.

Bicknoller is a pretty little village with a pub, the Bicknoller Inn (recommended), a 15th-century church and a shop (limited opening hours). There are bed and breakfasts in the nearby villages of Stogumber and Crowcombe (see www.quantockonline.co.uk for the latest information) but none in Bicknoller.

The West Somerset Railway near Bicknoller

From Bicknoller a delightful, steep climb on a good track up **Bicknoller Combe** leads to the main north–south ridge of the Quantocks (Day 12 Map 3). The next 9km along the ridge, heading south then southeast, give an excellent moorland walk with a choice of paths – the Trail tries to avoid those used by the off-road vehicles that appear to be officially tolerated on the Quantocks tracks. If you want to descend from the ridge for refreshment, there is a pub worth considering along the southwest foot of the hills – the Carew Arms in Crowcombe, 1.5km off-route from Crowcombe Combe Gate, though there is a stiff climb back up if you succumb to the temptation.

From Crowcombe Combe Gate the Trail climbs past Triscombe Quarry to **Wills Neck**, at 386m the highest point in the Quantocks, and an exceptional viewpoint – Bridgwater and the Mendips come into view here (Day 12 Map 4). (If the weather is poor, an alternative route from the col at Triscombe Stone avoids the summit – see map.)

About 2km after Wills Neck, the Trail skirts the summit of **Lydeard Hill** (Day 12 Map 5), then descends to the east, via Blaxhold Farm, Enmore and Goathurst (Day 12 Map 6), towards Bridgwater. At **Enmore**, the Tynte Arms inn is just off-route (unless you are following the bad weather alternative, which takes you past it), has accommodation, good beer and food, and there is also bed and breakfast 2km further along the road at Lexworthy Farmhouse, by another pub, the Enmore Inn.

Enmore's school, passed on the way into **Enmore**, was the first free elementary school in England, opened in 1810 and still in use. Enmore church, just off-route to the north, has a Norman doorway and a tower dating from about 1500.

By the road just before Goathurst, the Trail passes the **Temple of Harmony**, a folly completed in 1767 in the grounds of Halswell Park. The temple is based on the 1st-century temple of Fortuna Virilis in Rome, and is open to visitors on summer Sunday afternoons.

The road walking between Blaxhold Farm and **Goathurst** is not very inspiring, but the last 3km into **Bridgwater** is a lot better, through the Meads (meadows) to the southwest of the town (Day 12 Map 7), although care with route-finding is needed as some of the paths are invisible. Bridgwater has all facilities, including banks and accommodation.

Bridgwater, shabby little town on the slimy estuary Parrett, from whose mud bricks are made; a town of red brick buildings, billboards, and an absurdly lofty spire on a squat tower – hideous!

Jessie Barker Gardner, From Land's End to John O'Groat's, 1930

Bridgwater is not a pretty place, although it has a long history, since its strategic position at the crossing of the River Parrett has meant that a large proportion of traffic into and out of the southwest has come this way for centuries. Bridgwater was fortified in the 9th century, but the 14th-century St Mary's church is now the only remaining medieval building.

DAY 13

Bridgwater to Cheddar
The Somerset Levels

Distance	33km (20 miles)
Ascent	180m

Most of today's walking is only just above sea level on the Somerset Levels, land that was originally salt marsh and frequently flooded. Drainage work probably started at least 1500 years ago, much of it carried out by the monks of Glastonbury, Athelney and Muchelney. Although there are still floods from time to time, the Levels are now drained by a crisscross pattern of straight ditches and wider rivers, with pumping stations at intervals, and a continuous maintenance programme is needed to keep the system operational. Seawater floods used to reach a long way inland – in 1607 Glastonbury was completely surrounded by water when a sea wall gave way at Burnham. These days, drainage management is carried out to try to retain the traditional character of the Levels, which depends on seasonal freshwater flooding. The Levels will be allowed to continue to flood regularly, as they have done for hundreds of years.

The landscape is fascinating, but there are few public footpaths on the Levels, so the Trail follows quiet minor roads – you are likely to meet more tractors than cars.

Escape from Bridgwater (Day 13 Map 1) is not particularly pleasant, but the recommended route is a lot better than the more obvious one along the A372. A footbridge over the M5 motorway leads to the start of the Levels, where the land is flat and every field boundary is a drainage ditch. Walkers are scarce around here, so what footpaths there are tend to be invisible on the ground.

A footbridge over the wide King's Sedgemoor Drain leads to the village of **Bawdrip** (Day 13 Map 2), where there is a church, but no shop. The Knowle Inn (pub, no accommodation) is 1km west of the village on the A39.

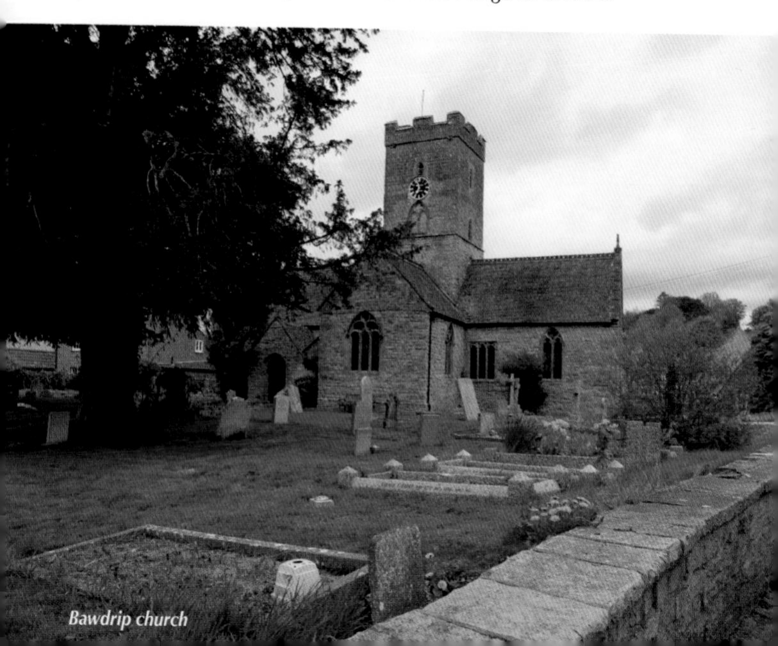

Bawdrip church

From Bawdrip, paths through the fields lead over a low ridge to **Cossington**, which has a church and a pub. From here you cross a couple of fields then join a minor road north (Bell Lane), down the hill and over the Levels again, crossing the River Brue, to reach **Westham** (Day 13 Map 3). At Gold Corner Bridge a big pumping station at the end of the Huntspill River gives an idea of the scale of the technology that keeps the Levels drained.

If you require the facilities at Mark (see below), you can take a shortcut early on Day 13 after crossing the River Brue – see Day 13 Map 3. Three options are shown on the map, but the best is the track that leaves the long straight section of road and takes you past Burnt House Farm B&B.

At Westham the Trail leaves the road to cross fields to **Blackford**, where there is a pub, the Sexeys Arms. Accommodation round here is scattered, but there is bed and breakfast at Burnt House Farm (tel 01278 641280, see shortcuts above) and the Old Barn (tel 01278 641552) in Mark, and one of the two pubs in Mark also has accommodation (the Pack Horse, tel 01278 641209). Mark is about 3km to the west of Blackford, and it also has a village shop/post office. There is an excellent cheap campsite at Splott Farm, 2km east of Blackford, and there is a bed and breakfast a bit closer to the route at Poplar Farm, 1km north of Blackford (ST 415 487, tel 01934 712087).

From Blackford a bridleway and invisible footpaths lead north, past **Middle Stoughton**, along the edge of the steep escarpment of **Brinscombe Hill** (Day 13 Map 4), covered in orchards overlooking more Levels, and across to **Axbridge** and Cheddar.

Dropping down from Brinscombe Hill (Day 13 Map 5) you then reach a bridge and follow the Cheddar Yeo riverbank into **Cheddar**, emerging conveniently at a campsite. (If you are in a hurry there is an alternative way into Cheddar, crossing the bridge over the Cheddar Yeo and walking along the road.) As well as the campsite (Cheddar Bridge Touring Park), Cheddar has a youth hostel, shops, pubs, banks and plenty of other accommodation.

Cheddar also has tourists who come to see the gorge, the caves and savour the Cheddar experience. It is the closest thing to Blackpool you will see on the route, surpassing even Land's End.

Cheddar Gorge is best seen from the road that winds up it, so if you are staying overnight, and the blisters are not too bad, walk up the B3135 to take it in. The vertical limestone cliffs on either side of the narrow gorge are 120m high in places, and it is one of the most spectacular places in England. (In the summer months I'd leave it as late in the evening as you can, when the gorge will be less busy.)

Here is a deep, frightful chasm in the mountain, in the hollow of which, the road goes, by which they travel towards Bristol; and out of the same hollow, springs a little river, which flows with such a full stream, that, it is said, it drives twelve mills within a quarter of a mile of the spring

Daniel Defoe, letting you know what the tourist shops replaced

DAY 14

Cheddar to Easton-in-Gordano
The Mendips and Cadbury Camp

Distance	45km (28 miles)
Ascent	920m

Cheddar is on the 'shore' of the Levels, and Cheddar Gorge cuts deep into the edge of the Mendips, which stretch inland for about 40km (25 miles) from the Bristol Channel. The Trail climbs up from Cheddar to cross the Mendips at their highest point, Beacon Batch (325m), then follows a lower ridge westwards before descending to more Levels north of the hills. The going is dead flat for most of the way north towards the coast, then a series of low ridges parallel to the coast gives good walking until the day's end, just before the mouth of the River Avon is reached at the edge of Bristol.

The exit from Cheddar is a steep one, climbing up to follow the southern edge of the gorge (Day 14 Map 1). At the top of the climb you meet the top of Jacob's Ladder stairs, which is an alternative way, up steps, from Cheddar (for which privilege you have to pay an admission fee). There is a wooden observation tower here (free), which gives good views of Cheddar and the Levels. As you continue through scrubland along the top of the gorge, in places you can peer down into the bottom.

After crossing the B3135, above the gorge, there is very pretty walking through the wooded limestone valleys of **Black Rock** and **Long Wood** Nature Reserves. Once out of the woods it's a stiff climb up to the moorland and **Beacon Batch** (Day 14 Map 2).

Cotswold Way/Heart of England Way alternative route
(See 'Alternative routes' at the beginning of Section 2.) If you want to follow this alternative, you should leave the main route of the Trail at the summit of Beacon Batch, and head northeast to pick up the Limestone Link at the foot of the hill and follow it eastwards to **Cold Ashton**, north of Bath, where it joins the Cotswold Way. *The Limestone Link* guidebook describes the route. Alternatively you can just follow the Limestone Link a few kilometres to **Compton Martin**, then follow the Monarch's Way through **Bristol** to join the Cotswold Way further north at **Little Sodbury**.

The main Trail route continues west from the summit of Beacon Batch along the ridge for a bit, then descends north into North Somerset (formerly part of the county of Avon), to pick up more good walking along a lower ridge heading west again. This is **Dolebury Warren**, National Trust land with the remains of an Iron Age fort at the far end of the ridge, and fine views to the north. There is a short further stretch in the Mendip foothills before dropping down to the plain at **Sandford** (Day 14 Map 3).

At Sandford if you turn right rather than left on the A368 there is a pub, the Railway Inn, owned by Thatcher's cider brewery next door – in fact the Trail goes through the orchard behind the brewery. There is bed and breakfast opposite the pub at Sandford Cottage (tel 01934 824839 or 07894 269929) and a shop five minutes further along the road.

For the next 6km from Sandford, the Trail takes advantage of another disused railway line, the Strawberry Line, which used to run from a junction at Yatton via Cheddar to Wells. It closed in 1965, and this section is now a cycle track.

At **Yatton** (Day 14 Map 4) the disused railway joins the railway from Bristol to Weston-super-Mare, so the Trail has to leave it to follow invisible paths through fields and meadows between the outskirts of Clevedon and Nailsea, towards Easton-in-Gordano and the Bristol Channel at the end of the day.

Before reaching the coast, the Trail meets the M5 motorway again (Day 14 Map 5), shadowing it along a low wooded ridge to **Cadbury Camp**, a big Iron Age hill fort, then dropping down to **Clapton in Gordano** (Day 14 Map 6), a small village with no accommodation but an excellent pub, the Black Horse (highly recommended, but no food in the evenings). If you're looking for somewhere to camp, the Black Horse is a good place to ask around – you may be allowed to pitch in the beer garden, or in a local customer's garden. (Clapton in Gordano sometimes has hyphens and sometimes doesn't, but I've stuck with the Ordnance Survey spelling.)

To reach the official stage end, push on a bit further, climbing back up to the ridge and crossing the deep wooded valley of **Bullock's Bottom** (Day 14 Map 7). The walking is mostly pleasant farmland, until you cross the busy A369 to reach **Easton-in-Gordano**.

There are a handful of pubs scattered around Easton and neighbouring Pill, including one where the route crosses the A369. Accommodation is harder to find though. The Days Inn hotel (tel 01275 373709) is 1km off-route along the A369 (see Day 14 Map 7) inside Gordano motorway services. There used to be a few bed and breakfasts in Easton and Pill, but at the time of writing none remain open. Easton itself is entirely made up of housing estates – if you want shops, etc, head for the centre of Pill (see Day 15 Map 1). Bradford Lodge bed and breakfast (tel 0117 982 3211) is just across the A4/B4054 roundabout at Avonmouth, only 0.5km off-route. To reach it, turn left rather than right when you leave the motorway bridge (Day 15 Map 1).

DAY 15

Easton-in-Gordano to Chepstow
Motorway bridges and other follies

Distance 29km (18 miles)
Ascent 370m

From Easton-in-Gordano there are ahead of you three formidable obstacles to an enjoyable walk to the start of the Offa's Dyke Path at Chepstow in Wales (the beginning of Section 3). These obstacles are the River Avon, the industrial and suburban sprawl in the City of Bristol, and the Bristol Channel.

The only bridge over the Avon downriver of the Clifton Suspension Bridge in Bristol is the M5 motorway bridge. The bridge is reached through a housing estate in Easton (Day 15 Map 1), and there is a foot and cycle path alongside the motorway. While nobody could call this sort of proximity to so much traffic pleasant, there are at least some interesting views to be had of the river valley and some of the outskirts of Bristol. There are shops near the north end of the bridge, and Shirehampton is only a five-minute walk away from here if you want banks, etc.

The bridge brings you out of North Somerset into the City of Bristol's territory – the second obstacle before the Bristol Channel. Following the coast to avoid the sprawl leads to a lot of road walking and a lot of industry, and is not very pleasant; further inland than the M5, and the industry gives way to housing estates, which are little better as walking territory. There is, however, a narrow green corridor through much of this, along Kings Weston Hill, after which only a short stretch in the housing estates leads to the edge of the city and countryside once more.

The climb up to **Kings Weston Hill** starts from a residential road near the north end of the bridge, and immediately you are in wooded parkland, with the city forgotten (Day 15 Map 2). The Trail continues along the ridge and on to climb up to the **Blaise Castle** folly, built by Thomas Farr in 1766 (it looks like a real castle at first glance). After this you drop down to the suburb of **Henbury**, where there is a hidden gem – the Hansel and Gretel cottages of **Blaise Hamlet**.

The **Blaise Hamlet cottages**, grouped around a green, were designed by John Nash in 1809, and housed pensioners from the Blaise Estate. The route passes a few metres from them and they shouldn't be missed.

As you cross the railway, leaving the last estate on the edge of Henbury (Day 15 Map 3), you enter the green belt land of South Gloucestershire (another part of the former county of Avon). The Trail now heads north to Aust, crossing the M5 for the last time before coming to the last hill of the day – **Spaniorum Hill**. This is the last good viewpoint before Aust, as for the next few kilometres it's back to sea level on more drained land. At the bottom of the hill is the village of **Easter Compton** (Day 15 Map 4), which has a welcoming pub, the Fox.

Little-used field paths and green lanes (Day 15 Map 5) lead past **Pilning** to **Aust**, where there is another pub and a motorway service station (Day 15 Map 6). The motorway used to be the M4, but is now the M48 (the new M4 bridge is further south). From Aust the M48 crosses the Bristol Channel, the third and greatest obstacle of the day, to reach Chepstow. Again, this bridge has a footpath and cycleway.

There is also…an ugly, dangerous, and very inconvenient ferry over the Severn, to the mouth of the Wye; namely, at Aust; the badness of the weather, and the sorry boats; at which, deterred us from crossing there

Daniel Defoe (so be thankful for the bridge)

The **M48 road bridge** was constructed in the 1960s. It's a suspension bridge with a main span of 1000 metres, side spans of 300 metres, and its towers are about 130m above sea level. It can be dangerous in windy weather, and sometimes has to be closed to traffic – this is one of the reasons the second crossing, the new M4 bridge, had to be built. Walking across it can be hard work if the weather is poor.

Chepstow Castle, on your left as you descend to the bridge

Halfway across the main span of the bridge is a **county boundary** – the Trail leaves South Gloucestershire and enters Gloucestershire proper. The bridge continues high above Beachley Point, and 2km after entering Gloucestershire, still on the bridge, the Trail enters Monmouthshire, Wales, as it crosses the River Wye.

After the path leaves the bridge (Day 15 Map 7), it roughly shadows the line of the River Wye, along the edge of housing estates and under the A48, for the short distance to the centre of **Chepstow** and the beginning of the Offa's Dyke Path.

Chepstow is a historic town on the Wye with accommodation and all the services you would expect of a small town, although there is no campsite nearby. Greenman backpackers hostel is in the centre of the town.

For the next four days you will be using your Offa's Dyke Path guidebook, so this is the end of the strip maps until Day 20.

DAY 16

Chepstow to Monmouth
The River Wye

Distance	28km (17 miles)
Ascent	960m

The Trail follows the Offa's Dyke Path up the beautiful Wye Valley all day today, and if you walk it on a sunny day in spring, the woodland is magical, covered in bluebells, wood anemones and other flowers. There are other bluebell woods on the route from Cornwall to Sutherland, but there are none to match the Wye Valley. There are also stretches of the old dyke along the valley edge, and the impressive ruins of Tintern Abbey below.

Leave Chepstow by crossing the old bridge over the Wye back into Gloucestershire and go straight on (without following the road round to the left). After a few yards the Offa's Dyke Path comes in from the right – keep straight on, following your guidebook.

Old Wye Bridge, Chepstow

The Trail follows the wooded valley edge on the eastern side of the Wye, passing high above Tintern Abbey. There is a riverside option from **Brockweir** to **Bigsweir Bridge**, which adds an extra 1km to the walk, but it is worth it scenically, and walking by the river is very easy (the stage length is measured this way as it's the option I'd recommend). Whichever route you choose, about 1km before Bigsweir Bridge you reach an important (but invisible) milestone – this point marks 25% of your journey completed.

For most of the way to the town of Monmouth you are in **Gloucestershire**, the River Wye forming the boundary between Wales and England; but in Redbrook, about 5km before reaching Monmouth, you leave Gloucestershire for good and re-enter **Wales**.

Monmouth ('…'tis rather a decayed than a flourishing town' – Defoe) is an ancient and attractive place, and has shops, banks and plenty of accommodation, including limited camping at Monmouth Caravan Park in the town (SO 502 129, on the B4233). You are advised to book camping in advance (tel 01600 714745).

DAY 17

Monmouth to Pandy
The River Trothy

Distance	26km (16 miles)
Ascent	610m

Follow your Offa's Dyke Path guidebook for a second day, now in rolling hills through farmland up the River Trothy. It's a pleasant enough day's walking, but there's nothing to compare to yesterday's delights, or tomorrow's for that matter. Even Offa's Dyke itself is elsewhere – it heads north from Monmouth and you don't meet it again until Kington, on Day 19.

Today is best seen as a link between the Wye Valley and the Black Mountains – farmland walking with only the spectacular ruins of 12th-century White Castle to enliven the day.

White Castle, Monmouthshire

White Castle is well worth exploring, with most of the walls still standing and the moat full of water. It drives home very effectively how impregnable these Norman fortresses must have been in their time.

There is no longer an inn at **Llantilio Crossenny** (Llandeilo Gresynni), but there is now a pub, the Hogs Head, 2km further on at **Great Treadam** – it has limited opening hours though, so plan ahead if you want to catch it open. The Hunter's Moon Inn at **Llangattock Lingoed**, 3.5 km from Pandy, has accommodation. As the day progresses, the whaleback mountains ahead beckon, until you reach the foot of them at the day's end at **Pandy**.

Pandy is a scattered community stretched along the A465 trunk road, in the shadow of the Black Mountains. There are a few bed and breakfasts here and three pubs, of which the Rising Sun (0.5km south of the A465 crossing point) has a campsite.

DAY 18

Pandy to Hay-on-Wye
The Black Mountains

Distance	26km (16 miles)
Ascent	750m

This is the third of four days on the Offa's Dyke Path, and you're in the hills all day. These hills are the Black Mountains, part of the Brecon Beacons National Park, although the Brecon Beacons proper are further west, separated from the Black Mountains by the River Usk. The Black Mountains are much higher than any hills so far encountered, but the day is an easy one if the weather is reasonable. After the initial climb up from Pandy, the route follows the Hatterrall ridge all day – the path is clear and the ridge gentle. The views are also very good, as you would expect from a high ridge along the edge of the hills, with a height of 703m attained at the highest point, approaching Hay-on-Wye. This is the highest on the End to End Trail so far, and the highest reached in Wales.

The day starts in Monmouthshire, then follows the border between Monmouthshire and Herefordshire along the **Hatterrall ridge**. Before the high point of the ridge, the northernmost corner of Monmouthshire is reached, and from here you have Powys on your left and Herefordshire on your right. Hay-on-Wye is in Powys (just), and also marks the northern tip of the national park.

There are all facilities and plenty of accommodation in **Hay-on-Wye**, which is a small town of great character, the main danger being the second-hand bookshops. Remember that you will have to carry anything you buy, unless you can get it posted home. There is camping and hostel accommodation at the Baskerville Hall Hotel across the river.

DAY 19

Hay-on-Wye to Knighton
Hergest Ridge and the Dyke

Distance	45km (28 miles)
Ascent	1450m

This is a long day, and a stop in Kington is an option, splitting this leg into sections of 23km (15 miles) and 22km (13 miles). Alternatively, camping is possible at Rockbridge Park, Discoed, near Presteigne. Staying here would split the 68km (42 miles) between Hay and Craven Arms (Day 20) into two reasonable days instead of a long and a short one.

The Trail follows the Offa's Dyke Path again all day. The way out of Hay-on-Wye crosses the River Wye for the last time, and briefly follows it north (downstream!) before leaving it to strike north across farmland to **Newchurch** and **Gladestry**. The stretch to Kington is more interesting, climbing up to over 400m along **Hergest Ridge**, crossing the old racecourse on the summit plateau.

Kington is another border town, this time on the English side. It has rather less character than Monmouth, Hay and Knighton, however, although it has a youth hostel, a campsite and some good pubs.

From Kington to Knighton the line of the ancient dyke is followed across hilly farmland – the dyke's direction is indicated by a ditch and ridges through the fields, often with a line of trees growing along it. The route crosses the border between Powys and Herefordshire four times during the day.

Knighton is just on the Powys side of the border, and has a railway station, pubs, bed and breakfasts, shops, post office, banks and an Indian restaurant. There is a tourist information centre on the edge of the town, and camping is available nearby at Panpwnton Farm.

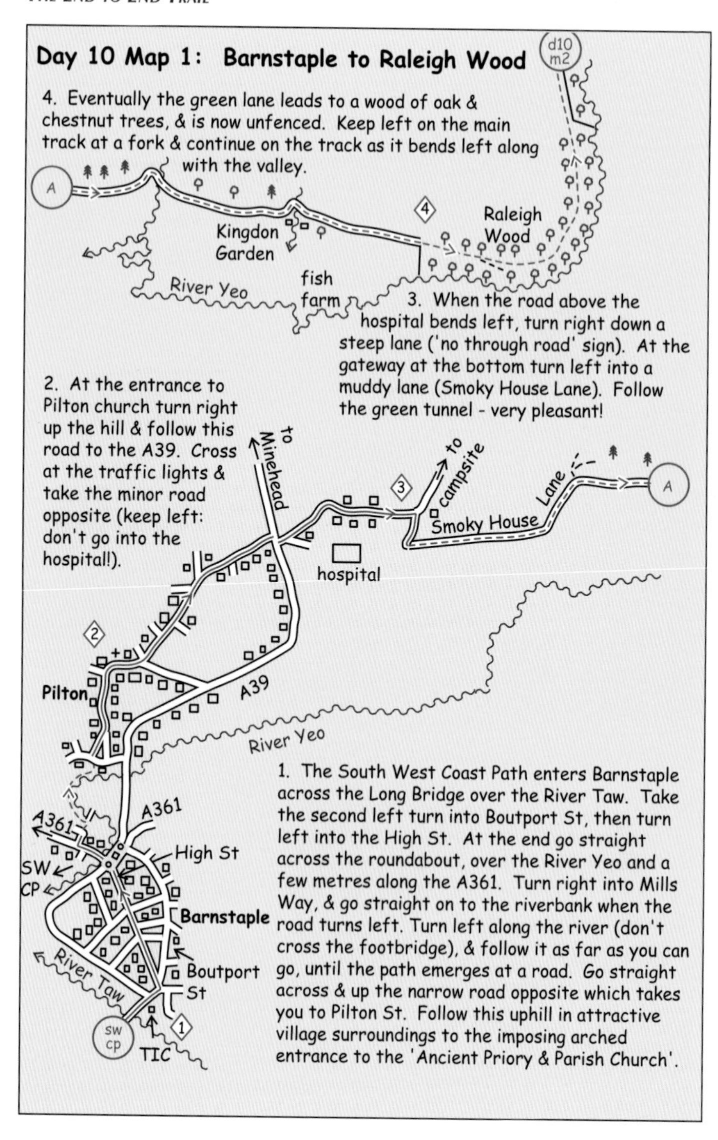

Day 10 Map 1: Barnstaple to Raleigh Wood
d10 m2
4. Eventually the green lane leads to a wood of oak & chestnut trees, & is now unfenced. Keep left on the main track at a fork & continue on the track as it bends left along with the valley.
A
Kingdon Garden
Raleigh Wood
River Yeo
fish farm
3. When the road above the hospital bends left, turn right down a steep lane ('no through road' sign). At the gateway at the bottom turn left into a muddy lane (Smoky House Lane). Follow the green tunnel - very pleasant!
2. At the entrance to Pilton church turn right up the hill & follow this road to the A39. Cross at the traffic lights & take the minor road opposite (keep left: don't go into the hospital!).
to Minehead
to campsite
Smoky House Lane
A
hospital
Pilton
A39
River Yeo
1. The South West Coast Path enters Barnstaple across the Long Bridge over the River Taw. Take the second left turn into Boutport St, then turn left into the High St. At the end go straight across the roundabout, over the River Yeo and a few metres along the A361. Turn right into Mills Way, & go straight on to the riverbank when the road turns left. Turn left along the river (don't cross the footbridge), & follow it as far as you can go, until the path emerges at a road. Go straight across & up the narrow road opposite which takes you to Pilton St. Follow this uphill in attractive village surroundings to the imposing arched entrance to the 'Ancient Priory & Parish Church'.
A361
A361
High St
SW CP
Barnstaple
River Taw
Boutport St
sw cp
TIC

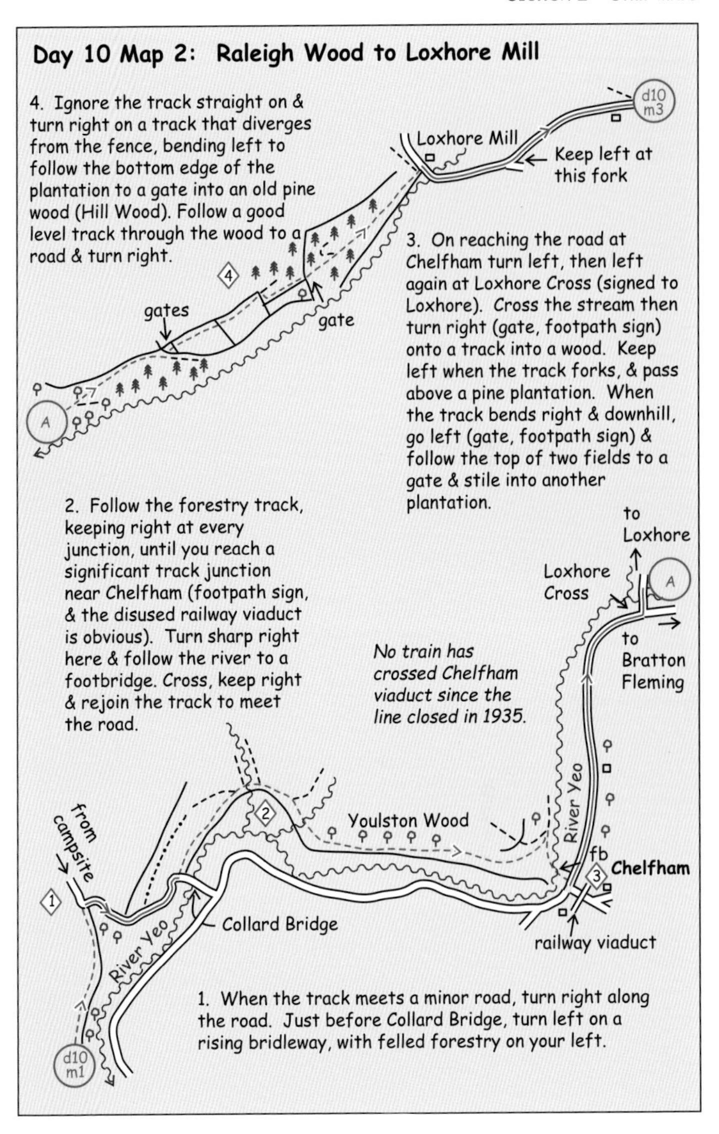
Day 10 Map 2: Raleigh Wood to Loxhore Mill
4. Ignore the track straight on & turn right on a track that diverges from the fence, bending left to follow the bottom edge of the plantation to a gate into an old pine wood (Hill Wood). Follow a good level track through the wood to a road & turn right.
d10 m3
Loxhore Mill
Keep left at this fork
4
gates
gate
3. On reaching the road at Chelfham turn left, then left again at Loxhore Cross (signed to Loxhore). Cross the stream then turn right (gate, footpath sign) onto a track into a wood. Keep left when the track forks, & pass above a pine plantation. When the track bends right & downhill, go left (gate, footpath sign) & follow the top of two fields to a gate & stile into another plantation.
A
2. Follow the forestry track, keeping right at every junction, until you reach a significant track junction near Chelfham (footpath sign, & the disused railway viaduct is obvious). Turn sharp right here & follow the river to a footbridge. Cross, keep right & rejoin the track to meet the road.
to Loxhore
Loxhore Cross
A
to Bratton Fleming
No train has crossed Chelfham viaduct since the line closed in 1935.
from campsite
1
2
Youlston Wood
River Yeo
fb
3
Chelfham
River Yeo
Collard Bridge
railway viaduct
d10 m1
1. When the track meets a minor road, turn right along the road. Just before Collard Bridge, turn left on a rising bridleway, with felled forestry on your left.

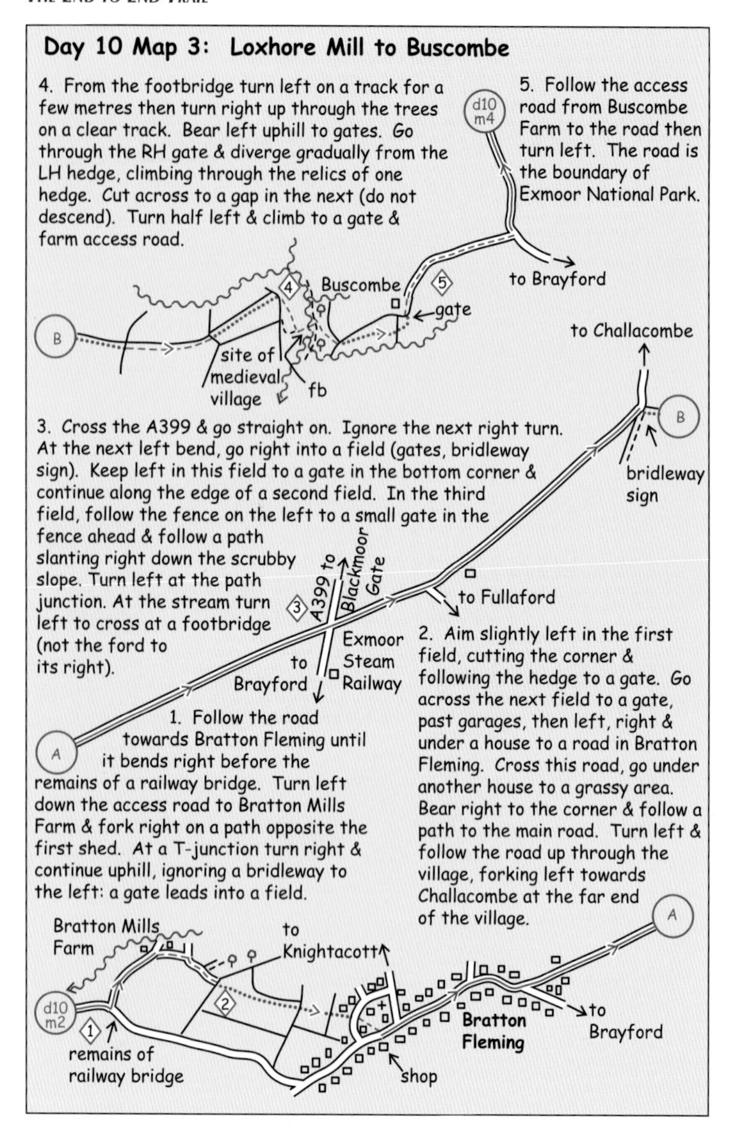
Day 10 Map 3: Loxhore Mill to Buscombe
4. From the footbridge turn left on a track for a few metres then turn right up through the trees on a clear track. Bear left uphill to gates. Go through the RH gate & diverge gradually from the LH hedge, climbing through the relics of one hedge. Cut across to a gap in the next (do not descend). Turn half left & climb to a gate & farm access road.
d10 m4
5. Follow the access road from Buscombe Farm to the road then turn left. The road is the boundary of Exmoor National Park.
Buscombe
to Brayford
gate
B
site of medieval village
fb
to Challacombe
3. Cross the A399 & go straight on. Ignore the next right turn. At the next left bend, go right into a field (gates, bridleway sign). Keep left in this field to a gate in the bottom corner & continue along the edge of a second field. In the third field, follow the fence on the left to a small gate in the fence ahead & follow a path slanting right down the scrubby slope. Turn left at the path junction. At the stream turn left to cross at a footbridge (not the ford to its right).
B
bridleway sign
A399 to Blackmoor Gate
to Fullaford
Exmoor Steam Railway
to Brayford
2. Aim slightly left in the first field, cutting the corner & following the hedge to a gate. Go across the next field to a gate, past garages, then left, right & under a house to a road in Bratton Fleming. Cross this road, go under another house to a grassy area. Bear right to the corner & follow a path to the main road. Turn left & follow the road up through the village, forking left towards Challacombe at the far end of the village.
A
1. Follow the road towards Bratton Fleming until it bends right before the remains of a railway bridge. Turn left down the access road to Bratton Mills Farm & fork right on a path opposite the first shed. At a T-junction turn right & continue uphill, ignoring a bridleway to the left: a gate leads into a field.
A
Bratton Mills Farm
to Knightacott
d10 m2
remains of railway bridge
Bratton Fleming
to Brayford
shop

Day 10 Map 4: Buscombe to South Regis Common

At the eastern end of South Regis Common the route is joined by the Tarka Trail, waymarked with the print of an otter's paw.

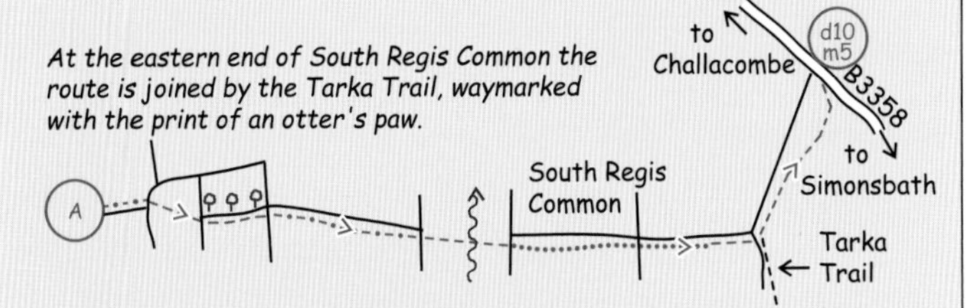

2. The track out of Challacombe climbs up along a ridge & then along the flank of South Regis Common: the first Exmoor moorland on the walk. There is a clear track initially, then you pass a shed, following the right edge of this field & the next. At the field corner go through the righthand gate then aim slightly right to a gate at the near end of a line of mature beech trees. Follow an old track with the line of trees on your left. From here the route over South Regis Common is easy to follow: just keep the field boundary on your left. The boundary is an old 'mound' hedge, some of it with a fence, some with trees, but always easy to follow. The path sometimes wanders right to avoid wet areas. When you meet a clear cross-track, turn left along it to cross the B3358 at gates.

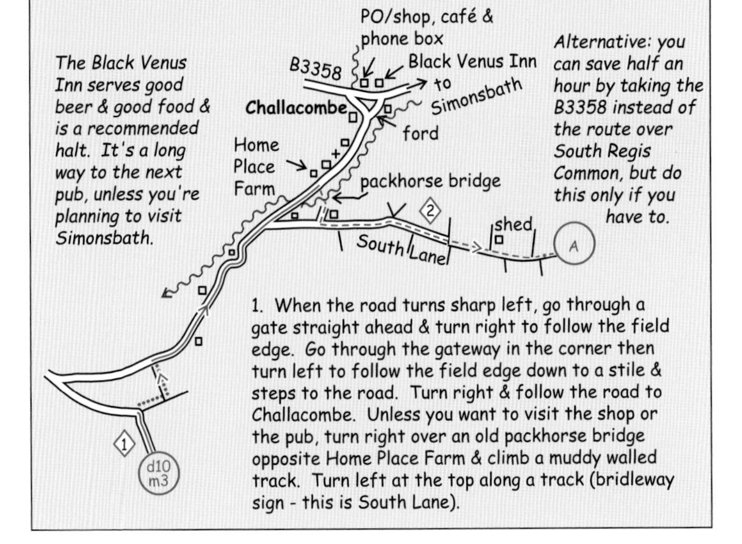

The Black Venus Inn serves good beer & good food & is a recommended halt. It's a long way to the next pub, unless you're planning to visit Simonsbath.

Alternative: you can save half an hour by taking the B3358 instead of the route over South Regis Common, but do this only if you have to.

1. When the road turns sharp left, go through a gate straight ahead & turn right to follow the field edge. Go through the gateway in the corner then turn left to follow the field edge down to a stile & steps to the road. Turn right & follow the road to Challacombe. Unless you want to visit the shop or the pub, turn right over an old packhorse bridge opposite Home Place Farm & climb a muddy walled track. Turn left at the top along a track (bridleway sign - this is South Lane).

Day 10 Map 5: South Regis Common to Exe Head

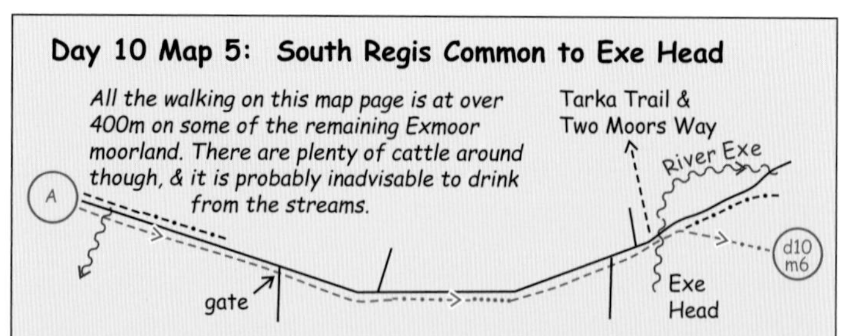

2. When you reach a gate, go through it & continue past Pinkery Pond (a reservoir), with the fence now on your right. Continue past the pond & on to a pair of gates on your right. Go through the second gate & continue, with the fence now on your left. (At the next gate a path goes left from a gate to the Ordnance column on Chains Barrow, which you can visit if you wish.) Continue through three gates to Exe Head, the source of the River Exe. Cross the stream on a cart track, which bends right & soon ends. Keep straight on from the end of the cart track on a grassy track (100 degrees), contouring the slope.

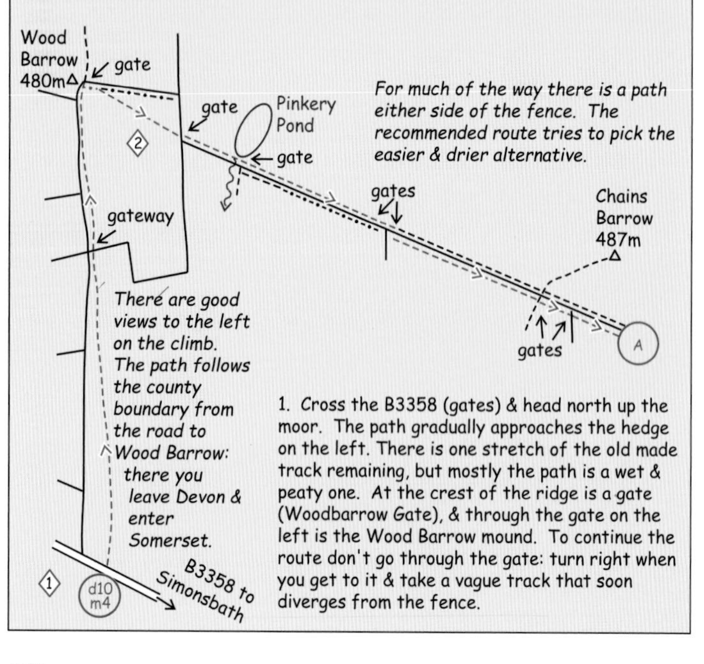

1. Cross the B3358 (gates) & head north up the moor. The path gradually approaches the hedge on the left. There is one stretch of the old made track remaining, but mostly the path is a wet & peaty one. At the crest of the ridge is a gate (Woodbarrow Gate), & through the gate on the left is the Wood Barrow mound. To continue the route don't go through the gate: turn right when you get to it & take a vague track that soon diverges from the fence.

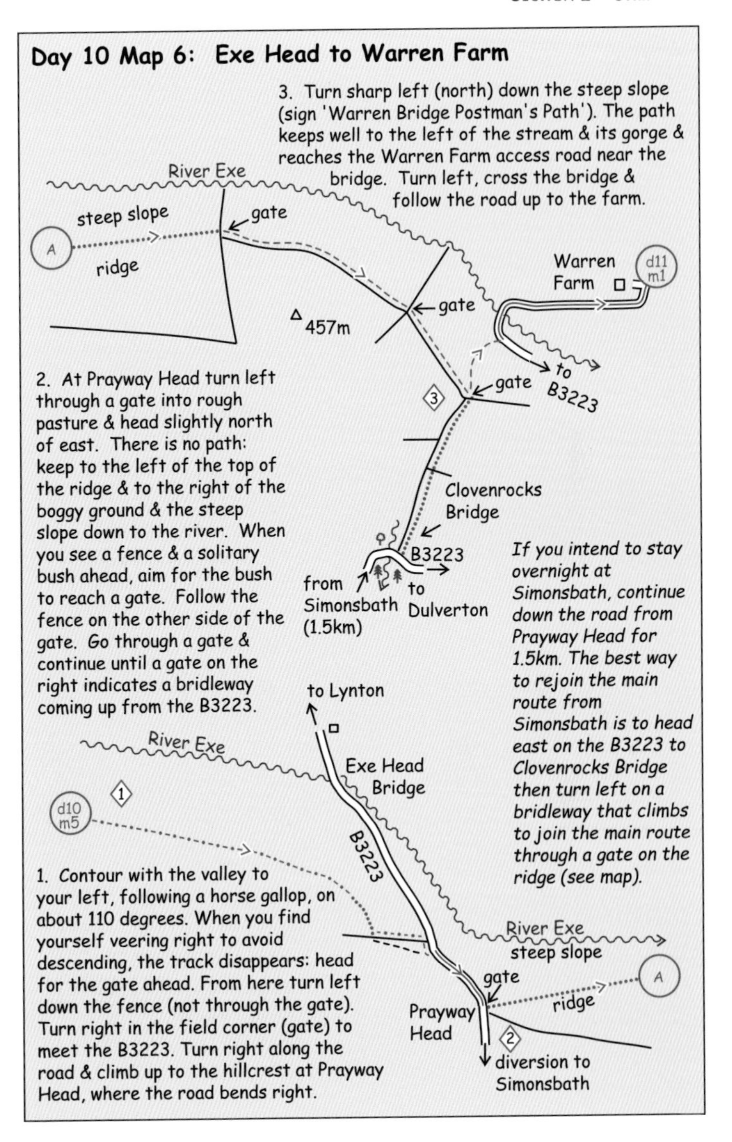

Day 10 Map 6: Exe Head to Warren Farm
3. Turn sharp left (north) down the steep slope (sign 'Warren Bridge Postman's Path'). The path keeps well to the left of the stream & its gorge & reaches the Warren Farm access road near the bridge. Turn left, cross the bridge & follow the road up to the farm.
River Exe
steep slope
gate
A
ridge
Warren Farm
d11 m1
457m
gate
to B3223
2. At Prayway Head turn left through a gate into rough pasture & head slightly north of east. There is no path: keep to the left of the top of the ridge & to the right of the boggy ground & the steep slope down to the river. When you see a fence & a solitary bush ahead, aim for the bush to reach a gate. Follow the fence on the other side of the gate. Go through a gate & continue until a gate on the right indicates a bridleway coming up from the B3223.
3
gate
Clovenrocks Bridge
B3223
from Simonsbath (1.5km)
to Dulverton
If you intend to stay overnight at Simonsbath, continue down the road from Prayway Head for 1.5km. The best way to rejoin the main route from Simonsbath is to head east on the B3223 to Clovenrocks Bridge then turn left on a bridleway that climbs to join the main route through a gate on the ridge (see map).
to Lynton
River Exe
Exe Head Bridge
1
d10 m5
B3223
1. Contour with the valley to your left, following a horse gallop, on about 110 degrees. When you find yourself veering right to avoid descending, the track disappears: head for the gate ahead. From here turn left down the fence (not through the gate). Turn right in the field corner (gate) to meet the B3223. Turn right along the road & climb up to the hillcrest at Prayway Head, where the road bends right.
River Exe
steep slope
gate
A
ridge
Prayway Head
2
diversion to Simonsbath

Day 11 Map 1: Warren Farm to Almsworthy Common

2. At the road turn left & follow it as far as a cattle grid. Turn right after the cattle grid on a good track signposted 'Exford 3' with a fence & field boundary on the right.

to Porlock

cattle grid

d11 m2

gates

Larkbarrow Corner

to campsite (2km)

A

If it's not too windy you should by now be getting used to the constant singing of skylarks above you. These birds are much more difficult to spot on the ground.

1. When the access road turns left into the Warren Farm farmyard, go through the gate ahead ('Public Bridleway Larkbarrow Corner 2'). Follow the cart track through another gate, then about 100 metres further on take the left fork through a gate on the left. Continue in your original direction on a good track, now with the field boundary on the right. Follow the path along the field boundary, cutting the corner at one point. From the head of Rams Combe a track heads off across the moor to the northeast: follow it to a field corner near Larkbarrow Corner. It is easy to follow. Go through the gate then take the path ahead (60 degrees). Keep in the same direction, ignoring a fork left, to join the road at a gate in the field corner.

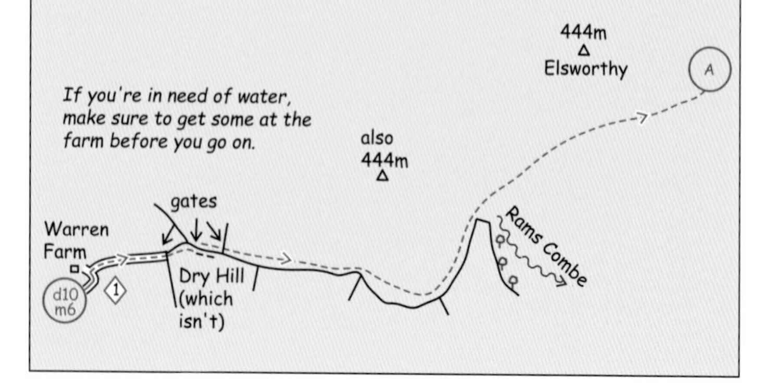

Day 11 Map 2: Almsworthy Common to Little Rowbarrow

Sign formerly on Great Rowbarrow: 'Bronze Age Cairns 3500-4000 years old. Please respect.' The views from here & along the ridge are extensive & very fine indeed: a great place to be on a clear day.

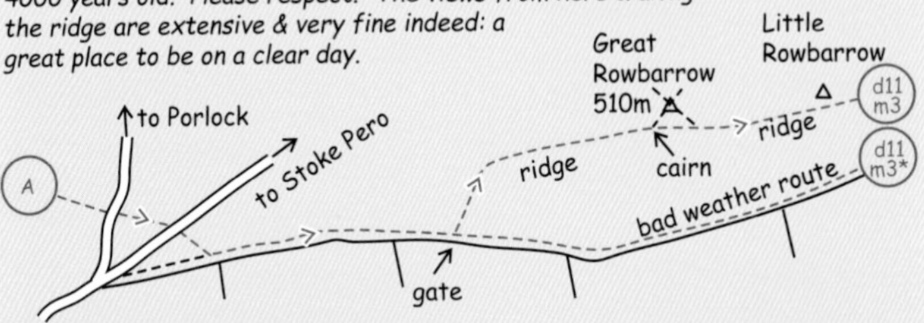

2. The path crosses the northern slope of Exford Common on a bearing averaging about 110 degrees, although it follows the contours of the slope. Cross two minor unfenced roads to turn left on a good track alongside the hedge that forms the southern boundary of the unenclosed moorland. Follow this track past a slight bend to the right, then turn left up a small path through the heather opposite a gate. This path leads to the ridge & along it to the cairn on Great Rowbarrow. From here a good track eastwards gives a glorious ridge walk to Dunkery Beacon.

In poor weather you can avoid the ridge walk by continuing along the track by the hedge to the south of the ridge (marked 'bad weather route' on the map). This leads to Dunkery Gate (Day 11 Map 3) where the main route is rejoined.

d11
m1
1
Almsworthy
Common
to
Porlock
2
gates
A
Exford
Common
464m
to
Exford

1. Follow the track along the edge of Almsworthy Common to gates where a lane starts. Don't go down the lane but continue along the edge of the moor to reach the road. Turn left along the road for about 150 metres then turn right (east) across Exford Common on a clear path (not marked on older OS maps). Ignore a minor left fork shortly after leaving the road.

Day 11 Map 3: Little Rowbarrow to Little Quarme Wood

3. When the track down the Avill valley leaves the wood at a gate continue along it until it crosses a side stream, then immediately take an old sunken path that forks right (uphill). At the road, cross & follow a good track climbing steeply through Little Quarme Wood ('Public Bridleway Wheddon Cross').

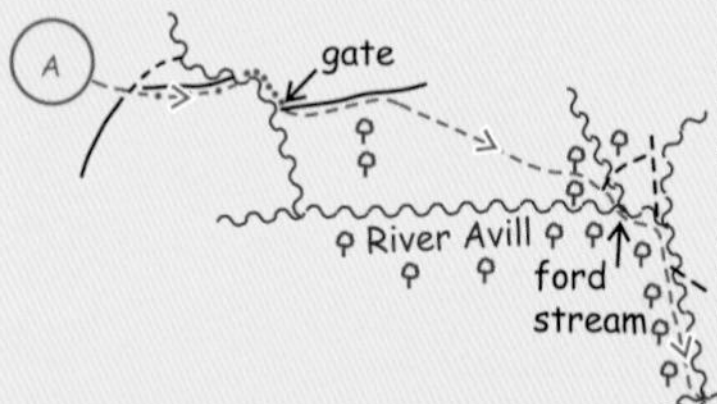

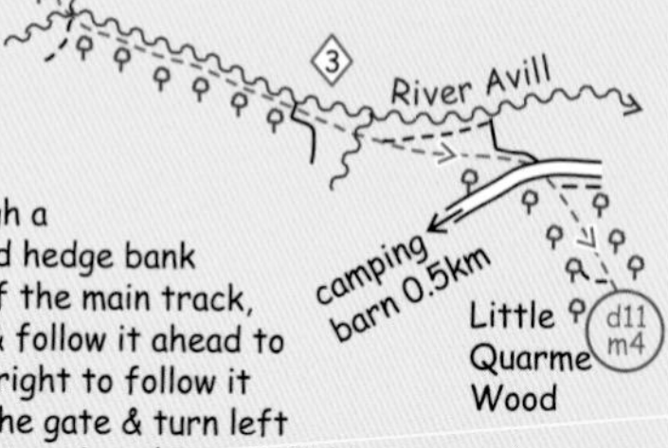

A
gate
River Avill
ford
stream
3
River Avill
camping barn 0.5km
Little Quarme Wood
d11 m4

2. At Dunkery Gate turn right down the road for a few metres, then before the bridge turn left on a cart track (sign 'Wheddon X 3'). Go through a gate into rough pasture. When a ruined hedge bank comes up from the right, fork right off the main track, go through the gap in the hedge bank & follow it ahead to a stream. Cross the stream then turn right to follow it down to a gate (no path). Go through the gate & turn left to follow the hedge bank. Go through a gap in a decrepit field boundary (trees & mound), & continue for a few metres until you can join a track that descends to the right. As the track nears the valley bottom it enters the trees. When a bridleway signed to Spangate goes left across a side stream keep straight on (signed 'Drapers Way') to ford the River Avill & follow a good track through the woods down the valley. Ignore the turns to Brockwell & Combeshead: keep to the valley, with the river on your left.

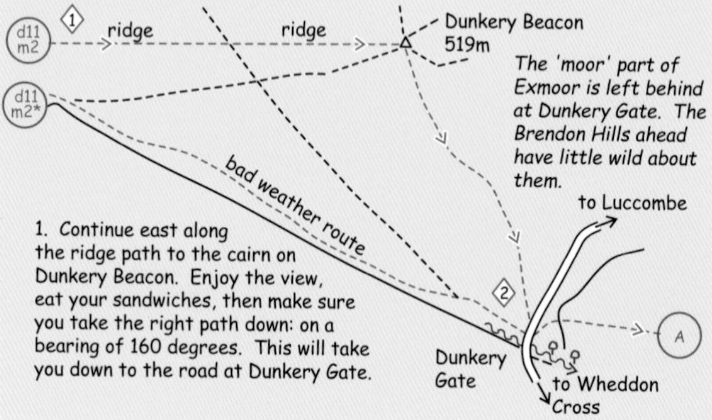

d11 m2
1
ridge
ridge
Dunkery Beacon 519m
d11 m2*
bad weather route

The 'moor' part of Exmoor is left behind at Dunkery Gate. The Brendon Hills ahead have little wild about them.

to Luccombe
2
A
Dunkery Gate
to Wheddon Cross

1. Continue east along the ridge path to the cairn on Dunkery Beacon. Enjoy the view, eat your sandwiches, then make sure you take the right path down: on a bearing of 160 degrees. This will take you down to the road at Dunkery Gate.

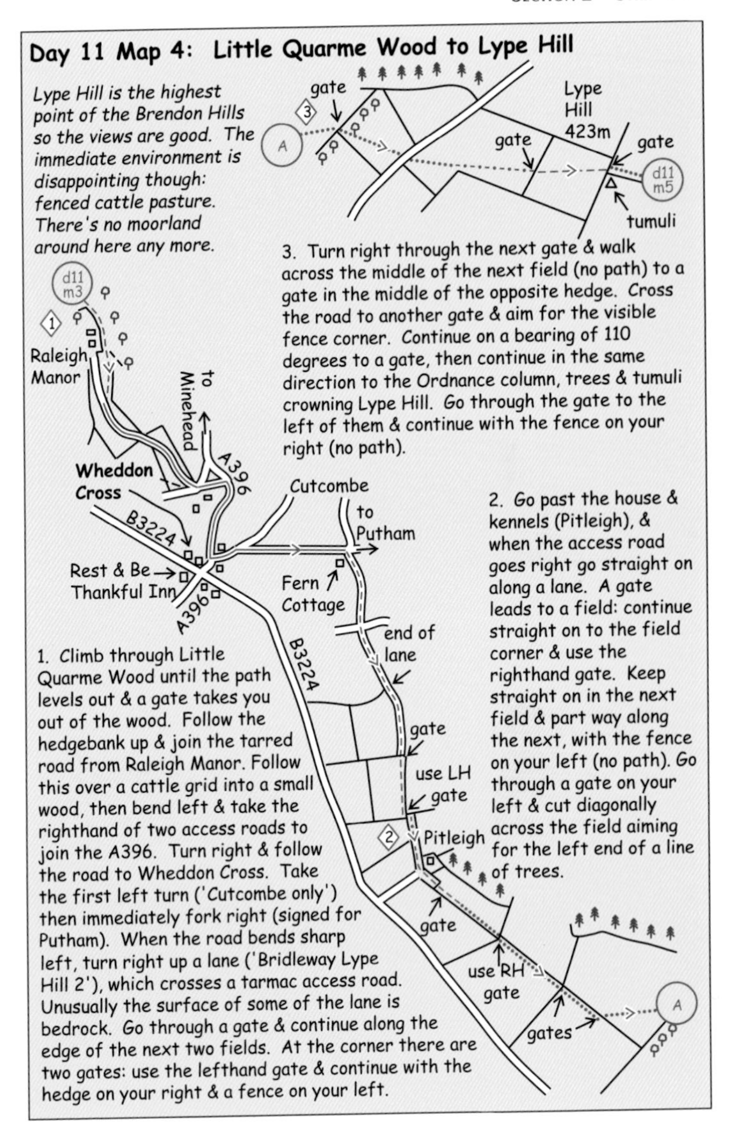
Day 11 Map 4: Little Quarme Wood to Lype Hill
Lype Hill is the highest point of the Brendon Hills so the views are good. The immediate environment is disappointing though: fenced cattle pasture. There's no moorland around here any more.
gate
3
A
Lype Hill 423m
gate
gate
d11 m5
tumuli
3. Turn right through the next gate & walk across the middle of the next field (no path) to a gate in the middle of the opposite hedge. Cross the road to another gate & aim for the visible fence corner. Continue on a bearing of 110 degrees to a gate, then continue in the same direction to the Ordnance column, trees & tumuli crowning Lype Hill. Go through the gate to the left of them & continue with the fence on your right (no path).
d11 m3
1
Raleigh Manor
to Minehead
A396
Wheddon Cross
Cutcombe
to Putham
B3224
Rest & Be Thankful Inn
A396
Fern Cottage
end of lane
B3224
2. Go past the house & kennels (Pitleigh), & when the access road goes right go straight on along a lane. A gate leads to a field: continue straight on to the field corner & use the righthand gate. Keep straight on in the next field & part way along the next, with the fence on your left (no path). Go through a gate on your left & cut diagonally across the field aiming for the left end of a line of trees.
gate
use LH gate
2
Pitleigh
gate
use RH gate
gates
A
1. Climb through Little Quarme Wood until the path levels out & a gate takes you out of the wood. Follow the hedgebank up & join the tarred road from Raleigh Manor. Follow this over a cattle grid into a small wood, then bend left & take the righthand of two access roads to join the A396. Turn right & follow the road to Wheddon Cross. Take the first left turn ('Cutcombe only') then immediately fork right (signed for Putham). When the road bends sharp left, turn right up a lane ('Bridleway Lype Hill 2'), which crosses a tarmac access road. Unusually the surface of some of the lane is bedrock. Go through a gate & continue along the edge of the next two fields. At the corner there are two gates: use the lefthand gate & continue with the hedge on your right & a fence on your left.

Day 11 Map 5: Lype Hill to Kingsbridge

2. Pass the pub on your left then turn right at the T-junction. In 40 metres fork left uphill into a lane (bridleway signs). Continue up this lane, keeping straight on when the farm access track turns left into a field, through gates & over the crest of the hill until the lane ends at a field corner (gate). Continue along the ridge (no path) with the hedge on your left: a lovely stretch of walking with good views.

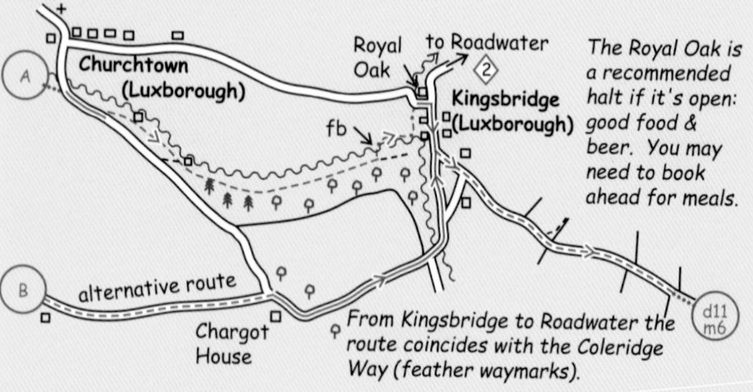

1. From Lype Hill the paths are mostly invisible: gates show the way. Go ahead to a gate, then ahead (east) across a field to another. Bear slightly left to another gate, go through & follow the fence on your right to another gate. Go through & head right (east) to the bottom field corner where an old track heads down towards the valley (signed to Luxborough). Take care on the descent, as the rocky surface can be very slippery in the wet. A good track goes right though a gate on the descent: this is a faster but inferior route to Kingsbridge. The main route continues down the old lane to meet another in the valley: keep right of the overgrown section on the descent. Turn right, then right again into a field immediately before a ford. Cross two fields to a road, turn right along the road, then left along the drive to Thorney Cottage (signed to Luxborough). Continue on the path through the woods past the cottage, eventually turning left off it over a footbridge into a field on the left. Keep by the stream initially, then at the end climb to a stile, a house, a short access road & the Royal Oak.

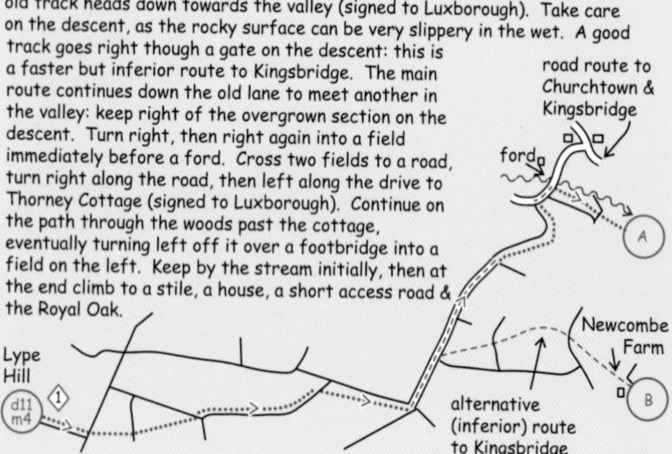

Day 11 Map 6: Kingsbridge to Roadwater

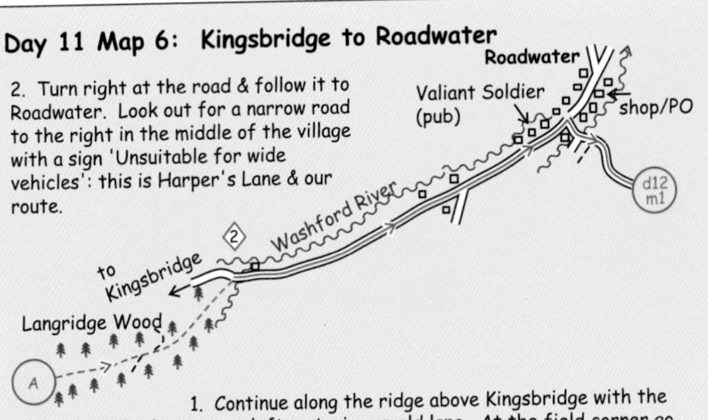

1. Continue along the ridge above Kingsbridge with the hedge on your left, entering an old lane. At the field corner go through the gate with a barn on your right & continue ahead to meet a lane. Go through the gate straight ahead into a field (signed to Roadwater) & head straight across, keeping left of a line of grassy mounds (no visible path). Keep left of the field corner to go through a small gate, & continue, with a hedge on your right. Go through a gate in the field corner, then turn right & diverge from the hedge (150 degrees) between gorse bushes. Keep right of the highest point to reach a gate & road.
Turn left immediately on a cart track signed to to Roadwater & follow it through one field to a gate & along the edge of the next. The path disappears briefly, but continue along the field edge as it bends right, to reach a stile at the corner. Follow the left edge of the next field to gates into the forestry & a good forestry track.
When the track bends left, fork right on a lesser track (footpath sign). Eventually another track comes in from the right, then the track forks again: keep right & continue to the road.

The cist in Langridge Wood is just to the right of the path.

It is a prehistoric buried stone chamber with a big capstone.

Day 12 Map 1: Roadwater to Monksilver

2. The path above the stream to Monksilver is not always clear to follow, although the general direction is obvious. Initially keep above the stream & trees. About halfway to Monksilver you need to descend to a gate & cross a side stream.

3. A gate then leads to a field: climb up the steep bank ahead, bearing left to a stile & a clear path in the trees, with a fence on the right. When a gap gives access to the field on the right ('Permitted footpath'), take this & follow the field edge.

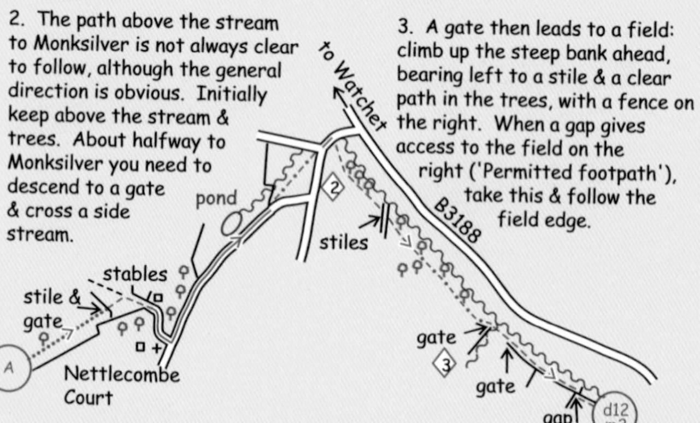

1. Climb steeply up the road from Roadwater. Turn left at a stile into a wood (signed to Chidgley) & follow the path to the top of the wood. At the end of the path enter the field on the right, & keep left to cross a stile. Follow the hedge round to the right (no path) & uphill, over a stile, & up around the top edge of a wood. Diverge from the trees slightly to cross a road then follow a cart track up the next field. A gap leads through trees, then continue uphill with a hedge on the left. The field levels out: cut the final corner to a stile (footpath junction & sign: head for Nettlecombe). Go straight on along the right edge of two fields (excellent views ahead & to the left, including Flat Holm & Steep Holm islands), then a fenced track leads to the B3190. Cross to a stile (signed to Nettlecombe) & bear left in the wood (no path), descending slightly to a gate in the fence angle. Cross the parkland, keeping parallel to the fence to your right until a gate leads to one of the drives of Nettlecombe Court (now a field centre). Follow the drive to the right through a gate & down to the main access road by the house & church. Turn left along the road. When the road bends right after a pond, go straight on (gate) along the original line of the road, now a grassy track. A gate leads to a road: go straight on then right over a stile (signed to Monksilver).

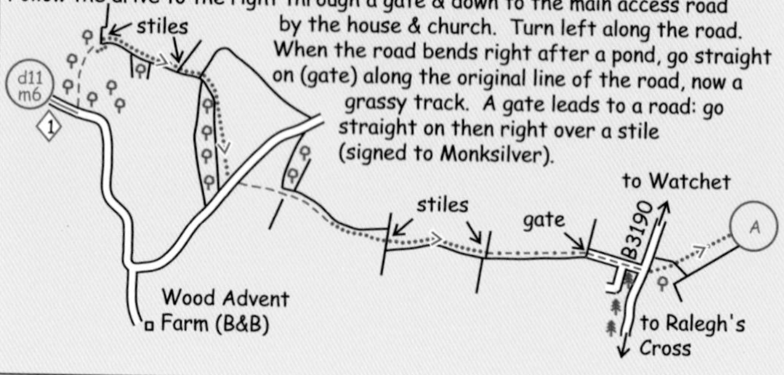

Day 12 Map 2: Monksilver to Bicknoller

4. Walk up the drive, through a gate, then take the small gate on the right into a field. Aim half left to a footbridge. Turn left to a stile then across the next field to a big oak, a bridge & the field corner (stile). Cut the corner to a stile, cross the railway, & aim half left in the next field to stiles leading to a lane & the A358.

5. Cross the A358 & follow Dashwoods Lane into Bicknoller. Keep left at the triangle & straight on at the crossroads up Hill Lane.

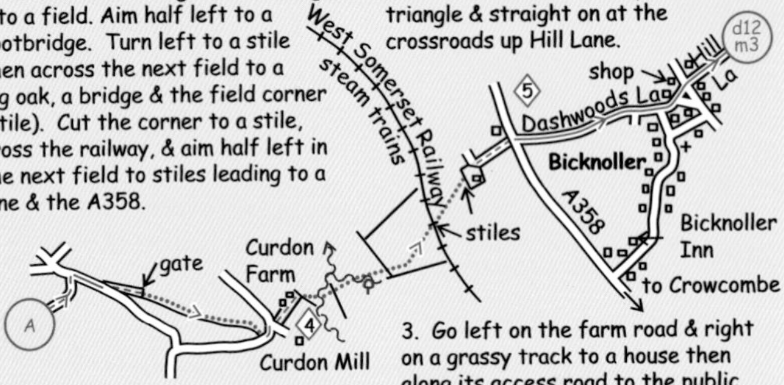

West Somerset Railway steam trains

shop
Dashwoods La
Hill La
Bicknoller
A358
Bicknoller Inn
to Crowcombe
stiles
gate
Curdon Farm
Curdon Mill
d12 m3
A

3. Go left on the farm road & right on a grassy track to a house then along its access road to the public road. Turn right, then fork left (footpath sign) down a grassy lane & along a field edge to its corner. A gate & steps lead to the road - take care here. Turn left along the road, then on the bend turn right towards Curdon Farm (not sharp right to Curdon Mill).

2. In the fourth field after Monksilver aim slightly left across the field to a gateway. Don't go through: turn left along the grassy track to the next field corner & turn right on a track into the wood then along a field edge. A gap leads to a wooded track, then a gate to a field. Bend left on the old grassy track to approach the farm. Don't go through the big gate ahead: take the small gate to the right then keep right of the pond to reach the farm access road.

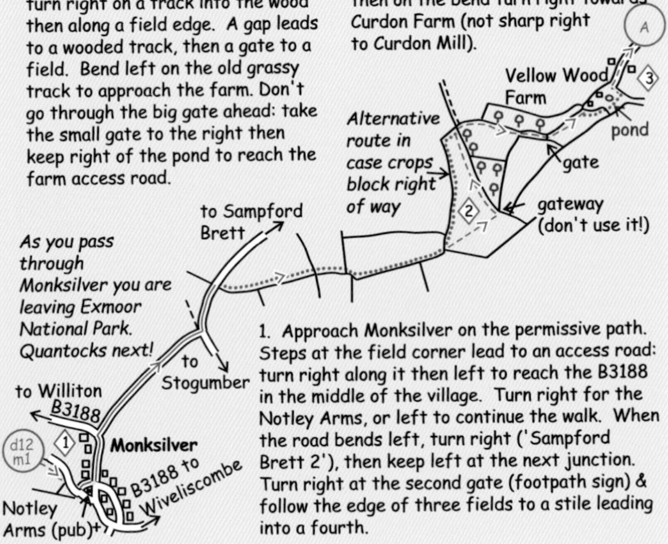

Vellow Wood Farm
pond
gate
gateway (don't use it!)

Alternative route in case crops block right of way

to Sampford Brett

As you pass through Monksilver you are leaving Exmoor National Park. Quantocks next!

to Stogumber
to Williton
B3188
Monksilver
B3188 to Wiveliscombe
Notley Arms (pub)
d12 m1

1. Approach Monksilver on the permissive path. Steps at the field corner lead to an access road: turn right along it then left to reach the B3188 in the middle of the village. Turn right for the Notley Arms, or left to continue the walk. When the road bends left, turn right ('Sampford Brett 2'), then keep left at the next junction. Turn right at the second gate (footpath sign) & follow the edge of three fields to a stile leading into a fourth.

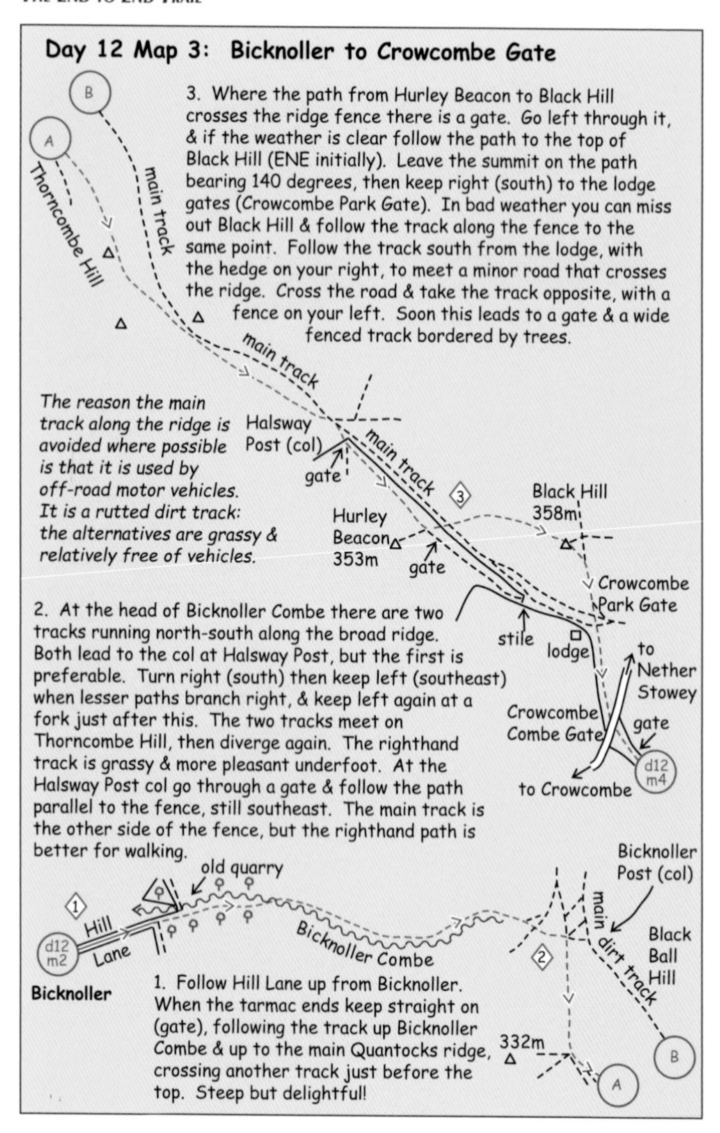
Day 12 Map 3: Bicknoller to Crowcombe Gate
3. Where the path from Hurley Beacon to Black Hill crosses the ridge fence there is a gate. Go left through it, & if the weather is clear follow the path to the top of Black Hill (ENE initially). Leave the summit on the path bearing 140 degrees, then keep right (south) to the lodge gates (Crowcombe Park Gate). In bad weather you can miss out Black Hill & follow the track along the fence to the same point. Follow the track south from the lodge, with the hedge on your right, to meet a minor road that crosses the ridge. Cross the road & take the track opposite, with a fence on your left. Soon this leads to a gate & a wide fenced track bordered by trees.
The reason the main track along the ridge is avoided where possible is that it is used by off-road motor vehicles. It is a rutted dirt track: the alternatives are grassy & relatively free of vehicles.
2. At the head of Bicknoller Combe there are two tracks running north-south along the broad ridge. Both lead to the col at Halsway Post, but the first is preferable. Turn right (south) then keep left (southeast) when lesser paths branch right, & keep left again at a fork just after this. The two tracks meet on Thorncombe Hill, then diverge again. The righthand track is grassy & more pleasant underfoot. At the Halsway Post col go through a gate & follow the path parallel to the fence, still southeast. The main track is the other side of the fence, but the righthand path is better for walking.
1. Follow Hill Lane up from Bicknoller. When the tarmac ends keep straight on (gate), following the track up Bicknoller Combe & up to the main Quantocks ridge, crossing another track just before the top. Steep but delightful!
B
A
Thorncombe Hill
main track
main track
Halsway Post (col)
gate
main track
3
Black Hill 358m
Hurley Beacon 353m
gate
Crowcombe Park Gate
stile
lodge
to Nether Stowey
Crowcombe Combe Gate
gate
d12 m4
to Crowcombe
Bicknoller Post (col)
old quarry
1
Hill Lane
d12 m2
Bicknoller
Bicknoller Combe
main dirt track
Black Ball Hill
2
332m
A
B

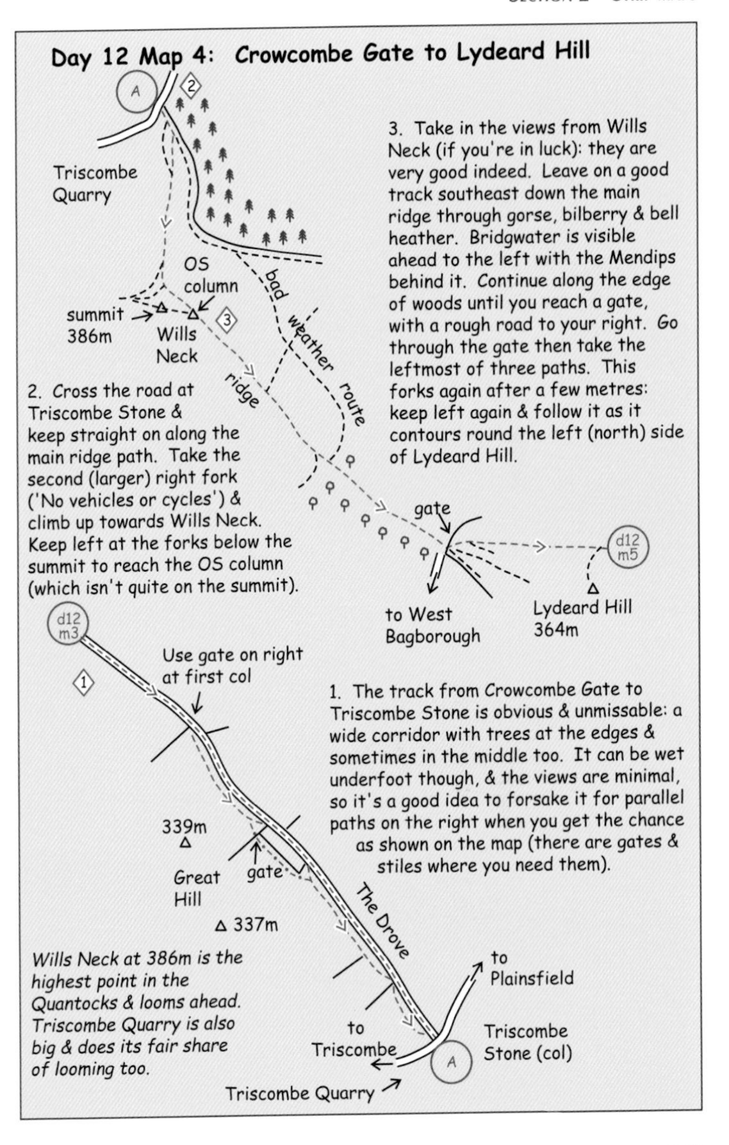
Day 12 Map 4: Crowcombe Gate to Lydeard Hill
A
2
Triscombe
Quarry
3. Take in the views from Wills Neck (if you're in luck): they are very good indeed. Leave on a good track southeast down the main ridge through gorse, bilberry & bell heather. Bridgwater is visible ahead to the left with the Mendips behind it. Continue along the edge of woods until you reach a gate, with a rough road to your right. Go through the gate then take the leftmost of three paths. This forks again after a few metres: keep left again & follow it as it contours round the left (north) side of Lydeard Hill.
OS
column
bad
weather
route
summit
386m
Wills
Neck
3
ridge
2. Cross the road at Triscombe Stone & keep straight on along the main ridge path. Take the second (larger) right fork ('No vehicles or cycles') & climb up towards Wills Neck. Keep left at the forks below the summit to reach the OS column (which isn't quite on the summit).
gate
d12
m5
to West
Bagborough
Lydeard Hill
364m
d12
m3
Use gate on right
at first col
1
1. The track from Crowcombe Gate to Triscombe Stone is obvious & unmissable: a wide corridor with trees at the edges & sometimes in the middle too. It can be wet underfoot though, & the views are minimal, so it's a good idea to forsake it for parallel paths on the right when you get the chance as shown on the map (there are gates & stiles where you need them).
339m
Great
Hill
gate
337m
The Drove
Wills Neck at 386m is the highest point in the Quantocks & looms ahead. Triscombe Quarry is also big & does its fair share of looming too.
to
Plainsfield
to
Triscombe
Triscombe
Stone (col)
A
Triscombe Quarry

Day 12 Map 5: Lydeard Hill to Blaxhold Farm

3. Turn right at the road then immediately left (footpath sign). Follow the hedge up the field to a stile in the top right corner. Go through & continue, now with a hedge on your left. At the end of the field cross a stile into a road. Almost opposite, to your right, a footpath sign indicates the way into a farmyard then along a good access track at right angles to the road (don't head for the farmhouse). Pass a bungalow, then at the next farm (Great Holwell, now derelict) turn left through the farmyard then right through a gate into a field. A grassy track diverges gradually from the hedge on the left: follow it through a gate & above a covert. The track peters out here: climb steeply up right to an electricity pole & then a hidden stile at the top of the field. Cross this, then go left through a gate & continue with the hedge on your left.

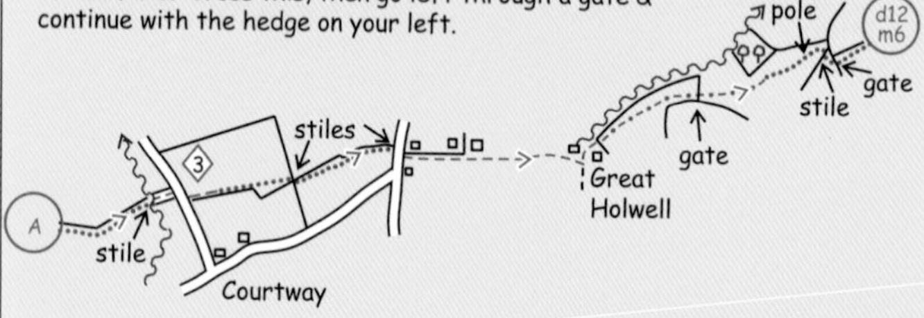

2. Turn right at the gate & follow the field edge. The second field is a big cultivated prairie: follow its edge past one gate on the right, then just after the hedge bends slightly to the left there is a second gate. Turn right through this gate (or climb it) & go ahead with a hedge on your left. Turn right at the road, then when it bends right turn left into the farmyard (kissing gate, footpath sign). Bear left to a two-part gate (footpath sign) into a field. Cross a fence (stile) then follow the hedge round to the left until you see a gate ahead: cut across to it (bearing 60 degrees). Don't go through the gate: turn right & follow the edge of the big field downhill to a stile, ford & short lane leading to a road.

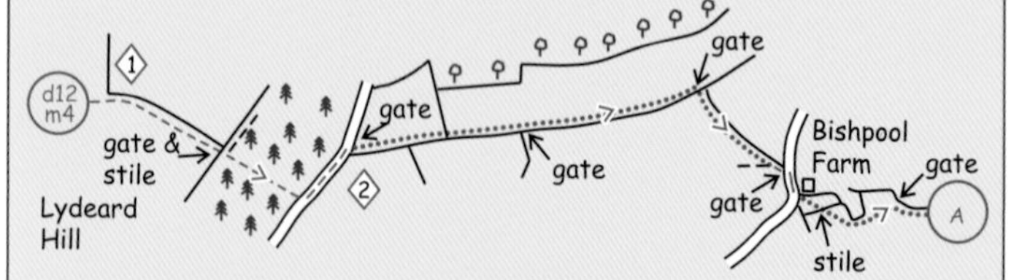

1. Follow the path round the north of Lydeard Hill: it is joined by a fence on the left. A gate leads to a forestry plantation & a good track through the trees. You have now left the Quantocks moorland behind you. At the far edge of the wood turn left along a lane then look out for a gate & footpath sign on the right.

Day 12 Map 6: Blaxhold Farm to Goathurst

3. Follow the road from Cobbs Cross Farm round a righthand bend, then turn left at the next junction. Turn left in the middle of Goathurst, signed to Bridgwater. The road bends left, then just before a house on the left, turn right (kissing gate & footpath sign) & follow the field edge, with a wood & a lane on your left.

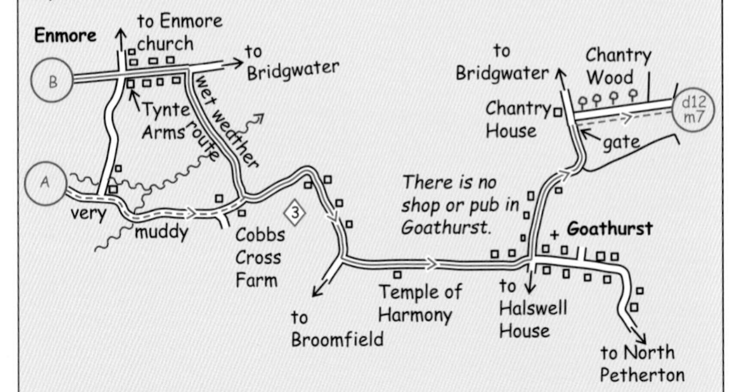

2. Continue on the road for just over 1km to a school & a right turn. Here you have a choice to make. If the weather is dry & you don't want to visit the pub, then turn right & follow the road down, across a stream & round a lefthand bend. When the road bends right, turn left along a lane in a green tunnel. This leads to the entrance to the Black Rock outdoor centre: bend left on the main track to reach Cobbs Cross Farm where you keep straight on to regain tarmac. Unfortunately the lane can get very muddy, so in wet weather stick to the main road, past the pub (Tynte Arms), then take the next right turn to rejoin the main route at a bend in the road by Cobbs Cross Farm.

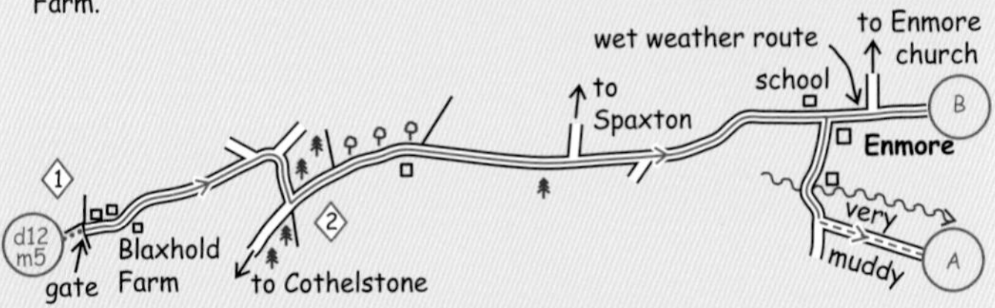

1. Follow the hedge to the field corner, where a gate leads to the end of a tarmac road & a house. Follow the tarmac past Blaxhold Farm to the public road & turn sharp left. Take care: although it is an unclassified road it is busy & the traffic is fast.

Day 12 Map 7: Goathurst to Bridgwater

Bridgwater is not a pretty place: you need to go through it as it is the lowest point at which the River Parrett is bridged. Luckily you can get quite close to the town centre before joining a road or meeting houses.

River Parrett

d13 m1

Bridgwater

4. Once the road is joined in Bridgwater, go straight on across traffic lights (Penel Orlieu), bear right at a roundabout & keep more or less straight on through the town centre, along High St, Cornhill & Fore St to reach the Town Bridge across the River Parrett.

Bridgwater & Taunton Canal

field used for fairs & circuses

allotments

gate & bridge

wide drain

Cross footbridge on left then go immediately through gate on right to regain original line

gate

fb & gate

use LH gateway

3. The path through the meadows is not always obvious: follow the map carefully. It is very pleasant, apart from a few nettles. Most of the way it follows a stream above which has grown a hedge.

A

gate & stile

fb, then aim away from hedge/stream to LH gateway in opposite hedge

A

fb

solar farm

farm

fb

Some of the hedges on this map page are accompanied by a stream: there are many more of these to come tomorrow.

gate

fb

d12 m6

Flatgate Cottages

stile in hedge (overgrown)

1. At the far end of the long field, turn right then cross a stile on the left & continue with the stream/hedge on your right. If this field is blocked with crops, take the alternative route via Oakenford Farm (if you can fight through the hedge).

Oakenford Farm

2. If the second field can be crossed easily, follow the stream then cut across to a gate (aim left of the house). Turn right along the road, then just after a farm access road turn left (gateway) past stables & into a field. Follow the right edge of the field to a footbridge.

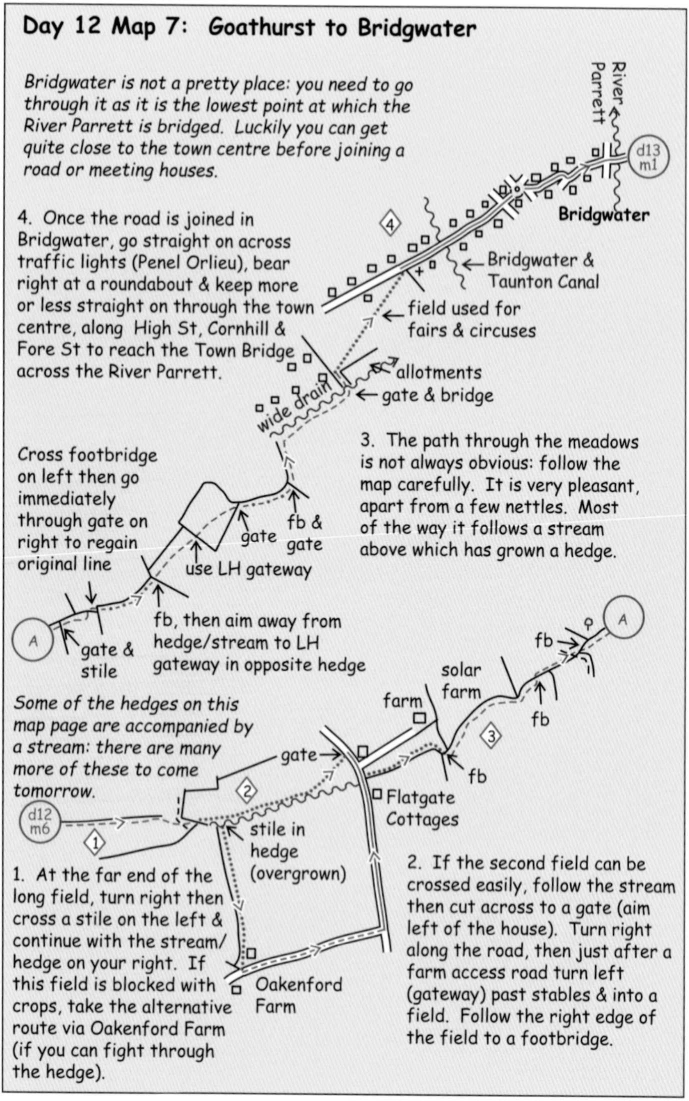

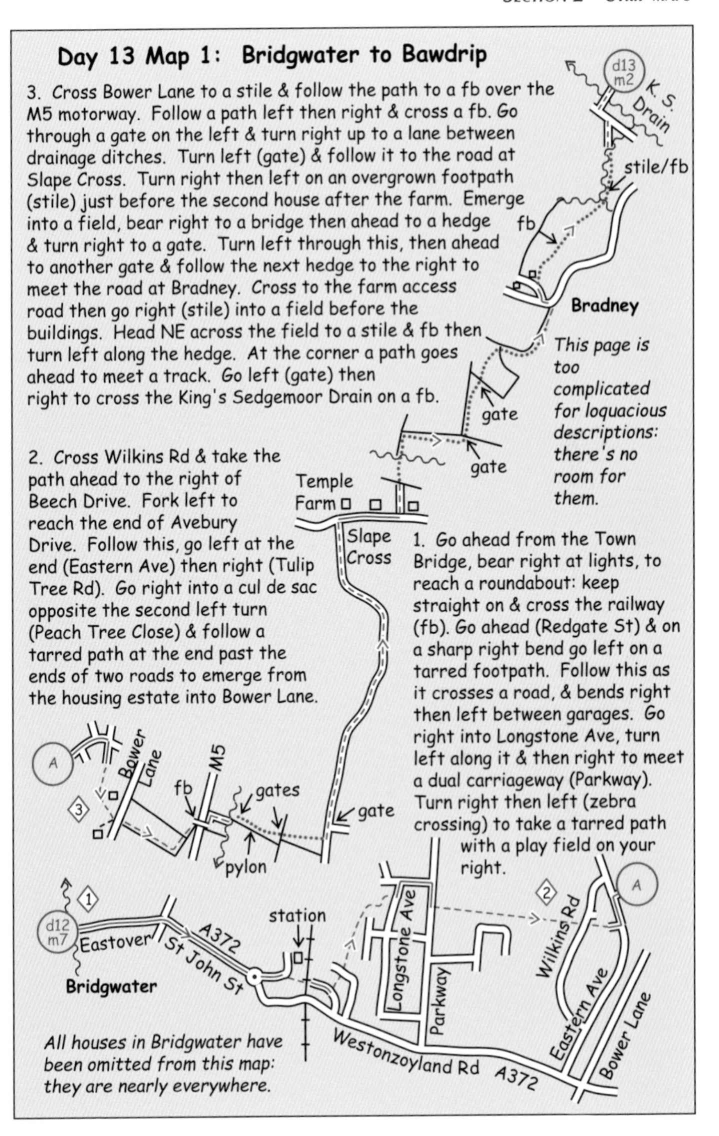
Day 13 Map 1: Bridgwater to Bawdrip
3. Cross Bower Lane to a stile & follow the path to a fb over the M5 motorway. Follow a path left then right & cross a fb. Go through a gate on the left & turn right up to a lane between drainage ditches. Turn left (gate) & follow it to the road at Slape Cross. Turn right then left on an overgrown footpath (stile) just before the second house after the farm. Emerge into a field, bear right to a bridge then ahead to a hedge & turn right to a gate. Turn left through this, then ahead to another gate & follow the next hedge to the right to meet the road at Bradney. Cross to the farm access road then go right (stile) into a field before the buildings. Head NE across the field to a stile & fb then turn left along the hedge. At the corner a path goes ahead to meet a track. Go left (gate) then right to cross the King's Sedgemoor Drain on a fb.
2. Cross Wilkins Rd & take the path ahead to the right of Beech Drive. Fork left to reach the end of Avebury Drive. Follow this, go left at the end (Eastern Ave) then right (Tulip Tree Rd). Go right into a cul de sac opposite the second left turn (Peach Tree Close) & follow a tarred path at the end past the ends of two roads to emerge from the housing estate into Bower Lane.
1. Go ahead from the Town Bridge, bear right at lights, to reach a roundabout: keep straight on & cross the railway (fb). Go ahead (Redgate St) & on a sharp right bend go left on a tarred footpath. Follow this as it crosses a road, & bends right then left between garages. Go right into Longstone Ave, turn left along it & then right to meet a dual carriageway (Parkway). Turn right then left (zebra crossing) to take a tarred path with a play field on your right.
This page is too complicated for loquacious descriptions: there's no room for them.
All houses in Bridgwater have been omitted from this map: they are nearly everywhere.
d13 m2
K. S. Drain
stile/fb
fb
Bradney
gate
gate
Temple Farm
Slape Cross
A
Bower Lane
M5
fb
gates
3
gate
pylon
1
d12 m7
Eastover
A372
St John St
station
Bridgwater
Longstone Ave
Parkway
2
A
Wilkins Rd
Eastern Ave
Bower Lane
Westonzoyland Rd
A372

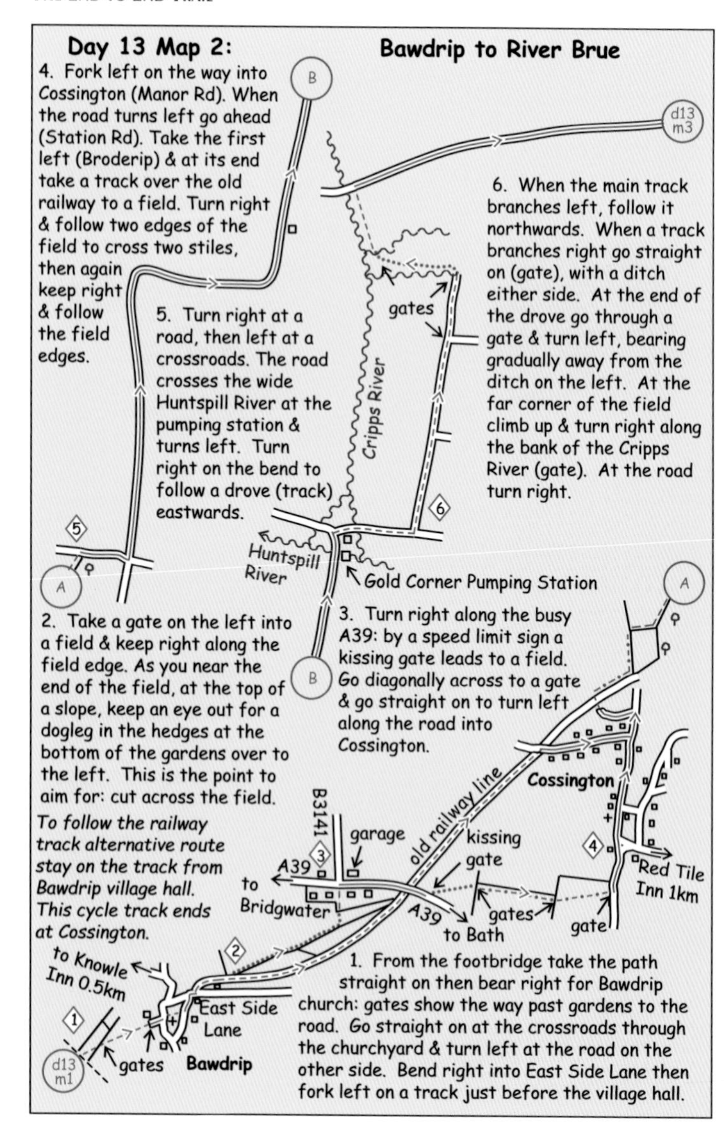
Day 13 Map 2:
Bawdrip to River Brue
4. Fork left on the way into Cossington (Manor Rd). When the road turns left go ahead (Station Rd). Take the first left (Broderip) & at its end take a track over the old railway to a field. Turn right & follow two edges of the field to cross two stiles, then again keep right & follow the field edges.
B
d13 m3
6. When the main track branches left, follow it northwards. When a track branches right go straight on (gate), with a ditch either side. At the end of the drove go through a gate & turn left, bearing gradually away from the ditch on the left. At the far corner of the field climb up & turn right along the bank of the Cripps River (gate). At the road turn right.
gates
5. Turn right at a road, then left at a crossroads. The road crosses the wide Huntspill River at the pumping station & turns left. Turn right on the bend to follow a drove (track) eastwards.
Cripps River
6
5
Huntspill River
A
Gold Corner Pumping Station
A
2. Take a gate on the left into a field & keep right along the field edge. As you near the end of the field, at the top of a slope, keep an eye out for a dogleg in the hedges at the bottom of the gardens over to the left. This is the point to aim for: cut across the field.
B
3. Turn right along the busy A39: by a speed limit sign a kissing gate leads to a field. Go diagonally across to a gate & go straight on to turn left along the road into Cossington.
Cossington
B3141
old railway line
To follow the railway track alternative route stay on the track from Bawdrip village hall. This cycle track ends at Cossington.
garage
kissing gate
3
A39
to Bridgwater
4
Red Tile Inn 1km
A39
to Bath
gates
gate
2
to Knowle Inn 0.5km
1. From the footbridge take the path straight on then bear right for Bawdrip church: gates show the way past gardens to the road. Go straight on at the crossroads through the churchyard & turn left at the road on the other side. Bend right into East Side Lane then fork left on a track just before the village hall.
1
East Side Lane
d13 m1
gates
Bawdrip

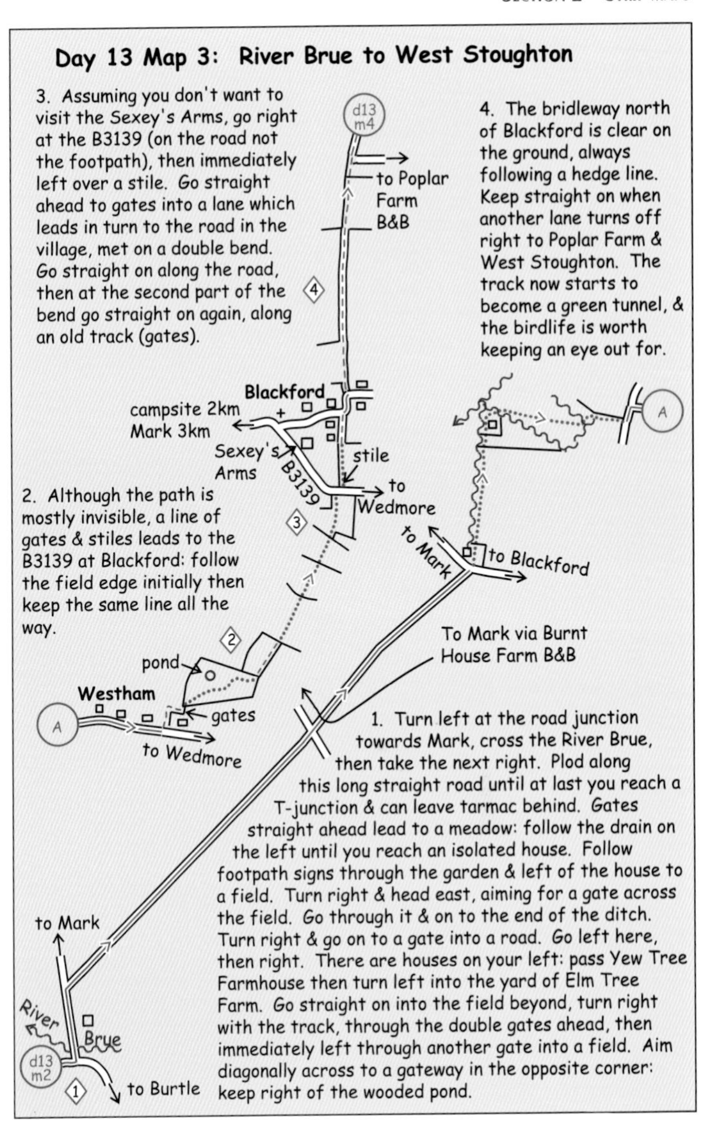
Day 13 Map 3: River Brue to West Stoughton
3. Assuming you don't want to visit the Sexey's Arms, go right at the B3139 (on the road not the footpath), then immediately left over a stile. Go straight ahead to gates into a lane which leads in turn to the road in the village, met on a double bend. Go straight on along the road, then at the second part of the bend go straight on again, along an old track (gates).
d13 m4
to Poplar Farm B&B
4
4. The bridleway north of Blackford is clear on the ground, always following a hedge line. Keep straight on when another lane turns off right to Poplar Farm & West Stoughton. The track now starts to become a green tunnel, & the birdlife is worth keeping an eye out for.
Blackford
campsite 2km
Mark 3km
Sexey's Arms
B3139
stile
to Wedmore
A
2. Although the path is mostly invisible, a line of gates & stiles leads to the B3139 at Blackford: follow the field edge initially then keep the same line all the way.
3
to Mark
to Blackford
2
To Mark via Burnt House Farm B&B
pond
Westham
A
gates
to Wedmore
1. Turn left at the road junction towards Mark, cross the River Brue, then take the next right. Plod along this long straight road until at last you reach a T-junction & can leave tarmac behind. Gates straight ahead lead to a meadow: follow the drain on the left until you reach an isolated house. Follow footpath signs through the garden & left of the house to a field. Turn right & head east, aiming for a gate across the field. Go through it & on to the end of the ditch. Turn right & go on to a gate into a road. Go left here, then right. There are houses on your left: pass Yew Tree Farmhouse then turn left into the yard of Elm Tree Farm. Go straight on into the field beyond, turn right with the track, through the double gates ahead, then immediately left through another gate into a field. Aim diagonally across to a gateway in the opposite corner: keep right of the wooded pond.
to Mark
River
Brue
d13 m2
1
to Burtle

Day 13 Map 4: West Stoughton to Brinscombe Hill

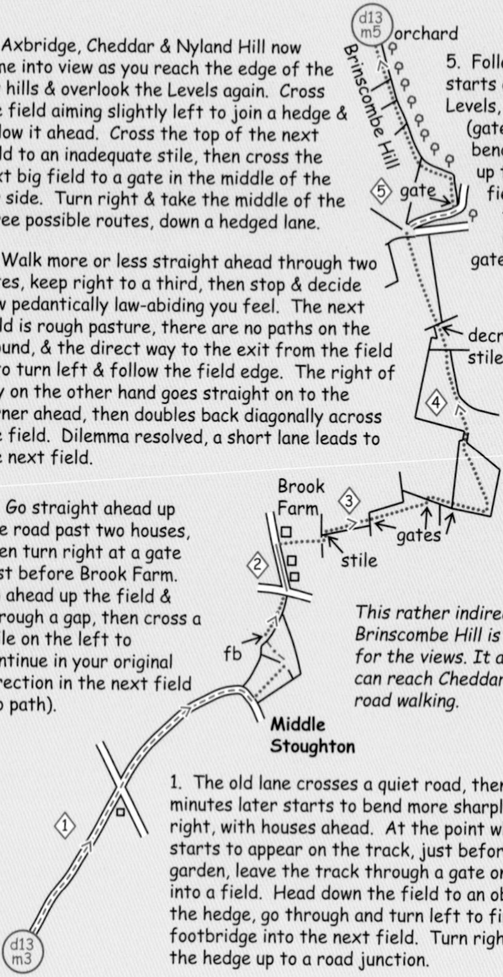

d13 m5

orchard

Brinscombe Hill

4. Axbridge, Cheddar & Nyland Hill now come into view as you reach the edge of the low hills & overlook the Levels again. Cross the field aiming slightly left to join a hedge & follow it ahead. Cross the top of the next field to an inadequate stile, then cross the next big field to a gate in the middle of the far side. Turn right & take the middle of the three possible routes, down a hedged lane.

5. Follow the lane as it starts downhill to the Levels, but turn left (gate) when the lane bends left, & climb up to follow the field edges along the crest of Brinscombe Hill: gates show the way.

gate

3. Walk more or less straight ahead through two gates, keep right to a third, then stop & decide how pedantically law-abiding you feel. The next field is rough pasture, there are no paths on the ground, & the direct way to the exit from the field is to turn left & follow the field edge. The right of way on the other hand goes straight on to the corner ahead, then doubles back diagonally across the field. Dilemma resolved, a short lane leads to the next field.

decrepit stile

Brook Farm

gates

stile

2. Go straight ahead up the road past two houses, then turn right at a gate just before Brook Farm. Go ahead up the field & through a gap, then cross a stile on the left to continue in your original direction in the next field (no path).

fb

This rather indirect route along Brinscombe Hill is well worthwhile for the views. It also means you can reach Cheddar with almost no road walking.

Middle Stoughton

1. The old lane crosses a quiet road, then a few minutes later starts to bend more sharply to the right, with houses ahead. At the point where tarmac starts to appear on the track, just before the first garden, leave the track through a gate on the left into a field. Head down the field to an obvious gap in the hedge, go through and turn left to find a footbridge into the next field. Turn right & follow the hedge up to a road junction.

d13 m3

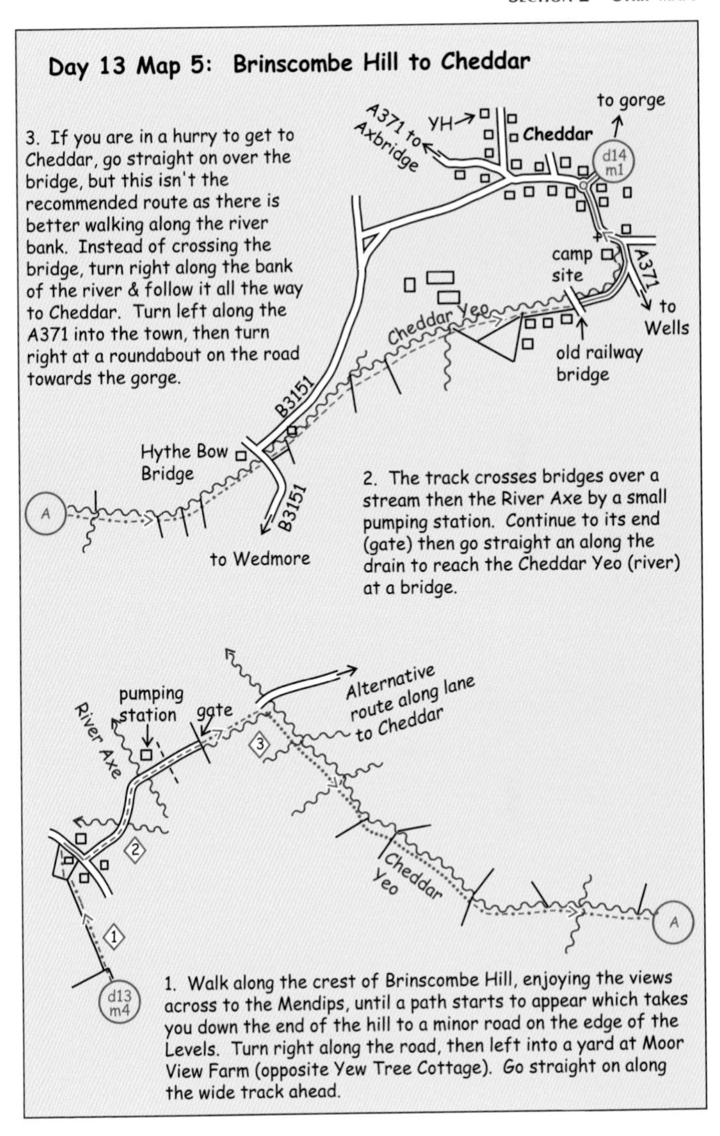
Day 13 Map 5: Brinscombe Hill to Cheddar
3. If you are in a hurry to get to Cheddar, go straight on over the bridge, but this isn't the recommended route as there is better walking along the river bank. Instead of crossing the bridge, turn right along the bank of the river & follow it all the way to Cheddar. Turn left along the A371 into the town, then turn right at a roundabout on the road towards the gorge.
A371 to Axbridge
YH
Cheddar
to gorge
d14 m1
camp site
A371
to Wells
Cheddar Yeo
old railway bridge
B3151
Hythe Bow Bridge
A
B3151
to Wedmore
2. The track crosses bridges over a stream then the River Axe by a small pumping station. Continue to its end (gate) then go straight an along the drain to reach the Cheddar Yeo (river) at a bridge.
pumping station
gate
River Axe
Alternative route along lane to Cheddar
3
2
Cheddar Yeo
A
1
d13 m4
1. Walk along the crest of Brinscombe Hill, enjoying the views across to the Mendips, until a path starts to appear which takes you down the end of the hill to a minor road on the edge of the Levels. Turn right along the road, then left into a yard at Moor View Farm (opposite Yew Tree Cottage). Go straight on along the wide track ahead.

Day 14 Map 1: Cheddar to Beacon Batch

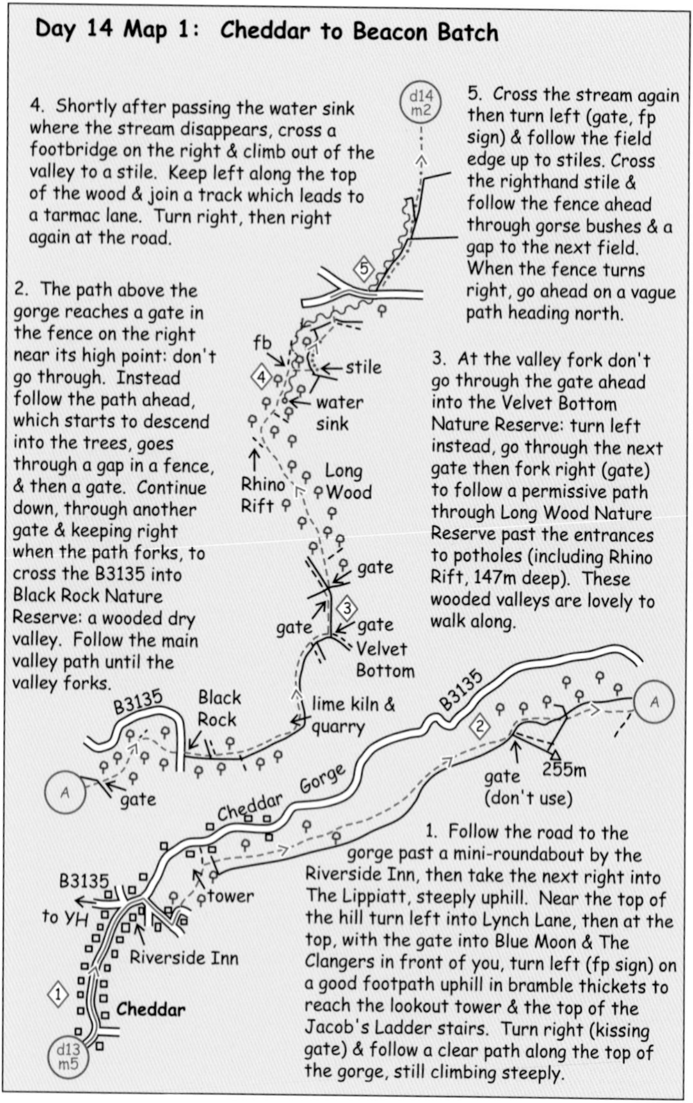

1. Follow the road to the gorge past a mini-roundabout by the Riverside Inn, then take the next right into The Lippiatt, steeply uphill. Near the top of the hill turn left into Lynch Lane, then at the top, with the gate into Blue Moon & The Clangers in front of you, turn left (fp sign) on a good footpath uphill in bramble thickets to reach the lookout tower & the top of the Jacob's Ladder stairs. Turn right (kissing gate) & follow a clear path along the top of the gorge, still climbing steeply.

2. The path above the gorge reaches a gate in the fence on the right near its high point: don't go through. Instead follow the path ahead, which starts to descend into the trees, goes through a gap in a fence, & then a gate. Continue down, through another gate & keeping right when the path forks, to cross the B3135 into Black Rock Nature Reserve: a wooded dry valley. Follow the main valley path until the valley forks.

3. At the valley fork don't go through the gate ahead into the Velvet Bottom Nature Reserve: turn left instead, go through the next gate then fork right (gate) to follow a permissive path through Long Wood Nature Reserve past the entrances to potholes (including Rhino Rift, 147m deep). These wooded valleys are lovely to walk along.

4. Shortly after passing the water sink where the stream disappears, cross a footbridge on the right & climb out of the valley to a stile. Keep left along the top of the wood & join a track which leads to a tarmac lane. Turn right, then right again at the road.

5. Cross the stream again then turn left (gate, fp sign) & follow the field edge up to stiles. Cross the righthand stile & follow the fence ahead through gorse bushes & a gap to the next field. When the fence turns right, go ahead on a vague path heading north.

d14 m2
fb
stile
water sink
Rhino Rift
Long Wood
gate
gate
gate
Velvet Bottom
Black Rock
lime kiln & quarry
B3135
B3135
A
A
gate
Cheddar Gorge
gate (don't use)
255m
tower
B3135
to YH
Riverside Inn
Cheddar
d13 m5

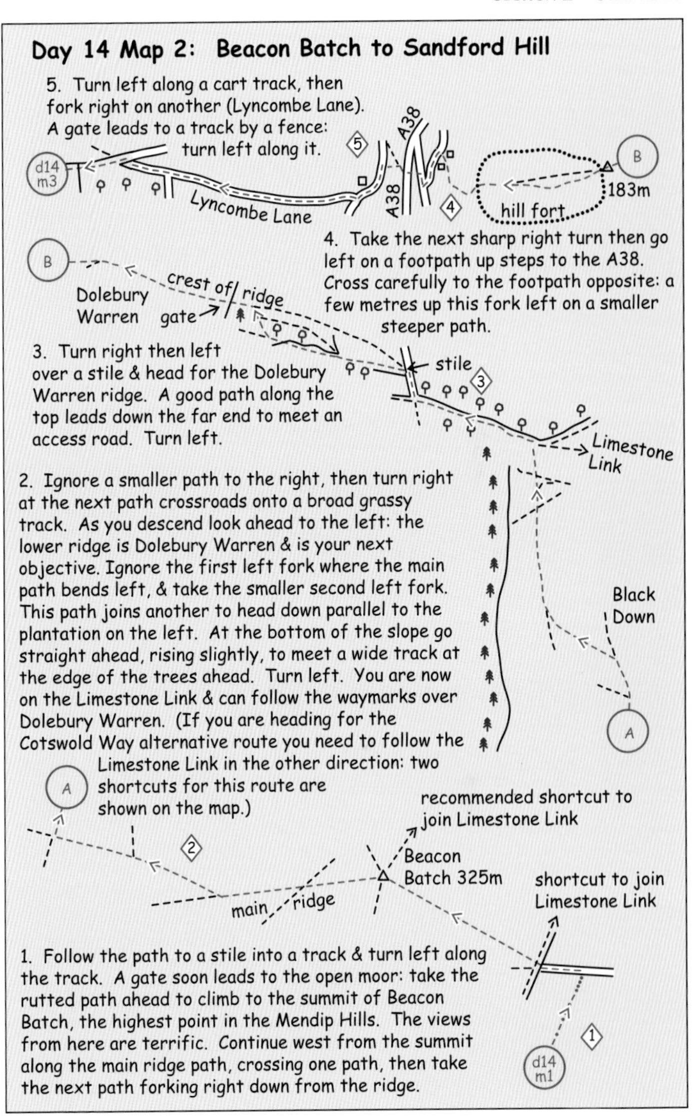
Day 14 Map 2: Beacon Batch to Sandford Hill
5. Turn left along a cart track, then fork right on another (Lyncombe Lane). A gate leads to a track by a fence: turn left along it.
d14 m3
Lyncombe Lane
A38
A38
B
183m
hill fort
4. Take the next sharp right turn then go left on a footpath up steps to the A38. Cross carefully to the footpath opposite: a few metres up this fork left on a smaller steeper path.
B
crest of ridge
Dolebury Warren
gate
stile
3. Turn right then left over a stile & head for the Dolebury Warren ridge. A good path along the top leads down the far end to meet an access road. Turn left.
Limestone Link
2. Ignore a smaller path to the right, then turn right at the next path crossroads onto a broad grassy track. As you descend look ahead to the left: the lower ridge is Dolebury Warren & is your next objective. Ignore the first left fork where the main path bends left, & take the smaller second left fork. This path joins another to head down parallel to the plantation on the left. At the bottom of the slope go straight ahead, rising slightly, to meet a wide track at the edge of the trees ahead. Turn left. You are now on the Limestone Link & can follow the waymarks over Dolebury Warren. (If you are heading for the Cotswold Way alternative route you need to follow the Limestone Link in the other direction: two shortcuts for this route are shown on the map.)
Black Down
A
A
recommended shortcut to join Limestone Link
Beacon Batch 325m
main ridge
shortcut to join Limestone Link
1. Follow the path to a stile into a track & turn left along the track. A gate soon leads to the open moor: take the rutted path ahead to climb to the summit of Beacon Batch, the highest point in the Mendip Hills. The views from here are terrific. Continue west from the summit along the main ridge path, crossing one path, then take the next path forking right down from the ridge.
d14 m1

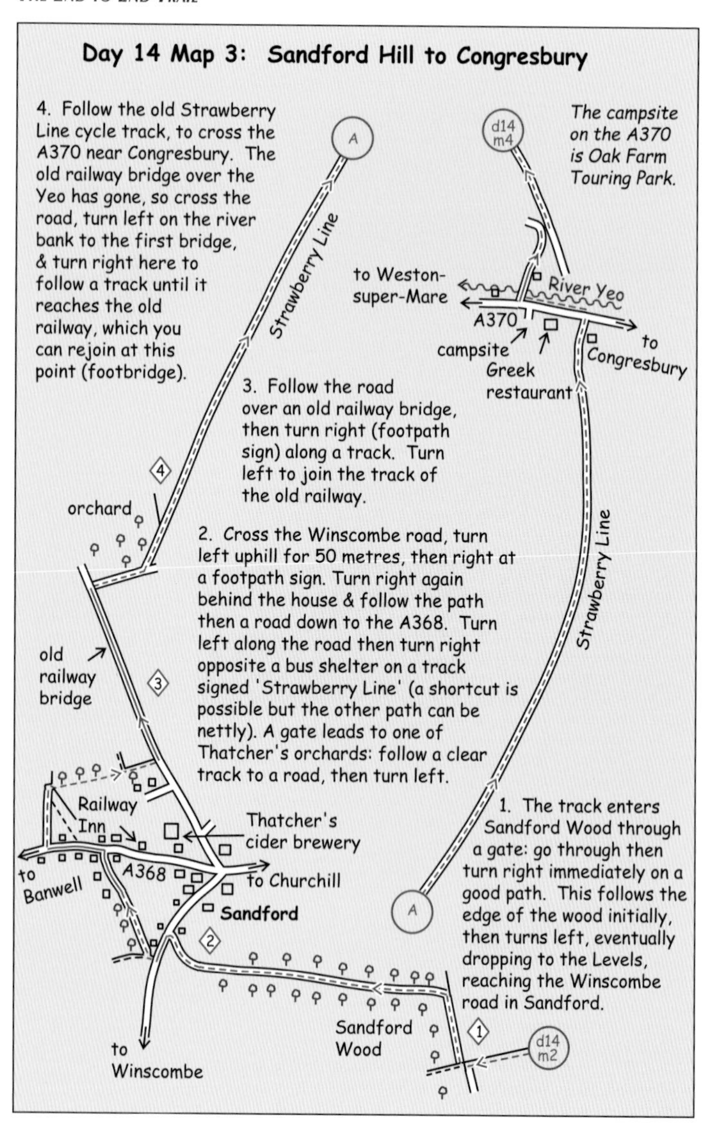
Day 14 Map 3: Sandford Hill to Congresbury
4. Follow the old Strawberry Line cycle track, to cross the A370 near Congresbury. The old railway bridge over the Yeo has gone, so cross the road, turn left on the river bank to the first bridge, & turn right here to follow a track until it reaches the old railway, which you can rejoin at this point (footbridge).
A
d14 m4
The campsite on the A370 is Oak Farm Touring Park.
Strawberry Line
to Weston-super-Mare
River Yeo
A370
campsite
Greek restaurant
to Congresbury
3. Follow the road over an old railway bridge, then turn right (footpath sign) along a track. Turn left to join the track of the old railway.
4
orchard
2. Cross the Winscombe road, turn left uphill for 50 metres, then right at a footpath sign. Turn right again behind the house & follow the path then a road down to the A368. Turn left along the road then turn right opposite a bus shelter on a track signed 'Strawberry Line' (a shortcut is possible but the other path can be nettly). A gate leads to one of Thatcher's orchards: follow a clear track to a road, then turn left.
Strawberry Line
old railway bridge
3
Railway Inn
Thatcher's cider brewery
to Banwell
A368
to Churchill
Sandford
2
1. The track enters Sandford Wood through a gate: go through then turn right immediately on a good path. This follows the edge of the wood initially, then turns left, eventually dropping to the Levels, reaching the Winscombe road in Sandford.
A
Sandford Wood
1
d14 m2
to Winscombe

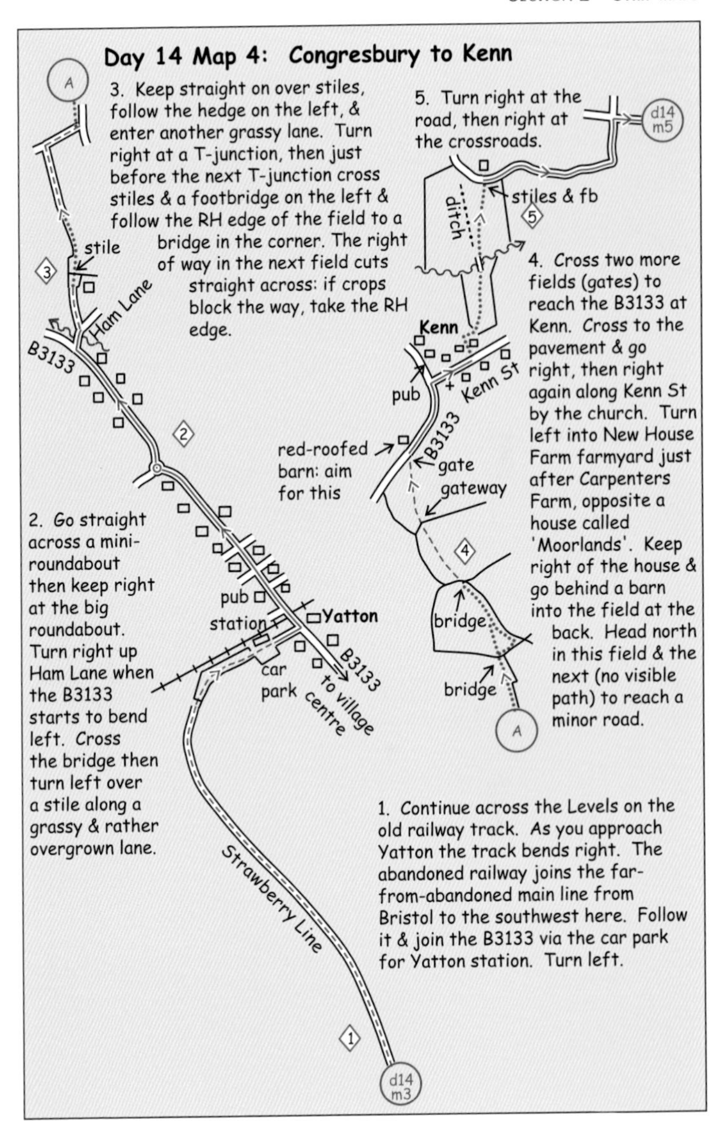
Day 14 Map 4: Congresbury to Kenn
3. Keep straight on over stiles, follow the hedge on the left, & enter another grassy lane. Turn right at a T-junction, then just before the next T-junction cross stiles & a footbridge on the left & follow the RH edge of the field to a bridge in the corner. The right of way in the next field cuts straight across: if crops block the way, take the RH edge.
5. Turn right at the road, then right at the crossroads.
d14 m5
stiles & fb
ditch
stile
Ham Lane
B3133
Kenn
pub
Kenn St
4. Cross two more fields (gates) to reach the B3133 at Kenn. Cross to the pavement & go right, then right again along Kenn St by the church. Turn left into New House Farm farmyard just after Carpenters Farm, opposite a house called 'Moorlands'. Keep right of the house & go behind a barn into the field at the back. Head north in this field & the next (no visible path) to reach a minor road.
red-roofed barn: aim for this
gate
gateway
2. Go straight across a mini-roundabout then keep right at the big roundabout. Turn right up Ham Lane when the B3133 starts to bend left. Cross the bridge then turn left over a stile along a grassy & rather overgrown lane.
pub
station
Yatton
car park
B3133
to village centre
bridge
bridge
Strawberry Line
1. Continue across the Levels on the old railway track. As you approach Yatton the track bends right. The abandoned railway joins the far-from-abandoned main line from Bristol to the southwest here. Follow it & join the B3133 via the car park for Yatton station. Turn left.
d14 m3

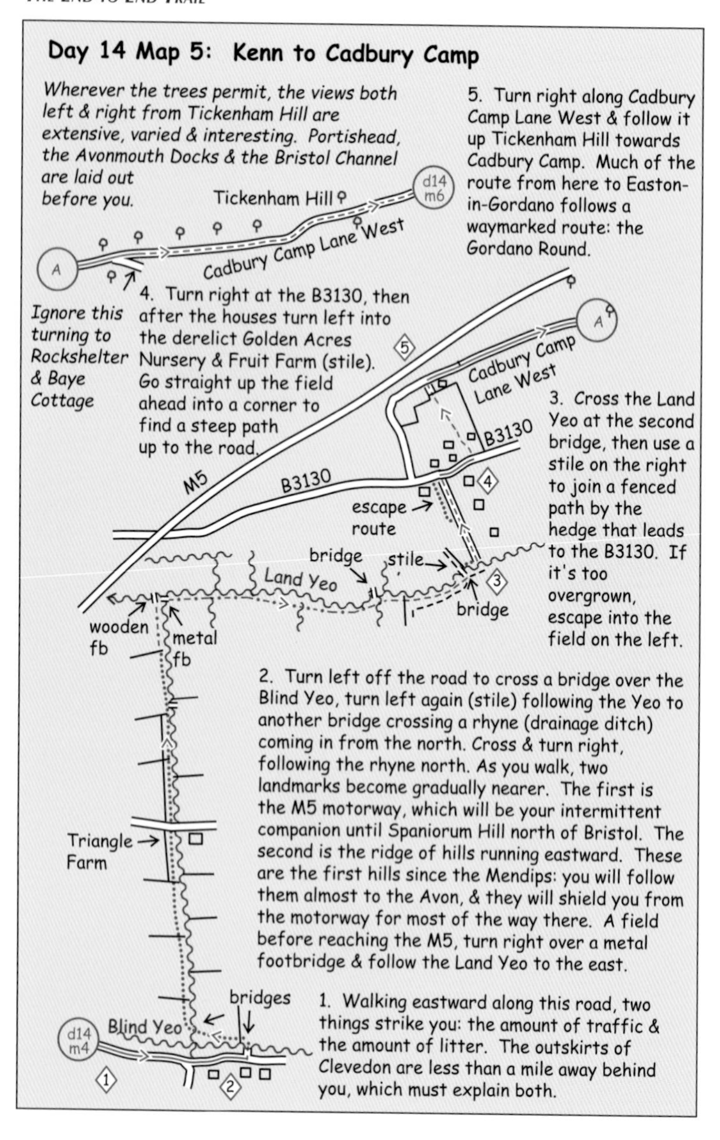
Day 14 Map 5: Kenn to Cadbury Camp
Wherever the trees permit, the views both left & right from Tickenham Hill are extensive, varied & interesting. Portishead, the Avonmouth Docks & the Bristol Channel are laid out before you.
Tickenham Hill
d14 m6
Cadbury Camp Lane West
A
Ignore this turning to Rockshelter & Baye Cottage
4. Turn right at the B3130, then after the houses turn left into the derelict Golden Acres Nursery & Fruit Farm (stile). Go straight up the field ahead into a corner to find a steep path up to the road.
5. Turn right along Cadbury Camp Lane West & follow it up Tickenham Hill towards Cadbury Camp. Much of the route from here to Easton-in-Gordano follows a waymarked route: the Gordano Round.
5
A
Cadbury Camp Lane West
B3130
M5
B3130
4
escape route
3. Cross the Land Yeo at the second bridge, then use a stile on the right to join a fenced path by the hedge that leads to the B3130. If it's too overgrown, escape into the field on the left.
bridge
stile
Land Yeo
3
bridge
wooden fb
metal fb
2. Turn left off the road to cross a bridge over the Blind Yeo, turn left again (stile) following the Yeo to another bridge crossing a rhyne (drainage ditch) coming in from the north. Cross & turn right, following the rhyne north. As you walk, two landmarks become gradually nearer. The first is the M5 motorway, which will be your intermittent companion until Spaniorum Hill north of Bristol. The second is the ridge of hills running eastward. These are the first hills since the Mendips: you will follow them almost to the Avon, & they will shield you from the motorway for most of the way there. A field before reaching the M5, turn right over a metal footbridge & follow the Land Yeo to the east.
Triangle Farm
bridges
d14 m4
Blind Yeo
1
2
1. Walking eastward along this road, two things strike you: the amount of traffic & the amount of litter. The outskirts of Clevedon are less than a mile away behind you, which must explain both.

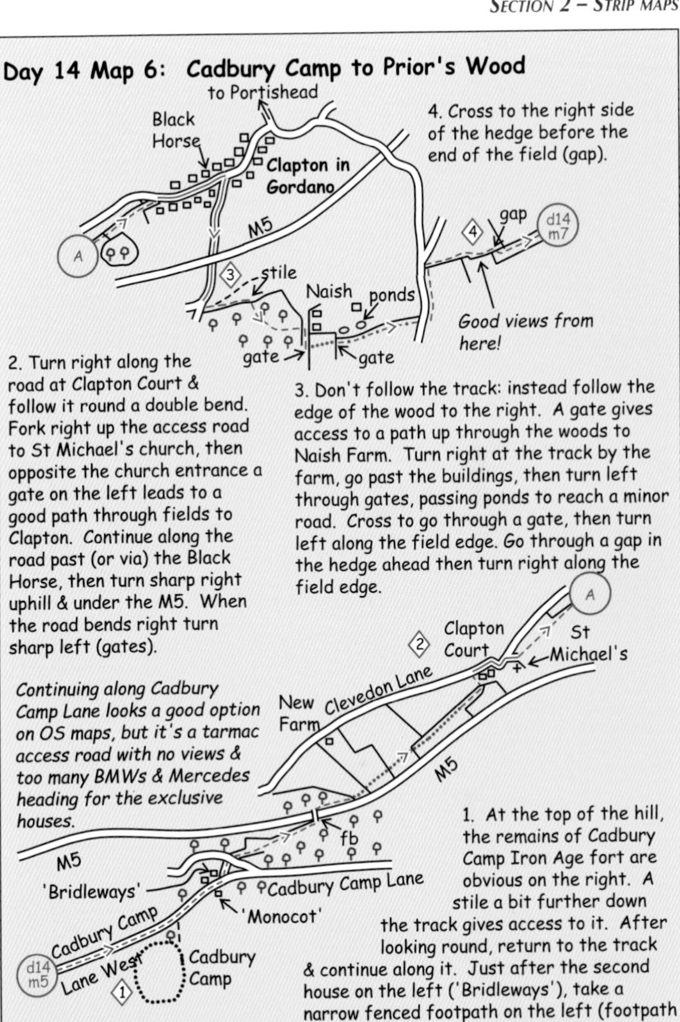
Day 14 Map 6: Cadbury Camp to Prior's Wood
to Portishead
Black Horse
Clapton in Gordano
M5
A
3
stile
Naish
ponds
gate
gate
4. Cross to the right side of the hedge before the end of the field (gap).
4
gap
d14 m7
Good views from here!
2. Turn right along the road at Clapton Court & follow it round a double bend. Fork right up the access road to St Michael's church, then opposite the church entrance a gate on the left leads to a good path through fields to Clapton. Continue along the road past (or via) the Black Horse, then turn sharp right uphill & under the M5. When the road bends right turn sharp left (gates).
3. Don't follow the track: instead follow the edge of the wood to the right. A gate gives access to a path up through the woods to Naish Farm. Turn right at the track by the farm, go past the buildings, then turn left through gates, passing ponds to reach a minor road. Cross to go through a gate, then turn left along the field edge. Go through a gap in the hedge ahead then turn right along the field edge.
A
Clapton Court
2
St Michael's
New Farm
Clevedon Lane
M5
Continuing along Cadbury Camp Lane looks a good option on OS maps, but it's a tarmac access road with no views & too many BMWs & Mercedes heading for the exclusive houses.
fb
M5
'Bridleways'
Cadbury Camp Lane
'Monocot'
Cadbury Camp Lane West
d14 m5
1
Cadbury Camp
1. At the top of the hill, the remains of Cadbury Camp Iron Age fort are obvious on the right. A stile a bit further down the track gives access to it. After looking round, return to the track & continue along it. Just after the second house on the left ('Bridleways'), take a narrow fenced footpath on the left (footpath sign). This leads to another lane: cross it & follow the signed path opposite to cross a footbridge over the M5. A path along the edge of a small wood leads to a field, then stiles & gates indicate the line of an invisible footpath diverging gradually from the M5 to reach the road by Clapton Court farm.

Day 14 Map 7: Prior's Wood to Easton-in-Gordano

5. Continue ahead on the road until the tarmac ends, then along the unmade lane beyond (gate). Just before the track enters a wood, leave it for a parallel path in the field to the right (stile, avoiding the wet bridleway). A stile gives access to the wood: continue, then turn right at a junction (fp sign). Follow field edges & cross an old lane to reach the A369 & Easton-in-Gordano.

4. The path continues down the other side of the hill to a gate into a field, & descends to a small gate into an old lane. This leads to the tarmac of Failand Lane. Cross into the field opposite (gate & stile) & go half left to a stile by the lefthand of two visible gates & onto a tarred access road.

3. Follow the path through the wood & past a ruin to descend to a gate into Mill Lane. Cross the tarmac to a gate & stile, & follow a clear path slightly right & up to turn left on a concrete access road. After a gate & stile in the corner the concrete turns right: leave it to keep left by the fence to stiles in the next corner. Continue in the same direction in the next field to reach a stile into the pines ahead on Windmill Hill.

Easton-in-Gordano
d15 m1
to Portishead & Days Inn
pub
A369
to Bristol
Hails Wood
to Portbury
Failand Lane
Mill Lane
to Portbury
Windmill Hill 122m
A

2. Aim half left across the field (60 degrees, aiming for the right end of a line of trees), & when a house comes into sight aim just left of it. Join an access road at a stile & turn right along it until you can turn left at a crossroads on the drive of The Downs School, curving round school buildings. Ignore a fp sign on your left & go through a car park to gates into a sports field. Go diagonally across this to a stile (120 degrees, no path), then keep left in the next field, cutting the corner (if practical) to a stile at the bottom of a dip into a scrubby wood on a clear path.

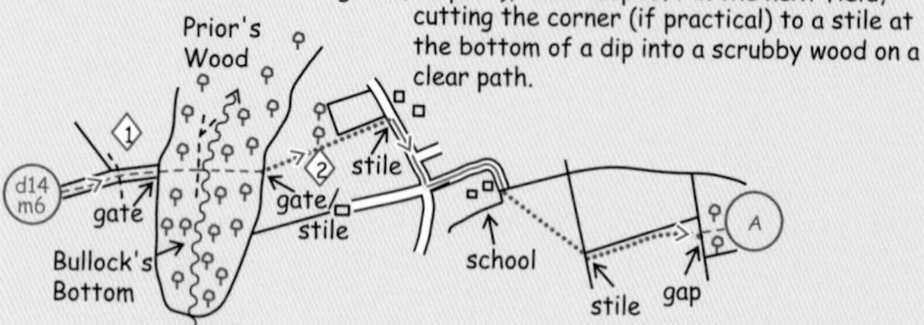

1. The path enters a wood & descends on into Prior's Wood Nature Reserve. At the valley floor go straight across a track, cross the stream & climb steeply up through the wood eastwards to a gate & stile into a large field.

Day 15 Map 1: Easton-in-Gordano to Shirehampton

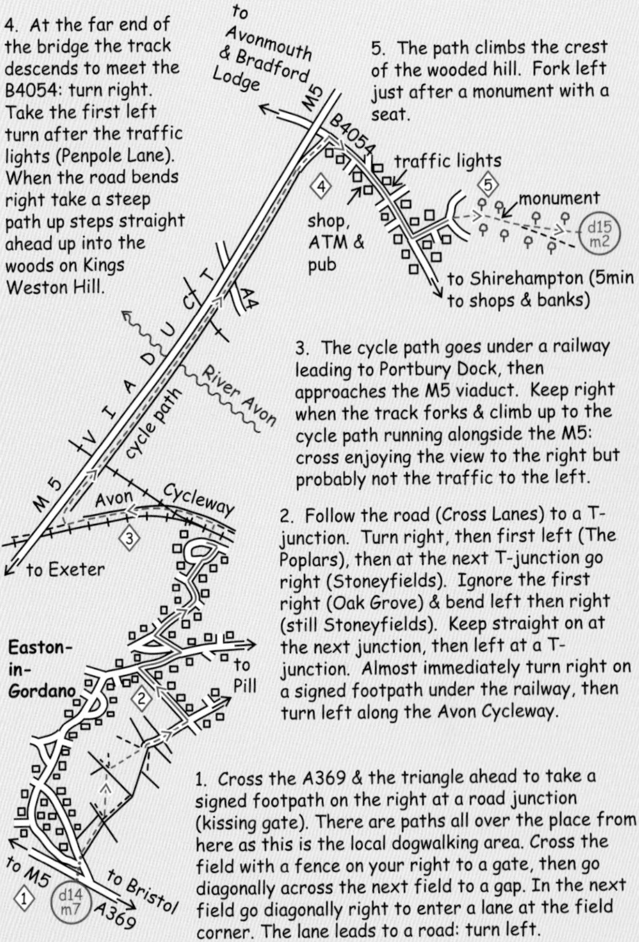

4. At the far end of the bridge the track descends to meet the B4054: turn right. Take the first left turn after the traffic lights (Penpole Lane). When the road bends right take a steep path up steps straight ahead up into the woods on Kings Weston Hill.

5. The path climbs the crest of the wooded hill. Fork left just after a monument with a seat.

3. The cycle path goes under a railway leading to Portbury Dock, then approaches the M5 viaduct. Keep right when the track forks & climb up to the cycle path running alongside the M5: cross enjoying the view to the right but probably not the traffic to the left.

2. Follow the road (Cross Lanes) to a T-junction. Turn right, then first left (The Poplars), then at the next T-junction go right (Stoneyfields). Ignore the first right (Oak Grove) & bend left then right (still Stoneyfields). Keep straight on at the next junction, then left at a T-junction. Almost immediately turn right on a signed footpath under the railway, then turn left along the Avon Cycleway.

1. Cross the A369 & the triangle ahead to take a signed footpath on the right at a road junction (kissing gate). There are paths all over the place from here as this is the local dogwalking area. Cross the field with a fence on your right to a gate, then go diagonally across the next field to a gap. In the next field go diagonally right to enter a lane at the field corner. The lane leads to a road: turn left.

to Avonmouth & Bradford Lodge
M5
B4054
traffic lights
monument
d15 m2
shop, ATM & pub
to Shirehampton (5min to shops & banks)
A4
M5 VIADUCT
cycle path
River Avon
Avon Cycleway
to Exeter
Easton-in-Gordano
to Pill
to M5
to Bristol
A369
d14 m7

Day 15 Map 2: Shirehampton to Henbury

4. Follow the drive round the left side of the museum to join the road in Henbury. Turn left, then right downhill (Hallen Rd). Look for a gate in the wall on the left, & a sign. This is the entrance to Blaise Hamlet, which should not be passed by without a visit.

5. After visiting Blaise Hamlet, continue down Hallen Rd, turn right at the end, then left along the B4055 (Station Rd). A shop/PO on the left is the last general store the Trail passes before Chepstow.

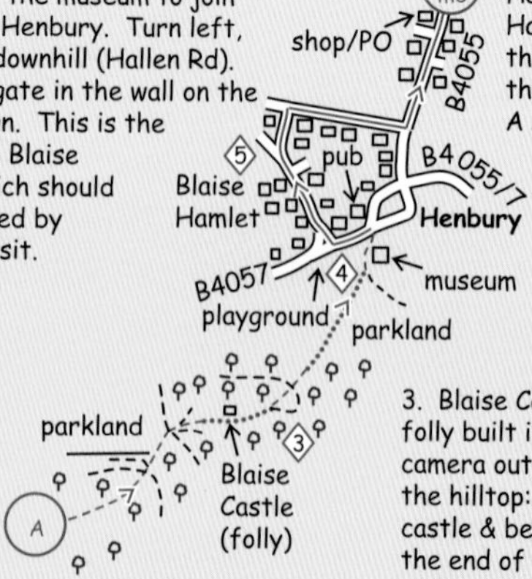

3. Blaise Castle is a picturesque folly built in 1766: get the camera out! There is no path on the hilltop: keep right of the castle & bear slightly right to the end of the clearing. Two paths descend through the trees from here: take the left one & drop steeply through the trees (crossing the other path), emerging in a tangle of paths into parkland at the bottom of the hill. Cross the park to the museum (the obvious big house).

2. After crossing the B4057 keep straight on (to right of the house) to regain the path along the ridge. Keep left when the path forks. Follow this path along the clearing on the ridge until just before the end of the clearing it descends left down steps through the wood. Cross a track near the bottom of the hill & bend slightly left to follow the right edge of the parkland (briefly). Re-enter the wood & go straight across another track. Ignore the first right fork (a dead end), & take the second. Climb steeply up to a hilltop clearing & Blaise Castle.

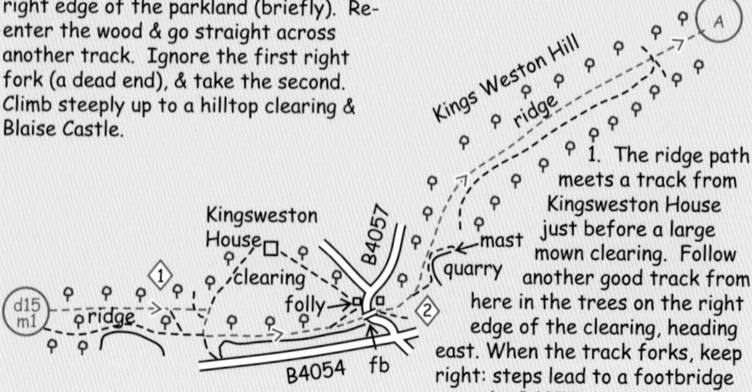

1. The ridge path meets a track from Kingsweston House just before a large mown clearing. Follow another good track from here in the trees on the right edge of the clearing, heading east. When the track forks, keep right: steps lead to a footbridge over the B4057.

Day 15 Map 3: Henbury to Easter Compton

1. The B4055 through Henbury bends slightly right. Take the next left (Greenlands Way), & turn left again almost immediately. At a T-junction go straight on (footpath sign) up a lane & over the railway. Cross stiles into the field on the right: signs & gates show the way to the road at Norton Farm.

2. Turn left on the minor road at Norton Farm & follow it until it crosses the M5: the last time the Trail crosses it. Turn right into a field immediately you are over the bridge (remains of stile), and cross a muddy quad bike circuit diagonally to a gate (no visible path). If you can't cross the quad bike track safely, use the lane further up the road.

3. Climb over the gate & turn left on the access lane for a few metres, then a footbridge on the right lets you into the big field. Cross a belt of greater willowherb to reach the field proper, then follow the field edge, with a wood on your left.

4. At the end of the wood continue straight on, keeping the overgrown hedge on your left. Go through a narrow belt of woodland on a good path, then continue along the left edge of the next field. Go a little right at the end of this field to a gap in a hedge. Cut straight across the next field towards a kissing gate & cross a track.

5. Cross the next field to another kissing gate, & it becomes obvious you are on a hill, albeit a modest one, as the M4 Severn Bridge comes into view. Go through the gate & turn half right to descend diagonally to a gate.

6. Follow field edges to a road, with the M48 bridge coming into view as you descend. Turn right along the road then left just before the first house (footbridge & footpath sign). Enter a field & cut half right across it to a gate then follow the field edge to cross another road into the churchyard opposite. Go through the lychgate & graveyard to a gate, & follow a clear path across a field to Easter Compton. Turn left along the B4055.

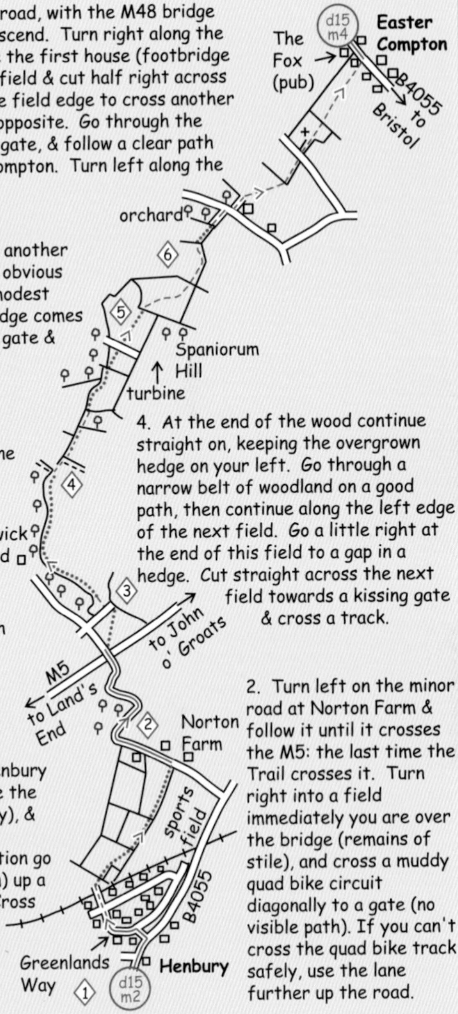

Easter Compton
d15 m4
The Fox (pub)
B4055 to Bristol
orchard
Spaniorum Hill
turbine
Berwick Wood
to John o' Groats
M5
to Land's End
Norton Farm
sports field
B4055
Greenlands Way
Henbury
d15 m2

Day 15 Map 4: Easter Compton to Pilning

Depending on how active the local council and/or footpath volunteers have been, the section from Easter Compton to the railway can be a bit awkward to follow, although it's generally a lot better now than it was when this book was originally published. An alternative route on minor roads is possible to the west if you need it.

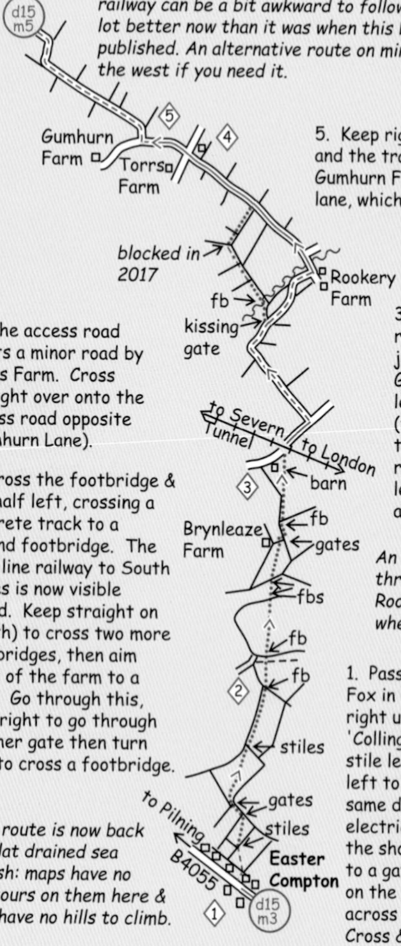

d15 m5

Gumhurn Farm

Torrs Farm

5

4

5. Keep right when the tarmac ends and the track divides (left goes to Gumhurn Farm). Continue along the lane, which gradually gets grassier.

blocked in 2017

fb

kissing gate

Rookery Farm

4. The access road meets a minor road by Torrs Farm. Cross straight over onto the access road opposite (Gumhurn Lane).

3. Past Brynleaze Farm aim right of the barn ahead to join a minor road (gates). Go under the railway & turn left at the first farm track (footpath sign). Follow the track when it bends to the right. At Rookery Farm go left & join the tarmac access road.

to Severn Tunnel

to London

3

barn

2. Cross the footbridge & aim half left, crossing a concrete track to a second footbridge. The main line railway to South Wales is now visible ahead. Keep straight on (north) to cross two more footbridges, then aim right of the farm to a gate. Go through this, turn right to go through another gate then turn left to cross a footbridge.

Brynleaze Farm

fb

gates

An alternative right of way through fields west of Rookery Farm was blocked when visited in 2017.

fbs

fb

fb

2

1. Pass (or pass through) the Fox in Easter Compton then turn right up the drive to 'Collingwood' (footpath sign). A stile leads to a field: aim half left to stiles & continue in the same direction past an electricity pole to a gate. Cross the short end of the next field to a gate (ignore the two gates on the right). Cut diagonally across the next field to stiles. Cross & follow the hedge & drain to a footbridge.

stiles

to Pilning

gates

stiles

The route is now back on flat drained sea marsh: maps have no contours on them here & you have no hills to climb.

B4055

Easter Compton

d15 m3

1

Day 15 Map 5: Pilning to Aust

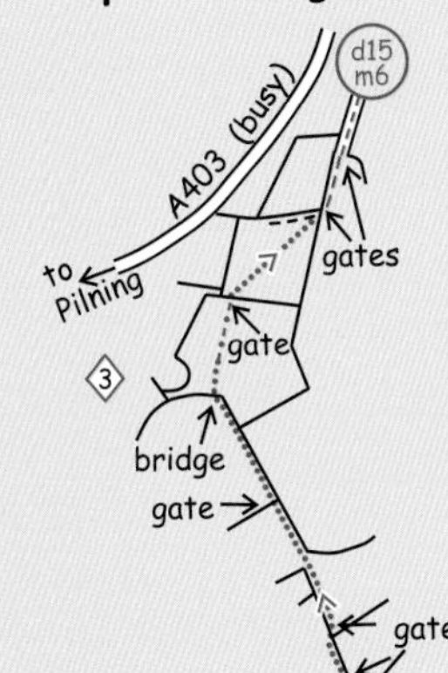

3. Cross the bridge over the rhine & cut across the big field to a visible gate. The Severn Bridge is in sight again now, not that far away. In the next field aim diagonally across the field to the right (NE), not straight ahead (N) to the more obvious gate. Go through a gate & follow a farm track to the left until another gate leads to a hedged lane, with Aust church now visible ahead.

2. Aim right of the buildings of Bilsham Farm, & go through the lefthand of the two gates ahead of you. Keep the hedge on your right to the next gate & footbridge, then continue, hedge now on your left. Go through a wide gap ahead & go on, now with the hedge & Lords Rhine (a drainage ditch) on the right again. Continue in the next field until you reach a bridge across the rhine (note they spell rhine with an 'i' around here - it was a 'y' earlier).

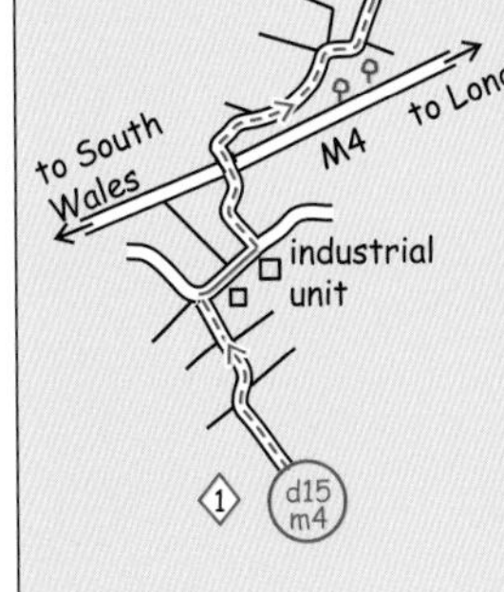

1. Follow the lane until it meets a road on a bend. Turn right, then left on a track opposite industrial premises. Follow this lane over the M4 motorway & round two double bends. On the next righthand bend, approaching Holm Farm, turn left over a footbridge & cut diagonally across the field to a gate in the far left corner. Continue with a hedge on your left, past a gate, until stiles on the left let you cross a road to the field opposite.

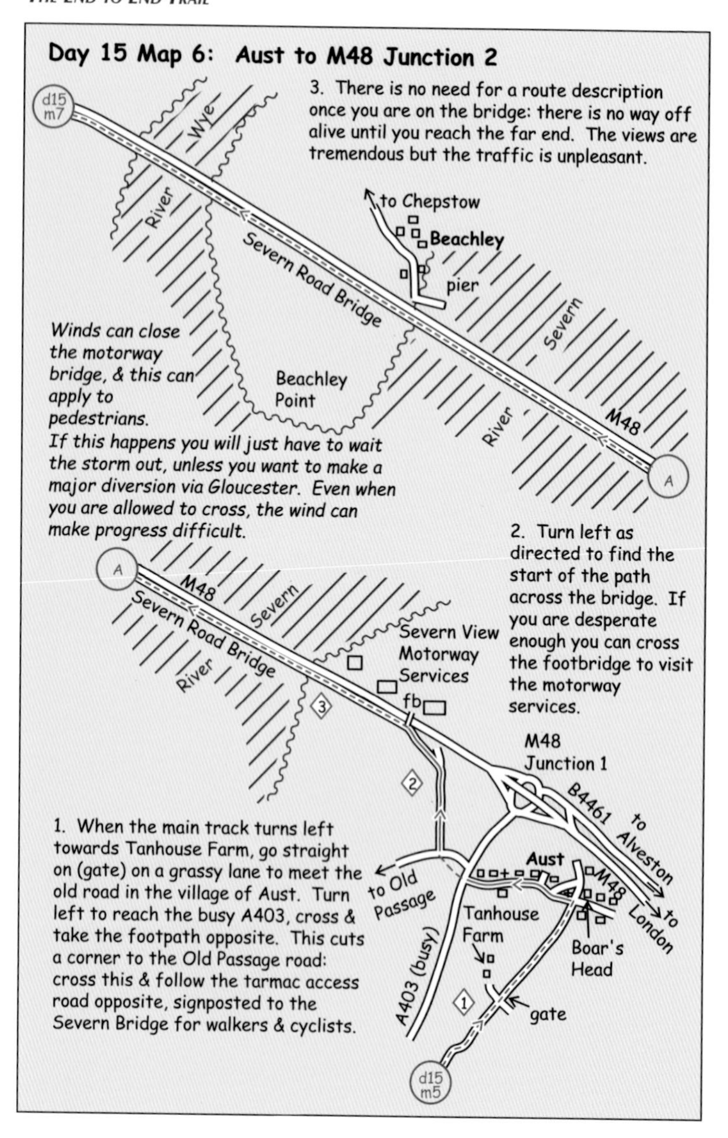
Day 15 Map 6: Aust to M48 Junction 2
3. There is no need for a route description once you are on the bridge: there is no way off alive until you reach the far end. The views are tremendous but the traffic is unpleasant.
d15 m7
River Wye
to Chepstow
Beachley
pier
Severn Road Bridge
River Severn
M48
A
Winds can close the motorway bridge, & this can apply to pedestrians.
If this happens you will just have to wait the storm out, unless you want to make a major diversion via Gloucester. Even when you are allowed to cross, the wind can make progress difficult.
Beachley Point
2. Turn left as directed to find the start of the path across the bridge. If you are desperate enough you can cross the footbridge to visit the motorway services.
A
M48
Severn Road Bridge
River Severn
Severn View Motorway Services
fb
3
2
M48 Junction 1
B4461 to Alveston
M48 to London
1. When the main track turns left towards Tanhouse Farm, go straight on (gate) on a grassy lane to meet the old road in the village of Aust. Turn left to reach the busy A403, cross & take the footpath opposite. This cuts a corner to the Old Passage road: cross this & follow the tarmac access road opposite, signposted to the Severn Bridge for walkers & cyclists.
to Old Passage
Aust
Tanhouse Farm
Boar's Head
A403 (busy)
1
gate
d15 m5

Day 15 Map 7: M48 Junction 2 to Chepstow

4. You are now in the centre of Chepstow: keep straight on, forking left along Bank St, Hocker Hill St & Bridge St to reach the Old Wye Bridge. Cross it & go straight on up a tarmac path & in a few metres the Offa's Dyke Path joins you from the right.

3. Keep straight on, on what becomes a fenced path between factories & a quarry. Emerge into a wood, taking the lefthand path & following it into the end of Wye Crescent. This leads to Hardwick Ave: turn left & go straight ahead when the road (& the Wales Coast Path) bends right. An underpass takes you under the A48: continue along Hardwick Terrace & turn right along Steep St & Moor St.

2. Continue on a good path from the end of the playing field. Follow this round the edge of the housing estate, crossing another path (stile on right), & along the edge of a wood. The path drops down to the fence along the bottom of the wood. When the main path loops back up left, continue ahead on the smaller path. Cross another path then keep right of houses ahead on a small path before climbing up to turn right along Raglan Way. Go left at the T-junction then right along a lane before no. 31 Victoria Rd.

1. The path descends from the M48: turn right under the motorway & follow Wales Coast Path signs along Caerwent Lane into the Thornwell housing estate. Turn right at a T-junction (Denbigh Drive), then again (Tenby Lane) to playing fields & a pavilion. Turn left before the pitch (footpath sign).

SECTION 3

Shropshire, Staffordshire and the Peak: Knighton to Hebden Bridge

Start	Knighton
Finish	Hebden Bridge
Distance	292km (182 miles)
Road walking	16%. The longest stretches are along minor lanes crossing low-lying farmland in Shropshire and Staffordshire, including quite a lot on the Staffordshire Way.
Days	9 (main schedule), or 12 (alternative schedule)
Maps and guides	*The whole section:* this guide, Section 3 strip maps

To reach the southern Pennines from the Welsh border hills means crossing a stretch of lowland farming country wherever you cut across. The route chosen for the Trail heads diagonally northeastwards from Knighton through the Shropshire hills, crossing the Clun and the Onny (tributaries of the River Teme that itself feeds the Severn near Worcester). It then follows the long ridge of Wenlock Edge to Much Wenlock, crosses the River Severn at Coalport just below Ironbridge, and continues east-northeast across farmland to meet the waymarked Staffordshire Way by the Shropshire Union Canal near Penkridge, south of Stafford.

The Staffordshire Way crosses Cannock Chase (where the Cotswold Way/ Heart of England Way alternative – see Section 2, 'Alternative routes' – rejoins the route), and continues northeast to Uttoxeter. Here you meet the River Dove, which the Trail follows upstream (northwards) for over 30km (20 miles) to Rocester in the Peak District. At Rocester the Staffordshire Way is abandoned for the Limestone Way – again a waymarked route. At Thorpe, 5km north of Ashbourne, the Trail leaves the Limestone Way to join the line of the Alternative Pennine Way (not waymarked), and follows it all the way to Hebden Bridge in West Yorkshire.

If you want to keep to the hills from Land's End to John o' Groats, then following the Pennines is the only way to go through the north of England. There used to be only one waymarked path, the Pennine Way, starting in Edale and finishing at Kirk Yetholm, in Scotland. This is a good route, but there are horrendous peat bogs at both ends, and serious erosion problems that don't need adding to. There's also a good chance you've already done it.

Section 3 Overview Map – Knighton to Hebden Bridge

A second waymarked route, the Pennine Bridleway, runs from near Matlock in Derbyshire to finish near Kirkby Stephen in Cumbria. This route has been designed principally for cyclists and horseriders, though, and it involves a fair amount of road walking and made surfaces.

The only other complete documented route is the Alternative Pennine Way (APW), devised by Denis Brook and Phil Hinchliffe. This avoids most of the peat bogs of the Dark Peak and the Cheviots, at either end of the Pennine Way, and while it tends not to follow the highest ground, it generally keeps to hilly country and avoids the Pennine Way crowds. Although it is not waymarked, surely this is an advantage rather than a disadvantage, and the APW would be the recommended route all the way to Jedburgh in Scotland, if the guidebook to it were generally available. Unfortunately it is long out of print, so the End to End Trail uses just the two ends to avoid the main Pennine Way peat bog areas, and joins the Pennine Way at Hebden Bridge, now safely beyond the Peak District morasses.

Maps

1:25,000 Explorer maps

- 201 Knighton & Presteigne
- 203 Ludlow (very briefly)
- 217 The Long Mynd & Wenlock Edge
- 242 Telford, Ironbridge & The Wrekin
- 244 Cannock Chase & Chasewater
- 259 Derby
- 24 The Peak District – White Peak Area
- 1 The Peak District – Dark Peak Area (later two-sided editions)
- 21 South Pennines (later two-sided editions)

1:50,000 Landranger maps

- 148 Presteigne & Hay-on-Wye
- 137 Church Stretton & Ludlow
- 138 Kidderminster & Wyre Forest (briefly)
- 127 Stafford & Telford
- 128 Derby & Burton upon Trent
- 119 Buxton & Matlock
- 110 Sheffield & Huddersfield
- 104 Leeds & Bradford (briefly)
- 103 Blackburn & Burnley

Guidebook

- *The Alternative Pennine Way* by Denis Brook and Phil Hinchliffe (Cicerone, 1992) (out of print)

Recommendations

Get Landranger 148 (see Section 2, 'Recommendations'), and Explorers 217, 242, 244, 259, 24, 1 and 21. This minimises the number of maps and gives good detail for most of Section 3.

Accommodation

The best sources of accommodation are the following tourist information centres:

- Church St, **Church Stretton** SY6 6DQ, tel 01694 723133 www.shropshiretourism.co.uk
- Shropshire Hills Discovery Centre, School Rd, **Craven Arms** SY7 9RS, tel 01588 676060 www.shropshirehillsdiscoverycentre.co.uk
- Coach Rd, Coalbrookdale, **Ironbridge** TF8 7DQ, tel 01952 884391 www.discovertelford.co.uk/visitironbridge
- The Museum, High St, **Much Wenlock** TF13 6HR, tel 01952 727679
- Gatehouse Theatre, Eastgate St, **Stafford** ST16 2LT, tel 01785 619619 www.visitstafford.org
- There is also more accommodation listed in **Staffordshire** at www.enjoystaffordshire.com
- Town Hall Yard, **Ashbourne** DE6 1ES, tel 01335 343666 www.visitpeakdistrict.com
- Old Market Hall, Bridge St, **Bakewell** DE45 1DS, tel 01629 816558 www.visitpeakdistrict.com
- Fairholmes, **Bamford**, Hope Valley S33 0AQ, tel 01433 650953 www.visitpeakdistrict.com
- Holmfirth Library, 47 Huddersfield Rd, **Holmfirth** HD9 3JH, tel 01484 414868 www.kirklees.gov.uk
- Butlers Wharf, New Rd, **Hebden Bridge** HX7 8AF, tel 01422 843831 www.hebdenbridge.co.uk
- Additionally, for the following areas, you should check out the corresponding websites: **Shifnal** (Day 22) www.shropshire-guide.co.uk; **Penkridge** (Day 22) www.penkridge.org.uk; **Abbots Bromley** (Day 23) www.abbotsbromley.com; **Youlgreave** (Day 25) www.youlgrave.org.uk. For the end of Day 27, check out www.holmfirth.org.

Planning ahead is particularly recommended for accommodation at the following stage ends (Note: 'A' in stage numbers indicates a stage end on the alternative schedule – see Appendix A):

- **Kemberton** (Day 22, Day A30)
- **Penkridge** (Day 22)
- **Abbots Bromley** (Day 23)
- **North Lees campsite**, near Hathersage (Day 26): often full, so booking is advisable (tel 01433 650838)
- **Moscar** (Day 27, Day A36): you will have to go off-route to find accommodation
- **Flouch** (Day 27, Day A37)
- **White Gate** (Day 27), if you're not camping

If you want to stay overnight in **Uttoxeter** (Day 24), bear in mind that accommodation may be difficult to find if you are there at the time of a horseracing meeting.

Equipment shops

- Day 22: (off-route) Tactree, Unit 3 Deer Park Court, **Telford** TF2 7NA, tel 01952 565670
- Day 22: (off-route) Millets, 11–12 Gaolgate Street, **Stafford** ST16 2BG, tel 01785 336397
- Day 24: There are a number of shops in **Ashbourne** (off-route)
- Day 26: There are a number of shops in **Bakewell** (off-route)
- Day 26: There are three outdoor shops in **Hathersage**
- Day 28: Mountain Wild, 19c Crown Street, **Hebden Bridge** HX7 8EH, tel 01422 844500
- Day 28: Alpine Outdoors, 42–44 Market Street, **Hebden Bridge** HX7 6AA, tel 01422 845673

Alternative routes

You can cut across from Offa's Dyke to the Pennines further north, if you wish, and I have outlined two good ways to do this. There are plenty of other alternatives, and if you want to investigate those, the best place to start is the Long Distance Walkers Association website www.ldwa.org.uk.

The South Cheshire option

This alternative means you get to walk about 80% of the Offa's Dyke Path rather than 50%, but miss out on the Peak limestone country and gritstone edges. It only grazes the edge of the Peak District, which is its main disadvantage, although it doesn't make a significant difference to the distance covered. If you want to take this route, you leave the Offa's Dyke Path at Bronygarth near Chirk, taking the waymarked Maelor Way east across farmland to Grindley Brook near Whitchurch, on the Cheshire–Shropshire border (a major crossroads of little-walked footpaths). From Grindley Brook another waymarked route, the South Cheshire Way, enables you to maintain your easterly direction to its end at Mow Cop, north of Stoke-on-Trent. At Mow Cop join the Gritstone Trail, and follow it north to its end at Disley. The Gritstone Trail is a great 56km (35-mile) route along the edge of the Peak District hills, well-waymarked and giving excellent views across the Cheshire plain. At Disley you are now not far from the Pennine Way. The simplest way to get there is to follow the Peak Forest Canal towpath to New Mills, then the Sett Valley Trail along a disused railway line to Hayfield, and climb William Clough to join the Pennine Way on Mill Hill. Alternatively, it's not much further to head east from Hayfield to the start of the Pennine Way at Edale. You can rejoin the main End to End Trail further north at Wessenden Head if you wish.

Guidebooks

- *Walking Offa's Dyke Path* by Mike Dunn (Cicerone, 2016)
- *Guide to the Maelor Way*, available from Wrexham Tourist Information Centre, Lambpit Street, Wrexham LL11 1AY, tel 01978 292015 www.wrexham.gov.uk
- *The South Cheshire Way: Grindley Brook to Mow Cop*, Mid-Cheshire Footpath Society; available via www.mcfs.org.uk
- A leaflet about the Gritstone Trail can be downloaded from Cheshire East Council website: visit www.cheshireeast.gov.uk and enter 'Gritstone Trail' in the Search box

The North Cheshire option

The Offa's Dyke Path ends at Prestatyn on the North Wales coast, so if you want to walk the whole of it, you need a route that will take you east from Prestatyn to the Pennines, where you can link either to the main Trail route, or the Pennine Way. Most of this link will be through lowland farmland across northeast Wales and Cheshire, and it adds significantly to the distance covered – Knighton to Hebden Bridge via Prestatyn and Edale is about 400km (250 miles), which is about 110km (70 miles) further than the main route of the End to End Trail.

From Prestatyn, the Wales Coast Path will take you to the English border on the outskirts of Chester. The North Cheshire Way has an alternative start at Chester railway station, and you can follow this route all the way across Cheshire to its end at Disley. You are now only 13km from the Pennine Way on Mill Hill: the South Cheshire option above outlines how to get there. The Wales Coast Path and the North Cheshire Way are both waymarked routes.

Guidebooks

- *Walking Offa's Dyke Path* by Mike Dunn (Cicerone, 2016)
- *The Wales Coast Path* by Paddy Dillon (Cicerone, 2015; reprinted 2016)
- *The North Cheshire Way*, Mid-Cheshire Footpath Society (2006); available via www.mcfs.org.uk

The complete Pennine Way

If you haven't already walked the Pennine Way, and if walking every inch of it is a 'must' for your Land's End to John o' Groats walk, then it is quite straightforward to vary the route to accommodate this. Leave the Alternative Pennine Way at Youlgreave and rejoin the Limestone Way, which has taken a much longer route between Thorpe and Youlgreave than the Trail. Follow the Limestone Way to its end at Castleton, then climb the tourist path over Mam Tor ridge to the start of the Pennine Way at Edale. It's about 33km from Youlgreave to Edale. From Edale, the Pennine Way will take you to Kirk Yetholm in the Scottish Borders, and from there the waymarked St Cuthbert's Way allows you to rejoin the main route of the End to End Trail near Jedburgh.

Guidebooks

- *The Limestone Way* published by Derbyshire Dales District Council; available from www.derbyshiredales.gov.uk
- *The Pennine Way* by Paddy Dillon (Cicerone, 4th edition, 2017)
- *St Oswald's Way and St Cuthbert's Way* by Rudolf Abraham (Cicerone, 2013)

The complete Alternative Pennine Way

The Alternative Pennine Way (APW) is a good route and a lot quieter than the Pennine Way, but to follow the whole of it, from Ashbourne to Jedburgh, you will need a copy of the out-of-print guidebook, since the route is not waymarked. Although it favours valleys rather than the high moorland, this doesn't mean it is easier – there are plenty of hills to climb to get from one valley to the next. (If you want to start at the very beginning of the APW, you will also have to find your way into Ashbourne.)

Guidebook

- *The Alternative Pennine Way* by Denis Brook and Phil Hinchliffe (Cicerone, 1992) (out of print)

Butterley Reservoir, approaching Marsden (Day 28)

DAY 20

Knighton to Craven Arms
The Shropshire hills

Distance	23km (14 miles)
Ascent	690m

This is a short day through the hills of southwest Shropshire. The Trail follows pleasant, quiet paths and tracks, over hummocky hills and through forestry plantations, before meeting the River Onny near picturesque Stokesay Castle and following the river to the small town of Craven Arms. There are no shops, pubs or cafés between the beginning and the end of the stage.

As you cross the railway bridge at Knighton station, the path leaves Wales for the last time and enters Shropshire (Day 20 Map 1). Initially a woodland track follows the Teme valley downstream, but soon you head into the hills, over a shoulder to the hamlet of **Stowe**, with its wooden church tower, and then over **Stow Hill** and down to the quiet Redlake valley (Day 20 Map 2). A steep climb up the other side of the valley leads to tracks through the forestry on **Hopton Titterhill** and down to the village of **Hopton Castle**, the ruined castle being clearly visible ahead (Day 20 Map 3). There are no facilities at Hopton Castle apart from the church, but it's a pretty place

The **castle** itself was originally built in the 13th century, and added to in the 14th and 16th centuries, although the mound it was built on is a 'motte', more typical of 11th- and 12th-century castles. The castle was attacked and ruined during the Civil War, and never rebuilt. It featured in the television programme *Time Team* in 2010, and is now open to the public.

After Hopton Castle, invisible footpaths lead over a low ridge to **Abcott** and **Clungunford**, where you pass another church. Climb up the road out of Clungunford and turn left at the T-junction.

You are now heading north on a minor road that used to be the line of a major **Roman highway** – now called Welsh Watling Street – which ran from Caerleon near Cardiff via Usk, Monmouth and Leintwardine to Wroxeter, and on to Chester. (The other Watling Street, mostly transformed by Thomas Telford into what is now the A5, ran from London to meet up with Welsh Watling Street at Wroxeter. The Trail crosses that Watling Street the day after tomorrow.)

After a short walk on the Roman road (Day 20 Map 4) the Trail turns right and crosses a broad, wooded shoulder on paths to descend towards **Stokesay Castle**.

Stokesay Castle is a spectacular 13th-century fortified manor house with an equally spectacular timber-framed gatehouse. The castle was sympathetically restored in the 19th century, and is open to the public daily except winter weekdays, courtesy of English Heritage. At Stokesay Castle you cross the waymarked Shropshire Way, a route you will meet again (and follow) later on tomorrow.

From Stokesay Castle you cross the A49 and follow the River Onny to **Craven Arms**. Craven Arms is a small town that grew up around what was once a major railway junction, and is now a minor railway junction (the Heart of Wales line branches off here). It has shops, a bank, a railway station and accommodation, and information is available at the Shropshire Hills Discovery Centre, which is an official tourist information point.

DAY 21

Craven Arms to Ironbridge
Wenlock Edge

Distance	36km (23 miles)
Ascent	760m

Wenlock Edge, formed by a tilted layer of limestone, is a wooded escarpment facing northwest and running for 30km (18 miles). Today's route follows it virtually all day, mainly through woods or along the edge of woods at the crest of the escarpment. There are extensive views all day, although along some stretches you can only spot them occasionally through gaps in the trees. The Long Mynd and the neighbouring hills east and northeast of Church

Stretton dominate on the left for the first half of the day; later the views open out a long way across Shropshire. On the right, the mass of Brown Clee Hill, with its radio masts, is the most obvious landmark. Underfoot there is a clear path virtually all day. There are many paths on Wenlock Edge, and plenty of visitors, and the Trail's route has been selected to try to give the best combination of pleasant immediate environment and views.

There are two waymarked long-distance paths that follow part of the Edge – the Shropshire Way and the Jack Mytton Way. If you are walking this part in the middle of the day, the Plough at Wistanstow is recommended. It is the brewery tap of Wood's Brewery and is 1km off-route from the footbridge over Quinny Brook near Strefford. There are no other shops or sources of refreshment close to the route between Craven Arms and Much Wenlock (Day 21 Map 6), 29km (18 miles) away.

Between Craven Arms (Day 21 Map 1) and Ironbridge there is only one real climb all day, which is the initial stiff pull from **Strefford**, diagonally up a muddy track from the bottom to the top of **Wenlock Edge**. This initial stretch along the top follows a good track and is easy underfoot. As with the rest of the day, the woods are delightful – ancient woodland that used to be coppiced, full of woodland flowers and birdlife.

The Shropshire Way joins the route (Day 21 Map 2), as the Trail continues along the Edge. Cross the two roads at **Burwood** and continue along a quieter path along the top, initially in the woods and later along field edges at the top of the woods.

The Wrekin from Wenlock Edge

Before reaching the next road at **Roman Bank** (Day 21 Map 3), a track rises up through the woods to join the Trail – along this runs the Jack Mytton Way, a waymarked long-distance bridleway that attracts many horseriders.

The **Jack Mytton Way** has been very successful, and as a result many stretches turned into deep mudbaths, which is probably unpleasant for horses, and certainly not what walkers have in mind when they head out to the country. Horses have churned up other paths along the Edge, but it is the Jack Mytton Way that seems to have suffered the most. Work has been done on the worst stretches, however, and it is now a lot better than it used to be.

The Trail follows the Jack Mytton Way only where it has to. From just before Roman Bank, through **Coats Wood**, to the next road near **Wilderhope Manor** (Day 21 Map 4), there is no real alternative.

From Wilderhope Manor to Presthope and beyond, the Edge is National Trust property, with open access for walkers, which means you can follow any path, not just rights of way. Although there are still a few muddy bits, from here the Trail parts temporarily with the Shropshire Way and also avoids many of the paths most frequented by horseriders, finding lesser-used paths in the woods rather than the main highways. The route passes close to Wilderhope Manor youth hostel (where you can also camp), and even if you are not staying there you may want to have a look at this historic manor house.

For much of the way from Wilderhope to Presthope (Day 21 Maps 4 and 5) the obvious line along the top of the Edge is taken by the B4371, so the Trail follows paths lower down the escarpment.

Along this section, the Jack Mytton Way mostly follows the disused railway line that used to run from Craven Arms to Much Wenlock, and on to Buildwas near Ironbridge. This is the fastest option, and not muddy, as the trackbed is well ballasted, as you would expect of a railway. (The trains stopped rumbling in 1962, after taking a Beeching's Powder – thank you to Maurice Dodd and his cartoon strip 'The Perishers' for that old joke.) Although this option is included on the strip maps and is a good walk, the old railway bed is not the best route, unless you are in a hurry, as there are other paths that are quieter and prettier – as shown on the strip maps.

Above the path between Easthope and Presthope is a limestone outcrop called **Ippikin's Rock** (Day 21 Map 4), on which you may see the occasional rock climber, although the rocks are not of any great height.

Above Ippikin's Rock, on the B4371, the Wenlock Edge Inn has been closed for many years, so don't be tempted to check it out. A little further along, the Trail passes the access road to Lower Hill Farm, where there is a very good little campsite (SO 581 977).

From the small car park at **Presthope** (Day 21 Map 5), the B4371 leaves the top of the Edge, so the Trail reclaims it, and follows it until rejoining the Jack Mytton Way and the Shropshire Way. The Trail leaves the Edge along a lane into **Much Wenlock** (Day 21 Map 6), following the narrow High Street to the 16th-century Guildhall and past the ruins of Wenlock Priory. There are many other old buildings worth looking at in this pretty little town, and it has plenty of shops, accommodation and other facilities. There is no longer a bank, but there is a cash machine at the garage (look right as you enter the town centre). There are campsites nearby, off the B4371 to the west and the A4169 to the north.

The 12th- and 13th-century **Wenlock Priory** was built on the site of the 7th-century St Milburga's Abbey. Much Wenlock is an ancient market town that grew around the priory.

From Much Wenlock to Ironbridge, the route follows the Shropshire Way, apart from a short stretch on the way out of Much Wenlock, to avoid unnecessary road walking. The route passes Audience Meadow, the location of a conference between Charles I and the Roundheads in 1642 (Day 21 Map 7). The Shropshire Way takes you through farmland and then below **Benthall Edge**, the last stretch

The Iron Bridge

of the continuation to the northeast of Wenlock Edge before the Severn Gorge outside Ironbridge (the motorway bridge over the Severn estuary seems a world away).

The final part of the day follows another disused railway through the woods alongside the Severn to end at the historic **Iron Bridge**. Across the bridge is the small town of **Ironbridge**, with accommodation and many old houses, shops and pubs, although the Trail itself does not go over the bridge. (There is a youth hostel at Coalport, 2.5km further along the route – see Day 22 Map 1.)

The **Iron Bridge** was completed in 1779, and was the first bridge in the world to use cast iron structurally, crossing the Severn in a single arch with a span of over 30 metres. It was built when the area was one of the most important of the Industrial Revolution, pioneering the use of coke instead of charcoal for iron smelting on an industrial scale. There were also a lot of pottery, tile and brick works, although virtually all the heavy industry has gone now, leaving a valley full of fascinating relics of its industrial past in an attractive wooded setting.

DAY 22

Ironbridge to Penkridge
Crossing the watershed

Distance	40km (25 miles)
Ascent	410m

Although today features the first time the main watershed is crossed since Exmoor, it is mostly easy walking through flat farmland. After leaving the interesting and atmospheric Severn Gorge at the beginning of the day, much of the countryside is pleasant enough, but not inspiring. The high point is King Charles's Wood near Kemberton, and the rest is really just the farmland you need to cross to bridge the gap between Wenlock Edge and Cannock Chase on your way to the southern end of the Peak District.

From the outskirts of Ironbridge you follow the disused railway along the valley on the south bank of the Severn for a couple of kilometres to a pub by a footbridge over the river (Day 22 Map 1). The Boat Inn is a basic and traditional pub that presumably used to serve the needs of the workers in the tile works.

The **footbridge** was originally put up in 1922, replacing Coalport Ferry (a boat sank here in 1799, drowning 29 people), and commemorates the dead of World War I. It was taken away by road for renovation in 2000 and put back later in the year.

Across the river and then the canal, the path climbs up alongside the Hay Inclined Plane. (Coalport youth hostel is just along the road to the right from here.)

The **Inclined Plane** is a steep railway line up the valley side that was used to transport boats down to the River Severn from a canal leading from coalmines. Boats were floated onto a cradle, which was then winched out of the water and down the rails. The height difference between canal and river was 63m, which would have needed 27 locks to connect them in a more orthodox manner. The Plane was operational from 1792 until 1894.

Once past the Inclined Plane and through the woods up the hillside, the interest fades (Day 22 Map 2). There is a pub in **Kemberton**, and bed and breakfast at Church Farm. After this comes a delightful walk up by the stream in **King Charles's Wood** to Evelith Mill. (If you want to find accommodation in Shifnal, you can follow paths north from here.) From Evelith Mill, lanes and cart tracks take you quickly east (Day 22 Map 3), under the M54 and across the A41 to **Tong Norton** (Day 22 Map 4).

At Tong Norton there is a pub (the Bell Inn) and a petrol station with a limited shop – the only shop before Penkridge. If you want an overnight stay around here your options are limited, and unfortunately the Bell Inn has no accommodation. Your best bet, if you are not staying in Kemberton or camping courtesy of a friendly farm, is to divert to Shifnal, where bed and breakfast is available (see Day 22 Map 3). It's worth checking out www.shropshire-guide.co.uk for the latest accommodation options.

Paths and lanes lead from Tong Norton to the site of **White Ladies Priory** and then on to **Boscobel House**, where there is a café (open from 8.30am on days when the House is open – see below).

All that remains of **White Ladies Priory** are the ruins of its 12th-century church. Charles II hid at the priory in 1651 after being defeated at the Battle of Worcester. He then moved on to **Boscobel House** 1.5km further along the Trail, famously hiding in an oak tree, then a priest's hole, which can still be seen on payment of the entry fee, courtesy of English Heritage. The original oak has gone, but a descendant has been planted in its place, and a descendant of that one as well. Entry to the grounds is free, and opening hours from

White Ladies Priory

Easter to the end of October are 10am–4pm Wednesday to Sunday. There is a permissive path joining the Priory and the House, but the end at Boscobel House is only open when the House is open.

By Boscobel House you cross the main **watershed** of Britain for the first time since Exmoor. On the west side, the streams flow into the River Worfe, which joins the Severn to the south; on the east side, the streams flow into the River Penk (which you meet at the end of the day), which flows north into the Sow, which flows east into the Trent, which eventually makes up its mind and flows north into the Humber. In fact the route from here lies entirely on the eastern side of the watershed all the way to the end of this section at Hebden Bridge and beyond. This is also where you cross the county boundary from Shropshire into Staffordshire.

The Trail goes via lanes and a cultivated field, past **Belvide Reservoir**, across the A5 (the more famous Roman Watling Street, as opposed to the Welsh Watling Street, encountered on Day 20), to meet the Staffordshire Way at the **Shropshire Union Canal** (Day 22 Map 5) before reaching **Lapley**.

For the rest of the day, to Penkridge (Day 22 Map 6), the Trail follows the Staffordshire Way (waymarked with the symbol of a knot), and continues to follow it all day the next day and part of the next, to eventually leave it on Day 24 at Rocester.

From Lapley, route-finding is easy to the small town of **Penkridge** (although there is rather too much road walking). Penkridge has a railway station, shops, banks and pubs. There are hotels and a bed and breakfast in Penkridge, and there is a campsite 2km to the east at Pillaton Hall Farm (tel 01785 715177). Although it has a two nights minimum stay policy for bookings, walkers can stay for single nights, but be aware it is expensive for single campers (£24 per tent in 2018). For the latest accommodation information, check www.penkridge.org.uk before you set out.

Penkridge is on an old coaching route, and this ancient market town was given its charter in 1244 by Henry III. Defoe called it 'a small but ancient town', and was surprised at the size of the horse fair there when he arrived for a three-day stay. The old coaching route is now the busy A449 connecting Stafford to Wolverhampton, so the west side of the town is rather dominated by traffic.

DAY 23

Penkridge to Abbots Bromley
Towpaths and Cannock Chase

Distance	26km (16 miles)
Ascent	300m

Today's walking along the Staffordshire Way starts off on one canal towpath, crosses some farmland to get to Cannock Chase (what is left of an ancient Royal Forest), then at the other side of the Chase takes you to a second canal, this time heading southeast – not often on the Trail does the route head so blatantly in the wrong direction. When the towpath is left for more fields and lanes, you head more or less northeast to Abbots Bromley. The canal towpaths are very pleasant to walk, easy underfoot, and the narrowboats provide a bit of colour and companionship. Cannock Chase is a big expanse of woodland, plantations and heathland that is very popular with walkers and mountain bikers, and fortunately the Staffordshire Way takes you through some of the best of it, avoiding forestry plantations. The remaining farmland is pleasant enough on the whole, but not what I go on walking holidays for.

The Trail leaves Penkridge along the **Staffordshire and Worcestershire Canal** (Day 23 Map 1). This is a classic narrowboat canal, completed in 1772, and running from the Severn at Stourport to join the Trent and Mersey Canal north of Cannock Chase. Despite the noise of the M6 motorway that crosses the canal, this is a beautiful stretch of water to walk along, overhung by trees, and some of the old canal bridges ought to be in paintings.

The towpath walking is over all too soon, and followed by a less pleasant trudge along the edges of huge cultivated fields. Lanes lead to **Bednall**, which has little worth stopping for (it is mainly a dormitory village with many modern houses), but, thankfully, just across the A34 is Cannock Chase, where you meet much better walking country (Day 23 Map 2). The last bit of the Heart of England Way crosses the Trail on the Chase, so this is where the Cotswold Way/Heart of England Way alternative – see Section 2, 'Alternative routes' – rejoins the main Trail.

Cannock Chase is entered at a wood of tall pines, but this is atypical of what the route sees of the Chase. After crossing a road you are on heathland – a mixture of heather, bracken and birch trees that is more characteristic of the next few kilometres.

The Trail descends into the Oldacre Valley, then climbs up again and crosses over to the Sherbrook Valley, which you follow north on a popular track until you reach the **Stepping Stones** (Day 23 Map 2).

You have a choice of route here. The main recommended route leaves the Staffordshire Way at the Stepping Stones, going via the **Seven Springs** car park (Day 23 Map 3) to reach the Trent and Mersey Canal at Bridge 72. Alternatively, you can take a longer route via Shugborough. This keeps to the Staffordshire Way from the Stepping Stones, going north to visit Shugborough Hall before turning back southeast along the Trent and Mersey Canal to reach Bridge 72. The Shugborough route is included on the strip maps, but is not the recommended route because it involves an extra 2km of unnecessary road walking, both on the busy A513 and the busy Shugborough estate roads.

Shugborough Hall, built in the 1690s and the home of the Earl of Lichfield, is probably worth a visit if you like country houses, but in my opinion the view of it from the route doesn't justify the additional road walking. The ancient **Essex Bridge** over the River Trent, used by the Staffordshire Way near Shugborough, is the longest packhorse bridge in England, and the best thing to be seen on the Shugborough route.

Whether you choose the main Trail route or the Shugborough alternative, you end up at **Bridge 72**, heading the 'wrong way' along the **Trent and Mersey Canal** (Day 23 Map 3). There are opportunities just off-route for pub lunch stops in **Little Haywood**, near Bridge 72, and at the Wolseley Arms near Bridge 70.

Colwich Lock, Trent and Mersey Canal

The **Trent and Mersey Canal** was built at the same time as the Staffordshire and Worcestershire Canal, linking Merseyside with the Trent Navigation. It runs through Stoke-on-Trent and the Cheshire salt mining area (characterised by towns ending in 'wich', such as Northwich and Middlewich). The key drivers for its construction were the pottery and salt industries, which wanted cheaper transportation of their raw materials, such as coal and iron, and of their products. Josiah Wedgwood cut the first sod in 1766, the canal was completed in 1777, and it was financially very successful. Like the Staffs and Worcs, it is a narrowboat canal, with locks only 2 metres wide.

The canal starts to become drearier as the trees disappear and the power station at Rugeley starts to loom near. With relief leave the canal at **Bridge 68** (Day 23 Map 4) and start heading in the right direction again. The Staffordshire Way bypasses most of the village of **Colton** through fields to its west, but there are two pubs in the village, both just off-route.

Intricate route-finding is the order of the day all the way from Colton to Abbots Bromley. Although stiles help to make the route relatively easy to follow, there are few Staffordshire Way signs, and for much of the way there is no visible path through the fields (follow the strip maps closely to trace the route).

Cross a ridge at Medleywood Barn (Day 23 Map 5), and suddenly **Blithfield Reservoir** is spread out ahead, covered with small boats if it is a weekend. More bobbing and weaving through the fields leads to **Abbots Bromley**.

Abbots Bromley is a pretty little village with shops and pubs. There is some bed and breakfast accommodation in and around Abbots Bromley, but it's limited, so you need to plan ahead to be sure of a bed.

Abbots Bromley's main claim to fame is the **Horn Dance**, enacted each September, when six local men wearing ancient reindeer antlers dance round the parish all day, drinking beer to keep them going. (The antlers are kept in the church for the rest of the year.)

DAY 24

Abbots Bromley to Thorpe
The River Dove

Distance	34km (21 miles)
Ascent	640m

Today the Trail follows the Staffordshire Way north across farmland to Uttoxeter, then up the broad floodplain of the River Dove to Rocester. At Rocester the Trail leaves the Staffordshire Way (which follows the River Churnet northwest instead) to continue up the Dove, then follows a tributary stream parallel to and west of the Dove, mostly following the waymarked Limestone Way. The day ends by crossing the Dove again and entering the Peak District National Park, just before the village of Thorpe, close to the tourist haunt of Dovedale.

The section from Abbots Bromley to Uttoxeter is not the best of walking, particularly the section through **Bagot's Park** (Day 24 Maps 1 and 2). The path here follows the edge of huge, prairie-like fields of crops, and it seems to take forever to get anywhere. It's possibly the low point of the whole Trail, and **Uttoxeter** is likely to be reached with some relief.

Uttoxeter has a railway station, banks, shops and accommodation. If you are there at the time of a horseracing meeting, accommodation may be difficult to find – try to plan ahead.

From Uttoxeter the day improves, although it is not until you are approaching Thorpe, at the end of the day, that any real sign of the Peak District raises the curtain on what is to come. The Staffordshire Way leaves Uttoxeter via a small industrial estate and car parks for the racecourse, then crosses floodplain meadows to meet the River Dove and the A50 trunk road (Day 24 Map 3). This is a very busy dual carriageway linking the M6 and M1 motorways, but a pedestrian underpass spares walkers any physical danger, although that doesn't make the road any more pleasant – the old Dove Bridge next to the modern one is a reminder of when driving was a less frenetic business.

All the way from its source on Axe Edge near Buxton to its confluence with the Trent near Burton, the Dove forms the boundary between Staffordshire and Derbyshire, and crossing the A50 bridge the Trail enters Derbyshire for the first time. From here you follow the river north, up to field edges at the top of the escarpment, then back down past a shooting club to follow quiet farm tracks and riverside paths towards **Rocester** (Day 24 Map 4).

Rocester's JCB factory is prominent ahead on the left as you near the village, with the Weaver Hills beyond. These hills are the start of limestone country, and being outside the Peak National Park have been quarried extensively.

At Rocester Bridge the Trail re-enters Staffordshire and heads along the road towards the village, leaving the Staffordshire Way by turning right into West View immediately after Tutbury Mill. This is the start of the Limestone Way, although there are no waymarks to indicate this. From here, bypassing the centre of Rocester, the Trail mainly follows the Limestone Way to Thorpe, where the day's walking ends.

Rocester is dominated by the JCB factory; most of the buildings are post-war, and the village centre is worth visiting only if you need the pub, a shop or accommodation.

There are virtually no visible signs of the Roman settlement or the old abbey at **Rocester**, but the Trail does pass Tutbury Mill, one of many early textile mills set up by Richard Arkwright in and around the Peak District.

The Trail is invisible for most of the next 2km, through fields on the ridge between the Churnet and Dove valleys, before descending to the Dove again, where the riverside path is very pleasant (Day 24 Map 5). At the B5033 bridge you leave the Dove, heading up towards Ellastone along a tributary running parallel to it (Day 24 Map 6).

Before turning left up the road towards Ellastone, it is worth considering visiting the ancient church and manor house at **Norbury**, a few hundred metres along the road to the right. Norbury Manor is a 13th-century medieval hall, and next to it is the 14th-century church of St Mary and St Barlok. You will probably only be able to view them from the outside, as the church is usually locked. The Naylor brothers visited the church here in 1871: 'On arrival at Ellastone we left our luggage at the substantially built inn there while we went to visit Norbury Church, which was well worth seeing.'

At **Ellastone** as at Rocester, the Trail misses the centre of the village. There is a pub, the Duncombe Arms, just off-route (see Day 24 Map 6).

Ellastone isn't particularly picturesque, but it is the setting for George Eliot's **Adam Bede**. The village is renamed Hayslope in the novel, and Adam Bede himself was based on George Eliot's grandfather, who was the local blacksmith and wheelwright.

East of Ellastone, the Trail passes through **Calwich Park**, the former grounds of Calwich Abbey, and shortly afterwards leaves the Limestone Way for a while for a better alternative. The Limestone Way follows field edges above Ordley Brook valley, but there is an excellent route along the wooded valley bottom that is a lot better (Day 24 Map 7). Although it is occasionally wet underfoot, the wood is delightful to walk through and mostly very easy walking.

The path emerges from the trees briefly to descend a minor road down **Ordley Bank** and rejoin the stream – this is the first time the flavour of the Peak District is tasted, with steep slopes, bracken and stone walls. The path up the stream from here is less frequented and a bit overgrown, but eventually climbs out of the valley to Ellishill Farm.

Tricky route-finding on invisible field paths leads up over the ridge, crossing the A52 at **Swinscoe**, where there is a pub, the Dog and Partridge. From the top of the next ridge, the cone of Thorpe Cloud and the narrow exit from Dovedale are clearly visible ahead – something to look forward to for tomorrow.

Dropping down from the ridge you rejoin the Limestone Way (Day 24 Map 8), then a switchback down and up again onto a second ridge leads to Coldwall Farm, where an old road is joined, now just a track, which leads down to cross the River Dove into Derbyshire again at Coldwall Bridge. This is also where you enter the Peak District National Park, and it's another place worth lingering, if you have time.

A riverside footpath to the left just before the bridge is the best way to Ilam youth hostel, otherwise **Thorpe** village is just ahead, with a pub and bed and breakfasts. There is also a campsite about 1.5km from Thorpe at Ashbourne Heights. (If you are camping here, there is another pub, the Blue Bell Inn, on the A515 at SK 172 516, which is closer to the campsite than the Old Dog in Thorpe.)

Thorpe is a strangely scattered village – it has attractive stone houses, a church, a pub, a hotel, and even used to have a railway station, but it doesn't seem to have a village centre.

DAY 25

Thorpe to Youlgreave
The limestone dales

Distance	26km (16 miles)
Ascent	630m

Today the Trail follows the Alternative Pennine Way all day (and continues to do so until the end of Day 28), but remember that this is not a waymarked route, so you will need to follow carefully the OS maps and the strip maps at the end of this section.

For much of the day the route is along the bottom of some of the Peak District's many limestone dales; these valley bottoms are usually the best places to walk in the Peak limestone areas. The higher ground above them is usually not particularly high in absolute terms, and provides good farmland, which means that paths mainly follow field edges. The valleys, on the other hand, are typically steep-sided and U-shaped, with a bottom not wide enough to bother with intensive farming. In addition, the more spectacular dales have outcrops, and sometimes high cliffs of pale-grey limestone lining their sides, and they tend to be quieter and wilder than the uplands, and used for pasture or left to woodland. Often they are dry, since the streams that carved them through ice-age permafrost have long since gone underground in the porous limestone. These valleys make excellent walking country, and what they lack in distant views is more than made up for by the immediate surroundings. Inevitably they are popular with walkers and day-trippers, and the first on the route, Dovedale (a Site of Special Scientific Interest), is the busiest of them all, with a huge car park at the southern end that has been known to experience gridlock on sunny summer Sundays.

The route from Thorpe, for the next three and a half days as far as Marsden (Day 28), is almost entirely within or along the boundary of the Peak District National Park. The environment here is traditionally rural and well protected

– of all the national parks, only the Peak District and Lake District authorities have direct control of the planning permission process in their areas.

There is an alternative route from Thorpe to Biggin following the Tissington Trail, a disused railway line, but although quicker, it's far inferior scenically, and disused railways are monotonous underfoot. The start is shown on Day 24 Map 8, and its junction with the recommended route of the Trail is shown on Day 25 Map 2.

The recommended route of the Trail takes a short walk from Thorpe down **Lin Dale** to reach the stepping stones in **Dovedale** (Day 25 Map 1). Thorpe Cloud is an excellent viewpoint, and well repays the short but brutally steep climb up the path from the stepping stones. From the stepping stones the Trail follows Dovedale north to **Milldale**. There is a small shop at Milldale, selling essentials such as ice cream and chocolate, and there is a camping barn at Alstonefield, about 1km to the northwest.

Dovedale is a classic limestone valley, perhaps the most spectacular in the country, and draws large numbers of visitors. It has attracted people for centuries – Isaac Walton was here in the 17th century, and Samuel Johnson and Byron also visited. The valley is deep and wooded, between limestone cliffs and pinnacles covered in rock climbs, with the River Dove playing its full part as an archetypal sparkling limestone stream (apart from staying resolutely above ground).

If I ever regretted being a cyclist it was along this section. The sweet pastoral Dove has an irresistible pulling power after the slightest introduction. But it is only for the walker, and it would be excusable for the cyclist and the motorist to throw their machines over the hedge, take to shoe leather and sample the exquisite walk from Alsop-on-le-Dale to Thorpe Cloud by the riverside

William Dawson, Land's End to John o' Groats, 1934

The route continues north up Mill Dale, the continuation of the Dove valley above Milldale village (Day 25, Map 2). It is slightly quieter now, but there are still plenty of hikers at weekends. The valley eventually forks, and you turn right to follow the side valley of **Biggin Dale**, still immaculate walking country.

Biggin Dale gradually becomes shallower, then you meet a minor road leading east through the small village of **Biggin**, where the Waterloo Inn is nicely placed for a **pub lunch**, with a spacious beer garden at the front and a **campsite** at the back.

From Biggin the Trail continues east along lanes and field paths (Day 25 Map 3). At **Gotham** the route briefly joins the High Peak Trail, which follows the trackbed of the Cromford and High Peak Railway, with Gotham Curve reputed to have been the tightest railway curve in Britain.

The **Cromford and High Peak Railway** was one of the earliest railways, opened in 1831. It was designed as part of the canal network, joining the Cromford Canal to the Peak Forest Canal at Whaley Bridge, and incorporated a number of steep inclines up which trucks had to be winched.

A pleasant kilometre along the High Peak Trail, then a less inspiring stretch on roads, and you drop down on a footpath into **Gratton Dale**, another fascinating, deep, wooded limestone valley.

At the foot of the dale a short climb up the hillside along a minor road (Day 25 Map 4) leads to very different type of country, with an invisible and soggy path crossing a gritstone boulder field towards Youlgreave (there will be plenty more grit tomorrow!). The gritstone area is soon passed, and the last limestone dale of the day, **Bradford Dale**, leads to the pretty village of **Youlgreave**. If you plan to camp, a footpath to the campsite at Hopping Farm begins where the route meets the river: see strip map and details below.

The Fountain, Youlgreave

(If you are heading for Edale and the start of the Pennine Way, you don't need to go through the centre of Youlgreave unless you need its facilities. See Day 25 Map 4 for the recommended point at which to leave the Alternative Pennine Way in Bradford Dale and rejoin the Limestone Way to Castleton, from where a climb over the Mam Tor ridge leads to Edale.)

Youlgreave (it is a matter of opinion whether the name of the village is spelled Youlgreave or Youlgrave – I've used the former to be consistent with the Ordnance Survey) is a classic Peak District village with old stone cottages crowded together and hugging the narrow roads. It has accommodation (check out www.youlgrave.org.uk), including a youth hostel and hotels. The nearest campsite is at Hopping Farm (SK 204 631, tel 01629 636302). Call at the farm, not at the bigger Camping and Caravan Club site next door, which does not cater for walkers. Youlgreave also has a post office, a couple of shops, and what looks like a monument opposite the youth hostel, but is actually the original water supply to the village, piped to here in 1829.

DAY 26

Youlgreave to Hathersage
The gritstone edges

Distance	29km (18 miles)
Ascent	860m

Today the Trail continues to follow the Alternative Pennine Way, heading northeast out of limestone country. At Baslow it picks up the line of gritstone edges that runs northwards for the rest of the day, above the east side of the Derwent valley, to Hathersage and Stanage Edge. A diversion from Stanage Edge down to the village of Hathersage is necessary at the end of the day to find accommodation, returning to the Edge the next morning.

From Youlgreave the route crosses **Lathkill Dale**, then through farmland to cross the River Wye close to Haddon Hall (Day 26 Map 1), and continues over low hills and through woods, via **Calton Pastures**, to descend to **Edensor** and the parklands of Chatsworth House (Day 26 Map 2).

Haddon Hall dates back to the Norman Conquest, and was the home of William Peverel, the illegitimate son of William the Conqueror. The hall was never allowed to fall into ruin, and was sympathetically restored by the Duke of Rutland in the 1920s and 30s.

Chatsworth is principally an 18th-century creation, built for the first Duke of Devonshire, and designed for show rather than defence, with an extensive landscaped park. Defoe expressed his astonishment that anyone would attempt to create something like the Chatsworth Estate in such a place, 'where the mountains insult the clouds, intercept the sun, and would threaten, were earthquakes frequent here, to bury the very towns, much more the house, in their ruins'.

Am I alone in thinking the Chatsworth House buildings are hideously ugly? From the hillside above Edensor they look to me more like a Victorian hospital than an elegant country house. By contrast, the buildings in the estate village of Edensor are delightful – all different, and all the woodwork painted in the same shade of Chatsworth Blue. The original Edensor village was largely demolished, resited and rebuilt when the park was landscaped.

Elihu Burritt visited both Haddon and Chatsworth on his walk to John o' Groats in 1863, and called them the 'two most representative buildings in the kingdom'. They are both open to visitors.

Edensor

A stroll alongside the River Derwent through Chatsworth's parkland leads to the village of **Baslow**, which has pubs, shops and accommodation.

From here the scenery changes. A steep climb up a rough lane brings you to **Baslow Edge**, the first of the gritstone edges, outcrops of hard, grey sandstone. By far the longest line of these in Britain runs due north from here for over 16km, overlooking the River Derwent, from Baslow to Moscar. The edges vary from nothing to 25m or more in height, and include some of the most popular rock climbing in the country. The walking along the top of the edges is usually easy, as the gritty rock forms well-drained and even paths. The views, particularly to the west, are extensive.

After Baslow Edge come **Curbar** and **Froggatt Edges** (Day 26 Map 3), both important rock-climbing areas, so expect to hear the clanking of metal coming up from below. Shortly after the end of Froggatt Edge, the Trail passes the excellent Grouse Inn, then diverges a bit from the top of the escarpment to cross, on an old estate road, what used to be the parkland of the **Longshaw Estate** (Day 26 Map 4). This used to be the Duke of Rutland's shooting land, but now belongs to the National Trust. (Note: The road numbering in this area was changed in 2000 due to rerouting of the A625, so older maps don't show the correct numbers.)

Crossing the A6187 near Burbage Bridge, a path climbs up the gritstone moorland to the outcrop of **Carl Wark**. On Carl Wark there is an ancient boulder wall, thought to be part of the defences for an Iron Age fort. Beyond Carl Wark, the Trail ascends to the higher outcrop of **Higger Tor**, then crosses two moorland roads and climbs to follow the longest of the gritstone edges – **Stanage Edge** (Day 26 Map 5) – to round off the day.

If there is mist on the Edge and you are planning to stay at Hathersage for the night, it is best to turn left along the second moorland road (Day 26 Map 4 – bad weather route) rather than continue the climb up to Stanage Edge. In mist it is difficult to identify the top of the descent from Stanage Edge to Hathersage.

Stanage Edge has been climbed on for over a hundred years, although it wasn't until after World War II that it started to become popular. Now, justifiably, it is one of the most popular venues in the country, with nearly a thousand documented routes, and hundreds of climbers swarm all over it on dry summer weekends. Even when the Edge is engulfed in mist, it is by no means unusual to hear the 'clank, clank' of climbers groping their way up the greasy rock below you.

The Trail route for the main schedule (ie the one reflected in the stage distances) drops down from Stanage Edge (just after Stanage Plantation and just before reaching the Long Causeway) to head for the North Lees campsite above

Hathersage (SK 235 833, which is where the length of this stage has been measured to), returning to the same point on the Edge the next morning. The campsite is the closest legitimate accommodation to the Trail around here (unofficial camping is not allowed in the national park). The campsite is small and often full, so booking is recommended (tel 01433 650838).

An alternative is to continue beyond the campsite to **Hathersage** village and stay there (even if you stay at the campsite you are likely to want to visit Hathersage to eat, drink and/or shop). Hathersage has a youth hostel, bed and breakfasts, shops, a bank, and outdoor shops, including the excellent Outside and its equally excellent café upstairs. It is a pleasant village, though marred slightly by the busy road through the middle, and Robin Hood's Little John is supposed to be buried in the churchyard here. Descent to Hathersage adds about 2km to the day, and the same again the next morning.

On the way down to Hathersage you pass **North Lees Hall**, reputed to be the model for Thornfield Hall, the home of Mr Rochester in Charlotte Brontë's *Jane Eyre*. In 1845 the author spent three weeks in Hathersage while writing the novel.

The Alternative Pennine Way as originally described doesn't drop down to Hathersage, but continues along Stanage Edge to a stage end at **Moscar** on the A57 (Day 27 Map 1). Unfortunately there is nowhere to stay at Moscar, and it is not a suitable place to camp (and again, wild camping isn't allowed in the national park), so if you don't want to stay at North Lees or Hathersage there are three options.

1. Drop down the **Long Causeway** from Stanage Edge to the village of **Bamford** (see Day 27 Map 1, number 1), which has accommodation and pubs, and camping at Swallowholme Caravan Park. This adds about 3km to today's walk, and makes little difference to tomorrow's.
2. Continue to **Moscar**, follow the A57 west, then take a minor road to the Strines Inn (Day 27 Map 1, SK 222 906, tel 0114 285 1247). This 13th-century pub has excellent accommodation (four-poster bed, coal fire in your room), but is not cheap. If you stay there, you can take a shortcut up to Derwent Edge tomorrow (Day 27 Map 2). This option adds nearly 7km to today, but reduces tomorrow's tally by 9km.
3. Again continue to **Moscar**, follow the A57 west (or, better, a parallel track just north of the A57), this time until you reach the Ladybower Inn (SK 204 865, tel 01433 651241), another pub with accommodation. (Again there is a route up to Derwent Edge to rejoin the Trail tomorrow.) This adds 6km to today and shortens tomorrow by the same distance.

DAY 27

Hathersage to White Gate
The Yorkshire Peak

Distance	39km (24 miles)
Ascent	1240m

Today's journey is quieter and less eventful, leaving Derbyshire and the busier areas of the Peak District for Yorkshire and the more industrialised region between the Manchester and West Yorkshire conurbations. There is no pub until Holme (tomorrow), and apart from some basics available at the pub there are no shops until you reach Marsden (tomorrow), so stock up in Hathersage before you leave.

It's an excellent day's walking, along the rest of Stanage Edge, and then across Derwent Moor to follow Derwent Edge, high above the flooded Derwent valley, then dropping down to the valley and following the shore of Howden Reservoir. From the head of the valley, and now in a very remote spot, an excellent path climbs up onto the moorland and north over the undulating and featureless peat moors. This path descends from the moor to cross the A628 trunk road, then the route follows another disused railway line (the Trans Pennine Trail, a coast to coast cycling and horseriding route from Southport to Humberside) westwards to the isolated hamlet of Dunford Bridge. There is no accommodation here, so the stage end is a bit further on at White Gate, where there is a campsite and a bed and breakfast (but nowhere nearby to get an evening meal): see suggestions at the end of Day 27.

From Hathersage there is a strenuous start to the day (Day 26 Map 5), climbing back up to rejoin the Trail following the Alternative Pennine Way along the top of **Stanage Edge** (Day 27 Map 1). It's worth the effort, though, to resume striding along the Edge, past the Ordnance Survey column on **High Neb** (458m) to **Stanage End**, at the end of Stanage Edge, and across the moor to the A57 at **Moscar**. In fact wherever you spent the night, you will start by climbing back up to the moors.

Sheffield is only a few kilometres away to the right, and to the left the A57 drops down again to the Derwent valley before starting its long climb up to the notorious **Snake Pass**. This route to Glossop and Manchester is frequently closed by snow and ice in winter, and passes few houses between here and Glossop.

From Moscar there is another stiff climb through the grouse-shooting country of the **Derwent Moors**, and you are on **Derwent Edge**, the last and highest of the line of gritstone edges (Day 27 Map 2). From here until you reach the Derwent valley reservoirs it is possible that you may be diverted from the main route by grouse shooting on certain days of the year – see Day 27 Maps 2 and 3 for alternative routes.

There are some grotesquely shaped **gritstone pinnacles** on and by Derwent Edge – the Wheel Stones and the Cakes of Bread are particularly bizarre. As soon as you see them the reasons for the names are obvious!

The ridge climbs to 538m at **Back Tor**, and to reach the OS column there you will need to scramble up the rocky top.

Back Tor is the highest point on the route since the Black Mountains near Hay-on-Wye, and won't be exceeded until Fountains Fell north of Malham on Day 30. Over to the left are the higher peat moors of Kinder Scout and the start of the Pennine Way – be thankful that you are not floundering in peat groughs in the middle of the Kinder plateau! – and the transmission mast on Holme Moss (passed on Day 28) is visible.

Further along, by the cairn at **Lost Lad**, there is a brass panoramic plaque that identifies the rest of the hills around you. After the descent from Derwent Edge, beyond Lost Lad (Day 27 Map 3), rather than continue along the moors north, where there are poor paths and boggy ground, the Trail descends with the Alternative Pennine Way into the Derwent valley, joining an untarred road up the valley past **Howden Reservoir** and on to a packhorse bridge at **Slippery Stones**.

The **Derwent Reservoir** was the scene for the testing of Barnes Wallace's bouncing bombs, both in reality and in the 1954 film *The Dam Busters*. The Derwent dam and the higher Howden dam were completed during World War I.

Derwent and Howden reservoirs, seen from the descent

At **Slippery Stones** the old packhorse bridge looks as though it's been there for centuries, although in fact it was only rebuilt here in 1959 after being removed from Derwent village, now drowned in Ladybower Reservoir, which was completed in 1945.

From Slippery Stones an old packhorse track climbs up out of the valley to the northeast (Day 27 Maps 3 and 4), then over the moor via **Mickleden Edge** to the head of **Langsett Reservoir** and the A628 trunk road.

At Langsett village, 1.5km down the valley, at the foot of the reservoir, the Waggon and Horses (tel 01226 763147) has inn accommodation. To reach Langsett, turn right along either of the two paths in the wood after crossing the River Porter, and follow the reservoir shore (Day 27 Map 5).

From the point where you cross the A628, the 'Flouch Hotel' used to be a few minutes east along the line of the old road, but has long been closed. There is accommodation at the Dog and Partridge Inn, 1.5km along the A628 to the west, but it's not cheap.

A few minutes beyond the A628, across a low moor called **Low Moor**, you are in the Don valley. Alongside the River Don is the disused Woodhead railway line between Manchester and Sheffield. This section has been recycled as part of the Trans Pennine Trail, and our route follows it west up the valley to the hamlet of **Dunford Bridge**.

Dunford Bridge is where the railway used to disappear into the **Woodhead Tunnels**. The three tunnels are 5km long, and have all been closed to traffic since 1981. The first opened in 1845, at a cost of 26 men killed. The second opened in 1852, with 28 more dead, many from cholera. The third tunnel opened in 1954 as part of electrification of the line, and even this project resulted in the loss of six more lives.

There is a stiff climb up from Dunford Bridge to the dam of **Winscar Reservoir**. The reservoir was completed in 1975 and looms over the hamlet like a scene from a disaster movie. The dam started leaking in early 2001, and the reservoir had to be drained for emergency remedial work.

Really this stage ought to end either at Dunford Bridge or at the next obvious stopping place, Holme village, 9km further on (Day 28 Map 1). Unfortunately, at the time of writing there is no accommodation in either village. The Stanhope Arms in Dunford Bridge closed down some years ago, as did the hotel in Holme. Instead the stage ends between the two where it crosses a minor road at **White Gate** (Day 27 Map 6). Here there is a campsite (Whitegate Leisure Camping and Caravan Site, tel 01484 688080 or 07786 707890 www.whitegateleisure.co.uk), and just down the road is a bed and breakfast (Coddy's Farm, tel 07714 588822 www.coddysfarm.co.uk). If you are camping you may be able to get breakfast at Coddy's Farm if you book it in advance. Alternatively, the best plan is to search online for the latest information (try www.kirklees.gov.uk and www.holmfirth.org) before you set out.

The nearest alternative B&Bs are: Corn Loft House, 146 Woodhead Road, Holmbridge (tel 01484 683147), 1km off-route – see Day 28 Map 1; and Waterhouse Farm, Shaw Lane, Hinchliffe Mill (tel 01484 685098), 1km further down the valley from Holmbridge.

DAY 28

White Gate to Hebden Bridge
Reservoirs and moor edges

Distance	40km (25 miles)
Ascent	1300m

Today is the last day on the Alternative Pennine Way (APW), which the Trail has been following since Day 25. This is the day you walk out of the Peak District and into the West Yorkshire Pennines, but rather than join the Pennine Way just yet, the route follows the APW on an intricate itinerary along the eastern flank of the Pennine spine (which separates Greater Manchester and south Lancashire from the West Yorkshire woollen mill towns of Huddersfield and Halifax). This means you avoid some of the more unsavoury peat bogs on the Pennine Way, such as the infamous Black Hill, and you also get better views.

From the start of the day at White Gate it is fairly hard work for a few kilometres, crossing the many minor valleys that feed into Holmfirth (Day 28 Map 1). The walking is good, though, past small reservoirs, and through plantations and typical West Yorkshire drystone wall hill country. There is a pub with a limited shop at **Holme**, where the route crosses the A6024.

At **Wessenden Head** (Day 28 Map 2), the highest point of the day at 451m, you cross the A635 Saddleworth Moor road, and meet the Pennine Way for the first time, although you don't start following it yet. (If you're lucky, there will be a tea van here as well.)

From **Leyzing Clough** (below Wessenden Head Reservoir) down to the small mill town of Marsden, the Trail follows the APW along the line of Deer Hill Conduit (which feeds Deer Hill Reservoir), before dropping steeply down into **Marsden** (Day 28 Map 3). The path along the conduit is virtually level and gives marvellous views over the reservoirs in the valley and over Marsden.

Marsden itself is an attractive old town, with shops, accommodation and pubs, including the Riverhead Brewery Tap in Peel Street, which brews its own beer. They also have a dining room upstairs. The nearest camping is behind the Carriage House pub, on the A62 (SE 028 102).

On the way out of Marsden you cross the Huddersfield Narrow Canal, and if you have time a short detour to the left brings you to the eastern end of the Standedge Tunnel, which has now been reopened to narrowboats.

From Marsden to Hebden Bridge is a switchback across valley after valley. Some of the crossings are above the intake walls across moorland, and some are within the stone-walled pasture areas; it is all good walking, though, and the views are excellent. There are reservoirs all over the place, feeding the surrounding towns.

In the first valley the Trail drops steeply to cross the dam of **Deanshead Reservoir**. In the second, just before Booth Wood Reservoir, you cross the M62 at the point where it divides to run either side of Stott Hall Farm (Day 28 Map 4).

In the third valley (Day 28 Map 5) you diverge from the original line of the APW, which crosses the dam of Baitings Reservoir then skirts Great Manshead Hill on minor roads. The Trail follows a better route, along the south shore of the reservoir and straight over the top of **Manshead Hill** (417m) on what is now a permissive footpath. (Don't worry about this route missing the two pubs by the other side of Baitings dam, marked on old maps – they are now both private houses.) The route of the APW is shown on the strip map as a bad weather alternative.

After rejoining the APW at a crossroads of paths and descending again, the fourth valley is Cragg Vale (Day 28 Map 6), which has old stone terraced houses scattered along it, and also a pub, the Hinchliffe Arms, whose door the route passes.

After crossing **Bell House Moor**, the fifth valley is the deep, narrow Calder Valley, where the path drops steeply down to enter **Hebden Bridge** (Day 28 Map 7). Hebden Bridge is a thriving community of great character, with all the services a walker needs (although there is no longer a bank). There are three campsites about 3km to the west, close to the Pennine Way.

The **Calder Valley** has been occupied ever since the valley bottom was drained when the Rochdale Canal was constructed. Mills were built in the main valley and the neighbouring side valleys in the early part of the Industrial Revolution, to avoid the regulations affecting less remote areas, and to exploit the water power of the streams. The valley is so narrow that there was little land to build on – the river, railway and canal use up the whole of the valley bottom in places.

In **Hebden Bridge**, terraces of back-to-back houses were built on slopes so steep that there was room for a second terrace below the back-to-backs on the lower side of the slope, with a walkway giving access to the 'upstairs' houses. In the 1960s this was a rundown area, and houses could barely be given away.

Day 20 Map 1: Knighton to Stow Hill

Say goodbye to Wales as you cross the railway bridge in Knighton & enter Shropshire. If you think you have escaped the hills at the same time you will be disappointed: this page is nearly all uphill.

4. The track through the woods emerges from the trees to meet a better track. Turn left (gate & stile) & follow the main track uphill. Keep right at a track junction by a pond then keep left to the top of the field (gate & stile).

3. Go through the gate straight ahead & continue, now with the hedge on your right, climbing the shoulder of the hill. At the top, cross a track & bear left downhill with a fence now on your left to a stile. Cross this & follow a vague track down to ford the stream left of the houses. Cross the track & climb steeply up the field past a ruin (no path) to a gate on the right. Follow the track uphill through the woods.

Stowe Church is ahead to the right with its distinctive wooden panelled tower.

2. Cross the Teme & the railway then bend right with the main road. After 50 metres a broad signed path forks left into the woods: follow this until it forks as it nears the road again. Fork right, descend to a forestry track & turn left. After a few metres the track bends sharp left: at the apex turn right (steps & gate) into the field ahead. Bear gradually away from the road (no visible path) to a footbridge then a kissing gate. Cross the road, go through the gate opposite & follow the hedge.

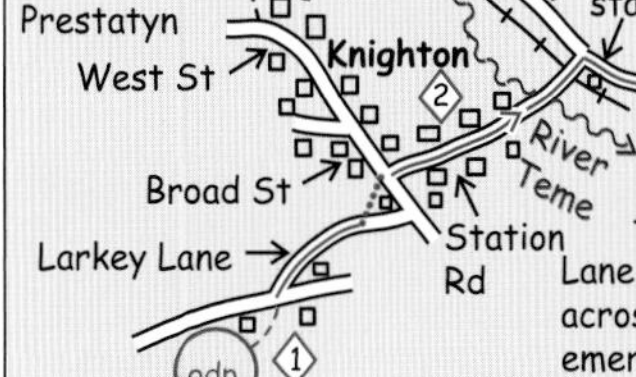

1. When the Offa's Dyke Path meets the first road in Knighton, go down Larkey Lane almost immediately opposite. Cut left across a car park & go through an arch to emerge in Broad St. The Offa's Dyke Path turns left here, but our route goes right then immediately left along Station Rd.

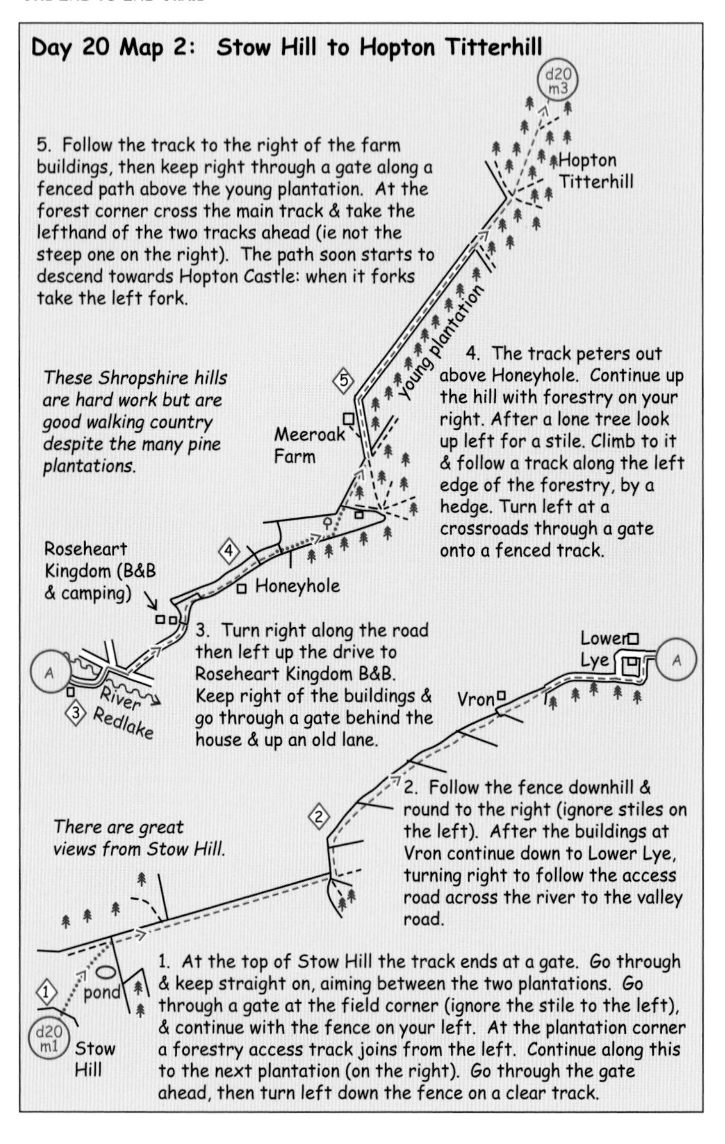
Day 20 Map 2: Stow Hill to Hopton Titterhill
d20 m3
Hopton Titterhill
5. Follow the track to the right of the farm buildings, then keep right through a gate along a fenced path above the young plantation. At the forest corner cross the main track & take the lefthand of the two tracks ahead (ie not the steep one on the right). The path soon starts to descend towards Hopton Castle: when it forks take the left fork.
young plantation
4. The track peters out above Honeyhole. Continue up the hill with forestry on your right. After a lone tree look up left for a stile. Climb to it & follow a track along the left edge of the forestry, by a hedge. Turn left at a crossroads through a gate onto a fenced track.
These Shropshire hills are hard work but are good walking country despite the many pine plantations.
5
Meeroak Farm
4
Roseheart Kingdom (B&B & camping)
Honeyhole
3. Turn right along the road then left up the drive to Roseheart Kingdom B&B. Keep right of the buildings & go through a gate behind the house & up an old lane.
A
River Redlake
3
Lower Lye
A
Vron
2
2. Follow the fence downhill & round to the right (ignore stiles on the left). After the buildings at Vron continue down to Lower Lye, turning right to follow the access road across the river to the valley road.
There are great views from Stow Hill.
1
pond
d20 m1
Stow Hill
1. At the top of Stow Hill the track ends at a gate. Go through & keep straight on, aiming between the two plantations. Go through a gate at the field corner (ignore the stile to the left), & continue with the fence on your left. At the plantation corner a forestry access track joins from the left. Continue along this to the next plantation (on the right). Go through the gate ahead, then turn left down the fence on a clear track.

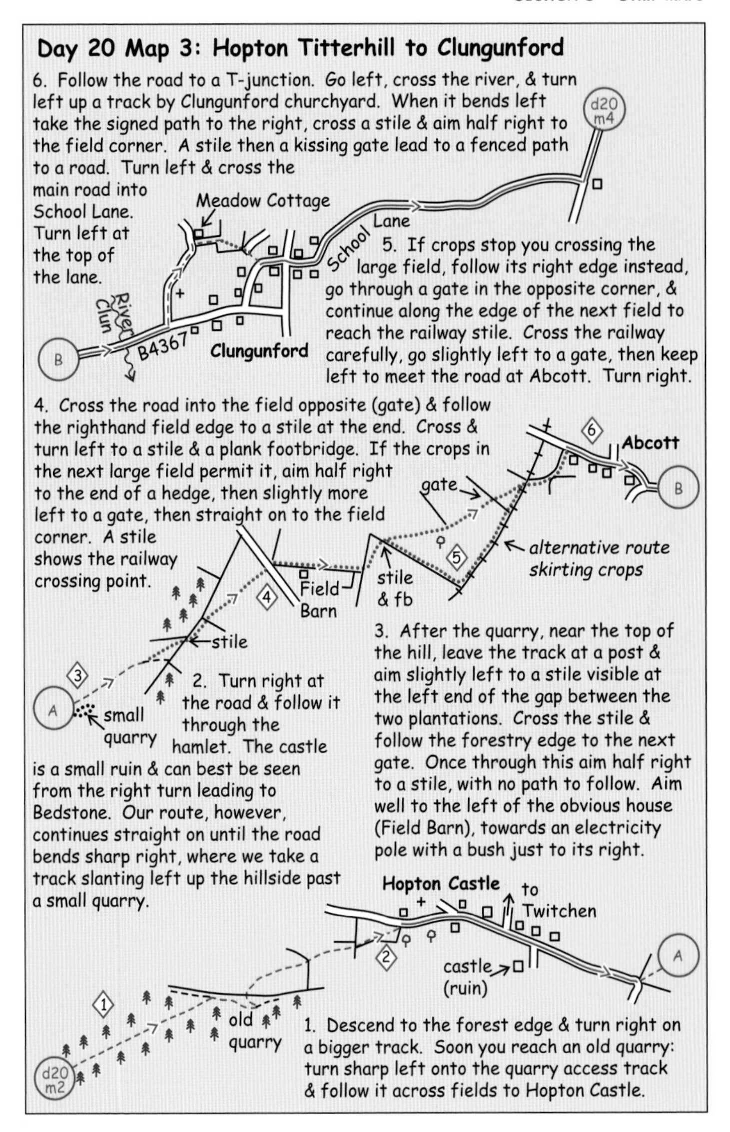
Day 20 Map 3: Hopton Titterhill to Clungunford
6. Follow the road to a T-junction. Go left, cross the river, & turn left up a track by Clungunford churchyard. When it bends left take the signed path to the right, cross a stile & aim half right to the field corner. A stile then a kissing gate lead to a fenced path to a road. Turn left & cross the main road into School Lane. Turn left at the top of the lane.
d20 m4
Meadow Cottage
School Lane
5. If crops stop you crossing the large field, follow its right edge instead, go through a gate in the opposite corner, & continue along the edge of the next field to reach the railway stile. Cross the railway carefully, go slightly left to a gate, then keep left to meet the road at Abcott. Turn right.
River Clun
B4367
Clungunford
B
4. Cross the road into the field opposite (gate) & follow the righthand field edge to a stile at the end. Cross & turn left to a stile & a plank footbridge. If the crops in the next large field permit it, aim half right to the end of a hedge, then slightly more left to a gate, then straight on to the field corner. A stile shows the railway crossing point.
6
Abcott
B
gate
alternative route skirting crops
5
Field Barn
stile & fb
4
stile
3
A
small quarry
2. Turn right at the road & follow it through the hamlet. The castle is a small ruin & can best be seen from the right turn leading to Bedstone. Our route, however, continues straight on until the road bends sharp right, where we take a track slanting left up the hillside past a small quarry.
3. After the quarry, near the top of the hill, leave the track at a post & aim slightly left to a stile visible at the left end of the gap between the two plantations. Cross the stile & follow the forestry edge to the next gate. Once through this aim half right to a stile, with no path to follow. Aim well to the left of the obvious house (Field Barn), towards an electricity pole with a bush just to its right.
Hopton Castle
to Twitchen
2
castle (ruin)
A
1
old quarry
d20 m2
1. Descend to the forest edge & turn right on a bigger track. Soon you reach an old quarry: turn sharp left onto the quarry access track & follow it across fields to Hopton Castle.

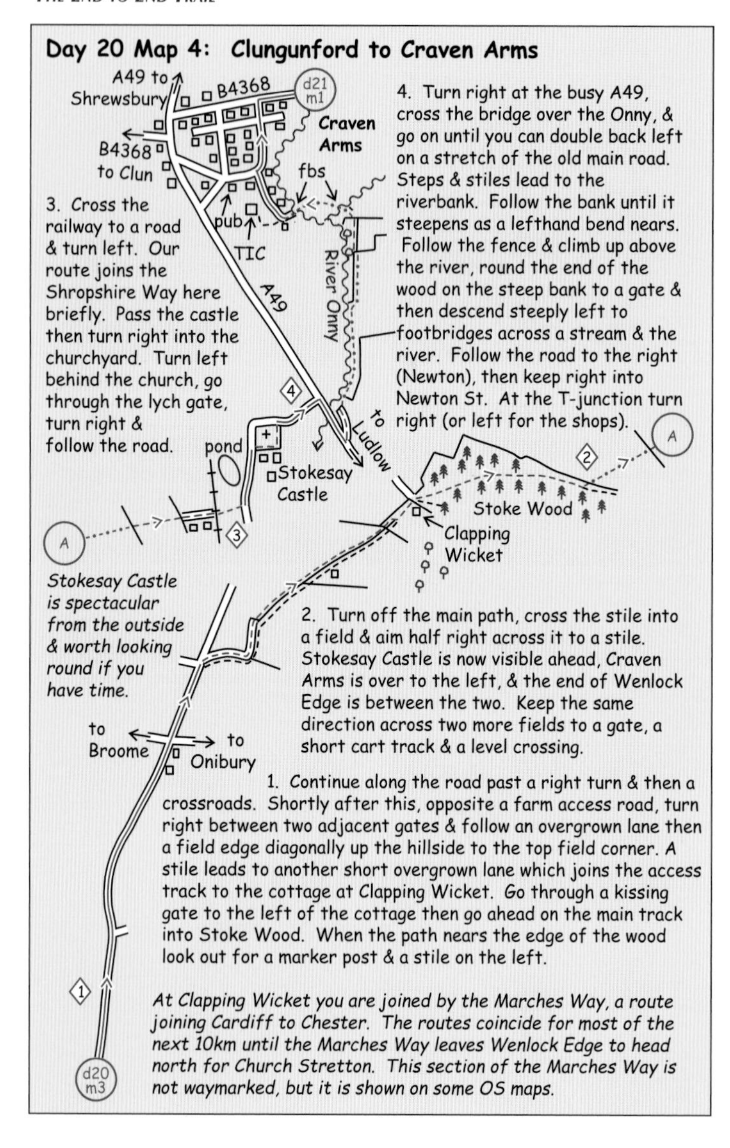

Day 20 Map 4: Clungunford to Craven Arms
A49 to Shrewsbury
B4368
d21 m1
Craven Arms
B4368 to Clun
fbs
pub
TIC
A49
River Onny
to Ludlow
pond
Stokesay Castle
Stoke Wood
Clapping Wicket
A
to Broome
to Onibury
d20 m3
4. Turn right at the busy A49, cross the bridge over the Onny, & go on until you can double back left on a stretch of the old main road. Steps & stiles lead to the riverbank. Follow the bank until it steepens as a lefthand bend nears. Follow the fence & climb up above the river, round the end of the wood on the steep bank to a gate & then descend steeply left to footbridges across a stream & the river. Follow the road to the right (Newton), then keep right into Newton St. At the T-junction turn right (or left for the shops).
3. Cross the railway to a road & turn left. Our route joins the Shropshire Way here briefly. Pass the castle then turn right into the churchyard. Turn left behind the church, go through the lych gate, turn right & follow the road.
Stokesay Castle is spectacular from the outside & worth looking round if you have time.
2. Turn off the main path, cross the stile into a field & aim half right across it to a stile. Stokesay Castle is now visible ahead, Craven Arms is over to the left, & the end of Wenlock Edge is between the two. Keep the same direction across two more fields to a gate, a short cart track & a level crossing.
1. Continue along the road past a right turn & then a crossroads. Shortly after this, opposite a farm access road, turn right between two adjacent gates & follow an overgrown lane then a field edge diagonally up the hillside to the top field corner. A stile leads to another short overgrown lane which joins the access track to the cottage at Clapping Wicket. Go through a kissing gate to the left of the cottage then go ahead on the main track into Stoke Wood. When the path nears the edge of the wood look out for a marker post & a stile on the left.
At Clapping Wicket you are joined by the Marches Way, a route joining Cardiff to Chester. The routes coincide for most of the next 10km until the Marches Way leaves Wenlock Edge to head north for Church Stretton. This section of the Marches Way is not waymarked, but it is shown on some OS maps.

Day 21 Map 1: Craven Arms to Strefford

From the top of the Edge a tower is prominent on Callow Hill to the southeast. This is Flounders Folly, built in 1838, & recently restored.

Wistanstow is 1km off-route & is the home of the Plough Inn & Wood's Brewery.

4. Once in the woods the path becomes a muddy sunken lane slanting up the steep slope. Ignore a left fork & a minor right fork to continue up to join a good path along the top of the Edge.

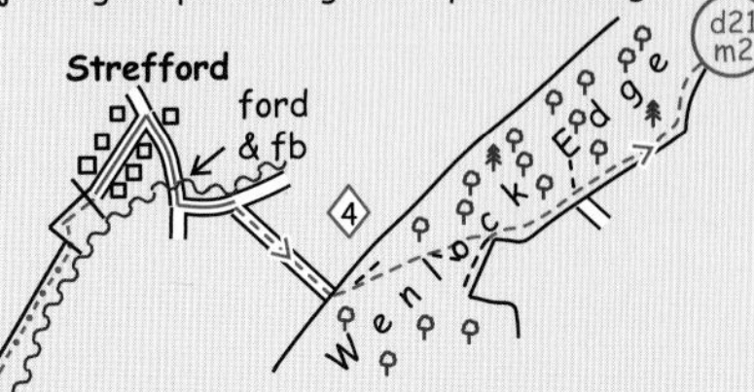

3. In the next field keep straight ahead to cross a footbridge in the corner. Turn left, cross a second bridge, & turn right to follow Quinny Brook to the hamlet of Strefford, which has some interesting old timber-framed houses. In Strefford turn right at the T-junction, turn left immediately after the ford, then in 50 metres turn right to climb up to Wenlock Edge on a hedged path.

2. Cross a stile on your left & continue in your original direction, now with the hedge on your right. Keep straight on through a gateway to the next field corner, where a kissing gate leads to a clear path through a wood (ignore the parallel track to your left). Leave the wood at a stile & cross the bottom of a field to a stile into a coppice. When you reach houses go straight on (gateway) & follow the path north across the fields to a stile.

1. Leave Craven Arms eastwards on the B4368 (Corvedale Rd). Just before the bridge over the Onny, a car park & a gate on the left both lead to another gate & a pleasant stroll along the riverbank northwards. This is a permissive footpath. Follow the river past the church and weir at Halford until a kissing gate leads to a lane & a bridge across the river. Cross & follow a good footpath that cuts diagonally right to meet an access road. Turn right along this, then sharp left after School House over stiles to follow the field edge behind two houses.

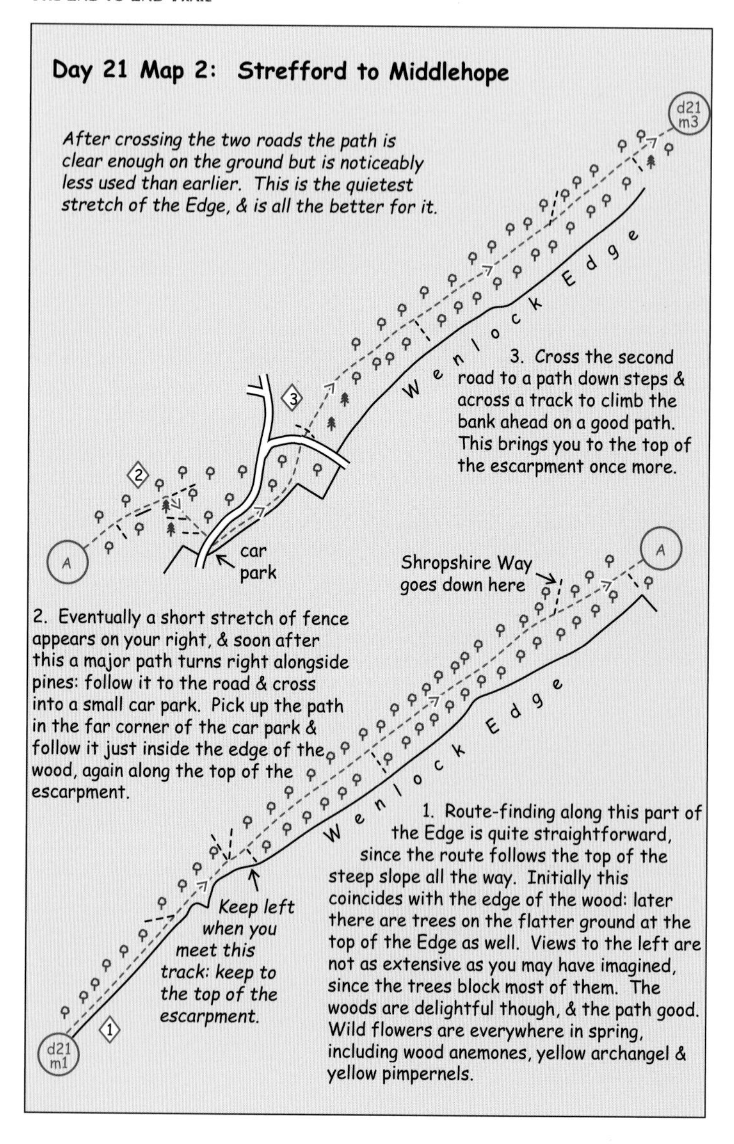

Day 21 Map 2: Strefford to Middlehope
d21 m3
After crossing the two roads the path is clear enough on the ground but is noticeably less used than earlier. This is the quietest stretch of the Edge, & is all the better for it.
Wenlock Edge
3. Cross the second road to a path down steps & across a track to climb the bank ahead on a good path. This brings you to the top of the escarpment once more.
3
2
A
car park
Shropshire Way goes down here
A
2. Eventually a short stretch of fence appears on your right, & soon after this a major path turns right alongside pines: follow it to the road & cross into a small car park. Pick up the path in the far corner of the car park & follow it just inside the edge of the wood, again along the top of the escarpment.
Wenlock Edge
1. Route-finding along this part of the Edge is quite straightforward, since the route follows the top of the steep slope all the way. Initially this coincides with the edge of the wood: later there are trees on the flatter ground at the top of the Edge as well. Views to the left are not as extensive as you may have imagined, since the trees block most of them. The woods are delightful though, & the path good. Wild flowers are everywhere in spring, including wood anemones, yellow archangel & yellow pimpernels.
Keep left when you meet this track: keep to the top of the escarpment.
1
d21 m1

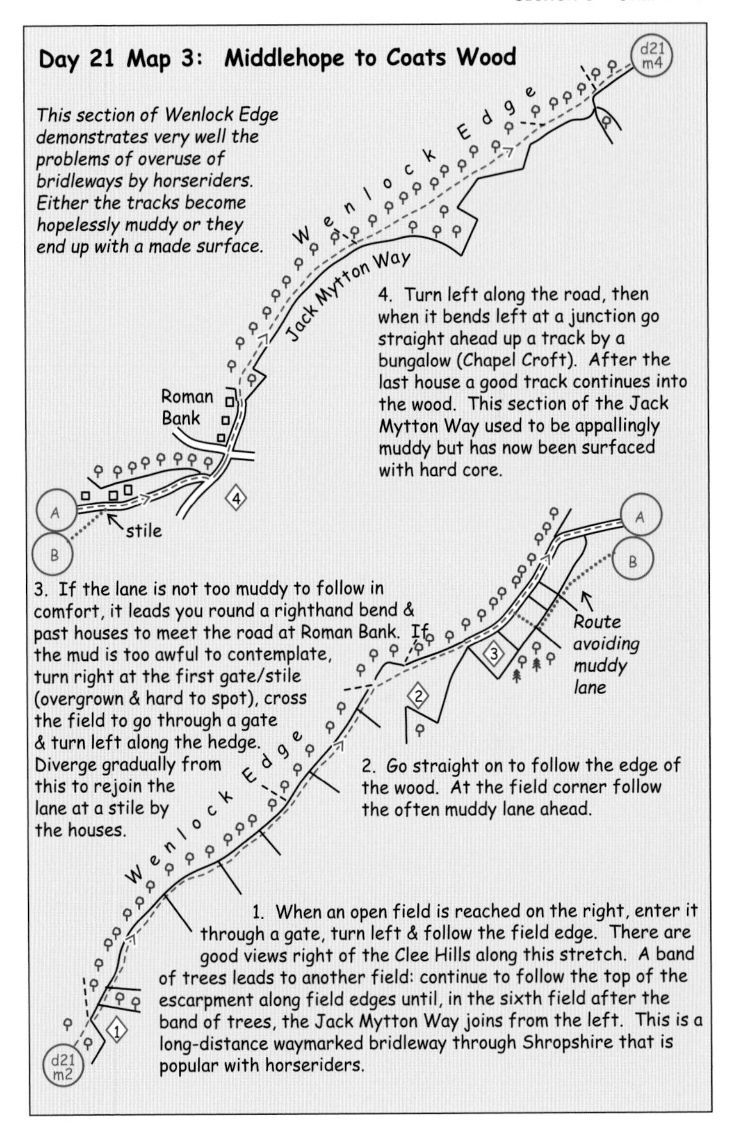
Day 21 Map 3: Middlehope to Coats Wood
d21 m4
This section of Wenlock Edge demonstrates very well the problems of overuse of bridleways by horseriders. Either the tracks become hopelessly muddy or they end up with a made surface.
Wenlock Edge
Jack Mytton Way
4. Turn left along the road, then when it bends left at a junction go straight ahead up a track by a bungalow (Chapel Croft). After the last house a good track continues into the wood. This section of the Jack Mytton Way used to be appallingly muddy but has now been surfaced with hard core.
Roman Bank
4
A
B
stile
A
B
3. If the lane is not too muddy to follow in comfort, it leads you round a righthand bend & past houses to meet the road at Roman Bank. If the mud is too awful to contemplate, turn right at the first gate/stile (overgrown & hard to spot), cross the field to go through a gate & turn left along the hedge. Diverge gradually from this to rejoin the lane at a stile by the houses.
3
Route avoiding muddy lane
2
Wenlock Edge
2. Go straight on to follow the edge of the wood. At the field corner follow the often muddy lane ahead.
1. When an open field is reached on the right, enter it through a gate, turn left & follow the field edge. There are good views right of the Clee Hills along this stretch. A band of trees leads to another field: continue to follow the top of the escarpment along field edges until, in the sixth field after the band of trees, the Jack Mytton Way joins from the left. This is a long-distance waymarked bridleway through Shropshire that is popular with horseriders.
1
d21 m2

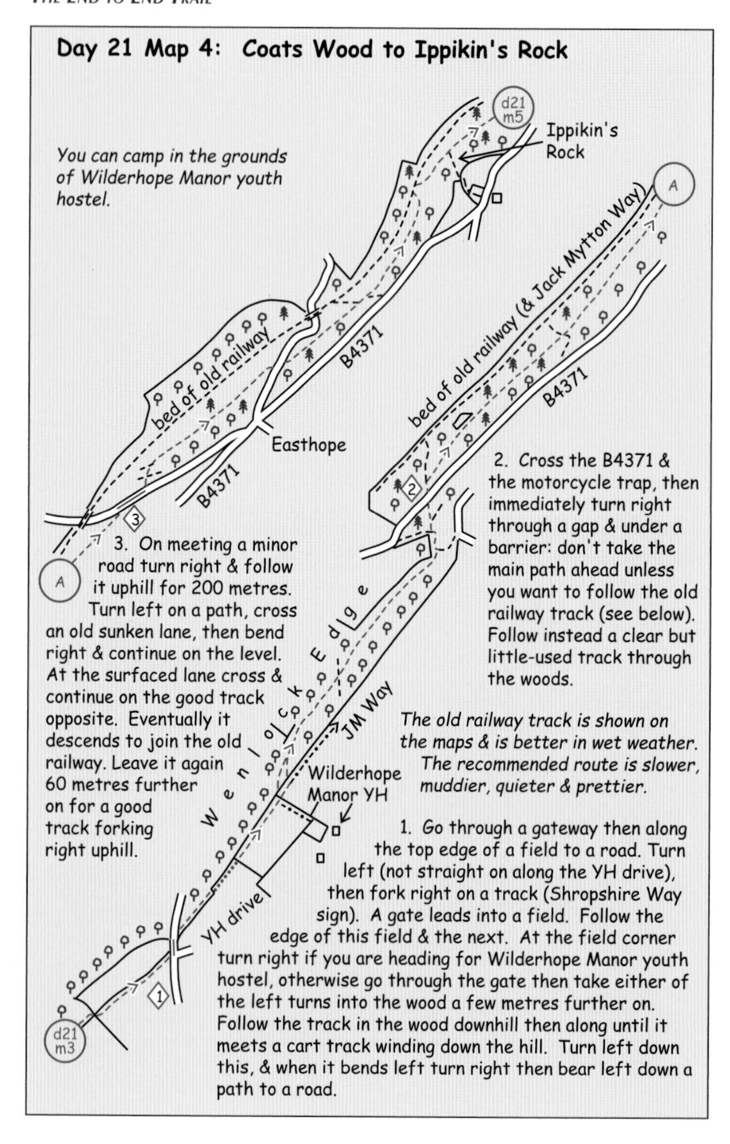
Day 21 Map 4: Coats Wood to Ippikin's Rock
You can camp in the grounds of Wilderhope Manor youth hostel.
d21 m5
Ippikin's Rock
A
bed of old railway
B4371
bed of old railway (& Jack Mytton Way)
B4371
Easthope
B4371
2. Cross the B4371 & the motorcycle trap, then immediately turn right through a gap & under a barrier: don't take the main path ahead unless you want to follow the old railway track (see below). Follow instead a clear but little-used track through the woods.
A
3. On meeting a minor road turn right & follow it uphill for 200 metres. Turn left on a path, cross an old sunken lane, then bend right & continue on the level. At the surfaced lane cross & continue on the good track opposite. Eventually it descends to join the old railway. Leave it again 60 metres further on for a good track forking right uphill.
Wenlock Edge
JM Way
The old railway track is shown on the maps & is better in wet weather. The recommended route is slower, muddier, quieter & prettier.
Wilderhope Manor YH
1. Go through a gateway then along the top edge of a field to a road. Turn left (not straight on along the YH drive), then fork right on a track (Shropshire Way sign). A gate leads into a field. Follow the edge of this field & the next. At the field corner turn right if you are heading for Wilderhope Manor youth hostel, otherwise go through the gate then take either of the left turns into the wood a few metres further on. Follow the track in the wood downhill then along until it meets a cart track winding down the hill. Turn left down this, & when it bends left turn right then bear left down a path to a road.
YH drive
d21 m3

Day 21 Map 5: Ippikin's Rock to Blakeway Coppice

3. Two paths lead northeast towards Much Wenlock from inside Presthope car park. Take the one further from the road, keeping left when in doubt, climbing up to the crest of Wenlock Edge again. Follow a permissive footpath above a big quarried area with a pool in it (the pool isn't shown on older OS maps). A bridleway climbs up from the left to join you on the crest, then a path forks left downhill - don't take it. The views into the distance are good, but the mess created by quarrying dominates the scene on your right.

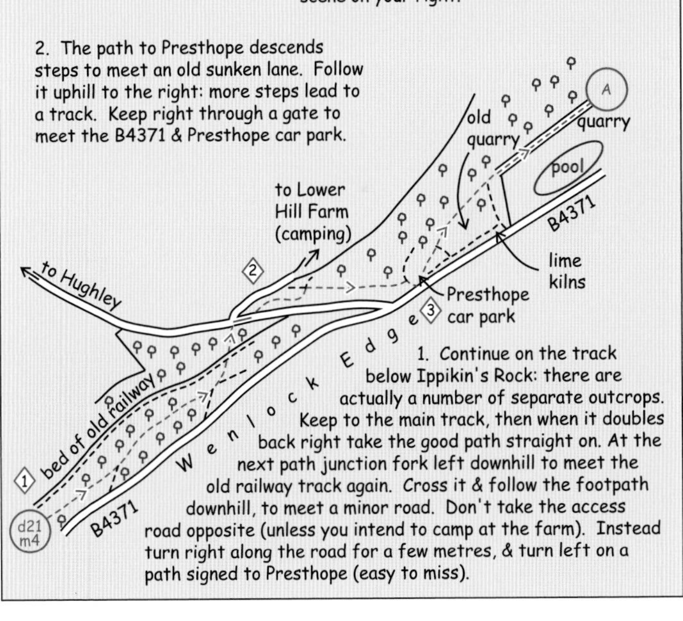

2. The path to Presthope descends steps to meet an old sunken lane. Follow it uphill to the right: more steps lead to a track. Keep right through a gate to meet the B4371 & Presthope car park.

1. Continue on the track below Ippikin's Rock: there are actually a number of separate outcrops. Keep to the main track, then when it doubles back right take the good path straight on. At the next path junction fork left downhill to meet the old railway track again. Cross it & follow the footpath downhill, to meet a minor road. Don't take the access road opposite (unless you intend to camp at the farm). Instead turn right along the road for a few metres, & turn left on a path signed to Presthope (easy to miss).

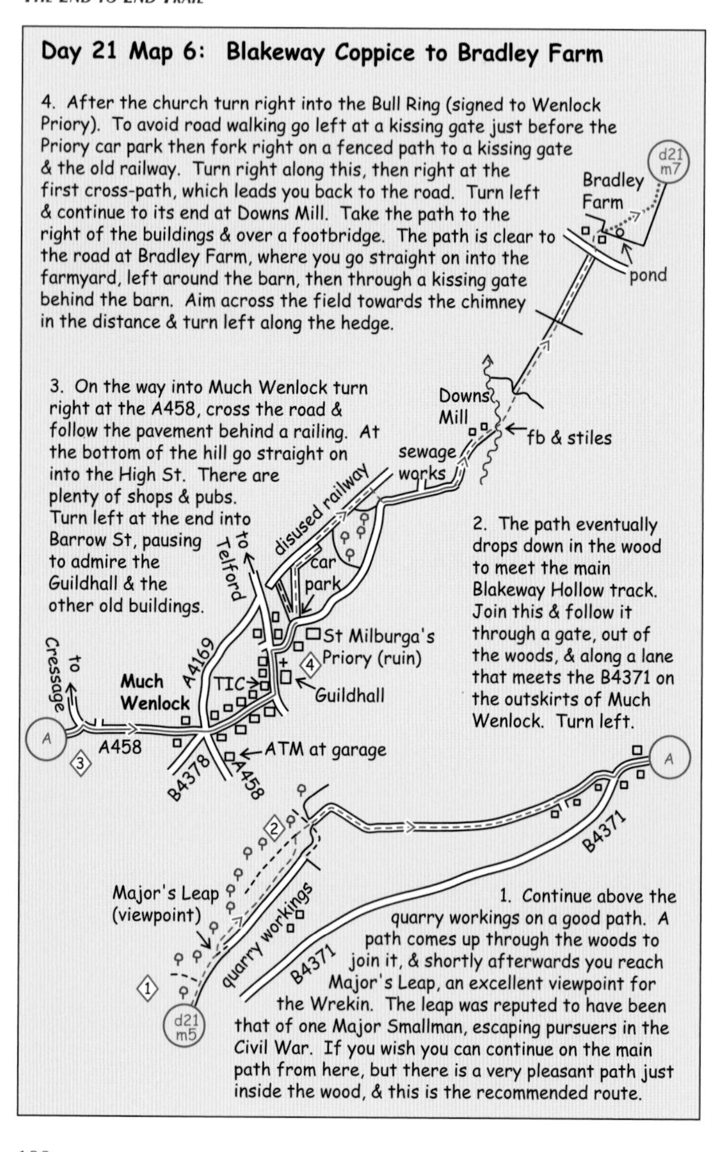

Day 21 Map 6: Blakeway Coppice to Bradley Farm
4. After the church turn right into the Bull Ring (signed to Wenlock Priory). To avoid road walking go left at a kissing gate just before the Priory car park then fork right on a fenced path to a kissing gate & the old railway. Turn right along this, then right at the first cross-path, which leads you back to the road. Turn left & continue to its end at Downs Mill. Take the path to the right of the buildings & over a footbridge. The path is clear to the road at Bradley Farm, where you go straight on into the farmyard, left around the barn, then through a kissing gate behind the barn. Aim across the field towards the chimney in the distance & turn left along the hedge.
d21 m7
Bradley Farm
pond
3. On the way into Much Wenlock turn right at the A458, cross the road & follow the pavement behind a railing. At the bottom of the hill go straight on into the High St. There are plenty of shops & pubs. Turn left at the end into Barrow St, pausing to admire the Guildhall & the other old buildings.
Downs Mill
fb & stiles
sewage works
disused railway
to Telford
car park
2. The path eventually drops down in the wood to meet the main Blakeway Hollow track. Join this & follow it through a gate, out of the woods, & along a lane that meets the B4371 on the outskirts of Much Wenlock. Turn left.
to Cressage
A4169
St Milburga's Priory (ruin)
4
Much Wenlock
TIC
Guildhall
A
A458
3
B4378
A458
ATM at garage
A
B4371
2
Major's Leap (viewpoint)
quarry workings
B4371
1
d21 m5
1. Continue above the quarry workings on a good path. A path comes up through the woods to join it, & shortly afterwards you reach Major's Leap, an excellent viewpoint for the Wrekin. The leap was reputed to have been that of one Major Smallman, escaping pursuers in the Civil War. If you wish you can continue on the main path from here, but there is a very pleasant path just inside the wood, & this is the recommended route.

Day 21 Map 7: Bradley Farm to Ironbridge

There are a lot of paths on Benthall Edge. The route shown follows the Shropshire Way, so you can follow the waymarks.

power station

River Severn

Ironbridge

deep quarry

Benthall Edge

d22 m1

A

4. Go straight on at the path crossroads (signposted to Ironbridge). This path runs parallel to a disused railway & eventually descends to meet it. Join the railway & follow it to the road & Ironbridge. To continue the route go straight on across the car park, or turn left across the old bridge to visit the town.

3. The path meets a track at a hairpin bend: keep right on the upper track. When this turns right to a gate, go straight on instead (gate, Shropshire Way sign) & follow the path through the wood. Keep left at a fork, heading downhill. You will pass two paths going left.

A

Audience Meadow

Vineyards Farm

Woodhouse Farm

Audience Wood

Wyke

gate

gate

d21 m6

2. Keep left in Wyke, then when the road bends right go ahead on the access road to Vineyards Farm. At the farm follow the grassy track uphill to a stile then a kissing gate. Follow the field edge from here, until a stile leads into woodland.

1. Follow the hedge to a kissing gate & on to a second kissing gate & a stream on your right. Go through & cross the field diagonally (50 degrees) past the lefthand solitary tree & on towards the distant chimney. At a kissing gate in the field corner by the farm enter a lane then follow the access road. Turn right at the public road.

Day 22 Map 1: Ironbridge to Brickkiln Coppice

3. Cross the river, then turn right along the canal to a footbridge: cross this & climb to the road. Ironbridge (Coalport) youth hostel is a short distance along the road to the right. To continue the walk turn left along the road, then turn right up a zigzag path just before the Shakespeare Inn, signed 'Silkin Way'. At a T-junction turn left (signed 'Blists Hill'), then right up steps just before the bridge under the Hay Inclined Plane. Climb steeply alongside the railway incline until a stile on the right gives access to an overgrown field. Cut diagonally up the field past a marker post (no visible path initially) to a gate into the wood. (If the first part of this is too overgrown continue to the top of the incline, turn right through a gate, descend this path 20 metres to the post & turn left.) Turn right & follow the path along the edge of the wood. The path soon rises through the wood to join the line of an old track. Keep straight on at a path junction (signed 'S. Maddock') to emerge from the woods onto a golf course. Turn right (no path) & follow the edge of the golf course then a short path to a road: turn left.

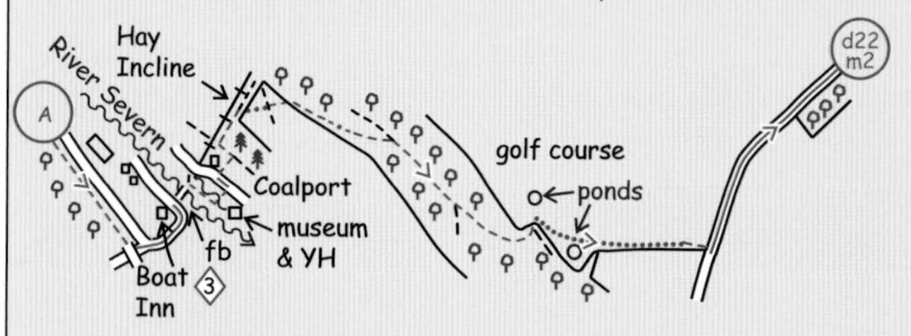

2. Follow the trackbed under two bridges to the restored level crossing gates at the road at Jackfield. From here the line of the railway has been taken into local gardens, so bear right (not sharp right) along the road, keeping straight on along Church Rd when the main road bends right. Follow the road alongside the Tile Museum, then fork right on a track on the line of the old railway. Look out for steps on the right: go down them, under the bridge & down the road to the Boat Inn & a footbridge over the river.

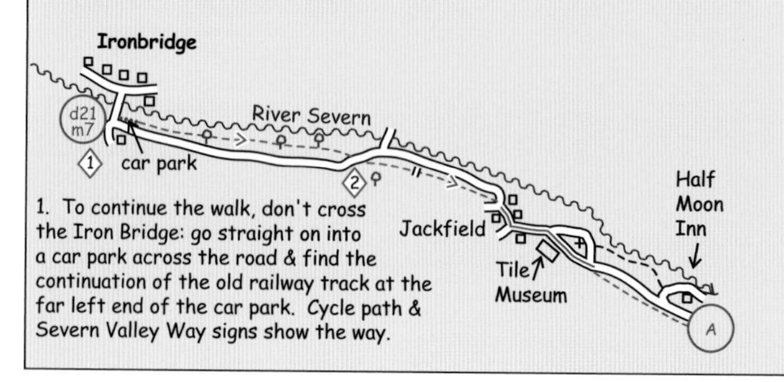

1. To continue the walk, don't cross the Iron Bridge: go straight on into a car park across the road & find the continuation of the old railway track at the far left end of the car park. Cycle path & Severn Valley Way signs show the way.

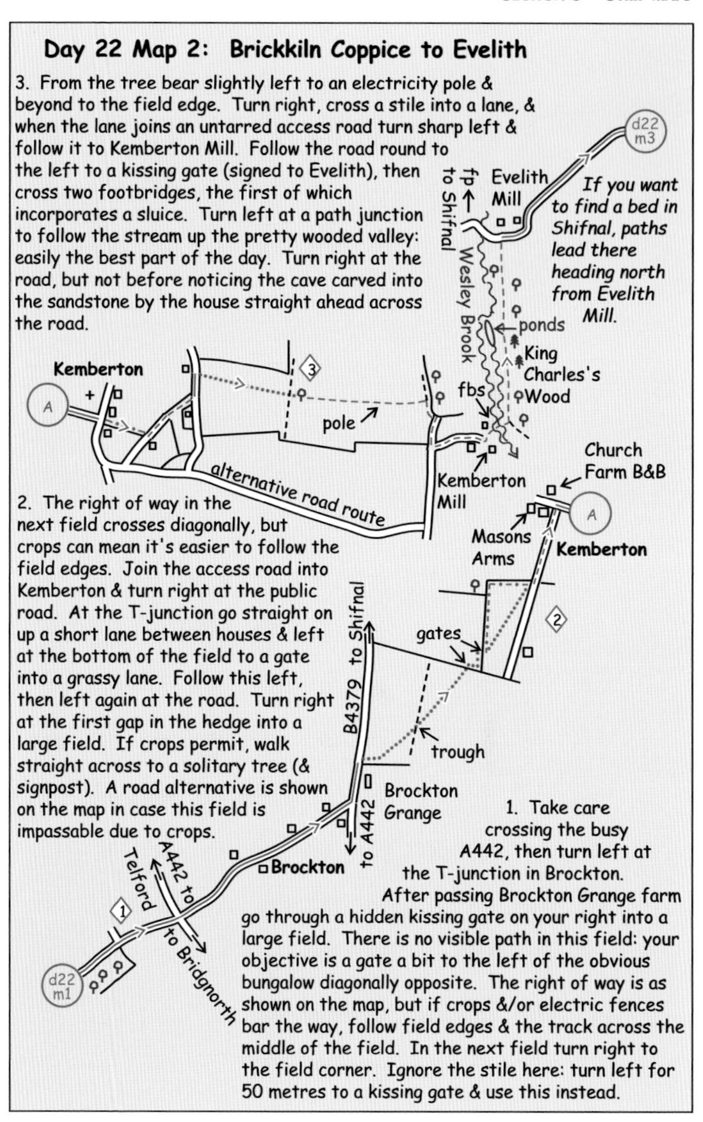
Day 22 Map 2: Brickkiln Coppice to Evelith
3. From the tree bear slightly left to an electricity pole & beyond to the field edge. Turn right, cross a stile into a lane, & when the lane joins an untarred access road turn sharp left & follow it to Kemberton Mill. Follow the road round to the left to a kissing gate (signed to Evelith), then cross two footbridges, the first of which incorporates a sluice. Turn left at a path junction to follow the stream up the pretty wooded valley: easily the best part of the day. Turn right at the road, but not before noticing the cave carved into the sandstone by the house straight ahead across the road.
d22 m3
fp to Shifnal
Evelith Mill
If you want to find a bed in Shifnal, paths lead there heading north from Evelith Mill.
Wesley Brook
ponds
King Charles's Wood
Kemberton
A
3
pole
fbs
Kemberton Mill
alternative road route
Church Farm B&B
A
Masons Arms
Kemberton
2. The right of way in the next field crosses diagonally, but crops can mean it's easier to follow the field edges. Join the access road into Kemberton & turn right at the public road. At the T-junction go straight on up a short lane between houses & left at the bottom of the field to a gate into a grassy lane. Follow this left, then left again at the road. Turn right at the first gap in the hedge into a large field. If crops permit, walk straight across to a solitary tree (& signpost). A road alternative is shown on the map in case this field is impassable due to crops.
B4379 to Shifnal
gates
2
trough
Brockton Grange
to A442
Brockton
A442 to Telford
to Bridgnorth
1
d22 m1
1. Take care crossing the busy A442, then turn left at the T-junction in Brockton. After passing Brockton Grange farm go through a hidden kissing gate on your right into a large field. There is no visible path in this field: your objective is a gate a bit to the left of the obvious bungalow diagonally opposite. The right of way is as shown on the map, but if crops &/or electric fences bar the way, follow field edges & the track across the middle of the field. In the next field turn right to the field corner. Ignore the stile here: turn left for 50 metres to a kissing gate & use this instead.

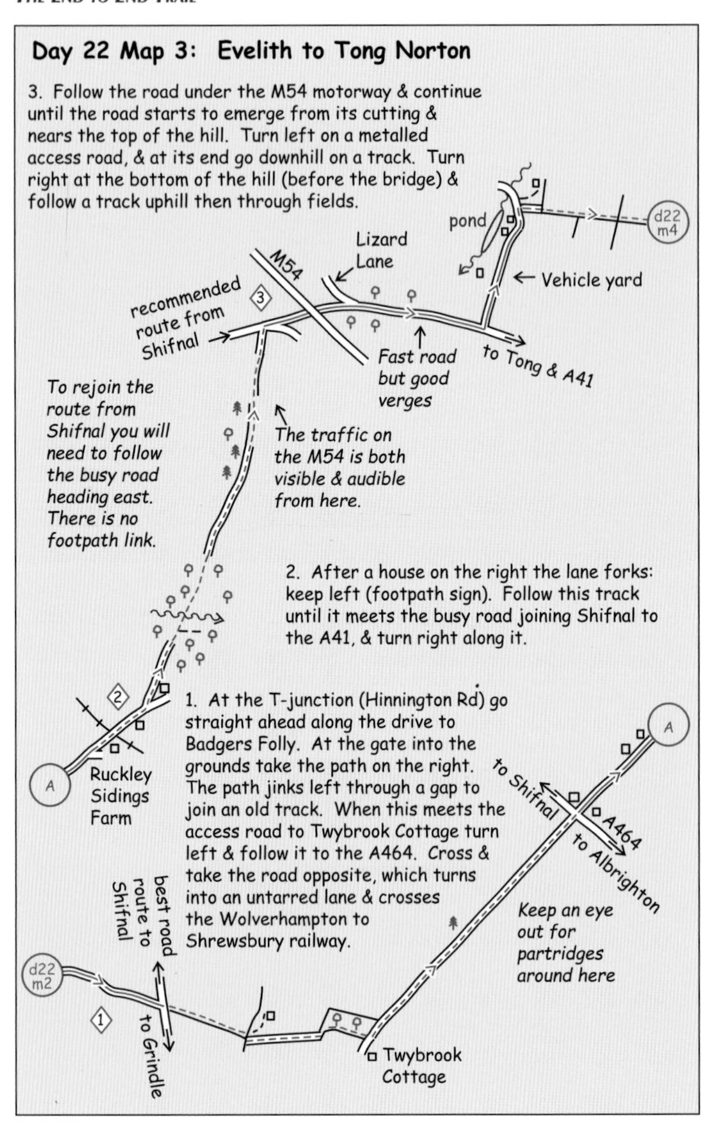
Day 22 Map 3: Evelith to Tong Norton
3. Follow the road under the M54 motorway & continue until the road starts to emerge from its cutting & nears the top of the hill. Turn left on a metalled access road, & at its end go downhill on a track. Turn right at the bottom of the hill (before the bridge) & follow a track uphill then through fields.
pond
d22 m4
Lizard Lane
M54
Vehicle yard
recommended route from Shifnal
3
Fast road but good verges
to Tong & A41
To rejoin the route from Shifnal you will need to follow the busy road heading east. There is no footpath link.
The traffic on the M54 is both visible & audible from here.
2. After a house on the right the lane forks: keep left (footpath sign). Follow this track until it meets the busy road joining Shifnal to the A41, & turn right along it.
2
1. At the T-junction (Hinnington Rd) go straight ahead along the drive to Badgers Folly. At the gate into the grounds take the path on the right. The path jinks left through a gap to join an old track. When this meets the access road to Twybrook Cottage turn left & follow it to the A464. Cross & take the road opposite, which turns into an untarred lane & crosses the Wolverhampton to Shrewsbury railway.
A
A
Ruckley Sidings Farm
to Shifnal
A464
to Albrighton
best road route to Shifnal
Keep an eye out for partridges around here
d22 m2
1
to Grindle
Twybrook Cottage

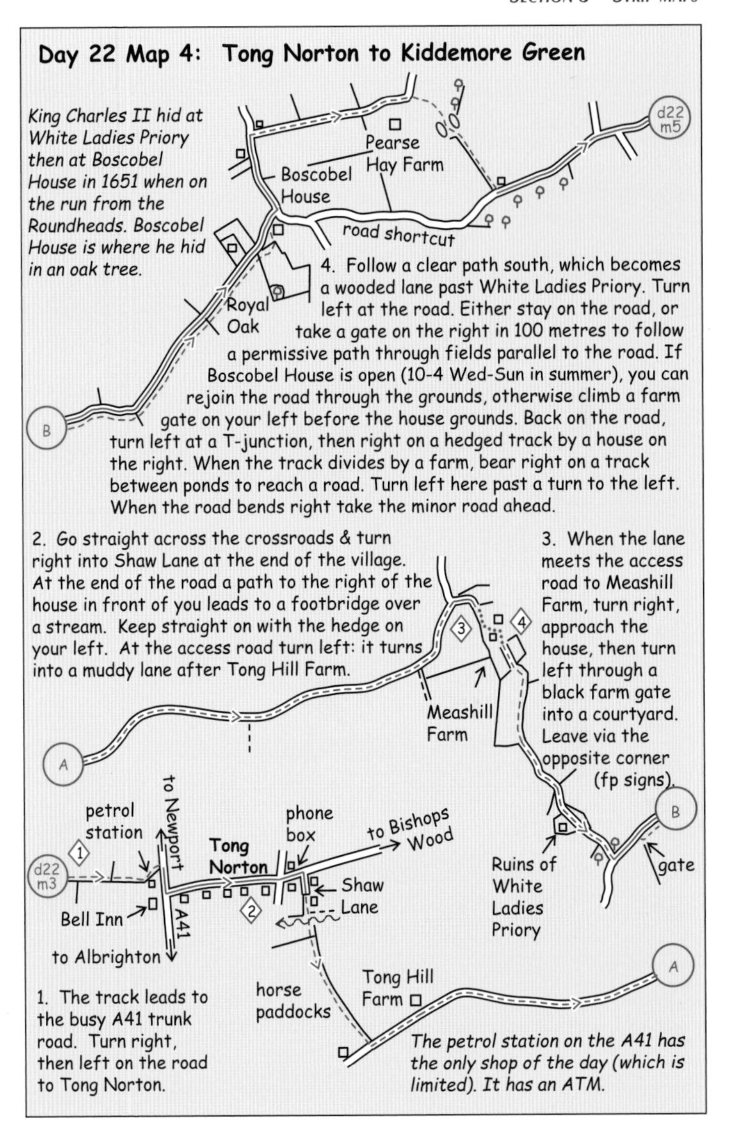
Day 22 Map 4: Tong Norton to Kiddemore Green
King Charles II hid at White Ladies Priory then at Boscobel House in 1651 when on the run from the Roundheads. Boscobel House is where he hid in an oak tree.
d22 m5
Pearse Hay Farm
Boscobel House
road shortcut
Royal Oak
B
4. Follow a clear path south, which becomes a wooded lane past White Ladies Priory. Turn left at the road. Either stay on the road, or take a gate on the right in 100 metres to follow a permissive path through fields parallel to the road. If Boscobel House is open (10-4 Wed-Sun in summer), you can rejoin the road through the grounds, otherwise climb a farm gate on your left before the house grounds. Back on the road, turn left at a T-junction, then right on a hedged track by a house on the right. When the track divides by a farm, bear right on a track between ponds to reach a road. Turn left here past a turn to the left. When the road bends right take the minor road ahead.
2. Go straight across the crossroads & turn right into Shaw Lane at the end of the village. At the end of the road a path to the right of the house in front of you leads to a footbridge over a stream. Keep straight on with the hedge on your left. At the access road turn left: it turns into a muddy lane after Tong Hill Farm.
3. When the lane meets the access road to Meashill Farm, turn right, approach the house, then turn left through a black farm gate into a courtyard. Leave via the opposite corner (fp signs).
3
4
Meashill Farm
A
B
to Newport
petrol station
1
d22 m3
Bell Inn
A41
to Albrighton
Tong Norton
2
phone box
to Bishops Wood
Shaw Lane
Ruins of White Ladies Priory
gate
A
horse paddocks
Tong Hill Farm
1. The track leads to the busy A41 trunk road. Turn right, then left on the road to Tong Norton.
The petrol station on the A41 has the only shop of the day (which is limited). It has an ATM.

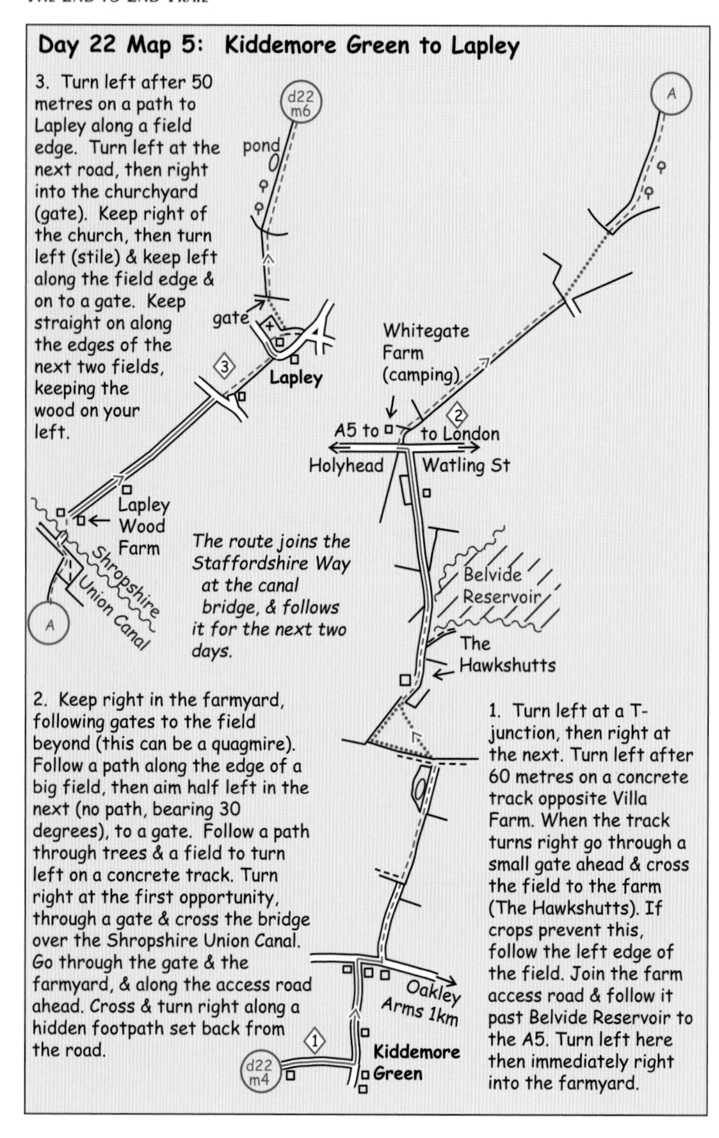

Day 22 Map 5: Kiddemore Green to Lapley
3. Turn left after 50 metres on a path to Lapley along a field edge. Turn left at the next road, then right into the churchyard (gate). Keep right of the church, then turn left (stile) & keep left along the field edge & on to a gate. Keep straight on along the edges of the next two fields, keeping the wood on your left.
d22 m6
pond
gate
Lapley
A
Whitegate Farm (camping)
A5 to Holyhead
to London
Watling St
Lapley Wood Farm
Shropshire Union Canal
A
The route joins the Staffordshire Way at the canal bridge, & follows it for the next two days.
Belvide Reservoir
The Hawkshutts
2. Keep right in the farmyard, following gates to the field beyond (this can be a quagmire). Follow a path along the edge of a big field, then aim half left in the next (no path, bearing 30 degrees), to a gate. Follow a path through trees & a field to turn left on a concrete track. Turn right at the first opportunity, through a gate & cross the bridge over the Shropshire Union Canal. Go through the gate & the farmyard, & along the access road ahead. Cross & turn right along a hidden footpath set back from the road.
1. Turn left at a T-junction, then right at the next. Turn left after 60 metres on a concrete track opposite Villa Farm. When the track turns right go through a small gate ahead & cross the field to the farm (The Hawkshutts). If crops prevent this, follow the left edge of the field. Join the farm access road & follow it past Belvide Reservoir to the A5. Turn left here then immediately right into the farmyard.
Oakley Arms 1km
Kiddemore Green
d22 m4

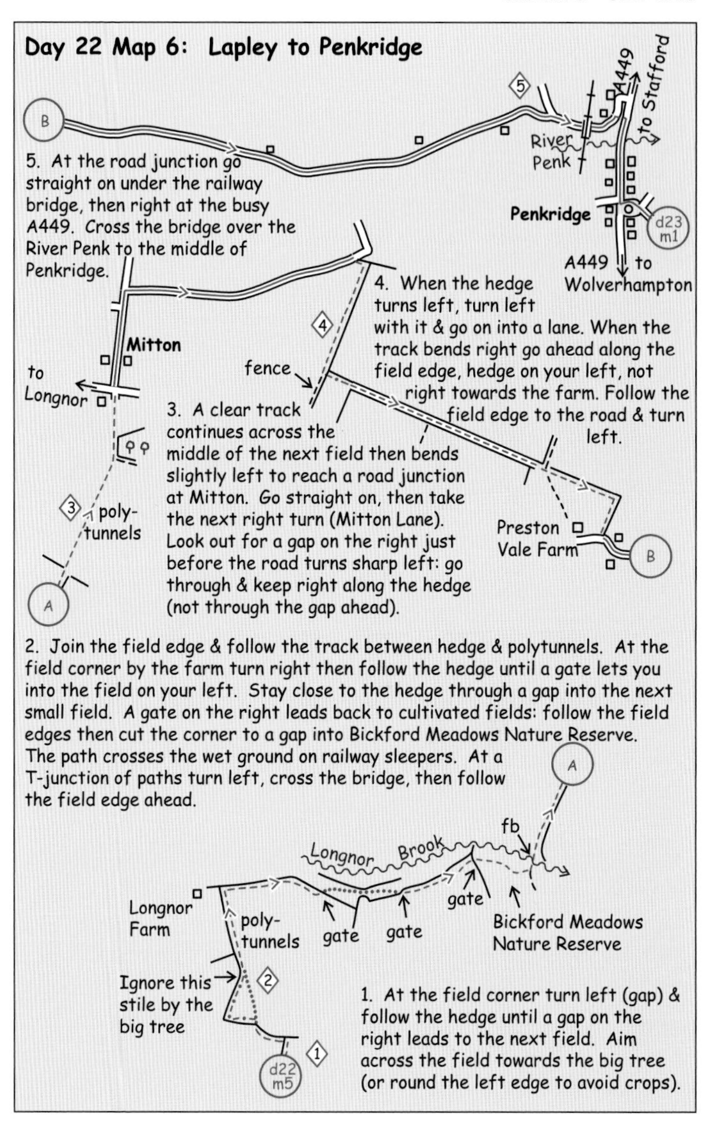
Day 22 Map 6: Lapley to Penkridge
B
A449
to Stafford
River Penk
Penkridge
d23 m1
A449 to Wolverhampton
5. At the road junction go straight on under the railway bridge, then right at the busy A449. Cross the bridge over the River Penk to the middle of Penkridge.
4. When the hedge turns left, turn left with it & go on into a lane. When the track bends right go ahead along the field edge, hedge on your left, not right towards the farm. Follow the field edge to the road & turn left.
Mitton
to Longnor
fence
3. A clear track continues across the middle of the next field then bends slightly left to reach a road junction at Mitton. Go straight on, then take the next right turn (Mitton Lane). Look out for a gap on the right just before the road turns sharp left: go through & keep right along the hedge (not through the gap ahead).
poly-tunnels
Preston Vale Farm
B
A
2. Join the field edge & follow the track between hedge & polytunnels. At the field corner by the farm turn right then follow the hedge until a gate lets you into the field on your left. Stay close to the hedge through a gap into the next small field. A gate on the right leads back to cultivated fields: follow the field edges then cut the corner to a gap into Bickford Meadows Nature Reserve. The path crosses the wet ground on railway sleepers. At a T-junction of paths turn left, cross the bridge, then follow the field edge ahead.
A
fb
Longnor Brook
Longnor Farm
poly-tunnels
gate
gate
gate
Bickford Meadows Nature Reserve
Ignore this stile by the big tree
d22 m5
1. At the field corner turn left (gap) & follow the hedge until a gap on the right leads to the next field. Aim across the field towards the big tree (or round the left edge to avoid crops).

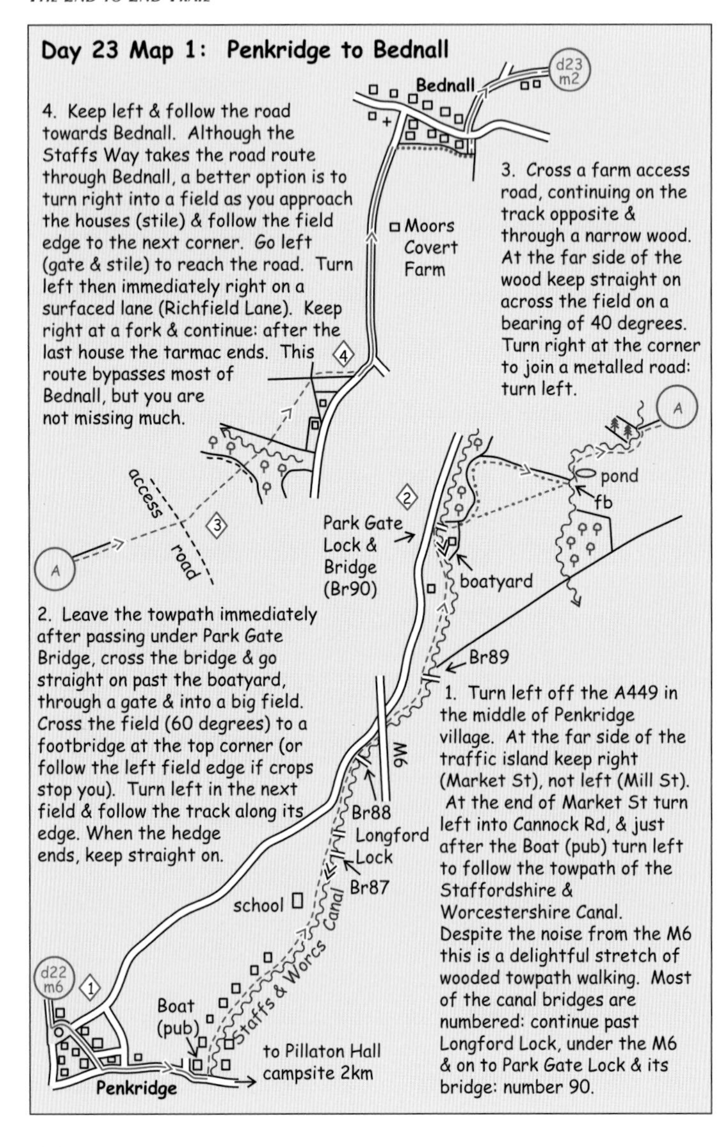

Day 23 Map 1: Penkridge to Bednall
d23 m2
Bednall
4. Keep left & follow the road towards Bednall. Although the Staffs Way takes the road route through Bednall, a better option is to turn right into a field as you approach the houses (stile) & follow the field edge to the next corner. Go left (gate & stile) to reach the road. Turn left then immediately right on a surfaced lane (Richfield Lane). Keep right at a fork & continue: after the last house the tarmac ends. This route bypasses most of Bednall, but you are not missing much.
Moors Covert Farm
3. Cross a farm access road, continuing on the track opposite & through a narrow wood. At the far side of the wood keep straight on across the field on a bearing of 40 degrees. Turn right at the corner to join a metalled road: turn left.
4
A
pond
fb
access road
3
2
Park Gate Lock & Bridge (Br90)
boatyard
A
2. Leave the towpath immediately after passing under Park Gate Bridge, cross the bridge & go straight on past the boatyard, through a gate & into a big field. Cross the field (60 degrees) to a footbridge at the top corner (or follow the left field edge if crops stop you). Turn left in the next field & follow the track along its edge. When the hedge ends, keep straight on.
Br89
1. Turn left off the A449 in the middle of Penkridge village. At the far side of the traffic island keep right (Market St), not left (Mill St). At the end of Market St turn left into Cannock Rd, & just after the Boat (pub) turn left to follow the towpath of the Staffordshire & Worcestershire Canal. Despite the noise from the M6 this is a delightful stretch of wooded towpath walking. Most of the canal bridges are numbered: continue past Longford Lock, under the M6 & on to Park Gate Lock & its bridge: number 90.
M6
Br88
Longford Lock
Br87
school
Staffs & Worcs Canal
d22 m6
1
Boat (pub)
to Pillaton Hall campsite 2km
Penkridge

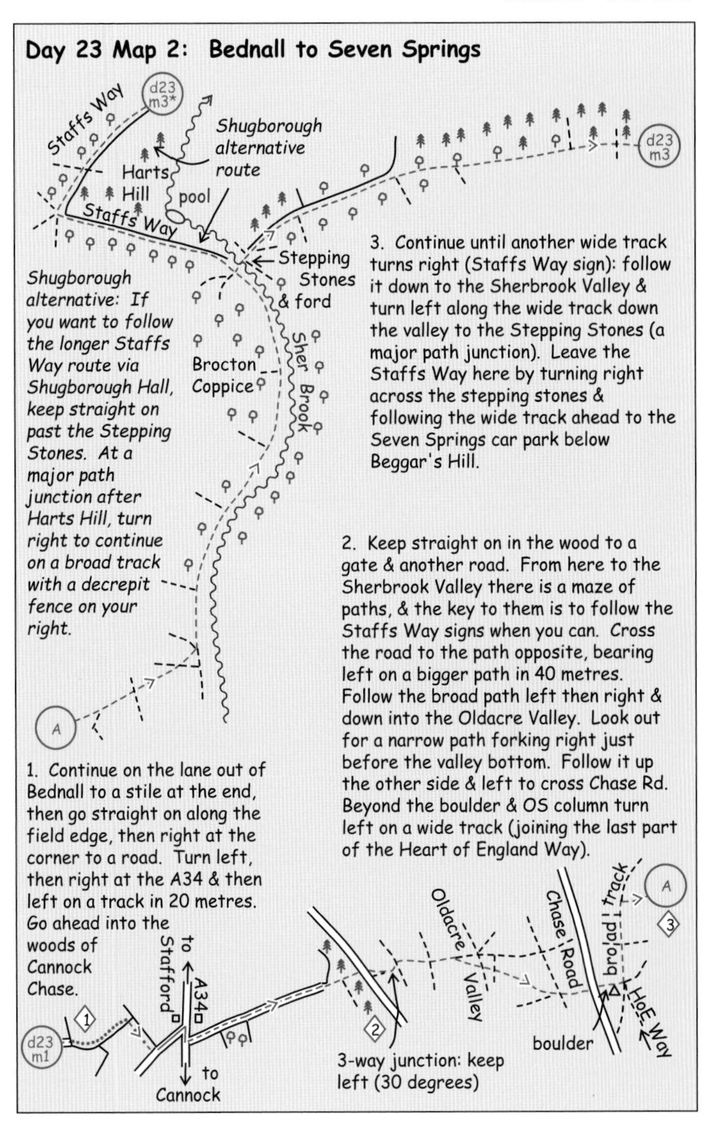

Day 23 Map 2: Bednall to Seven Springs
Staffs Way
d23 m3*
Shugborough alternative route
Harts Hill
pool
Staffs Way
Stepping Stones & ford
d23 m3
3. Continue until another wide track turns right (Staffs Way sign): follow it down to the Sherbrook Valley & turn left along the wide track down the valley to the Stepping Stones (a major path junction). Leave the Staffs Way here by turning right across the stepping stones & following the wide track ahead to the Seven Springs car park below Beggar's Hill.
Shugborough alternative: If you want to follow the longer Staffs Way route via Shugborough Hall, keep straight on past the Stepping Stones. At a major path junction after Harts Hill, turn right to continue on a broad track with a decrepit fence on your right.
Brocton Coppice
Sher Brook
2. Keep straight on in the wood to a gate & another road. From here to the Sherbrook Valley there is a maze of paths, & the key to them is to follow the Staffs Way signs when you can. Cross the road to the path opposite, bearing left on a bigger path in 40 metres. Follow the broad path left then right & down into the Oldacre Valley. Look out for a narrow path forking right just before the valley bottom. Follow it up the other side & left to cross Chase Rd. Beyond the boulder & OS column turn left on a wide track (joining the last part of the Heart of England Way).
A
1. Continue on the lane out of Bednall to a stile at the end, then go straight on along the field edge, then right at the corner to a road. Turn left, then right at the A34 & then left on a track in 20 metres. Go ahead into the woods of Cannock Chase.
to Stafford
A34
to Cannock
d23 m1
1
2
3-way junction: keep left (30 degrees)
Oldacre Valley
Chase Road
boulder
broad track
HoE Way
A
3

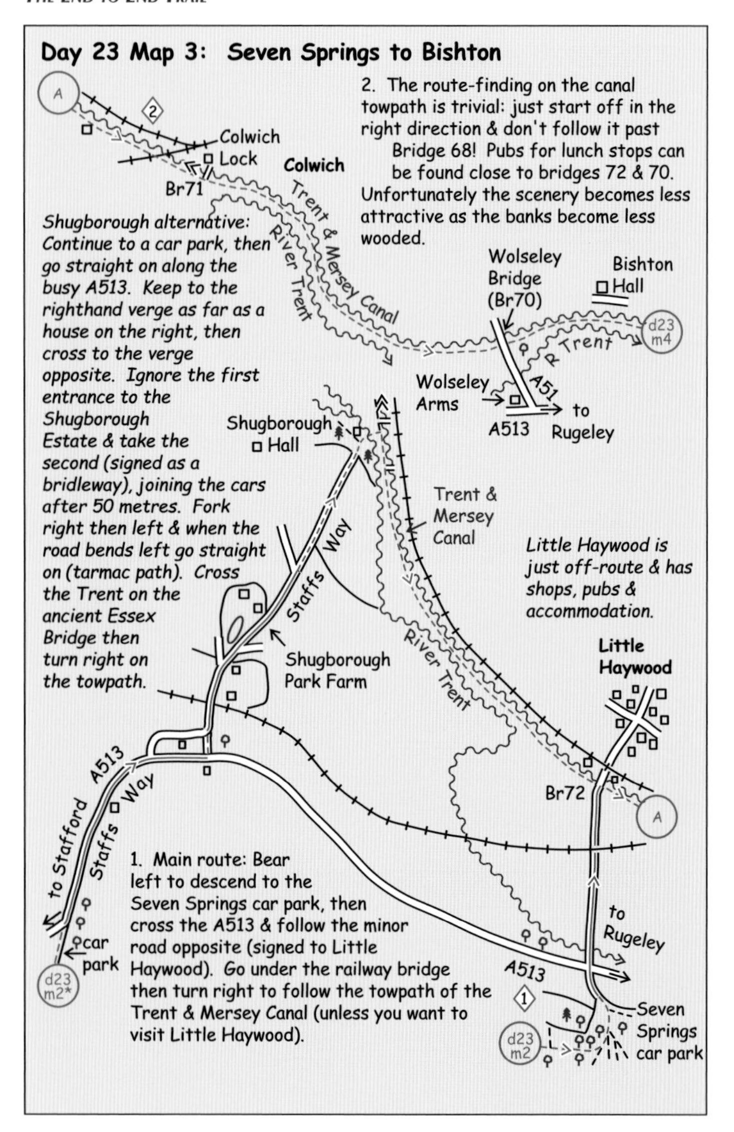
Day 23 Map 3: Seven Springs to Bishton
2. The route-finding on the canal towpath is trivial: just start off in the right direction & don't follow it past Bridge 68! Pubs for lunch stops can be found close to bridges 72 & 70. Unfortunately the scenery becomes less attractive as the banks become less wooded.
A
2
Colwich Lock
Colwich
Br71
Trent & Mersey Canal
River Trent
Shugborough alternative: Continue to a car park, then go straight on along the busy A513. Keep to the righthand verge as far as a house on the right, then cross to the verge opposite. Ignore the first entrance to the Shugborough Estate & take the second (signed as a bridleway), joining the cars after 50 metres. Fork right then left & when the road bends left go straight on (tarmac path). Cross the Trent on the ancient Essex Bridge then turn right on the towpath.
Wolseley Bridge (Br70)
Bishton Hall
d23 m4
R Trent
Wolseley Arms
A51
A513
to Rugeley
Shugborough Hall
Trent & Mersey Canal
Staffs Way
Little Haywood is just off-route & has shops, pubs & accommodation.
Shugborough Park Farm
River Trent
Little Haywood
A513
Br72
A
to Stafford
Staffs Way
car park
d23 m2*
1. Main route: Bear left to descend to the Seven Springs car park, then cross the A513 & follow the minor road opposite (signed to Little Haywood). Go under the railway bridge then turn right to follow the towpath of the Trent & Mersey Canal (unless you want to visit Little Haywood).
to Rugeley
A513
1
Seven Springs car park
d23 m2

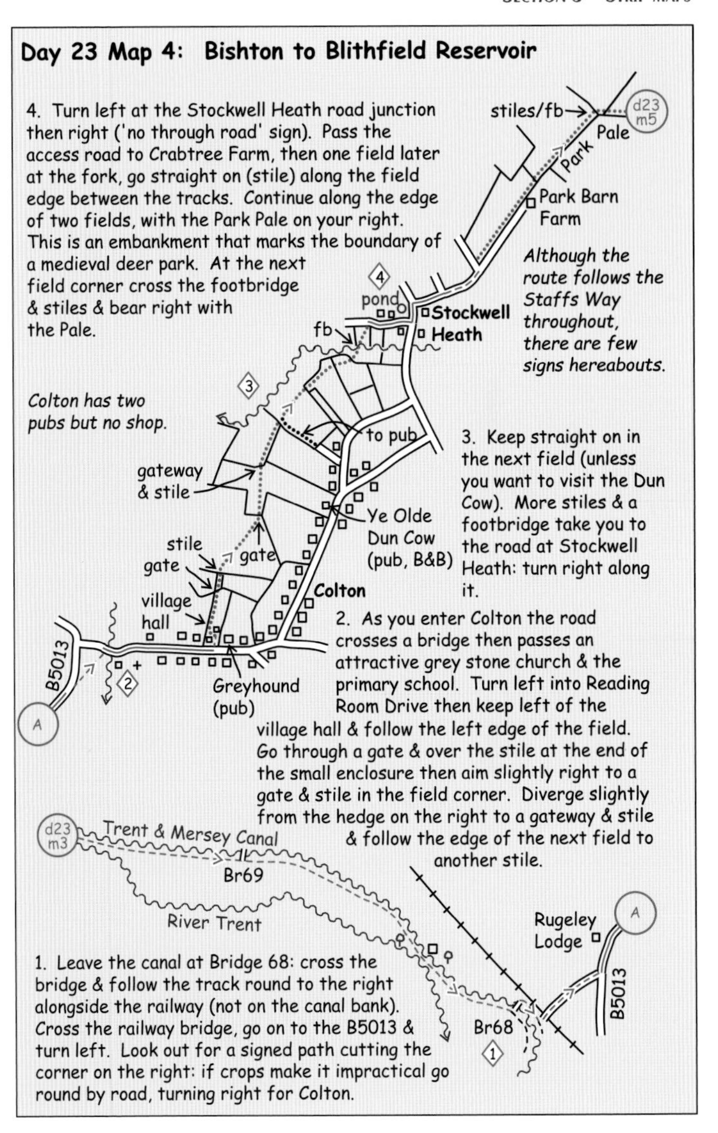
Day 23 Map 4: Bishton to Blithfield Reservoir
4. Turn left at the Stockwell Heath road junction then right ('no through road' sign). Pass the access road to Crabtree Farm, then one field later at the fork, go straight on (stile) along the field edge between the tracks. Continue along the edge of two fields, with the Park Pale on your right. This is an embankment that marks the boundary of a medieval deer park. At the next field corner cross the footbridge & stiles & bear right with the Pale.
stiles/fb
d23 m5
Park
Pale
Park Barn Farm
Although the route follows the Staffs Way throughout, there are few signs hereabouts.
4
pond
Stockwell Heath
fb
3
Colton has two pubs but no shop.
to pub
3. Keep straight on in the next field (unless you want to visit the Dun Cow). More stiles & a footbridge take you to the road at Stockwell Heath: turn right along it.
gateway & stile
Ye Olde Dun Cow (pub, B&B)
stile
gate
gate
Colton
village hall
B5013
2
Greyhound (pub)
A
2. As you enter Colton the road crosses a bridge then passes an attractive grey stone church & the primary school. Turn left into Reading Room Drive then keep left of the village hall & follow the left edge of the field. Go through a gate & over the stile at the end of the small enclosure then aim slightly right to a gate & stile in the field corner. Diverge slightly from the hedge on the right to a gateway & stile & follow the edge of the next field to another stile.
d23 m3
Trent & Mersey Canal
Br69
River Trent
Rugeley Lodge
A
B5013
Br68
1
1. Leave the canal at Bridge 68: cross the bridge & follow the track round to the right alongside the railway (not on the canal bank). Cross the railway bridge, go on to the B5013 & turn left. Look out for a signed path cutting the corner on the right: if crops make it impractical go round by road, turning right for Colton.

Day 23 Map 5: Blithfield Reservoir to Abbots Bromley

3. Follow the cart track below the dam until it approaches a gate & joins the road across the dam, by a water company building. You could go through the gate & turn right on the road, but that's not the right of way. That leaves the track for a stile to the right, then crosses grass in the next field to join the road. Turn right, then left at the first opportunity along a track. At the end turn right (stile) & follow the field edge with a ditch on your left then a footpath straight on through fields to a road junction. Turn right, then at the first opportunity sharp left (stile) & follow the right edge of the field to a stile into a lane. Continue past the sewage works & cross a stile on the left into a field when the lane bends right. Ignore the footbridge to your left: instead keep the stream on your left, & aim for a stile to the right of the church. Keep right in the churchyard & exit through the lychgate. Take the first left turn which brings you out in the centre of Abbots Bromley, opposite Schoolhouse Lane.

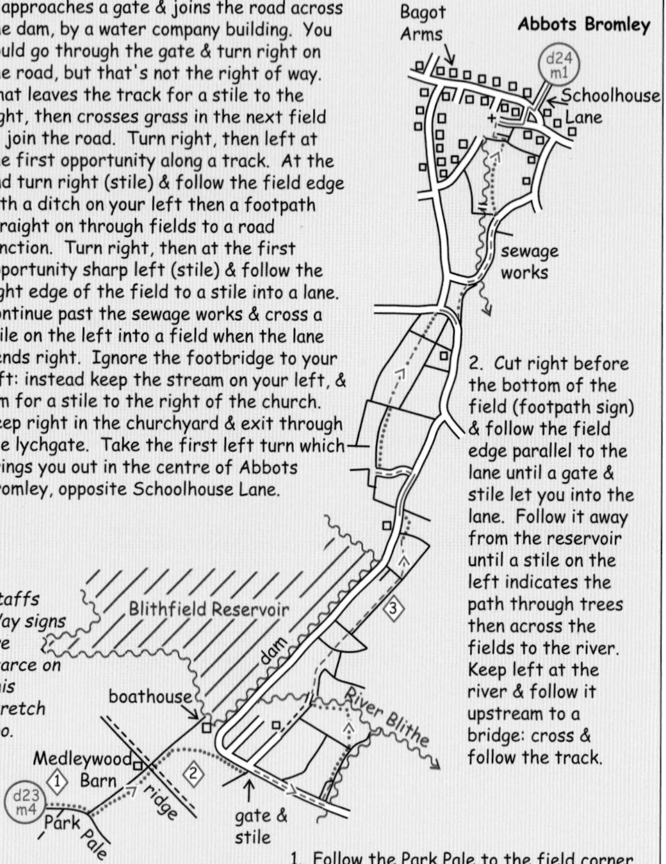

2. Cut right before the bottom of the field (footpath sign) & follow the field edge parallel to the lane until a gate & stile let you into the lane. Follow it away from the reservoir until a stile on the left indicates the path through trees then across the fields to the river. Keep left at the river & follow it upstream to a bridge: cross & follow the track.

Staffs Way signs are scarce on this stretch too.

1. Follow the Park Pale to the field corner, cross the stile & turn left up the hill to Medleywood Barn. At the barn Blithfield Reservoir comes into view, complete with sailing dinghies. Keep straight on down towards the dam & boathouse.

You could of course take a shortcut across the dam, but despite the volume of traffic it is not a right of way.

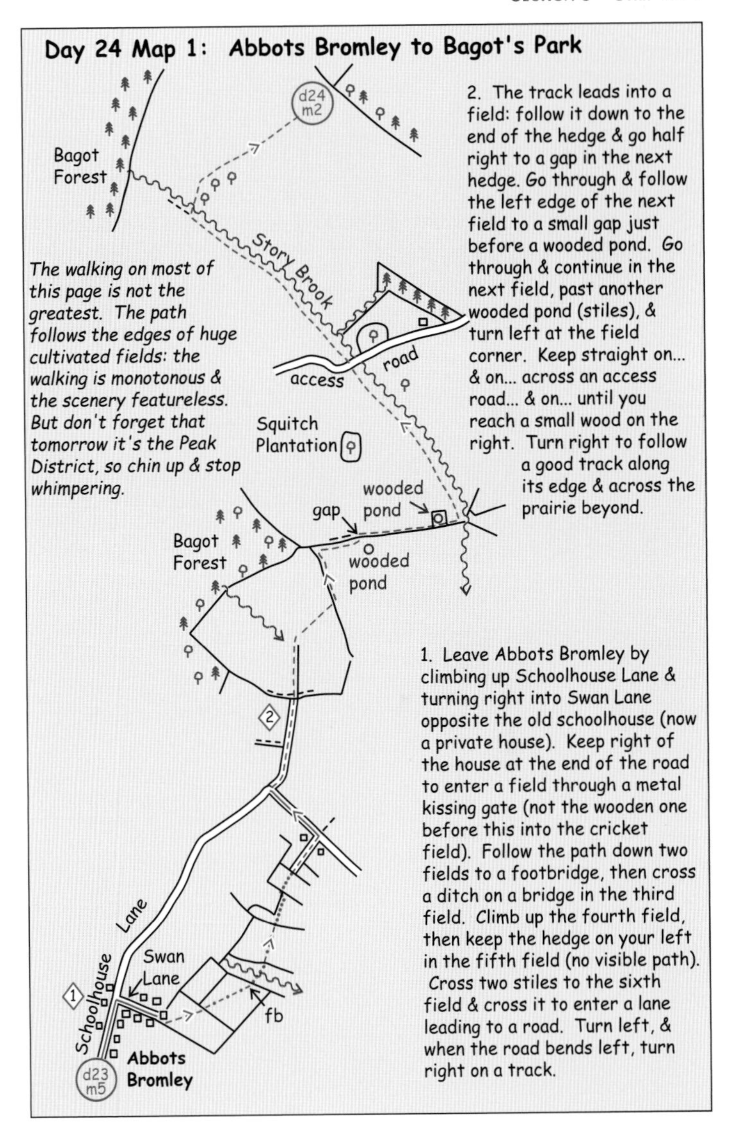
Day 24 Map 1: Abbots Bromley to Bagot's Park
d24 m2
Bagot Forest
2. The track leads into a field: follow it down to the end of the hedge & go half right to a gap in the next hedge. Go through & follow the left edge of the next field to a small gap just before a wooded pond. Go through & continue in the next field, past another wooded pond (stiles), & turn left at the field corner. Keep straight on... & on... across an access road... & on... until you reach a small wood on the right. Turn right to follow a good track along its edge & across the prairie beyond.
Story Brook
The walking on most of this page is not the greatest. The path follows the edges of huge cultivated fields: the walking is monotonous & the scenery featureless. But don't forget that tomorrow it's the Peak District, so chin up & stop whimpering.
access road
Squitch Plantation
wooded pond
gap
Bagot Forest
wooded pond
2
1. Leave Abbots Bromley by climbing up Schoolhouse Lane & turning right into Swan Lane opposite the old schoolhouse (now a private house). Keep right of the house at the end of the road to enter a field through a metal kissing gate (not the wooden one before this into the cricket field). Follow the path down two fields to a footbridge, then cross a ditch on a bridge in the third field. Climb up the fourth field, then keep the hedge on your left in the fifth field (no visible path). Cross two stiles to the sixth field & cross it to enter a lane leading to a road. Turn left, & when the road bends left, turn right on a track.
Schoolhouse Lane
Swan Lane
1
fb
d23 m5
Abbots Bromley

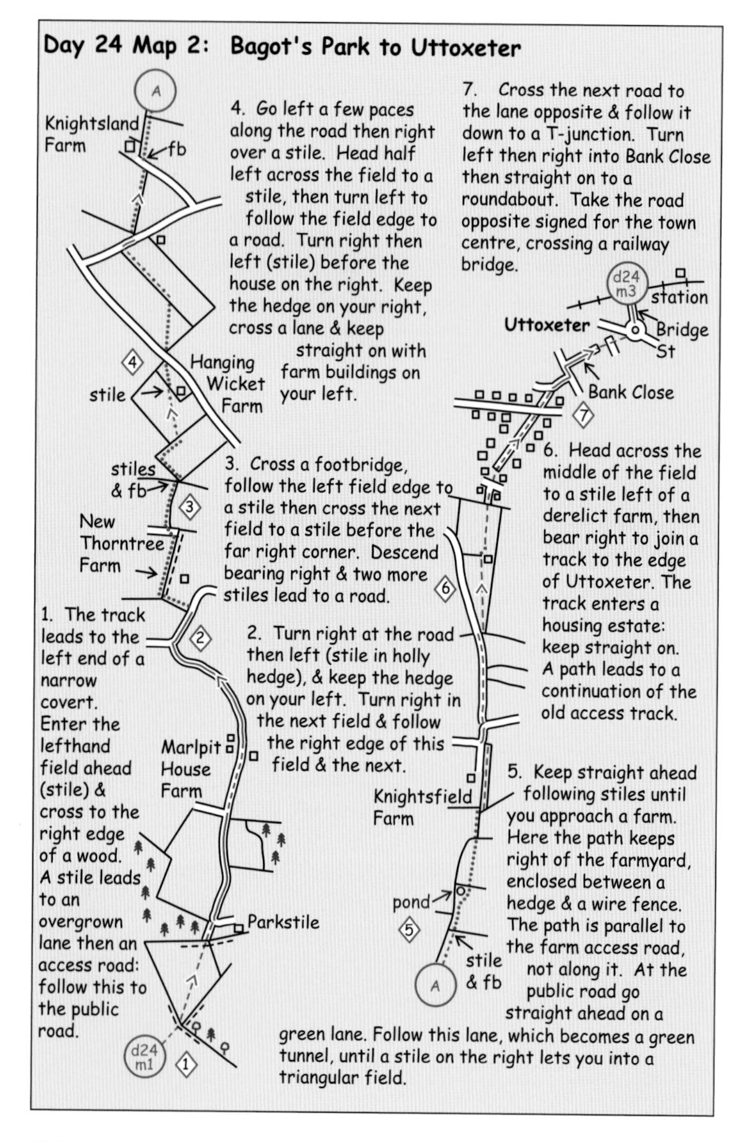
Day 24 Map 2: Bagot's Park to Uttoxeter
A
Knightsland Farm
fb
4. Go left a few paces along the road then right over a stile. Head half left across the field to a stile, then turn left to follow the field edge to a road. Turn right then left (stile) before the house on the right. Keep the hedge on your right, cross a lane & keep straight on with farm buildings on your left.
7. Cross the next road to the lane opposite & follow it down to a T-junction. Turn left then right into Bank Close then straight on to a roundabout. Take the road opposite signed for the town centre, crossing a railway bridge.
d24 m3
station
Uttoxeter
Bridge St
Bank Close
4
Hanging Wicket Farm
stile
7
6. Head across the middle of the field to a stile left of a derelict farm, then bear right to join a track to the edge of Uttoxeter. The track enters a housing estate: keep straight on. A path leads to a continuation of the old access track.
stiles & fb
3. Cross a footbridge, follow the left field edge to a stile then cross the next field to a stile before the far right corner. Descend bearing right & two more stiles lead to a road.
3
New Thorntree Farm
6
1. The track leads to the left end of a narrow covert. Enter the lefthand field ahead (stile) & cross to the right edge of a wood. A stile leads to an overgrown lane then an access road: follow this to the public road.
2
2. Turn right at the road then left (stile in holly hedge), & keep the hedge on your left. Turn right in the next field & follow the right edge of this field & the next.
Marlpit House Farm
5. Keep straight ahead following stiles until you approach a farm. Here the path keeps right of the farmyard, enclosed between a hedge & a wire fence. The path is parallel to the farm access road, not along it. At the public road go straight ahead on a green lane. Follow this lane, which becomes a green tunnel, until a stile on the right lets you into a triangular field.
Knightsfield Farm
pond
Parkstile
5
stile & fb
A
d24 m1
1

Day 24 Map 3: Uttoxeter to Eaton Hall Farm

4. Cross the meadow (20 degrees, past a post) to join the riverbank. Take the lefthand gap in the field corner & keep straight on to climb the field ahead. At the top keep to the left edge of the field & into an overgrown lane at its end. Turn left at the corner of the next field (footpath sign) & follow its left edge along the top of the escarpment. Turn left on the access track to Doveridge Clay Sports Club & follow it down the slope.

3. Cross the rivers Tean & Dove on the cycle path, then leave it immediately to descend right to a pedestrian underpass by the Dove. In the wood the other side of the A50, turn right at a path junction (away from the A50), to reach a stile into a meadow.

2. At the end of the track go left (stile), not through the gate ahead. Keep left to the field corner (stile to the right). Head across the field past a pylon to a stile just left of the end of the hedge on the right. Cross an access road, & another stile leads to the cycle path by the very busy A50: turn right.

1. Turn right at the roundabout after the railway bridge & follow Brookside Rd to its end. Black gates & a footpath sign show the way on a track across grass - car park access for the racecourse. Bend left round a large industrial building then straight on to a stile into pasture. Cut across to a gate & stile just left of the house. Turn right on the access road & the short track beyond.

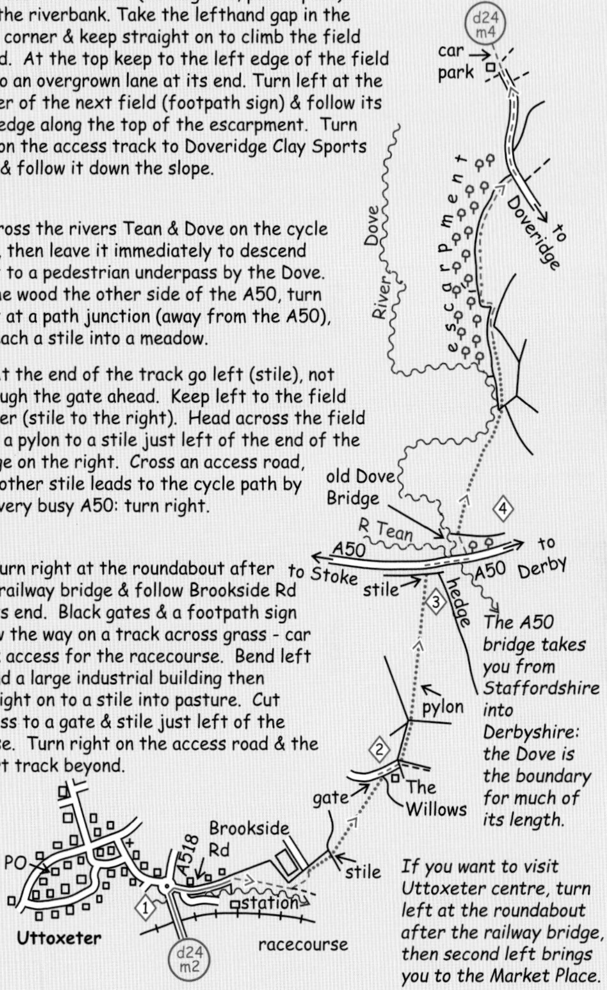

The A50 bridge takes you from Staffordshire into Derbyshire: the Dove is the boundary for much of its length.

If you want to visit Uttoxeter centre, turn left at the roundabout after the railway bridge, then second left brings you to the Market Place.

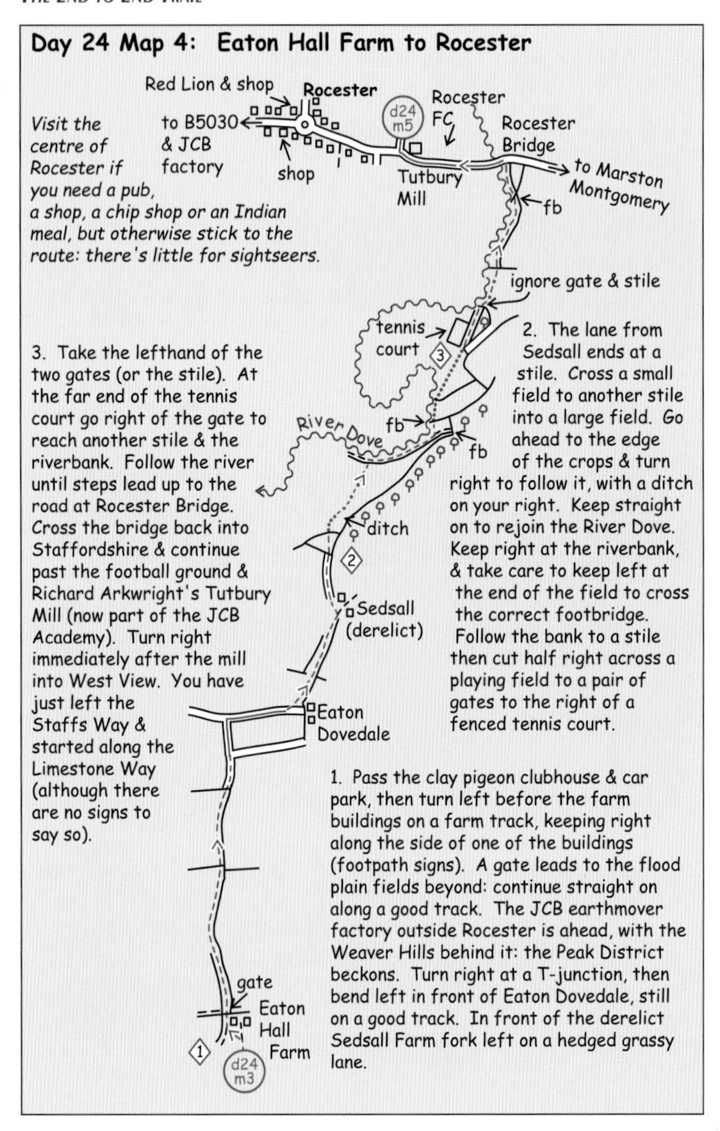
Day 24 Map 4: Eaton Hall Farm to Rocester
Red Lion & shop
Rocester
Rocester FC
Rocester Bridge
d24 m5
to B5030 & JCB factory
shop
Tutbury Mill
to Marston Montgomery
fb
Visit the centre of Rocester if you need a pub, a shop, a chip shop or an Indian meal, but otherwise stick to the route: there's little for sightseers.
ignore gate & stile
tennis court
3
2. The lane from Sedsall ends at a stile. Cross a small field to another stile into a large field. Go ahead to the edge of the crops & turn right to follow it, with a ditch on your right. Keep straight on to rejoin the River Dove. Keep right at the riverbank, & take care to keep left at the end of the field to cross the correct footbridge. Follow the bank to a stile then cut half right across a playing field to a pair of gates to the right of a fenced tennis court.
3. Take the lefthand of the two gates (or the stile). At the far end of the tennis court go right of the gate to reach another stile & the riverbank. Follow the river until steps lead up to the road at Rocester Bridge. Cross the bridge back into Staffordshire & continue past the football ground & Richard Arkwright's Tutbury Mill (now part of the JCB Academy). Turn right immediately after the mill into West View. You have just left the Staffs Way & started along the Limestone Way (although there are no signs to say so).
River Dove
fb
fb
ditch
2
Sedsall (derelict)
Eaton Dovedale
1. Pass the clay pigeon clubhouse & car park, then turn left before the farm buildings on a farm track, keeping right along the side of one of the buildings (footpath signs). A gate leads to the flood plain fields beyond: continue straight on along a good track. The JCB earthmover factory outside Rocester is ahead, with the Weaver Hills behind it: the Peak District beckons. Turn right at a T-junction, then bend left in front of Eaton Dovedale, still on a good track. In front of the derelict Sedsall Farm fork left on a hedged grassy lane.
gate
Eaton Hall Farm
1
d24 m3

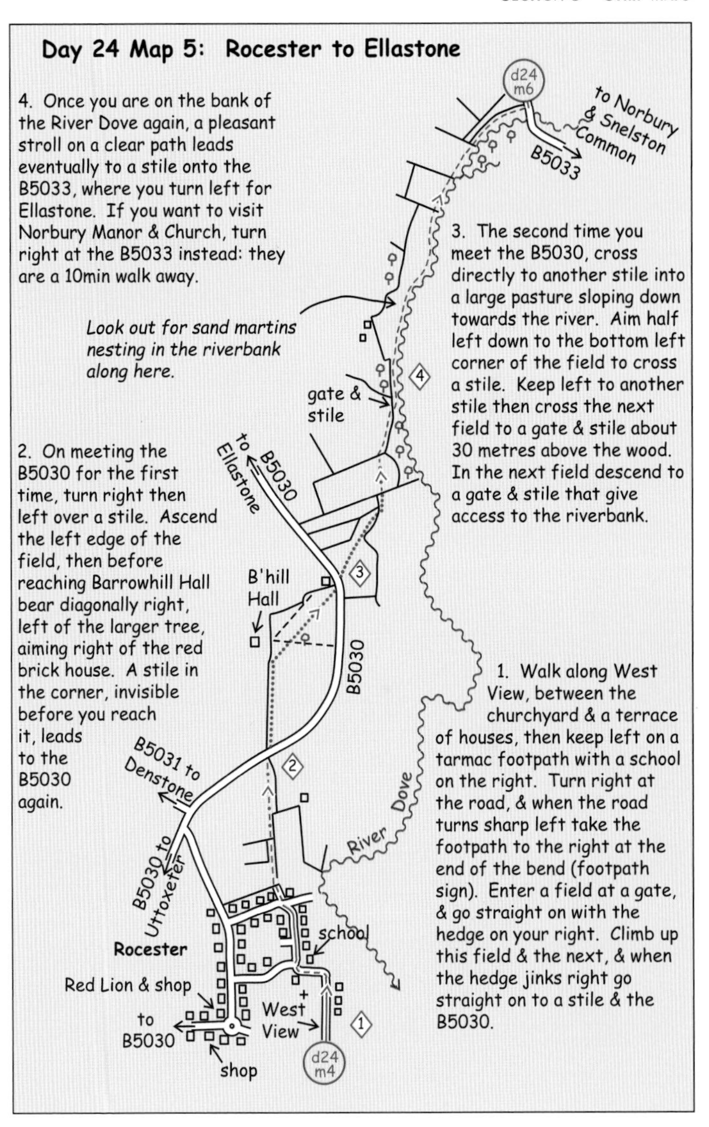
Day 24 Map 5: Rocester to Ellastone
4. Once you are on the bank of the River Dove again, a pleasant stroll on a clear path leads eventually to a stile onto the B5033, where you turn left for Ellastone. If you want to visit Norbury Manor & Church, turn right at the B5033 instead: they are a 10min walk away.
Look out for sand martins nesting in the riverbank along here.
2. On meeting the B5030 for the first time, turn right then left over a stile. Ascend the left edge of the field, then before reaching Barrowhill Hall bear diagonally right, left of the larger tree, aiming right of the red brick house. A stile in the corner, invisible before you reach it, leads to the B5030 again.
3. The second time you meet the B5030, cross directly to another stile into a large pasture sloping down towards the river. Aim half left down to the bottom left corner of the field to cross a stile. Keep left to another stile then cross the next field to a gate & stile about 30 metres above the wood. In the next field descend to a gate & stile that give access to the riverbank.
1. Walk along West View, between the churchyard & a terrace of houses, then keep left on a tarmac footpath with a school on the right. Turn right at the road, & when the road turns sharp left take the footpath to the right at the end of the bend (footpath sign). Enter a field at a gate, & go straight on with the hedge on your right. Climb up this field & the next, & when the hedge jinks right go straight on to a stile & the B5030.
d24 m6
to Norbury & Snelston Common
B5033
gate & stile
to Ellastone
B5030
B'hill Hall
B5030
B5031 to Denstone
B5030 to Uttoxeter
River Dove
Rocester
school
Red Lion & shop
to B5030
West View
shop
d24 m4

Day 24 Map 6: Ellastone to Motcarn Sprink

3. The access road down from the Hutts Farm doubles back on itself. There is a stile on this bend, indicating the line of the Limestone Way, which follows a ridge through fields for the next few kilometres. The End to End Trail follows the wooded valley instead: continue along the road for 25 metres to a second stile. Descend the steep pathless slope to a footbridge & climb a clear path opposite to join a good path. Turn right & follow it up the valley & into the woods.

d24 m7

Ordley Brook

to Stanton

Ousley Cross

fb

Limestone Way

3

The Hutts Farm

barn

stiles

Motcarn Sprink, whatever it may be, is up in the woods to the left just before the end of this map page (according to the OS).

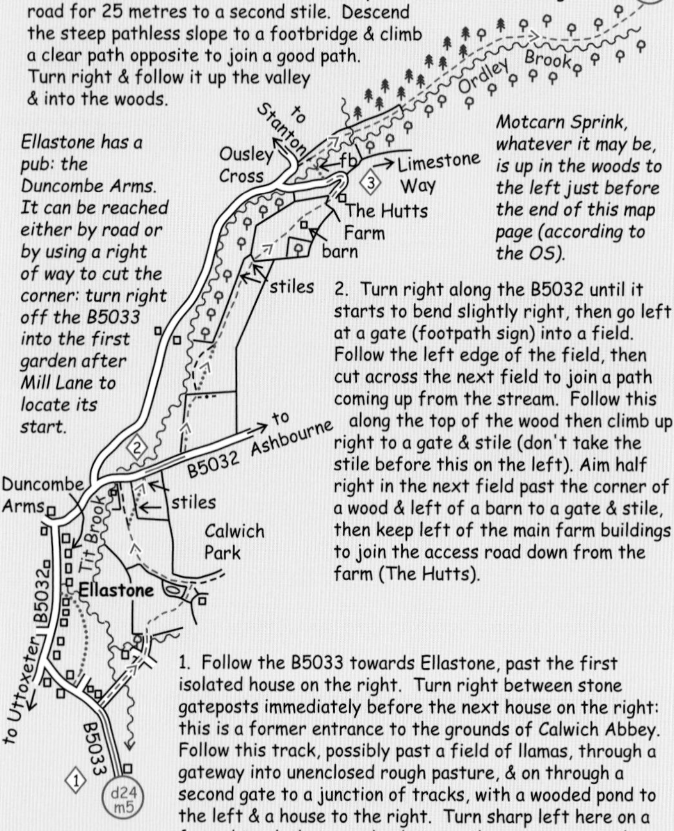

Ellastone has a pub: the Duncombe Arms. It can be reached either by road or by using a right of way to cut the corner: turn right off the B5033 into the first garden after Mill Lane to locate its start.

2. Turn right along the B5032 until it starts to bend slightly right, then go left at a gate (footpath sign) into a field. Follow the left edge of the field, then cut across the next field to join a path coming up from the stream. Follow this along the top of the wood then climb up right to a gate & stile (don't take the stile before this on the left). Aim half right in the next field past the corner of a wood & left of a barn to a gate & stile, then keep left of the main farm buildings to join the access road down from the farm (The Hutts).

to Ashbourne

B5032

2

Duncombe Arms

Tit Brook

stiles

Calwich Park

Ellastone

B5032

to Uttoxeter

B5033

1

d24 m5

1. Follow the B5033 towards Ellastone, past the first isolated house on the right. Turn right between stone gateposts immediately before the next house on the right: this is a former entrance to the grounds of Calwich Abbey. Follow this track, possibly past a field of llamas, through a gateway into unenclosed rough pasture, & on through a second gate to a junction of tracks, with a wooded pond to the left & a house to the right. Turn sharp left here on a fenced track that soon leads to another pasture. As the lodge & its enclosure grow nearer, look for a stile to the right: leave the track to cross this stile & cut the corner of the field beyond to another stile & the B5032.

Day 24 Map 7: Motcarn Sprink to Swinscoe

1. The path along Ordley Brook is mostly easy to follow, although there are parts that are very wet underfoot. Apart from this, the wood is a very pleasant place to walk, & far preferable to the Limestone Way route on the ridge to the right. Eventually a gate marks the end of the old wood & the path climbs slightly through wooded pasture with more recent planting to meet a road.

2. Turn right downhill on the minor road until it crosses the stream, then turn left (stile) to continue walking up by the stream. This section is less frequented & once back in the woods the path is rudimentary in places. It is close to the stream until it peters out between the stream & a steep bank on your right. At this point the path is actually up to your right on this bank: it left the stream path obscurely a short distance behind you.

3. Once you have found the path in the wood again it climbs gradually up from the stream to leave the wood at a stile. Follow the top of the wood briefly, then slant up the steep field along the line of an old disused track, aiming right of Ellishill Farm, visible ahead. Join a track along the top of the field & follow it to the farm.

4. Join the road at Ellishill Farm, then go left through a small gate. Cross the field to a stile, turn half left to another, then half right to the next. From here aim between the barn & the house to join the access road at Leasow Farm.

5. Leave the Leasow Farm road almost immediately as it bends left, over a stile straight ahead. Cross the field to a stile visible in front of a group of houses at Swinscoe: keep left initially to avoid a marshy dip. An alley leads to a road: turn right to reach the A52 & then turn left.

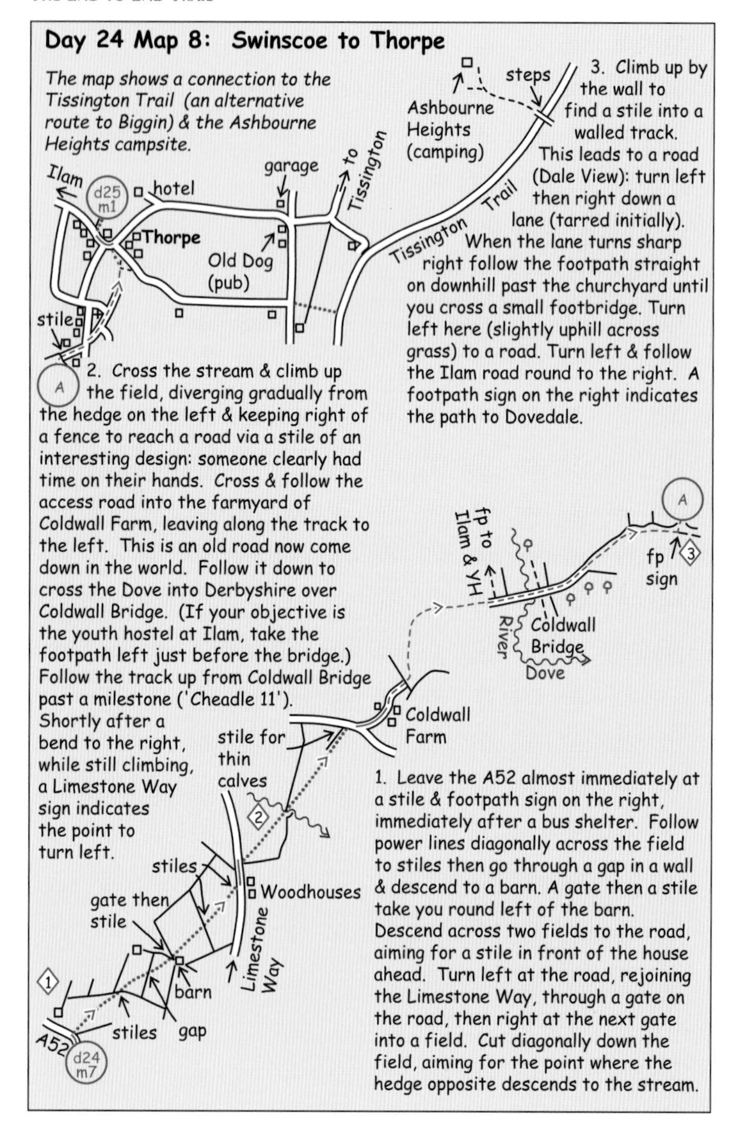
Day 24 Map 8: Swinscoe to Thorpe
The map shows a connection to the Tissington Trail (an alternative route to Biggin) & the Ashbourne Heights campsite.
steps
Ashbourne Heights (camping)
3. Climb up by the wall to find a stile into a walled track. This leads to a road (Dale View): turn left then right down a lane (tarred initially). When the lane turns sharp right follow the footpath straight on downhill past the churchyard until you cross a small footbridge. Turn left here (slightly uphill across grass) to a road. Turn left & follow the Ilam road round to the right. A footpath sign on the right indicates the path to Dovedale.
Ilam
d25 m1
hotel
garage
to Tissington
Tissington Trail
Thorpe
Old Dog (pub)
stile
A
2. Cross the stream & climb up the field, diverging gradually from the hedge on the left & keeping right of a fence to reach a road via a stile of an interesting design: someone clearly had time on their hands. Cross & follow the access road into the farmyard of Coldwall Farm, leaving along the track to the left. This is an old road now come down in the world. Follow it down to cross the Dove into Derbyshire over Coldwall Bridge. (If your objective is the youth hostel at Ilam, take the footpath left just before the bridge.) Follow the track up from Coldwall Bridge past a milestone ('Cheadle 11'). Shortly after a bend to the right, while still climbing, a Limestone Way sign indicates the point to turn left.
fp to Ilam & YH
A
fp sign
3
Coldwall Bridge
River Dove
Coldwall Farm
stile for thin calves
2
1. Leave the A52 almost immediately at a stile & footpath sign on the right, immediately after a bus shelter. Follow power lines diagonally across the field to stiles then go through a gap in a wall & descend to a barn. A gate then a stile take you round left of the barn. Descend across two fields to the road, aiming for a stile in front of the house ahead. Turn left at the road, rejoining the Limestone Way, through a gate on the road, then right at the next gate into a field. Cut diagonally down the field, aiming for the point where the hedge opposite descends to the stream.
stiles
Woodhouses
gate then stile
Limestone Way
1
barn
A52
stiles
gap
d24 m7

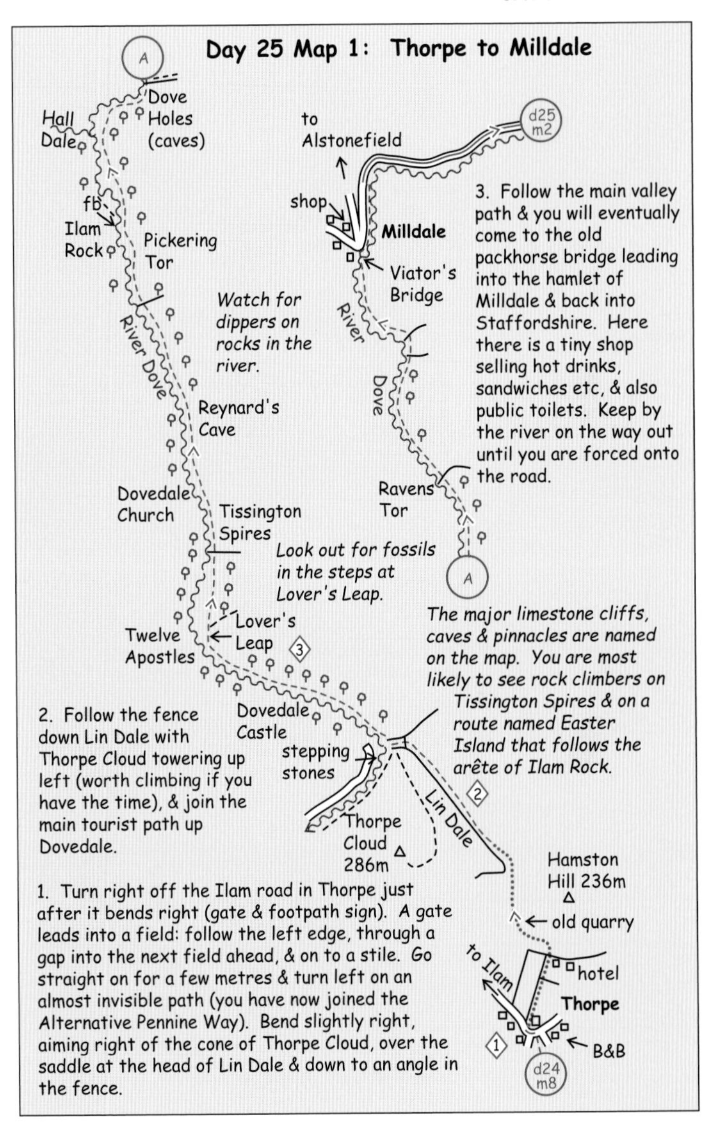
Day 25 Map 1: Thorpe to Milldale
A
Dove Holes (caves)
Hall Dale
to Alstonefield
d25 m2
shop
fb
Ilam Rock
Pickering Tor
Milldale
Viator's Bridge
3. Follow the main valley path & you will eventually come to the old packhorse bridge leading into the hamlet of Milldale & back into Staffordshire. Here there is a tiny shop selling hot drinks, sandwiches etc, & also public toilets. Keep by the river on the way out until you are forced onto the road.
Watch for dippers on rocks in the river.
River Dove
River Dove
Reynard's Cave
Dovedale Church
Tissington Spires
Ravens Tor
Look out for fossils in the steps at Lover's Leap.
A
Lover's Leap
3
Twelve Apostles
The major limestone cliffs, caves & pinnacles are named on the map. You are most likely to see rock climbers on Tissington Spires & on a route named Easter Island that follows the arête of Ilam Rock.
2. Follow the fence down Lin Dale with Thorpe Cloud towering up left (worth climbing if you have the time), & join the main tourist path up Dovedale.
Dovedale Castle
stepping stones
Lin Dale
2
Thorpe Cloud 286m
Hamston Hill 236m
old quarry
1. Turn right off the Ilam road in Thorpe just after it bends right (gate & footpath sign). A gate leads into a field: follow the left edge, through a gap into the next field ahead, & on to a stile. Go straight on for a few metres & turn left on an almost invisible path (you have now joined the Alternative Pennine Way). Bend slightly right, aiming right of the cone of Thorpe Cloud, over the saddle at the head of Lin Dale & down to an angle in the fence.
to Ilam
hotel
Thorpe
1
B&B
d24 m8

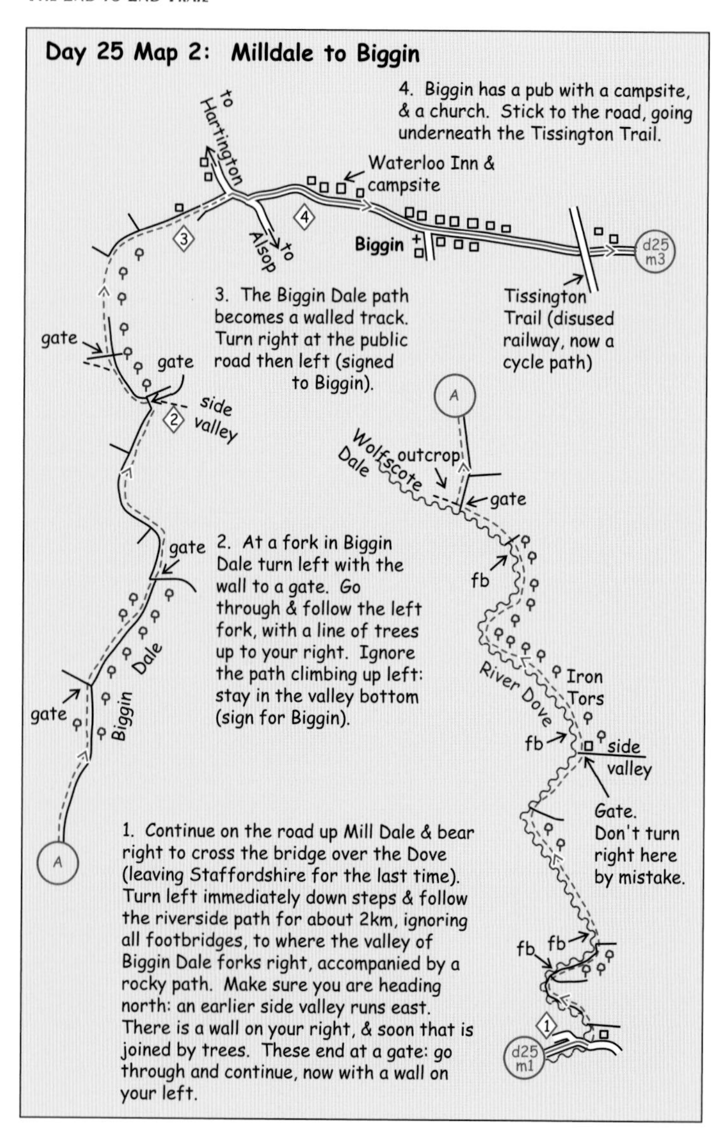
Day 25 Map 2: Milldale to Biggin
4. Biggin has a pub with a campsite, & a church. Stick to the road, going underneath the Tissington Trail.
to Hartington
Waterloo Inn & campsite
4
3
to Alsop
Biggin
d25 m3
3. The Biggin Dale path becomes a walled track. Turn right at the public road then left (signed to Biggin).
Tissington Trail (disused railway, now a cycle path)
gate
gate
side valley
2
A
Wolfscote Dale
outcrop
gate
gate
2. At a fork in Biggin Dale turn left with the wall to a gate. Go through & follow the left fork, with a line of trees up to your right. Ignore the path climbing up left: stay in the valley bottom (sign for Biggin).
fb
Biggin Dale
gate
River Dove
Iron Tors
fb
side valley
Gate. Don't turn right here by mistake.
A
1. Continue on the road up Mill Dale & bear right to cross the bridge over the Dove (leaving Staffordshire for the last time). Turn left immediately down steps & follow the riverside path for about 2km, ignoring all footbridges, to where the valley of Biggin Dale forks right, accompanied by a rocky path. Make sure you are heading north: an earlier side valley runs east. There is a wall on your right, & soon that is joined by trees. These end at a gate: go through and continue, now with a wall on your left.
fb
fb
1
d25 m1

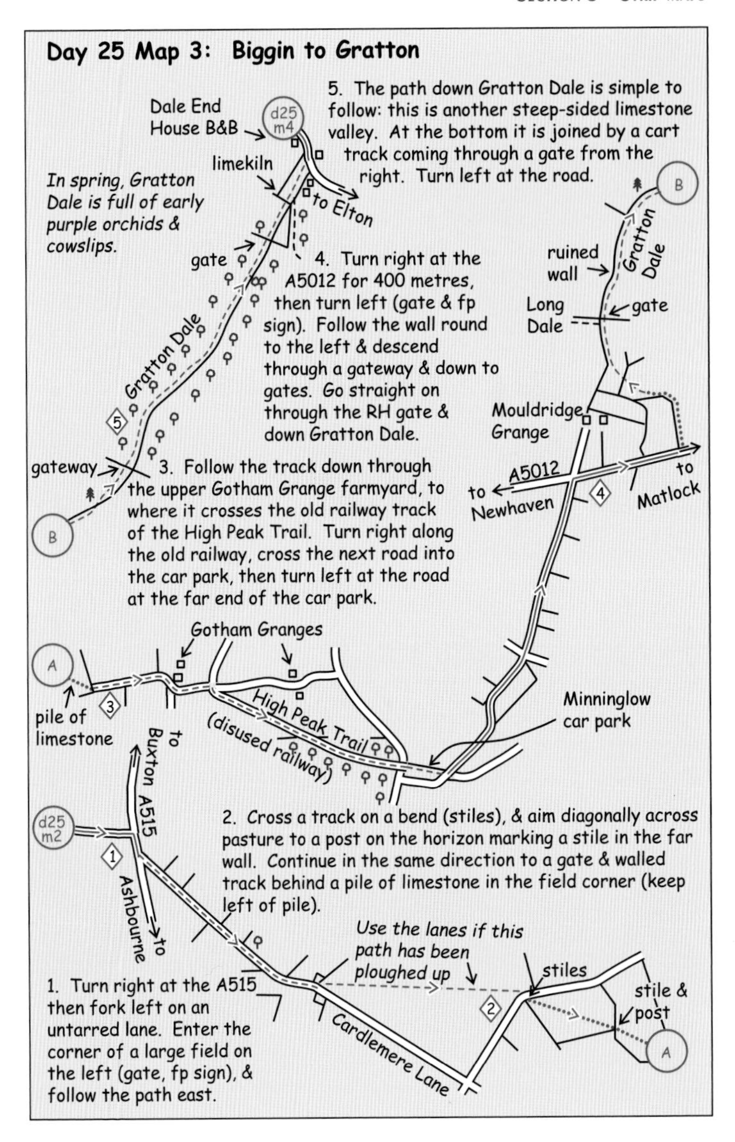
Day 25 Map 3: Biggin to Gratton
5. The path down Gratton Dale is simple to follow: this is another steep-sided limestone valley. At the bottom it is joined by a cart track coming through a gate from the right. Turn left at the road.
Dale End House B&B
d25 m4
limekiln
to Elton
In spring, Gratton Dale is full of early purple orchids & cowslips.
gate
4. Turn right at the A5012 for 400 metres, then turn left (gate & fp sign). Follow the wall round to the left & descend through a gateway & down to gates. Go straight on through the RH gate & down Gratton Dale.
B
ruined wall
Gratton Dale
Long Dale
gate
Gratton Dale
5
Mouldridge Grange
gateway
3. Follow the track down through the upper Gotham Grange farmyard, to where it crosses the old railway track of the High Peak Trail. Turn right along the old railway, cross the next road into the car park, then turn left at the road at the far end of the car park.
B
A5012
to Newhaven
4
to Matlock
Gotham Granges
A
3
pile of limestone
to Buxton A515
High Peak Trail (disused railway)
Minninglow car park
d25 m2
1
Ashbourne to
2. Cross a track on a bend (stiles), & aim diagonally across pasture to a post on the horizon marking a stile in the far wall. Continue in the same direction to a gate & walled track behind a pile of limestone in the field corner (keep left of pile).
Use the lanes if this path has been ploughed up
stiles
stile & post
2
A
1. Turn right at the A515 then fork left on an untarred lane. Enter the corner of a large field on the left (gate, fp sign), & follow the path east.
Cardlemere Lane

Day 25 Map 4: Gratton to Youlgreave

1. Keep right when the road forks & climb up past Gratton Grange Farm to the start of a double bend where the road steepens: turn left off the road here on an overgrown walled path (fp sign). A stile leads to a field, with overhead power lines indicating the approximate direction. The gap in the next fence is slightly left of the power lines, although keeping right of them until you get there avoids wet ground. This is a gritstone boulder field: a brief taste of things to come tomorrow.

2. Aim just right of the power lines to a gate & stile. Go straight on from here, with the power lines, & when they bend right follow the line of trees & ditch ahead to join a farm access road. Turn right along the road, then after 30 metres leave it by a stile on the right.

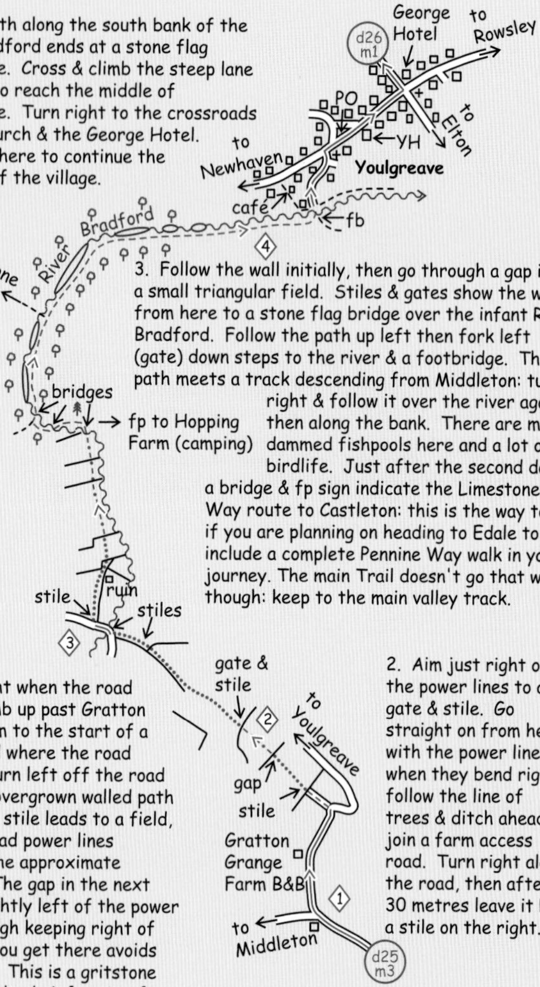

3. Follow the wall initially, then go through a gap into a small triangular field. Stiles & gates show the way from here to a stone flag bridge over the infant River Bradford. Follow the path up left then fork left (gate) down steps to the river & a footbridge. The path meets a track descending from Middleton: turn right & follow it over the river again then along the bank. There are many dammed fishpools here and a lot of birdlife. Just after the second dam a bridge & fp sign indicate the Limestone Way route to Castleton: this is the way to go if you are planning on heading to Edale to include a complete Pennine Way walk in your journey. The main Trail doesn't go that way though: keep to the main valley track.

4. The path along the south bank of the River Bradford ends at a stone flag footbridge. Cross & climb the steep lane opposite to reach the middle of Youlgreave. Turn right to the crossroads by the church & the George Hotel. Turn left here to continue the walk out of the village.

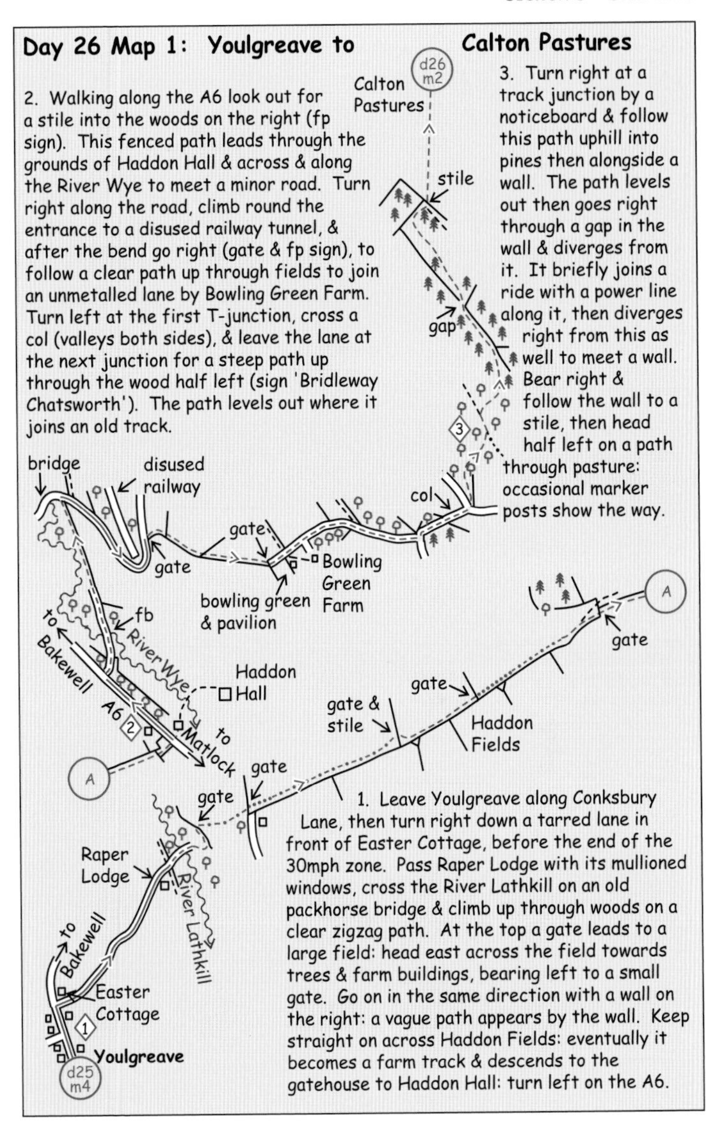
Day 26 Map 1: Youlgreave to Calton Pastures
d26 m2
Calton Pastures
2. Walking along the A6 look out for a stile into the woods on the right (fp sign). This fenced path leads through the grounds of Haddon Hall & across & along the River Wye to meet a minor road. Turn right along the road, climb round the entrance to a disused railway tunnel, & after the bend go right (gate & fp sign), to follow a clear path up through fields to join an unmetalled lane by Bowling Green Farm. Turn left at the first T-junction, cross a col (valleys both sides), & leave the lane at the next junction for a steep path up through the wood half left (sign 'Bridleway Chatsworth'). The path levels out where it joins an old track.
3. Turn right at a track junction by a noticeboard & follow this path uphill into pines then alongside a wall. The path levels out then goes right through a gap in the wall & diverges from it. It briefly joins a ride with a power line along it, then diverges right from this as well to meet a wall. Bear right & follow the wall to a stile, then head half left on a path through pasture: occasional marker posts show the way.
stile
gap
3
bridge
disused railway
col
gate
gate
Bowling Green Farm
bowling green & pavilion
fb
to Bakewell
River Wye
Haddon Hall
A6
2
to Matlock
A
A
gate
gate
gate & stile
Haddon Fields
gate
gate
1. Leave Youlgreave along Conksbury Lane, then turn right down a tarred lane in front of Easter Cottage, before the end of the 30mph zone. Pass Raper Lodge with its mullioned windows, cross the River Lathkill on an old packhorse bridge & climb up through woods on a clear zigzag path. At the top a gate leads to a large field: head east across the field towards trees & farm buildings, bearing left to a small gate. Go on in the same direction with a wall on the right: a vague path appears by the wall. Keep straight on across Haddon Fields: eventually it becomes a farm track & descends to the gatehouse to Haddon Hall: turn left on the A6.
Raper Lodge
River Lathkill
to Bakewell
Easter Cottage
1
Youlgreave
d25 m4

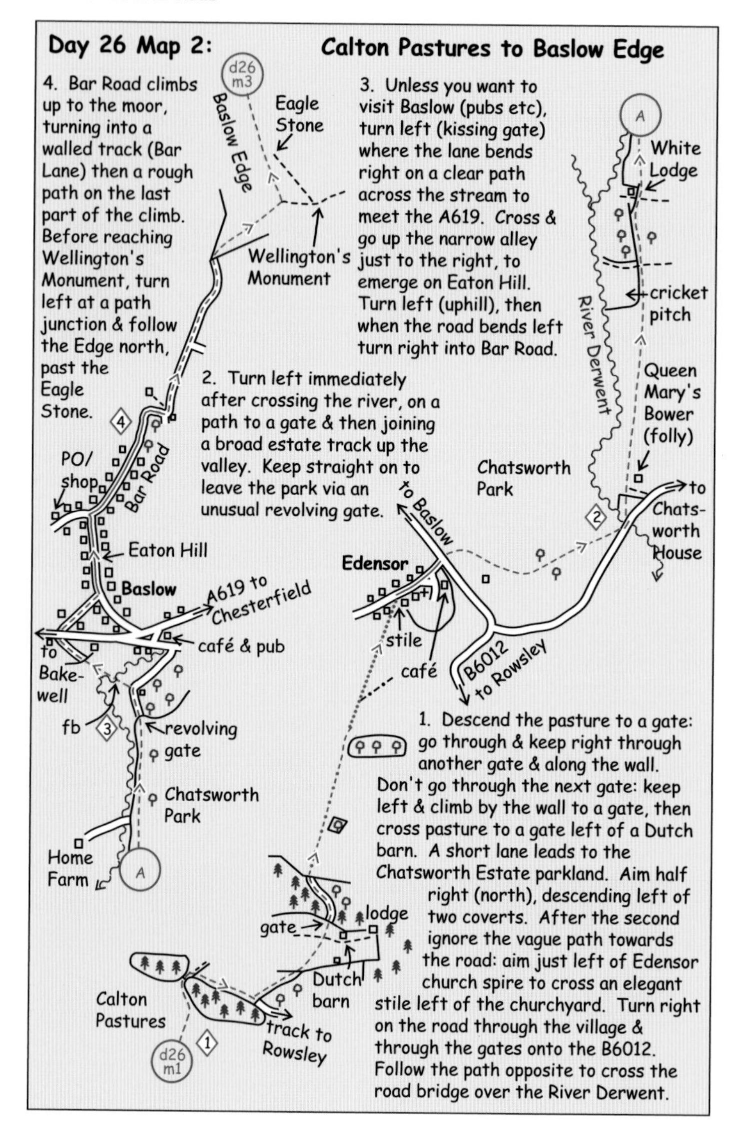
Day 26 Map 2:
Calton Pastures to Baslow Edge
d26 m3
Baslow Edge
Eagle Stone
Wellington's Monument
4. Bar Road climbs up to the moor, turning into a walled track (Bar Lane) then a rough path on the last part of the climb. Before reaching Wellington's Monument, turn left at a path junction & follow the Edge north, past the Eagle Stone.
3. Unless you want to visit Baslow (pubs etc), turn left (kissing gate) where the lane bends right on a clear path across the stream to meet the A619. Cross & go up the narrow alley just to the right, to emerge on Eaton Hill. Turn left (uphill), then when the road bends left turn right into Bar Road.
A
White Lodge
cricket pitch
River Derwent
Queen Mary's Bower (folly)
to Chatsworth House
2. Turn left immediately after crossing the river, on a path to a gate & then joining a broad estate track up the valley. Keep straight on to leave the park via an unusual revolving gate.
Chatsworth Park
to Baslow
PO/ shop
Bar Road
Eaton Hill
Baslow
A619 to Chesterfield
café & pub
to Bakewell
fb
revolving gate
Chatsworth Park
Home Farm
A
Edensor
stile
café
B6012 to Rowsley
1. Descend the pasture to a gate: go through & keep right through another gate & along the wall. Don't go through the next gate: keep left & climb by the wall to a gate, then cross pasture to a gate left of a Dutch barn. A short lane leads to the Chatsworth Estate parkland. Aim half right (north), descending left of two coverts. After the second ignore the vague path towards the road: aim just left of Edensor church spire to cross an elegant stile left of the churchyard. Turn right on the road through the village & through the gates onto the B6012. Follow the path opposite to cross the road bridge over the River Derwent.
lodge
gate
Dutch barn
Calton Pastures
track to Rowsley
d26 m1

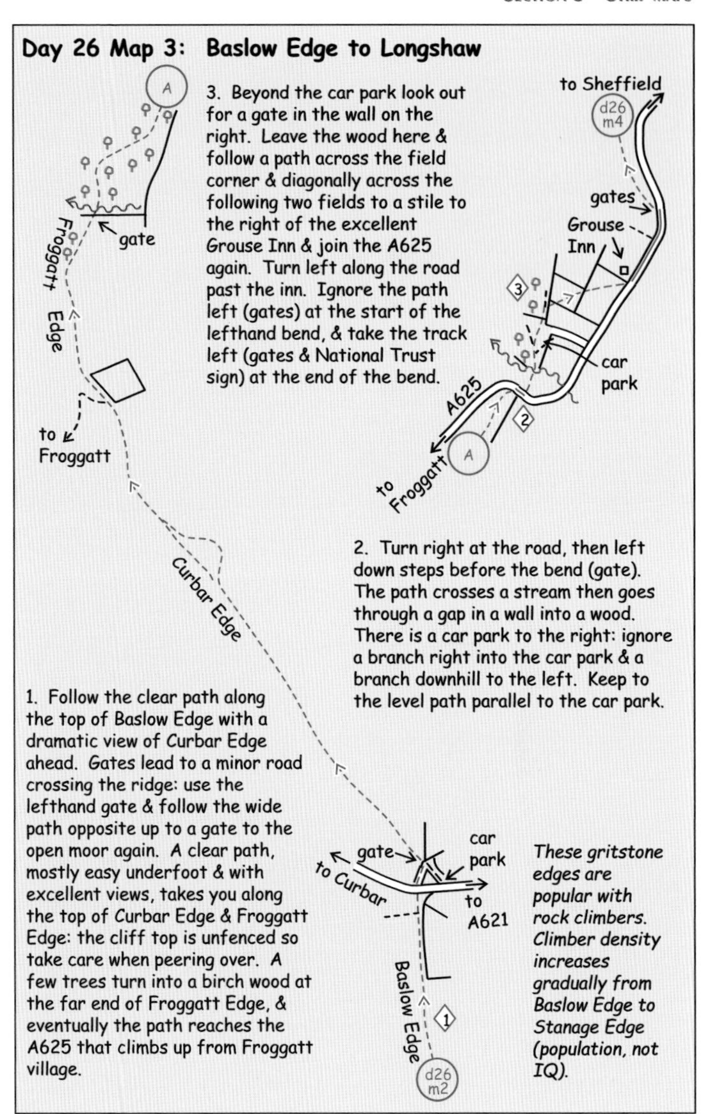
Day 26 Map 3: Baslow Edge to Longshaw
A
3. Beyond the car park look out for a gate in the wall on the right. Leave the wood here & follow a path across the field corner & diagonally across the following two fields to a stile to the right of the excellent Grouse Inn & join the A625 again. Turn left along the road past the inn. Ignore the path left (gates) at the start of the lefthand bend, & take the track left (gates & National Trust sign) at the end of the bend.
to Sheffield
d26 m4
gates
Grouse Inn
3
car park
A625
2
A
to Froggatt
gate
Froggatt Edge
to Froggatt
Curbar Edge
2. Turn right at the road, then left down steps before the bend (gate). The path crosses a stream then goes through a gap in a wall into a wood. There is a car park to the right: ignore a branch right into the car park & a branch downhill to the left. Keep to the level path parallel to the car park.
1. Follow the clear path along the top of Baslow Edge with a dramatic view of Curbar Edge ahead. Gates lead to a minor road crossing the ridge: use the lefthand gate & follow the wide path opposite up to a gate to the open moor again. A clear path, mostly easy underfoot & with excellent views, takes you along the top of Curbar Edge & Froggatt Edge: the cliff top is unfenced so take care when peering over. A few trees turn into a birch wood at the far end of Froggatt Edge, & eventually the path reaches the A625 that climbs up from Froggatt village.
gate
car park
to Curbar
to A621
Baslow Edge
1
d26 m2
These gritstone edges are popular with rock climbers. Climber density increases gradually from Baslow Edge to Stanage Edge (population, not IQ).

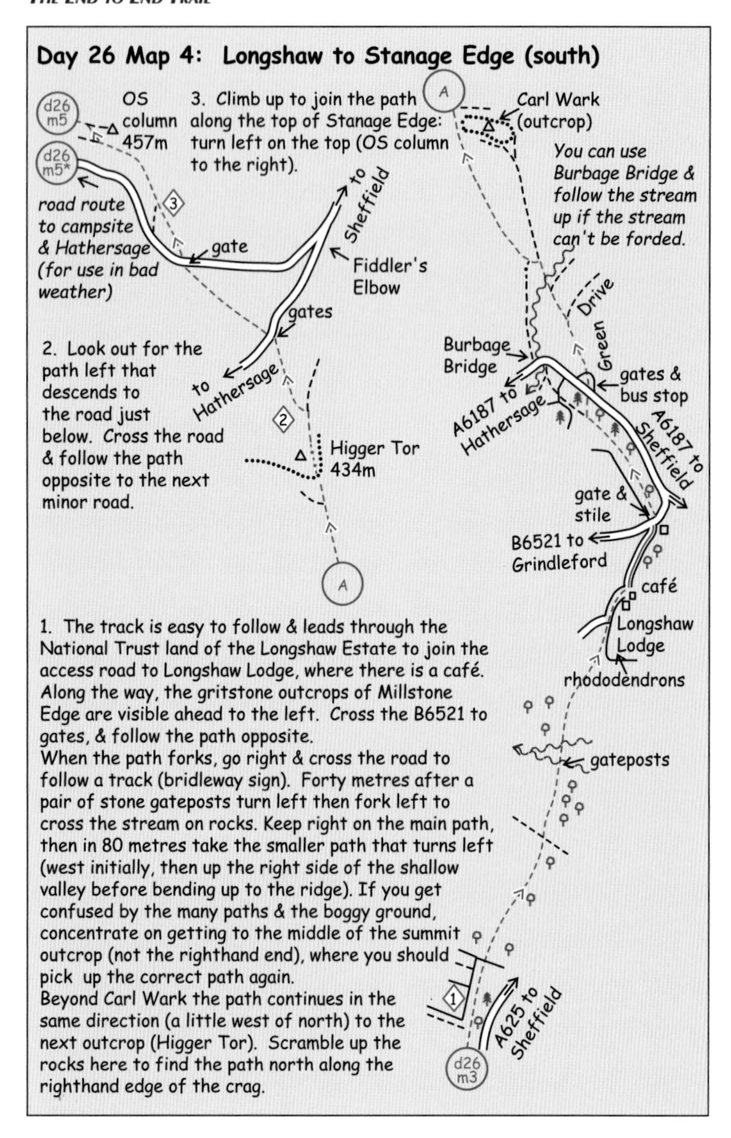
Day 26 Map 4: Longshaw to Stanage Edge (south)
d26 m5
d26 m5*
OS column 457m
3. Climb up to join the path along the top of Stanage Edge: turn left on the top (OS column to the right).
road route to campsite & Hathersage (for use in bad weather)
gate
to Sheffield
Fiddler's Elbow
gates
to Hathersage
2. Look out for the path left that descends to the road just below. Cross the road & follow the path opposite to the next minor road.
Higger Tor 434m
A
Carl Wark (outcrop)
You can use Burbage Bridge & follow the stream up if the stream can't be forded.
Green Drive
Burbage Bridge
gates & bus stop
A6187 to Hathersage
A6187 to Sheffield
gate & stile
B6521 to Grindleford
café
Longshaw Lodge
rhododendrons
gateposts
A625 to Sheffield
d26 m3
1. The track is easy to follow & leads through the National Trust land of the Longshaw Estate to join the access road to Longshaw Lodge, where there is a café. Along the way, the gritstone outcrops of Millstone Edge are visible ahead to the left. Cross the B6521 to gates, & follow the path opposite.
When the path forks, go right & cross the road to follow a track (bridleway sign). Forty metres after a pair of stone gateposts turn left then fork left to cross the stream on rocks. Keep right on the main path, then in 80 metres take the smaller path that turns left (west initially, then up the right side of the shallow valley before bending up to the ridge). If you get confused by the many paths & the boggy ground, concentrate on getting to the middle of the summit outcrop (not the righthand end), where you should pick up the correct path again.
Beyond Carl Wark the path continues in the same direction (a little west of north) to the next outcrop (Higger Tor). Scramble up the rocks here to find the path north along the righthand edge of the crag.

Day 26 Map 5: Stanage Edge (south) to Stanage Plantation

1. Main route: Follow the top of Stanage Edge on a good path. When you are above the far edge of Stanage Plantation the wall on your right ends & you need to climb the fence ahead. A few metres after this look for a flagged path dropping down left & cutting back into the trees. Descend to North Lees on this, returning the same way tomorrow. (If you meet a broad track joining from the right you have gone past the descent path: retrace your steps.)

2. Descent to North Lees campsite: Follow the flagged path down. After the plantation it divides three ways: keep left to meet the road at a toilet block. Take the path ahead to join the main track down through a wood. A gate leads to a field: a few metres after this a stile on the left indicates a private route to the campsite; otherwise stay on the main path to a gate, along a walled lane round a dogleg, to follow the North Lees access road.

3. North Lees to Hathersage: Turn left up the road & right (gate & fp sign) on a path to Cowclose Farm. Follow the fence on your left above the farm on a path leading to a gate into a meadow: go ahead, fence on your right. Continue along the bottom edge of a long field to a gate at its end. A path then drops diagonally right (gap): join the hedge below & follow it to a footbridge & steeply up again to turn right on a track to the church. Turn left & follow the road down.

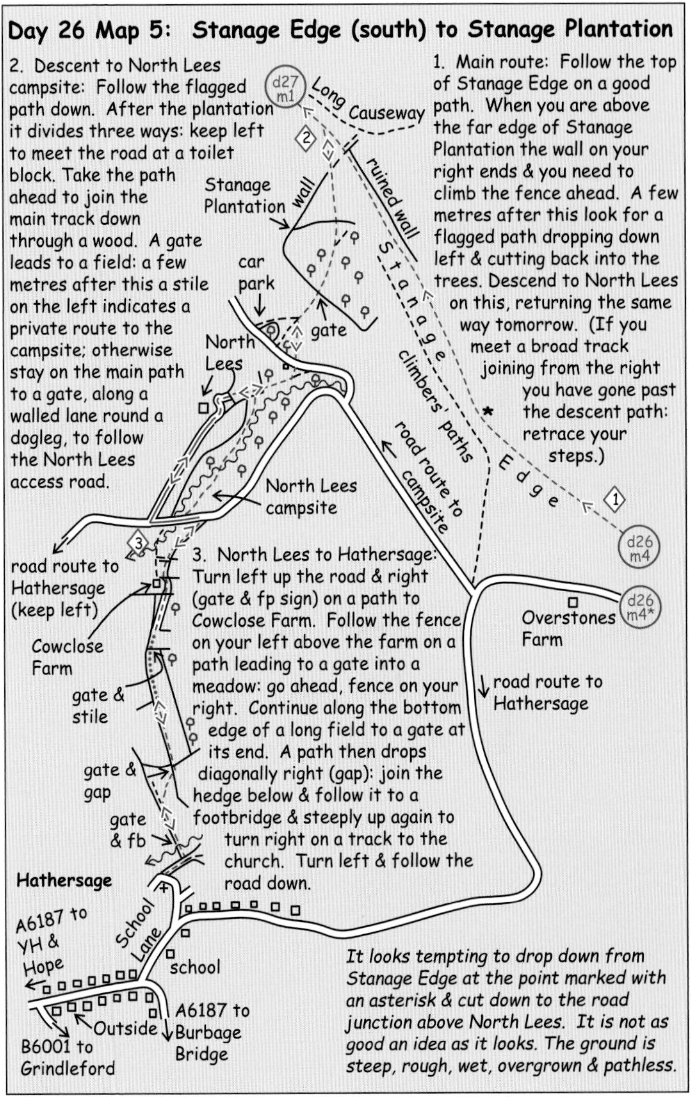

Long Causeway
ruined wall
wall
Stanage Plantation
car park
gate
North Lees
North Lees campsite
Stanage Edge
climbers' paths
road route to campsite
d27 m1
d26 m4
d26 m4*
Overstones Farm
road route to Hathersage
road route to Hathersage (keep left)
Cowclose Farm
gate & stile
gate & gap
gate & fb
Hathersage
School Lane
school
A6187 to YH & Hope
Outside
A6187 to Burbage Bridge
B6001 to Grindleford

It looks tempting to drop down from Stanage Edge at the point marked with an asterisk & cut down to the road junction above North Lees. It is not as good an idea as it looks. The ground is steep, rough, wet, overgrown & pathless.

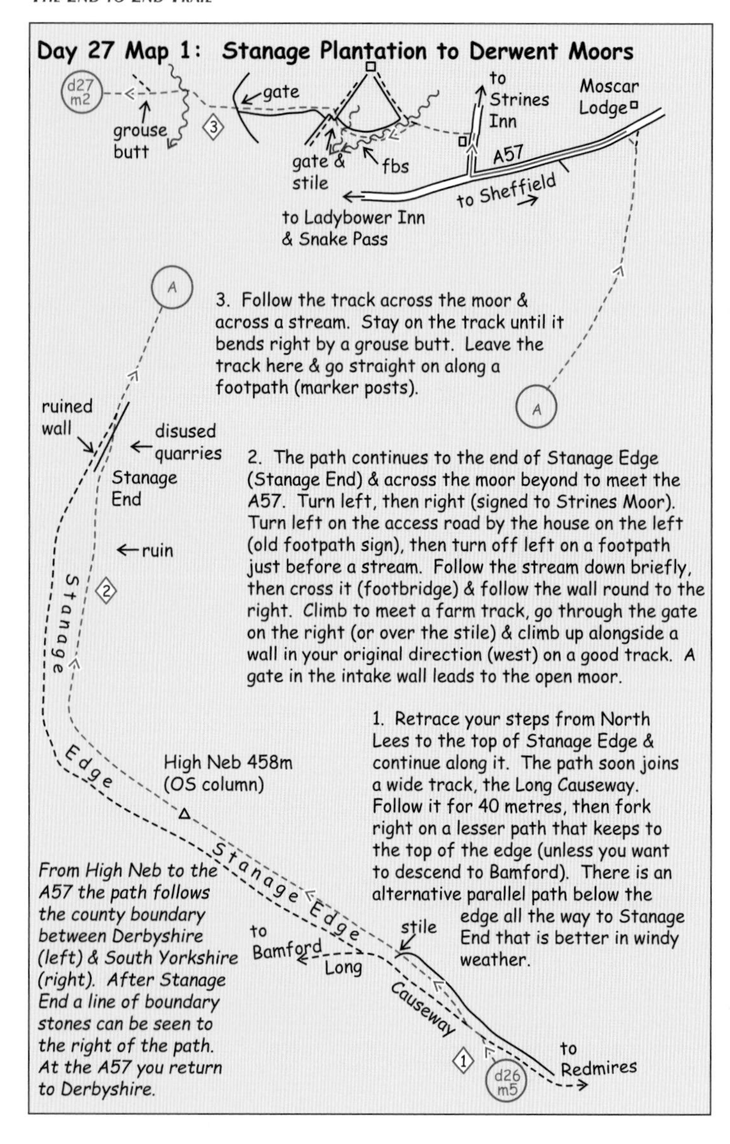
Day 27 Map 1: Stanage Plantation to Derwent Moors
d27 m2
grouse butt
3
gate
gate & stile
fbs
to Strines Inn
Moscar Lodge
A57
to Sheffield
to Ladybower Inn & Snake Pass
A
3. Follow the track across the moor & across a stream. Stay on the track until it bends right by a grouse butt. Leave the track here & go straight on along a footpath (marker posts).
A
ruined wall
disused quarries
Stanage End
2. The path continues to the end of Stanage Edge (Stanage End) & across the moor beyond to meet the A57. Turn left, then right (signed to Strines Moor). Turn left on the access road by the house on the left (old footpath sign), then turn off left on a footpath just before a stream. Follow the stream down briefly, then cross it (footbridge) & follow the wall round to the right. Climb to meet a farm track, go through the gate on the right (or over the stile) & climb up alongside a wall in your original direction (west) on a good track. A gate in the intake wall leads to the open moor.
ruin
Stanage
2
1. Retrace your steps from North Lees to the top of Stanage Edge & continue along it. The path soon joins a wide track, the Long Causeway. Follow it for 40 metres, then fork right on a lesser path that keeps to the top of the edge (unless you want to descend to Bamford). There is an alternative parallel path below the edge all the way to Stanage End that is better in windy weather.
Edge
High Neb 458m (OS column)
Stanage Edge
From High Neb to the A57 the path follows the county boundary between Derbyshire (left) & South Yorkshire (right). After Stanage End a line of boundary stones can be seen to the right of the path. At the A57 you return to Derbyshire.
to Bamford
Long
Causeway
stile
1
d26 m5
to Redmires

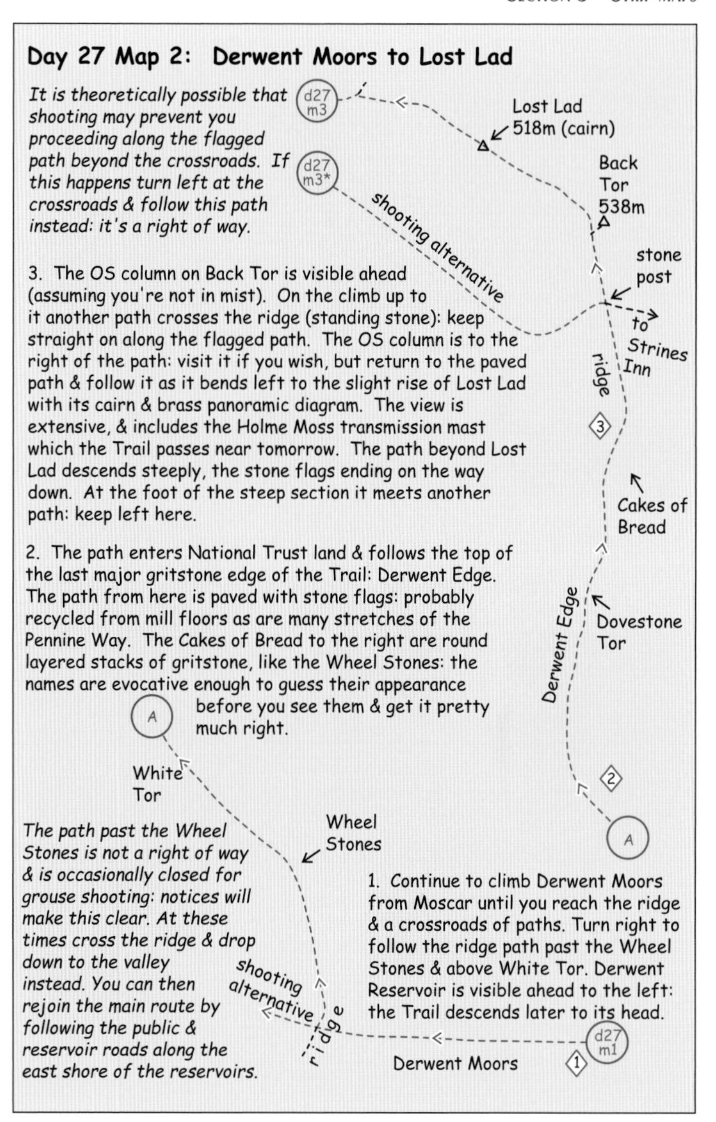
Day 27 Map 2: Derwent Moors to Lost Lad
It is theoretically possible that shooting may prevent you proceeding along the flagged path beyond the crossroads. If this happens turn left at the crossroads & follow this path instead: it's a right of way.
d27 m3
d27 m3*
Lost Lad 518m (cairn)
Back Tor 538m
shooting alternative
stone post
to Strines Inn
ridge
3. The OS column on Back Tor is visible ahead (assuming you're not in mist). On the climb up to it another path crosses the ridge (standing stone): keep straight on along the flagged path. The OS column is to the right of the path: visit it if you wish, but return to the paved path & follow it as it bends left to the slight rise of Lost Lad with its cairn & brass panoramic diagram. The view is extensive, & includes the Holme Moss transmission mast which the Trail passes near tomorrow. The path beyond Lost Lad descends steeply, the stone flags ending on the way down. At the foot of the steep section it meets another path: keep left here.
3
Cakes of Bread
2. The path enters National Trust land & follows the top of the last major gritstone edge of the Trail: Derwent Edge. The path from here is paved with stone flags: probably recycled from mill floors as are many stretches of the Pennine Way. The Cakes of Bread to the right are round layered stacks of gritstone, like the Wheel Stones: the names are evocative enough to guess their appearance before you see them & get it pretty much right.
Derwent Edge
Dovestone Tor
A
White Tor
2
A
The path past the Wheel Stones is not a right of way & is occasionally closed for grouse shooting: notices will make this clear. At these times cross the ridge & drop down to the valley instead. You can then rejoin the main route by following the public & reservoir roads along the east shore of the reservoirs.
Wheel Stones
1. Continue to climb Derwent Moors from Moscar until you reach the ridge & a crossroads of paths. Turn right to follow the ridge path past the Wheel Stones & above White Tor. Derwent Reservoir is visible ahead to the left: the Trail descends later to its head.
shooting alternative
ridge
d27 m1
Derwent Moors
1

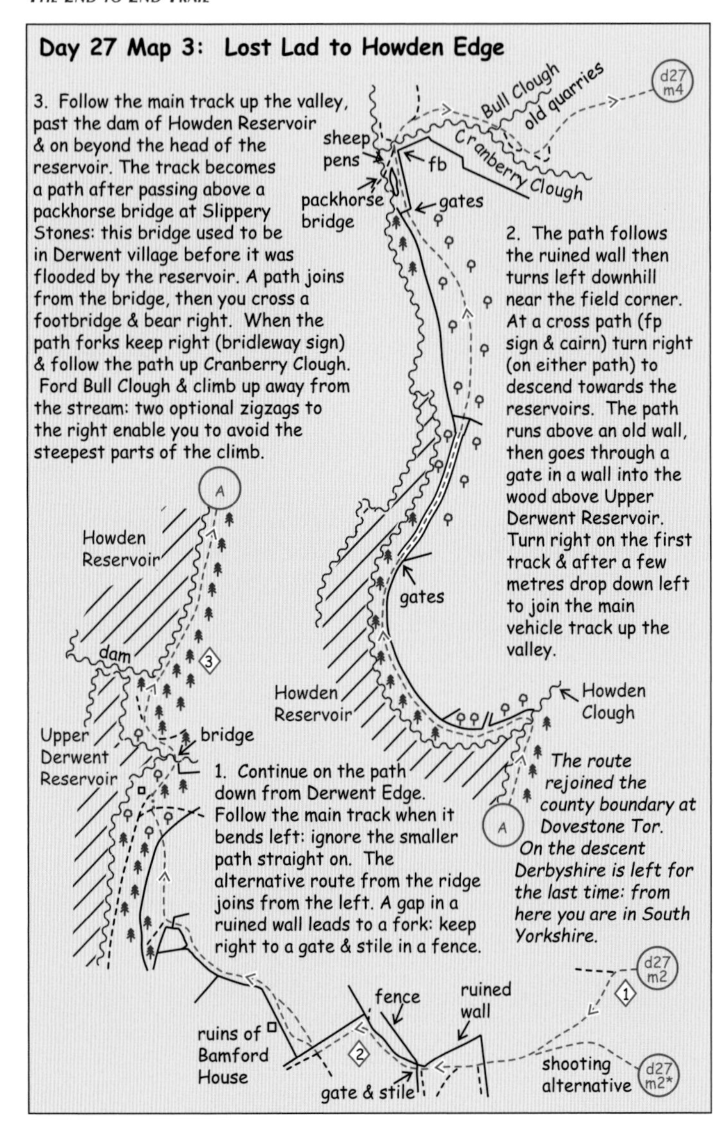
Day 27 Map 3: Lost Lad to Howden Edge
3. Follow the main track up the valley, past the dam of Howden Reservoir & on beyond the head of the reservoir. The track becomes a path after passing above a packhorse bridge at Slippery Stones: this bridge used to be in Derwent village before it was flooded by the reservoir. A path joins from the bridge, then you cross a footbridge & bear right. When the path forks keep right (bridleway sign) & follow the path up Cranberry Clough. Ford Bull Clough & climb up away from the stream: two optional zigzags to the right enable you to avoid the steepest parts of the climb.
sheep pens
fb
packhorse bridge
gates
Bull Clough
old quarries
Cranberry Clough
d27 m4
2. The path follows the ruined wall then turns left downhill near the field corner. At a cross path (fp sign & cairn) turn right (on either path) to descend towards the reservoirs. The path runs above an old wall, then goes through a gate in a wall into the wood above Upper Derwent Reservoir. Turn right on the first track & after a few metres drop down left to join the main vehicle track up the valley.
A
Howden Reservoir
dam
3
gates
Howden Reservoir
Howden Clough
bridge
Upper Derwent Reservoir
1. Continue on the path down from Derwent Edge. Follow the main track when it bends left: ignore the smaller path straight on. The alternative route from the ridge joins from the left. A gap in a ruined wall leads to a fork: keep right to a gate & stile in a fence.
The route rejoined the county boundary at Dovestone Tor. On the descent Derbyshire is left for the last time: from here you are in South Yorkshire.
A
d27 m2
1
fence
ruined wall
ruins of Bamford House
2
gate & stile
shooting alternative
d27 m2*

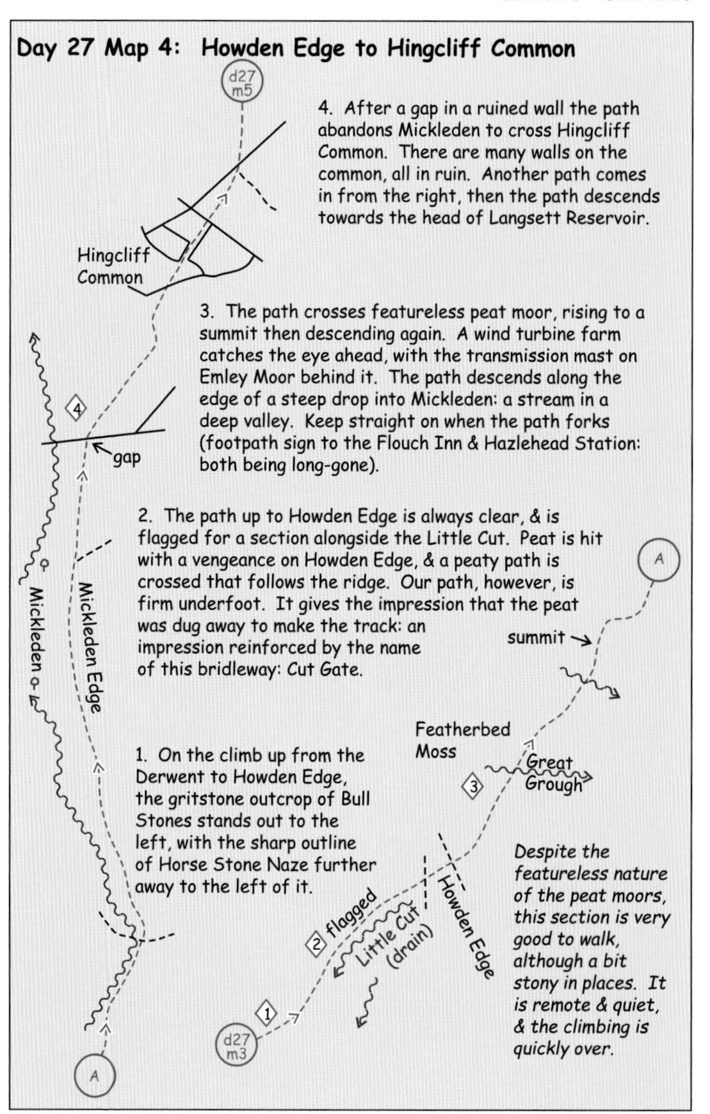
Day 27 Map 4: Howden Edge to Hingcliff Common
d27 m5
4. After a gap in a ruined wall the path abandons Mickleden to cross Hingcliff Common. There are many walls on the common, all in ruin. Another path comes in from the right, then the path descends towards the head of Langsett Reservoir.
Hingcliff Common
3. The path crosses featureless peat moor, rising to a summit then descending again. A wind turbine farm catches the eye ahead, with the transmission mast on Emley Moor behind it. The path descends along the edge of a steep drop into Mickleden: a stream in a deep valley. Keep straight on when the path forks (footpath sign to the Flouch Inn & Hazlehead Station: both being long-gone).
4
gap
2. The path up to Howden Edge is always clear, & is flagged for a section alongside the Little Cut. Peat is hit with a vengeance on Howden Edge, & a peaty path is crossed that follows the ridge. Our path, however, is firm underfoot. It gives the impression that the peat was dug away to make the track: an impression reinforced by the name of this bridleway: Cut Gate.
A
summit
Mickleden
Mickleden Edge
Featherbed Moss
1. On the climb up from the Derwent to Howden Edge, the gritstone outcrop of Bull Stones stands out to the left, with the sharp outline of Horse Stone Naze further away to the left of it.
Great Grough
3
Despite the featureless nature of the peat moors, this section is very good to walk, although a bit stony in places. It is remote & quiet, & the climbing is quickly over.
flagged
2
Little Cut (drain)
Howden Edge
1
d27 m3
A

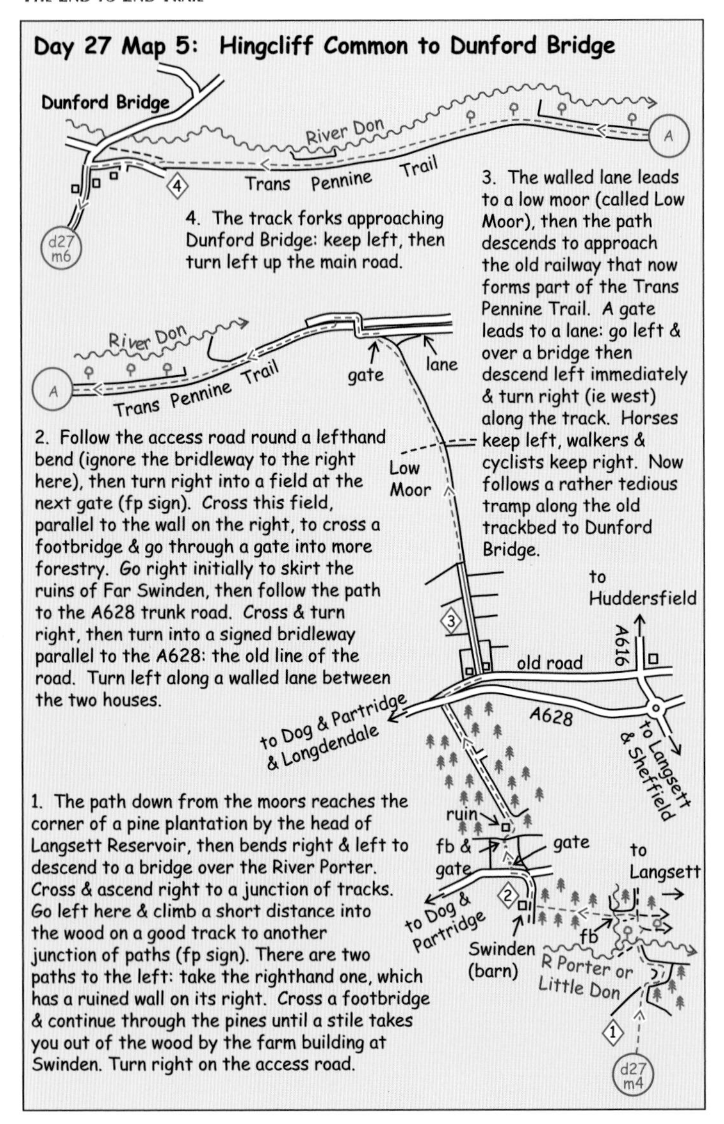

Day 27 Map 5: Hingcliff Common to Dunford Bridge
Dunford Bridge
River Don
Trans Pennine Trail
A
d27 m6
4. The track forks approaching Dunford Bridge: keep left, then turn left up the main road.
3. The walled lane leads to a low moor (called Low Moor), then the path descends to approach the old railway that now forms part of the Trans Pennine Trail. A gate leads to a lane: go left & over a bridge then descend left immediately & turn right (ie west) along the track. Horses keep left, walkers & cyclists keep right. Now follows a rather tedious tramp along the old trackbed to Dunford Bridge.
River Don
gate
lane
Trans Pennine Trail
2. Follow the access road round a lefthand bend (ignore the bridleway to the right here), then turn right into a field at the next gate (fp sign). Cross this field, parallel to the wall on the right, to cross a footbridge & go through a gate into more forestry. Go right initially to skirt the ruins of Far Swinden, then follow the path to the A628 trunk road. Cross & turn right, then turn into a signed bridleway parallel to the A628: the old line of the road. Turn left along a walled lane between the two houses.
Low Moor
to Huddersfield
A616
old road
A628
to Dog & Partridge & Longdendale
to Langsett & Sheffield
1. The path down from the moors reaches the corner of a pine plantation by the head of Langsett Reservoir, then bends right & left to descend to a bridge over the River Porter. Cross & ascend right to a junction of tracks. Go left here & climb a short distance into the wood on a good track to another junction of paths (fp sign). There are two paths to the left: take the righthand one, which has a ruined wall on its right. Cross a footbridge & continue through the pines until a stile takes you out of the wood by the farm building at Swinden. Turn right on the access road.
ruin
fb & gate
gate
to Langsett
to Dog & Partridge
Swinden (barn)
fb
R Porter or Little Don
d27 m4

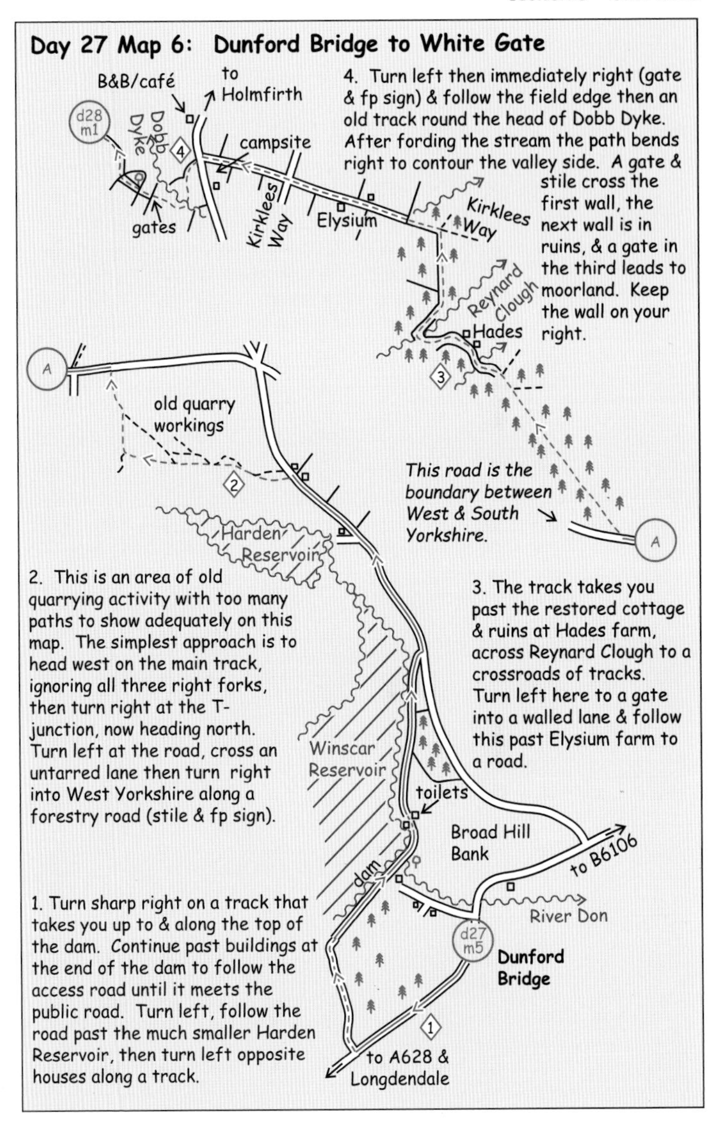
Day 27 Map 6: Dunford Bridge to White Gate
B&B/café
to Holmfirth
d28 m1
Dobb Dyke
4
campsite
gates
Kirklees Way
Elysium
Kirklees Way
4. Turn left then immediately right (gate & fp sign) & follow the field edge then an old track round the head of Dobb Dyke. After fording the stream the path bends right to contour the valley side. A gate & stile cross the first wall, the next wall is in ruins, & a gate in the third leads to moorland. Keep the wall on your right.
Reynard Clough
Hades
3
A
old quarry workings
2
This road is the boundary between West & South Yorkshire.
A
Harden Reservoir
2. This is an area of old quarrying activity with too many paths to show adequately on this map. The simplest approach is to head west on the main track, ignoring all three right forks, then turn right at the T-junction, now heading north. Turn left at the road, cross an untarred lane then turn right into West Yorkshire along a forestry road (stile & fp sign).
3. The track takes you past the restored cottage & ruins at Hades farm, across Reynard Clough to a crossroads of tracks. Turn left here to a gate into a walled lane & follow this past Elysium farm to a road.
Winscar Reservoir
toilets
Broad Hill Bank
to B6106
dam
River Don
d27 m5
Dunford Bridge
1. Turn sharp right on a track that takes you up to & along the top of the dam. Continue past buildings at the end of the dam to follow the access road until it meets the public road. Turn left, follow the road past the much smaller Harden Reservoir, then turn left opposite houses along a track.
1
to A628 & Longdendale

Day 28 Map 1: White Gate to Marsden Clough

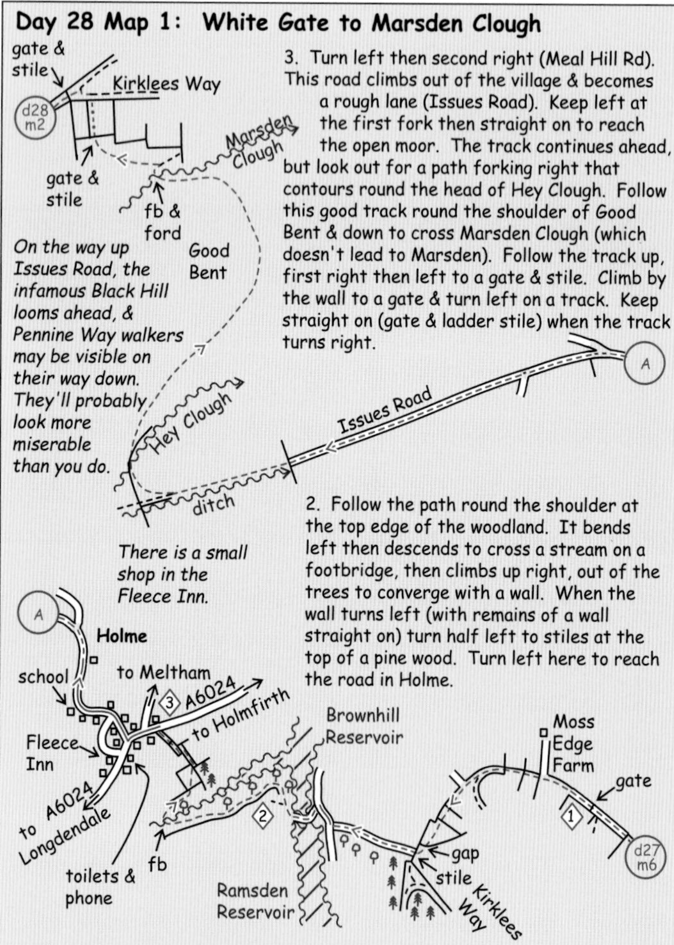

3. Turn left then second right (Meal Hill Rd). This road climbs out of the village & becomes a rough lane (Issues Road). Keep left at the first fork then straight on to reach the open moor. The track continues ahead, but look out for a path forking right that contours round the head of Hey Clough. Follow this good track round the shoulder of Good Bent & down to cross Marsden Clough (which doesn't lead to Marsden). Follow the track up, first right then left to a gate & stile. Climb by the wall to a gate & turn left on a track. Keep straight on (gate & ladder stile) when the track turns right.

On the way up Issues Road, the infamous Black Hill looms ahead, & Pennine Way walkers may be visible on their way down. They'll probably look more miserable than you do.

2. Follow the path round the shoulder at the top edge of the woodland. It bends left then descends to cross a stream on a footbridge, then climbs up right, out of the trees to converge with a wall. When the wall turns left (with remains of a wall straight on) turn half left to stiles at the top of a pine wood. Turn left here to reach the road in Holme.

There is a small shop in the Fleece Inn.

1. The path contours round the hill shoulder: ignore a track down to a farm & a left fork that climbs uphill. On the descent the path leaves the righthand wall briefly then descends right to a gap & a stile. Go down the track (now on the Kirklees Way). Continue past a picnic area to turn right at the reservoir road, then turn left on a fenced footpath across the dam of Ramsden Reservoir. A clear path now slants up right through trees.

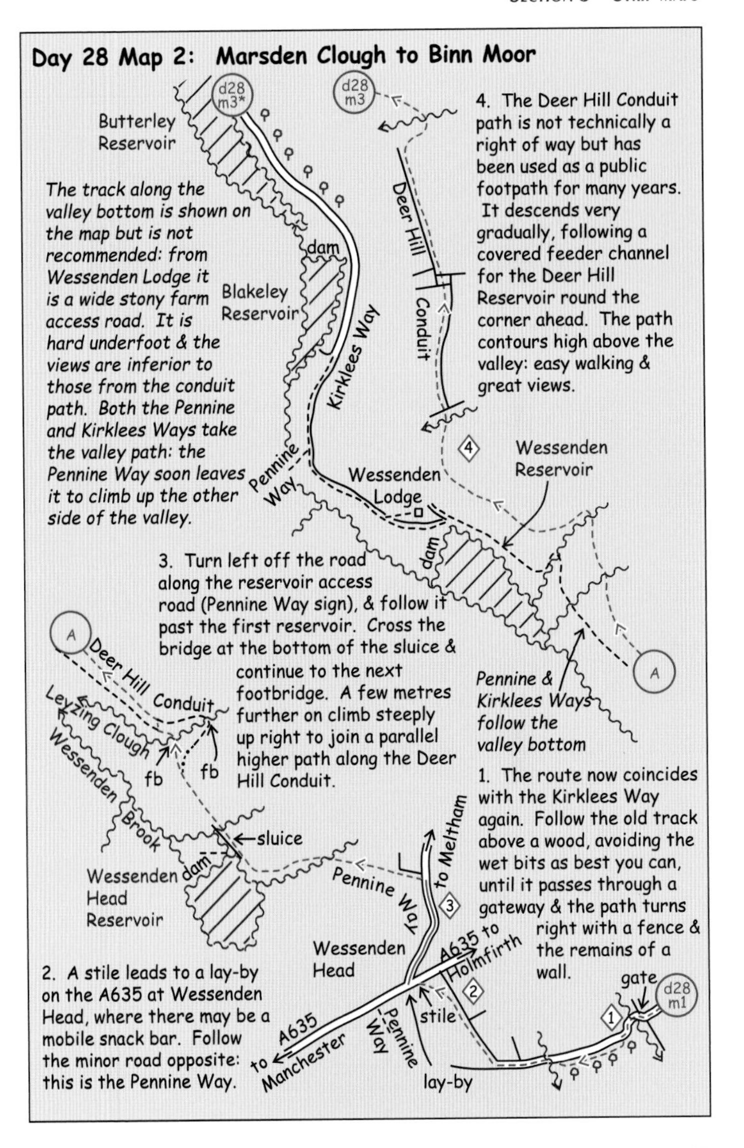

Day 28 Map 2: Marsden Clough to Binn Moor
d28 m3*
d28 m3
Butterley Reservoir
The track along the valley bottom is shown on the map but is not recommended: from Wessenden Lodge it is a wide stony farm access road. It is hard underfoot & the views are inferior to those from the conduit path. Both the Pennine and Kirklees Ways take the valley path: the Pennine Way soon leaves it to climb up the other side of the valley.
dam
Blakeley Reservoir
Kirklees Way
Deer Hill
Conduit
4. The Deer Hill Conduit path is not technically a right of way but has been used as a public footpath for many years. It descends very gradually, following a covered feeder channel for the Deer Hill Reservoir round the corner ahead. The path contours high above the valley: easy walking & great views.
4
Wessenden Reservoir
Pennine Way
Wessenden Lodge
dam
3. Turn left off the road along the reservoir access road (Pennine Way sign), & follow it past the first reservoir. Cross the bridge at the bottom of the sluice & continue to the next footbridge. A few metres further on climb steeply up right to join a parallel higher path along the Deer Hill Conduit.
A
Deer Hill Conduit
Leyzing Clough
Wessenden Brook
fb
fb
A
Pennine & Kirklees Ways follow the valley bottom
sluice
dam
Wessenden Head Reservoir
Pennine Way
to Meltham
3
1. The route now coincides with the Kirklees Way again. Follow the old track above a wood, avoiding the wet bits as best you can, until it passes through a gateway & the path turns right with a fence & the remains of a wall.
Wessenden Head
A635 to Holmfirth
2
gate
d28 m1
1
2. A stile leads to a lay-by on the A635 at Wessenden Head, where there may be a mobile snack bar. Follow the minor road opposite: this is the Pennine Way.
A635
to Manchester
Pennine Way
stile
lay-by

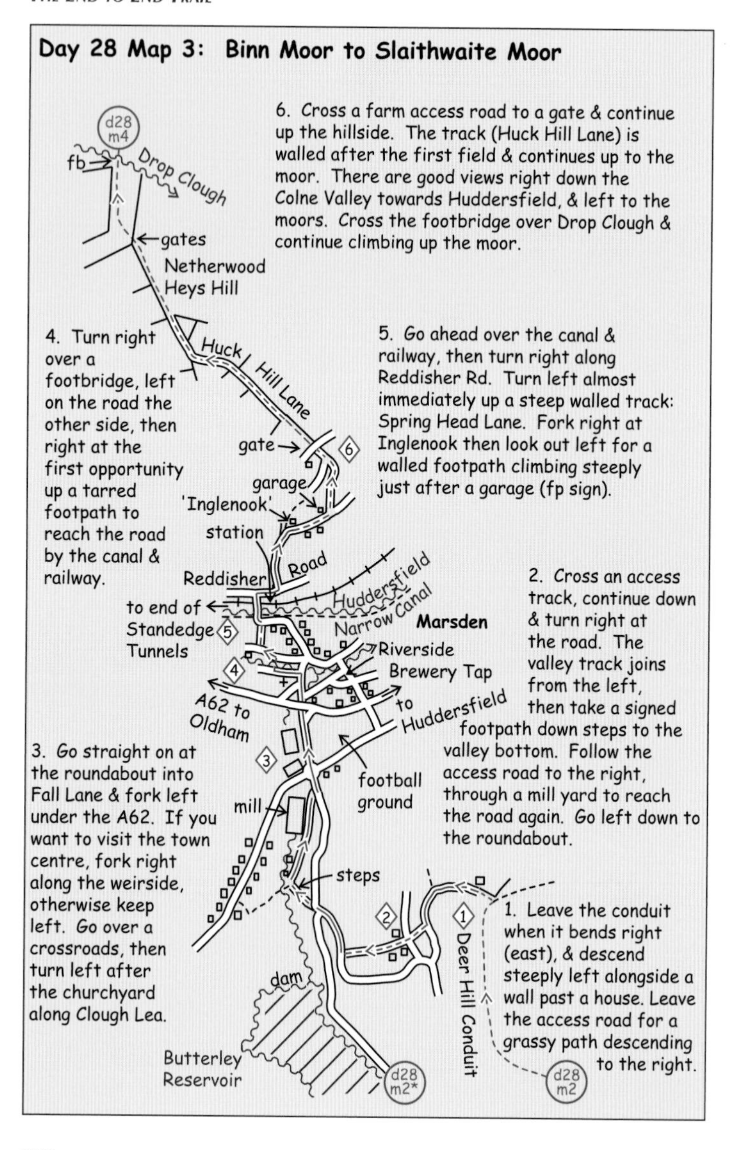
Day 28 Map 3: Binn Moor to Slaithwaite Moor
6. Cross a farm access road to a gate & continue up the hillside. The track (Huck Hill Lane) is walled after the first field & continues up to the moor. There are good views right down the Colne Valley towards Huddersfield, & left to the moors. Cross the footbridge over Drop Clough & continue climbing up the moor.
d28 m4
fb
Drop Clough
gates
Netherwood Heys Hill
4. Turn right over a footbridge, left on the road the other side, then right at the first opportunity up a tarred footpath to reach the road by the canal & railway.
Huck Hill Lane
5. Go ahead over the canal & railway, then turn right along Reddisher Rd. Turn left almost immediately up a steep walled track: Spring Head Lane. Fork right at Inglenook then look out left for a walled footpath climbing steeply just after a garage (fp sign).
gate
6
garage
'Inglenook'
station
Reddisher Road
Huddersfield Narrow Canal
2. Cross an access track, continue down & turn right at the road. The valley track joins from the left, then take a signed footpath down steps to the valley bottom. Follow the access road to the right, through a mill yard to reach the road again. Go left down to the roundabout.
to end of Standedge Tunnels
5
Marsden
Riverside Brewery Tap
4
A62 to Oldham
to Huddersfield
3. Go straight on at the roundabout into Fall Lane & fork left under the A62. If you want to visit the town centre, fork right along the weirside, otherwise keep left. Go over a crossroads, then turn left after the churchyard along Clough Lea.
3
football ground
mill
steps
2
1
1. Leave the conduit when it bends right (east), & descend steeply left alongside a wall past a house. Leave the access road for a grassy path descending to the right.
Deer Hill Conduit
dam
Butterley Reservoir
d28 m2*
d28 m2

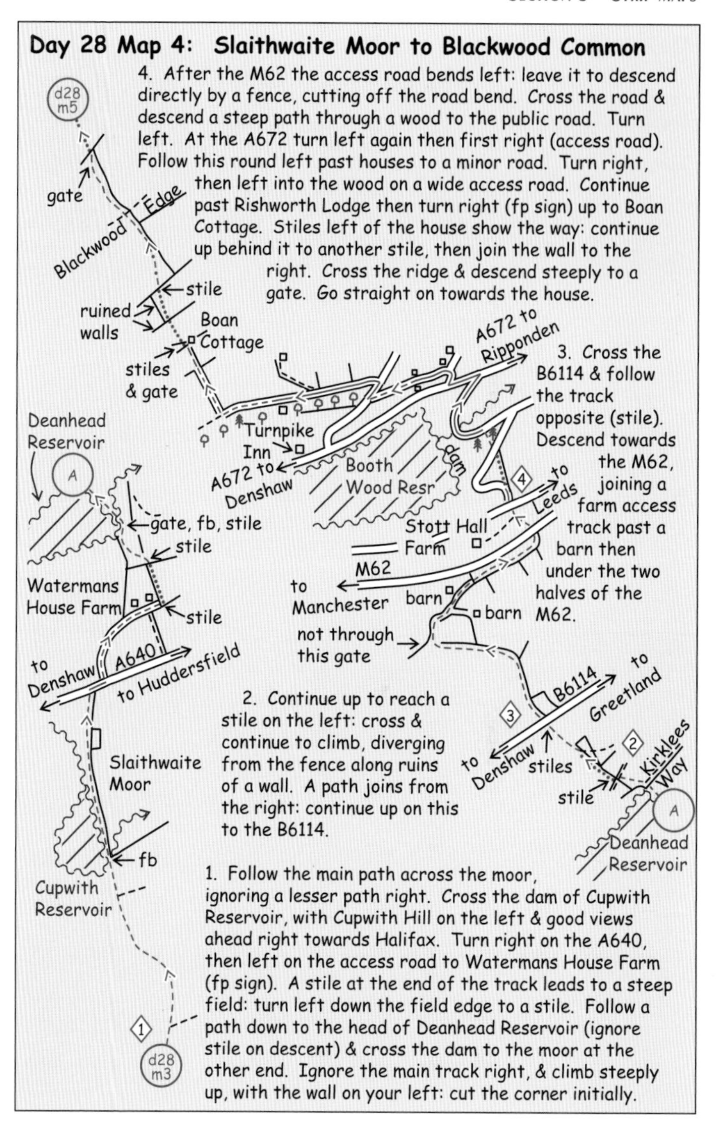

Day 28 Map 4: Slaithwaite Moor to Blackwood Common
4. After the M62 the access road bends left: leave it to descend directly by a fence, cutting off the road bend. Cross the road & descend a steep path through a wood to the public road. Turn left. At the A672 turn left again then first right (access road). Follow this round left past houses to a minor road. Turn right, then left into the wood on a wide access road. Continue past Rishworth Lodge then turn right (fp sign) up to Boan Cottage. Stiles left of the house show the way: continue up behind it to another stile, then join the wall to the right. Cross the ridge & descend steeply to a gate. Go straight on towards the house.
3. Cross the B6114 & follow the track opposite (stile). Descend towards the M62, joining a farm access track past a barn then under the two halves of the M62.
2. Continue up to reach a stile on the left: cross & continue to climb, diverging from the fence along ruins of a wall. A path joins from the right: continue up on this to the B6114.
1. Follow the main path across the moor, ignoring a lesser path right. Cross the dam of Cupwith Reservoir, with Cupwith Hill on the left & good views ahead right towards Halifax. Turn right on the A640, then left on the access road to Watermans House Farm (fp sign). A stile at the end of the track leads to a steep field: turn left down the field edge to a stile. Follow a path down to the head of Deanhead Reservoir (ignore stile on descent) & cross the dam to the moor at the other end. Ignore the main track right, & climb steeply up, with the wall on your left: cut the corner initially.
d28 m5
gate
Blackwood Edge
stile
ruined walls
Boan Cottage
stiles & gate
Deanhead Reservoir
A
Turnpike Inn
A672 to Denshaw
Booth Wood Resr
dam
A672 to Ripponden
4
to Leeds
Stott Hall Farm
M62
to Manchester
barn
barn
not through this gate
gate, fb, stile
stile
Watermans House Farm
stile
to Denshaw
A640
to Huddersfield
B6114
to Greetland
3
to Denshaw
stiles
2
stile
Kirklees Way
A
Deanhead Reservoir
Slaithwaite Moor
fb
Cupwith Reservoir
1
d28 m3

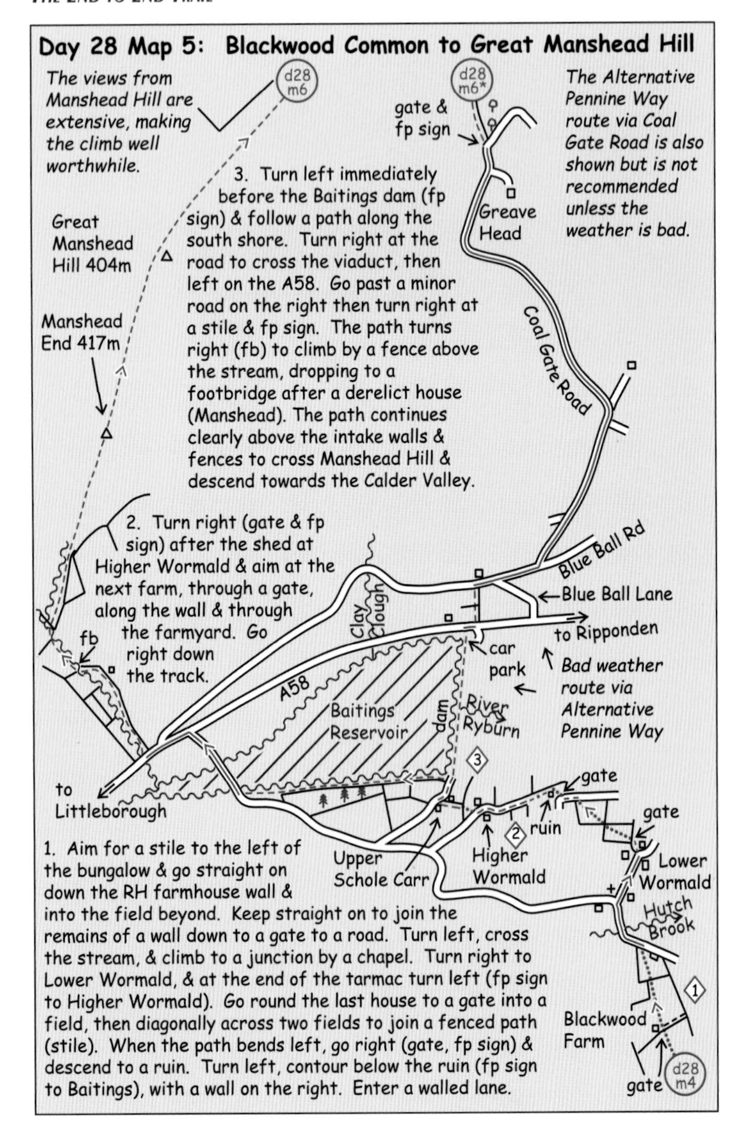
Day 28 Map 5: Blackwood Common to Great Manshead Hill
The views from Manshead Hill are extensive, making the climb well worthwhile.
d28 m6
d28 m6*
gate & fp sign
The Alternative Pennine Way route via Coal Gate Road is also shown but is not recommended unless the weather is bad.
3. Turn left immediately before the Baitings dam (fp sign) & follow a path along the south shore. Turn right at the road to cross the viaduct, then left on the A58. Go past a minor road on the right then turn right at a stile & fp sign. The path turns right (fb) to climb by a fence above the stream, dropping to a footbridge after a derelict house (Manshead). The path continues clearly above the intake walls & fences to cross Manshead Hill & descend towards the Calder Valley.
Great Manshead Hill 404m
Greave Head
Manshead End 417m
Coal Gate Road
2. Turn right (gate & fp sign) after the shed at Higher Wormald & aim at the next farm, through a gate, along the wall & through the farmyard. Go right down the track.
Blue Ball Rd
Blue Ball Lane
Clay Clough
to Ripponden
fb
car park
Bad weather route via Alternative Pennine Way
A58
Baitings Reservoir
dam
River Ryburn
3
gate
to Littleborough
2
ruin
gate
Upper Schole Carr
Higher Wormald
Lower Wormald
Hutch Brook
1. Aim for a stile to the left of the bungalow & go straight on down the RH farmhouse wall & into the field beyond. Keep straight on to join the remains of a wall down to a gate to a road. Turn left, cross the stream, & climb to a junction by a chapel. Turn right to Lower Wormald, & at the end of the tarmac turn left (fp sign to Higher Wormald). Go round the last house to a gate into a field, then diagonally across two fields to join a fenced path (stile). When the path bends left, go right (gate, fp sign) & descend to a ruin. Turn left, contour below the ruin (fp sign to Baitings), with a wall on the right. Enter a walled lane.
1
Blackwood Farm
gate
d28 m4

Day 28 Map 6: Great Manshead Hill to Cragg Vale

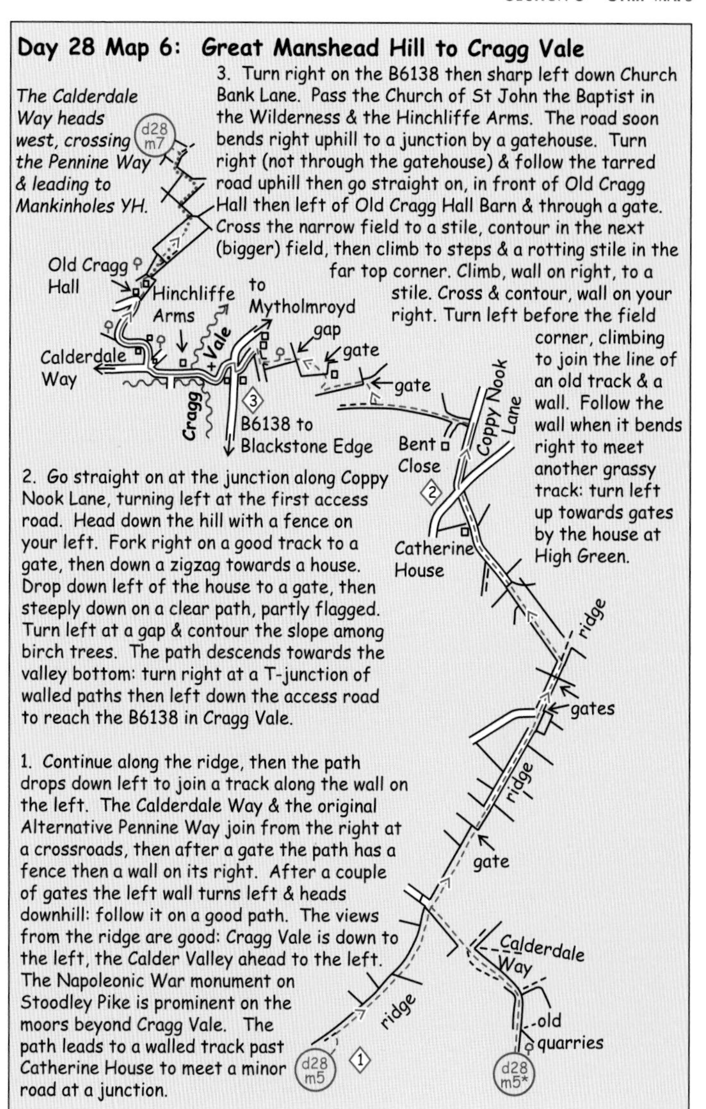

3. Turn right on the B6138 then sharp left down Church Bank Lane. Pass the Church of St John the Baptist in the Wilderness & the Hinchliffe Arms. The road soon bends right uphill to a junction by a gatehouse. Turn right (not through the gatehouse) & follow the tarred road uphill then go straight on, in front of Old Cragg Hall then left of Old Cragg Hall Barn & through a gate. Cross the narrow field to a stile, contour in the next (bigger) field, then climb to steps & a rotting stile in the far top corner. Climb, wall on right, to a stile. Cross & contour, wall on your right. Turn left before the field corner, climbing to join the line of an old track & a wall. Follow the wall when it bends right to meet another grassy track: turn left up towards gates by the house at High Green.

2. Go straight on at the junction along Coppy Nook Lane, turning left at the first access road. Head down the hill with a fence on your left. Fork right on a good track to a gate, then down a zigzag towards a house. Drop down left of the house to a gate, then steeply down on a clear path, partly flagged. Turn left at a gap & contour the slope among birch trees. The path descends towards the valley bottom: turn right at a T-junction of walled paths then left down the access road to reach the B6138 in Cragg Vale.

1. Continue along the ridge, then the path drops down left to join a track along the wall on the left. The Calderdale Way & the original Alternative Pennine Way join from the right at a crossroads, then after a gate the path has a fence then a wall on its right. After a couple of gates the left wall turns left & heads downhill: follow it on a good path. The views from the ridge are good: Cragg Vale is down to the left, the Calder Valley ahead to the left. The Napoleonic War monument on Stoodley Pike is prominent on the moors beyond Cragg Vale. The path leads to a walled track past Catherine House to meet a minor road at a junction.

Day 28 Map 7: Cragg Vale to Hebden Bridge

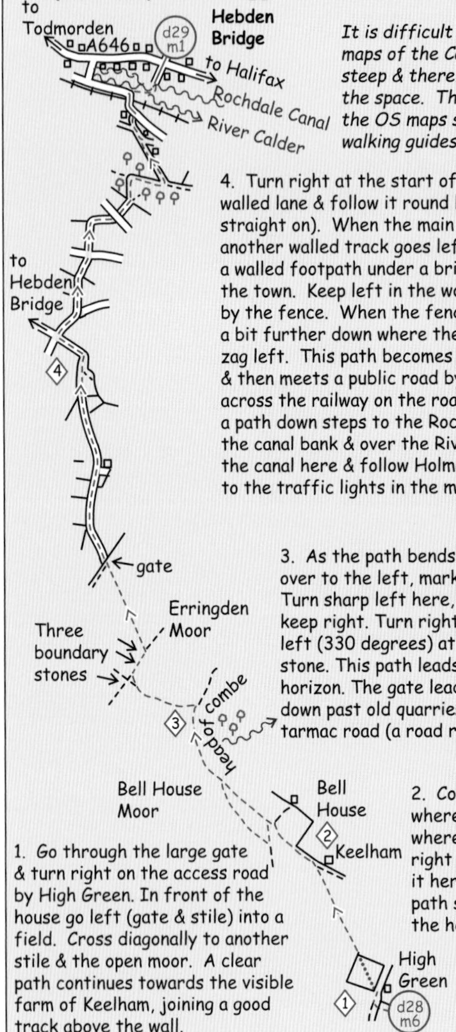

to Todmorden
A646
d29 m1
Hebden Bridge
to Halifax
Rochdale Canal
River Calder

It is difficult to show enough detail on maps of the Calder Valley: the sides are steep & there is too much to fit into the space. That's my excuse anyway: the OS maps suffer from it as well as walking guides.

4. Turn right at the start of the tarmac on another walled lane & follow it round left (not the grassy track straight on). When the main track turns right & another walled track goes left, go straight ahead down a walled footpath under a bridge & into a wood above the town. Keep left in the wood, taking the sunken path by the fence. When the fence zigs right follow it, then a bit further down where there is a choice of paths, zag left. This path becomes an access road for houses & then meets a public road by the railway. Turn left across the railway on the road bridge, then go right on a path down steps to the Rochdale Canal. Go right along the canal bank & over the River Calder to a lock. Cross the canal here & follow Holme St past the post office to the traffic lights in the middle of Hebden Bridge.

to Hebden Bridge

gate

Erringden Moor

Three boundary stones

head of combe

3. As the path bends right look out for a post over to the left, marking a path to Mytholmroyd. Turn sharp left here, & when the path forks keep right. Turn right at the path junction, then left (330 degrees) at the second boundary stone. This path leads to a gate visible on the horizon. The gate leads to a walled lane: follow it down past old quarries to reach the end of a tarmac road (a road route to Hebden Bridge).

Bell House Moor

Bell House

Keelham

2. Continue on the track beyond where the wall turns right, to where the track itself bends right towards Bell House. Leave it here for a partly flagged wet path straight on that contours to the head of a wooded combe.

1. Go through the large gate & turn right on the access road by High Green. In front of the house go left (gate & stile) into a field. Cross diagonally to another stile & the open moor. A clear path continues towards the visible farm of Keelham, joining a good track above the wall.

High Green

d28 m6

There is an alternative route shown that is slightly drier (preferable in wet conditions).

SECTION 4

The Pennines and Cheviots:
Hebden Bridge to Jedburgh

Start	Hebden Bridge
Finish	Jedburgh
Distance	330km (205 miles)
Road walking	12%. This is not much for a long-distance footpath, reflecting the success of the Pennine Way in avoiding roads. The longest road stretches are along Roman Dere Street in Scotland on Day 39, the last day of this section.
Days	11 (main schedule), or 14 (alternative schedule)
Maps and guides	*Hebden Bridge to Widdop (Holme Ends):* this guide, strip maps Day 29 Maps 1 and Map 2; *Widdop (Holme Ends) to Chew Green:* Pennine Way guide; *Chew Green to Jedburgh:* this guide, strip maps Day 39 Maps 1 and Map 2
Note	The map scale changes from 1:25,000 to 1:50,000 from Chew Green.

Just beyond Hebden Bridge the Trail joins the Pennine Way, and follows it for about 310km (190 miles) along the hills that form the spine of the north of England. The Pennine Way was the first official long-distance path in the UK, opened in 1965. These days it is not as popular as Wainwright's Coast to Coast Walk or the West Highland Way, but you will still meet many fellow walkers, and there is a good, clear path almost all the way.

The terrain is varied and nearly all very good to walk. The Yorkshire Dales are beautiful, with a contrast between the bleaker gritstone moorland and the green limestone areas. This is drystone wall country, and the valleys are intricately laid out with ancient small fields whose boundaries have been unchanged for centuries.

There is a lot of high moorland, and the weather up there can be poor – rain, mist and wind are normal. On the other hand, when the sun shines, nearly every day is magnificent. As you go further north, the scale of the scenery becomes bigger – the hills sprawl more and the villages are sparser, until you meet the fascinating remains of Hadrian's Wall, by far the most impressive Roman relic in Britain.

Section 4 Overview Map – Hebden Bridge to Jedburgh
EDINBURGH
St Abb's Head
R Tweed
Holy Island
Northumberland Coast
R Clyde
Upper Tweeddale
Eildon & Leaderfoot
R Teviot
Jedburgh
NORTHUMBERLAND
Byrness
R Annan
R Nith
Kielder Water
R North Tyne
Bellingham
R Esk
Dumfries
Newcastle upon Tyne
Tynemouth
South Shi
Nith Estuary
Greenhead
Hexham
R Tyne
Gateshead
SOLWAY FIRTH
Carlisle
Solway Coast
R South Tyne
Sunderla
R Eden
Alston
North Pennines
R Wear
THE PENNINES
R Derwent
Hartlepool
Workington
Dufton
Middleton in Teesdale
Stockton-on-Tees
Whitehaven
Ullswater
CUMBRIA
Darlington
Middlesbro
St Bees Head
LAKE DISTRICT
Wast Water
R Tees
Keld
NOR YORK M
Coniston Water
Windermere
Hawes
R Lune
YORKSHIRE DALES
Barrow-in-Furness
Morecambe Bay
Horton in Ribblesdale
NORTH YORKSHIRE
Nidderdale
Lancaster
Forest of Bowland
LANCASHIRE
Skipton
Harrogate
Thorton in Craven
Leeds
Blackpool
R Ribble
Preston
Burnley
Bradford
R Aire
Blackburn
Hebden Bridge
Southport
Huddersfield
Bolton
Barnsley
MANCHESTER
White Gate
N
0
20
km
0
10 miles

Continuing north, the moors are even bleaker, habitation scarce, and much of what was moorland has been planted with pines to form the vast Kielder Forest. In the Cheviot Hills, at the Scottish border, the Pennine Way crosses the Roman road Dere Street, and here the Trail leaves the Pennine Way and follows Dere Street into Scotland, and out of the hills to the border town of Jedburgh, and the end of Section 4.

This section is nearly all on the eastern side of the main watershed. Only twice, for overnight stops in Horton and Dufton, does the route cross to the western side.

Maps

1:25,000 Explorer maps

- 21 South Pennines (later two-sided editions)
- 2 Yorkshire Dales (Southern & Western Areas)
- 30 Yorkshire Dales (Northern & Central Areas)
- 31 North Pennines
- 43 Hadrian's Wall
- 42 Kielder Water & Forest
- 16 The Cheviot Hills

1:50,000 Landranger maps

- 103 Blackburn & Burnley
- 98 Wensleydale & Upper Wharfedale
- 91 Appleby-in-Westmorland
- 86 Haltwhistle & Brampton
- 80 Cheviot Hills & Kielder Water
- 74 Kelso & Coldstream

Guidebook

- *The Pennine Way* by Paddy Dillon (Cicerone, 4th edition, 2017). This is another good Cicerone guide, including a booklet containing all the OS 1:25,000 mapping for the route.

Recommendations

Get Paddy Dillon's *Pennine Way* guide, and Explorer 16 for the last section into Jedburgh. The 1:25,000 map booklet gives enough coverage on the Pennine Way, provided you are not planning to vary the route. The path is usually clear, and generally well waymarked in more complex valley farmland.

If you're planning to use an alternative Pennine Way guidebook, don't rely solely on a guide with narrow strip maps – you do need OS maps as well to be safe on some sections of the Pennine Way. Take either set of maps: there is little advantage in taking 1:25,000 maps rather than 1:50,000, unless you are doing without a guidebook altogether.

Accommodation

Since virtually all this section is on the Pennine Way, you can take advantage of other people's work in compiling an accommodation list. The key source is the official National Trails website at www.nationaltrail.co.uk. It's worth downloading this list.

Hebden Bridge and Jedburgh aren't on the Pennine Way, so you may need these tourist information centres:

- Butlers Wharf, New Rd, **Hebden Bridge** HX7 8AF, tel 01422 843831 www.hebdenbridge.co.uk
- Murrays Green, **Jedburgh** TD8 6BE, tel 01835 863170 www.visitscotland.com

You should consider booking ahead for the following stage ends, where accommodation is limited:

- **Thornton in Craven** (Day 29), unless you're camping
- **Byrness** (Day 38)

Equipment shops

- Day 30: Goredale Outdoor and Gifts, **Malham** BD23 4DA, tel 01729 830285
- Day 30: Pen-y-ghent Café & Outdoor Shop, **Horton in Ribblesdale** BD24 0HE, tel 01729 860333 (open Wed–Sun)
- Day 31: Three Peaks Outdoor Leisure, Riverside House, Town Foot, **Hawes** DSL8 3NH, tel 01969 667443
- Day 31: Stewart R Cunningham Outdoor Centre, Market Place, **Hawes** DL8 3QX, tel 01969 667595
- Day 35: Hi-Pennine Outdoor Shop, Market Square, **Alston** CA9 3QN, tel 01434 381389

Alternative routes

The Pennine Way and the Alternative Pennine Way

As described at the beginning of Section 3, you can follow the Pennine Way all the way to its end at Kirk Yetholm, in the Scottish Borders, if you wish, and from here the waymarked St Cuthbert's Way allows you to rejoin the main route of the Trail near Jedburgh.

From Day 30 to Day 38 the Trail follows the Pennine Way, but as the Alternative Pennine Way (APW) and the Pennine Way cross and approach each other frequently, there are also many points where you can switch between the two. For instance, if you decide to follow the APW, it could still be tempting to climb Cross Fell, which is the highest point in the Pennines, and is on the Pennine Way.

Dere Street Roman road near Oxnam (Day 39)

DAY 29

Hebden Bridge to Thornton in Craven
Clog country

Distance	36km (22 miles)
Ascent	1260m

Once Hebden Bridge has been left behind, the day follows side valleys, moorland and pasture up the western edge of the Yorkshire hills.

For the first 6km from Hebden Bridge, the Trail follows the deep, wooded valley of Hebden Dale, an area known locally as **Hardcastle Crags**, although there aren't actually many crags (Day 29 Map 1). It is a lovely valley to walk along (although it gets busy on sunny weekends), and has been a local recreation area for generations. Much of it is owned by the National Trust. (The Pennine Way avoids Hardcastle Crags, presumably for fear of adding to the Sunday crowds.)

On emerging from the woods below Blake Dean (Day 29 Map 2), the Trail joins the Pennine Way on the reservoir track at **Holme Ends**, close to the Pack Horse Inn, an old and remote pub that the locals call the Ridge.

The strip maps in this guide stop here for the time being, and you will need a Pennine Way guidebook as far as the Scottish border, just beyond Byrness on Day 39.

From Holme Ends, the reservoir access road takes you up to the **Walshaw Dean reservoirs**, then a good path through heather crosses the moor over **Dean Stones Edge** to the Worth valley above Keighley – this is Brontë country. (There is a pub, the Old Silent Inn, outside Stanbury 1km off-route to the east, on Hob Lane in the Worth valley.)

From the Worth valley, the Pennine Way climbs up onto **Ickornshaw Moor**, crossing into North Yorkshire near Wolf Stones. (Although the Trail doesn't enter Lancashire at all, you are only about 300 metres from it here – the Lancashire–Yorkshire border crosses Wolf Stones, as does the main watershed.)

Ickornshaw Moor is a featureless mound of moorland, and was one of the last parts of the Pennine Way along which a visible path was established. The descent from the moor to **Cowling** and **Ickornshaw** marks the end of the best part of the day. Although the farmland that follows is mainly pasture, and pleasant enough, it isn't a patch on Hardcastle Crags or the moors.

Cowling has accommodation, shops, a pub and a chip shop, all along the main road to the right, while neighbouring Ickornshaw has a bunkhouse and a campsite. Further along, at the end of the day, **Thornton in Craven** has only a campsite, but there is a bed and breakfast and a hostel at Earby to the south, and a campsite at East Marton, 3km to the north.

DAY 30

Thornton in Craven to Horton in Ribblesdale
Airedale and Pen-y-ghent

Distance	40km (25 miles)
Ascent	1170m

This is a day of two halves, all but the start of it in the Yorkshire Dales National Park.

The first part potters merrily from Thornton in Craven up the River Aire to its source in the limestone playground of Malham. On the way you go through the pretty village of **Gargrave**, which has a cash machine and shops. The day gradually gets better and better as the limestone bones of the land come closer and closer to the surface, until around **Malham** they are exposed completely. Streams disappear and reappear, the vegetation is lush, and the rocks themselves break out, most spectacularly at the cliff of Malham Cove (on route) and the gorge of Gordale Scar (just off-route).

Malham is a wonderful place, but gets very busy on summer weekends. If you are there midweek and don't already know the area, break here overnight and spend some time exploring. There is a large youth hostel and two pubs with accommodation, including the Lister Arms, which in earlier days memorably discouraged walkers with a 'no boots, no stockinged feet' sign on the door. There are also two campsites.

The second half of the day, from Malham, climbs up above **Malham Cove**, across bare limestone pavements up to Malham Tarn, then on to the hills of Fountains Fell and Pen-y-ghent. The first part is classic limestone country – spectacular stuff – walking across huge limestone blocks, round a dry waterfall, and

Malham Cove

past a stream that disappears under a wall. **Malham Tarn** is bleak by comparison, although the planted estate around Malham Tarn House makes up for this a bit.

There's no mercy after this, though. **Fountains Fell** is high (the Pennine Way crosses near the summit, at about 650m), big and bleak, and **Pen-y-ghent** is even higher (694m), although a lot less extensive and much more interesting to climb. Pen-y-ghent is also avoidable if you need a break – a path leads straight down into Horton from SD 836 728 on the shoulder of Pen-y-ghent. Walking Land's End to John o' Groats entitles you to miss out bits of the Pennine Way in an emergency, although it would be a pity to miss out Pen-y-ghent.

Horton in Ribblesdale is a small village largely dependent on walkers and cavers for its living. There are two pubs: the Crown has accommodation and the Golden Lion has a bunkhouse next door. The Pen-y-ghent café (open Wed–Sun) acts as a tourist information centre for walkers, and there are also bed and breakfasts and a good campsite.

DAY 31

Horton in Ribblesdale to Hawes
Ribblesdale and Cam High Road

Distance	22km (14 miles)
Ascent	540m

This is a relatively short day, mainly on good tracks with easy gradients, and tomorrow is even shorter, so if you are going particularly well you could consider running the two days into one.

A cart track leads north out of Horton, gradually climbing up the east side of **Ribblesdale**, past a number of potholes. The track climbs to the summit of a pass over to Langstrothdale, where the Pennine Way and our Trail leave it to cut across west and join an old packhorse road bound for Hawes. Continuing north, the Pennine Way crosses Ling Gill and climbs onto **Cam Fell** to join **Cam High Road**: a Roman road that rises to 588m across the hills.

After 1km on this old road you should pause briefly to take in the fact that you have completed **half your journey**. This is the midpoint of the End to End Trail, and despite the fact that you'd almost have been in John o' Groats by now had you walked a direct route, you'll have to admit that the scenery here is probably rather better than that 18km underneath the Isle of Man.

After 4km on the Roman road, the Pennine Way takes a track forking left off Cam High Road along a ridge to the north, and descends to **Wensleydale** and the small town of **Hawes**. Hawes is a traditional Dales town, still acting as the focal point for a wide community (as well as tourists). It is a relaxing place to stop and has shops and banks. There is plenty of accommodation, including a youth hostel, and two campsites nearby. (The local Wensleydale cheese is very good – buy some to help boost the local economy.)

DAY 32

Hawes to Keld
Great Shunner Fell and Swaledale

Distance	20km (12 miles)
Ascent	740m

Today is really all about crossing Great Shunner Fell. This is a huge area of high moorland, and the Pennine Way crosses its summit, reaching your highest point so far at 716m. (Great Shunner Fell is just a few metres higher than is reached by the Offa's Dyke Path in the Black Mountains on Day 18.)

The climb starts a couple of kilometres from Hawes and is pretty unremitting. You climb higher and higher out of Wensleydale along a long, exposed ridge to the top of **Great Shunner Fell**, and the descent to the village of **Thwaite** is almost as long.

Thwaite is in **Swaledale**, a little way to the west of the main valley, and rather than follow Thwaite Beck east to the Swale, then follow the river upstream to Keld, the Pennine Way follows a far superior course, high above the river. This means a stiff climb up from Thwaite, but the views down to and across the valley bottom between here and Keld more than justify the effort. The walking is good as well, along terraces high on the steep valley side.

In due course the path descends gradually to meet the Swale at the hamlet of **Keld** – the nearest thing to a major crossroads in British long-distance walking. Here the Pennine Way crosses Wainwright's Coast to Coast Walk, and in summer the population of Keld seems to be made up mainly of long-distance walkers. As you near Keld, the waterfalls of Kisdon Force are below to your right, and are well worth the short diversion.

Keld is a lovely spot, unspoilt despite the walkers, who have in fact probably contributed a lot to keeping the old stone buildings in active use. There is plenty of accommodation here for such a small village, including two campsites: one in the village and another (with a bunkhouse as well) just outside it (both campsites are notorious for midges, so beware). The former youth hostel, Keld Lodge, has accommodation and also a public bar and restaurant. The village campsite shop sells basic provisions, including beer and wine.

Kisdon Force, Keld

DAY 33

Keld to Middleton-in-Teesdale
The Durham moors

Distance	33km (21 miles)
Ascent	800m

It's farewell to the Yorkshire Dales, and hello to wet feet in all probability. It's moorland all day, and the first half is famously wet underfoot, not having (as yet) been paved with stone flags like the wet parts of the southern Pennine Way.

The first section as far as the **Tan Hill Inn** runs parallel to a road, so there is an alternative if needed. The Tan Hill Inn is the highest pub in England, and is only there because there used to be a mining industry here, many traces of which can still be seen. There is bed and breakfast available here and a bunkhouse, or you can camp by the inn.

At Tan Hill the Pennine Way finally leaves the Yorkshire Dales National Park, and North Yorkshire, and enters Durham. Sodden **Sleightholme Moor** can also be avoided, if necessary, by following the road east from Tan Hill then forking left on the Sleightholme Moor Road.

The Trail meets a road at Sleightholme Farm, then crosses the River Greta and the A66 Penrith to Scotch Corner trunk road. It's still pretty remote moorland, though, and this is followed by another moorland crossing to **Baldersdale**. This section is a bit drier underfoot than earlier in the day, and a bit more enjoyable. There used to be accommodation in Baldersdale, but now there is none, so don't get caught out here late in the day.

There are two more climbs and descents to complete the day. As for Day 28 (around Huddersfield) the valleys run east–west across the route, so it's up out of Baldersdale, down into **Lunedale**, up again, then back down to **Teesdale** and the quiet town of **Middleton-in-Teesdale**.

Middleton has shops, pubs, a bank (Barclays – open on Mondays, Tuesdays and Fridays) and accommodation, and there is a campsite on the right before you cross the river to the town. There's also a bunkhouse and campsite by the river at Low Way Farm, 4km further up the valley (on route), with a pub (the Strathmore Arms) close by.

DAY 34

Middleton-in-Teesdale to Dufton
Upper Teesdale and High Cup

Distance	32km (20 miles)
Ascent	710m

Admittedly we are going in the wrong direction all day, but believe me it's worth it – this is one of the best days of the whole Trail, and arguably the very best day on the Pennine Way.

It starts with a riverside walk along the River Tees – in spring and early summer there are wild flowers everywhere along here, including globe flowers, early purple orchids and fairy foxgloves. There are also waterfalls – **Low Force** and **High Force**, the latter being spectacular in wet weather – and a youth hostel, a pub and a bed and breakfast at **Langdon Beck**, if you want to make an overnight stop hereabouts.

Continuing up the river heading west, the rural and pastoral gradually give way to upland scenery – look out for spring gentians in the turf. Just before reaching **Cauldron Snout** waterfall there is a short, difficult section across boulders, and this is a good excuse for a lunch stop by the waterfall, where the Tees tumbles down from **Cow Green Reservoir**.

The Trail leaves Durham for Cumbria as it crosses the river above the waterfall. Beyond here, past remote Birkdale Farm, it's back to the moors, climbing to nearly 600m above and beside Maize Beck.

The main watershed is eventually reached on a wide, flat rocky plateau, then suddenly you become aware of the huge U-shaped valley scooped out of the hillside ahead. This is **High Cup**, about 300m deep, 3km long, and with very steep sides topped off with a line of crags. If it is clear enough there is a terrific view across the Vale of Eden to the Lake District. This is a place to stop for a while and enjoy just being there. Once you can drag yourself away, an easy descent into **Dufton** follows.

Dufton is a small, unspoilt village on the edge of the wide Vale of Eden, clustering around a wide, tree-lined main-street-cum-green. It has a youth hostel, bed and breakfasts, a campsite and an excellent pub, the Stag Inn. There is

High Cup, looking back before descending to Dufton

Dufton

no shop. The village economy is largely dependent on walkers, so spend your money here. (The YHA threatened to close the youth hostel rather than spend money on it, but it was reprieved with the aid of a local action committee and generous grants.)

DAY 35

Dufton to Alston
Cross Fell

Distance	31km (19 miles)
Ascent	1070m

Physically this is the high point of the Trail. The Pennine Way crosses the summit of Cross Fell, which at 893m is the highest point on the Pennine Way as well as on the End to End Trail, and the highest mountain in England outside the Lake District.

In good weather this is a tremendous day, particularly the ascents, but if the weather is poor it could also be the psychological low point of your walk – Cross Fell is notorious for bad weather and strong winds. It is also big and remote, and can feel very bleak and exposed. Unlike most of the Pennine Way, there isn't a clear path all the way, and you should not attempt this section in bad weather unless you know how to navigate by map and compass.

The climb up from Dufton is steady and hard work. Gradually you haul your way up to **Green Fell** (800m), then **Great Dun Fell** (848m, with an ugly radar station on its summit), then across bleak, pathless terrain to **Little Dun Fell** (842m), and then up to **Cross Fell**. A short descent leads to an old track that heads eventually down past relics of old mining activity (including Greg's Hut, now an MBA bothy) to **Garrigill** and the River South Tyne. Garrigill is a quiet little village with a shop/post office and a pub.

The last stretch follows the river north to Alston, an easy riverside stroll, but not as memorable as yesterday morning's walk up the Tees. **Alston** is another unspoilt small town you don't want to leave. It has shops, bed and breakfasts, a campsite and a youth hostel.

DAY 36

Alston to Greenhead
The South Tyne

Distance	26km (16 miles)
Ascent	610m

This is a fairly easy day, not too long and not particularly hilly. Shortly after leaving Alston, a footbridge across Gilderdale Burn takes you out of Cumbria and into Northumberland, the most northerly English county.

For most of the day the Pennine Way follows the River South Tyne northwards, mainly along the hillside on the west side of the valley, and briefly along the riverbank on the approach to **Slaggyford** – this bit is particularly good. (There is a pub, the Kirkstyle Inn, five minutes off-route due east from **Burnstones**, 2km beyond Slaggyford.)

Soon after this, the **Maiden Way** is joined, an old Roman road heading for a fort near Greenhead, although the Pennine Way reaches Greenhead by a slightly more circuitous route, abandoning the Maiden Way for some featureless moors to the west. Here there is a rare opportunity to lose the Pennine Way on the descent, as the path disappears in places.

The Pennine Way doesn't go through Greenhead village, but an invisible footpath leads there across fields, from NY 653 644, where the Pennine Way turns sharp left. Get out your compass if you want to follow this footpath to **Greenhead**. (Walking along the A69 is best avoided, as it is a fast and busy trunk road connecting Carlisle and Newcastle.)

Greenhead is a small village with a range of accommodation in the village and nearby, including a campsite, a camping barn, a hotel (the Greenhead Hotel) and a hostel (which used to be a YHA hostel but is now run by the hotel). The hotel is largely a locals' haunt, but serves food and is welcoming to visitors.

DAY 37

Greenhead to Bellingham
Hadrian's Wall and Wark Forest

Distance	35km (22 miles)
Ascent	950m

The Pennine Way changes direction at Greenhead to follow Hadrian's Wall eastwards. Even without the Roman wall this would be an excellent walk, as it follows the crests of a series of rock ridges. The views are good and the walking interesting, although it's a bit of a switchback, and when you add the Roman remains, the result is one of the best bits of the whole Trail.

Hadrian's Wall is well preserved along a lot of this stretch due to its remoteness – less of the stone has been taken for building. There are a number of milecastles along the part of Hadrian's Wall followed by the Pennine Way, and a lot of major ditch-work is obvious.

Hadrian's Wall was built by the Roman Emperor Hadrian around AD120, and he visited Britain to oversee its construction. The objective was to protect the Roman Empire from marauding invaders from the north, and it was the high-water mark of the empire. The Romans had no control north of this line for any significant length of time, and it marked the boundary of the empire for nearly 300 years.

Milecastle, Hadrian's Wall

About 12km from Greenhead, and just off-route to the south, are the **Twice Brewed Inn** (accommodation, camping) and the Sill youth hostel. The hostel is large and well equipped. Not far away there is another campsite, a bunkhouse and more bed and breakfasts.

After following the wall a little further, the Pennine Way turns left at **Cuddy's Crags** to head north, and although the rest of the day is pleasant enough, it can't compete with Hadrian and his wall.

First there is a soggy section of rough pasture between Greenlee and Broomlee Loughs, then the rest of the day follows pretty nondescript low moorland, three sections of which are planted with conifers. This is **Wark Forest**, part of the huge Kielder Forest Park.

There is a campsite at **Stonehaugh** and a bunkhouse and limited camping at Shitlington Crag Farm (NY 829 808), otherwise all the accommodation is in the small and quiet town of **Bellingham**, by the River North Tyne. Bellingham has campsites, bed and breakfasts, a bunkhouse, shops, a post office and a cash machine at the Co-op.

DAY 38

Bellingham to Byrness
Northumberland moors and Kielder Forest

Distance	24km (15 miles)
Ascent	550m

This is a day of featureless, boggy moorland followed by a trudge on forestry roads. In bad weather it feels like typical Pennine Way purgatory, and you may start wondering what you've done to deserve it.

The moors north of Bellingham are bleak. The Pennine Way gradually climbs up to around 370m across bog and heather, crossing the tops of **Deer Play**, **Whitley Pike**, **Padon Hill** and **Brownrigg Head**. All of these are wide, flat hills (the name 'Whitley Pike' giving entirely the wrong impression) and it's also wet underfoot in places.

Near Brownrigg Head the forestry is met again, and after following its edge for a while the Trail enters the trees of **Kielder Forest** – and that's it for scenery. The path joins a forestry road, and you'll see nothing but pine trees for the rest of the day.

The forestry road takes the Pennine Way down into **Redesdale**, then a riverside path heads up the valley to a campsite/bed and breakfast at **Cottonshopeburnfoot**. A bit further up the valley is the hamlet of **Byrness** on the A68 trunk road. You meet the road by a hotel (the Byrness Hotel), and just down the road there is a bed and breakfast and the Forest View Inn, which has accommodation, a bunkhouse and a small camping area. The Byrness Hotel appears to be no longer operating full-time as an inn, but may still have accommodation available.

Deep in the forestry, 3km to the north of Byrness at NT 768 056, there is also a small but comfortable MBA bothy: **Spithope**. If you want to stay there, ignore the bridleways shown on your OS map, and instead follow the A68 northwest for about 700 metres to where an untarred access road turns right. Go straight along this until you see the bothy close by on your right, across the stream, then look out for the path to it. To rejoin the Trail, return to the track & turn right up the valley. Turn sharp left at a track junction (NT 769 069) then when the track bends left leave it, going straight on to cross the fence out of the forestry. Turn right along the fence to meet the Pennine Way and turn left.

Spithope bothy

DAY 39

Byrness to Jedburgh
The Cheviots and Dere Street

Distance	31km (19 miles)
Ascent	800m

This is a significant day in your progress from End to End. It is the day you leave the Pennine Way, after following it for 10 days and 310km (190 miles), and also the day the Trail leaves England and enters Scotland. The journey will have a different feel from here on, the cultural and building traditions being quite distinct on the two sides of the border.

From Byrness to Chew Green continue to follow your Pennine Way guidebook. From Byrness there is a brutally steep climb up through the forestry to the top of **Byrness Hill** (427m). Just before the top of the hill the Pennine Way finally emerges from the pines and onto the Cheviot Hills, to follow a ridge north, over **Houx Hill** and **Ravens Knowe** (527m), but this is no rocky Lake District ridge – the Cheviots appear to be made of equal quantities of peat, water and bath sponges. Some of the wettest parts have now been paved, but some haven't, and it's still quite possible to end up in a morass up to your thighs (he said with feeling).

A little beyond Ravens Knowe the border fence is reached – go through the gate and you are in Scotland. The Pennine Way soon crosses back into Northumberland again at **Chew Green** (Day 39 Map 1), where there are the remains of a Roman army camp. Through the camp passes Dere Street, a Roman road older than Hadrian's Wall, and the Pennine Way follows **Dere Street** north for 2km as far as another gate in the border fence at **Black Halls**, between Brownhart Law and Blackhall Hill, and this is where you finally leave the Pennine Way. (It stays on the English side of the fence, soon heading northeast, aiming for the Cheviot, and eventually descending into Scotland to end at the village of Kirk Yetholm.)

The Trail follows Dere Street to Jedburgh, instead, missing out most of the Cheviot peat bogs, so put away your Pennine Way guidebook and turn to the strip map pages in this guide again. (Note: The strip maps are at a scale of 1:50,000 from here on.)

Dere Street originally ran from York to the Forth near Edinburgh, via the fort at Trimontium near Melrose, and was built during the governorship of Agricola, who governed Roman Britain from AD79 to AD83, 40 years before Hadrian built his wall. Agricola built the road as he advanced in AD81. This was a two-pronged advance, the other route being along the Western Way, which you cross above West Linton on Day 43.

Pass through the gate at Black Halls and out of England for the last time on the Trail. Follow the path along the fence, and when it forks, keep left to follow a path across the flank of **Blackhall Hill**. This is not the line of Dere Street, which went round the back of Blackhall Hill, but the line of the old road here has now become difficult to follow, so is not recommended. The two lines reunite by a gate.

The track now follows the crest of a saddle between White Hope and Twise Hope streams, then at the next saddle descends between Woden Law and Langside Law to the road junction at **Tow Ford**, and out of the Cheviot Hills. On the descent, the three hills – the Roman 'Trimontium' – of the Eildon Hills above Melrose can be seen straight ahead: the Trail crosses them at the end of tomorrow.

From Tow Ford, Dere Street is a tarmac road for a short way, then at the next road junction becomes a path again, following a rough pasture ridge with good views of the Cheviots to the right and the Eildons to the left.

The track passes Cunzierton Hill (Day 39 Map 2), then meets a road just before Shibden Hill. Dere Street is covered in tarmac again for about 3km, but luckily it's a quiet road. After that there is a delightful stretch of track up hill and down dale, in a dead straight line, some of it accompanied by a line of mature beech trees.

Dere Street doesn't visit Jedburgh, but the Trail does, so if you plan to do so also, you will need to turn left into the trees after the second road crossing (see Day 39 Map 2) and follow a minor road into town.

Jedburgh is one of the main border towns, and has all services and plenty of accommodation, as well as restaurants and takeaways. I can recommend Belters Bar for food: book ahead to be sure of a seat.

Jedburgh has plenty of history, and the ruins of the abbey are worth visiting if you have time. It was founded by King David I in 1118 for Augustinian canons, and destroyed by the Earl of Hertford in 1545.

Historic Jedburgh I remember well because its castle looks so new that it might have been built by Marks and Spencer

Theo Lang, Cross Country, 1948

Twise Hope and Streethouse Wood, Cheviot Hills

Day 29 Map 1: Hebden Bridge to Gibson Mill

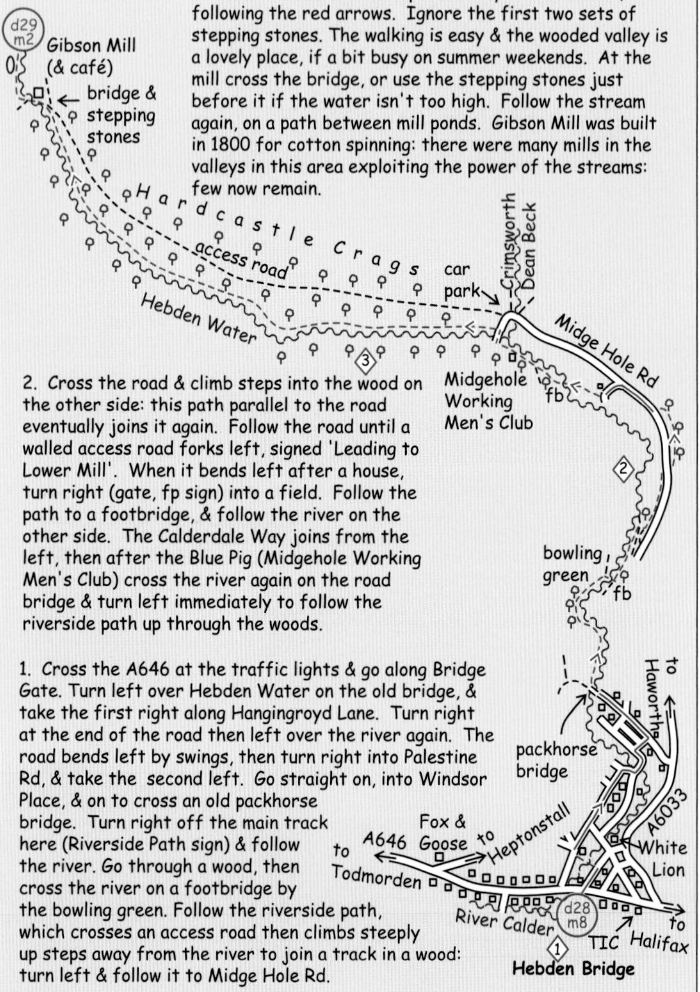

3. Follow Hebden Water up the valley to Gibson Mill, following the red arrows. Ignore the first two sets of stepping stones. The walking is easy & the wooded valley is a lovely place, if a bit busy on summer weekends. At the mill cross the bridge, or use the stepping stones just before it if the water isn't too high. Follow the stream again, on a path between mill ponds. Gibson Mill was built in 1800 for cotton spinning: there were many mills in the valleys in this area exploiting the power of the streams: few now remain.

2. Cross the road & climb steps into the wood on the other side: this path parallel to the road eventually joins it again. Follow the road until a walled access road forks left, signed 'Leading to Lower Mill'. When it bends left after a house, turn right (gate, fp sign) into a field. Follow the path to a footbridge, & follow the river on the other side. The Calderdale Way joins from the left, then after the Blue Pig (Midgehole Working Men's Club) cross the river again on the road bridge & turn left immediately to follow the riverside path up through the woods.

1. Cross the A646 at the traffic lights & go along Bridge Gate. Turn left over Hebden Water on the old bridge, & take the first right along Hangingroyd Lane. Turn right at the end of the road then left over the river again. The road bends left by swings, then turn right into Palestine Rd, & take the second left. Go straight on, into Windsor Place, & on to cross an old packhorse bridge. Turn right off the main track here (Riverside Path sign) & follow the river. Go through a wood, then cross the river on a footbridge by the bowling green. Follow the riverside path, which crosses an access road then climbs steeply up steps away from the river to join a track in a wood: turn left & follow it to Midge Hole Rd.

d29 m2
Gibson Mill (& café)
bridge & stepping stones
Hardcastle Crags
access road
Hebden Water
car park
Crimsworth Dean Beck
Midge Hole Rd
Midgehole Working Men's Club
fb
bowling green
fb
to Haworth
packhorse bridge
A6033
White Lion
Fox & Goose
to Heptonstall
A646
to Todmorden
River Calder
d28 m8
TIC
to Halifax
Hebden Bridge

Day 29 Map 2: Gibson Mill to Widdop (Holme Ends)

2. After crossing the footbridge below Blake Dean follow the path for a few paces then turn right up steps & through a gate in a wall. Here you have a choice: (a) To continue the walk, turn right to follow the track up by Alcomden Water until it joins a reservoir access road. You can now put these maps away until you reach the Scottish border, & get out your Pennine Way guide, as the End to End Trail follows the Pennine Way for the rest of its time in England. Or (b): If you are thirsty, & you have carefully planned to be here at a suitable time of day, climb very steeply up the bank ahead of you to reach the Widdop road on a hairpin bend. Follow the road up to reach the Pack Horse Inn (known locally as the Ridge), which serves good food. To regain your route afterwards continue along the road & turn right along the Pennine Way.

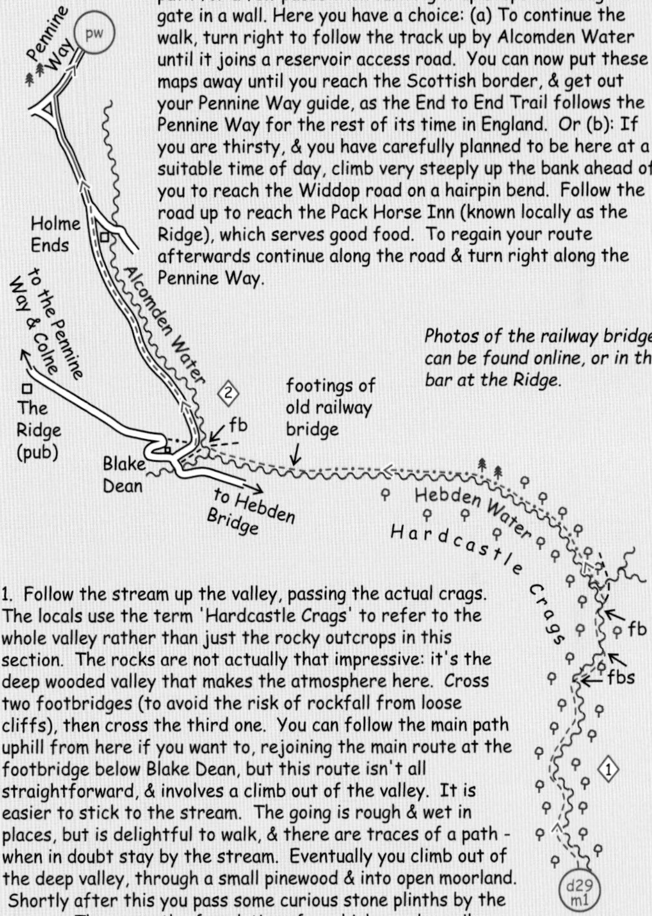

Photos of the railway bridge can be found online, or in the bar at the Ridge.

1. Follow the stream up the valley, passing the actual crags. The locals use the term 'Hardcastle Crags' to refer to the whole valley rather than just the rocky outcrops in this section. The rocks are not actually that impressive: it's the deep wooded valley that makes the atmosphere here. Cross two footbridges (to avoid the risk of rockfall from loose cliffs), then cross the third one. You can follow the main path uphill from here if you want to, rejoining the main route at the footbridge below Blake Dean, but this route isn't all straightforward, & involves a climb out of the valley. It is easier to stick to the stream. The going is rough & wet in places, but is delightful to walk, & there are traces of a path - when in doubt stay by the stream. Eventually you climb out of the deep valley, through a small pinewood & into open moorland. Shortly after this you pass some curious stone plinths by the stream. These are the foundations for a high wooden railway bridge, completed in 1901 for the construction of the Walshaw Dean reservoirs you will walk past shortly.

Day 39 Map 1: Chew Green to Cunzierton Hill

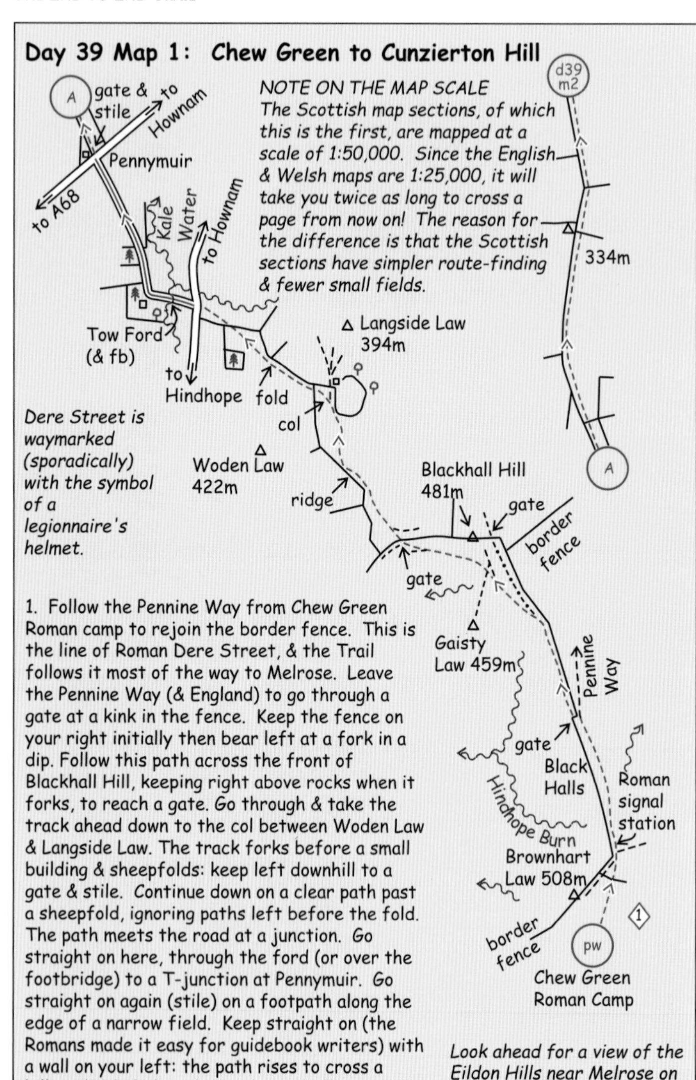

NOTE ON THE MAP SCALE
The Scottish map sections, of which this is the first, are mapped at a scale of 1:50,000. Since the English & Welsh maps are 1:25,000, it will take you twice as long to cross a page from now on! The reason for the difference is that the Scottish sections have simpler route-finding & fewer small fields.

Dere Street is waymarked (sporadically) with the symbol of a legionnaire's helmet.

1. Follow the Pennine Way from Chew Green Roman camp to rejoin the border fence. This is the line of Roman Dere Street, & the Trail follows it most of the way to Melrose. Leave the Pennine Way (& England) to go through a gate at a kink in the fence. Keep the fence on your right initially then bear left at a fork in a dip. Follow this path across the front of Blackhall Hill, keeping right above rocks when it forks, to reach a gate. Go through & take the track ahead down to the col between Woden Law & Langside Law. The track forks before a small building & sheepfolds: keep left downhill to a gate & stile. Continue down on a clear path past a sheepfold, ignoring paths left before the fold. The path meets the road at a junction. Go straight on here, through the ford (or over the footbridge) to a T-junction at Pennymuir. Go straight on again (stile) on a footpath along the edge of a narrow field. Keep straight on (the Romans made it easy for guidebook writers) with a wall on your left: the path rises to cross a hilltop (334m) then descends gradually.

Look ahead for a view of the Eildon Hills near Melrose on the descent to Tow Ford.

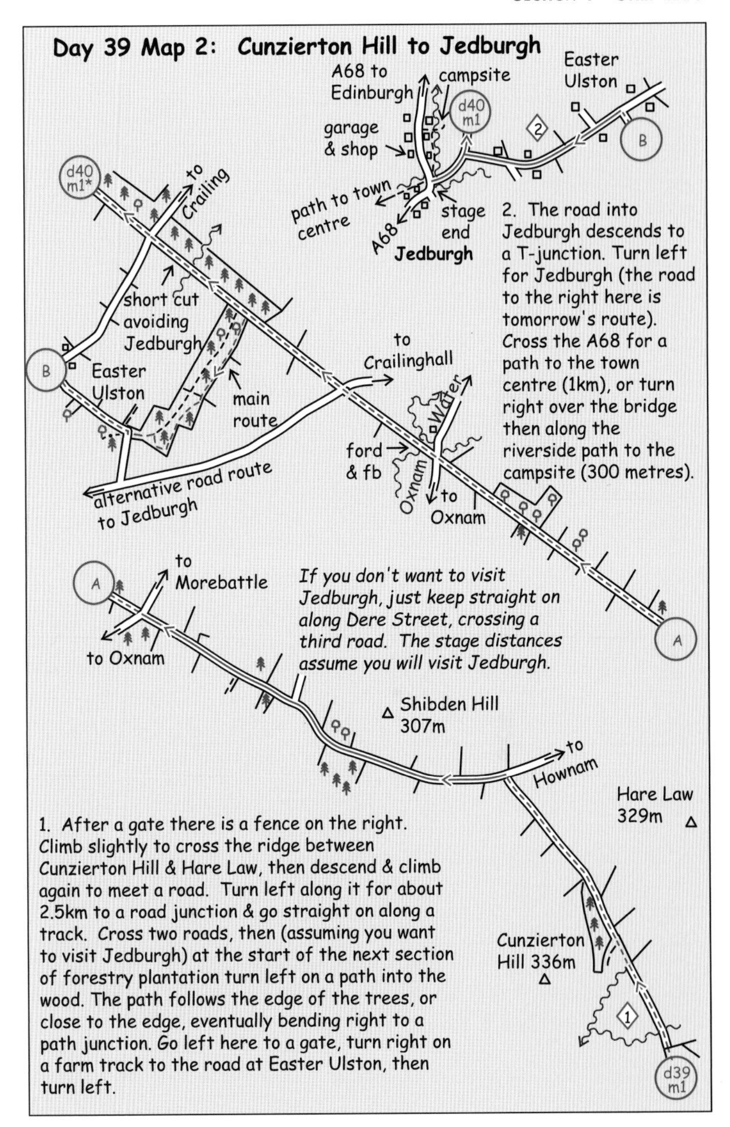
Day 39 Map 2: Cunzierton Hill to Jedburgh
A68 to Edinburgh
campsite
Easter Ulston
d40 m1
garage & shop
B
d40 m1*
to Crailing
path to town centre
A68
stage end
Jedburgh
2. The road into Jedburgh descends to a T-junction. Turn left for Jedburgh (the road to the right here is tomorrow's route). Cross the A68 for a path to the town centre (1km), or turn right over the bridge then along the riverside path to the campsite (300 metres).
short cut avoiding Jedburgh
to Crailinghall
B
Easter Ulston
main route
Oxnam Water
ford & fb
alternative road route to Jedburgh
to Oxnam
A
to Morebattle
to Oxnam
If you don't want to visit Jedburgh, just keep straight on along Dere Street, crossing a third road. The stage distances assume you will visit Jedburgh.
A
Shibden Hill 307m
to Hownam
Hare Law 329m
1. After a gate there is a fence on the right. Climb slightly to cross the ridge between Cunzierton Hill & Hare Law, then descend & climb again to meet a road. Turn left along it for about 2.5km to a road junction & go straight on along a track. Cross two roads, then (assuming you want to visit Jedburgh) at the start of the next section of forestry plantation turn left on a path into the wood. The path follows the edge of the trees, or close to the edge, eventually bending right to a path junction. Go left here to a gate, turn right on a farm track to the road at Easter Ulston, then turn left.
Cunzierton Hill 336m
d39 m1

SECTION 5

Southern Scotland and the West Highland Way: Jedburgh to Fort William

Start	Jedburgh
Finish	Fort William
Distance	341km (212 miles)
Road walking	12%. The longest stretches of road are around Peebles and West Linton in the Tweed Valley, not (as you might have expected) in the Forth–Clyde lowlands. There is, however, a lot of tarmac to walk here, on the canal towpaths and the disused railway.
Days	10 (main schedule), or 14 (alternative schedule)
Maps and guides	*Jedburgh to Carbeth:* this guide, strip maps Day 40 Map 1 to Day 45 Map 2; *Carbeth to Fort William:* West Highland Way guide

Section 5 takes the Trail from the Scottish border to Fort William in the heart of the Highlands. The general direction is northwest, initially parallel to or alongside the River Tweed, then crossing the rolling Southern Upland hills to descend to the Forth–Clyde lowlands. The lowlands have seen a lot of industrial development over the past 200 years, but the Trail misses the worst of this, threading its way between Edinburgh and Glasgow on canal towpaths and along a disused railway line to reach Loch Lomond, then following the West Highland Way north into the mountains.

From Jedburgh to where it joins the West Highland Way, north of Glasgow, the Trail mainly follows documented routes, and most of it is waymarked or follows towpaths. On Day 40, St Cuthbert's Way follows Roman Dere Street into Tweeddale, then from Maxton follows the River Tweed itself to Newtown St Boswells before crossing the Eildon Hills to end in Melrose. Here the Trail picks up the Southern Upland Way and heads westward for Day 41. The Southern Upland Way is a waymarked national trail, and it crosses the hills to Traquair, with the Tweed once more close by.

At Traquair you leave the Southern Upland Way and join the Cross Borders Drove Road, a newly established waymarked route. This follows an old cattle-droving route over the hills to Peebles, and then northwest over the Pentland Hills

Section 5 Overview Map – Jedburgh to Fort William
Inverness
Glen Affric
N
0
20
km
0
10 miles
HIGHLAND REGION
SCOTLAND
CAIRNGORMS
The Cairngorm Mountains
GRAMPIAN MOUNTAINS
Fort William
Kinlochleven
Loch Rannoch & Glen Lyon
Loch Tummel
TAY
R Tay
Ben Nevis & Glen Coe
Bridge of Orchy
PERTH & KINROSS
R Earn (Comrie to St Fillans)
Dundee
Perth
Firth of Tay
St Andrews Bay
Crianlarich
LOCH LOMOND & THE TROSSACHS
Inverarnan
Fife Ness
Loch Leven
STERLING
Drymen
Stirling
Kirkcaldy
FIRTH OF FORTH
Greenock
Kilsyth
Falkirk
EDINBURGH
Linlithgow
Glasgow
East Kilbride
W Linton
ISLE OF ARRAN
Irvine
Kilmarnock
Peebles
Melrose
Traquair
Upper Tweeddale
Eildon & Leaderfoot
Selkirk
BORDERS
Ayr
Jedburgh
Hawick
Byrness
GALLOWAY
River Don
River Dee
R Spey
R Nairn
R Beauly
Loch Ness
R Moriston
Loch Cluanie
Loch Lochy
R Spean
Loch Treig
Loch Ericht
R Tummel
Loch Rannoch
R Lyon
L Lyon
Loch Tay
L Earn
R Earn
Loch Katrine
R Teith
R Forth
Loch Leven
Loch Lomond
Loch Long
Firth of Clyde
R Clyde
R Tweed
R Teviot
R Annan
R Nith
R Esk
Loch Doon
Kielder Water

to its end at Little Vantage. The Trail then crosses Corston Hill to meet the mid-Scotland sprawl at Mid Calder.

Here the character of the route changes – a patchwork of countryside and industrial Scotland lies between you and the West Highland Way. Walkers are not particularly provided for, and there are many signs of present and past industrial activity, although on the other hand there are plenty of small towns for restocking with provisions.

From Mid Calder the Almondell Country Park takes you down the beautiful wooded Almond valley to meet the newly reopened Union Canal, linking Edinburgh to the Forth and Clyde Canal at Falkirk. The Union Canal towpath is followed to Falkirk, then the Forth and Clyde towpath on towards Glasgow. By the end of the 20th century, both these canals had fallen into disrepair and were closed to boats, but they were reopened in 2001 at a cost of £78 million. A unique new boatlift (the Falkirk Wheel) was built: this came into operation in 2002, linking the two canals once again. Both they and the old railway that follows have been made into cycle tracks, and are now surfaced with tarmac. While this is not ideal for walkers, it does mean that you can get a good speed up along this stretch.

You forsake the canals at Kirkintilloch for a disused railway track northwest along the valley to Lennoxtown and Strathblane, to join the West Highland Way at Carbeth, a few kilometres north of its start at Milngavie (thus avoiding going all the way into Glasgow).

The route then follows the West Highland Way up the east side of Loch Lomond and north to Glencoe and Fort William. The West Highland Way was the first long-distance trail in Scotland, opening in 1980, and it attracts a lot of walkers. It largely follows the same valleys and passes as the main road from Glasgow to Fort William as far as the Kingshouse Hotel above Glencoe. From here it cuts across the hills to Kinlochleven, then follows side valleys northwards to Fort William, the walkers' capital of the Highlands.

Melrose Abbey

Ben Nevis looms above Fort William, or rather it does when the cloud is high enough to see it. Since this is the highest mountain in Great Britain it is worth taking a day off from the Trail to climb it.

You will probably need to do some serious shopping in Fort William anyway, since it is the last chance to stock up properly. You will need plenty of fuel and food, particularly dried food. The only shops on or near the route after Fort William are at Kinlochewe (end of Day 53) and at Watten (end of Day 60), unless you are taking the alternative route via Lairg. Ben Nevis in the morning and shopping in the afternoon could be a good plan.

Maps

1:25,000 Explorer maps

- 16 The Cheviot Hills
- 338 Galashiels, Selkirk & Melrose
- 337 Peebles & Innerleithen
- 336 Biggar & Broughton (briefly)
- 344 Pentland Hills
- 349 Falkirk, Cumbernauld & Livingston
- 342 Glasgow (briefly)
- 348 Campsie Fells
- 38 Loch Lomond South
- 39 Loch Lomond North
- 377 Loch Etive & Glen Orchy
- 384 Glen Coe & Glen Etive
- 392 Ben Nevis & Fort William

1:50,000 Landranger maps

- 74 Kelso & Coldstream
- 73 Peebles, Galashiels & Selkirk
- 72 Upper Clyde Valley
- 65 Falkirk & Linlithgow
- 64 Glasgow
- 57 Stirling & the Trossachs
- 56 Loch Lomond & Inveraray
- 50 Glen Orchy & Loch Etive
- 41 Ben Nevis

Note that the Ordnance Survey has renumbered some of these maps, giving some confusion here. Explorers 338 and 337 used to be combined as Explorer 44 (Tweed Valley). Explorers 38 and 39 used to be numbered 347 and 364. These are not the same as the even older Explorers 38 and 39, which were strip maps of the West Highland Way.

Guidebooks

- *Exploring the Edinburgh to Glasgow Canals* by Hamish Brown (Mercat Press, 2nd edition, 2006) (now out of print)
- *The West Highland Way* by Terry Marsh (Cicerone, 4th edition, 2016; reprinted 2019). This guidebook comes with a 1:25,000 OS map booklet (which is also available separately).

Recommendations

If you haven't already got some of the 1:25,000 maps, then get Explorer 16 or Landranger 74, and Landrangers 73, 72, 65 and 64. There is little additional benefit in having the other 1:25,000 maps to get you to the West Highland Way, and it's not worth buying OS maps for the WHW itself as navigation is pretty easy. You might want to consider getting the Harvey's strip map for the WHW, but the obvious solution is to buy Terry Marsh's guidebook with its separate 1:25,000 map booklet.

Hamish Brown's book about the canals adds a lot to the experience of walking them, and I recommend it highly if you can find a second-hand copy, despite it now being a bit out of date.

Accommodation

The following tourist information centres (TICs) are your best sources of information as far as the West Highland Way. They all share a common website at www.visitscotland.com:

- Murrays Green, **Jedburgh** TD8 6BE, tel 01835 863170
- 23 High Street, **Peebles** EH45 8AG, tel 01721 728095
- The Falkirk Wheel, Lime Road, Tamfourhill, **Falkirk** FK1 4RS, tel 01324 620244
- 156a/158 Buchanan Street, **Glasgow** G1 2LL, tel 0141 566 4083
- There is also a TIC in Fort William: 15 High St, **Fort William** PH33 6DH, tel 01397 701801

An accommodation guide to the **Southern Upland Way** is available online at www.southernuplandway.gov.uk, and this contains the best information for Melrose and Traquair. Accommodation in and around **Linlithgow** is listed on the town's website www.linlithgow.info; and similarly, for **Kilsyth**, check out www.kilsyth.org.uk. **The John Muir Way** website https://johnmuirway.org has a comprehensive accommodation guide, and a lot of this is relevant to the End to End Trail, from Linlithgow to Strathblane.

Finding out about accommodation along the **West Highland Way** is not very easy (at the time of writing). There is an accommodation guide on the WHW website www.westhighlandway.org, but it is by no means comprehensive.

Bear in mind that a permit is required for wild camping in many areas around Loch Lomond (Days 45 and 46). These can be bought online up to eight weeks in advance: see www.lochlomond-trossachs.org.

A few stage end points have more limited accommodation, so you should consider booking ahead for these (Note: 'A' in stage numbers indicates a stage end on the alternative schedule – see Appendix A):

- **West Linton** (Day 42)
- **Broxburn** (Day 43, Day A58)
- **Kilsyth** (Day 44)
- **Lennoxtown** (Day 45, Day A60)
- **Inverarnan** (Day 46), unless you are camping
- **Bridge of Orchy** (Day 47), unless you are wild camping
- **Kingshouse** (Day 48, Day A65)

Although there are bed and breakfasts and bunkhouses all along the West Highland Way, supply often cannot meet the demand at peak times, even at other stage ends not listed above. Either book ahead or carry camping equipment just in case.

Equipment shops

- Day 42: Out and About, 2 Elcho Street Brae, **Peebles** EH45 8HU, tel 01721 723590
- Days 43 and 45: There are plenty of outdoor shops in the centres of **Edinburgh** and **Glasgow** (both off-route)
- Day 44: The Outdoor Store, 29 Cow Wynd, **Falkirk** FK1 1PU, tel 01324 633244
- Day 47: Green Welly Stop, **Tyndrum** FK20 8RY, tel 01838 400271
- Day 49: **Fort William** has plenty of shops, the highlight being Nevisport at the end of the High Street, PH33 6EU, tel 01397 704921

Alternative routes

The John Muir Way

This is a waymarked east–west route between Helensburgh and Dunbar, following the Forth–Clyde gap. From Linlithgow to the West Highland Way its route is either the same as or close to the line of the End to End Trail, and it provides a series of variations on the route for Day 44, if you wish to take them. While the End to End Trail mainly follows the quickest route along the canals and then an old railway line, the John Muir Way takes in more local attractions, so is slower. It does get you off the tarmac for a while though, so it is worth considering these options. Be careful when following the waymarking though, as it can be confusing due to this being a cycle route as well as a walking route, with two separate sets of variations off the towpaths.

Guidebook

- *John Muir Way* by Sandra Bardwell and Jacquetta Megarry (Rucksack Readers, 2014)

Via Milngavie

The recommended route of the End to End Trail misses out the first few kilometres of the West Highland Way. If you want to walk the whole of the WHW, then this alternative, between Kirkintilloch and Drymen via Milngavie, where the WHW starts, is recommended. It adds 7km in distance, and about half of that is additional road walking.

From Kirkintilloch, keep on the Forth and Clyde Canal towpath for another 7km towards Glasgow (Day 45 Map 1). You will pass the stables at Glasgow Bridge (now a restaurant), another bridge carrying the A807, then another at Cadder (church on right). At the next bridge (NS 605 716) leave the canal and turn right on Balmuildy Road. Follow the road round three corners (the line of the Roman Antonine Wall is now on your right) to meet the main road (A879 Balmore Road). The site of Balmuildy Fort is on your right, although there isn't much to see. Turn right, cross the River Kelvin, then turn right off the road to follow the Kelvin Walkway, a waymarked path by the river. After 1km the River Allander joins from the left – the waymarked route follows the Allander all the way to the centre of Milngavie and the start of the West Highland Way. Follow the West Highland Way to Carbeth, where the main route of the End to End Trail joins it.

Not the West Highland Way

If the weather is good enough, there is an alternative route that runs parallel with the West Highland Way, taking to the mountain tops rather than the valleys. The route follows the West Highland Way closely enough to enable you to mix and match days from each. This mountain alternative is not a waymarked route, and follows remote mountain tops where there are not always well-defined paths. It is not a route to follow if you are not experienced in such a mountain environment.

Guidebook

- *Not the West Highland Way* by Ronald Turnbull (Cicerone, 2010)

Avoiding the West Highland Way: Alternative routes from Drymen to Fort William

If you are feeling antisocial and want to avoid the West Highland Way altogether, there are alternative routes possible further to the east that will link Drymen with Fort William. There are a number of options to get from Drymen to Killin (about three days from Fort William) at the head of Loch Tay, in Perthshire, which should be possible in a couple of days if you are following the End to End Trail main schedule. The easiest option (excluding roads of course) is to follow the Rob Roy Way via Aberfoyle, Callander and Lochearnhead. This follows forestry tracks and valley paths. The route isn't waymarked, but there is a guidebook (see below) and a website (www.robroyway.com).

There are other alternative routes if you want to be more adventurous. The Menteith Hills, northeast of Loch Lomond, make a good hill route variation between Aberfoyle and Callander, or you could instead head from Aberfoyle through the forestry past Loch Drunkie and down to Brig o' Turk, then follow routes across the hills to Balquhidder and Killin. The route from Brig o' Turk to Killin is described in *Scottish Hill Tracks* (see below).

From Killin to Fort William, again there are routes described in *Scottish Hill Tracks* that should see you there in three days. The first day takes you over the Lairig Breisleich pass into Glen Lyon, then over another bealach (pass) from Innerwick to reach the head of Loch Rannoch. The second day takes the road west nearly to Rannoch station, then by Loch Eigheach and the historic Road to the Isles over to Loch Ossian and Corrour. On the third day you can follow the popular route west along Glen Nevis to Fort William. Alternatively you could miss out Fort William altogether, and head north via the Lairig Leacach and down to Spean Bridge, which is about 6km by road from Gairlochy, where you can rejoin the main route of the Trail part way through Day 50.

All these alternatives will be a lot quieter than the West Highland Way, and will give a taste of what is to come beyond Fort William.

Guidebooks

- *The Rob Roy Way* by Jacquetta Megarry (Rucksack Readers, 3rd edition, 2012)
- *Scottish Hill Tracks*, edited by DJ Bennet and CD Stone (Scottish Rights of Way and Access Society, 5th edition, 2012)

Eastern routes from the Lowlands to Inverness

There are many alternative routes possible through the Scottish Highlands, and in particular if you want to take an eastern route north from Inverness, there are more direct routes possible from the Edinburgh and Glasgow areas than via Fort William. You can cross the Forth road bridge west of Edinburgh, head north to Perth (mainly on roads), then northwest on hill tracks to Aberfeldy and on to Pitlochry. A short way up Glen Garry takes you to Blair Atholl and the start of the track up Glen Tilt and into the Cairngorms. From Linn of Dee you can continue north over the high pass of the Lairig Ghru (833m), or alternatively take a lower route into Glen Feshie to the west. You can then follow what's left of one of General Wade's roads, parallel to the A9 as far as Tomatin, then minor roads to the west of the A9 enable you to reach Inverness with minimal main-road walking. The new John o' Groats Trail will then take you the rest of the way to John o' Groats: see the start of Section 6 for more information on this.

You may also want to consider heading north from closer to Glasgow. Paths lead from Kilsyth across the Kilsyth and Gargunnock hills to Kippen on the River Forth. From there it's not far on the B822 to Callander, and from there you can take a path northeast over to Glen Artney and down a track to Comrie in Strath Earn. Tracks north of the valley can be followed east to join the A822 at the Falls of Monzie, north of Crieff. Another of General Wade's roads heads north from here to Aberfeldy, where you can join the route described above.

If you want to take any of these options, you should study your OS maps and all four of the books listed below. Christine Roche's book is an account of her journey rather than a guidebook, but the route she took was worked out with care, and sufficient detail is included to make it reasonably easy to follow.

Guidebooks

- *Land's End to John O'Groats: A Thousand Mile Walking Route* by Mike Salter (Folly Publications, 2006)
- *Follow the Spring North* by Christine Roche (Trafford Publishing, 2004)
- *Land's End to John o'Groats: A Choice of Footpaths for Walking the Length of Britain* by Andrew McCloy (Hodder & Stoughton, 1994)
- *Scottish Hill Tracks*, edited by DJ Bennet and CD Stone (Scottish Rights of Way and Access Society, 5th edition, 2012)

DAY 40

Jedburgh to Melrose
St Cuthbert's Way

Distance	29km (18 miles)
Ascent	630m

Once you've regained Dere Street from Jedburgh, today's route follows St Cuthbert's Way all day to its end at Melrose, so follow the 'St Cuthbert's cross' waymarks. This is a very good day's walk, varied and interesting, passing through some lovely countryside. (The other end of St Cuthbert's Way is on Holy Island, off the Northumberland coast, and the whole of this walk is highly recommended.)

The route back to Dere Street via **Mount Ulston** is on a quiet access road followed by a footpath, and brings you back to the Roman road on the slope down to Jed Water and the River Teviot (Day 40 Map 1). On reaching the valley bottom, if you are hungry there is the Caddy Mann tearoom/restaurant, just east of Jedfoot Bridge on the A698.

The **Waterloo Monument** on Peniel Heugh is a prominent landmark. Begun in 1815, it collapsed in 1816 before it was finished, and was finally completed in 1824. It is dedicated to 'The Duke of Wellington and the British Army'.

There's no sign of Dere Street on the ground after crossing **Jedfoot Bridge** – it was obliterated by the landscaping of the Monteviot Estate, which you are now approaching. Monteviot House, the seat of the Earls of Ancrum and the earlier Earls of Lothian, was built in 1740 and largely rebuilt in 1840.

St Cuthbert's Way follows Jed Water to its confluence with the River Teviot, then follows the river up through parkland to cross an elegant suspension footbridge (**Monteviot Bridge**). It then continues on a tortuous route through the **Monteviot House** parkland and Divet Ha' Wood, until the line of Dere Street reappears in the wood. In the grounds of Monteviot House is the Harestanes

Visitor Centre, which has a good café. The visitor centre is open 10am–5pm from April to October, with more limited opening the rest of the year.

Dere Street continues northwest across the landscape, mainly in a wide enclosure of its own, too broad to call a lane. (Turn aside to read the famous inscription on Lady Lilliard's Stone, and hope you don't meet anyone as fierce on the rest of your journey – particularly if you're English).

Gradually the line of the Roman road converges with that of the A68 trunk road (Day 40 Map 2). The path runs in trees parallel to the A68, then meets a minor road going right to Maxton. Turn right here (St Cuthbert's Way), rather than continuing on the path ahead through the woods (Dere Street).

After parting from Dere Street the route to Melrose is a lot less direct, but for the most part is worth the extra distance. At **Maxton**, St Cuthbert's Way meets the River Tweed and follows the bank as it meanders round towards Melrose.

The **Tweed** is one of the longest rivers in Britain, about 160km (100 miles), and the entire river channel is a Site of Special Scientific Interest (SSSI). This is another bit of classic riverside walking to be savoured, even if you don't have time to dawdle. The wild flowers, trees and meadows are delightful, and the river itself is a pleasure to walk beside.

St Cuthbert's Way forsakes the Tweed temporarily to walk the streets of **St Boswells**, which has shops and refreshments, but little else here to make the diversion worthwhile. If you need neither, St Boswells can be avoided by staying close to the river, which is the route shown on Day 40 Map 2.

Shortly after passing the suspension footbridge across to Dryburgh Abbey, St Cuthbert's Way leaves the Tweed and heads west-southwest up the side valley of Bowden Burn, before passing through **Newtown St Boswells** (which also has little to offer the visitor). It continues along a minor road and a pleasant track (Day 40 Map 3), before crossing Bowden Burn to the pretty little village of **Bowden**, at the foot of the **Eildon Hills**.

Here...arose to the still, blue bosom of the sky the three great Eildon Hills, with their heads crowned with heather as with an emerald diadem

Elihu Burritt, A Walk from London to John O'Groat's, 1864

All that now remains between you and the day's end at Melrose is a group of three hills, and the route crosses the col between the two highest. The climb is steady and reasonably easy, partly through woodland. If you want to belt up one of the hills, the left one is the higher (Eildon Mid Hill, 422m) and the righthand one has the Roman signal station on it (Eildon Hill North, 404m). (And before you descend to Melrose and tell people where you've been, it would be as well to take on board that Eildons is pronounced 'Eeldons' and not 'Isledons'.)

The views are very good from the col, and you'll probably be keen to get down to the fleshpots of Melrose just below, which is where St Cuthbert's Way ends.

Melrose is the second of the principal border towns on route (Jedburgh is the first), and it gets a lot of tourists, so tends to be quite expensive and accommodation often fills up. There is, however, a campsite close to the town centre. The Ship Inn has good food and is not too expensive. Burts Hotel and the Kings Arms Hotel are also worth a look for both food and accommodation. There's also a good Italian restaurant hidden up a side street.

Melrose Abbey, in the middle of the town, is where the town started, and the abbey ruins are very photogenic and atmospheric, worth visiting in the evening sunshine (if there is any). The abbey was founded in 1136, in the reign of King David I, by Cistercian monks from Rievaulx, in Yorkshire. By the end of the 14th century, English raids had pretty much destroyed it, and most of the ruins that remain are 15th and 16th century. It was abandoned in 1545. It is open all year to visitors.

DAY 41

Melrose to Traquair
The Southern Upland Way

Distance	29km (18 miles)
Ascent	990m

Today the Trail follows the Southern Upland Way all day. This long-distance path is a connoisseur's route, running from coast to coast across southern Scotland, and generally more or less at right angles to the Trail, but for this section it runs east–west and makes a convenient link in the chain of our route. It crosses high moorland, rising to 520m crossing Minch Moor, and can be exposed, so treat this stretch with respect. Like other Scottish Great Trails, the Southern Upland Way is waymarked with a thistle inside a hexagon.

The first part of the day follows the bank of the River Tweed (Day 41 Map 1), and is as good as the riverside stretch yesterday. This is followed by a rather less scenic march alongside a railway line through an industrial estate. The railway reopened in 2015, being part of the old Waverley line from Carlisle to Edinburgh.

Once you leave the railway, things improve markedly. There is another short stretch by the river, then the Southern Upland Way starts to climb over the hills in the direction of Yair Bridge. However, for some unaccountable reason it then changes its mind and drops down again into the valley to wander around Galashiels municipal park, before climbing back up Gala Hill. There is no point in this, so instead the End to End Trail takes a shorter and more pleasant route through forestry on the south side of **Gala Hill**. The two routes converge shortly afterwards and climb steadily up fields to cross a pass by **Hog Hill** at about 200m (Day 41 Map 2), dropping back down through coverts to cross the Tweed again at **Yair Bridge**.

From Yair Bridge there is a steady climb through forestry, alongside Shorthope Burn, to the high moors, culminating in the summit of the **Three Brethren** (464m), crowned by three large cairns. The views from here are extensive, with the Eildons yet again unmistakable in the panorama, as they seem to be from every angle.

Having gained the height up to the heather moors, the benefit isn't wasted – the path heads west without dropping below 400m until the end of the day. **Brown Knowe** is at 523m (Day 41 Map 3), then there is a climb, along ancient **Minchmoor Road**, up a corridor of moorland between forestry to a similar height on the shoulder of **Minch Moor**. The summit, at 567m, is an easy 10-minute climb from here, and well worth the detour for the views. (Minchmoor Road was used by Edward I of England and his army in 1296 on the way to Peebles as they rampaged through Scotland.)

From Minch Moor it is a simple descent on Minchmoor Road to **Traquair**, but there is no longer any accommodation here. Unless you are wild camping, you

The Three Brethren

will have to walk 2km along the B709 to **Innerleithen** (crossing the Tweed again). There is a 'bothy' in Traquair marked on the OS map, but this is actually a holiday self-catering cottage, not a real bothy. At Innerleithen there are shops, a campsite and hotels, including the Traquair Arms, which serves meals in the bar.

Traquair hamlet dates back to Roman times. Its main claim to fame is Traquair House, believed to be the oldest continuously inhabited house in Scotland. It was a royal hunting lodge, and parts of it are over 1000 years old – the last monarch to hunt from here was Mary Queen of Scots in 1566. It has a working 18th-century brewery, a maze, a priest's room with a hidden staircase, and is open to visitors on summer afternoons. The famous Bear Gates into the estate haven't been opened for hundreds of years, the reason for this depending on which guidebook you read.

DAY 42

Traquair to West Linton
Peebles and White Meldon

Distance	36km (22 miles)
Ascent	1060m

Yesterday, on the descent to Traquair, the Southern Upland Way was joined by the Cross Borders Drove Road. This is an 84km (52-mile) route for walkers, cyclists and horseriders running from Little Vantage through West Linton and Traquair to Hawick, following (more or less) a route historically used to drive cattle south to market. It follows hills rather than valleys, and is waymarked with the outline of what looks to be a young bull. For this edition, the main End to End Trail route has been rerouted to follow the Cross Borders Drove Road from Traquair to Little Vantage.

There is an alternative option for the first part of the route as far as Peebles, as there is now a tarmac cycle path along the old railway line by the River Tweed from Innerleithen to Peebles. This provides an easier but less adventurous alternative, particularly attractive if you are staying overnight in Innerleithen rather than Traquair. Both routes are shown on the strip maps.

The main route heads southwest along the main road out of Traquair (Day 42 Map 1), then west on a quiet minor road. You then climb up onto the moorland on an old track that is a bit vague at first, but soon becomes clear. It climbs up and round the head of the Kirk Burn valley and Cardrona Forest to reach the summit of **Kirkhope Law**, at 537m. The views from here are great. The drove road now descends to skirt the top of **Kailzie Hill** and then drops down along the **Craig Head** ridge to **Peebles**, which is a magnificent stretch of walking between old droving walls.

Alternative route to Peebles

The alternative route to Peebles starts with a 2km road walk to **Innerleithen** (Day 41 Map 3). As you enter the town, the cycle path is signed on your left, although you can actually take an alternative path along the river if you wish – turn off the B719 as soon as you've crossed the River Tweed, and join the railway a bit further along. The railway closed in 1962, and a new footbridge across the Tweed had to be built before it could be reopened for walkers and cyclists. The route is straightforward as far as the village of **Cardrona** (Day 42 Map 2). Follow the signs through the village to a roundabout, where there is a café, and then the cycle path resumes at the far side of the roundabout and takes you to **Peebles**. On the way you will notice the ruins of 16th-century Horsbrugh Castle above you on the right, and quite possibly a lot of sand martins, nesting in burrows in the sandy banks of the river.

The River Tweed flows through the centre of Peebles, and the whole town has something of an old-fashioned air. It is the last of the three border towns the Trail passes through, and bigger and busier than Jedburgh and Melrose. It is another ancient town of character, having been given its charter by King David II in 1367, and there are shops, banks and all services here, including a campsite beside the Trail on the way out of town.

Once out of the town, the Trail follows a good track over the shoulder of **Hamilton Hill** (Day 42 Map 3) and down to cross Kidston Burn. The next section is a bit scrappy, zigzagging along farm tracks and a bit of road, until you enter a forestry plantation and climb over a ridge. Good forestry tracks take you nearly to the edge of the plantation (Day 42 Map 4), then you must look out for a small path on the right that takes you out of the trees by Flemington Burn, in a quiet hill valley. Almost immediately you turn right along Fingland Burn, on a good path. You cross a pass in a narrow band of forestry on a very wet path, then at last you can descend to the valley of Lyne Water. The A701 is reached near **Romannobridge**, 5km by road from West Linton. The Trail avoids the first half of this road walking along paths and tracks to the east, but if you are in a hurry take the road.

West Linton is an attractive village that markets itself for walkers, holding walking festivals, and the church has some intricate woodcarvings that are worth seeing. Bed and breakfast accommodation is limited, so it is a good idea to book ahead. I can recommend The Meadows B&B at 4 Robinsland Drive EH46 7JD, tel 01968 661798. There are shops and a post office, and also a hotel (the Gordon Arms), which has accommodation and serves evening meals.

DAY 43

West Linton to Linlithgow
The Pentland Hills and the Union Canal

Distance	44km (27 miles)
Ascent	750m

Today the Trail leaves the Border hills and enters the industrial lowlands of the Forth and Clyde valleys. This is a long day, but most of it is particularly easy walking. The first part of the day crosses the Pentland Hills on an ancient droving route, over a pass going by the evocative name of Cauldstane Slap. The Pentlands are the last range of Border hills to cross, and the last moorland until Loch Lomond. You are still on the waymarked Cross Borders Drove Road, as far as its end at Little Vantage where you cross the A70.

Once you've descended Corston Hill, what follows is two days of walking through the Scottish industrial heartland, but it's surprising how rural most of this is. So much of the old heavy industry has gone, and although evidence of it usually remains, it is overgrown with regenerated woodland and grass. The Trail follows stream, river, canals and a disused railway track. The roads, factories and housing estates are there, but you will see only a little of them from the route.

After the initial steep lane climbing out of West Linton, the gradient is easy, following Agricola's **Roman road**, the Western Way invasion route (now a tarmac farm access road), for a short distance (Day 43 Map 1). The route up to **Baddinsgill** is varied and interesting, on a track above the upper Lyne Water valley. Beyond Baddinsgill the moors become wild and bleak. The summit of **Cauldstane Slap** (435m) is a pretty godforsaken place, and marks your exit from the Borders region and entry into West Lothian.

The descent to cross the Water of Leith and the A70 is less interesting than the ascent (Day 43 Map 2), but Edinburgh and Arthur's Seat come into view for the first time, to the right on the way down, in compensation. The best views of the day, however, are from the top of **Corston Hill**, the last hill on the Trail for a long way.

It may be only 348m high, but **Corston Hill** is right on the edge of high ground, so the views are a lot more extensive than its height suggests. Ahead is the Almond valley, full of past and present industry. Look right and the valley meets the Firth of Forth, the river meeting the sea between the Forth bridges and Edinburgh, all set out below you. Also, closer at hand, are the first of the pink piles of the shale bings, slag heaps from the defunct 19th-century industry that extracted oil from the shale strata.

The descent from Corston Hill follows a line of old boundary stones to join a quiet access road to the valley and the A71 (Day 43 Map 3). Across the road there used to be a shale quarry, now the start of the Almondell and Calderwood Country Park, and what used to be desolation is now quiet and pretty woodland along the Linhouse Water valley. There is even a snack van in the car park by the A71 most days of the week. The path down to Mid Calder winds through woodland and clearings, and feels as if it is miles from civilisation, although in fact it is only 300 metres from a housing estate at one point. The stream and path descend to go under the B7015 at Mid Calder.

Mid Calder has a couple of pubs, a handful of shops, a post office and an Indian restaurant, and there is bed and breakfast accommodation in nearby East Calder if you need to stop overnight around here.

Continuing on the path down the river, Linhouse Water soon joins the River Almond, and good paths follow the wooded valley down towards the Firth of Forth. This part of the country park is a popular local recreation area, and rightly so – once you're past Mid Calder sewage works, the rest of it is really very pretty.

A footbridge takes you across to the lefthand bank, then under a disused railway (Camp Viaduct: if you are planning an overnight stop at Uphall, there is a cycle track along this old railway line that takes you straight there). Just after the viaduct an artificial channel branches off the river. This feeds the Union Canal, nearly 5km downstream, and the Trail follows it all the way, apart from a few stretches where it is culverted. The feeder crosses the river, accompanied by a footbridge, and the Trail continues down the righthand bank of the river, then gradually rises above it. There is a campsite just above you on the right along here (see Day 43 Map 3): Linwater Caravan Park (tel 0131 333 3326 www.linwater.co.uk). When Lin's Mill Aqueduct comes into view, carrying the canal high across the valley, it becomes clear why the feeder channel left the river so far back. At Lin's Mill the Trail joins the **Union Canal** to follow its tarmac towpath.

The **Union Canal** was opened in 1822, joining Edinburgh to the Forth and Clyde Canal to give a fast new communications and trading link between Glasgow and Edinburgh. It started to become redundant soon afterwards, however, as the first railway link between the two cities opened in the early 1840s, and a proposed link to the Firth of Forth at the Edinburgh end was never built. The canal was closed to navigation in 1933 and not reopened until 2001. This reopening was funded by the National Lottery Millennium Fund, and included building a new bridge for the M8 motorway south of Broxburn.

The initial crossing of **Lin's Mill Aqueduct** is spectacular – the views of the valley are lovely, although anyone with no head for heights may have other things to think about. After that the day becomes a bit more humdrum, as walking along the canal can't touch the River Almond for quality walking. The towpath through the housing estates of **Broxburn** is the low point of the day (Day 43 Map 4), and possibly slightly more risky than Cross Fell in poor weather. If you are walking alone and concerned about your personal security, taking a road route between Bridges 23 and 27 is a safer option.

Shale bings and the Union Canal, Niddry

Broxburn has shops and banks, but like many of the villages and towns on the Trail today and tomorrow, it has seen better days. The decline in industry in recent decades is nowhere more obvious than around here. If you are after bed and breakfast accommodation, you can either head west for 2km along the A899 to the Oatridge Hotel in Uphall (that's Up-hall, not Uffall), or push on 3km to Winchburgh.

Things look up from **Bridge 27**, where you leave the Broxburn estates for the shale bings ('bing' is a corruption of 'ben', as in Ben Nevis). This must have been grim when the shale was still being worked (for oil), but has now become pleasantly rural, with the added bonus of plenty of industrial archaeological remains.

Just before Winchburgh, **Niddry Castle** is to the right of the canal, on the other side of the railway. It's old, built in 1490, but not very big, and not open to the public. The canal passes through the middle of **Winchburgh**, but you hardly see anything of the village as the canal is in a deep cutting.

The canal continues in its own wooded world for another 5 or 6km, then surfaces into more open country after **Philpstoun** for the last stretch to Linlithgow. This area isn't industrial – the nearby surroundings are pleasant farmland, and the distant views of the Ochil Hills to the north are good.

Linlithgow town centre has its attractions, but also some horrendous post-war additions that should never have been given planning approval. There are pubs, shops, banks, and a range of accommodation, including a campsite just across the M9 (take the A706 Bo'ness road).

Linlithgow Castle

Linlithgow is an ancient and royal town. King David I built a house here in the 12th century, and subsequent kings built the royal palace, in which Mary Queen of Scots was born. It wasn't until the union of the monarchies in 1603 that its importance started to decline. The palace was gutted by fire in 1746, but is still an impressive ruin, set on the shore of Linlithgow Loch in the heart of the town, and well worth visiting.

Linlithgow, whose every stone spoke volumes of the storied past
Robert and John Naylor, From John o' Groat's to Land's End, 1916

DAY 44

Linlithgow to Kilsyth
Canal towpaths

Distance	33km (20 miles)
Ascent	290m

This is the easiest walking of the whole Trail, being on tarmac towpaths nearly all day. There aren't even any locks until the end of the Union Canal, so it's absolutely level all the way to Falkirk.

The first stretch is a continuation of the rural environment on the way into Linlithgow yesterday, and includes another spectacular aqueduct, this time over the River Avon, which is where you also leave West Lothian Unitary Authority (UA) for Falkirk UA (Day 44 Map 1). It gets a bit more urban through **Polmont**, and the young offenders' institution on the other bank isn't the most photogenic sight of the day.

Shortly before Falkirk, there is the option to leave the canal and take the John Muir Way to visit Callendar House and its grounds. Callendar House dates from the 14th century, and is well worth a visit if you have the time. The John Muir Way then crosses the canal to go through Bantaskine Estate Park, before heading for the Falkirk Wheel to rejoin the main End to End Trail route.

Towards the end of the Union Canal, after Bridge 61 on the approach to Falkirk, it disappears into a 631-metre **tunnel**, dug purely to appease the wealthy industrialist William Forbes, who objected to the canal being visible from his estate. The tunnel is the first high point of the day, being old and atmospheric. Water sprays out of cracks in the roof, boats nose their way past you, and at the far end the light gradually turns from a pinprick to an archway out into the daylight again. The lights in the tunnel give little illumination, but there is a railing to stop you from falling into the water (carrots the night before may be a sensible precaution).

If you want to visit **Falkirk**, leave the canal after the tunnel. Falkirk is the biggest town on the whole Trail (if you don't count Bristol) and has all services, but it's not worth visiting as a tourist.

Just west of Falkirk (Day 44 Map 2), the Union Canal joins the **Forth and Clyde Canal** at the **Falkirk Wheel** (where there is a visitor centre and café).

The two **canals** used to be joined via a stair of 11 locks at Camelon, down to a canal basin by the Union Inn – the remains of them are still visible. In 2001 the canals were both reopened, and a new connection between them was completed in 2002, 1.5km further west from the original locks. Now, instead of a flight of locks, a unique new boatlift called the **Falkirk Wheel** carries boats a height of 25m up and down from one canal to the other (thanks to National Lottery funding).

Falkirk Tunnel on the Union Canal

Note that occasionally, usually in February and November, the pedestrian tunnel under the railway from the locks on the Union Canal leading to the Wheel may be shut for maintenance. If you are unlucky and find it locked, cross the locks to follow a path and track, and cross the railway on the B816 instead.

It is possible to join the Forth and Clyde towpath at the Falkirk Wheel, as there is a swing footbridge here to take you across the canal (open 6am to 8pm). The main Trail route doesn't go this way though: instead, it visits the Roman wall.

Just west of the Falkirk Wheel, around Rough Castle, are the best-preserved sections of the Roman **Antonine Wall**. This was a turf-built wall across the Forth–Clyde gap. For a couple of decades from its construction in AD142–3, it formed a northern barrier of the Roman Empire, before the legions fell back again to Hadrian's Wall.

The Trail heads west through woods from the Falkirk Wheel to the **Rough Castle** site, descending to rejoin the Trail on the Forth and Clyde towpath at **Bonnybridge**.

Daniel Defoe was already pushing the idea of a canal in the 1720s, and the **Forth and Clyde Canal** eventually opened in 1790, linking the coasts via the two rivers after which it was named. This meant cheap bulk transport of goods and people across the country for the first time, without the long detour round the north coast. As with most canals, traffic declined with the development of railways, and it eventually closed altogether in 1963, reopening along with the Union Canal in 2001, almost 40 years later.

The **Forth and Clyde Canal** climbs on its way west, passing under the very busy M80 motorway. (The Castlecary House Hotel – accommodation – is just off-route to the left near the M80 bridge.)

At **Wyndford Lock** you join the highest stretch of the canal, at a mere 48m above sea level. The next stretch is long and straight, and the canal is wider than normal – this was Dullatur Bog, now given a more upmarket name as **Dullatur Marsh Nature Reserve**. Building the canal across here was a major feat, as the embankment it is on had to be built up 16m before it settled properly into the bog. At some point along here, the canal crosses the main watershed between the River Carron and the River Kelvin, and just to prove the point, Kelvinhead is just to the right, claiming to be the source of the River Kelvin, which flows west into the Clyde.

If you are staying at Kilsyth, turn right either at **Craigmarloch Bridge** (where there is no longer a drawbridge) or at **Auchinstarry Bridge** (where there is no longer a swingbridge).

Kilsyth itself is a rundown and desolate town, deserted by the coalmining industry that built it. There are a handful of bed and breakfasts in and around the town, and food is available at a hotel (the Coachman) on the A803 (NS 716 781). Alternatively, you can push on to **Twechar**, where there is bed and breakfast available at the farm.

DAY 45

Kilsyth to Drymen
Below the Campsie Fells

Distance	38km (24 miles)
Ascent	450m

The view to the right for most of the day is dominated by the Campsie Fells – a steep escarpment rises to the north to a high plateau of moorland hills about 500m high. The Trail follows the valleys, however, pushing on to join the West Highland Way at Carbeth towards the end of the day. (The strip maps guide you to Carbeth, then you will need your West Highland Way guidebook for the stretch to Drymen.)

The Forth and Clyde Canal passes into East Dunbartonshire just after Auchinstarry Bridge, and the Trail follows it past **Twechar** to **Kirkintilloch**, the next town down the valley (Day 45 Map 1). The canal and the River Kelvin continue down to Glasgow and the Clyde, but the Trail avoids the city by heading northwest from Kirkintilloch (leaving the canal at Hillhead Bridge), up the side valley of Glazert Water, along the toes of the Campsies. The Trail follows the **Strathkelvin Railway Path** – a disused railway that ran from Kirkintilloch to a junction at Gartness, near Drymen – all the way to Strathblane. Overnight options in the area are limited: there is at least one bed and breakfast in Kirkintilloch, there are hotels in **Milton of Campsie** and **Lennoxtown** (Day 45 Map 2), and an upmarket bed and breakfast in Campsie Glen.

Dunglass, approaching Strathblane

The old railway bed has been turned into an official cycle path with a tarmac surface, and it makes a change from the canal towpath. But despite the mainly rural situation, and the views of the Campsies, walking the railway is, as usual, inferior to walking a canal. Without water the wildlife is less varied, and the more distant views are more often obscured by trees.

Approaching Strathblane and just before passing **Dunglass** – a small but striking rocky hill that is probably a volcanic plug – you leave East Dunbartonshire for Stirlingshire. **Strathblane** has a hotel, the Kirkhouse Inn, which makes a good lunch stop.

You have to leave the line of the old railway at Strathblane, then John Muir Way signs take you the next 3km along paths and tracks, mainly through trees.

The Trail joins the West Highland Way at **Carbeth** by the B821, so from here until the end of this section you will need your West Highland Way guidebook. (This part of the West Highland Way is just an overture really. It is pleasant, but the WHW doesn't really get into its stride until tomorrow.)

Suddenly you will find yourself part of a crowd, after probably having had little company but a few dog walkers since you left Peebles on Day 42. The West Highland Way is very popular, and attracts a lot of people who have never walked a long-distance path before. You are joining these tyros as they complete the first 8km of their walk, and some will already be tired and sore and wondering what they've let themselves in for. You, on the other hand, have been walking every day for weeks. This is where you may well realise for the first time just how fit you have become – even when you think you are taking it easy, you will probably be overtaking people all day every day, so give them a bit of encouragement on your way past!

At **Gartness**, close to the site of the old railway junction, the West Highland Way leaves the old railway track and takes to minor roads to climb over the last hill and down into **Drymen** (which rhymes with 'women' not 'piemen').

Drymen is a pretty village, providing well for the many walkers that pass through. There are shops, accommodation and pubs, and a bunkhouse in a converted church hall (tel 07734 394315 www.kipinthekirk.co.uk). The campsite is at Easter Drumquhassie Farm, which is on the route nearly 3km before Drymen, which is a bit inconvenient if you want to eat, drink or shop in Drymen.

There used to be an alternative rough camping site a bit further on in the forestry, at NS 453 918, but this area has now been felled so you'll have to leave the forestry before you can find anywhere to pitch. There are no facilities here, but if all you want is somewhere to put up your tent after an evening in Drymen, it is ideal, and recommended for a good head start for what is a very long day tomorrow (see introduction to Day 46). Note that there are by-laws restricting wild camping in many places near Loch Lomond and part of the way to Crianlarich to the north of the loch, with hefty fines possible if you get it wrong. As long as you camp between leaving the forestry and reaching Conic Hill, you are outside the restricted area: for full details go to www.lochlomond-trossachs.org.

DAY 46

Drymen to Inverarnan
Loch Lomond

Distance	46km (29 miles)
Ascent	1600m

This is indeed a very long day. From Drymen, the West Highland Way climbs up into the Garadhban forestry (look out for a first glimpse of Loch Lomond as you near the far edge of the plantations), over Conic Hill and up the eastern shore of Loch Lomond, through Rowardennan and Inversnaid, to Inverarnan. On the map it appears to be easy, flat walking after the initial climb over Conic Hill, but this is misleading. The northern half of the lochside path is hard work in many places, being rocky and slow to follow. The advantage of an early start from the rough camping site in the forestry outside Drymen is a strong argument against bed and breakfast in Drymen itself at the end of Day 45, unless you choose to split Day 46 into two, with an overnight stop at Rowardennan.

From Drymen, the West Highland Way soon enters **Garadhban Forest**, much of which has now been felled. On leaving the forestry, you are on moorland, crossing the Burn of Mar, and climbing over **Conic Hill** (361m), an aptly named, steep-sided and rocky hill (the path doesn't go to the summit, and you probably haven't got time to either). The views of Loch Lomond are stunning. The path descends through another plantation, then via a big car park to **Balmaha** on the shore of Loch Lomond.

If you are unlucky, you will have to miss out on the excellent Conic Hill excursion and follow the B837 from Milton of Buchanan to Balmaha, as each spring the high-level route is closed to the public for four weeks at lambing time.

Balmaha is a haunt of day-trippers and best left behind quickly. The views across Loch Lomond are tremendous the whole way to Rowardennan, but for

Loch Lomond

Rowardennan youth hostel, Loch Lomond

much of it the route is either too close to the road, or follows tortuous diversions to avoid it. **Rowardennan** has a hotel, a youth hostel and bed and breakfasts. There is also a wild camping area, for which you must buy a permit beforehand – see www.lochlomond-trossachs.org. You can book online, up to eight weeks in advance, and spaces are limited.

After Rowardennan things improve, as there is no public road. Either follow an untarred private road for the next few kilometres, which is fast and easy to walk, or take the alternative route at a lower level, which is harder going, requiring scrambling through boulders in places. The lower route has now been reinstated as an official West Highland Way alternative route. It leaves the road about 300 metres beyond Ptarmigan Lodge.

The vehicle track ends just after the two routes join again, and the path onwards is slow and rocky in places. At **Inversnaid** a footbridge crosses Arklet Water next to waterfalls, and you are at the Inversnaid Hotel, serviced by a road that follows Arklet Water down from Loch Arklet. The hotel allows walkers into the bar, and is the only place for refreshments between Rowardennan and Inverarnan, above the head of Loch Lomond.

From Inversnaid the route continues along the loch shore, or close to it, and is delightful if you are not in a hurry. It is hard work and slow, though, clambering through rocky areas on steep slopes.

Two kilometres beyond Inversnaid is the **three-quarter mark** of the Trail, a message you may find hard to get across to anyone 'down south' who thinks you are already in the far north.

Opposite the island of I Vow, the path leaves Stirlingshire and enters Argyll and Bute (which for some reason claims the slopes on the east side of the valley for a short stretch as far as Inverarnan). Towards the end of the loch the difficulties ease, and from here the route is both easy and delightful, across rough pasture and through woodland. It re-enters Stirlingshire just before reaching Beinglas Farm and the bridge across the River Falloch, which gives access to the Drovers Inn at **Inverarnan**.

Beinglas Farm has a campsite and some wooden chalets for those carrying no tent. There is a small shop and a bar/restaurant as well, and the breakfasts are recommended. Evening meals can also be obtained at the nearby Drovers Inn, an inn of (Scottish) character that is definitely worth a visit. There is limited bed and breakfast accommodation at Inverarnan, so plan ahead if you don't intend to camp.

DAY 47

Inverarnan to Bridge of Orchy
Glen Falloch and Strath Fillan

Distance	30km (18 miles)
Ascent	770m

This is the second of four full days of being sociable on the West Highland Way. Now there is no longer Loch Lomond to separate the walkers from the rest of the traffic, the fact that the West Highland Way, the Fort William railway and the busy A82 all share the same valleys has much more impact today. Having said that, the day is surprisingly good, although there is nothing particularly challenging about it. The walking is easy, on good paths and tracks, the gradients are easy and route-finding is also easy.

Initially the path from Beinglas Farm follows the bank of the River Falloch, a pleasant riverside stroll with the road and the railway on the opposite bank. Soon you cross all three to join General Wade's 18th-century military road, built to pacify and control the Highlanders, and now a well-built cart track climbing above the A82.

In the first half of the 18th century there was a lot of Scottish resistance to the rule of the House of Hanover and the London parliament. In 1724, King George I sent **General George Wade** to the Highlands to assess the situation there and report back on what should be done about it. One of the key messages of Wade's report was the need for an improved network of forts, and connecting roads along which troops could be moved more effectively.

Wade went on to plan a network of **roads and forts**, supervising the building of the first 250 miles (400km) of road himself before handing over construction to William Caulfeild in about 1740. These roads were well built and often underlie today's roads in the Highlands. Where the modern road takes a different line, the old road often makes a good route for walkers, and the West Highland Way follows Wade's roads in a number of places. Caulfeild's roads are also often referred to as 'General Wade's roads'.

At the head of Glen Falloch the A82 crosses a low pass, and the main Scottish watershed, over to Crianlarich and Strath Fillan. The old military road also crosses the watershed, on a slightly higher line, then instead of continuing to follow the old road straight down into Strath Fillan, the West Highland Way leaves to follow paths through forestry along the side of the valley, eventually descending to Strath Fillan valley bottom further upstream. The path then wanders easily up to **Tyndrum**, avoiding the road, with a railway to each side.

Tyndrum itself is a place to pass through as quickly as possible, dominated as it is by a large coach-party hotel, and what is best described as a motorway service station gone astray, although it does include an outdoor shop. There is, however, plenty of accommodation in Tyndrum, including a bunkhouse and camping. Unless you have already sorted out somewhere to stay at Bridge of Orchy, Tyndrum is your best bet for an overnight stop.

From Tyndrum the railways each go their own way, west to Oban and north to Fort William, and the main road divides as well, the A85 heading west to Oban and the A82 north. The West Highland Way heads north too, back on General Wade's road. Together with the A82 and the railway, it climbs back into Argyll and Bute, crossing to the west side of the main watershed again at a pass at 315m, then descending a side valley into **Glen Orchy**. (Be thankful that the old road sticks closer to the quiet railway than to the busy A82.)

Bridge of Orchy is just a hamlet, with no facilities other than one hotel, one bed and breakfast, some camping pods and a railway station. Both the Bridge of Orchy Hotel and the station used to have bunkhouses, but both have closed, resulting in a serious shortage of affordable beds. If you can't get into the B&B or a camping pod, and you don't want to camp wild (by the bridge over the River Orchy), then cut the day short at Tyndrum. If you want a camping pod, they sleep two, and if you're on your own you'll have to pay for the whole pod.

DAY 48

Bridge of Orchy to Kinlochleven
Black Mount and the Devil's Staircase

Distance	34km (21 miles)
Ascent	960m

This is the third day on the West Highland Way, and the route continues to follow the old military road all day, apart from a stretch on a parallel drove road from Victoria Bridge to just before Bà Bridge.

From Bridge of Orchy, the A82 and the railway head north and pass to the east of Loch Tulla, before separating to take different routes across the huge, undulating peat bog of Rannoch Moor. Here, the A82 heads north and the railway northwest, and they don't meet again until Fort William. General Wade's road takes a third route, round the western side of Loch Tulla, then along the western margin of Rannoch Moor.

From Bridge of Orchy, General Wade strangely took his road over the northern shoulder of **Ben Inverveigh**, rather than following the more natural lower route taken by the modern minor road to the Inveroran Hotel and Victoria Bridge, at the western tip of **Loch Tulla**. The climb through forestry is easy enough, though, as it was engineered with reasonable gradients. Botanists should keep their eyes open for chickweed wintergreen along here.

From **Victoria Bridge** there is an excellent cart track (the drove road) heading north across remote moorland. For the first few kilometres this doesn't actually follow the line of Wade's road, which follows a parallel line up the hill to the left. Along here the main watershed is crossed again, imperceptibly, and at the same time the Trail enters the old county of Inverness-shire, and the modern

Highland region of Scotland. From here to John o' Groats, the Trail is entirely in the Highland region, which covers a huge area of largely unpopulated country. The drove road and the military road merge before the crossing of the River Bà at **Bà Bridge**, a beautiful and remote spot.

The old road crosses a pass (and the watershed one more time) and descends towards the A82 again, joining the road to the **White Corries** ski lift on the approach to the A82.

If the road wasn't here this would be as remote a location as any in the Highlands – a big, marshy area at the head of Glen Etive, many miles from anything other than mountains, heather and bog. In fact it has been an important route to the sea to the west for hundreds of years, and the **Kingshouse Hotel** has been here for at least 250 of those years. The Naylor brothers passed through on their walk south in 1871:

> We walked on to a place which had figured on mileposts for a long distance named 'Kingshouse'. Here we expected to find a village, but as far as we could see there was only one fairly large house there, and that an inn.

There's little more than that here now, and it's still a small oasis in a big wet desert. Apart from hotel rooms, there is also a bunkhouse here. Camping is permitted near the hotel, but there are no camping facilities other than those of the hotel bar.

The modern road to the sea from the Kingshouse goes west and down Glen Coe, and these days the route north crosses Loch Leven on the Ballachulish Bridge (there used to be a ferry). Being a military man, and short on high-tech bridge technology, General Wade instead made pretty much a beeline from the Kingshouse for the head of Loch Leven – Kinlochleven, which is now a small town. The route he took, and which the Trail follows, climbs steeply up the side of the valley a little west of the Kingshouse, a route known as the **Devil's Staircase**. It climbs to a sharp col at a height of 548m, the highest point on the West Highland Way. From here, without warning, the mountains to the north are suddenly all laid out ahead, the biggest of them being the biggest in the country – Ben Nevis. This is one of the best moments of the Trail, provided the weather is good enough to see the view.

From the col at the top of the Devil's Staircase the old road descends as it traverses the hillside, joining a vehicle track servicing Blackwater Reservoir, and eventually reaching **Kinlochleven**. There is plenty of accommodation, including campsites and a bunkhouse, and an indoor ice-climbing centre is housed in the old aluminium works.

Kinlochleven is not a particularly pretty town, having been built around an aluminium plant, for which Blackwater Reservoir was built to generate electricity. The plant has closed, and any passing tourist trade vanished when the Ballachulish Bridge across Loch Leven replaced the ferry in 1975. The town has reinvented itself to attract the tourist trade in its own right, aided by the West Highland Way.

DAY 49

Kinlochleven to Fort William
The Mamores and Glen Nevis

Distance	24km (15 miles)
Ascent	710m

This is the last day on the West Highland Way, and is a relatively short and easy one.

The line of Wade's road climbs up out of Kinlochleven and follows a deep trench between Beinn na Caillich on the left and the Munros of the Mamores on the right, crossing a minor watershed on the way. The valley bends north and heads for Fort William, and so does the old road, but it soon becomes a tarred motor

Ben Nevis, from the approach to Glen Nevis

Descent into Glen Nevis

road. Rather than follow this, the West Highland Way crosses northeast through forestry into the next valley, **Glen Nevis**, to the foot of Ben Nevis. In clear weather the views of the Ben on the descent are tremendous – it's a big mountain!

The route follows forestry tracks down the glen, and there are two alternative West Highland Way routes down to join the valley road, although it is actually best to take neither, unless you are heading for the youth hostel. Where the second West Highland Way alternative turns right off the forestry road (NN 118 727), keep straight on, and this will take you to the valley road further north, avoiding unnecessary walking on this busy road.

When you do join the Glen Nevis road, follow it down to the roundabout (formerly the end of the West Highland Way). Keep left here and follow the main road into **Fort William** (the A82 again).

Fort William has supermarkets, outdoor shops, a tourist information centre and loads of accommodation. The nearest campsite is in Glen Nevis near the youth hostel. The most impressive of the outdoor shops is Nevisport at the end of the High Street. The town will probably be full of visitors, many of them walkers and climbers. Fort William is the most important town serving the needs of visitors to the mountains, and before beginning Section 6 you will want to take as much advantage of it as you can.

Day 40 Map 1: Jedburgh to Hiltonshill

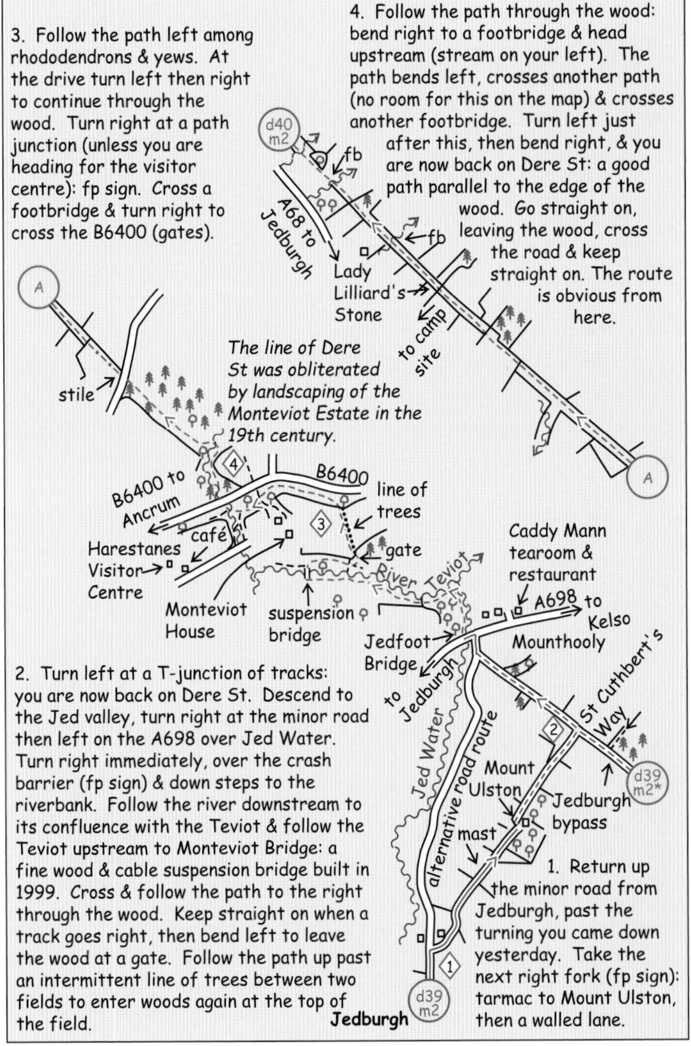

4. Follow the path through the wood: bend right to a footbridge & head upstream (stream on your left). The path bends left, crosses another path (no room for this on the map) & crosses another footbridge. Turn left just after this, then bend right, & you are now back on Dere St: a good path parallel to the edge of the wood. Go straight on, leaving the wood, cross the road & keep straight on. The route is obvious from here.

3. Follow the path left among rhododendrons & yews. At the drive turn left then right to continue through the wood. Turn right at a path junction (unless you are heading for the visitor centre): fp sign. Cross a footbridge & turn right to cross the B6400 (gates).

d40 m2
fb
A68 to Jedburgh
fb
Lady Lilliard's Stone
to camp site
A
stile

The line of Dere St was obliterated by landscaping of the Monteviot Estate in the 19th century.

A
4
B6400 to Ancrum
B6400
line of trees
café
3
gate
Harestanes Visitor Centre
River Teviot
Caddy Mann tearoom & restaurant
Monteviot House
suspension bridge
A698 to Kelso
Jedfoot Bridge
Mounthooly
to Jedburgh
St Cuthbert's Way
Jed Water
alternative road route
2
Mount Ulston
Jedburgh bypass
d39 m2*
mast
1
d39 m2
Jedburgh

2. Turn left at a T-junction of tracks: you are now back on Dere St. Descend to the Jed valley, turn right at the minor road then left on the A698 over Jed Water. Turn right immediately, over the crash barrier (fp sign) & down steps to the riverbank. Follow the river downstream to its confluence with the Teviot & follow the Teviot upstream to Monteviot Bridge: a fine wood & cable suspension bridge built in 1999. Cross & follow the path to the right through the wood. Keep straight on when a track goes right, then bend left to leave the wood at a gate. Follow the path up past an intermittent line of trees between two fields to enter woods again at the top of the field.

1. Return up the minor road from Jedburgh, past the turning you came down yesterday. Take the next right fork (fp sign): tarmac to Mount Ulston, then a walled lane.

Day 40 Map 2: Hiltonshill to Newtown St Boswells

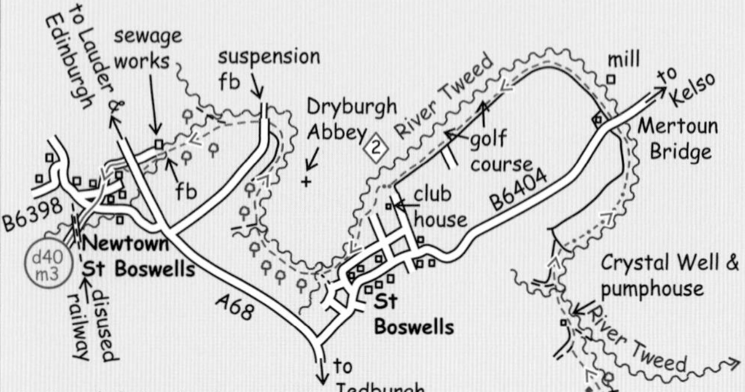

2. Keep left by the fence until you reach a tarmac access road leading left up to the clubhouse. St Cuthbert's Way turns left up this for a pretty pointless excursion through the streets of St Boswells: unless you need a shop it's best to keep straight on here, above a golf green, then drop down near to the river (not up the steps). You will then find a good path up into the woods along the river. Follow this, keeping right at every opportunity, & St Cuthbert's Way will rejoin you the other side of the town. Follow the Tweed upstream, past the ruins of Dryburgh Abbey (on the opposite side) to reach an elegant suspension footbridge. Don't cross: turn left on the road then immediately right & steeply up (footpath sign). The path soon descends towards a stream: keep left here to follow the stream up through trees, across a footbridge & under the bypass to join an access road for a sewage works. Follow the road round bends between houses. Go straight across a crossroads (or right for the pub), down the short road opposite. Cross the main road & leave Newtown St Boswells on the road opposite, over a stream & under a disused railway.

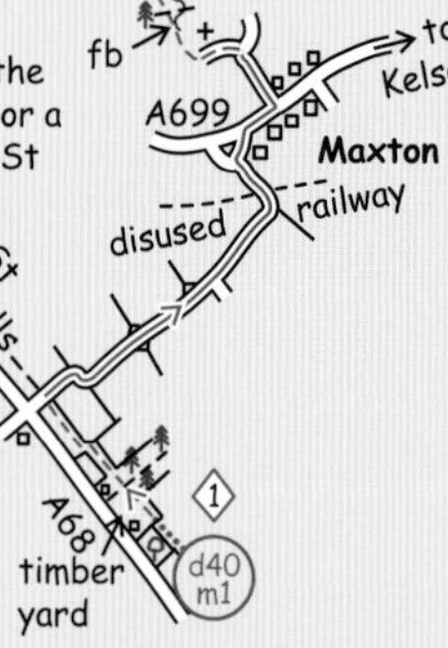

1. After a timber yard keep right at a fork & cross a track to a gate, then follow a fenced path. Go left at the field corner then right & continue to a minor road: turn right along it to Maxton, bearing right to reach the A699. Turn right then left, signed to the church. When the road bends right go straight on (path), keeping left of all buildings & passing the old church. The path leads into a wood, down steps, over a footbridge & across a track. At a junction of paths by a wall turn right, which takes you down more steps to the River Tweed. Follow the river up to Mertoun Bridge & beyond it, bending left to reach a golf course.

Day 40 Map 3: Newtown St Boswells to Melrose

5. Climb to the Eildon ridge. There are a lot of paths to choose from: St Cuthbert's Way signs show the way. Ignore the first forks left & right, keep right at the next fork, then almost immediately turn left on a small path to reach a saddle on the ridge. Cross the ridge path & descend to the right, contouring round more than you would expect from the map. When the main path goes steeply down left follow it down to the intake hedge & follow that right to a gate. Descend steeply on a fenced path to the B6359 & turn right into Melrose.

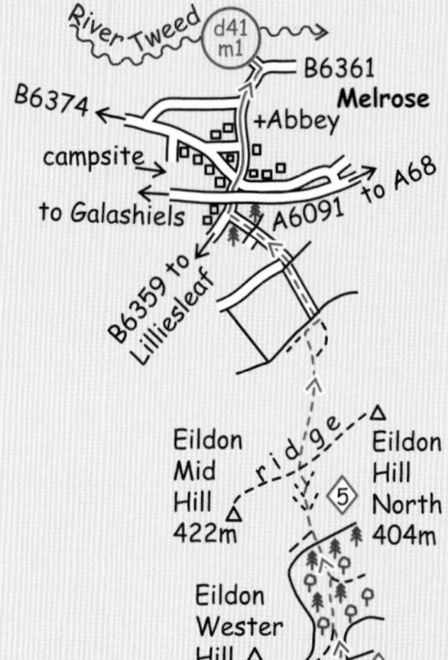

4. Field edges are visible on either side: level with the top of the lefthand field turn right at a path junction to follow the righthand field edge. Near the end of this field the path climbs left to meet a vehicle track: turn right on this. Climb to a track junction, go left, & climb to leave the trees at a gate in the fence.

3. Keep to the left when you get the option on the way up the field. At the end bend left then fork right to a gate into the trees. At the end of this small plantation follow a field edge then cross a track & go up steps into a larger wood. Turn right to follow a path parallel to the track (not up the long flight of steps). The path eventually bends left & starts to climb, crossing an old track.

2. Cross the burn on a footbridge & continue upstream. The path diverges from the stream & becomes a lane. Ignore a track to the right, then keep right at the fork just afterwards. At the road turn right up to Bowden & turn right on the B6398, then first left. The road bends left immediately: go straight ahead through a play area to a gate & up the narrow field ahead.

1. Follow the road until it turns sharp left at a farm. Go straight on here along a good track (gates), with a fence on the left & Bowden Burn below the trees to the right. The path goes through a gate then forks soon afterwards: take the smaller path descending right to the stream (not through the gateway ahead).

Day 41 Map 1: Melrose to Hog Hill

1. Leave Melrose along Abbey St, then go left on Chain Bridge Rd when the main road turns sharp right (see previous map). This leads to the Chain Bridge, where the Southern Upland Way joins you (marked with a thistle in a hexagon). Don't cross: continue on the tarmac path then up steps & along a path above the river. At a residential road go right then right again (gate) to the riverside meadows. Follow the path to the B6374.

2. Cross the B6374 & take the tarmac path opposite (not the road to the nursery). Go right at a road then ahead at the T-junction on another tarmac path: a disused railway between factories, then by the newly reopened railway. Cross a bridge over the Tweed, climb to the road & turn left. Cross the stream then turn left into a wood (gate) before the road on the left. When the path leaves the trees follow either edge of the field beyond & go through a gap at the end of the field. Go left of a play area & car park, & under the bypass.

3. Continue on a clear path that rises & falls between road & river. Pass a red footbridge over the old railway to the right then descend to the river again, until the path meets the road.

4. Cross the road: a footpath opposite cuts the corner to a road. Turn right, cross the railway bridge & climb to the A7. Go right then left up steps to reach the old A7. Turn right, pass a drive, then go left up a walled track between gardens.

5. A gate leads to a field: keep ahead to field corner (gate) then turn right & keep climbing, wall on your right. After the next gate turn left & follow a track through trees over Gala Hill: keep left at every option.

6. Turn right at the road then left at the first path by a wall. A stile leads to a field: follow its right edge up to a Scots pine & veer left up the ridge to a stile into a wood. On the far side follow edges of two fields & in the next climb past a pile of stones to a post then a cairn on the skyline. Cross a stile & descend a dip to join a wall.

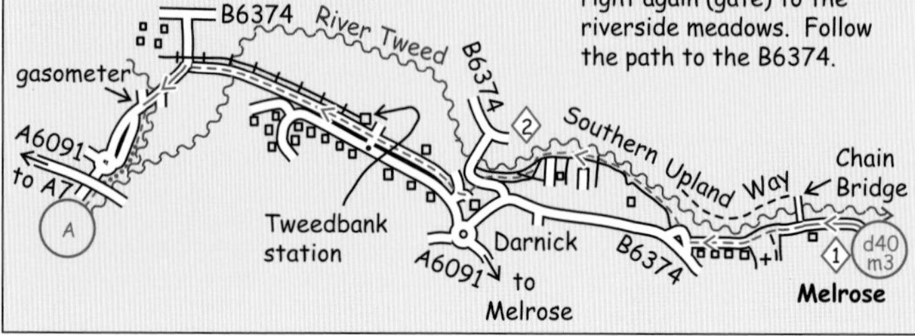

Day 41 Map 2: Hog Hill to Brown Knowe

The hills are clothed in a mixture of forestry plantations & heather moorland.

4. Turn left with the fence & forestry edge, & follow a good path past the end of the plantation. This is an old drove road & is generally level & dry underfoot. Gates & stiles show the way, passing right of the summit of Broomy Law, then between pines & another summit on the right, unnamed on OS maps. At the end of the pines is another gate & stile: continue, now with a wall on your right, climbing towards Brown Knowe.

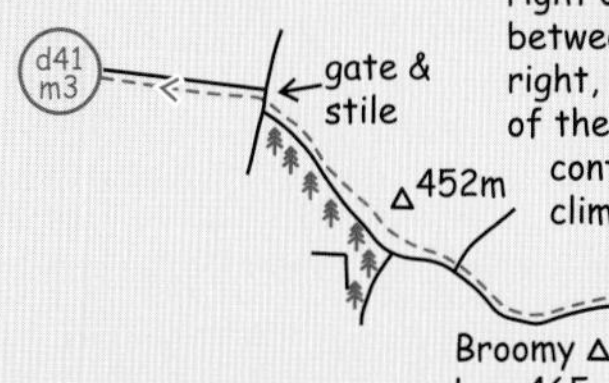

3. Follow the Yair road, pass a house & drive on the right, then keep left again at the next house & bend right uphill behind it. Turn sharp left (fp signs) into the trees on a wide path. This climbs all the time, reaching the edge of the trees & following a wall then a fence. Eventually it bends left into the regenerating woodland in the valley bottom. Continue up the valley: the stream is below to the left & a forestry track runs parallel beyond it. The path bends left & crosses both stream & track to climb steeply. Cross a second track, continuing to climb steeply, until you reach the top edge of the trees, with fence & moor on your left. Don't use the gate onto the moor: keep between fence & trees on a good path. Climb to the three cairns on the summit (the Three Brethren) & enjoy the views. This is the start of a very good high-level section of the Trail: spectacular & easy (in reasonable weather).

2. At the bottom edge of the wood go left down a track between fields to cross a road & enter another wood on a fenced track. Continue down towards the A707, forking right to avoid the farmyard. Turn left on the A707, bear right over Yair Bridge, then turn right: 'Private road to Yair').

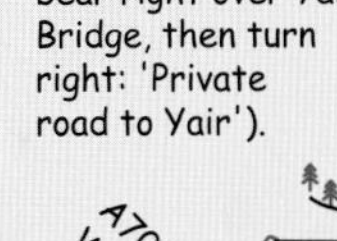

1. Continue down on a good track with Minch Moor looming ahead. Pass between two woods, head steeply down to cross a stream & straight on to join a track coming in from the right. Enter a wood (gate & stile) & continue on an unmade road.

Day 41 Map 3: Brown Knowe to Traquair & Innerleithen

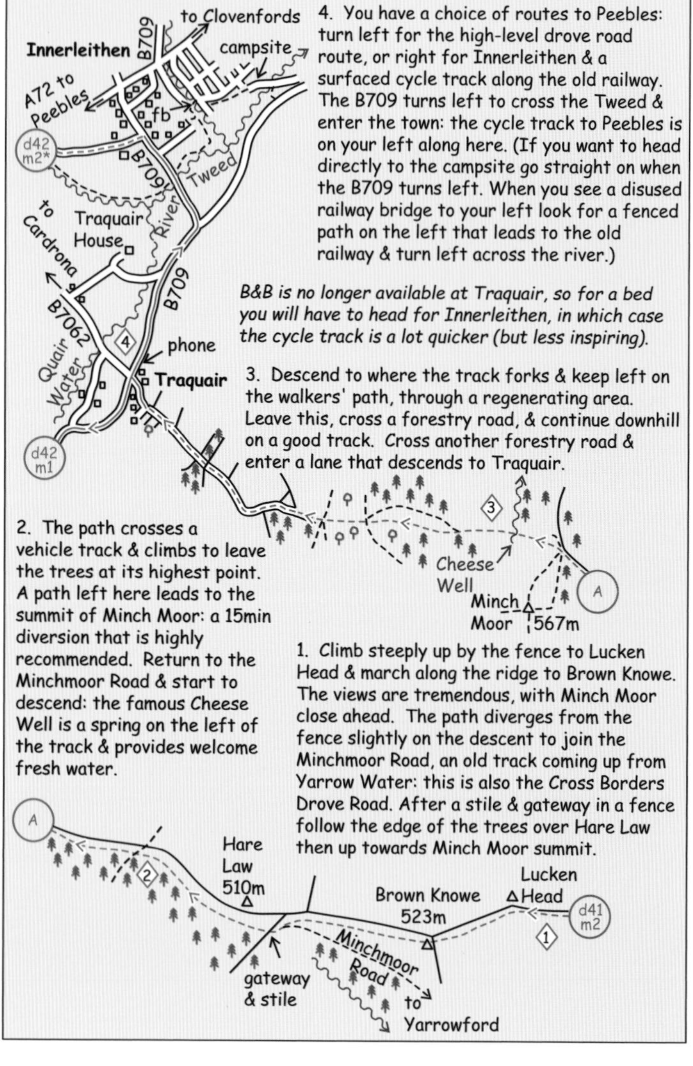

4. You have a choice of routes to Peebles: turn left for the high-level drove road route, or right for Innerleithen & a surfaced cycle track along the old railway. The B709 turns left to cross the Tweed & enter the town: the cycle track to Peebles is on your left along here. (If you want to head directly to the campsite go straight on when the B709 turns left. When you see a disused railway bridge to your left look for a fenced path on the left that leads to the old railway & turn left across the river.)

B&B is no longer available at Traquair, so for a bed you will have to head for Innerleithen, in which case the cycle track is a lot quicker (but less inspiring).

3. Descend to where the track forks & keep left on the walkers' path, through a regenerating area. Leave this, cross a forestry road, & continue downhill on a good track. Cross another forestry road & enter a lane that descends to Traquair.

2. The path crosses a vehicle track & climbs to leave the trees at its highest point. A path left here leads to the summit of Minch Moor: a 15min diversion that is highly recommended. Return to the Minchmoor Road & start to descend: the famous Cheese Well is a spring on the left of the track & provides welcome fresh water.

1. Climb steeply up by the fence to Lucken Head & march along the ridge to Brown Knowe. The views are tremendous, with Minch Moor close ahead. The path diverges from the fence slightly on the descent to join the Minchmoor Road, an old track coming up from Yarrow Water: this is also the Cross Borders Drove Road. After a stile & gateway in a fence follow the edge of the trees over Hare Law then up towards Minch Moor summit.

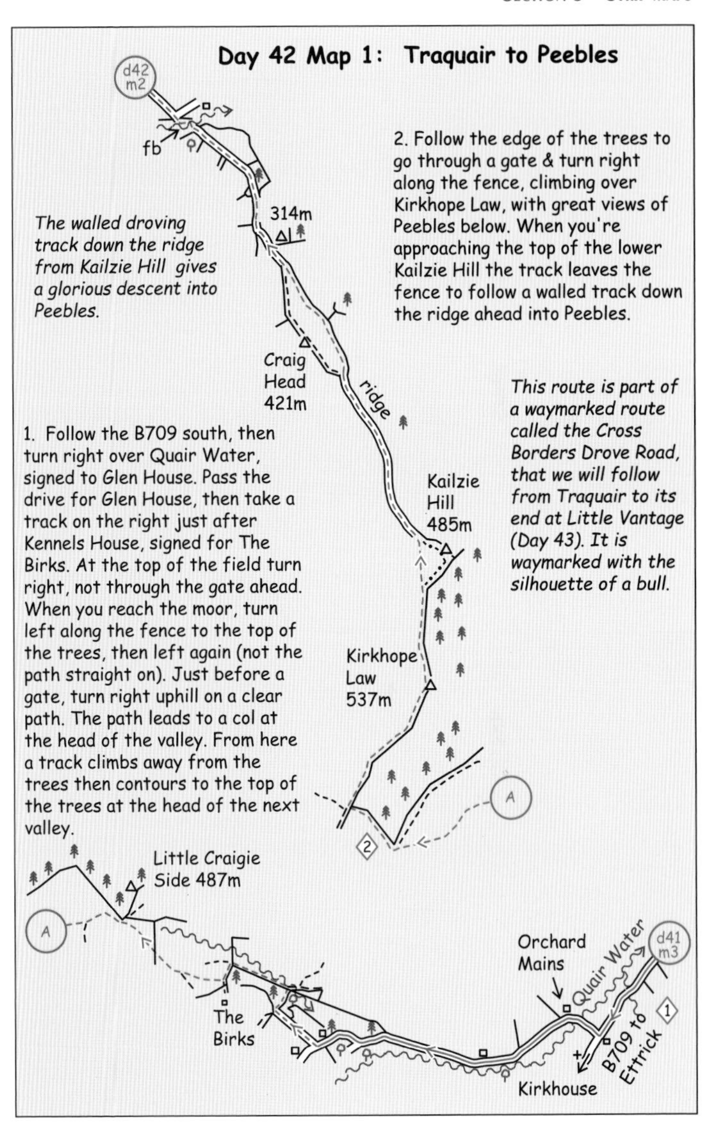
Day 42 Map 1: Traquair to Peebles
d42 m2
fb
314m
The walled droving track down the ridge from Kailzie Hill gives a glorious descent into Peebles.
2. Follow the edge of the trees to go through a gate & turn right along the fence, climbing over Kirkhope Law, with great views of Peebles below. When you're approaching the top of the lower Kailzie Hill the track leaves the fence to follow a walled track down the ridge ahead into Peebles.
Craig Head 421m
ridge
This route is part of a waymarked route called the Cross Borders Drove Road, that we will follow from Traquair to its end at Little Vantage (Day 43). It is waymarked with the silhouette of a bull.
1. Follow the B709 south, then turn right over Quair Water, signed to Glen House. Pass the drive for Glen House, then take a track on the right just after Kennels House, signed for The Birks. At the top of the field turn right, not through the gate ahead. When you reach the moor, turn left along the fence to the top of the trees, then left again (not the path straight on). Just before a gate, turn right uphill on a clear path. The path leads to a col at the head of the valley. From here a track climbs away from the trees then contours to the top of the trees at the head of the next valley.
Kailzie Hill 485m
Kirkhope Law 537m
A
2
Little Craigie Side 487m
A
The Birks
Orchard Mains
Quair Water
d41 m3
1
B709 to Ettrick
Kirkhouse

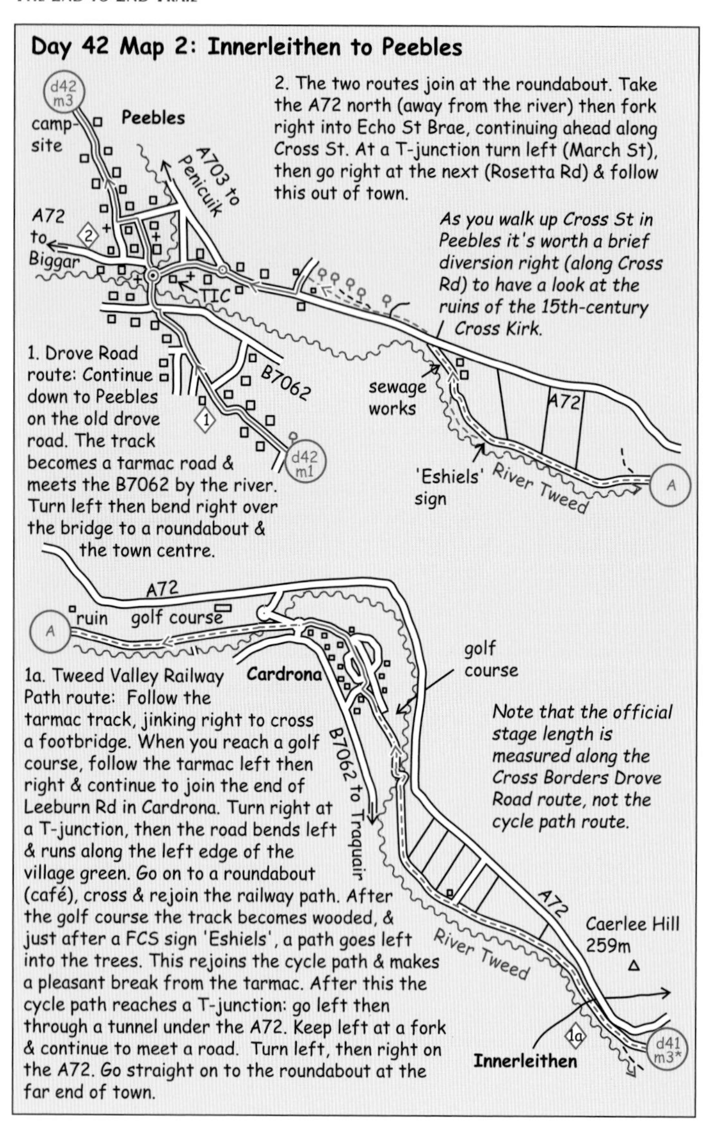

Day 42 Map 2: Innerleithen to Peebles
d42 m3
camp-site
Peebles
A703 to Penicuik
2. The two routes join at the roundabout. Take the A72 north (away from the river) then fork right into Echo St Brae, continuing ahead along Cross St. At a T-junction turn left (March St), then go right at the next (Rosetta Rd) & follow this out of town.
A72 to Biggar
2
TIC
As you walk up Cross St in Peebles it's worth a brief diversion right (along Cross Rd) to have a look at the ruins of the 15th-century Cross Kirk.
1. Drove Road route: Continue down to Peebles on the old drove road. The track becomes a tarmac road & meets the B7062 by the river. Turn left then bend right over the bridge to a roundabout & the town centre.
B7062
1
d42 m1
sewage works
A72
'Eshiels' sign
River Tweed
A
A72
A
ruin
golf course
Cardrona
golf course
1a. Tweed Valley Railway Path route: Follow the tarmac track, jinking right to cross a footbridge. When you reach a golf course, follow the tarmac left then right & continue to join the end of Leeburn Rd in Cardrona. Turn right at a T-junction, then the road bends left & runs along the left edge of the village green. Go on to a roundabout (café), cross & rejoin the railway path. After the golf course the track becomes wooded, & just after a FCS sign 'Eshiels', a path goes left into the trees. This rejoins the cycle path & makes a pleasant break from the tarmac. After this the cycle path reaches a T-junction: go left then through a tunnel under the A72. Keep left at a fork & continue to meet a road. Turn left, then right on the A72. Go straight on to the roundabout at the far end of town.
B7062 to Traquair
Note that the official stage length is measured along the Cross Borders Drove Road route, not the cycle path route.
A72
River Tweed
Caerlee Hill 259m
1a
Innerleithen
d41 m3*

Day 42 Map 3: Peebles to Courhope

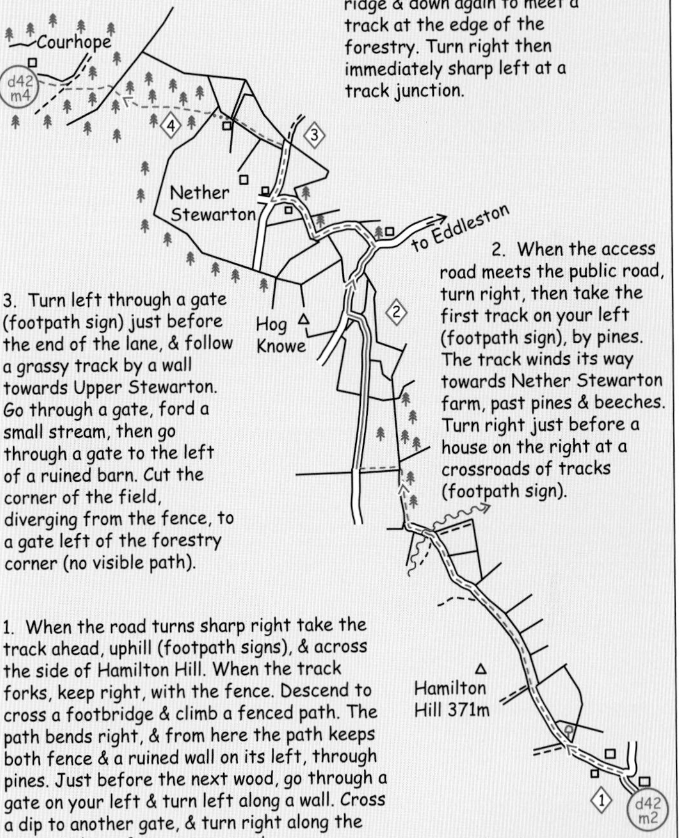

1. When the road turns sharp right take the track ahead, uphill (footpath signs), & across the side of Hamilton Hill. When the track forks, keep right, with the fence. Descend to cross a footbridge & climb a fenced path. The path bends right, & from here the path keeps both fence & a ruined wall on its left, through pines. Just before the next wood, go through a gate on your left & turn left along a wall. Cross a dip to another gate, & turn right along the Upper Kidston farm access road.

2. When the access road meets the public road, turn right, then take the first track on your left (footpath sign), by pines. The track winds its way towards Nether Stewarton farm, past pines & beeches. Turn right just before a house on the right at a crossroads of tracks (footpath sign).

3. Turn left through a gate (footpath sign) just before the end of the lane, & follow a grassy track by a wall towards Upper Stewarton. Go through a gate, ford a small stream, then go through a gate to the left of a ruined barn. Cut the corner of the field, diverging from the fence, to a gate left of the forestry corner (no visible path).

4. Follow a good path up through the trees, over the ridge & down again to meet a track at the edge of the forestry. Turn right then immediately sharp left at a track junction.

Courhope

d42 m4

Nether Stewarton

to Eddleston

Hog Knowe

Hamilton Hill 371m

d42 m2

The views are great from the track over Hamilton Hill.

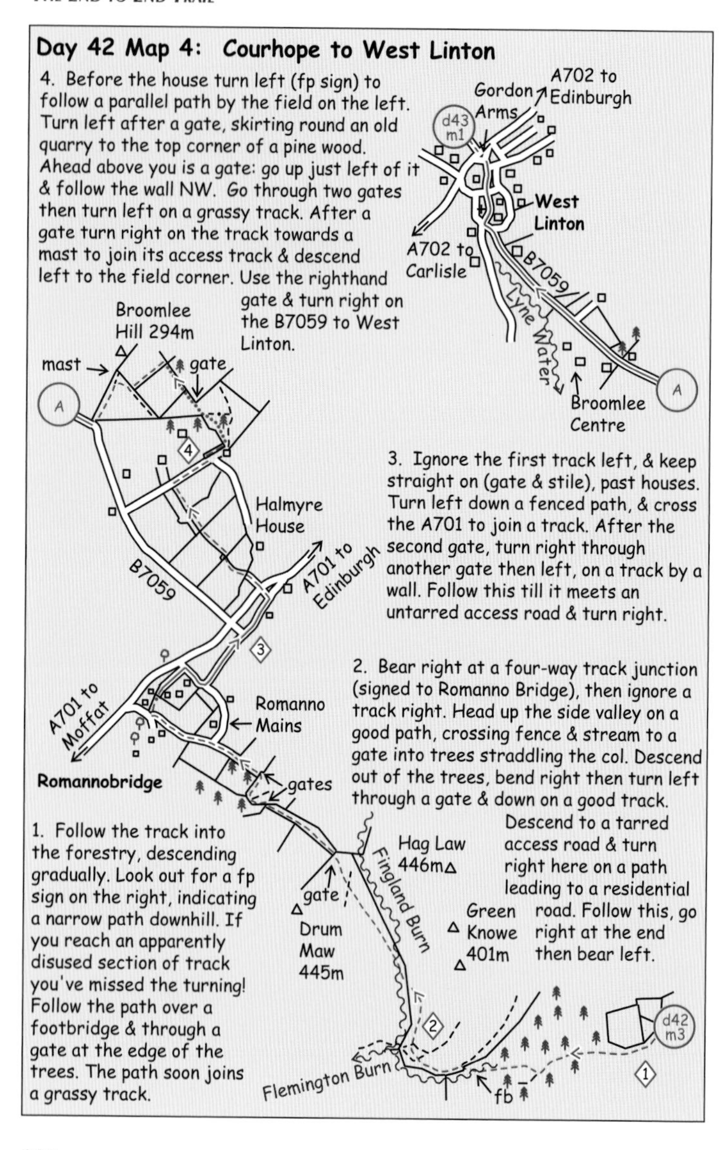
Day 42 Map 4: Courhope to West Linton
4. Before the house turn left (fp sign) to follow a parallel path by the field on the left. Turn left after a gate, skirting round an old quarry to the top corner of a pine wood. Ahead above you is a gate: go up just left of it & follow the wall NW. Go through two gates then turn left on a grassy track. After a gate turn right on the track towards a mast to join its access track & descend left to the field corner. Use the righthand gate & turn right on the B7059 to West Linton.
A702 to Edinburgh
Gordon Arms
d43 m1
West Linton
A702 to Carlisle
B7059
Lyne Water
Broomlee Centre
A
Broomlee Hill 294m
mast
gate
A
4
Halmyre House
B7059
A701 to Edinburgh
3. Ignore the first track left, & keep straight on (gate & stile), past houses. Turn left down a fenced path, & cross the A701 to join a track. After the second gate, turn right through another gate then left, on a track by a wall. Follow this till it meets an untarred access road & turn right.
3
A701 to Moffat
Romanno Mains
Romannobridge
gates
2. Bear right at a four-way track junction (signed to Romanno Bridge), then ignore a track right. Head up the side valley on a good path, crossing fence & stream to a gate into trees straddling the col. Descend out of the trees, bend right then turn left through a gate & down on a good track. Descend to a tarred access road & turn right here on a path leading to a residential road. Follow this, go right at the end then bear left.
1. Follow the track into the forestry, descending gradually. Look out for a fp sign on the right, indicating a narrow path downhill. If you reach an apparently disused section of track you've missed the turning! Follow the path over a footbridge & through a gate at the edge of the trees. The path soon joins a grassy track.
Hag Law 446m
Fingland Burn
gate
Drum Maw 445m
Green Knowe 401m
2
d42 m3
Flemington Burn
fb
1

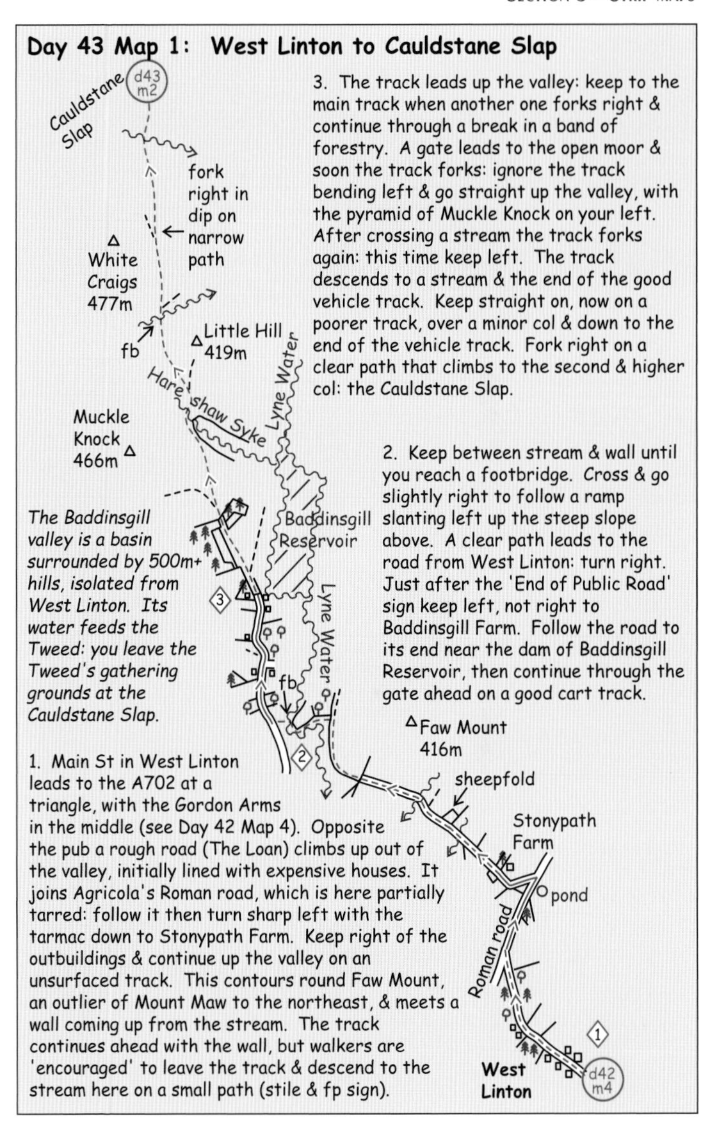
Day 43 Map 1: West Linton to Cauldstane Slap
d43 m2
Cauldstane Slap
fork right in dip on narrow path
White Craigs 477m
fb
Little Hill 419m
Lyne Water
Hareshaw Syke
Muckle Knock 466m
Baddinsgill Reservoir
3
Lyne Water
fb
2
Faw Mount 416m
sheepfold
Stonypath Farm
pond
Roman road
1
West Linton
d42 m4
3. The track leads up the valley: keep to the main track when another one forks right & continue through a break in a band of forestry. A gate leads to the open moor & soon the track forks: ignore the track bending left & go straight up the valley, with the pyramid of Muckle Knock on your left. After crossing a stream the track forks again: this time keep left. The track descends to a stream & the end of the good vehicle track. Keep straight on, now on a poorer track, over a minor col & down to the end of the vehicle track. Fork right on a clear path that climbs to the second & higher col: the Cauldstane Slap.
2. Keep between stream & wall until you reach a footbridge. Cross & go slightly right to follow a ramp slanting left up the steep slope above. A clear path leads to the road from West Linton: turn right. Just after the 'End of Public Road' sign keep left, not right to Baddinsgill Farm. Follow the road to its end near the dam of Baddinsgill Reservoir, then continue through the gate ahead on a good cart track.
The Baddinsgill valley is a basin surrounded by 500m+ hills, isolated from West Linton. Its water feeds the Tweed: you leave the Tweed's gathering grounds at the Cauldstane Slap.
1. Main St in West Linton leads to the A702 at a triangle, with the Gordon Arms in the middle (see Day 42 Map 4). Opposite the pub a rough road (The Loan) climbs up out of the valley, initially lined with expensive houses. It joins Agricola's Roman road, which is here partially tarred: follow it then turn sharp left with the tarmac down to Stonypath Farm. Keep right of the outbuildings & continue up the valley on an unsurfaced track. This contours round Faw Mount, an outlier of Mount Maw to the northeast, & meets a wall coming up from the stream. The track continues ahead with the wall, but walkers are 'encouraged' to leave the track & descend to the stream here on a small path (stile & fp sign).

Day 43 Map 2: Cauldstane Slap to Selm Muir

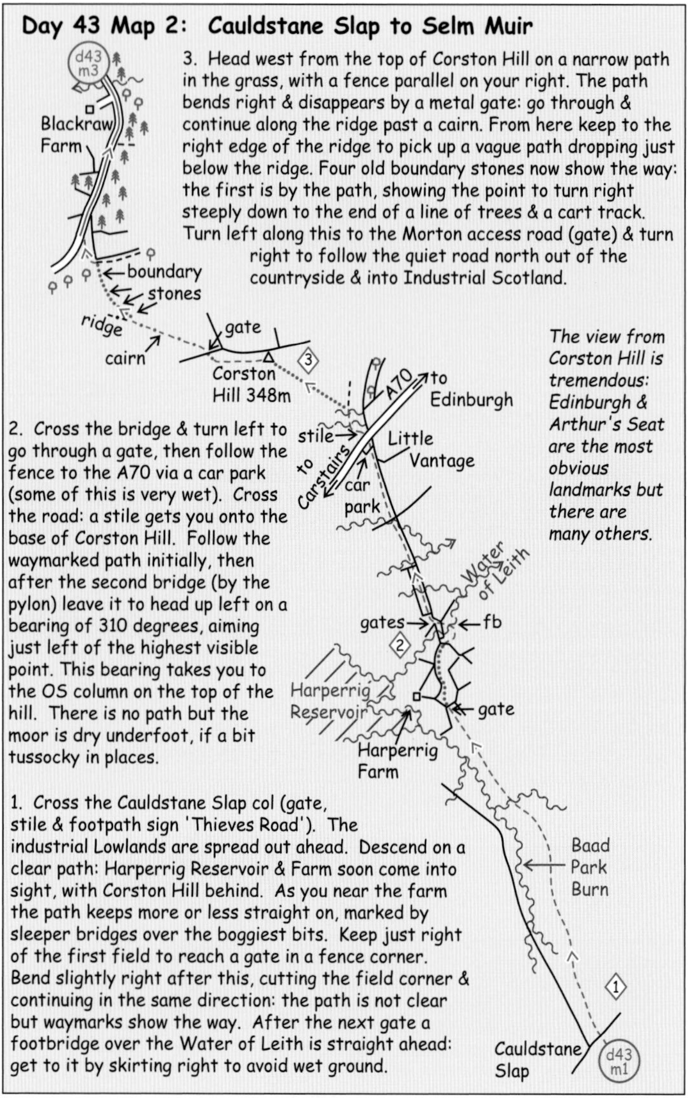

3. Head west from the top of Corston Hill on a narrow path in the grass, with a fence parallel on your right. The path bends right & disappears by a metal gate: go through & continue along the ridge past a cairn. From here keep to the right edge of the ridge to pick up a vague path dropping just below the ridge. Four old boundary stones now show the way: the first is by the path, showing the point to turn right steeply down to the end of a line of trees & a cart track. Turn left along this to the Morton access road (gate) & turn right to follow the quiet road north out of the countryside & into Industrial Scotland.

The view from Corston Hill is tremendous: Edinburgh & Arthur's Seat are the most obvious landmarks but there are many others.

2. Cross the bridge & turn left to go through a gate, then follow the fence to the A70 via a car park (some of this is very wet). Cross the road: a stile gets you onto the base of Corston Hill. Follow the waymarked path initially, then after the second bridge (by the pylon) leave it to head up left on a bearing of 310 degrees, aiming just left of the highest visible point. This bearing takes you to the OS column on the top of the hill. There is no path but the moor is dry underfoot, if a bit tussocky in places.

1. Cross the Cauldstane Slap col (gate, stile & footpath sign 'Thieves Road'). The industrial Lowlands are spread out ahead. Descend on a clear path: Harperrig Reservoir & Farm soon come into sight, with Corston Hill behind. As you near the farm the path keeps more or less straight on, marked by sleeper bridges over the boggiest bits. Keep just right of the first field to reach a gate in a fence corner. Bend slightly right after this, cutting the field corner & continuing in the same direction: the path is not clear but waymarks show the way. After the next gate a footbridge over the Water of Leith is straight ahead: get to it by skirting right to avoid wet ground.

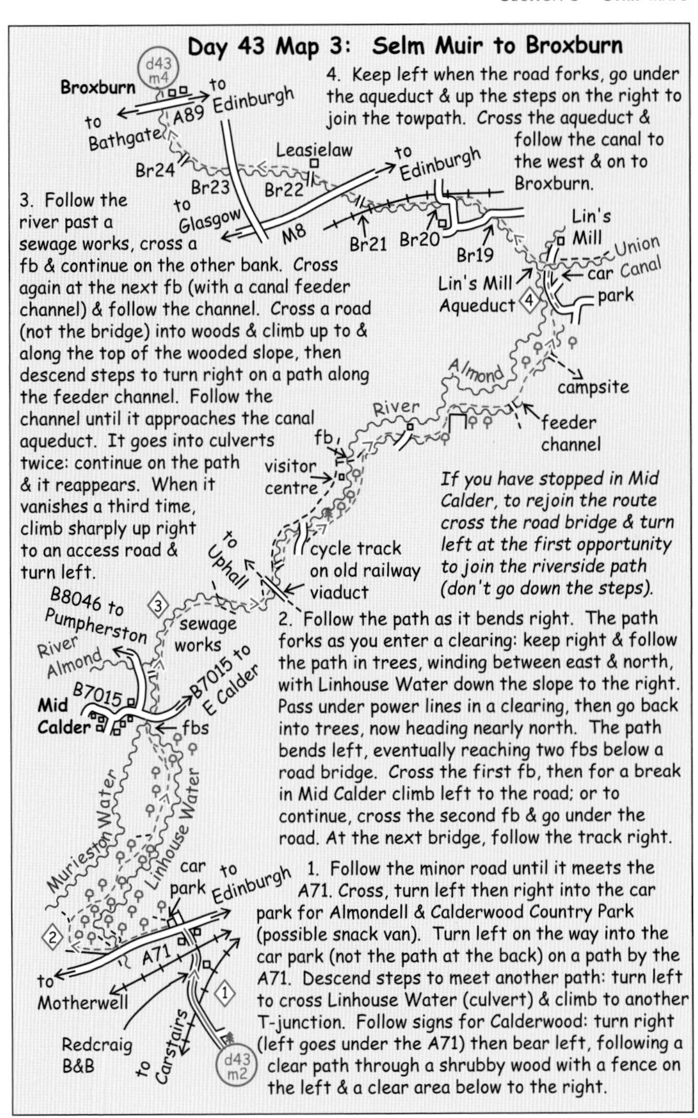
Day 43 Map 3: Selm Muir to Broxburn
4. Keep left when the road forks, go under the aqueduct & up the steps on the right to join the towpath. Cross the aqueduct & follow the canal to the west & on to Broxburn.
3. Follow the river past a sewage works, cross a fb & continue on the other bank. Cross again at the next fb (with a canal feeder channel) & follow the channel. Cross a road (not the bridge) into woods & climb up to & along the top of the wooded slope, then descend steps to turn right on a path along the feeder channel. Follow the channel until it approaches the canal aqueduct. It goes into culverts twice: continue on the path & it reappears. When it vanishes a third time, climb sharply up right to an access road & turn left.
If you have stopped in Mid Calder, to rejoin the route cross the road bridge & turn left at the first opportunity to join the riverside path (don't go down the steps).
2. Follow the path as it bends right. The path forks as you enter a clearing: keep right & follow the path in trees, winding between east & north, with Linhouse Water down the slope to the right. Pass under power lines in a clearing, then go back into trees, now heading nearly north. The path bends left, eventually reaching two fbs below a road bridge. Cross the first fb, then for a break in Mid Calder climb left to the road; or to continue, cross the second fb & go under the road. At the next bridge, follow the track right.
1. Follow the minor road until it meets the A71. Cross, turn left then right into the car park for Almondell & Calderwood Country Park (possible snack van). Turn left on the way into the car park (not the path at the back) on a path by the A71. Descend steps to meet another path: turn left to cross Linhouse Water (culvert) & climb to another T-junction. Follow signs for Calderwood: turn right (left goes under the A71) then bear left, following a clear path through a shrubby wood with a fence on the left & a clear area below to the right.
d43 m4
Broxburn
to Edinburgh
to Bathgate
A89
Leasielaw
to Edinburgh
Br24
Br23
Br22
to Glasgow
M8
Br21
Br20
Br19
Lin's Mill
Union Canal
car park
Lin's Mill Aqueduct
4
River Almond
campsite
feeder channel
fb
visitor centre
cycle track on old railway viaduct
to Uphall
3
B8046 to Pumpherston
sewage works
River Almond
B7015
B7015 to E Calder
Mid Calder
fbs
Murieston Water
Linhouse Water
car park
to Edinburgh
2
A71
to Motherwell
1
Redcraig B&B
to Carstairs
d43 m2

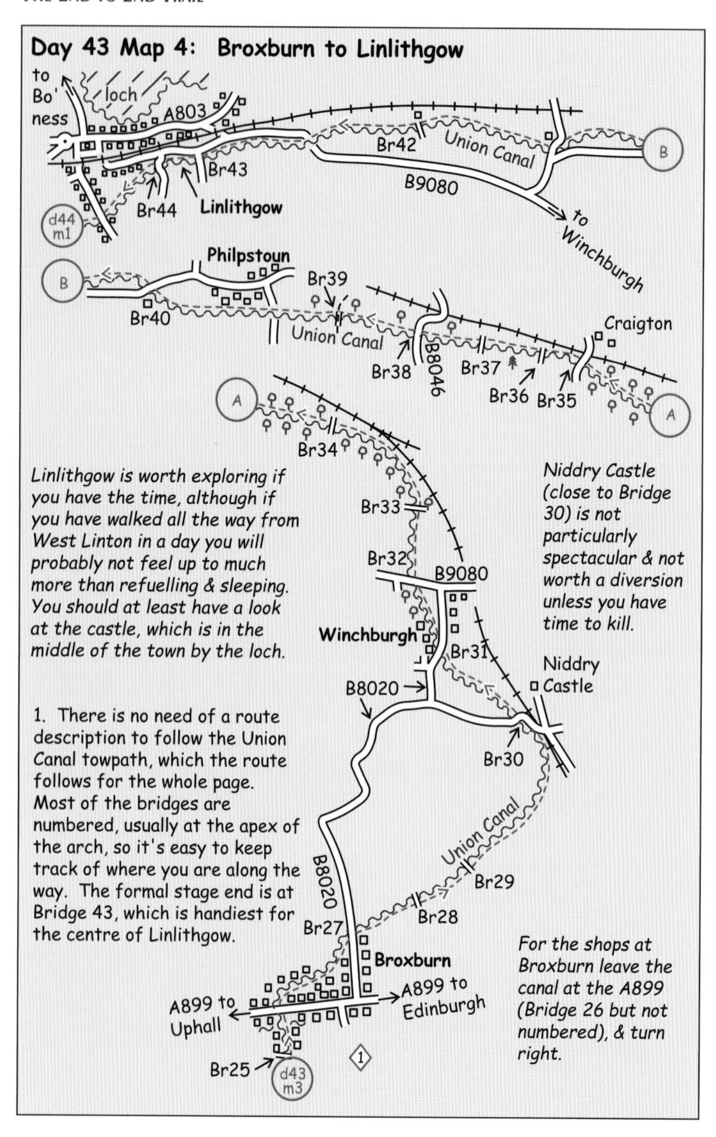

Linlithgow is worth exploring if you have the time, although if you have walked all the way from West Linton in a day you will probably not feel up to much more than refuelling & sleeping. You should at least have a look at the castle, which is in the middle of the town by the loch.

Niddry Castle (close to Bridge 30) is not particularly spectacular & not worth a diversion unless you have time to kill.

1. There is no need of a route description to follow the Union Canal towpath, which the route follows for the whole page. Most of the bridges are numbered, usually at the apex of the arch, so it's easy to keep track of where you are along the way. The formal stage end is at Bridge 43, which is handiest for the centre of Linlithgow.

For the shops at Broxburn leave the canal at the A899 (Bridge 26 but not numbered), & turn right.

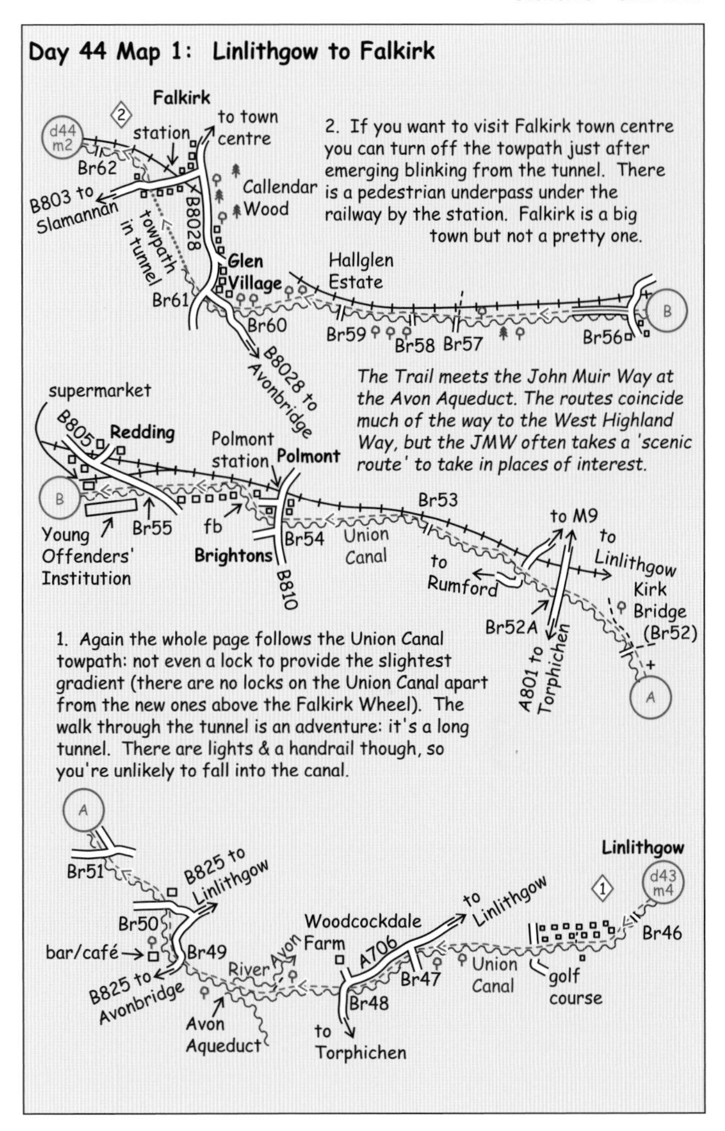

Day 44 Map 1: Linlithgow to Falkirk
Falkirk
d44 m2
2
station
to town centre
2. If you want to visit Falkirk town centre you can turn off the towpath just after emerging blinking from the tunnel. There is a pedestrian underpass under the railway by the station. Falkirk is a big town but not a pretty one.
Br62
B803 to Slamannan
Callendar Wood
B8028
towpath in tunnel
Glen Village
Hallglen Estate
Br61
Br60
Br59
Br58
Br57
Br56
B
B8028 to Avonbridge
The Trail meets the John Muir Way at the Avon Aqueduct. The routes coincide much of the way to the West Highland Way, but the JMW often takes a 'scenic route' to take in places of interest.
supermarket
B805
Redding
Polmont station
Polmont
B
Young Offenders' Institution
Br55
fb
Brightons
Br54
Union Canal
B810
Br53
to M9
to Linlithgow
to Rumford
Kirk Bridge (Br52)
Br52A
A801 to Torphichen
A
1. Again the whole page follows the Union Canal towpath: not even a lock to provide the slightest gradient (there are no locks on the Union Canal apart from the new ones above the Falkirk Wheel). The walk through the tunnel is an adventure: it's a long tunnel. There are lights & a handrail though, so you're unlikely to fall into the canal.
A
Br51
B825 to Linlithgow
Br50
bar/café
Br49
B825 to Avonbridge
River Avon
Avon Aqueduct
Woodcockdale Farm
A706
Br48
to Torphichen
Br47
to Linlithgow
Union Canal
golf course
Linlithgow
1
d43 m4
Br46

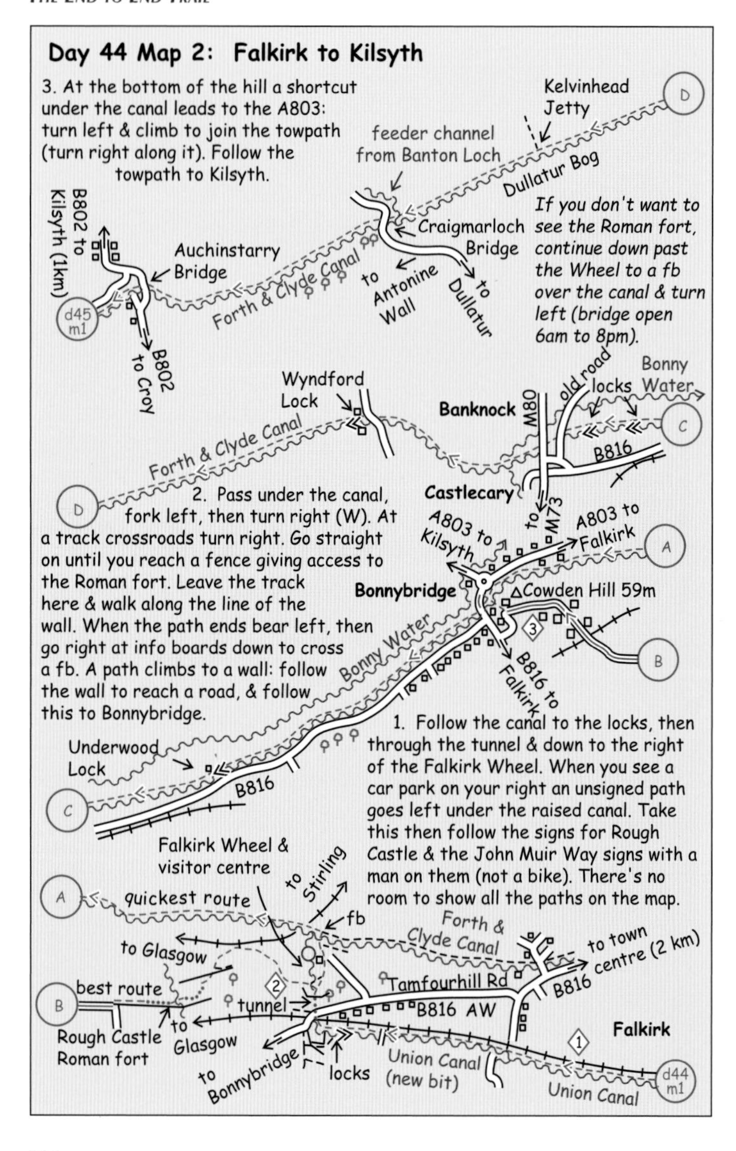
Day 44 Map 2: Falkirk to Kilsyth
3. At the bottom of the hill a shortcut under the canal leads to the A803: turn left & climb to join the towpath (turn right along it). Follow the towpath to Kilsyth.
Kelvinhead Jetty
feeder channel from Banton Loch
Dullatur Bog
If you don't want to see the Roman fort, continue down past the Wheel to a fb over the canal & turn left (bridge open 6am to 8pm).
B802 to Kilsyth (1km)
Auchinstarry Bridge
Craigmarloch Bridge
Forth & Clyde Canal
to Antonine Wall
to Dullatur
d45 m1
B802 to Croy
Wyndford Lock
Banknock
M80
old road
locks
Bonny Water
B816
Forth & Clyde Canal
Castlecary
2. Pass under the canal, fork left, then turn right (W). At a track crossroads turn right. Go straight on until you reach a fence giving access to the Roman fort. Leave the track here & walk along the line of the wall. When the path ends bear left, then go right at info boards down to cross a fb. A path climbs to a wall: follow the wall to reach a road, & follow this to Bonnybridge.
A803 to Kilsyth
to M73
A803 to Falkirk
Bonnybridge
Cowden Hill 59m
Bonny Water
B816 to Falkirk
Underwood Lock
B816
1. Follow the canal to the locks, then through the tunnel & down to the right of the Falkirk Wheel. When you see a car park on your right an unsigned path goes left under the raised canal. Take this then follow the signs for Rough Castle & the John Muir Way signs with a man on them (not a bike). There's no room to show all the paths on the map.
Falkirk Wheel & visitor centre
quickest route
to Stirling
fb
Forth & Clyde Canal
to Glasgow
to town centre (2 km)
best route
Tamfourhill Rd
B816
tunnel
B816 AW
Falkirk
Rough Castle Roman fort
to Glasgow
to Bonnybridge
locks
Union Canal (new bit)
Union Canal
d44 m1

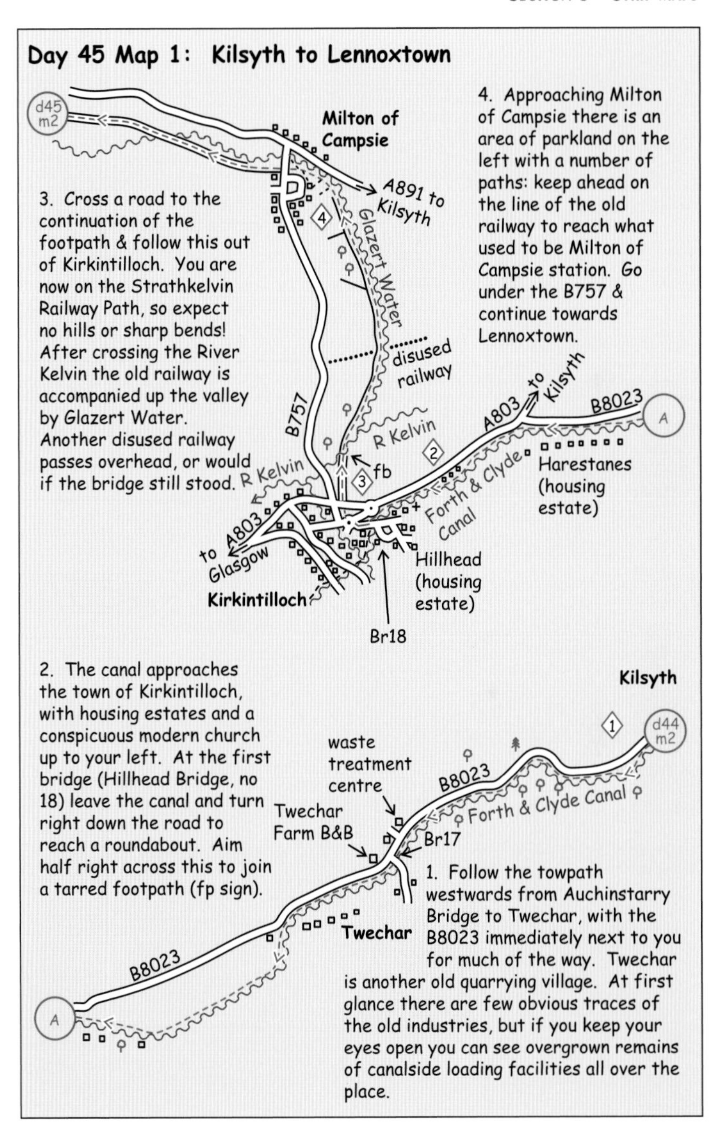
Day 45 Map 1: Kilsyth to Lennoxtown
d45 m2
Milton of Campsie
A891 to Kilsyth
4
Glazert Water
disused railway
B757
R Kelvin
to Kilsyth
A803
B8023
A
2
fb
3
Forth & Clyde Canal
Harestanes (housing estate)
R Kelvin
A803
to Glasgow
Kirkintilloch
Hillhead (housing estate)
Br18
Kilsyth
1
d44 m2
waste treatment centre
B8023
Forth & Clyde Canal
Twechar Farm B&B
Br17
Twechar
B8023
A
3. Cross a road to the continuation of the footpath & follow this out of Kirkintilloch. You are now on the Strathkelvin Railway Path, so expect no hills or sharp bends! After crossing the River Kelvin the old railway is accompanied up the valley by Glazert Water. Another disused railway passes overhead, or would if the bridge still stood.
4. Approaching Milton of Campsie there is an area of parkland on the left with a number of paths: keep ahead on the line of the old railway to reach what used to be Milton of Campsie station. Go under the B757 & continue towards Lennoxtown.
2. The canal approaches the town of Kirkintilloch, with housing estates and a conspicuous modern church up to your left. At the first bridge (Hillhead Bridge, no 18) leave the canal and turn right down the road to reach a roundabout. Aim half right across this to join a tarred footpath (fp sign).
1. Follow the towpath westwards from Auchinstarry Bridge to Twechar, with the B8023 immediately next to you for much of the way. Twechar is another old quarrying village. At first glance there are few obvious traces of the old industries, but if you keep your eyes open you can see overgrown remains of canalside loading facilities all over the place.

Day 45 Map 2: Lennoxtown to Carbeth

A81 to Aberfoyle
A81
whw
B821
Strathblane
West Highland Way
mast
B

2. The way is obvious until you approach Strathblane, where you are diverted right to join the A891. Turn left at the A891, then left at the A81, & next right along Dumbrock Rd. Turn left at the end of the houses on a footpath signed to Milngavie Rd.

3. Turn right at a road & continue as it bends right & becomes a climbing track. Follow the track past a mast & on through the woods, past a house, then take a good path sharp right, signed for the West Highland Way via Red Brae. This path descends to a gate: turn right here on a track, & you are now on the West Highland Way, which comes in from your left here. Turn left at the B821 & get your WHW guidebook out.

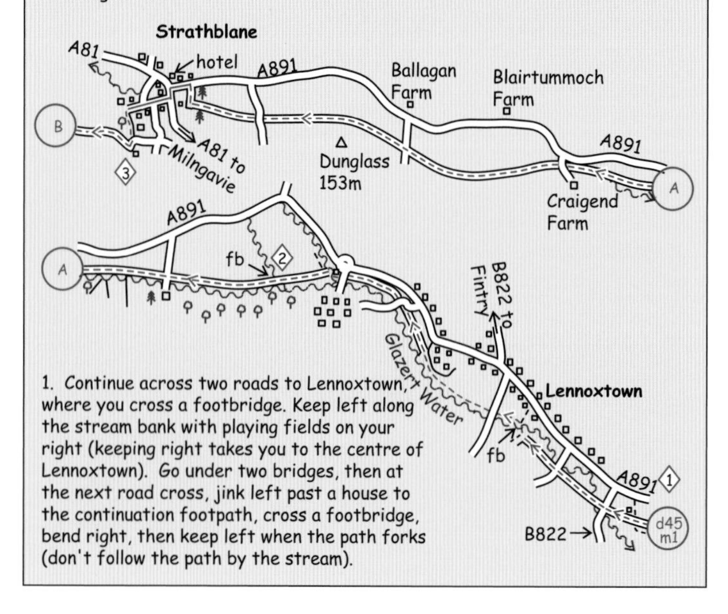

1. Continue across two roads to Lennoxtown, where you cross a footbridge. Keep left along the stream bank with playing fields on your right (keeping right takes you to the centre of Lennoxtown). Go under two bridges, then at the next road cross, jink left past a house to the continuation footpath, cross a footbridge, bend right, then keep left when the path forks (don't follow the path by the stream).

SECTION 6

The Northern Highlands and the Flow Country:
Fort William to John o' Groats

Start	Fort William
Finish	John o' Groats
Distance	394km (245 miles)
Road walking	11%. This is considerably less than the average for the rest of the route; there is not much need to walk on tarred roads in the north of Scotland.
Days	12 (main schedule), or 18 (alternative schedule)
Maps and guides	*The whole section:* this guide, Section 6 strip maps

From Fort William, the Trail leads northwards into the mountains, wild and largely uninhabited. In the 11 days from Fort William to Watten, at the end of Day 60, the only facilities passed are one small village with shops, four isolated hotels, a bunkhouse and a youth hostel. You also cross only 12 public roads in that time.

There are many streams and rivers to ford in this section, and alternative wet weather routes are described or indicated wherever possible, but be aware that in very wet weather even these may not be passable. If you are in any doubt about your mountain navigation and survival skills, a better course from Fort William would be to follow the Great Glen towards Inverness then the John o' Groats Trail up the east coast (see 'Alternative routes', below).

The valleys between Fort William and Kinlochewe, four days to the north, run mainly east–west, across the line of the Trail. This means that the route has to climb passes (bealachs) in and out of many remote glens over Days 50–53, a significant change from the valley walking of the West Highland Way. Remote though these glens are, there are usually a few walkers about on this stretch.

A long day (Day 54) along valleys and over passes through the 'Great Wilderness' of the Kinlochewe and Dundonnel forests leads to the A835 Ullapool trunk road at the head of Loch Broom. (For the benefit of those not familiar with the Highlands, don't expect trees in Highland forests – a forest is a game reserve, not a tree reserve.)

From Inverlael at the head of Loch Broom, the Trail leaves the west coast for good, heading northeast towards John o' Groats. A high pass crosses the main watershed, then tracks along glens lead down to the hotel at Oykel Bridge, and up

Section 6 Overview Map – Fort William to John o' Groats
N
0 20 km
0 10 miles
Cape Wrath
Strathy Point
Dunnet Head
West Mainland
Rora Head
HOY
Scapa Flow
S Walls
PENTLAND FI
John o' Groats
Thurso
Watten
Wick
Sinclair
Dail Righe
R Thurso
Kinbrace
L Naver
R Naver
Loch Loyal
Kyle of Tongue
L Hope
L Eriboll
North-west Sutherland
Eddrachillis Bay
Enard Bay
Assynt-Coigach
Overscaig
Crask
Loch Shin
Oykel Bridge
Lairg
R Shin
R Oykel
Ullapool
L Broom
Inverlael
R Carron
Dornoch Firth
MORAY FIR
HIGHLAND REGION
Fionn Loch
Loch Maree
Loch Fannich
Wester Ross
Kinlochewe
Black Wt
Cromarty Firth
Spey Bay
R Spey
R Beauly
R Nairn
Inverness
Loch Carron
Bendronaig Lodge
Loch Monar
R Farrar
R Glass
Loch Mullardoch
Kintail
Glen Affric
Loch Cluanie
R Moriston
Loch Ness
Aviemore
River Spey
CAIRNGORMS
The Cairngorm Mountains
Knoydart
Glen Garry
Loch Quoich
R Garry
Loch Lochy
Loch Arkaig
SCOTLAND
River Dee
Loch Eil
R Spean
Loch Shiel
Fort William
Loch Treig
Loch Ericht
GRAMPIAN MOUNTAINS
Loch Tummel
Loch Leven
Kinlochlevan
Loch Rannoch & Glen Lyon
R Tummel
TAY
Loch Rannoch
R Tay
Sunart
Loch Linnhe
Ben Nevis & Glen Coe

the River Oykel to the foot of the great Assynt massif. You will probably see few other walkers between here and John o' Groats.

An old stalkers' track skirts the eastern edge of Assynt above Glen Cassley, then the Trail leaves it to cut across a trackless pass to the head of Loch Shin. Continuing east, the last Highland pass leads to Loch Choire below Ben Klibreck, and then the mountains are left behind. Ahead are the lower Flow Country hills and peat bogs.

The track down from Loch Choire leads to the River Helmsdale, then a last climb over the unfrequented Knockfin Heights reaches the headwaters of the River Thurso. A path turns into a track then turns into a tarmac road as the river flows northeast. At this point the River Thurso turns north, so the Trail leaves it and the tarmac for a more direct and relatively tarmac-free route to Watten, meeting the east coast at Sinclair's Bay. The last stretch to Duncansby Head and John o' Groats follows the coast, initially on the beach then along spectacular cliff tops to finish.

Maps

1:50,000 Landranger maps

- 41 Ben Nevis, Fort William & Glen Coe
- 34 Fort Augustus
- 33 Loch Alsh, Glen Shiel
- 25 Glen Carron & Glen Affric
- 19 Gairloch & Ullapool
- 20 Beinn Dearg
- 16 Lairg, Loch Shin
- 15 Loch Assynt (not needed if you take the alternative route via Lairg)
- 17 Helmsdale & Strath of Kildonan
- 12 Thurso & Wick

Recommendations

You will need all these maps. Because of the nature of the terrain, there is little additional benefit in taking 1:25,000 maps, so, unlike for the earlier sections, I haven't listed any of these.

Accommodation

These tourist information centres (TICs) are on or reasonably close to the route, and all share a common website at www.visitscotland.com:

- 15 High St, **Fort William**, tel 01397 701801
- Cluanie Inn, **Cluanie**, tel 01320 340293
- Argyle Street, **Ullapool**, tel 01854 612486 (off-route, seasonal)

- Ferrycroft Visitor Centre, **Lairg**, tel 01549 402160
- McAllans, 66 High Street, **Wick**, tel 01955 602547
- County Road, **John o' Groats**, tel 01955 611373

These TICs will have local knowledge, but bear in mind that Visit Scotland maintain a single accommodation guide to cover the whole area. Accommodation is sparse, and advance research is recommended. For Days 53–55, the best accommodation guide is online at https://capewrathtrail guide.org.

For this section of the route, you will need to be equipped for wild camping and carry much of your food. Beds are few and far between, so it's a good idea to book ahead where you can. This particularly applies to the following stage ends (Note: 'A' in stage numbers indicates a stage end on the alternative schedule – see Appendix A):

- **Gairlochy** (Day 50, Day A68): if you want to camp by the lock, you'll need to get a key in advance for access to the toilets and showers (see Day 50 for details)
- **Glen Affric** (Day 51)
- **Kinlochewe** (Day 53)
- **Oykel Bridge** (Day 55)
- **Overscaig** (Day 56)
- **Crask** (Day 57)
- **Watten** (Day 60)
- **Keiss** (Day 61, Day A84)

Although there are bed and breakfasts along the final stretch from Keiss to John o' Groats, they often all fill up, so book ahead if you can. There is a campsite by the hotel and pier at John o' Groats.

Equipment shops

- Day 55 (off-route): North West Outdoors, West Argyle Street, **Ullapool** IV26 2TY, tel 01854 613383

Food shops

Chances to resupply are limited after Fort William and you will have to take care not to run out of provisions.

- Day 53: **Kinlochewe** has two general stores
- Day 56L: If you are taking the Lairg alternative route (see below), there are shops in **Lairg**
- Day 60: There is a village shop/post office in **Watten**
- Day 61: There are shops and a post office at **John o' Groats**

Alternative routes

Via Lairg

An alternative route from Oykel Bridge via Lairg (at the foot of Loch Shin) to Loch Choire is described, avoiding the Assynt massif and the trackless pass at the head of Loch Shin. The Lairg alternative is advised if the weather is bad, if you need to resupply, or if you just don't want to venture into a remote area. Unfortunately it involves a considerable amount of road walking on the first of the two days. The maps and description of the alternative route via Lairg are provided between Days 57 and 58, and are numbered 56L and 57L.

The Great Glen Way and the John o' Groats Trail

If the wilderness walking and remoteness from support and civilisation entailed by the recommended route north from Fort William are not really your sort of thing, the best option is to head northeast up the Great Glen towards Inverness. Then, once you are close to the east coast, go north to John o' Groats, following the coast. As far as the Dornoch Firth the scenery doesn't really compare with the main route through the mountains, but the last few days up the coast are spectacular. Don't be tempted onto the main roads for any of this, though. The busier roads really must be avoided as far as possible – the A82 up the Great Glen and the A9 and A99 further north are busy and dangerous.

From Fort William you can follow the Great Glen Way, a waymarked 117km (79-mile) walking route that follows the glen all the way to Inverness. The Great Glen is a straight valley along an ancient fault line from coast to coast across Scotland, with a line of lochs including Loch Lochy and Loch Ness. The Great Glen Way is on towpaths, forestry roads and minor public roads, and since it follows the valley it gives pretty easy walking.

From the end of the Great Glen Way at Inverness Castle, there is now a new trail north to John o' Groats – the John o' Groats Trail. A lot of this route has been created from scratch, particularly the northern half, where there were few existing walking routes. This Trail is 235km (147 miles) long, and gives a pretty direct route to John o' Groats, avoiding roads as much as is practical. You leave Inverness across the massive Kessock Bridge to the Black Isle, then cut across the Black Isle and the Easter Ross peninsula to Tain. For the rest of the way you follow the coast, with the second half of the Trail mainly along spectacular cliff tops. At the time of writing, in 2019, the route is still a work in progress. It can be followed now, waymarking is well underway, and there is a draft guidebook available (see below); however, there are still a few fences and burns to cross, some sections are very close to cliff edges, and there is one nastily steep slope to descend to cross a deep valley – steps are being constructed here though, so by the time you get there it should be fine. The John o' Groats Trail makes an excellent way to finish a Land's End to John o' Groats walk, and the rough edges will gradually be smoothed off as the work on the Trail proceeds.

You also have the option of leaving the Great Glen Way at Drumnadrochit and heading north from here over the hills to Beauly and on to Dingwall, joining the John o' Groats Trail above the Cromarty Bridge. This is a bit shorter than going through Inverness, reduces road walking, and avoids going through the city. Although this route is not included in the draft guidebook to the John o' Groats Trail, we are hoping to include a detailed route for this option in the forthcoming Cicerone edition.

Guidebooks

- *Walking The Great Glen Way* by Paddy Dillon (Cicerone, 2nd edition, 2016)
- *John o' Groats Trail* by Andy Robinson and Jay Wilson (draft edition, 2018). This is available via the John o' Groats Trail website www.jogt.org.uk, and will be replaced by a Cicerone edition in due course.

Aonach Meadhoin, A' Chralaig and Loch Cluanie (Day 51)

DAY 50

Fort William to Glen Garry (Loch Poulary)
The Great Glen and Glen Garry

Distance	38km (23 miles)
Ascent	930m

The journey into the wilder Highlands starts deceptively easily, along the Great Glen – as far as Loch Lochy the route coincides more or less with the Great Glen Cycle Route and the Great Glen Way footpath. It then heads up into the mountains, crossing the highest of the Trail's Scottish passes – the Bealach Carn na h-Urchaire – and dropping down into Glen Garry.

From Fort William, road walking is avoided for the most part on 3km of footpaths to reach the **Caledonian Canal** at **Neptune's Staircase** (Day 50 Map 1). You then follow the towpath for about 11km northeast to **Gairlochy** at the foot of Loch Lochy (Day 50 Map 2). If you want to break the journey overnight at Gairlochy, there is a bed and breakfast here (Dalcomera, tel 01397 712778 or 07752 892561), and also another bed and breakfast and a campsite (Gairlochy Holiday Park) at Mucomir, about 1.5km off-route along the B8004 to the southeast. Camping is also permitted by the lock at Gairlochy, although you can only gain access to the toilets and shower if you have a key, which you need to get in advance by post or at Fort William for a payment of £10. See www.greatglencanoetrail.info for details of how to do this.

THE CALEDONIAN CANAL

The Caledonian Canal follows the Great Glen (Glen Mor), which is a fault line running from coast to coast across the Highlands from Fort William to Inverness. For much of the way there were already natural lochs before the canal was dug – lochs Lochy, Oich, Ness and Dochfour. Joining them up with a canal suitable for seagoing vessels was first considered in 1726, although it wasn't until 1804 that work on building it started. The main justification for the canal was that it would give sailing ships a safer alternative to the dangerous Pentland Firth route round the north coast of Scotland, avoiding treacherous seas and even more treacherous French pirates. The canal is thus much bigger than a typical English canal designed for inland barge traffic. Each lock on the Caledonian Canal is at least 50 metres long and 12 metres wide. The point at which the route meets the canal is in the middle of Neptune's Staircase, an impressive flight of eight locks raising the canal most of the way from sea level to the level of Loch Lochy.

Construction proved difficult, and the canal wasn't opened all the way through until 1822, and even then it wasn't yet as deep as it was designed to be. Financially it wasn't a success – steamships had started to appear on the scene, and they had far less trouble with the Pentland Firth, and consequently weren't prepared to pay the canal dues. Unlike many canals, however, it managed to survive intact, and has remained open to shipping from sea to sea. It also makes a pleasant interlude on your journey through the Highlands, the towpath making for the easiest bit of walking you will get between Glasgow and John o' Groats. Moy Bridge, passed on the Trail, is the only surviving original bridge on the canal, and the bridge keeper used to have to row across to open the bridge fully.

Sailing ship La Grace, Caledonian Canal

Between Loch Lochy and Loch Arkaig the Trail follows a track through woods past **St Ciaran's church**, a pretty little building inaccessible by road, and then past **Achnacarry**, the home of the Camerons.

The Camerons forfeited their land after the 1745 Jacobite Rebellion, but had it returned to them in 1784. Donald Cameron of Lochiel then got rid of all his tenants, replacing them with sheep farmers from the lowlands. This was a classic example of the **clearance of the Highlands**, which took place in the 18th and 19th centuries. Once the autonomy of the clan chieftains was taken from them after 1745, they were little more than landowners, and many decamped south to Edinburgh or London and became absentee landlords. Instead of defending the territory of their extended families, they looked to maximise their incomes, and this led to the expulsion of the local population to make way for large sheep farms.

This happened throughout the Highlands, and in many of the glens that are now uninhabited, or nearly so, there are many old abandoned homesteads. Your route passes many of these sites – if the political situation had been different, perhaps some of the people would still be there. Many of the glens are not that different in character from the valleys of Northumberland or the English Lake District, which have retained a local farming population.

From the foot of Loch Lochy to the foot of **Loch Arkaig**, the walking is easy, on paths, tracks and tarmac. From here (Day 50 Map 3) the character of the walk changes, as does the whole journey – today and on Days 51–53 the route crosses pass after pass, from valley to valley.

Looking back to Loch Arkaig on the main route

At the road junction at the foot of Loch Arkaig you need to consider the state of the weather and how full the streams are before going any further. The most direct route, and the best in reasonable weather, is via the Bealach Carn na h-Urchaire. This is the main Trail route, and is described first. There are, however, two potential drawbacks with this route. The first is that it crosses a high pathless pass that is in places quite difficult underfoot. If the cloud is down and your navigation skills are limited, you should take the alternative route via Fedden, described below. The second disadvantage is that if the streams are running at all high, you may not be able to cross the streams once you have descended into Glen Garry, and this will mean a detour at the end of a long day. This is not as big an issue as it used to be though, due to the building of new bridges and paths. This means it is now possible to reach the valley from the pass reasonably easily without crossing any significant burns, as long as you follow the alternative 'flood route' shown on Day 50 Map 4.

Main route via the Bealach Carn na h-Urchaire (Day 50 Maps 3 and 4)

The main route from Loch Arkaig to Glen Garry crosses a major pass, the **Bealach Carn na h-Urchaire**, on the main watershed. At 648m this is the highest point of the Scottish part of the route, and the pass itself is wild and pathless. For about 4km it is very hard work because of the nature of the terrain – steep and peaty. David Paterson followed this route on his original 'Cape Wrath Trail' walk, and slept out on the pass without a tent. When I was there at the end of May one year, it was sleeting, and there was nowhere dry enough to consider sitting down, never mind sleeping.

> Despite the fact that you cross the Bealach Carn na h-Urchaire heading more or less northwest, you are actually crossing the **watershed** from west to east. The southern slopes feed into Loch Lochy and thence towards Fort William, and the northern slopes drain to Loch Ness and Inverness.

Descent from the pass is steep and difficult to start with, but you pick up a path before the confluence with the Allt an Fhithich. From here to the bottom of the glen, the walking is not too difficult but it is wet underfoot in its early stages. You also have two major streams to cross before reaching the valley forestry, which has mostly been felled. There is now a bridge across the Allt Choire a' Bhalachain, which has removed what used to be a nasty trap in wet weather.

Alternative wet weather descent from the Bealach Carn na h-Urchaire (Day 50 Map 4)

If the streams are high, it is possible to descend to Glen Garry without crossing any major streams, although this means walking slightly further and you may have to climb a deer fence. To do this, cross the Allt Ailein high up (see Day 50 Map 3), then follow it down to the fence (Day 50 Map 4), keeping the stream on your left. (You can avoid climbing the fence if the Allt Ailein is fordable below the fence: follow the main route through the gate then cross the burn.) A good path appears eventually, and when you reach a forestry track you turn left to rejoin the main route.

Alternative bad weather route via Fedden (Day 50 Maps 5, 6 and 4)

If the weather is already bad when you reach Loch Arkaig, you have the option of taking a less scenic but lower-level route to Glen Garry further east, climbing up **Gleann Cia-aig** to the ruined farmstead at **Fedden**, and descending through forestry. More forestry tracks then take you up **Glen Garry** to rejoin the main Trail route. The sole advantage of this option is that it only reaches an altitude of 400m, rather than the 648m of Bealach Carn na h-Urchaire. It has nearly as much climbing, just as much rough ground, and is 6.5km further than the main route.

There has been no accommodation in **Glen Garry**, since the Tomdoun Hotel and its bunkhouse closed down a few years ago. The best place to camp is near the bridge over the River Garry, where the main route emerges from the forestry, although this can be very midgy. There are also a couple of possible small camping areas by the road between the two birch groves further west.

Until 1962 the main road to Kyle of Lochalsh and Skye passed what was then the **Tomdoun Inn**, heading west, then turned sharp right after 250 metres by a chapel. In 1962 Loch Loyne was dammed to make a reservoir, the road north of Tomdoun was flooded, and a new road was built between Glen Garry and Loch Cluanie, further east, going round the foot of the new Loch Loyne reservoir. This left the Tomdoun Inn marooned, so its eventual closure is not really too surprising. Tomorrow the Trail meets up with the old road, which now looks like a cart track, on the other side of Glen Loyne, and follows it to Loch Cluanie.

DAY 51

Glen Garry (Loch Poulary) to Glen Affric

Four Glens

Distance	26km (16 miles)
Ascent	970m

Today the Trail heads due north, crossing three passes that link four glens running from east to west: Glen Garry, Glen Loyne, Strath Cluanie and Glen Affric. None of the passes are particularly high, and there is only a short stretch that doesn't follow a clear path. There is even a pub at lunchtime.

The path over from Glen Garry to **Glen Loyne** is easy to follow and easy underfoot, considering that it climbs to about 500m (Day 51 Map 1). Near the River Loyne the path disappears, however, close to where you need to cross the river. In normal weather the crossing is easy enough, but to quote *Scottish Hill Tracks*: 'This route is not possible if the River Loyne is in spate'. There is no alternative wet weather route for this section. The only guaranteed way of making progress in spate conditions would be to follow the A87 round the foot of Loch Loyne and along Loch Cluanie, which is not really much fun as a walking route, since the road is a busy one. If the River Loyne is too full to cross safely, it may be practical to follow the river upstream (westwards) for 2–3km and cross higher up, above some of the many tributaries feeding the spate, although I have not tried this and am not aware that anyone else has, either.

Once across the Loyne (and into the old county of Ross and Cromarty) there is a good path running along the lower slope of the hillside, leading down the valley to a ruined settlement near the head of Loch Loyne. From here a steep and mainly pathless climb up by a stream out of the valley brings you to the old Skye road, which is now a deserted and decaying track. Fast progress on the old

Glen Affric youth hostel

road takes you down to the A87 and the **Cluanie Inn** (Day 51 Map 2, tel 01809 335021).

The inn is open all day, is comfortable and serves bar meals. If you are looking for overnight accommodation, the only available beds are at the inn, which is comparatively upmarket. There are good camping spots between the road and the loch on the way east towards the Glen Affric track.

The track over to Glen Affric is a good one most of the way to the watershed, then it deteriorates into a very wet path. Following the path from here onwards is easy, but keeping feet dry is not. The path traverses well above the River Affric, dropping down to cross a bridge near **Alltbeithe** youth hostel, which is a great place to stop overnight. This is the only accommodation, indeed it is the only building in sight – upper Glen Affric is a remote place. Suitable ground for pitching a tent is scarce, but there are some pitches by the Allt Beithe Garbh to the west of the youth hostel, or you can camp by the hostel itself. There is also an MBA bothy a bit further up the glen.

DAY 52

Glen Affric to Bendronaig Lodge
The Falls of Glomach

Distance	34km (21 miles)
Ascent	900m

This is an excellent day's walking over passes and along valleys, the high point being the great chasm of the Falls of Glomach, one of the most atmospheric and impressive places in the British mountains. Some of the walking is not easy; in particular, the route down the west side of Gleann Gaorsaic to the falls is slow and hard work. The effort is well rewarded though, and the rest of the day is enjoyable, mostly on good paths and tracks. There are no tarmac roads to be seen on this stage, and you will probably see no cars at all, as there is no public access for cars to the estate road up Glen Elchaig.

Glen Affric is remote, but probably the busiest place you will see all day, because of the youth hostel and the number of Munros that surround it (a Munro is a Scottish mountain or top with a height of at least 3000ft, or 914.4m). Just about everyone else will be ticking Munros from their lists rather than following the glens and passes.

A little upstream from the hostel the main valley swings south, and a side valley comes in from the west – Gleann Gniomhaidh (Day 52 Map 1). There is a route from here all the way to the coast at Loch Duich, going over two passes. The Trail follows the first part of this path, initially alongside the Allt Beithe Garbh, then up the classically U-shaped **Gleann Gniomhaidh** between Beinn Fhada and Sgùrr nan Ceathreamhnan, over the peat hags and the main watershed at its head, and down slightly to **Loch a' Bhealaich** at the head of **Gleann Gaorsaic**. The path to the coast continues west over the Bealach an Sgàirne, but the End to End Trail leaves it here to head north down the glen, which joins Glen Elchaig in a few more kilometres.

The most direct way would be to keep to the east side of the valley and follow a path that cuts a corner to join Glen Elchaig at Carnach. It may give easier walking, as well, but the Falls of Glomach must not be missed, so the Trail takes the west side of the valley, along the shore of Loch a' Bhealaich to avoid the worst of the peat hags, then for most of the way keeping close to the stream and smaller lochs. There are occasional traces of an old stalking path, but the going is still difficult, as the path has been neglected for a long time. The bridges across side streams are no more, and detours are needed to keep out of the peat bogs. Eventually the valley narrows, bends west, and you arrive at the brink of the **Falls of Glomach** (Day 52 Map 2).

The Falls of Glomach

Leave your sack at the top near the warning sign and scramble down the dead-end path below to the viewpoints. The falls are over 200m high, including a sheer drop of 90m, and the gorge is massive – the scale is alpine rather than anything you would expect to find in Britain.

Back at the top again, follow the scrambly path to **Glen Elchaig**, not forgetting to keep looking round for views of the falls and the gorge. This path is probably the best place to view them from other than the viewpoint path. If you are carrying walking poles it is a good idea to pack them away for this section, as you will probably want to use your hands in places.

Alternative wet weather route

If the weather is bad there is an alternative route from Glen Elchaig to the Coulin Pass (Day 53 Map 2). It is outlined in *Scottish Hill Tracks* (see Appendix B). This route is recommended if the rivers are in spate, as there is a river crossing by Loch Cruoshie on the main route that could be difficult. This alternative follows Glen Elchaig westwards to **Nonach Lodge** (NG 935 310), follows paths north up **Glen Ling**, then east of Loch an Iasaich and down to **Loch Carron** at Attadale. The valley is then followed northeast, mostly on roads, to **Achnashellach**, and the Trail rejoined either just below the **Coulin Pass** (see Day 53), or the other side of it if you take the route up the River Lair from Achnashellach. **Strathcarron** is a possible overnight stop.

To follow the main route of the Trail, turn right to follow Glen Elchaig upstream to the northeast. The walking is now easy on an unmade access road, and you can at last start to get moving at a reasonable pace.

The road turns into a good path after the last house (Iron Lodge), then the valley and the path fork. The left fork takes you easily over a pass and down to

Glen Elchaig and Loch na Leitreach

the River Ling, to **Maol-bhuidhe** bothy and good wild camping by **Loch Cruoshie** (Day 52 Map 3) – and Glen Affric seemed remote!

The mountain straight ahead across the valley is Beinn Dronaig, and tonight's destination is the other side of it – the Trail goes round its righthand side. Cross the river just above Loch Cruoshie if you can – if there's too much water there is an easier crossing point 2.5km upstream (to the right). A pathless climb up to the shoulder of **Beinn Dronaig** crosses the main watershed again, then a good bridge over the stream leads to a clear track along the shore of **Loch Calavie** and over a low pass (and the watershed yet again).

The track descends slightly to the Uisge Dubh (Black Water), a tributary of the Ling, at a footbridge close to **Bendronaig Lodge**. Here there is a good bothy (maintained by the estate, not the MBA), or you can camp outside the bothy. This is a remote place – there are no other facilities, but there are plenty of red deer.

DAY 53

Bendronaig Lodge to Kinlochewe
Bealach Bhearnais and the Coulin Pass

Distance	33km (20 miles)
Ascent	1070m

Today the Trail crosses another high pass, the Bealach Bhearnais, the climb up to which is the highlight of the day. Descent into Glen Carron and its forestry follows, to cross the Kyle of Lochalsh road and railway. A short, steep path climbs up an old pony route through forestry to the low Coulin Pass, followed by a gradual descent to Coulin Loch and more forestry. You can follow the valley from here, along the lochs then along the A896 to Kinlochewe, but good tracks climb up through the forestry to cut the corner off, and that's the 'official' route. You descend from the moor again to reach Kinlochewe and civilisation at last. Make the most of it – it's the last for a long way.

From Bendronaig Lodge a hydro plant track then an old stalkers' track run up the valley to **Loch an Laoigh**, then a path climbs northeast high above the valley across the flank of **Beinn Tharsuinn** (Day 53 Map 1). It peters out about 2km

Uisge Dubh and Bendronaig Lodge

before the pass, and the next section up to the **Bealach Bhearnais** is rough and pathless. At almost 600m, the Bealach Bhearnais is a well-defined saddle pass, and only the Bealach na h-Urchaire is higher on the Scottish part of the Trail.

There is a good path down from the pass to a precarious wire bridge across the Allt a' Chonais, to join the Glenuaig Lodge access track down through the forestry into **Glen Carron** (Day 53 Map 2). Most of the plantation that the track goes through on the descent was cleared some years ago, and it is now regrowing.

In the valley bottom a level crossing over the Inverness to Kyle of Lochalsh railway leads to the busy A890 at **Craig** and the first traffic since Cluanie on Day 51.

Craig is just a few houses by a busy road, but it does have a bunkhouse – the only accommodation here. Check out the latest reviews online about the bunkhouse before booking, as there have been mixed reports of it – your alternative here is wild camping before crossing the railway. There is no pub or shop, and don't bother walking east to Achnashellach looking for them there, either, as the nearest are at Strathcarron and Achnasheen, both many miles away.

About 1km west along the A890 from Craig, a path leaves the road to climb steeply up through cleared forestry to join the main track up to the **Coulin Pass**. This path isn't marked on OS maps, but is the line of the original route, and was reopened in 1990, presumably largely thanks to the Scottish Rights of Way and Access Society. The Coulin Pass is a low one, at 286m – the hills north of Glen Carron are not as high as those to the south.

A good track descends to **Coulin** (Day 53 Map 3), joined on the way down by the Easan Dorcha track, an alternative route from Achnashellach. In the summer of 2018 this area was a bit of a mess due to the building of a new hydro scheme, but it should look a lot better again by the mid 2020s. On the descent you can see an area of forestry straight ahead behind **Loch Coulin** – the line of the Trail slants up through this and can be seen clearly. Above the trees, the track crosses a short stretch of moorland, then starts descending to enter the upper edge of another plantation, this one felled. Follow the track most of the way down to the valley road, then you can turn right on an old track that takes you to the edge of the forestry area. Once on the other side of the forestry, cover up your arms and legs as there is bracken to push through, and you may pick up a few ticks otherwise. A narrow path and some careful attention to the route description on Day 53 Map 3 lead you down the valley to **Kinlochewe**.

Kinlochewe has a couple of shops selling groceries. There is accommodation, and a hotel (the Kinlochewe Hotel, recommended, tel 01445 760253), which also has a comfortable bunkhouse. The caravan site in the village has a small number of tent pitches. Stock up well before leaving Kinlochewe, as the next shop is at Watten, at least seven days away (unless you take the alternative route via Lairg – Days 56L and 57L). Wild camping is practical around the Heights of Kinlochewe, and there is also a bothy at Leckie, NH 097 645, just over 2km off-route to the east from there.

DAY 54

Kinlochewe to Inverlael
The great wilderness

Distance	41km (25 miles)
Ascent	1510m

This isn't quite the longest day in terms of distance covered, but it takes longer to complete than any but the coastal switchback round Hartland Point on Day 8. You should expect today to take as long as Day 8, even if the weather is good, and longer if it isn't. You will need to start as early as possible from Kinlochewe, and then keep moving if you want to reach Inverlael in a day.

After the initial easy walking to Lochan Fada, the day is dominated by high mountains (if you are lucky with the weather). Lochan Fada is surrounded by Slioch, A' Mhaighdean, Beinn Tarsuinn and Mullach Coire Mhic Fhearchair. A pathless and rough section up to the Bealach na Croise leads to Loch an Nid, and then a walk north down the valley, with the great slabs on the lower slopes of Sgùrr Bàn dominating the view. Eventually the huge An Teallach massif comes into view ahead and continues to stamp its impact on the rest of the day's walking. A good vehicle track crosses from Strath na Sealga to the Dundonnell valley and the A832. From here, an old and neglected track climbs up and crosses the moors to drop down to the Ullapool road (A835) at Inverlael, near the head of Loch Broom.

From Kinlochewe the main route gets to the foot of Lochan Fada via a good vehicle track to the **Heights of Kinlochewe** and up **Gleann na Muice** (Day 54 Map 1). By the time you get near **Lochan Fada** the track is a path, but the going is easy.

(There is an alternative route from Kinlochewe, further to the west, up Gleann Bianasdail from the head of Loch Maree. There are two reasons it is not the preferred End to End Trail route: it is slower, and it involves crossing the outflow from Lochan Fada, which is not possible in times of spate.)

From Lochan Fada to the Bealach na Croise is less than 3km, but it is the only pathless section of the day and involves two steep climbs (Day 54 Map 2). First you must climb up from the loch and over featureless moor to descend to the stream flowing out of Coire Mhic Fhearchair. From here, cross the stream and ascend in prettier surroundings alongside a tributary stream to the **Bealach na Croise**.

The main route of the Trail follows a path from the pass down to Loch an Nid, although it is rough and not quick to walk down. It also involves wading the stream above the loch, which isn't possible if the streams are up, so if this is the case you are best advised to keep to the wet weather route to the right of the stream all the way down, although the ground is rough and pathless (see Day 54 Map 2).

On reaching **Loch an Nid**, review your plans. If it is any later than lunchtime, you should abandon any expectation of reaching Inverlael today, in which case staying where you are is an option worth considering. There is good camping ground by the loch, and the surroundings are idyllic. Otherwise, find your lunch and eat it on the move as you follow the path down the valley (Day 54 Map 3).

When the valley starts to bend left (to descend towards Loch na Sealga), a vehicle track cuts up out of the valley to the right. (At this point you have the option to descend the valley for 4km to the MBA bothy at Shenavall, if you want

Strath More and the River Broom, just before descending

to stay there overnight.) The vehicle track takes you easily across wet moorland to descend to the A832 at **Corrie Hallie** and the Dundonnell River (Day 54 Map 4).

Dundonnell feels very different from the environment of the past few days. For the first time since Fort William, the sea (Little Loch Broom) is very close, and the valley is much lusher and greener than anything seen so far in the Highlands. There are, however, no facilities for walkers and neither is there any obvious place to camp unobtrusively – this is a valley of neat fields full of sheep.

An old track connects the heads of Little Loch Broom and Loch Broom, and you pick this up at the edge of an old wood on the valley side. It climbs up out of the wood and the valley to cross moorland above the deep, wooded Allt a' Chairn valley, then over more undulating moorland to the edge of a steep escarpment down to **Strath More**, the River Broom and Inverlael. All the way across the moor there are stunning views of An Teallach behind you.

The path follows the escarpment edge briefly before dropping down and becoming intermittent on the way down to the valley. If you are planning to camp, fill your water bottle before you reach the valley bottom.

At **Inverlael** there are places where you can camp discreetly if you look carefully, and bed and breakfast is available at Clachan Farmhouse, 1km up the minor road towards Letters (NH 175 848, tel 01854 655209). There are more B&Bs a little further away, and a bunkhouse 3km to the south. If you need to get to 'civilisation', Ullapool is about 14km along the A835, and the route can be rejoined from there by taking a track east from Ullapool past Loch Achall and Loch an Daimh.

DAY 55

Inverlael to Oykel Bridge
Glen Douchary and Glen Einig

Distance	30km (19 miles)
Ascent	890m

Today the Trail leaves the west coast of Scotland for good and starts to head northeast towards John o' Groats. Initially on forestry tracks, a vehicle track climbs out of the valley, and then you are on your own across rough and difficult ground, with no path until you drop down to Glen Douchary, which is a desolate and lonely place. An estate track then takes you easily over a low pass and along Strath Mulzie, a long wide valley, to meet forestry tracks above Oykel Bridge. The descent down Glen Einig is now mainly in birch woods, which have replaced the former conifer plantation.

From the A835 Ullapool road, at the head of Loch Broom, a track crosses a field and enters the forestry in **Gleann na Sguaib** (Day 55 Map 1). Twin bridges cross the River Lael, which here runs in two deep, parallel slots it has carved from the bedrock. After a couple of kilometres following forestry tracks in the valley bottom, you reach a fork in the valley. Turn left to climb up out of the forestry, and out of the valley altogether on a good vehicle track.

The built track ends high up on the boggy moorland, and the next 4km across the moor and down to Glen Douchary are mainly pathless and difficult. Initially the way is a bit soggy underfoot east up to the pass, then the descent by the Allt na Lairige is rough going – the stream bank is too steep to follow, and the ground above it is difficult and peaty.

Eventually descend with relief to the broad valley of **Glen Douchary** and cross the river. Before going any further look upstream to the head of the valley, where there is an impressive rocky cirque (Cadha Dearg), flanked by Seana Bhraigh (927m) on the left and Meall Glac an Ruighe (859m) on the right.

Climb a short way up the valley side and join an estate track that starts wet but quickly improves. It takes you out of Glen Douchary and over to the next valley, **Strath Mulzie** (Day 55 Map 2). This is a wide grassy valley, with good places to camp. The going is very easy on a good track that eventually brings you to **Duag Bridge** (Day 55 Map 3), where two valleys meet to become **Glen Einig**. As well as the bridge there is a small MBA bothy here, the School House.

Shortly after Duag Bridge the Trail enters forestry and continues down Glen Einig on a forestry road to **Oykel Bridge**, where the River Einig joins the River Oykel.

At Oykel Bridge there is a road, the A837, which is not exactly a major arterial route, more a minor capillary. There is also a hotel (the Oykel Bridge Hotel, tel 01549 441218), which is reasonably upmarket and intended principally for fishermen (the Oykel is more used to fishermen than walkers). The hotel does bar meals, and has the only accommodation here, including some cheaper rooms for walkers. The best place to camp is by the river, below the bridge (at the start of Day 56L Map 1).

DAY 56

Oykel Bridge to the Overscaig Hotel
The Upper Oykel and Assynt

Distance	38km (24 miles)
Ascent	880m

This is the last day in the heart of the high mountains. The Trail follows the River Oykel north to the foot of the huge Ben More Assynt massif, then contours round its eastern flank on an old path. The objective is to get round the northeast end of Loch Shin, so once this path has taken the Trail far enough north, you need to turn off it to cross Glen Cassley. A climb over a pathless pass and a descent to the end of Loch Shin follow, then a short road walk above the loch to the Overscaig Hotel.

This is a long day in a remote setting, and there is nowhere to shelter if you find you can't make it all the way in a day. It is a good idea to be equipped for a night camping in Glen Cassley, just in case, and you should make sure someone knows where you are going. If the weather is bad or you need supplies, consider the Lairg alternative route (Days 56L and 57L, see below).

From Oykel Bridge (Day 56 Map 1), the A837 heads northwest along the left side of the valley (looking upstream), gradually diverging from the River Oykel. Luckily

THE MAIN ROUTE AND THE LAIRG ALTERNATIVE

At Oykel Bridge you have a decision to make on which route to follow. The direct route to John o' Groats is blocked by Loch Shin, 28km (18 miles) long and directly in your way, so the main Trail (Days 56 and 57) heads up the River Oykel and takes a remote mountain route round the northwest end of the loch, via the Overscaig Hotel, to the Crask Inn.

The main route will get you from Oykel Bridge to Kinbrace in three days, following the main schedule, with two long days and a short one in between. Oykel Bridge to Kinbrace in two days would be difficult, so you may as well break at the two inns (Overscaig and Crask). The main options are: (1) to split Day 56 in two and camp in Glen Cassley (Day 56 Map 3); (2) to extend Day 57 and camp at the head of Loch Choire (Day 58 Map 2); or (3) to follow the Lairg alternative route.

The Lairg alternative route (Days 56L and 57L) heads down the River Oykel, away from the mountains, to go round the southeast end of Loch Shin. The principal advantages of this route are: (1) if the weather is bad and you are not confident about navigating through pathless terrain with map and compass, it provides a route that is easier to follow; and (2) at the south-east end of Loch Shin is the small town of Lairg, which has all the facilities that you have probably been dreaming about for days, even shops.

The disadvantages of the Lairg alternative are: (1) there is a lot of road walking on the way; (2) there isn't the same mountain scenery; and (3) the navigation north of Lairg to Loch Choire is as tricky as any on the whole route. This last point means that, if your navigation skills are shaky, you will need to follow the A836 from Lairg to Crask rather than the route for Day 57L.

there is also an unmade vehicle track on the right side of the quiet valley. It is mainly used by fishermen, but is just as good for walkers. The main route crosses the bridge by the hotel, taking you out of Ross and Cromarty and into what used to be the county of Sutherland, the river forming the boundary.

As you walk along you will see what look like garden sheds here and there. These are huts provided as shelters for fishermen, and they make good emergency overnight shelters.

A big forestry plantation covers the upper reaches of **Glen Oykel**, but a wide strip along the riverbank has been left clear of trees. The track now continues further upstream than marked on OS maps, but eventually ends. The next stretch along the river is slower, but no less pleasant, on a rudimentary path through the tussocky grass, and there is a good place to camp here. A short climb up by

River Oykel, near Salachy

a stream leads to a forestry track, and in a short distance this leads to the shore of **Loch Ailsh**, with the Assynt mountains behind it (Day 56 Map 2). To the right, behind Benmore Lodge, is the steep end of the ridge of Sail an Ruathair – the Trail runs beneath it.

An estate road follows the loch shore to **Benmore Lodge**, then a track follows the river to where it divides. The right fork is the Allt Sail an Ruathair, and a path follows this up into a wide bowl, with Loch Sail an Ruathair to the left and the shoulder of Meall an Aonaich looming ahead. The path zigzags up this steep slope to cross the shoulder and continue its lonely way north, past **Loch Carn nan Conbhairean**, with Glen Cassley now apparent down to the right (Day 56 Map 3). A couple of kilometres past Loch Carn nan Conbhairean, the Trail meets the end of a vehicle track coming up from Glen Cassley.

Wet weather alternative

If the streams are high, you won't be able to cross the River Cassley by Loch na Sròine Luime, so turn right here and follow the wet weather alternative down into the glen, then turn left upstream to a bridge over the River Cassley by a hydro-electric **power station**. From here you can cross the bridge and follow the river upstream, to rejoin the main route of the Trail north of Loch na Sròine Luime. Alternatively, if you are feeling really miserable, you can follow the power station road over **Maovally** and reach **Loch Shin** that way.

Assuming the streams are fordable, the main Trail continues north from the vehicle track, still on the old path. When it starts to bend west, with the lochs of Glen Cassley visible below, the Trail leaves the path to cross the valley between the lochs, fording the river, and climbing up the pathless hillside to the northeast (Day 56 Map 4).

A pass is crossed under the crags of **Creag Riabhach Loch nan Sgaraig**, then a beeline down the slope northeast leads to the head of **Loch Shin** and the power station road. An easy stroll (or limp) finds the A838, another A-road with little traffic. Turn right down the road into the forestry to reach the **Overscaig Hotel** in 3km.

The Overscaig Hotel has a bar, food and accommodation (tel 01549 431203). There is also a bed and breakfast next door: Oak Lodge (tel 01549 431255 or 07866 040689). There is a place to camp by the forestry track just after you leave the A838 (although you will need to carry water in) – see Day 56 Map 4; alternatively, ask at the hotel.

DAY 57

The Overscaig Hotel to the Crask Inn
The quaking shortcut

Distance	16km (10 miles)
Ascent	400m

This is a very short day, but the Crask Inn is your last chance for a cooked meal and a proper bed before Watten at the end of Day 60, so it's where most people will stay overnight. The other option is to push on to camp or stay in the small bothy at the head of Loch Choire (Day 58 Map 2).

Day 57 consists of two very different sections. The first is a delightful stroll along a forestry track high above Loch Shin (Day 57 Map 1). To get to the track from the hotel you can follow a pathless ride up through the forestry and you're on the track in just a few minutes. The views are extensive, the track pleasant to walk on, and the alternative is dodging occasional fast cars on a narrow road (and you don't want to arrive at Crask too early anyway).

Ben Klibreck and the Crask Inn

The forestry track leads back to the A838 by **Fiag Bridge** (Day 57 Map 2). Here starts the second section – a pathless trudge across featureless peat bog to reach the Crask Inn. It's actually not as bad as it sounds or as it looks on the map though. The bog is blanket bog, but as peat goes it is fairly dry initially and fairly easy to walk on – there is little erosion. It can get very wet underfoot though, on the approach to Crask. The navigation is straightforward and the altitude low, so you will be unlucky if you end up in mist. You can see the Crask Inn for miles before you get there, but if you are tired it seems to take forever to reach.

The **Crask Inn** (tel 01549 411241) is a simple, old-fashioned pub with reasonably priced accommodation and food. It was gifted to the Scottish Episcopal Church by the previous owners, and walkers are made more than welcome, so it is recommended for an overnight stop. You can also camp in the garden.

DAY 56L

Oykel Bridge to Lairg
Lairg alternative

Distance	27km (17 miles)
Ascent	490m

The Lairg alternative is recommended if the weather is bad or if you need to resupply. The first part of the day is a pleasant riverside stroll, but most of the remainder is on roads.

From Oykel Bridge a track follows the north bank of the River Oykel downstream, and then a footbridge crosses the river (Day 56L Map 1). The footpath on the south side of the river is better than the one on the north bank from here. There are many signs of fly fishermen, including huts that make good emergency shelters.

At Langwell Farm the path ends and a cart track climbs along the valley side, descending again to meet the head of a minor road at Brae Farm. From here there is only tarmac to walk on down the valley, then across it to join the A837 and follow it to **Rosehall** and **Invercassley**. Here there is bed and breakfast accommodation and the Achness Hotel, which serves bar meals.

By going through the grounds of the derelict manor house on what could well be the original road up the valley, but is now a quiet, unsurfaced lane, the Trail avoids a stretch of road walking along the A839. After this, it's back to tarmac to climb out of the valley through forestry, to join the A839 (Day 56L Map 2) and follow it most of the way to Lairg. Road walking can be avoided for the last bit into Lairg by following an old path over the **Ord**, a small hill just outside Lairg.

Lairg is a small place but has plenty of facilities, since it is the largest town, indeed the only town, for a long way. There is a tourist information centre, and shops, pubs, bed and breakfasts, a campsite and a couple of cash machines (at the garage and in the High Street).

DAY 57L

Lairg to Loch Choire
Lairg alternative

Distance	29km (18 miles)
Ascent	600m

From Lairg there are two options for rejoining the main Trail. The first is a weary 20km grind north up the A836 to the Crask Inn – this doesn't need a route description, other than a warning not to turn left onto the A838 by mistake. You need to follow this route if your navigation skills aren't good. The second option is to follow forestry tracks through the hills north-northeast of Lairg, by Loch Beannach, to Dalnessie, then follow a little-used path north from here over the hills to descend to the head of Loch Choire. This is an excellent day's walk, but the catch is that the path from Dalnessie to Loch Choire is indeed 'little used', and not always easy to follow. In mist you would be more likely to lose it than not.

From Lairg, minor roads and a path climb out of the valley to a forestry access road past **Loch Dola** and into the forestry plantation (Day 57L Map 1). A brief descent down an old track leads to **Loch Tigh na Creige**, a loch now surrounded by the plantation. The track disappears, and you walk round the shore of the loch to a stile, wondering if there is a way out at all. A short walk along the bank of a stream then a short climb up through the trees and you are soon back on a proper forestry track, which is followed all the way to the edge of the plantation, passing **Loch Beannach**, and up to the isolated houses at **Dalnessie** (Day 57L Map 2). This is a bleak place in poor weather.

The path north from Dalnessie is an old one, and at one time was carefully built – there are signs of this all the way to Loch Choire. The Trail takes the left fork of the valley along the Allt Gobhlach then continues north at the head of the valley, climbing up onto the broad featureless ridge of **Meall an Fhuarain** (Day 57L Map 3).

Careful route-finding will lead to the correct way down the northern slopes, which are much more interesting than the featureless southern side, and down a side valley to the picturesque head of **Loch Choire**. This is an excellent place to camp, and there is also a small bothy here which makes a comfortable overnight stop. You are now back on the main Trail route, 11km into Day 58 (see Day 58 Map 2).

DAY 58

The Crask Inn to Kinbrace
Farewell to the Highlands

Distance	41km (25 miles)
Ascent	490m

Today's route crosses the last bealach, passes the last Munro, and follows the shore of the last mountain lochs in the last glen of the journey. The second half of the day follows an estate road out of the mountains and into upper Helmsdale and the Flow Country hills.

A wet path leads up **Srath a' Chraisg** from the Crask Inn. The valley is wide and featureless, with forestry to the right. As the outlying foothills of Ben Klibreck (961m) draw nearer, the path climbs the hillside and bends to the left to reach **Bealach Easach**, and you feel a very different atmosphere. The slopes are steep, the pass narrow, and the descent to **Loch a' Bhealaich** is to be savoured, not hurried over (Day 58 Map 1). The pass marks another crossing of the main watershed, since the water from Loch Choire flows to the north coast along Strathnaver – another sign that journey's end is approaching.

At the shore of **Loch Choire** (Day 58 Map 2) there is a choice to be made. Turn left and you will follow a good track along the northwest side of the loch to Loch Choire House. Much better, however, is the path on the southeast side, reached by turning right instead, which skirts round the head of the loch. There are bridges to cross the two streams, idyllic camping grounds, and a small bothy. This is where the Lairg alternative rejoins the main route of the Trail. From here the path along the loch potters through patches of old woodland and a constantly changing environment (the path on the northwest side is rather boring by comparison).

At the foot of the loch is **Loch Choire House**, quite impressive as shooting lodges go, and you can follow the estate access road from here to the B871 if you wish. The Trail, however, follows what is presumably the original line of the road for the first 3km. This old track keeps higher up the hillside and is much pleasanter to walk (Day 58 Map 2), although eventually it descends to meet the estate road again (Day 58 Map 3), and from here there is no alternative but to plod along it to **Loch Badanloch**, the River Helmsdale and the B871 (Day 58 Map 4). In the process, you cross the watershed imperceptibly again into the Helmsdale gathering grounds.

Kinbrace is a further 7km eastwards along the B871, but rather than take the road the Trail follows the line (more or less) of an old track above and parallel to the road – this is a pleasant route, and reaches Kinbrace avoiding most of the road walking. You should only take this option if the burns are low though, as the footbridge over Bannock Burn just outside the village is no longer usable. In dry conditions it is possible to ford the burn just upstream of the footbridge, or alternatively you can cross on a bridge a little further upstream, assuming you can cross Claggan Burn first.

Wild camping at Kinbrace

The day ends by the disused footbridge over Bannock Burn just outside the village. This is an excellent place to camp, and camping is the only option here. At **Kinbrace** there is a railway station, a 'main road' (the single track A897) and a school, but no shop or accommodation. Bannock Burn is downstream of farms, so you should not drink from it. Claggan Burn is probably safe to drink from – I'd risk it anyway.

DAY 59

Kinbrace to River Thurso (Dail Righe)
The Knockfin Heights and Glutt Water

Distance	26km (16 miles)
Ascent	420m

Today the Trail climbs up to the soggy plateau of the Knockfin Heights, then descends to follow Glutt Water from its source down the long valley until it becomes the River Thurso. Although the altitude is not great, the country is wild and remote. You are unlikely to see another walker, and may not see another person all day after crossing the road north of Kinbrace.

For the first 3km the Trail follows Bannock Burn up the valley north from Kinbrace, parallel to the road and railway (Day 59 Map 1). The walking is easy and pleasant, so there is little point in following the road instead. After crossing the railway and the A897 you follow the burn northwest, away from the road, across moorland, to reach the remains of the abandoned clearance village of **Knockfin**, at the base of the steep flank of the Knockfin Heights. As well as the ruins and some idyllic camping, there is a fully restored circular sheepfold, showing what all the others you have seen must have looked like at one time.

It is important to locate the ruined village before climbing onto the plateau, unless your navigation skills are pretty good. The Knockfin Heights consist of a featureless, flat plateau of wet peat bog covering a huge area. If you lose your way, you are likely to stay lost until you have descended into one valley or another and regained your bearings. The Trail follows a stream up from Knockfin to approach the Ordnance Survey column on the **Knockfin Heights** (438m) – about the only sure landmark on the whole plateau. It is only the summit in the sense that there are no obvious higher points among the acres of alternative candidates for the title.

Bannock Burn near Kinbrace

At the OS column the Trail leaves Sutherland and enters Caithness (Day 59 Map 2). Around the same point you cross the watershed again – Glutt Water flows eventually to the north coast at Thurso. From the top it is important to descend towards the east, not further south. On this featureless ground it is vital to rely on map and compass, even in clear weather, as poor judgement here could mean a descent into Berriedale before you have realised your mistake.

Once running water has been picked up between the peat hags, following it downhill eventually leads to valley scenery rather than moorland tops. For the first time all day, a track appears – this is stalking country.

Just before you meet the track, 'chalybeate springs' is marked on the 1:25,000 OS map. **Chalybeate**, according to the Oxford English Dictionary, means 'impregnated or flavoured with iron', so the springs appear to be a source of natural, if rather flat, Irn Bru. The spa at Harrogate is based on chalybeate springs, but so far the crowds have not flocked to Glutt Water with quite the same fervour.

The track passes a good hut with seating in it, that walkers are welcome to use for a lunch stop, then continues down to **Glutt Lodge** and its outbuildings.

Circular sheepfold at Knockfin

An untarred access road continues down the valley from Glutt Lodge, past the house at **Dalganachan**, where Glutt Water turns into the River Thurso. Shortly after this, and before Dalnawillan Lodge comes into view (Day 60 Map 1), you reach a flat, grassy field by the river. This is called **Dail Righe**, and is one of the best places to camp between Land's End and John o' Groats (you will have to share it with the varied birdlife though, and possibly deer too).

DAY 60

River Thurso (Dail Righe) to Watten
The River Thurso and Acharole

Distance	33km (21 miles)
Ascent	140m

Today the Trail continues on the access road down the Thurso valley, with the valley becoming wider and flatter all the time. Shortly after the road turns to tarmac, the Trail takes to the riverbank, following it in pleasant meadows to the point where a tributary, the Little River, joins it. You leave the Thurso here for a quarry track up the Little River in wild surroundings, fording the river to reach the A9 Thurso trunk road (there's a bridge option too). A forestry track and a pleasant stroll through meadows lead to the end of a minor road running down the valley into the village of Watten, and the end of the penultimate day.

From the recommended camping ground at Dail Righe, near Dalnawillan Lodge, the access road continues past **Dalnawillan** – the lodge itself is derelict, but a house and noisy kennels are still very much occupied (Day 60 Map 1).

As you continue downriver the valley opens out, with Loch More coming into view. The surroundings are still very much peat moors, but are becoming flatter and flatter – typical Flow Country. The road makes for easy walking. It passes a number of gravel pits, dug to make the road, but other features are few and far between.

Eventually the forestry at the end of **Loch More** is reached, and a short walk through the trees leads to the metalled public road from Lochmore Cottage. There is a stream just off-route in the forestry to replenish your water bottle. Reliable

River Thurso, below Strathmore Lodge

drinking water is hard to find between here and Watten, so don't pass this by unless you are sure you won't regret it later.

If you want to, you can stay on the tarmac – keep straight on and the road leads directly to Watten, today's objective. The Trail, however, takes to the riverbank after the first houses (**Strathmore Lodge**), following a much more interesting and enjoyable route (Day 60 Map 2). The ground by the River Thurso varies between rough moorland and green pastures, but the latter predominate, making this a very pleasant stretch after the long walk on the access road.

Just before the river changes direction from eastward to northwest, two bridges carry a track over it. This track continues southeast, parallel to the Little River, and leads to **Knockdoo quarries**, where a lot of sand and gravel has been extracted over the years. The first quarried area, a section about 1km long, is reached soon after crossing the Thurso. Quarrying was still taking place here in the 1990s, but there's been none in more recent years so the land has started to recover.

At the end of this section the track rises up an artificial ramp to continue across the moorland. This stretch has clearly had little traffic for a long time, and puts the smile back on your face. When you reach the next quarries, at the end of the track, it is plain they have not been active for many decades. Just before two flooded quarries, the track crosses a stream, so you can replenish your water here.

You now have to cross the Little River to get to the A9. Depending on how much water there is in the river you have two options: (1) if the water is low you can cross just before it turns south, to the ruined building at **Torran**, which is the shortest route; (2) if it is not absolutely clear that it is safe to cross here, then there's a bridge below **Tacher farm**, about 700 metres further south. If you want to camp around here, ask at the farm. The A9 is busy, and you have to follow it north until you can enter the forestry on the right (Day 60 Map 3), crossing the watershed for the last time, and also the Trail's last 100m contour in the process.

Once among the trees, the busy road is forgotten in moments. The forestry road is soon following the eastern edge of the plantation, with Halsary Burn alongside, and when the burn turns east away from the forestry, the Trail follows it. This is a lovely walk alongside a 'babbling brook', accompanied by yellow flags (irises) and marsh marigolds in season – a good place to camp if you want to stop.

At **Shielton**, the highest farm in the Acharole valley, the Trail joins the farm access road, which becomes a minor road to Watten. The road is quiet (and what appears to be a possible alternative route along the bank of the burn is not a through route). After passing two brochs and then **Achingale Mill**, the Trail takes to the meadows again for the last short stretch to the crossroads in **Watten**.

Brochs were tall Iron Age stone buildings, found only in Scotland, and the densest concentration of known brochs was here in Caithness. You will see the remains of more tomorrow as you walk north along the coast. They had hollow walls, and may have had an internal wooden structure as well. Most of the brochs in Caithness were excavated in the 19th century, but there is still a lot that is not understood about them.

Watten is a small village with a shop/post office, and the Brown Trout Hotel (tel 01955 621354), which stands at the crossroads. The hotel is the only accommodation actually in the village, and is not expensive. It can fill up with anglers, however, so phoning ahead is worth considering. There's also a bed and breakfast 1km along the A882 towards Wick (Loch Watten House, tel 01955 621223). Alternatively, you should be able to find somewhere discreet to camp by the Wick River a bit further along the Trail.

DAY 61

Watten to Duncansby Head and John o' Groats
The Butt

Distance	39km (24 miles)
Ascent	1020m

This is the last day. It is also the most varied day, one of the toughest days, and one of the very best days. Having said all that, it comes with a health warning. For half the day the Trail follows the cliff tops along the east coast, and for some of this there is no path. Between Keiss and Freswick Bay the route is mainly between the cliff-top fence and the cliff top, and these are occasionally uncomfortably close to each other. If you have no head for heights, it's probably not a good route to take. If you don't want to follow the cliff edge, the best option is to follow the road route north from Watten via Lyth – the road is quiet, but boring. If you head for the coast, then decide not to follow the cliffs, your only real option is the busy A99, but this would be a poor way to end your Land's End to John o' Groats journey.

Here is my journey's end, here is my butt,
And very sea-mark of my utmost sail.
William Shakespeare, Othello

From Watten the first section of the day follows the Wick river downstream (Day 61 Map 1). This is a popular fishing river, so it is possible to follow the bank for most of the way. Some of it is along the edge of crops, some through pasture, until you reach the hamlet of **Bilbster**. Here the Trail leaves the river to head northeast for Sinclair's Bay and the sea. It crosses the railway and follows the B874 for 2km to take a farm access track to the edge of the **Moss of Killimster**, a spectacularly soggy area of flat, heather-covered peat bog at an altitude of only 20m.

In the first edition of this guidebook, the Trail went across the middle of the Moss of Killimster, on difficult ground, very boggy and covered in tall reeds. For this edition, it's been rerouted round the eastern edge of the Moss. It's still quite wet underfoot, but a lot less so than the original route, and there are no reeds to fight through either. The price you have to pay is the extra 2km of road, and a barbed wire fence to cross.

The next short section is along the road from **Killimster** to Westerloch, from where the undersea pipeline assembly line is visible ahead (Day 61 Map 2). That's 'line' as in 'railway line' – 8km of dual railway tracks head inland in a straight line from the shore. Lengths of pipeline are brought up the A99 and added onto the end of the pipeline, which is mounted on bogies on the railway line.

The Trail reaches the A99 (formerly the A9) at **Westerloch**, by the pipeline works, crosses sand dunes, and suddenly you are on the beach – the sands of **Sinclair's Bay**. The next section is a pleasant stroll along the sands to Keiss, as the beach is long, scenic, sandy, and usually deserted. The sands end just before Keiss, and from the end of the beach a good track above the shore leads to the village.

Keiss has a pretty little harbour, a hotel (the Sinclair Bay Hotel) and other bed and breakfast accommodation. John o' Groats via the Trail is a long and strenuous way from here, so if you aren't going to make it today, then Keiss is probably the best place to stop for the night. If you want to camp, you can find a good place for a tent by the cliff-top path between the harbour and the castle.

From Keiss to Freswick Bay the Trail follows the cliff top, and as far as the picturesque ruins of **Keiss Castle** (Day 61 Map 3) there is a clear path.

> **Keiss Castle** is a typical Scottish cliff-top castle, and over 300 years old. Built on the cliff edge for defence, it was obviously designed to repel enemies. The newer 'Keiss Castle' inland from the ruin is also typical of its period. Many ugly buildings, such as this and the former John O'Groats House Hotel, were put up along the Caithness coast once the railway had made access easier, although this one actually predates the railway.

From Keiss Castle to **Freswick Bay** the cliffs are less frequented and there is no clear path. In summer, whenever a stream or field drain reaches the cliff edge, there is a patch of nettles, and sometimes there is little room between fence and cliff top to avoid them. Long trousers are essential.

Bucholly Castle

The cliff scenery, on the other hand, is some of the best in Britain. The situation of the ruins of **Bucholly Castle**, in particular, is astonishing, and the contorted strata below the castle just have to be seen. Every geo is also worth investigating. (For the uninitiated, a geo is an inlet in the cliffs, often very narrow. They are called 'zawns' in Wales and the southwest of England, and there are a lot of them along this eastern coast of Caithness, giving plenty of very atmospheric places to peer down into.)

At **Freswick Bay** the Trail passes Freswick Castle, a 17th-century fortified house built on the foundations of a 12th-century Viking building. Viking remains have been found in Freswick Bay, including that of the only known longhouse in Scotland.

At the far end of the beach the Trail abandons the cliffs briefly – a fence has been put up too close to the edge for comfort. You are soon back above the cliffs again though, on a pathless section round the headland to a quarry and **Skippie Geo** (Day 61 Map 4). Following the coast north from here to Duncansby Head is straightforward, if not always quick underfoot. Nowhere are you constrained uncomfortably between fence and cliff top. The cliff scenery continues to be spectacular to the end, and although alternative shortcuts away from the cliffs are sometimes possible, they are disappointing in comparison. There is a clear path most of the way, with alternatives as you get closer to Duncansby Head. Again, the best views are to be had from closer to the cliffs, which rise to over 60m.

From **Duncansby Head** the views to the north across the Pentland Firth are wonderful, and there is a panorama diagram showing which island is which. The nearest island is Stroma, with the Orkneys behind and the Pentland Skerries over to the right. Over to the left is St John's Point, with Dunnet Head behind it, the most northerly point of the Scottish mainland.

Duncansby Head is logically the end of the route, although the Trail continues to **John o' Groats**, following the coast to end at the pier and the former John O'Groats House Hotel.

The end: John o' Groats

Approached this way, John o' Groats feels less of an anticlimax than if approached by road, which is what cyclists and many walkers do. Principally, it is because you meet Duncansby Head, its Ordnance Survey column, its lighthouse and its cliffs before you meet the village itself.

As you reach John o' Groats the path forks – keep left to enter the campsite, or right for the pier and the hotel. If you want accommodation or a meal, there is a tourist information centre here, with addresses and phone numbers in the window. In any event, your best bet is to follow the road inland for a few minutes. Meals and accommodation are available at the Seaview Hotel, and there are bed and breakfasts close by. The John O'Groats House Hotel itself, after many years in a semi-derelict state, has now been converted into self-catering accommodation and renamed 'The Inn at John O'Groats'.

Sort out your accommodation, get something to eat, and have a drink or two, and if you want, you can register your achievement at the Seaview Hotel. You are entitled to sit back with a self-satisfied grin on your face – you've made it.

John o' Groats has a long history (although most of what is here now is due to the growing number of tourists over the past 100 years or so). James IV of Scotland wanted to set up a regular ferry service to connect his new territory, the Orkneys, to the Scottish mainland, to consolidate his hold on them. He engaged three Dutchmen, possibly brothers, to set up the ferry, and they turned up in the wilds of Caithness in 1496. They ran the ferry service to the Orkneys from the location that was most practical, close to the northeast corner of the mainland. One of the three Dutchmen was called Jan de Groot, which led to the wilderness location from which they ran the ferry becoming known as John o' Groats. Today it's still next to nothing in the middle of nowhere, but the ferry continues to run, half a millennium later.

The legend of Jan de Groot building an octagonal house with an octagonal table in it to resolve family hierarchy squabbles appears to be no more substantiated than King Arthur's suspiciously similar round table at Tintagel. Elihu Burritt found little evidence for it in 1863, which was before the new hotel was built nearby.

The Huna Inn is where Elihu Burritt and the Naylor brothers stayed on the earliest Land's End–John o' Groats walks. At that time there was nothing much at John O'Groats but the vague marks on the ground where Jan de Groot's house had been – the Huna Inn was 2km to the west by the shore of the Pentland Firth. In 1875, four years after the Naylors were here, the John O'Groats House Hotel opened.

There are various spellings of the name John o' Groats. For this guide, I have adopted the spelling used by the Ordnance Survey, with a lower case 'o' and a space before 'Groats'. The Inn at John O'Groats is an exception: I have used the spelling given on their website for this and for the inn's previous incarnation as the John O'Groats House Hotel.

How to leave John o' Groats

The rest of this book is about how to get to John o' Groats, but all you need is a short paragraph to get you away again. For times of the buses from John o' Groats to Wick and Inverness, check the Stagecoach website www.stagecoachbus.com and the John o' Groats Ferry website www.jogferry.co.uk before you set out. The bus stop is in the car park by the tourist information centre. There are four or five buses a day, but none on Sundays apart from two ferry coaches to Inverness in the summer months. From Wick you can catch a train south, but don't forget you're a long way north. It is likely to take you more than a day to get home, if home isn't in Scotland.

RECOGNITION OF YOUR FEAT

There is nothing 'official' about walking between Land's End and John o' Groats, but there is an organisation you can register your achievement with if you wish, whether you have walked, cycled or driven End to End. You will need to collect evidence of your journey, in the form of signatures of witnesses along your route.

The Land's End John o' Groats Association

This is an independent association run by its members. If you send them £15 for your first year's membership, together with evidence of your journey, they will send you a certificate, and a magazine three times a year. Continuing membership is £15 annually, there is an annual dinner and presentation weekend, and other social events. And you may even win a trophy – the Shanks Pony Trophy is awarded annually to 'the individual/s who achieve the best performance on foot'. For details go to www.lejog.org.

Registration

Arrangements for registration for the Association have changed from time to time, so check their websites for the latest information. You will need to pick up or download a form and follow instructions for collecting evidence of your journey along the way. You can register your finish at the Seaview Hotel in John o' Groats.

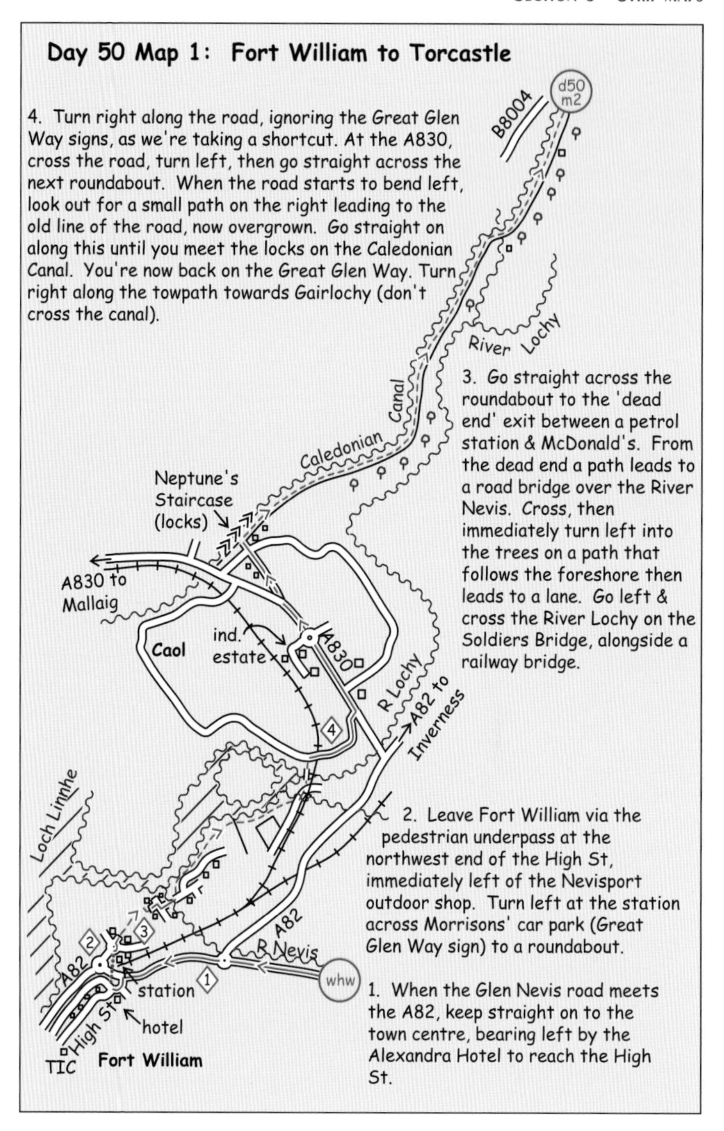
Day 50 Map 1: Fort William to Torcastle
d50 m2
B8004
4. Turn right along the road, ignoring the Great Glen Way signs, as we're taking a shortcut. At the A830, cross the road, turn left, then go straight across the next roundabout. When the road starts to bend left, look out for a small path on the right leading to the old line of the road, now overgrown. Go straight on along this until you meet the locks on the Caledonian Canal. You're now back on the Great Glen Way. Turn right along the towpath towards Gairlochy (don't cross the canal).
River Lochy
Caledonian Canal
3. Go straight across the roundabout to the 'dead end' exit between a petrol station & McDonald's. From the dead end a path leads to a road bridge over the River Nevis. Cross, then immediately turn left into the trees on a path that follows the foreshore then leads to a lane. Go left & cross the River Lochy on the Soldiers Bridge, alongside a railway bridge.
Neptune's Staircase (locks)
A830 to Mallaig
Caol
ind. estate
A830
R Lochy
A82 to Inverness
4
Loch Linnhe
2. Leave Fort William via the pedestrian underpass at the northwest end of the High St, immediately left of the Nevisport outdoor shop. Turn left at the station across Morrisons' car park (Great Glen Way sign) to a roundabout.
A82
R Nevis
2
3
1
whw
A82
station
hotel
High St
TIC
Fort William
1. When the Glen Nevis road meets the A82, keep straight on to the town centre, bearing left by the Alexandra Hotel to reach the High St.

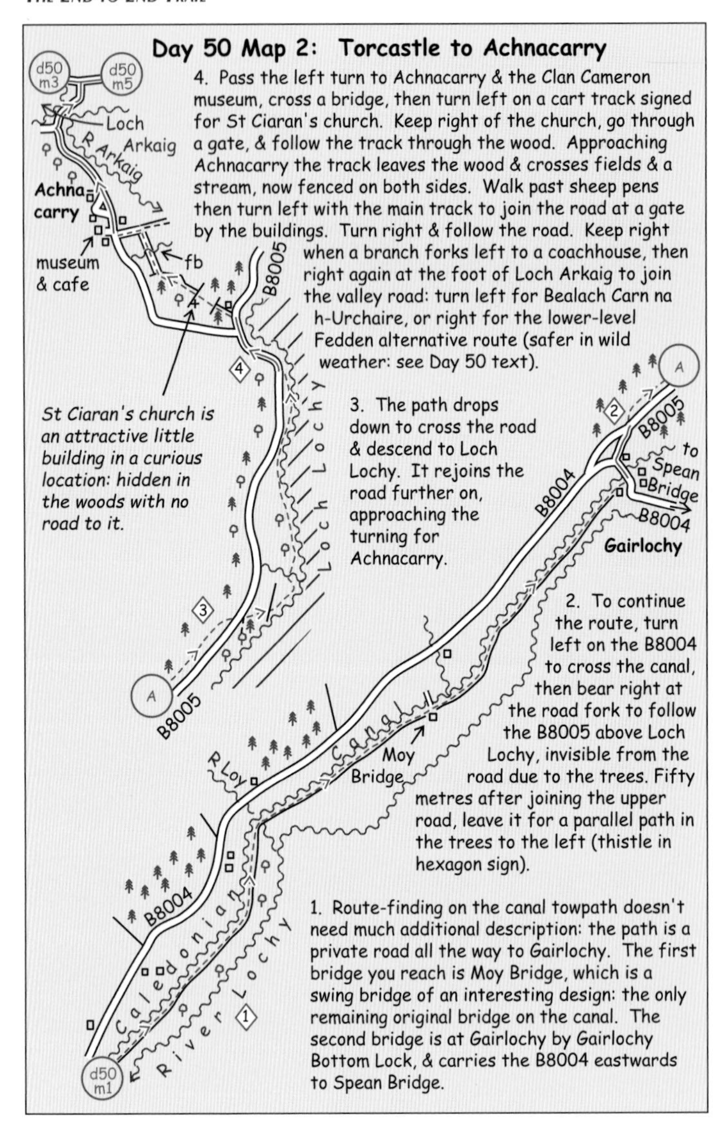

Day 50 Map 2: Torcastle to Achnacarry
d50 m3
d50 m5
Loch Arkaig
R Arkaig
Achnacarry
museum & cafe
fb
B8005
4. Pass the left turn to Achnacarry & the Clan Cameron museum, cross a bridge, then turn left on a cart track signed for St Ciaran's church. Keep right of the church, go through a gate, & follow the track through the wood. Approaching Achnacarry the track leaves the wood & crosses fields & a stream, now fenced on both sides. Walk past sheep pens then turn left with the main track to join the road at a gate by the buildings. Turn right & follow the road. Keep right when a branch forks left to a coachhouse, then right again at the foot of Loch Arkaig to join the valley road: turn left for Bealach Carn na h-Urchaire, or right for the lower-level Fedden alternative route (safer in wild weather: see Day 50 text).
St Ciaran's church is an attractive little building in a curious location: hidden in the woods with no road to it.
Loch Lochy
3. The path drops down to cross the road & descend to Loch Lochy. It rejoins the road further on, approaching the turning for Achnacarry.
A
B8005
B8004
to Spean Bridge
B8004
Gairlochy
2. To continue the route, turn left on the B8004 to cross the canal, then bear right at the road fork to follow the B8005 above Loch Lochy, invisible from the road due to the trees. Fifty metres after joining the upper road, leave it for a parallel path in the trees to the left (thistle in hexagon sign).
A
B8005
R Loy
Caledonian Canal
Moy Bridge
B8004
River Lochy
d50 m1
1. Route-finding on the canal towpath doesn't need much additional description: the path is a private road all the way to Gairlochy. The first bridge you reach is Moy Bridge, which is a swing bridge of an interesting design: the only remaining original bridge on the canal. The second bridge is at Gairlochy by Gairlochy Bottom Lock, & carries the B8004 eastwards to Spean Bridge.

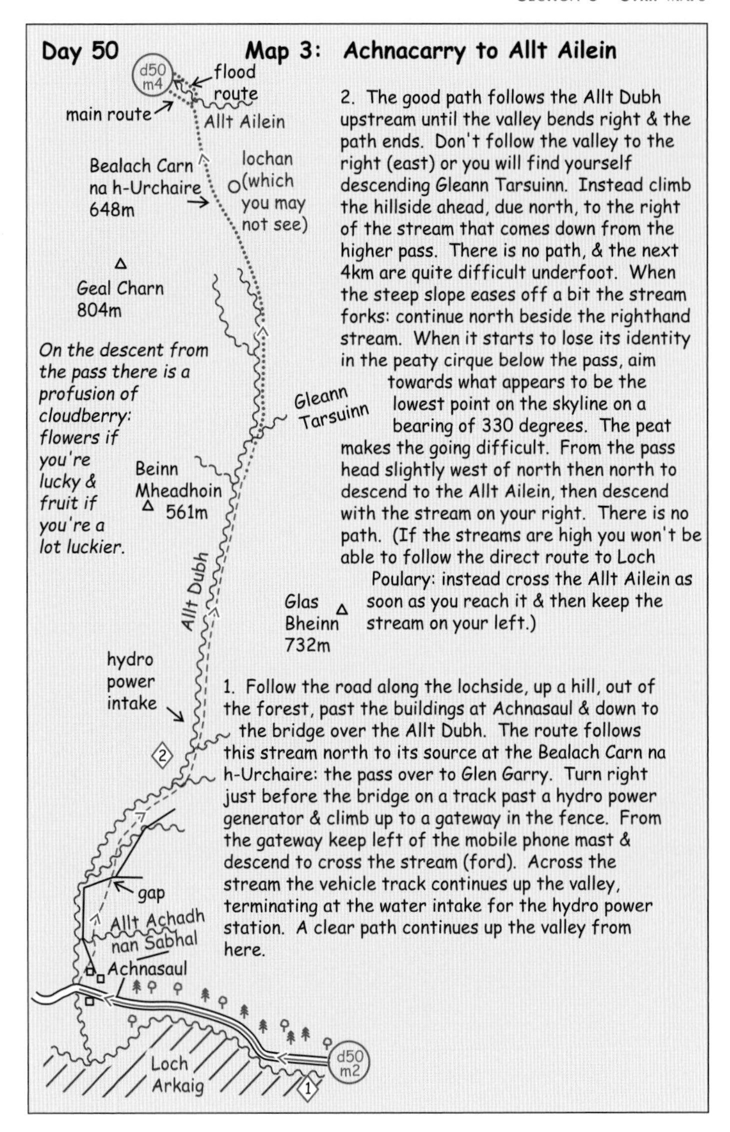
Day 50
Map 3: Achnacarry to Allt Ailein
d50 m4
flood route
main route
Allt Ailein
Bealach Carn na h-Urchaire 648m
lochan (which you may not see)
Geal Charn 804m
On the descent from the pass there is a profusion of cloudberry: flowers if you're lucky & fruit if you're a lot luckier.
Gleann Tarsuinn
Beinn Mheadhoin 561m
Allt Dubh
Glas Bheinn 732m
hydro power intake
2
gap
Allt Achadh nan Sabhal
Achnasaul
Loch Arkaig
d50 m2
1
2. The good path follows the Allt Dubh upstream until the valley bends right & the path ends. Don't follow the valley to the right (east) or you will find yourself descending Gleann Tarsuinn. Instead climb the hillside ahead, due north, to the right of the stream that comes down from the higher pass. There is no path, & the next 4km are quite difficult underfoot. When the steep slope eases off a bit the stream forks: continue north beside the righthand stream. When it starts to lose its identity in the peaty cirque below the pass, aim towards what appears to be the lowest point on the skyline on a bearing of 330 degrees. The peat makes the going difficult. From the pass head slightly west of north then north to descend to the Allt Ailein, then descend with the stream on your right. There is no path. (If the streams are high you won't be able to follow the direct route to Loch Poulary: instead cross the Allt Ailein as soon as you reach it & then keep the stream on your left.)
1. Follow the road along the lochside, up a hill, out of the forest, past the buildings at Achnasaul & down to the bridge over the Allt Dubh. The route follows this stream north to its source at the Bealach Carn na h-Urchaire: the pass over to Glen Garry. Turn right just before the bridge on a track past a hydro power generator & climb up to a gateway in the fence. From the gateway keep left of the mobile phone mast & descend to cross the stream (ford). Across the stream the vehicle track continues up the valley, terminating at the water intake for the hydro power station. A clear path continues up the valley from here.

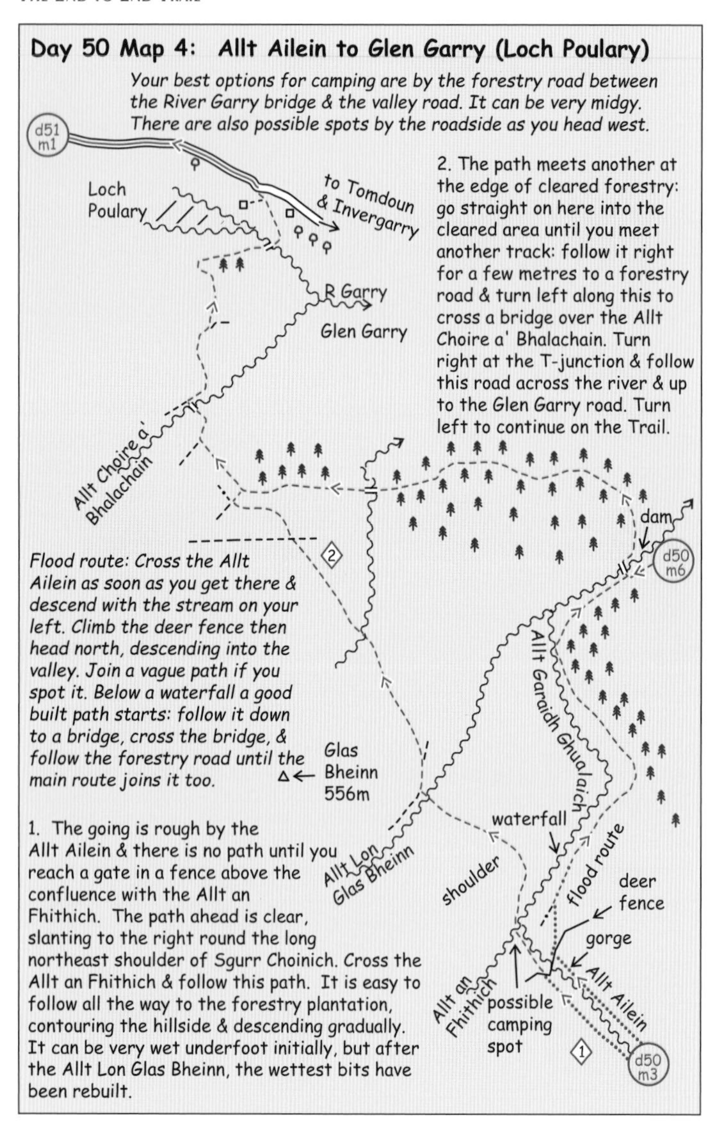

Day 50 Map 4: Allt Ailein to Glen Garry (Loch Poulary)
Your best options for camping are by the forestry road between the River Garry bridge & the valley road. It can be very midgy. There are also possible spots by the roadside as you head west.
d51 m1
Loch Poulary
to Tomdoun & Invergarry
2. The path meets another at the edge of cleared forestry: go straight on here into the cleared area until you meet another track: follow it right for a few metres to a forestry road & turn left along this to cross a bridge over the Allt Choire a' Bhalachain. Turn right at the T-junction & follow this road across the river & up to the Glen Garry road. Turn left to continue on the Trail.
R Garry
Glen Garry
Allt Choire a' Bhalachain
dam
d50 m6
2
Flood route: Cross the Allt Ailein as soon as you get there & descend with the stream on your left. Climb the deer fence then head north, descending into the valley. Join a vague path if you spot it. Below a waterfall a good built path starts: follow it down to a bridge, cross the bridge, & follow the forestry road until the main route joins it too.
Glas Bheinn 556m
Allt Garaidh Ghualaich
waterfall
flood route
1. The going is rough by the Allt Ailein & there is no path until you reach a gate in a fence above the confluence with the Allt an Fhithich. The path ahead is clear, slanting to the right round the long northeast shoulder of Sgurr Choinich. Cross the Allt an Fhithich & follow this path. It is easy to follow all the way to the forestry plantation, contouring the hillside & descending gradually. It can be very wet underfoot initially, but after the Allt Lon Glas Bheinn, the wettest bits have been rebuilt.
Allt Lon Glas Bheinn
shoulder
deer fence
gorge
Allt Ailein
Allt an Fhithich
possible camping spot
1
d50 m3

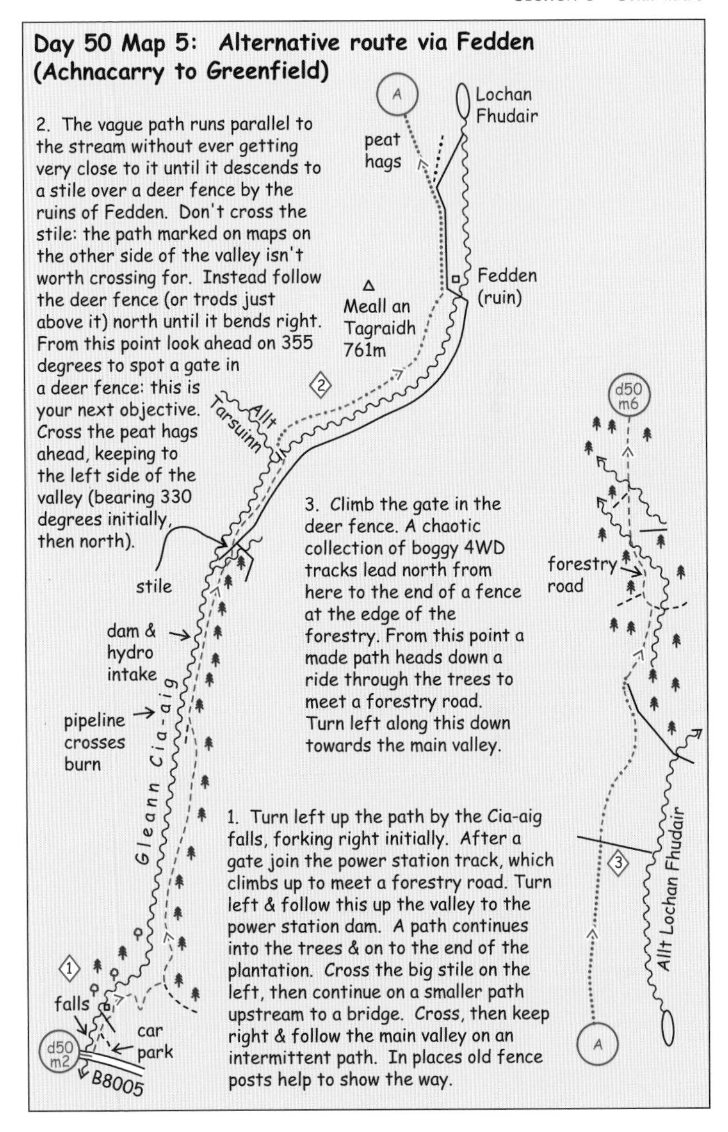
Day 50 Map 5: Alternative route via Fedden (Achnacarry to Greenfield)
2. The vague path runs parallel to the stream without ever getting very close to it until it descends to a stile over a deer fence by the ruins of Fedden. Don't cross the stile: the path marked on maps on the other side of the valley isn't worth crossing for. Instead follow the deer fence (or trods just above it) north until it bends right. From this point look ahead on 355 degrees to spot a gate in a deer fence: this is your next objective. Cross the peat hags ahead, keeping to the left side of the valley (bearing 330 degrees initially, then north).
A
Lochan Fhudair
peat hags
Fedden (ruin)
Meall an Tagraidh 761m
2
Allt Tarsuinn
d50 m6
3. Climb the gate in the deer fence. A chaotic collection of boggy 4WD tracks lead north from here to the end of a fence at the edge of the forestry. From this point a made path heads down a ride through the trees to meet a forestry road. Turn left along this down towards the main valley.
stile
forestry road
dam & hydro intake
pipeline crosses burn
Gleann Cia-aig
1. Turn left up the path by the Cia-aig falls, forking right initially. After a gate join the power station track, which climbs up to meet a forestry road. Turn left & follow this up the valley to the power station dam. A path continues into the trees & on to the end of the plantation. Cross the big stile on the left, then continue on a smaller path upstream to a bridge. Cross, then keep right & follow the main valley on an intermittent path. In places old fence posts help to show the way.
3
Allt Lochan Fhudair
1
falls
car park
d50 m2
B8005
A

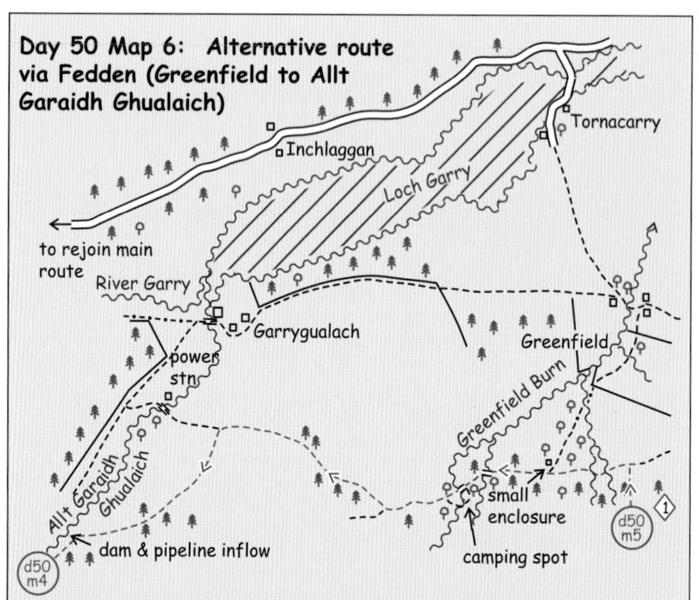

1. Continuation of the Fedden route: Follow the forestry road to a T-junction & turn left. Follow this road over two substantial bridges (there is an old track round the second of these to a ford that makes a good place to camp). Keep straight on at the first junction then when the road forks take the main fork left uphill to reach a bridge where you rejoin the main route.

If instead you want to get to the valley road as quickly as possible: Follow the forestry road to a T-junction & turn left. The track crosses two small streams then bends slightly left. In another 200 metres the trees on the left change from mature to younger trees. At this point turn sharp right (cairn) on a small path past a small fenced enclosure. Ford a stream, then the path disappears in a small but difficult felled area. Walk on 30 degrees until fallen trees stop you. Skirt them on the right then descend a short gully to the left (300 degrees). At the bottom bear right (north then 30 degrees), bear right round another area of brash to find the path again, to a gate, & follow it down to meet an untarred road by houses at Greenfield. Turn left across the bridge & follow the road to a big bridge across Loch Garry & the tarmac of the valley road. Turn left to Tomdoun & beyond to rejoin the main route at the end of Loch Poulary.

If the path through from the small enclosure to Greenfield has become impossible to follow, return to the forestry track & follow it east, then take the first sharp left which takes you to Greenfield, adding 3km to the day.

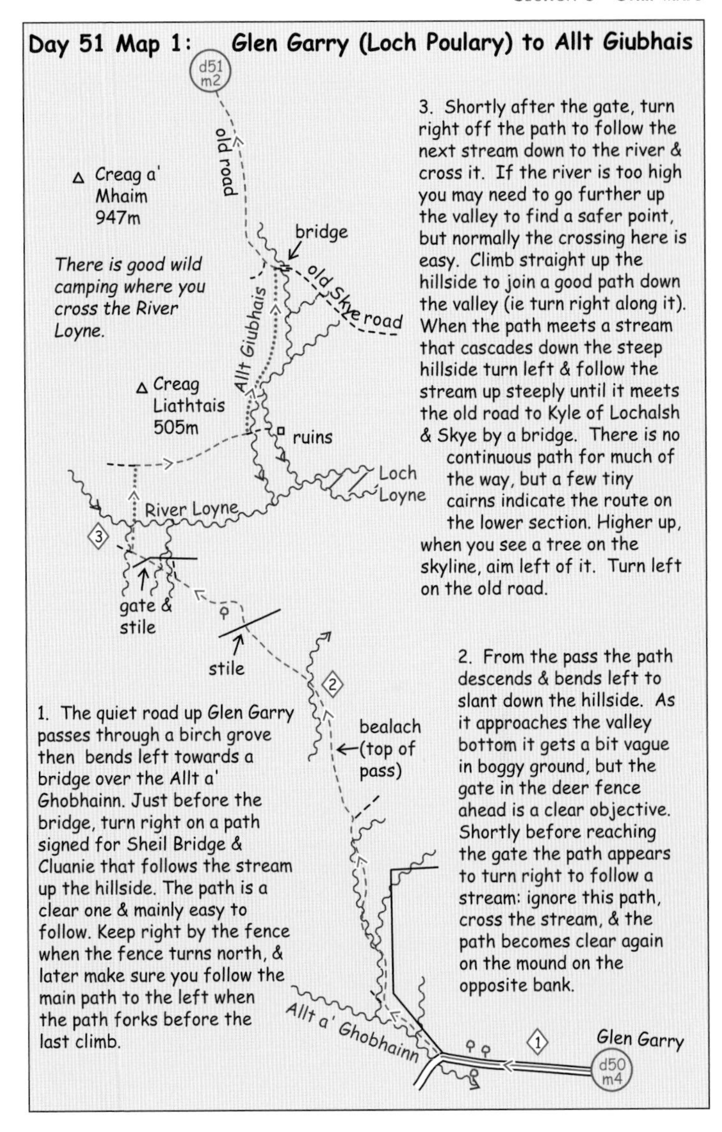
Day 51 Map 1: Glen Garry (Loch Poulary) to Allt Giubhais
d51 m2
old road
Creag a' Mhaim 947m
bridge
old Skye road
There is good wild camping where you cross the River Loyne.
Allt Giubhais
Creag Liathtais 505m
ruins
Loch Loyne
River Loyne
3
gate & stile
stile
2
bealach (top of pass)
Allt a' Ghobhainn
1
Glen Garry
d50 m4
3. Shortly after the gate, turn right off the path to follow the next stream down to the river & cross it. If the river is too high you may need to go further up the valley to find a safer point, but normally the crossing here is easy. Climb straight up the hillside to join a good path down the valley (ie turn right along it). When the path meets a stream that cascades down the steep hillside turn left & follow the stream up steeply until it meets the old road to Kyle of Lochalsh & Skye by a bridge. There is no continuous path for much of the way, but a few tiny cairns indicate the route on the lower section. Higher up, when you see a tree on the skyline, aim left of it. Turn left on the old road.
2. From the pass the path descends & bends left to slant down the hillside. As it approaches the valley bottom it gets a bit vague in boggy ground, but the gate in the deer fence ahead is a clear objective. Shortly before reaching the gate the path appears to turn right to follow a stream: ignore this path, cross the stream, & the path becomes clear again on the mound on the opposite bank.
1. The quiet road up Glen Garry passes through a birch grove then bends left towards a bridge over the Allt a' Ghobhainn. Just before the bridge, turn right on a path signed for Sheil Bridge & Cluanie that follows the stream up the hillside. The path is a clear one & mainly easy to follow. Keep right by the fence when the fence turns north, & later make sure you follow the main path to the left when the path forks before the last climb.

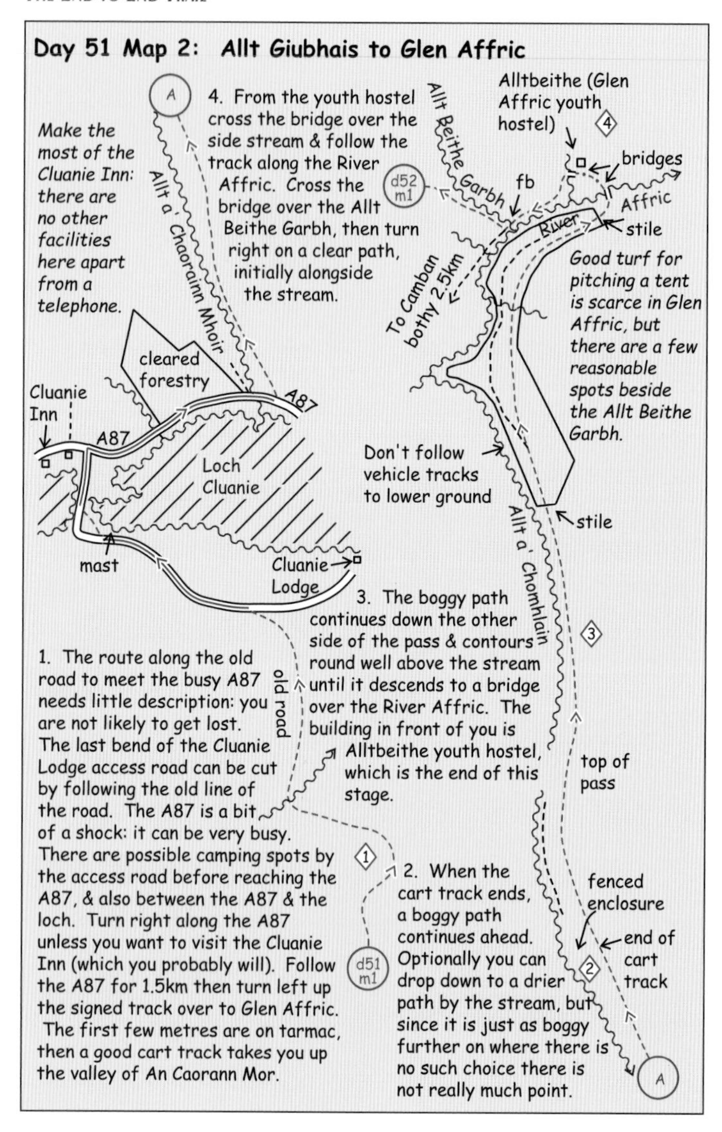

Day 51 Map 2: Allt Giubhais to Glen Affric
A
Make the most of the Cluanie Inn: there are no other facilities here apart from a telephone.
4. From the youth hostel cross the bridge over the side stream & follow the track along the River Affric. Cross the bridge over the Allt Beithe Garbh, then turn right on a clear path, initially alongside the stream.
d52 m1
Allt Beithe Garbh
Alltbeithe (Glen Affric youth hostel)
4
bridges
fb
Affric
River
stile
Good turf for pitching a tent is scarce in Glen Affric, but there are a few reasonable spots beside the Allt Beithe Garbh.
To Camban bothy 2.5km
Allt a' Chaorainn Mhoir
cleared forestry
Cluanie Inn
A87
A87
Loch Cluanie
Don't follow vehicle tracks to lower ground
stile
Allt a' Chomhlain
mast
Cluanie Lodge
3. The boggy path continues down the other side of the pass & contours round well above the stream until it descends to a bridge over the River Affric. The building in front of you is Alltbeithe youth hostel, which is the end of this stage.
3
old road
1. The route along the old road to meet the busy A87 needs little description: you are not likely to get lost. The last bend of the Cluanie Lodge access road can be cut by following the old line of the road. The A87 is a bit of a shock: it can be very busy. There are possible camping spots by the access road before reaching the A87, & also between the A87 & the loch. Turn right along the A87 unless you want to visit the Cluanie Inn (which you probably will). Follow the A87 for 1.5km then turn left up the signed track over to Glen Affric. The first few metres are on tarmac, then a good cart track takes you up the valley of An Caorann Mor.
top of pass
1
2. When the cart track ends, a boggy path continues ahead. Optionally you can drop down to a drier path by the stream, but since it is just as boggy further on where there is no such choice there is not really much point.
fenced enclosure
end of cart track
d51 m1
2
A

Day 52 Map 1: Glen Affric to the Falls of Glomach

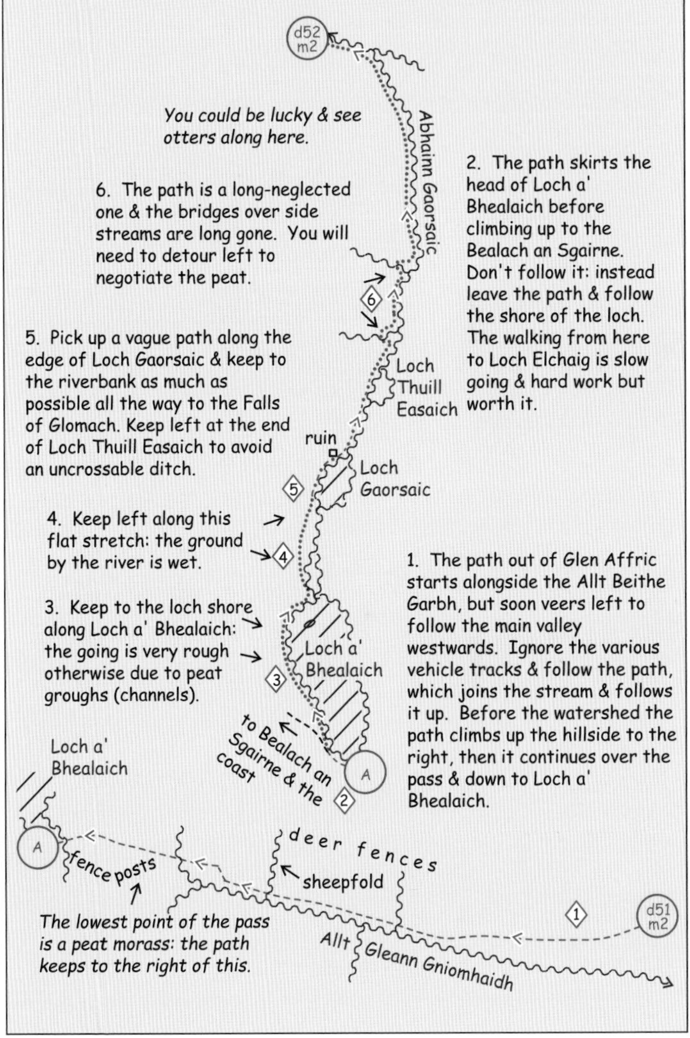

d52 m2

You could be lucky & see otters along here.

Abhainn Gaorsaic

2. The path skirts the head of Loch a' Bhealaich before climbing up to the Bealach an Sgairne. Don't follow it: instead leave the path & follow the shore of the loch. The walking from here to Loch Elchaig is slow going & hard work but worth it.

6. The path is a long-neglected one & the bridges over side streams are long gone. You will need to detour left to negotiate the peat.

5. Pick up a vague path along the edge of Loch Gaorsaic & keep to the riverbank as much as possible all the way to the Falls of Glomach. Keep left at the end of Loch Thuill Easaich to avoid an uncrossable ditch.

Loch Thuill Easaich

ruin

Loch Gaorsaic

4. Keep left along this flat stretch: the ground by the river is wet.

1. The path out of Glen Affric starts alongside the Allt Beithe Garbh, but soon veers left to follow the main valley westwards. Ignore the various vehicle tracks & follow the path, which joins the stream & follows it up. Before the watershed the path climbs up the hillside to the right, then it continues over the pass & down to Loch a' Bhealaich.

3. Keep to the loch shore along Loch a' Bhealaich: the going is very rough otherwise due to peat groughs (channels).

Loch a' Bhealaich

to Bealach an Sgairne & the coast

A

Loch a' Bhealaich

A

fence posts

deer fences

sheepfold

d51 m2

The lowest point of the pass is a peat morass: the path keeps to the right of this.

Allt Gleann Gniomhaidh

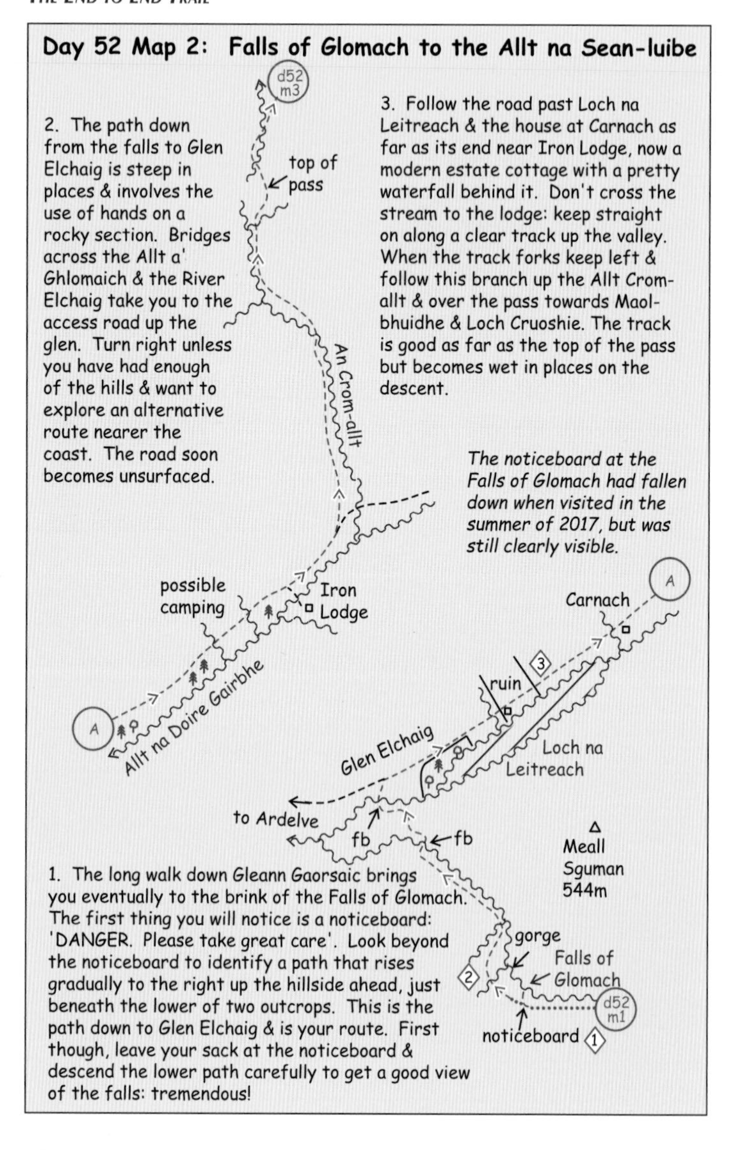
Day 52 Map 2: Falls of Glomach to the Allt na Sean-luibe
d52 m3
2. The path down from the falls to Glen Elchaig is steep in places & involves the use of hands on a rocky section. Bridges across the Allt a' Ghlomaich & the River Elchaig take you to the access road up the glen. Turn right unless you have had enough of the hills & want to explore an alternative route nearer the coast. The road soon becomes unsurfaced.
top of pass
3. Follow the road past Loch na Leitreach & the house at Carnach as far as its end near Iron Lodge, now a modern estate cottage with a pretty waterfall behind it. Don't cross the stream to the lodge: keep straight on along a clear track up the valley. When the track forks keep left & follow this branch up the Allt Crom-allt & over the pass towards Maol-bhuidhe & Loch Cruoshie. The track is good as far as the top of the pass but becomes wet in places on the descent.
An Crom-allt
The noticeboard at the Falls of Glomach had fallen down when visited in the summer of 2017, but was still clearly visible.
possible camping
Iron Lodge
A
Carnach
3
ruin
A
Allt na Doire Gairbhe
Glen Elchaig
Loch na Leitreach
to Ardelve
fb
fb
Meall Sguman 544m
1. The long walk down Gleann Gaorsaic brings you eventually to the brink of the Falls of Glomach. The first thing you will notice is a noticeboard: 'DANGER. Please take great care'. Look beyond the noticeboard to identify a path that rises gradually to the right up the hillside ahead, just beneath the lower of two outcrops. This is the path down to Glen Elchaig & is your route. First though, leave your sack at the noticeboard & descend the lower path carefully to get a good view of the falls: tremendous!
gorge
Falls of Glomach
2
d52 m1
noticeboard
1

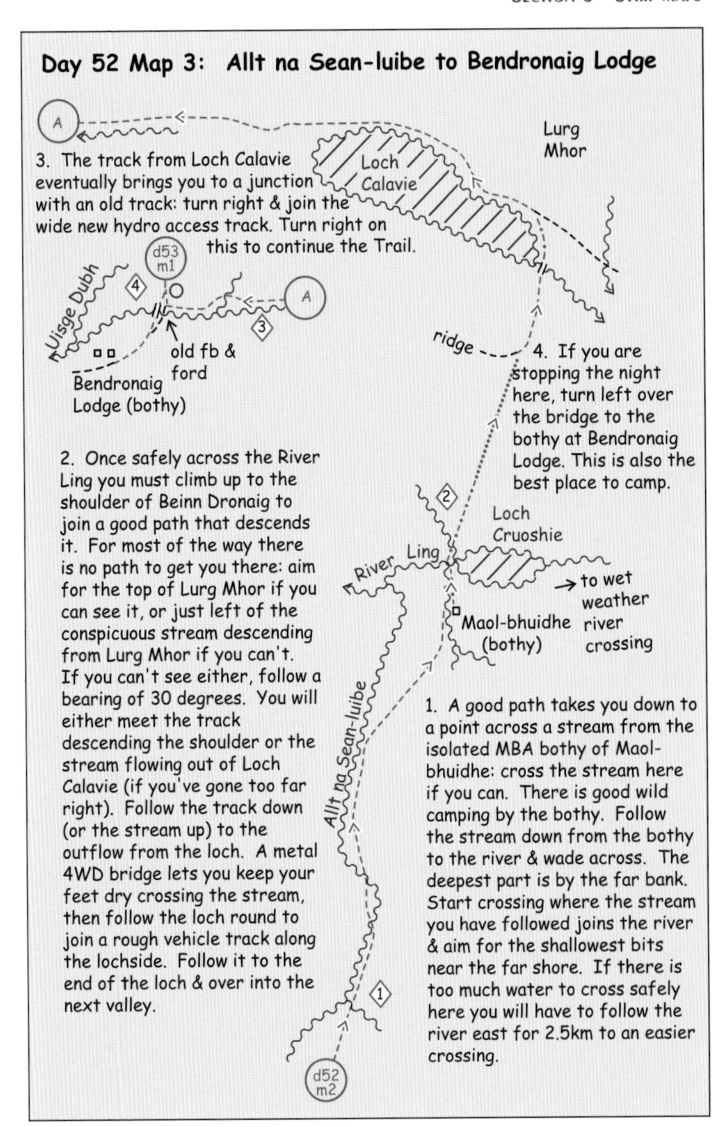
Day 52 Map 3: Allt na Sean-luibe to Bendronaig Lodge
A
Lurg
Mhor
3. The track from Loch Calavie eventually brings you to a junction with an old track: turn right & join the wide new hydro access track. Turn right on this to continue the Trail.
Loch
Calavie
d53
m1
4
Uisge Dubh
A
3
old fb &
ford
Bendronaig
Lodge (bothy)
ridge
4. If you are stopping the night here, turn left over the bridge to the bothy at Bendronaig Lodge. This is also the best place to camp.
2. Once safely across the River Ling you must climb up to the shoulder of Beinn Dronaig to join a good path that descends it. For most of the way there is no path to get you there: aim for the top of Lurg Mhor if you can see it, or just left of the conspicuous stream descending from Lurg Mhor if you can't. If you can't see either, follow a bearing of 30 degrees. You will either meet the track descending the shoulder or the stream flowing out of Loch Calavie (if you've gone too far right). Follow the track down (or the stream up) to the outflow from the loch. A metal 4WD bridge lets you keep your feet dry crossing the stream, then follow the loch round to join a rough vehicle track along the lochside. Follow it to the end of the loch & over into the next valley.
2
Loch
Cruoshie
River Ling
to wet
weather
river
crossing
Maol-bhuidhe
(bothy)
Allt na Sean-luibe
1. A good path takes you down to a point across a stream from the isolated MBA bothy of Maol-bhuidhe: cross the stream here if you can. There is good wild camping by the bothy. Follow the stream down from the bothy to the river & wade across. The deepest part is by the far bank. Start crossing where the stream you have followed joins the river & aim for the shallowest bits near the far shore. If there is too much water to cross safely here you will have to follow the river east for 2.5km to an easier crossing.
1
d52
m2

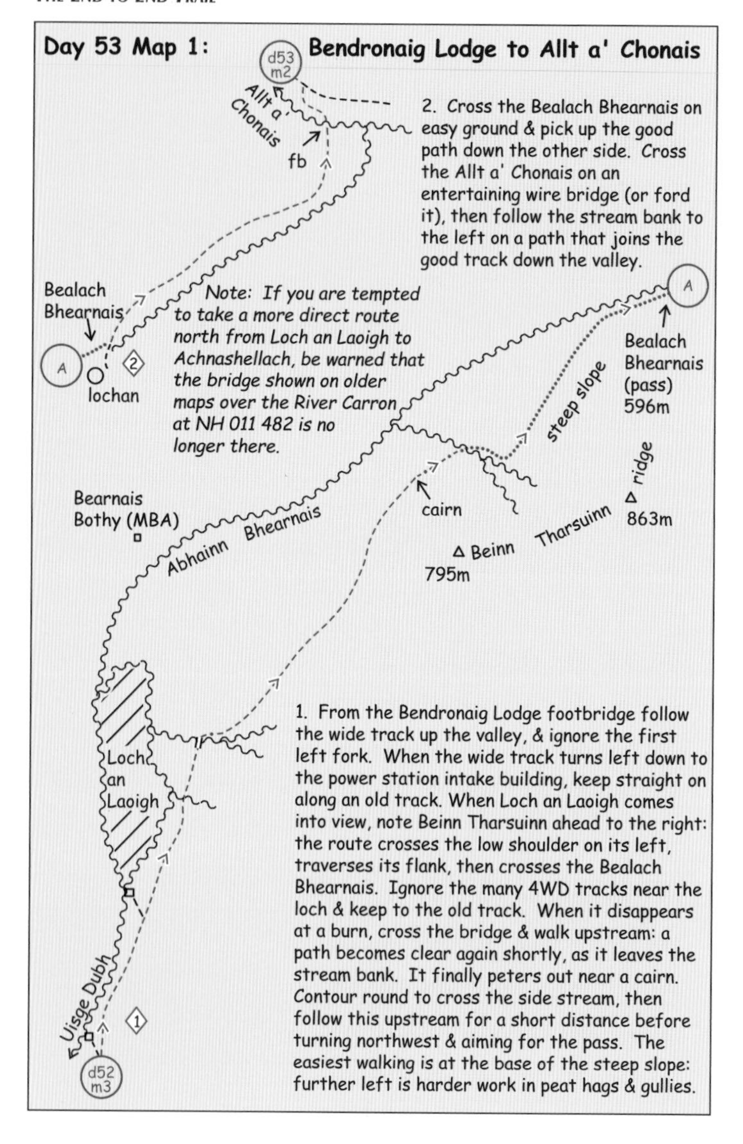
Day 53 Map 1:
Bendronaig Lodge to Allt a' Chonais
d53 m2
Allt a' Chonais
fb
2. Cross the Bealach Bhearnais on easy ground & pick up the good path down the other side. Cross the Allt a' Chonais on an entertaining wire bridge (or ford it), then follow the stream bank to the left on a path that joins the good track down the valley.
Bealach Bhearnais
A
lochan
2
Note: If you are tempted to take a more direct route north from Loch an Laoigh to Achnashellach, be warned that the bridge shown on older maps over the River Carron at NH 011 482 is no longer there.
A
Bealach Bhearnais (pass) 596m
steep slope
ridge
863m
cairn
Bearnais Bothy (MBA)
Abhainn Bhearnais
Beinn Tharsuinn
795m
Loch an Laoigh
1. From the Bendronaig Lodge footbridge follow the wide track up the valley, & ignore the first left fork. When the wide track turns left down to the power station intake building, keep straight on along an old track. When Loch an Laoigh comes into view, note Beinn Tharsuinn ahead to the right: the route crosses the low shoulder on its left, traverses its flank, then crosses the Bealach Bhearnais. Ignore the many 4WD tracks near the loch & keep to the old track. When it disappears at a burn, cross the bridge & walk upstream: a path becomes clear again shortly, as it leaves the stream bank. It finally peters out near a cairn. Contour round to cross the side stream, then follow this upstream for a short distance before turning northwest & aiming for the pass. The easiest walking is at the base of the steep slope: further left is harder work in peat hags & gullies.
Uisge Dubh
1
d52 m3

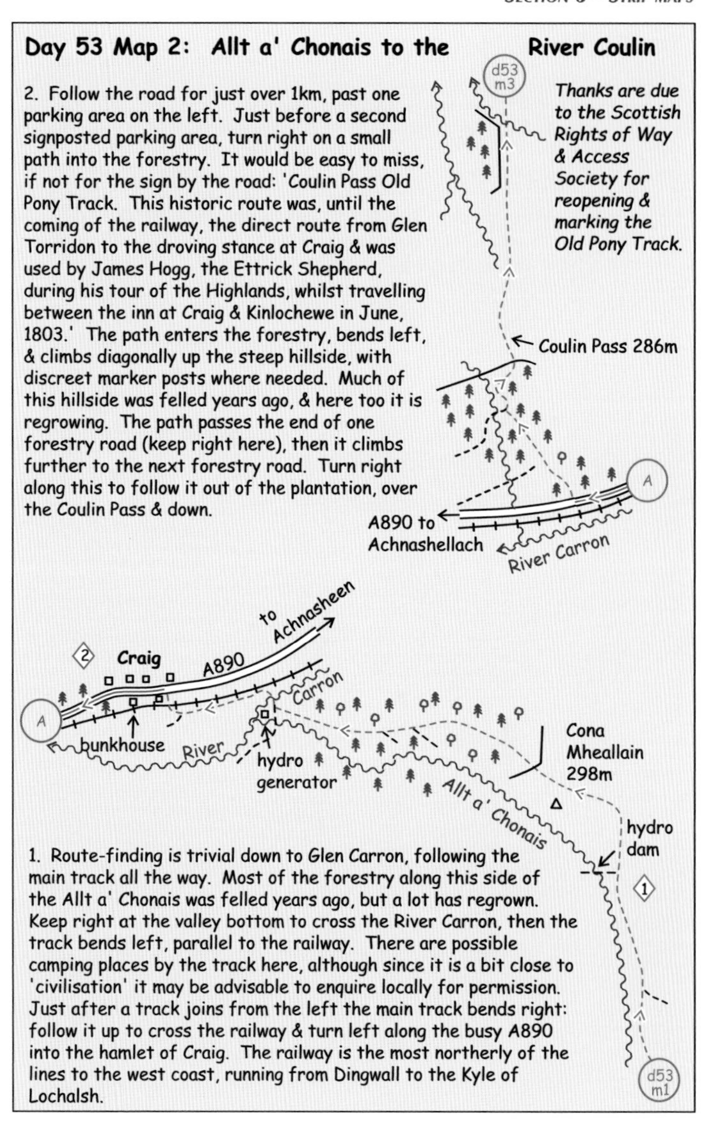
Day 53 Map 2: Allt a' Chonais to the River Coulin
2. Follow the road for just over 1km, past one parking area on the left. Just before a second signposted parking area, turn right on a small path into the forestry. It would be easy to miss, if not for the sign by the road: 'Coulin Pass Old Pony Track. This historic route was, until the coming of the railway, the direct route from Glen Torridon to the droving stance at Craig & was used by James Hogg, the Ettrick Shepherd, during his tour of the Highlands, whilst travelling between the inn at Craig & Kinlochewe in June, 1803.' The path enters the forestry, bends left, & climbs diagonally up the steep hillside, with discreet marker posts where needed. Much of this hillside was felled years ago, & here too it is regrowing. The path passes the end of one forestry road (keep right here), then it climbs further to the next forestry road. Turn right along this to follow it out of the plantation, over the Coulin Pass & down.
d53 m3
Thanks are due to the Scottish Rights of Way & Access Society for reopening & marking the Old Pony Track.
Coulin Pass 286m
A
A890 to Achnashellach
River Carron
to Achnasheen
2
Craig
A890
Carron
A
bunkhouse
River
hydro generator
Cona Mheallain 298m
Allt a' Chonais
hydro dam
1
1. Route-finding is trivial down to Glen Carron, following the main track all the way. Most of the forestry along this side of the Allt a' Chonais was felled years ago, but a lot has regrown. Keep right at the valley bottom to cross the River Carron, then the track bends left, parallel to the railway. There are possible camping places by the track here, although since it is a bit close to 'civilisation' it may be advisable to enquire locally for permission. Just after a track joins from the left the main track bends right: follow it up to cross the railway & turn left along the busy A890 into the hamlet of Craig. The railway is the most northerly of the lines to the west coast, running from Dingwall to the Kyle of Lochalsh.
d53 m1

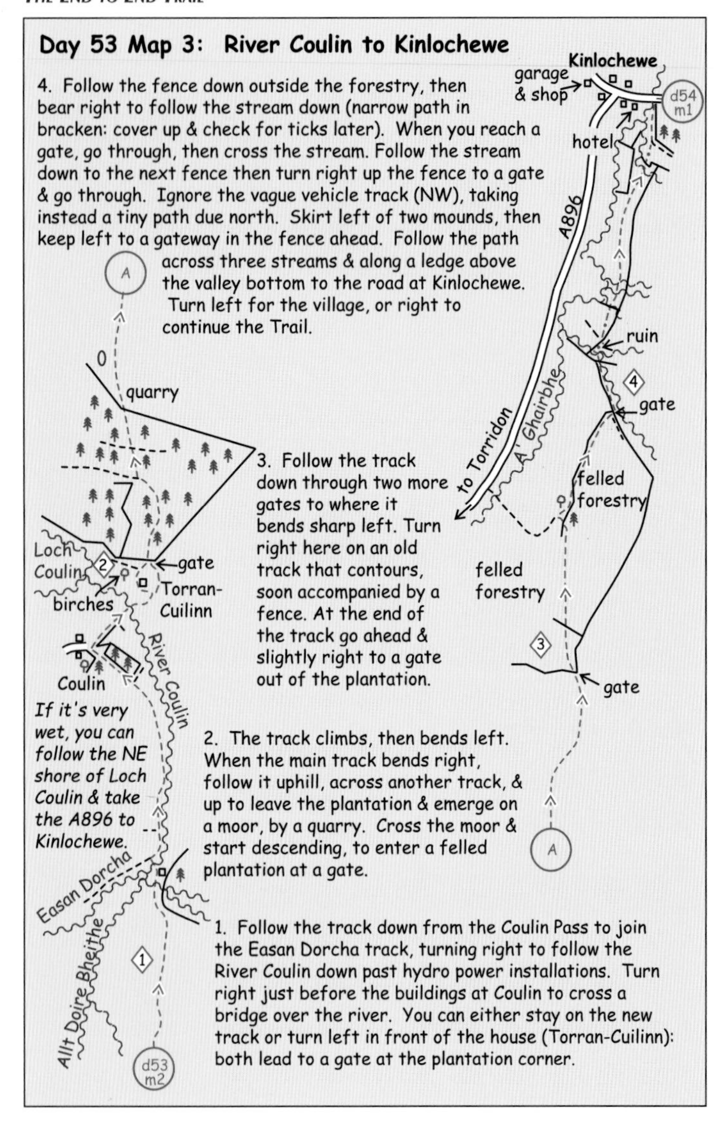

Day 53 Map 3: River Coulin to Kinlochewe
4. Follow the fence down outside the forestry, then bear right to follow the stream down (narrow path in bracken: cover up & check for ticks later). When you reach a gate, go through, then cross the stream. Follow the stream down to the next fence then turn right up the fence to a gate & go through. Ignore the vague vehicle track (NW), taking instead a tiny path due north. Skirt left of two mounds, then keep left to a gateway in the fence ahead. Follow the path across three streams & along a ledge above the valley bottom to the road at Kinlochewe. Turn left for the village, or right to continue the Trail.
Kinlochewe
garage & shop
hotel
d54 m1
A896
ruin
gate
A' Ghairbhe
to Torridon
felled forestry
felled forestry
gate
A
quarry
0
3. Follow the track down through two more gates to where it bends sharp left. Turn right here on an old track that contours, soon accompanied by a fence. At the end of the track go ahead & slightly right to a gate out of the plantation.
Loch Coulin
gate
Torran-Cuilinn
birches
River Coulin
Coulin
If it's very wet, you can follow the NE shore of Loch Coulin & take the A896 to Kinlochewe.
2. The track climbs, then bends left. When the main track bends right, follow it uphill, across another track, & up to leave the plantation & emerge on a moor, by a quarry. Cross the moor & start descending, to enter a felled plantation at a gate.
A
Easan Dorcha
Allt Doire Bheithe
1. Follow the track down from the Coulin Pass to join the Easan Dorcha track, turning right to follow the River Coulin down past hydro power installations. Turn right just before the buildings at Coulin to cross a bridge over the river. You can either stay on the new track or turn left in front of the house (Torran-Cuilinn): both lead to a gate at the plantation corner.
d53 m2

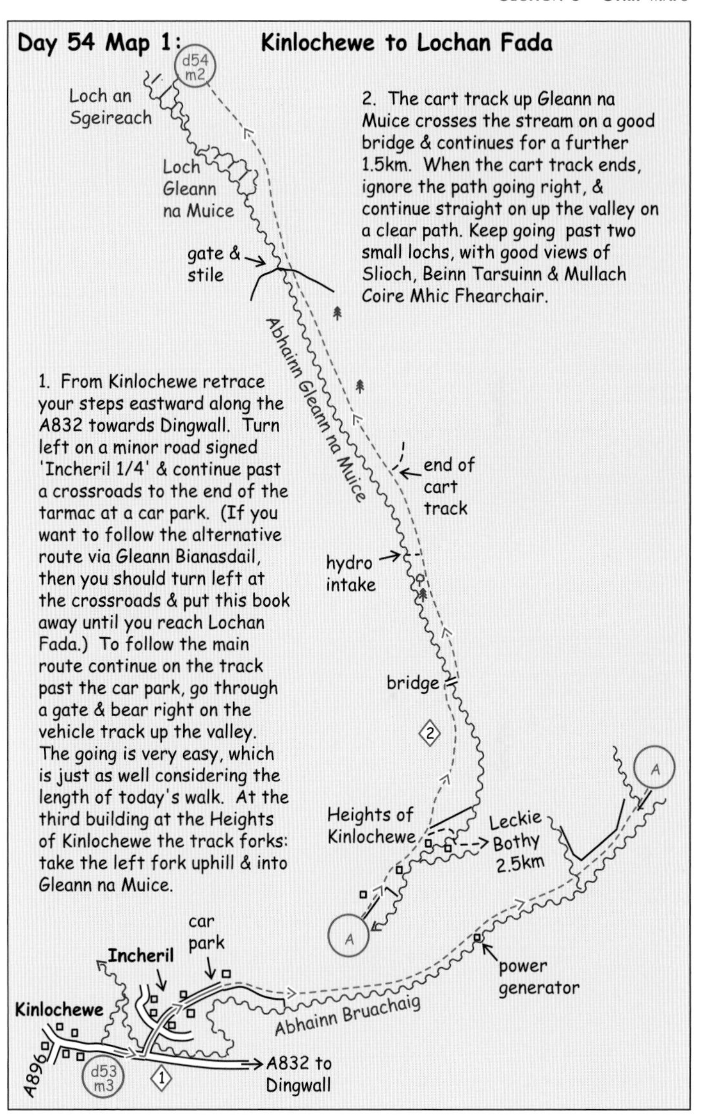
Day 54 Map 1: Kinlochewe to Lochan Fada
d54 m2
Loch an Sgeireach
Loch Gleann na Muice
gate & stile
Abhainn Gleann na Muice
end of cart track
hydro intake
bridge
2
Heights of Kinlochewe
Leckie Bothy 2.5km
A
A
power generator
car park
Incheril
Kinlochewe
A896
d53 m3
1
Abhainn Bruachaig
A832 to Dingwall
2. The cart track up Gleann na Muice crosses the stream on a good bridge & continues for a further 1.5km. When the cart track ends, ignore the path going right, & continue straight on up the valley on a clear path. Keep going past two small lochs, with good views of Slioch, Beinn Tarsuinn & Mullach Coire Mhic Fhearchair.
1. From Kinlochewe retrace your steps eastward along the A832 towards Dingwall. Turn left on a minor road signed 'Incheril 1/4' & continue past a crossroads to the end of the tarmac at a car park. (If you want to follow the alternative route via Gleann Bianasdail, then you should turn left at the crossroads & put this book away until you reach Lochan Fada.) To follow the main route continue on the track past the car park, go through a gate & bear right on the vehicle track up the valley. The going is very easy, which is just as well considering the length of today's walk. At the third building at the Heights of Kinlochewe the track forks: take the left fork uphill & into Gleann na Muice.

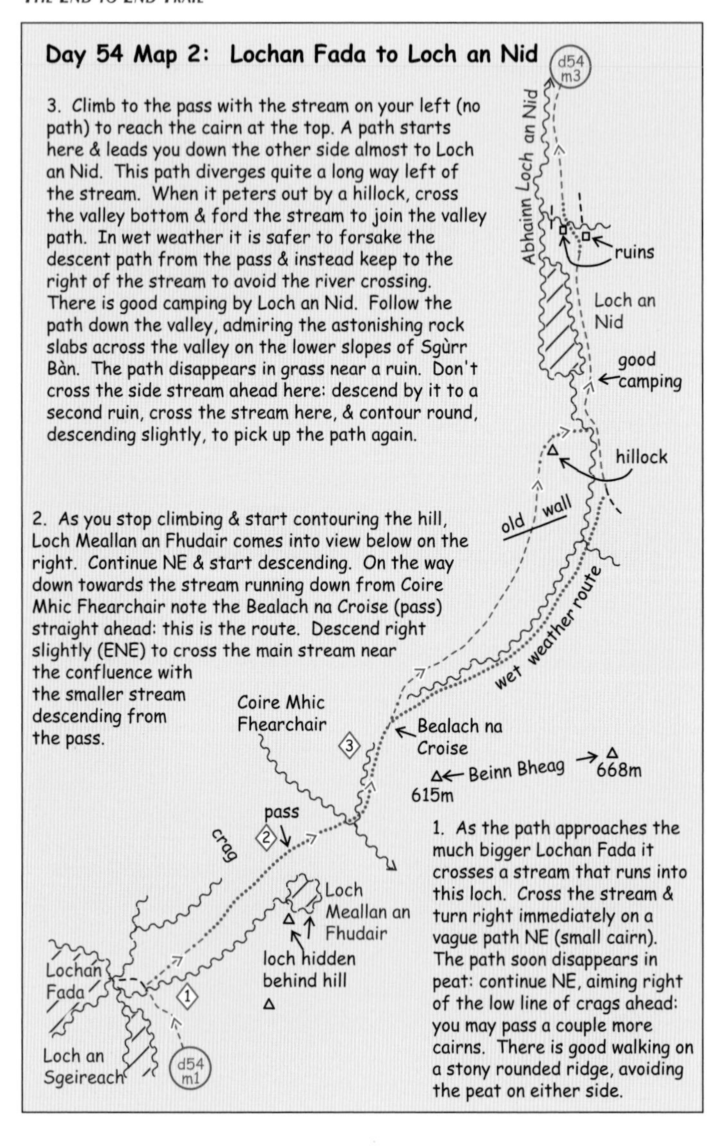

Day 54 Map 2: Lochan Fada to Loch an Nid
d54 m3
3. Climb to the pass with the stream on your left (no path) to reach the cairn at the top. A path starts here & leads you down the other side almost to Loch an Nid. This path diverges quite a long way left of the stream. When it peters out by a hillock, cross the valley bottom & ford the stream to join the valley path. In wet weather it is safer to forsake the descent path from the pass & instead keep to the right of the stream to avoid the river crossing. There is good camping by Loch an Nid. Follow the path down the valley, admiring the astonishing rock slabs across the valley on the lower slopes of Sgùrr Bàn. The path disappears in grass near a ruin. Don't cross the side stream ahead here: descend by it to a second ruin, cross the stream here, & contour round, descending slightly, to pick up the path again.
Abhainn Loch an Nid
ruins
Loch an Nid
good camping
hillock
old wall
2. As you stop climbing & start contouring the hill, Loch Meallan an Fhudair comes into view below on the right. Continue NE & start descending. On the way down towards the stream running down from Coire Mhic Fhearchair note the Bealach na Croise (pass) straight ahead: this is the route. Descend right slightly (ENE) to cross the main stream near the confluence with the smaller stream descending from the pass.
wet weather route
Coire Mhic Fhearchair
3
Bealach na Croise
Beinn Bheag
668m
615m
pass
2
crag
1. As the path approaches the much bigger Lochan Fada it crosses a stream that runs into this loch. Cross the stream & turn right immediately on a vague path NE (small cairn). The path soon disappears in peat: continue NE, aiming right of the low line of crags ahead: you may pass a couple more cairns. There is good walking on a stony rounded ridge, avoiding the peat on either side.
Loch Meallan an Fhudair
loch hidden behind hill
Lochan Fada
1
Loch an Sgeireach
d54 m1

Day 54 Map 3: Loch an Nid to Corrie Hallie

2. The track over to Dundonnell is a good one & there is no chance of going astray. You should be able to keep up a good pace, & you will need to if you want to reach Inverlael today!

3. The track comes down into the Dundonnell glen to a gate. Soon after this you reach the quiet A832 road: turn left & walk past a house (Corrie Hallie). There are no facilities near here, & there is nowhere obvious to pitch a tent.

1. Follow the path down the valley from Loch an Nid. The grey whale's back of Beinn a' Chlaidheimh (914m) comes into view ahead on the left, and then parts of the higher An Teallach massif. The cart track over to Dundonnell is visible long before you reach it, climbing out of the valley to the right when the valley bends left. As you get near to it a ruin is passed on your right. Ford a side stream just after this then cut right to join the Dundonnell track.

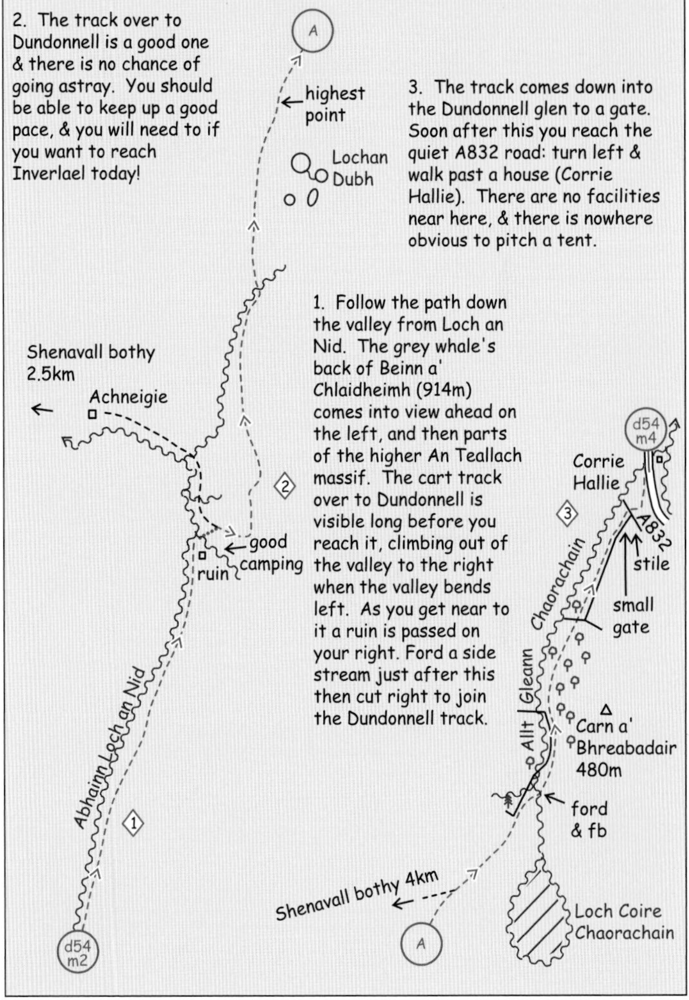

A
highest point
Lochan Dubh
Shenavall bothy 2.5km
Achneigie
good camping
ruin
Abhainn Loch an Nid
d54 m2
d54 m4
Corrie Hallie
A832
stile
small gate
Gleann Chaorachain
Allt
Carn a' Bhreabadair 480m
ford & fb
Shenavall bothy 4km
A
Loch Coire Chaorachain

Day 54 Map 4: Corrie Hallie to Inverlael

Turn round as you cross the moorland & take in the tremendous view behind you of An Teallach & its satellites standing on a huge plinth of grey slabs.

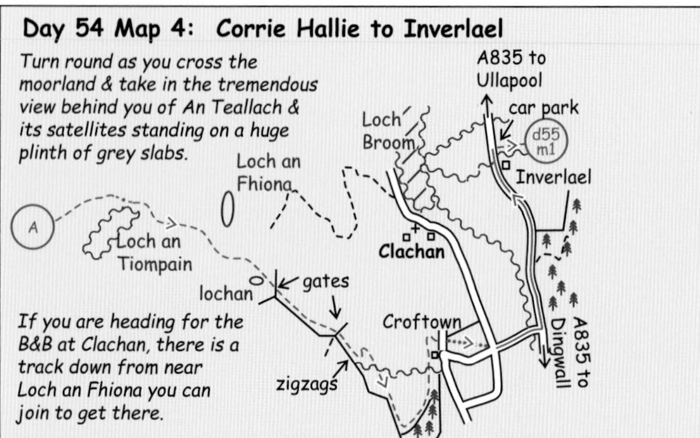

If you are heading for the B&B at Clachan, there is a track down from near Loch an Fhiona you can join to get there.

3. The track across the moorland from Dundonnell to Inverlael is a clear one, although it is little used now. Although wet in places it is easy to follow until it reaches the edge of the steep drop to the valley & Loch Broom. The path/track follows the edge of the escarpment for a while before starting to descend via zigzags. Continue slanting down, crossing a small burn. If you intend to camp in the valley this is the last chance to fill your water bottle, although the burn can dry up in very dry weather. Follow the path to the righthand end of the plantation visible ahead, then turn sharp left to follow the edge of the trees down steeply. Pass above cottages & some gorse bushes & follow the track as it doubles back right, descending to a gate ('Coffin Road' sign). Cross to the gate opposite then cross the field on 100 degrees to a gate in the far right corner & a road junction. Unless you are heading for Clachan B&B go straight on along the road to the A835, then turn left.

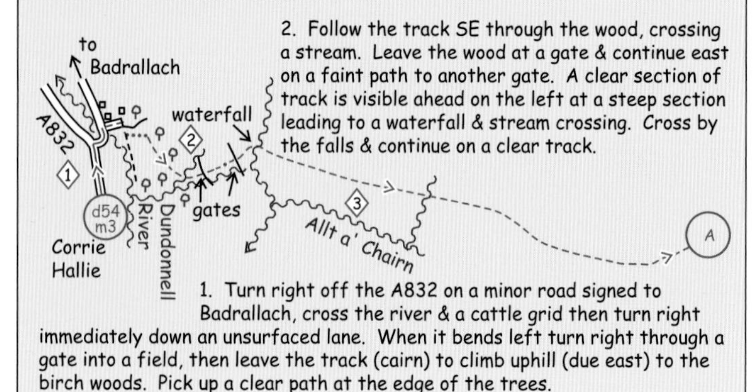

2. Follow the track SE through the wood, crossing a stream. Leave the wood at a gate & continue east on a faint path to another gate. A clear section of track is visible ahead on the left at a steep section leading to a waterfall & stream crossing. Cross by the falls & continue on a clear track.

1. Turn right off the A832 on a minor road signed to Badrallach, cross the river & a cattle grid then turn right immediately down an unsurfaced lane. When it bends left turn right through a gate into a field, then leave the track (cairn) to climb uphill (due east) to the birch woods. Pick up a clear path at the edge of the trees.

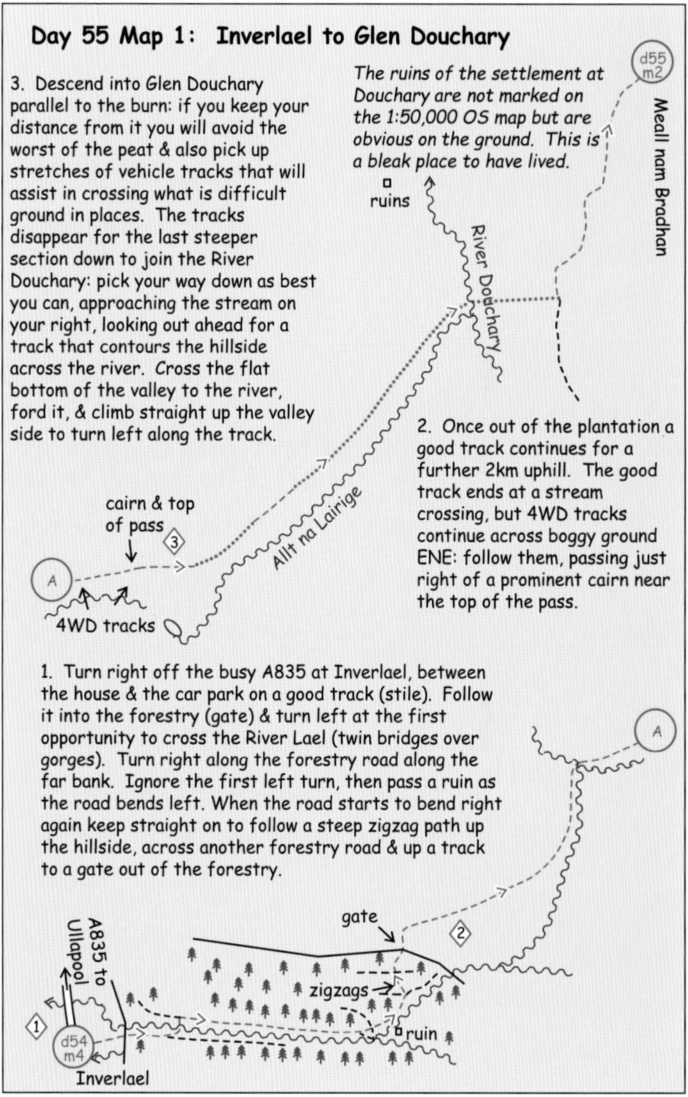

Day 55 Map 1: Inverlael to Glen Douchary

3. Descend into Glen Douchary parallel to the burn: if you keep your distance from it you will avoid the worst of the peat & also pick up stretches of vehicle tracks that will assist in crossing what is difficult ground in places. The tracks disappear for the last steeper section down to join the River Douchary: pick your way down as best you can, approaching the stream on your right, looking out ahead for a track that contours the hillside across the river. Cross the flat bottom of the valley to the river, ford it, & climb straight up the valley side to turn left along the track.

The ruins of the settlement at Douchary are not marked on the 1:50,000 OS map but are obvious on the ground. This is a bleak place to have lived.

d55 m2

Meall nam Bradhan

ruins

River Douchary

cairn & top of pass

3

Allt na Lairige

A

4WD tracks

2. Once out of the plantation a good track continues for a further 2km uphill. The good track ends at a stream crossing, but 4WD tracks continue across boggy ground ENE: follow them, passing just right of a prominent cairn near the top of the pass.

1. Turn right off the busy A835 at Inverlael, between the house & the car park on a good track (stile). Follow it into the forestry (gate) & turn left at the first opportunity to cross the River Lael (twin bridges over gorges). Turn right along the forestry road along the far bank. Ignore the first left turn, then pass a ruin as the road bends left. When the road starts to bend right again keep straight on to follow a steep zigzag path up the hillside, across another forestry road & up a track to a gate out of the forestry.

A

gate

2

A835 to Ullapool

zigzags

1

d54 m4

ruin

Inverlael

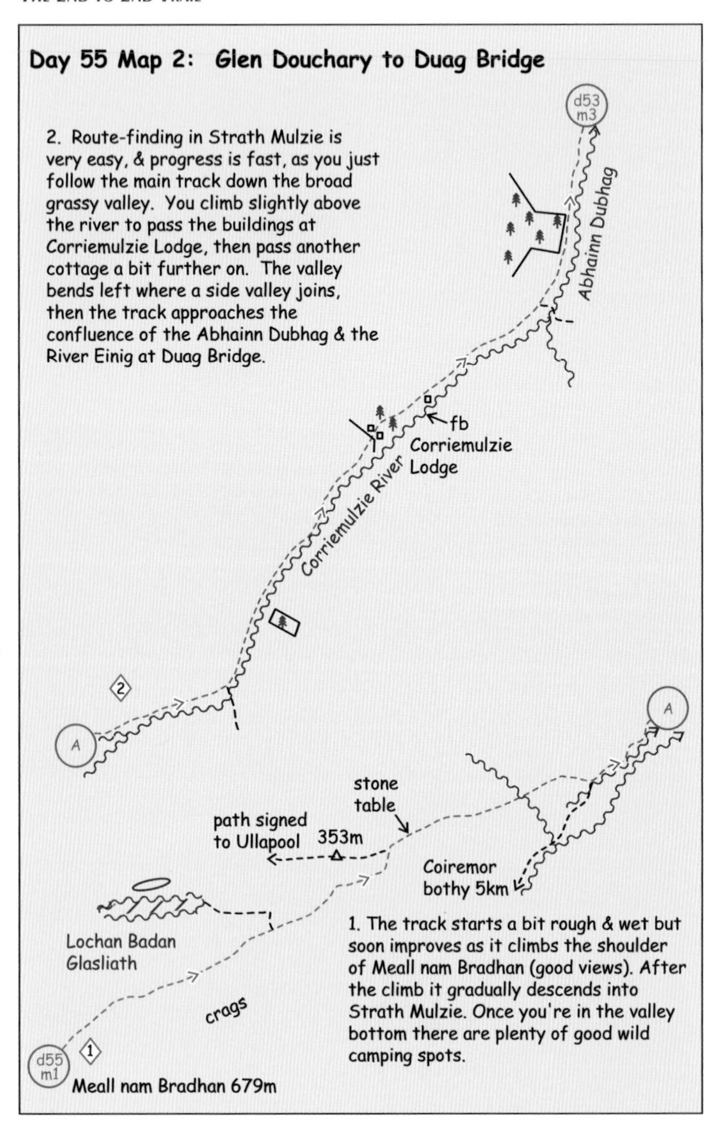

Day 55 Map 2: Glen Douchary to Duag Bridge
d53
m3
2. Route-finding in Strath Mulzie is very easy, & progress is fast, as you just follow the main track down the broad grassy valley. You climb slightly above the river to pass the buildings at Corriemulzie Lodge, then pass another cottage a bit further on. The valley bends left where a side valley joins, then the track approaches the confluence of the Abhainn Dubhag & the River Einig at Duag Bridge.
Abhainn Dubhag
fb
Corriemulzie Lodge
Corriemulzie River
2
A
A
stone table
path signed to Ullapool
353m
Coiremor bothy 5km
Lochan Badan Glasliath
1. The track starts a bit rough & wet but soon improves as it climbs the shoulder of Meall nam Bradhan (good views). After the climb it gradually descends into Strath Mulzie. Once you're in the valley bottom there are plenty of good wild camping spots.
crags
1
d55
m1
Meall nam Bradhan 679m

Day 55 Map 3: Duag Bridge to Oykel Bridge

2. The track eventually crosses a cattle grid: shortly after this bear left to cross a bridge over the river. Follow the track, keep right at a junction, & pass houses, now on a surfaced road, to meet the A837 at Oykel Bridge. Turn left for the hotel, right for the Lairg alternative route, or go straight on for the main route.

Oykel Bridge Hotel

d56 m1

A837

d56L m1

R Oykel

You can camp by the river: turn right at the A837 then right on a track down to the river (the start of Day 56L).

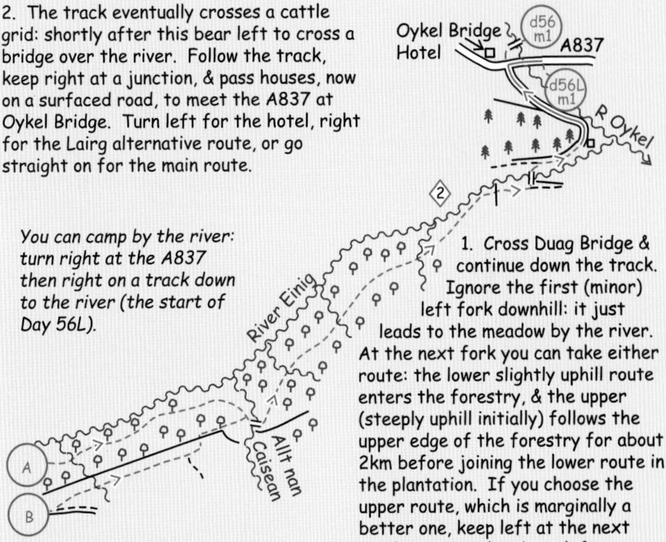

River Einig

1. Cross Duag Bridge & continue down the track. Ignore the first (minor) left fork downhill: it just leads to the meadow by the river. At the next fork you can take either route: the lower slightly uphill route enters the forestry, & the upper (steeply uphill initially) follows the upper edge of the forestry for about 2km before joining the lower route in the plantation. If you choose the upper route, which is marginally a better one, keep left at the next track junction then bear left through a gate into the plantation. Turn right at a junction with the lower route just before the bridge over the Allt nan Caisean.

Allt nan Caisean

A

B

The valley is heavily wooded with birches, regenerated after the pine plantation was felled.

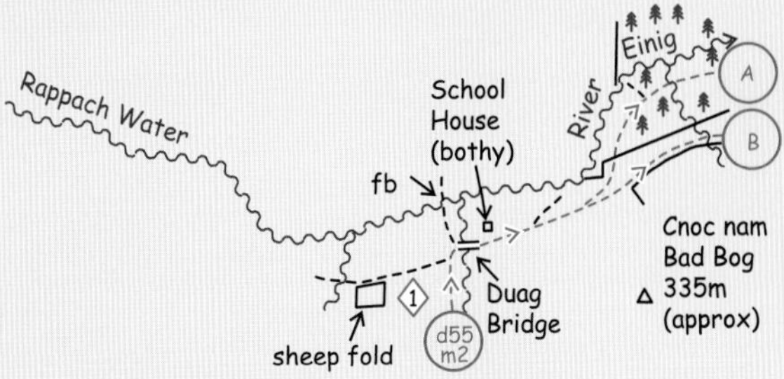

Rappach Water

School House (bothy)

fb

River Einig

A

B

Cnoc nam Bad Bog 335m (approx)

Duag Bridge

d55 m2

sheep fold

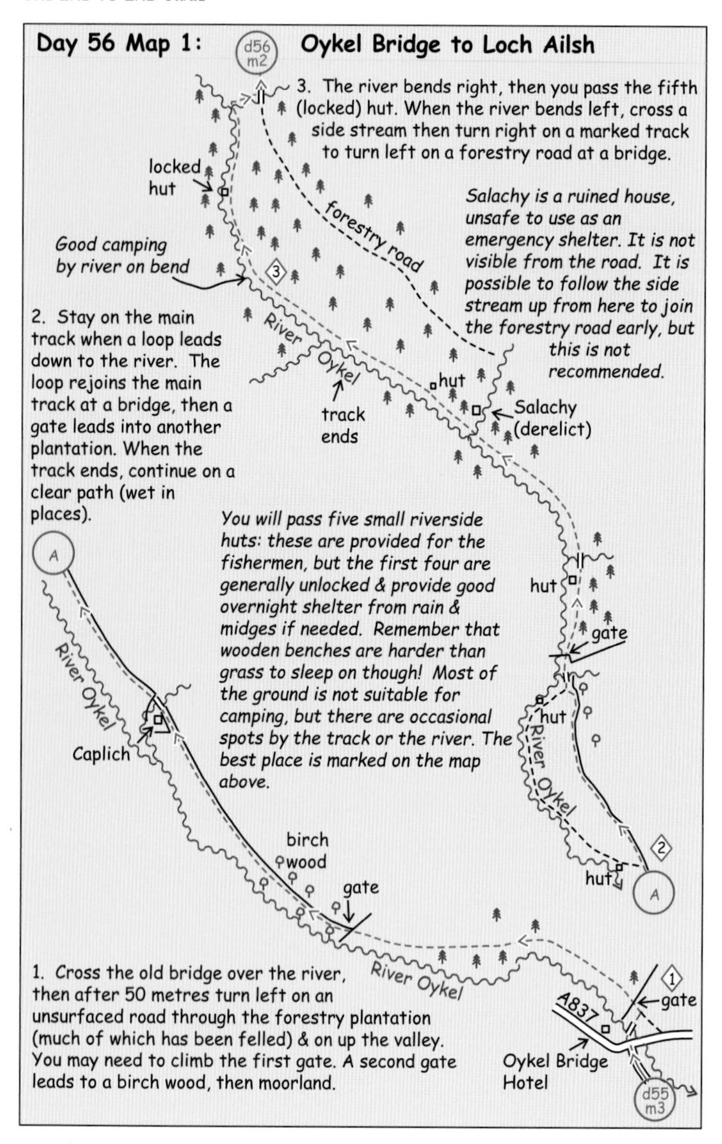
Day 56 Map 1:
d56 m2
Oykel Bridge to Loch Ailsh
3. The river bends right, then you pass the fifth (locked) hut. When the river bends left, cross a side stream then turn right on a marked track to turn left on a forestry road at a bridge.
locked hut
forestry road
Salachy is a ruined house, unsafe to use as an emergency shelter. It is not visible from the road. It is possible to follow the side stream up from here to join the forestry road early, but this is not recommended.
Good camping by river on bend
3
2. Stay on the main track when a loop leads down to the river. The loop rejoins the main track at a bridge, then a gate leads into another plantation. When the track ends, continue on a clear path (wet in places).
River Oykel
hut
track ends
Salachy (derelict)
You will pass five small riverside huts: these are provided for the fishermen, but the first four are generally unlocked & provide good overnight shelter from rain & midges if needed. Remember that wooden benches are harder than grass to sleep on though! Most of the ground is not suitable for camping, but there are occasional spots by the track or the river. The best place is marked on the map above.
A
hut
gate
River Oykel
Caplich
hut
River Oykel
2
birch wood
gate
hut
A
1. Cross the old bridge over the river, then after 50 metres turn left on an unsurfaced road through the forestry plantation (much of which has been felled) & on up the valley. You may need to climb the first gate. A second gate leads to a birch wood, then moorland.
River Oykel
1
gate
A837
Oykel Bridge Hotel
d55 m3

Day 56 Map 2: Loch Ailsh to Meall an Aonaich

Benmore Lodge is the last building you will see for many hours, & you may see no one else all day. This is very remote country, so make sure you are equipped for survival before you set out, & have told someone where you are going.

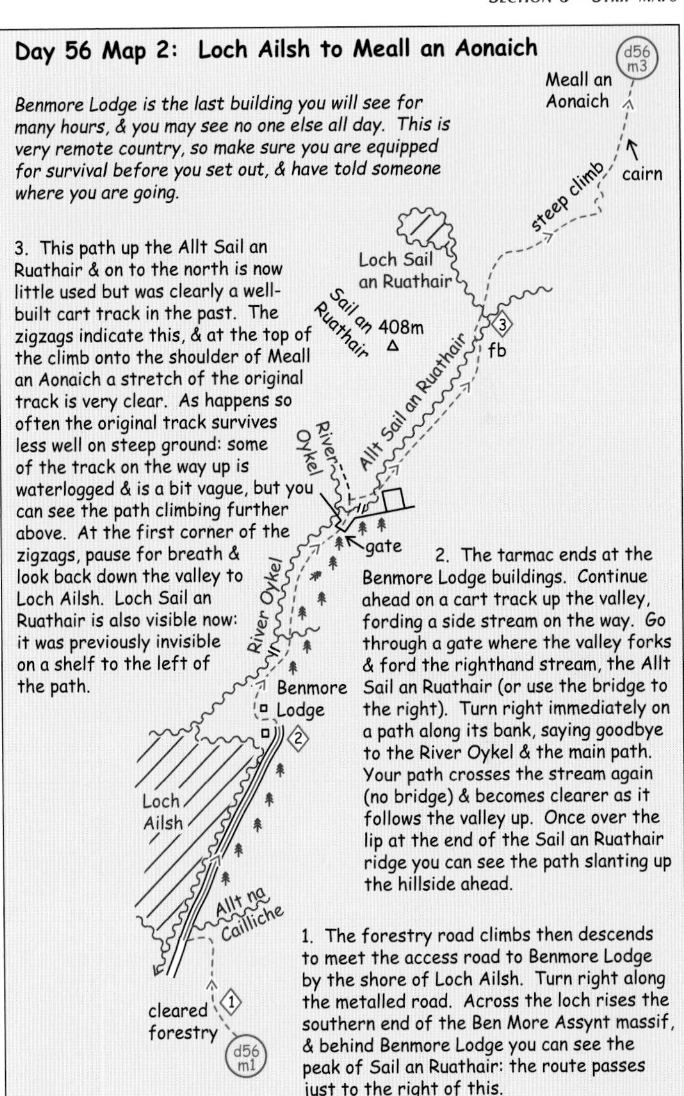

3. This path up the Allt Sail an Ruathair & on to the north is now little used but was clearly a well-built cart track in the past. The zigzags indicate this, & at the top of the climb onto the shoulder of Meall an Aonaich a stretch of the original track is very clear. As happens so often the original track survives less well on steep ground: some of the track on the way up is waterlogged & is a bit vague, but you can see the path climbing further above. At the first corner of the zigzags, pause for breath & look back down the valley to Loch Ailsh. Loch Sail an Ruathair is also visible now: it was previously invisible on a shelf to the left of the path.

2. The tarmac ends at the Benmore Lodge buildings. Continue ahead on a cart track up the valley, fording a side stream on the way. Go through a gate where the valley forks & ford the righthand stream, the Allt Sail an Ruathair (or use the bridge to the right). Turn right immediately on a path along its bank, saying goodbye to the River Oykel & the main path. Your path crosses the stream again (no bridge) & becomes clearer as it follows the valley up. Once over the lip at the end of the Sail an Ruathair ridge you can see the path slanting up the hillside ahead.

1. The forestry road climbs then descends to meet the access road to Benmore Lodge by the shore of Loch Ailsh. Turn right along the metalled road. Across the loch rises the southern end of the Ben More Assynt massif, & behind Benmore Lodge you can see the peak of Sail an Ruathair: the route passes just to the right of this.

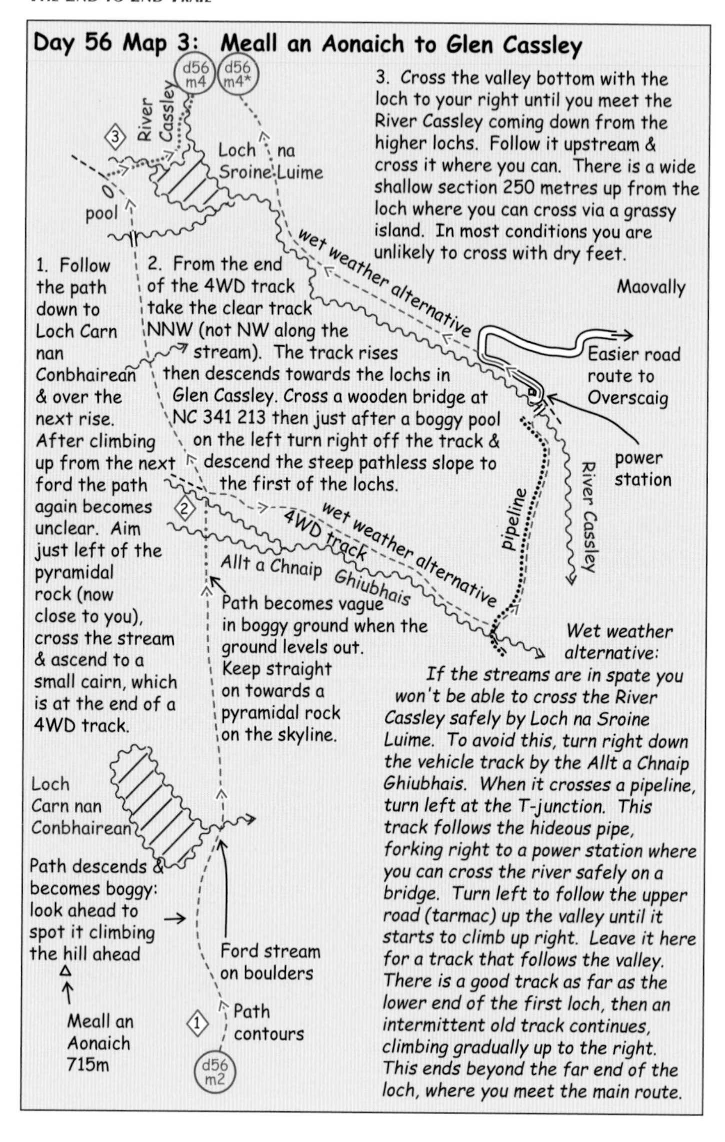
Day 56 Map 3: Meall an Aonaich to Glen Cassley
d56 m4
d56 m4*
3. Cross the valley bottom with the loch to your right until you meet the River Cassley coming down from the higher lochs. Follow it upstream & cross it where you can. There is a wide shallow section 250 metres up from the loch where you can cross via a grassy island. In most conditions you are unlikely to cross with dry feet.
River Cassley
Loch na Sroine Luime
pool
wet weather alternative
Maovally
1. Follow the path down to Loch Carn nan Conbhairean & over the next rise. After climbing up from the next ford the path again becomes unclear. Aim just left of the pyramidal rock (now close to you), cross the stream & ascend to a small cairn, which is at the end of a 4WD track.
2. From the end of the 4WD track take the clear track NNW (not NW along the stream). The track rises then descends towards the lochs in Glen Cassley. Cross a wooden bridge at NC 341 213 then just after a boggy pool on the left turn right off the track & descend the steep pathless slope to the first of the lochs.
Easier road route to Overscaig
power station
pipeline
River Cassley
wet weather alternative
4WD track
Allt a Chnaip Ghiubhais
Path becomes vague in boggy ground when the ground levels out. Keep straight on towards a pyramidal rock on the skyline.
Wet weather alternative:
If the streams are in spate you won't be able to cross the River Cassley safely by Loch na Sroine Luime. To avoid this, turn right down the vehicle track by the Allt a Chnaip Ghiubhais. When it crosses a pipeline, turn left at the T-junction. This track follows the hideous pipe, forking right to a power station where you can cross the river safely on a bridge. Turn left to follow the upper road (tarmac) up the valley until it starts to climb up right. Leave it here for a track that follows the valley. There is a good track as far as the lower end of the first loch, then an intermittent old track continues, climbing gradually up to the right. This ends beyond the far end of the loch, where you meet the main route.
Loch Carn nan Conbhairean
Path descends & becomes boggy: look ahead to spot it climbing the hill ahead
Ford stream on boulders
Meall an Aonaich 715m
Path contours
d56 m2

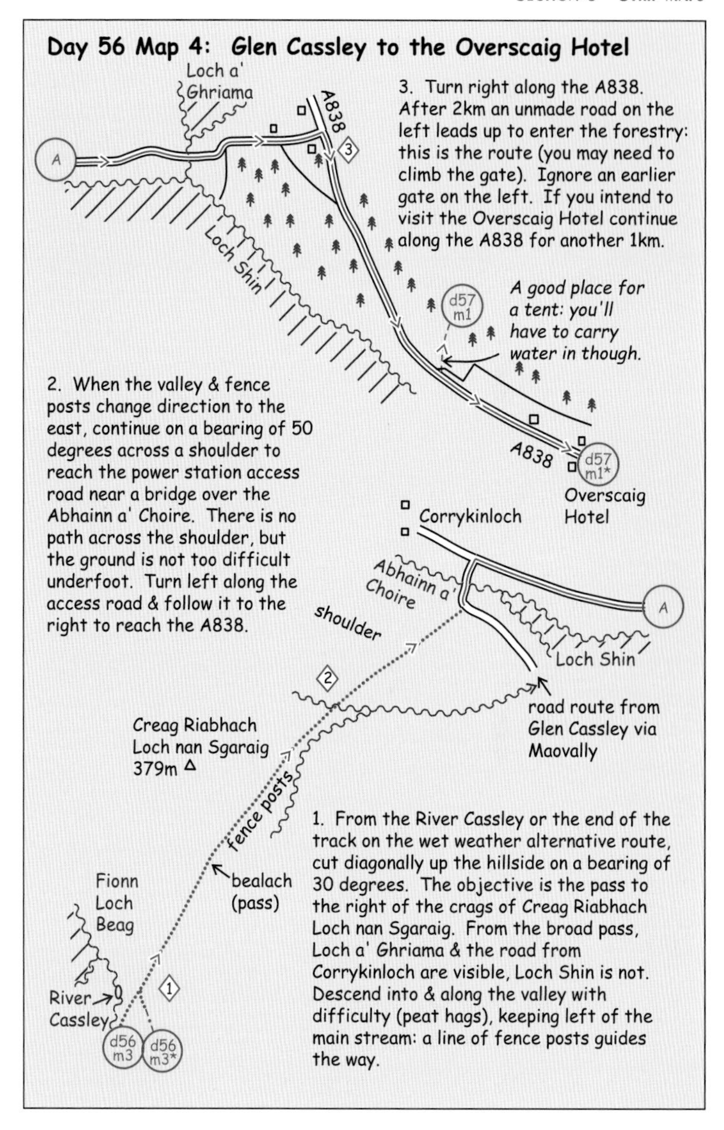

Day 56 Map 4: Glen Cassley to the Overscaig Hotel
Loch a' Ghriama
A838
3
A
Loch Shin
3. Turn right along the A838. After 2km an unmade road on the left leads up to enter the forestry: this is the route (you may need to climb the gate). Ignore an earlier gate on the left. If you intend to visit the Overscaig Hotel continue along the A838 for another 1km.
d57 m1
A good place for a tent: you'll have to carry water in though.
2. When the valley & fence posts change direction to the east, continue on a bearing of 50 degrees across a shoulder to reach the power station access road near a bridge over the Abhainn a' Choire. There is no path across the shoulder, but the ground is not too difficult underfoot. Turn left along the access road & follow it to the right to reach the A838.
A838
d57 m1*
Overscaig Hotel
Corrykinloch
Abhainn a' Choire
shoulder
A
Loch Shin
2
road route from Glen Cassley via Maovally
Creag Riabhach Loch nan Sgaraig 379m
fence posts
bealach (pass)
Fionn Loch Beag
1. From the River Cassley or the end of the track on the wet weather alternative route, cut diagonally up the hillside on a bearing of 30 degrees. The objective is the pass to the right of the crags of Creag Riabhach Loch nan Sgaraig. From the broad pass, Loch a' Ghriama & the road from Corrykinloch are visible, Loch Shin is not. Descend into & along the valley with difficulty (peat hags), keeping left of the main stream: a line of fence posts guides the way.
1
River Cassley
d56 m3
d56 m3*

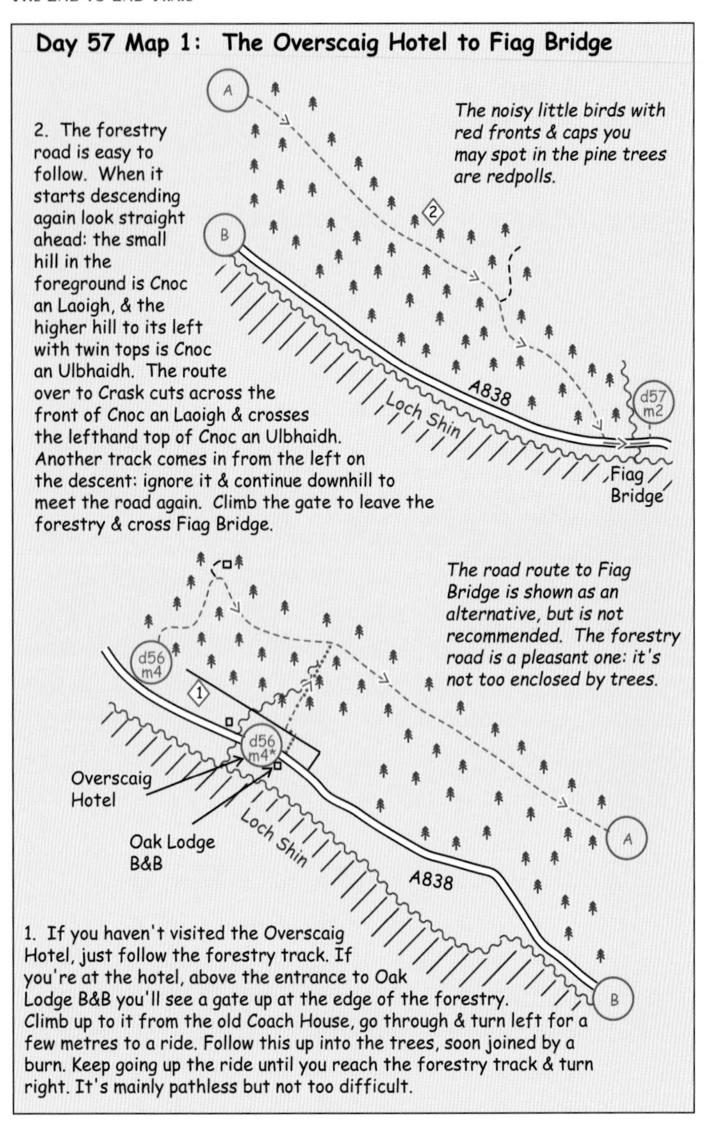
Day 57 Map 1: The Overscaig Hotel to Fiag Bridge
A
2. The forestry road is easy to follow. When it starts descending again look straight ahead: the small hill in the foreground is Cnoc an Laoigh, & the higher hill to its left with twin tops is Cnoc an Ulbhaidh. The route over to Crask cuts across the front of Cnoc an Laoigh & crosses the lefthand top of Cnoc an Ulbhaidh. Another track comes in from the left on the descent: ignore it & continue downhill to meet the road again. Climb the gate to leave the forestry & cross Fiag Bridge.
The noisy little birds with red fronts & caps you may spot in the pine trees are redpolls.
2
B
A838
Loch Shin
d57
m2
Fiag
Bridge
The road route to Fiag Bridge is shown as an alternative, but is not recommended. The forestry road is a pleasant one: it's not too enclosed by trees.
d56
m4
1
d56
m4*
Overscaig
Hotel
Oak Lodge
B&B
Loch Shin
A838
A
B
1. If you haven't visited the Overscaig Hotel, just follow the forestry track. If you're at the hotel, above the entrance to Oak Lodge B&B you'll see a gate up at the edge of the forestry. Climb up to it from the old Coach House, go through & turn left for a few metres to a ride. Follow this up into the trees, soon joined by a burn. Keep going up the ride until you reach the forestry track & turn right. It's mainly pathless but not too difficult.

Day 57 Map 2: Fiag Bridge to Crask

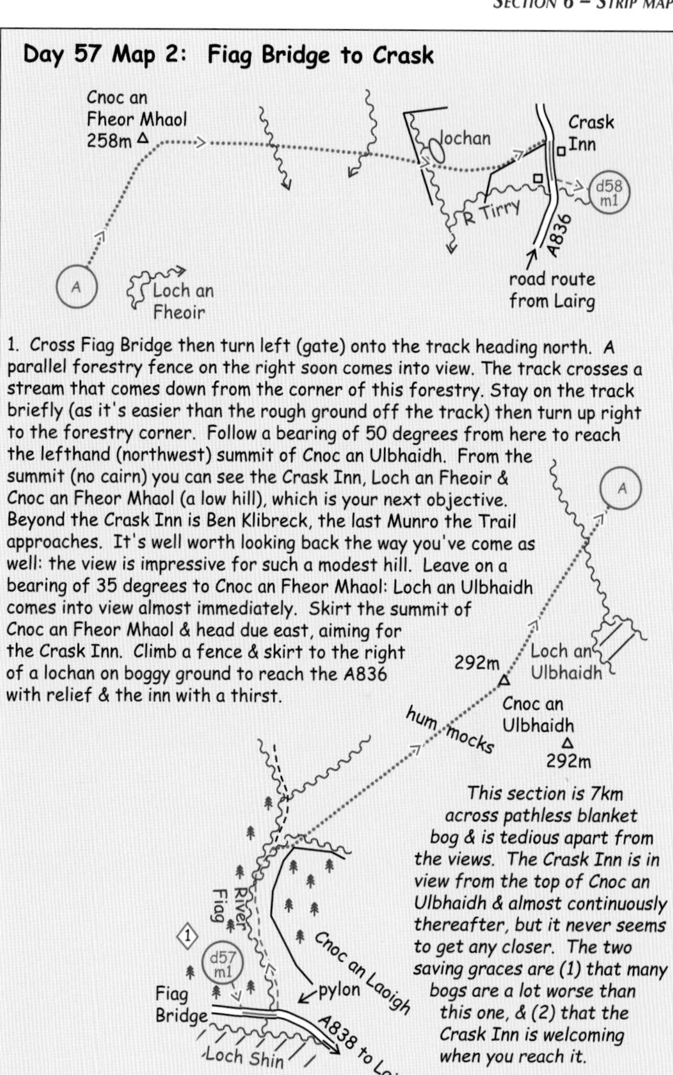

1. Cross Fiag Bridge then turn left (gate) onto the track heading north. A parallel forestry fence on the right soon comes into view. The track crosses a stream that comes down from the corner of this forestry. Stay on the track briefly (as it's easier than the rough ground off the track) then turn up right to the forestry corner. Follow a bearing of 50 degrees from here to reach the lefthand (northwest) summit of Cnoc an Ulbhaidh. From the summit (no cairn) you can see the Crask Inn, Loch an Fheoir & Cnoc an Fheor Mhaol (a low hill), which is your next objective. Beyond the Crask Inn is Ben Klibreck, the last Munro the Trail approaches. It's well worth looking back the way you've come as well: the view is impressive for such a modest hill. Leave on a bearing of 35 degrees to Cnoc an Fheor Mhaol: Loch an Ulbhaidh comes into view almost immediately. Skirt the summit of Cnoc an Fheor Mhaol & head due east, aiming for the Crask Inn. Climb a fence & skirt to the right of a lochan on boggy ground to reach the A836 with relief & the inn with a thirst.

This section is 7km across pathless blanket bog & is tedious apart from the views. The Crask Inn is in view from the top of Cnoc an Ulbhaidh & almost continuously thereafter, but it never seems to get any closer. The two saving graces are (1) that many bogs are a lot worse than this one, & (2) that the Crask Inn is welcoming when you reach it.

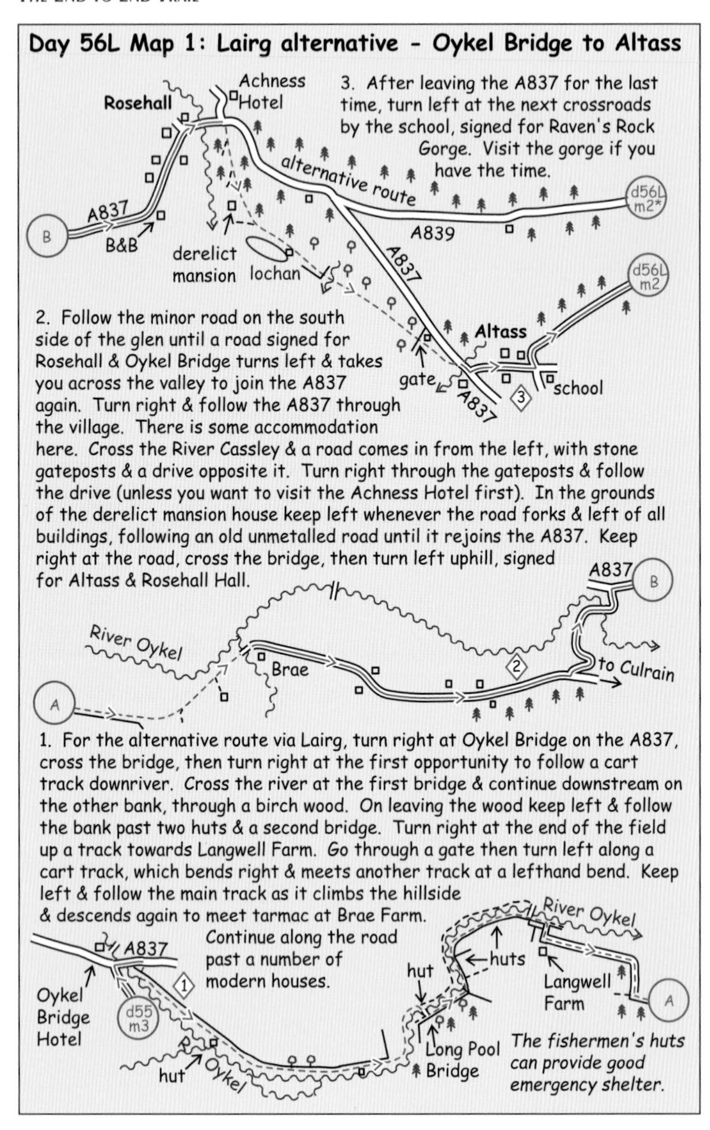
Day 56L Map 1: Lairg alternative - Oykel Bridge to Altass
Achness Hotel
Rosehall
3. After leaving the A837 for the last time, turn left at the next crossroads by the school, signed for Raven's Rock Gorge. Visit the gorge if you have the time.
alternative route
d56L m2*
A837
B&B
B
derelict mansion
lochan
A839
A837
d56L m2
2. Follow the minor road on the south side of the glen until a road signed for Rosehall & Oykel Bridge turns left & takes you across the valley to join the A837 again. Turn right & follow the A837 through the village. There is some accommodation here. Cross the River Cassley & a road comes in from the left, with stone gateposts & a drive opposite it. Turn right through the gateposts & follow the drive (unless you want to visit the Achness Hotel first). In the grounds of the derelict mansion house keep left whenever the road forks & left of all buildings, following an old unmetalled road until it rejoins the A837. Keep right at the road, cross the bridge, then turn left uphill, signed for Altass & Rosehall Hall.
Altass
gate
school
3
A837
A837
B
River Oykel
Brae
2
to Culrain
A
1. For the alternative route via Lairg, turn right at Oykel Bridge on the A837, cross the bridge, then turn right at the first opportunity to follow a cart track downriver. Cross the river at the first bridge & continue downstream on the other bank, through a birch wood. On leaving the wood keep left & follow the bank past two huts & a second bridge. Turn right at the end of the field up a track towards Langwell Farm. Go through a gate then turn left along a cart track, which bends right & meets another track at a lefthand bend. Keep left & follow the main track as it climbs the hillside & descends again to meet tarmac at Brae Farm.
Continue along the road past a number of modern houses.
A837
1
Oykel Bridge Hotel
d55 m3
hut
R. Oykel
hut
huts
River Oykel
Langwell Farm
A
Long Pool Bridge
The fishermen's huts can provide good emergency shelter.

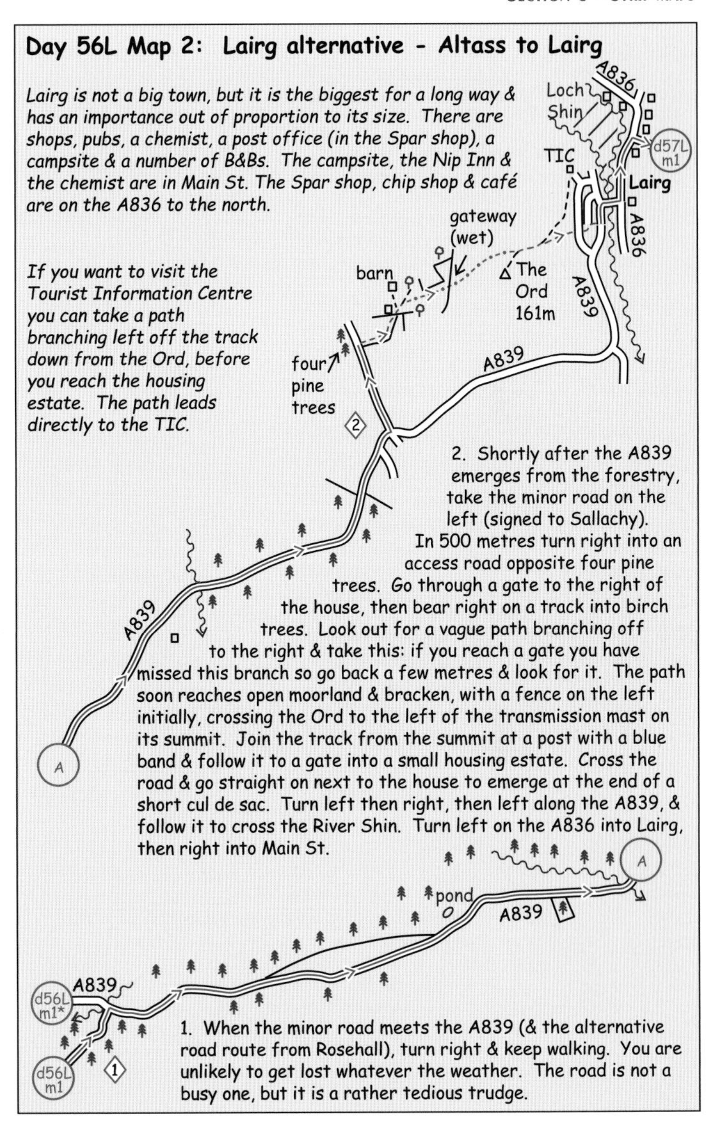
Day 56L Map 2: Lairg alternative - Altass to Lairg
Lairg is not a big town, but it is the biggest for a long way & has an importance out of proportion to its size. There are shops, pubs, a chemist, a post office (in the Spar shop), a campsite & a number of B&Bs. The campsite, the Nip Inn & the chemist are in Main St. The Spar shop, chip shop & café are on the A836 to the north.
If you want to visit the Tourist Information Centre you can take a path branching left off the track down from the Ord, before you reach the housing estate. The path leads directly to the TIC.
A836
Loch Shin
TIC
d57L m1
Lairg
A836
gateway (wet)
barn
The Ord 161m
A839
four pine trees
A839
2
2. Shortly after the A839 emerges from the forestry, take the minor road on the left (signed to Sallachy). In 500 metres turn right into an access road opposite four pine trees. Go through a gate to the right of the house, then bear right on a track into birch trees. Look out for a vague path branching off to the right & take this: if you reach a gate you have missed this branch so go back a few metres & look for it. The path soon reaches open moorland & bracken, with a fence on the left initially, crossing the Ord to the left of the transmission mast on its summit. Join the track from the summit at a post with a blue band & follow it to a gate into a small housing estate. Cross the road & go straight on next to the house to emerge at the end of a short cul de sac. Turn left then right, then left along the A839, & follow it to cross the River Shin. Turn left on the A836 into Lairg, then right into Main St.
A839
A
A
pond
A839
A839
d56L m1*
d56L m1
1
1. When the minor road meets the A839 (& the alternative road route from Rosehall), turn right & keep walking. You are unlikely to get lost whatever the weather. The road is not a busy one, but it is a rather tedious trudge.

Day 57L Map 1: Lairg alternative - Lairg to Loch Beannach

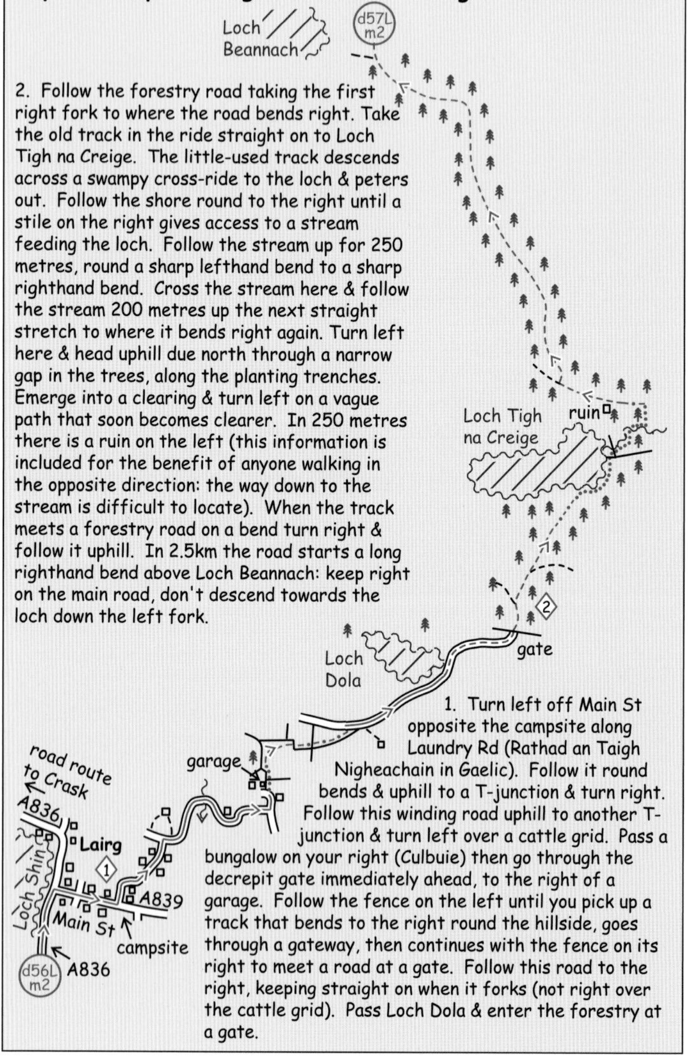

Loch Beannach
d57L m2

2. Follow the forestry road taking the first right fork to where the road bends right. Take the old track in the ride straight on to Loch Tigh na Creige. The little-used track descends across a swampy cross-ride to the loch & peters out. Follow the shore round to the right until a stile on the right gives access to a stream feeding the loch. Follow the stream up for 250 metres, round a sharp lefthand bend to a sharp righthand bend. Cross the stream here & follow the stream 200 metres up the next straight stretch to where it bends right again. Turn left here & head uphill due north through a narrow gap in the trees, along the planting trenches. Emerge into a clearing & turn left on a vague path that soon becomes clearer. In 250 metres there is a ruin on the left (this information is included for the benefit of anyone walking in the opposite direction: the way down to the stream is difficult to locate). When the track meets a forestry road on a bend turn right & follow it uphill. In 2.5km the road starts a long righthand bend above Loch Beannach: keep right on the main road, don't descend towards the loch down the left fork.

Loch Tigh na Creige
ruin
2
gate
Loch Dola

1. Turn left off Main St opposite the campsite along Laundry Rd (Rathad an Taigh Nigheachain in Gaelic). Follow it round bends & uphill to a T-junction & turn right. Follow this winding road uphill to another T-junction & turn left over a cattle grid. Pass a bungalow on your right (Culbuie) then go through the decrepit gate immediately ahead, to the right of a garage. Follow the fence on the left until you pick up a track that bends to the right round the hillside, goes through a gateway, then continues with the fence on its right to meet a road at a gate. Follow this road to the right, keeping straight on when it forks (not right over the cattle grid). Pass Loch Dola & enter the forestry at a gate.

road route to Crask
garage
A836
Lairg
1
Loch Shin
A839
Main St
campsite
A836
d56L m2

Day 57L (d57L m3) Map 2: Lairg alternative - Loch Beannach to Bun nan Tri-allt

From Dalnessie to Loch Choire the route follows an old track that has fallen into disuse & disrepair. In places it is difficult to follow & it could be tricky in mist across the top.

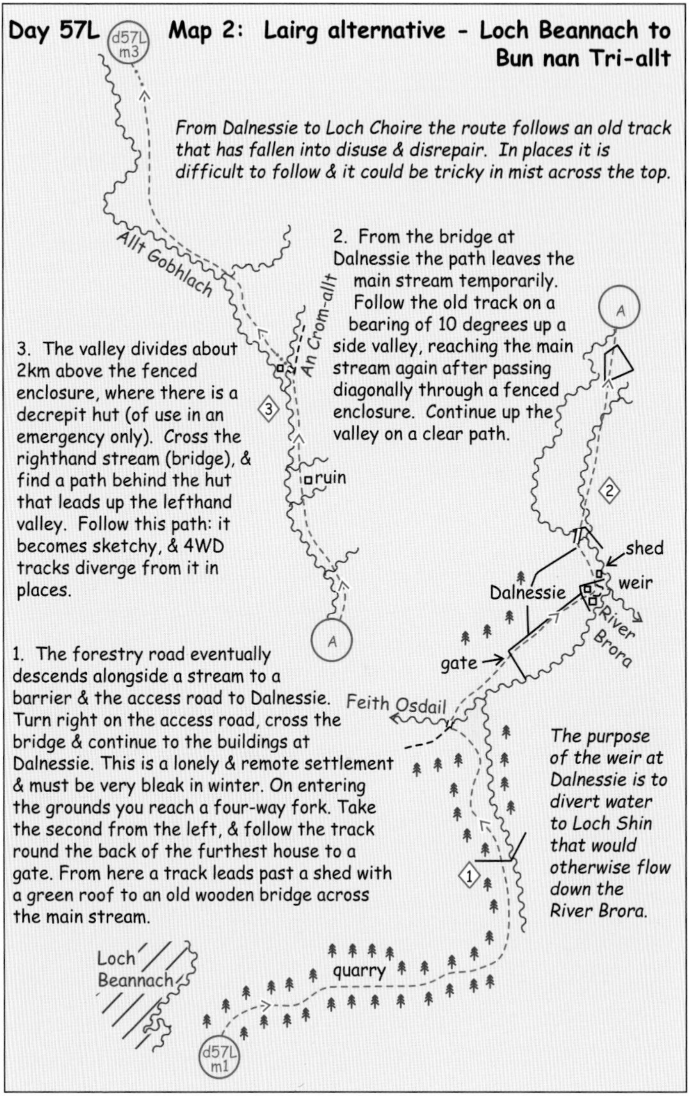

2. From the bridge at Dalnessie the path leaves the main stream temporarily. Follow the old track on a bearing of 10 degrees up a side valley, reaching the main stream again after passing diagonally through a fenced enclosure. Continue up the valley on a clear path.

3. The valley divides about 2km above the fenced enclosure, where there is a decrepit hut (of use in an emergency only). Cross the righthand stream (bridge), & find a path behind the hut that leads up the lefthand valley. Follow this path: it becomes sketchy, & 4WD tracks diverge from it in places.

1. The forestry road eventually descends alongside a stream to a barrier & the access road to Dalnessie. Turn right on the access road, cross the bridge & continue to the buildings at Dalnessie. This is a lonely & remote settlement & must be very bleak in winter. On entering the grounds you reach a four-way fork. Take the second from the left, & follow the track round the back of the furthest house to a gate. From here a track leads past a shed with a green roof to an old wooden bridge across the main stream.

The purpose of the weir at Dalnessie is to divert water to Loch Shin that would otherwise flow down the River Brora.

Day 57L Map 3: Lairg alternative - Bun nan Tri-allt to Loch Choire

The head of Loch Choire is a lovely place to stay overnight.

from Crask (main route)

Loch Choire

d58 m2

This wooden hut is Loch Choire bothy, & a good place to stay overnight. There is good drinking water at the burn a short distance back the way you came.

good camping

4. The burn enters a small gorge, & the path follows the gorge for a while, climbing to the right of the burn at the bottom of the gorge & continuing with the burn once more on your left. The path peters out in trees: continue down to the valley until you see a deer fence below you: follow the fence to the right to a gate, which you must climb. Walk forward for a short distance & turn right on a track to cross the next burn to a track junction: turn left & follow this track down to Loch Choire.

gate

3. On the far side of the summit plateau there is a boggy area in which the path weaves to some extent to avoid the wettest areas. It still keeps to a 30 degree bearing overall until it bends right to cross a burn at the remains of a bridge. Follow the burn down.

gorge

4

Meall an Fhuarain 503m

boggy area

remains of bridge

3

summit plateau

487m

2. On the climb towards the summit plateau the path crosses the burn (small cairn on either bank). It is important to find this crossing: the path from here isn't visible before you cross. Continue on an indistinct path, initially north then on about 30 degrees over the broad ridge.

cairns

2

1. At the head of the valley the burn divides into three (hence 'Bun nan Tri-allt'). The path stays with the middle burn (keep the burn on your left), initially northwards then bending to the right. It crosses to the other bank before the burn bends left, becoming more difficult to follow.

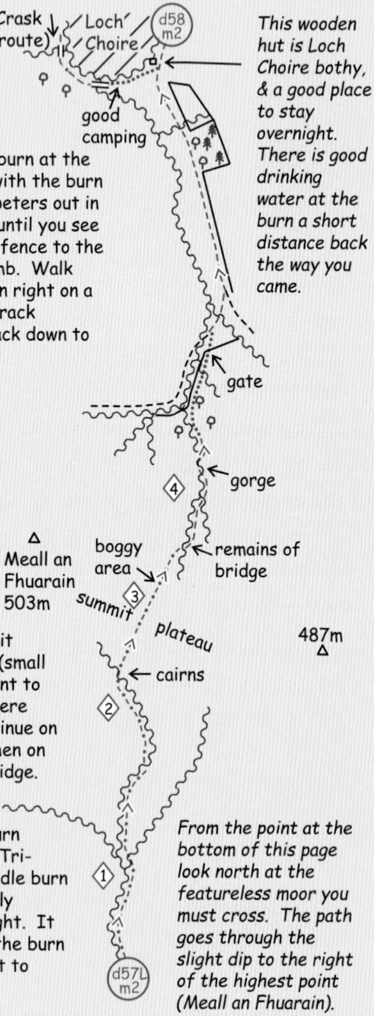

1

d57L m2

From the point at the bottom of this page look north at the featureless moor you must cross. The path goes through the slight dip to the right of the highest point (Meall an Fhuarain).

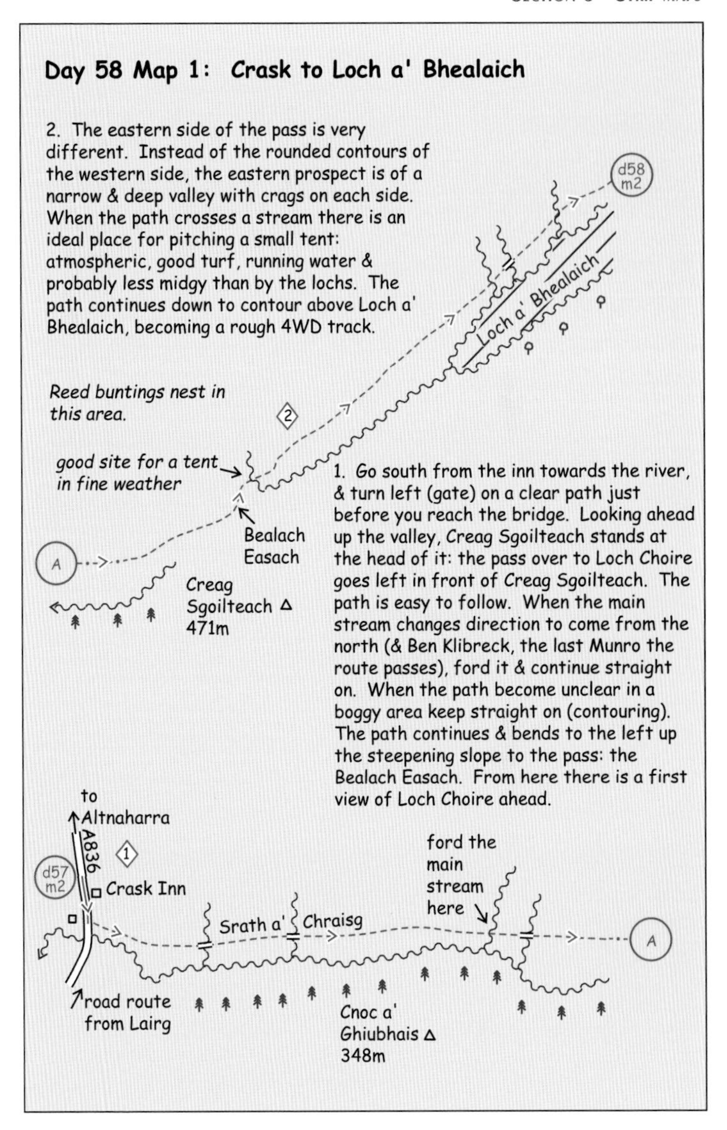
Day 58 Map 1: Crask to Loch a' Bhealaich
2. The eastern side of the pass is very different. Instead of the rounded contours of the western side, the eastern prospect is of a narrow & deep valley with crags on each side. When the path crosses a stream there is an ideal place for pitching a small tent: atmospheric, good turf, running water & probably less midgy than by the lochs. The path continues down to contour above Loch a' Bhealaich, becoming a rough 4WD track.
d58 m2
Loch a' Bhealaich
Reed buntings nest in this area.
2
good site for a tent in fine weather
Bealach Easach
A
Creag Sgoilteach 471m
1. Go south from the inn towards the river, & turn left (gate) on a clear path just before you reach the bridge. Looking ahead up the valley, Creag Sgoilteach stands at the head of it: the pass over to Loch Choire goes left in front of Creag Sgoilteach. The path is easy to follow. When the main stream changes direction to come from the north (& Ben Klibreck, the last Munro the route passes), ford it & continue straight on. When the path become unclear in a boggy area keep straight on (contouring). The path continues & bends to the left up the steepening slope to the pass: the Bealach Easach. From here there is a first view of Loch Choire ahead.
to Altnaharra
A836
1
d57 m2
Crask Inn
ford the main stream here
Srath a' Chraisg
A
road route from Lairg
Cnoc a' Ghiubhais 348m

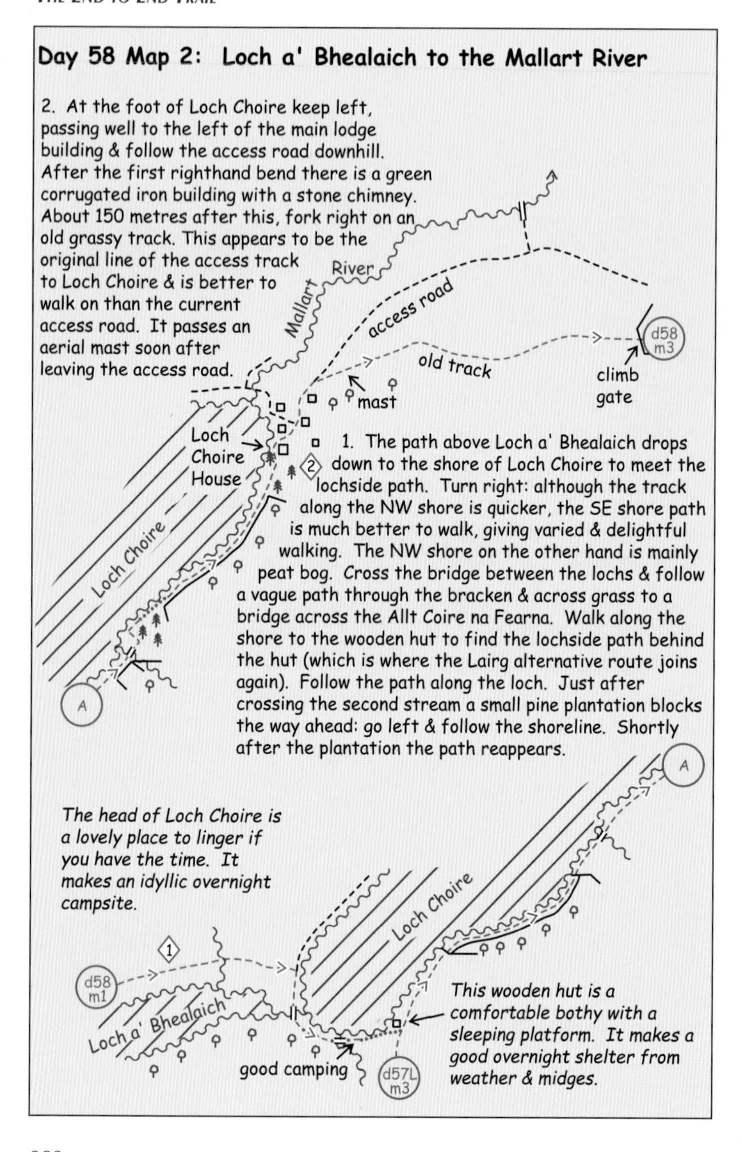
Day 58 Map 2: Loch a' Bhealaich to the Mallart River
2. At the foot of Loch Choire keep left, passing well to the left of the main lodge building & follow the access road downhill. After the first righthand bend there is a green corrugated iron building with a stone chimney. About 150 metres after this, fork right on an old grassy track. This appears to be the original line of the access track to Loch Choire & is better to walk on than the current access road. It passes an aerial mast soon after leaving the access road.
River
Mallart
access road
old track
d58
m3
climb
gate
mast
Loch
Choire
House
2
1. The path above Loch a' Bhealaich drops down to the shore of Loch Choire to meet the lochside path. Turn right: although the track along the NW shore is quicker, the SE shore path is much better to walk, giving varied & delightful walking. The NW shore on the other hand is mainly peat bog. Cross the bridge between the lochs & follow a vague path through the bracken & across grass to a bridge across the Allt Coire na Fearna. Walk along the shore to the wooden hut to find the lochside path behind the hut (which is where the Lairg alternative route joins again). Follow the path along the loch. Just after crossing the second stream a small pine plantation blocks the way ahead: go left & follow the shoreline. Shortly after the plantation the path reappears.
Loch Choire
A
A
The head of Loch Choire is a lovely place to linger if you have the time. It makes an idyllic overnight campsite.
1
d58
m1
Loch a' Bhealaich
Loch Choire
good camping
d57L
m3
This wooden hut is a comfortable bothy with a sleeping platform. It makes a good overnight shelter from weather & midges.

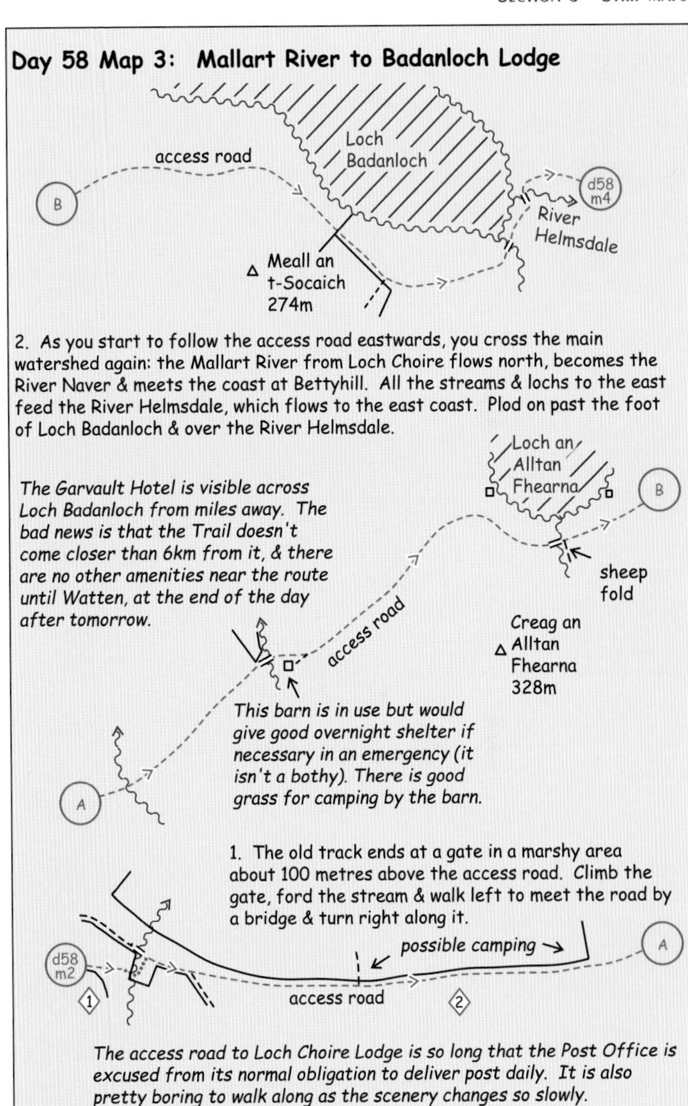

Day 58 Map 3: Mallart River to Badanloch Lodge
Loch Badanloch
access road
B
d58 m4
River Helmsdale
Meall an t-Socaich 274m
2. As you start to follow the access road eastwards, you cross the main watershed again: the Mallart River from Loch Choire flows north, becomes the River Naver & meets the coast at Bettyhill. All the streams & lochs to the east feed the River Helmsdale, which flows to the east coast. Plod on past the foot of Loch Badanloch & over the River Helmsdale.
Loch an Alltan Fhearna
B
The Garvault Hotel is visible across Loch Badanloch from miles away. The bad news is that the Trail doesn't come closer than 6km from it, & there are no other amenities near the route until Watten, at the end of the day after tomorrow.
sheep fold
access road
Creag an Alltan Fhearna 328m
This barn is in use but would give good overnight shelter if necessary in an emergency (it isn't a bothy). There is good grass for camping by the barn.
A
1. The old track ends at a gate in a marshy area about 100 metres above the access road. Climb the gate, ford the stream & walk left to meet the road by a bridge & turn right along it.
possible camping
A
d58 m2
1
access road
2
The access road to Loch Choire Lodge is so long that the Post Office is excused from its normal obligation to deliver post daily. It is also pretty boring to walk along as the scenery changes so slowly.

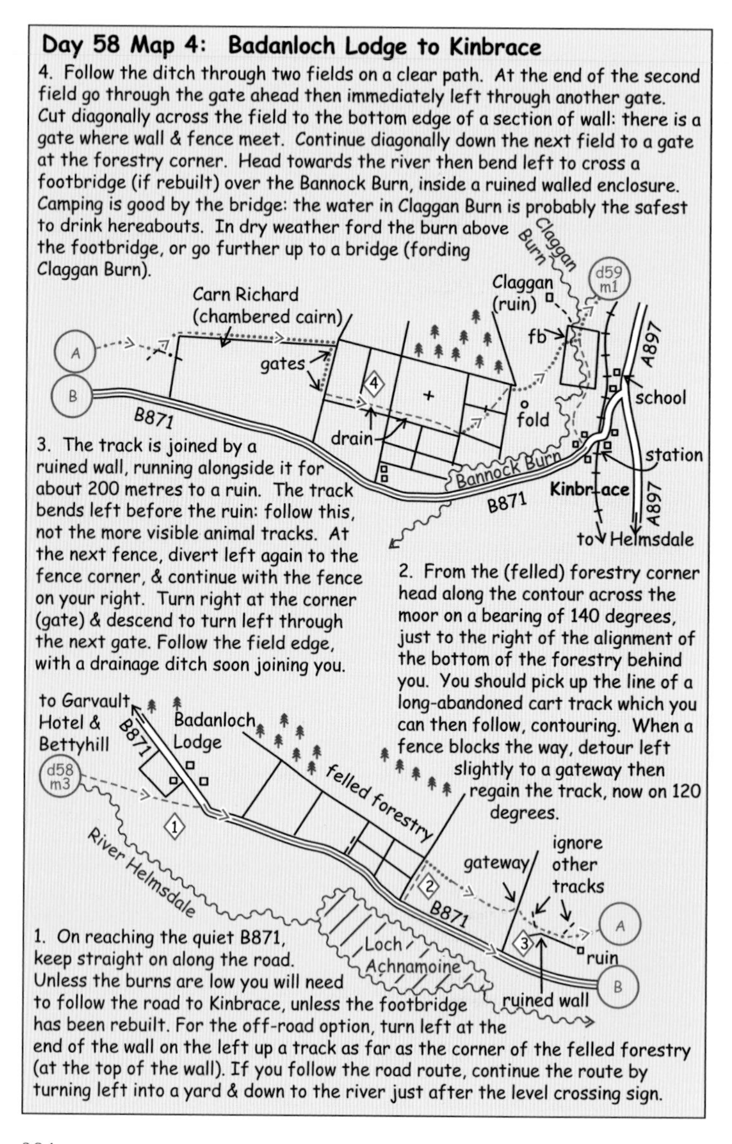
Day 58 Map 4: Badanloch Lodge to Kinbrace
4. Follow the ditch through two fields on a clear path. At the end of the second field go through the gate ahead then immediately left through another gate. Cut diagonally across the field to the bottom edge of a section of wall: there is a gate where wall & fence meet. Continue diagonally down the next field to a gate at the forestry corner. Head towards the river then bend left to cross a footbridge (if rebuilt) over the Bannock Burn, inside a ruined walled enclosure. Camping is good by the bridge: the water in Claggan Burn is probably the safest to drink hereabouts. In dry weather ford the burn above the footbridge, or go further up to a bridge (fording Claggan Burn).
Claggan Burn
d59 m1
Claggan (ruin)
Carn Richard (chambered cairn)
A
B
gates
fb
4
A897
school
B871
fold
drain
station
Bannock Burn
Kinbrace
B871
A897
to Helmsdale
3. The track is joined by a ruined wall, running alongside it for about 200 metres to a ruin. The track bends left before the ruin: follow this, not the more visible animal tracks. At the next fence, divert left again to the fence corner, & continue with the fence on your right. Turn right at the corner (gate) & descend to turn left through the next gate. Follow the field edge, with a drainage ditch soon joining you.
2. From the (felled) forestry corner head along the contour across the moor on a bearing of 140 degrees, just to the right of the alignment of the bottom of the forestry behind you. You should pick up the line of a long-abandoned cart track which you can then follow, contouring. When a fence blocks the way, detour left slightly to a gateway then regain the track, now on 120 degrees.
to Garvault Hotel & Bettyhill
B871
Badanloch Lodge
d58 m3
felled forestry
1
River Helmsdale
ignore other tracks
gateway
2
B871
A
Loch Achnamoine
3
ruin
B
ruined wall
1. On reaching the quiet B871, keep straight on along the road. Unless the burns are low you will need to follow the road to Kinbrace, unless the footbridge has been rebuilt. For the off-road option, turn left at the end of the wall on the left up a track as far as the corner of the felled forestry (at the top of the wall). If you follow the road route, continue the route by turning left into a yard & down to the river just after the level crossing sign.

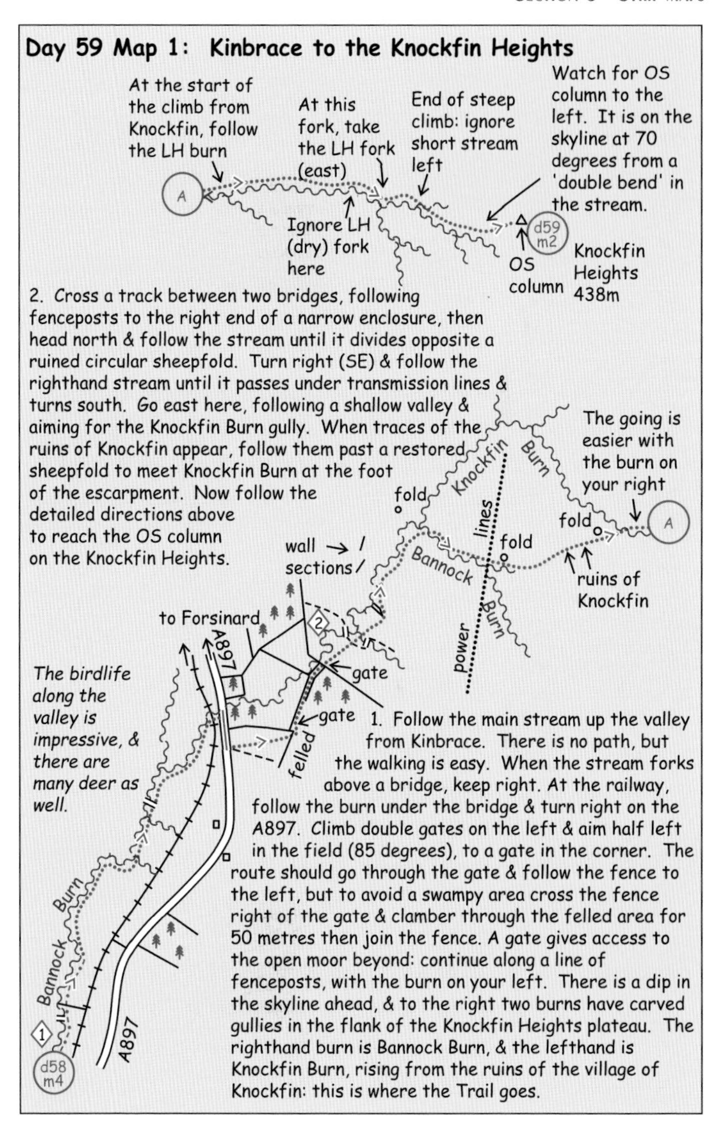
Day 59 Map 1: Kinbrace to the Knockfin Heights
At the start of the climb from Knockfin, follow the LH burn
At this fork, take the LH fork (east)
End of steep climb: ignore short stream left
Watch for OS column to the left. It is on the skyline at 70 degrees from a 'double bend' in the stream.
A
Ignore LH (dry) fork here
d59 m2
OS column
Knockfin Heights 438m
2. Cross a track between two bridges, following fenceposts to the right end of a narrow enclosure, then head north & follow the stream until it divides opposite a ruined circular sheepfold. Turn right (SE) & follow the righthand stream until it passes under transmission lines & turns south. Go east here, following a shallow valley & aiming for the Knockfin Burn gully. When traces of the ruins of Knockfin appear, follow them past a restored sheepfold to meet Knockfin Burn at the foot of the escarpment. Now follow the detailed directions above to reach the OS column on the Knockfin Heights.
The going is easier with the burn on your right
Knockfin Burn
fold
lines
fold
fold
A
ruins of Knockfin
Bannock Burn
power
wall sections
to Forsinard
A897
2
gate
gate
felled
The birdlife along the valley is impressive, & there are many deer as well.
1. Follow the main stream up the valley from Kinbrace. There is no path, but the walking is easy. When the stream forks above a bridge, keep right. At the railway, follow the burn under the bridge & turn right on the A897. Climb double gates on the left & aim half left in the field (85 degrees), to a gate in the corner. The route should go through the gate & follow the fence to the left, but to avoid a swampy area cross the fence right of the gate & clamber through the felled area for 50 metres then join the fence. A gate gives access to the open moor beyond: continue along a line of fenceposts, with the burn on your left. There is a dip in the skyline ahead, & to the right two burns have carved gullies in the flank of the Knockfin Heights plateau. The righthand burn is Bannock Burn, & the lefthand is Knockfin Burn, rising from the ruins of the village of Knockfin: this is where the Trail goes.
Bannock Burn
1
A897
d58 m4

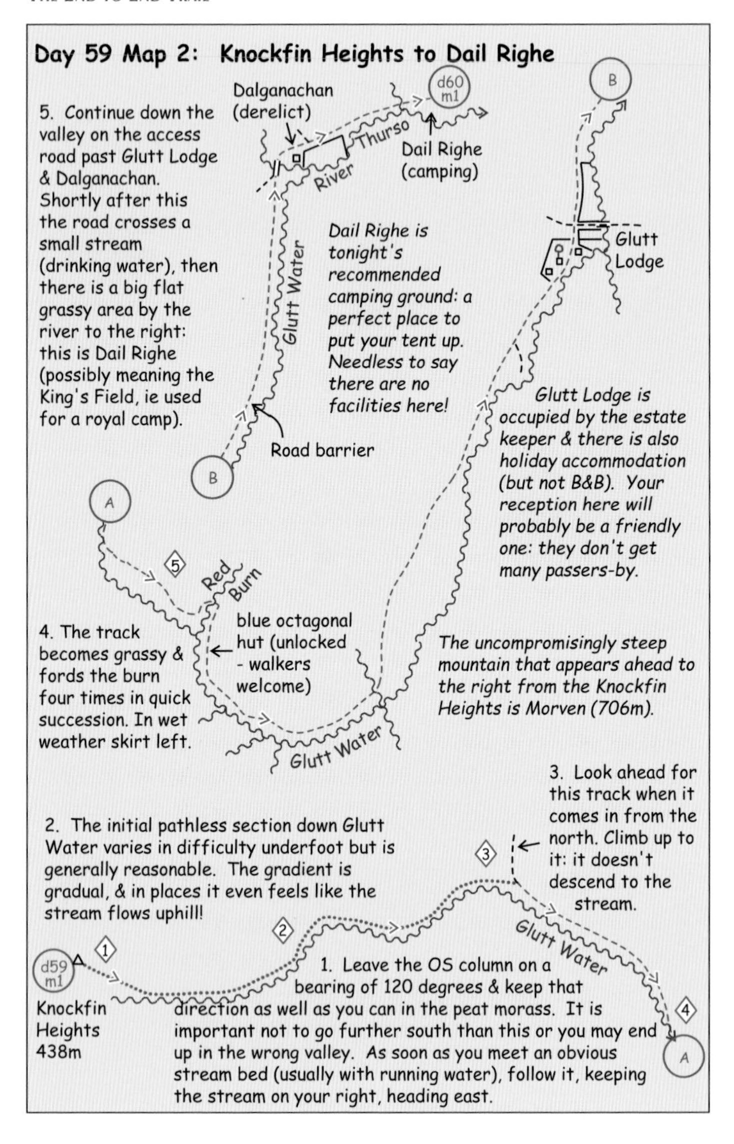
Day 59 Map 2: Knockfin Heights to Dail Righe
5. Continue down the valley on the access road past Glutt Lodge & Dalganachan. Shortly after this the road crosses a small stream (drinking water), then there is a big flat grassy area by the river to the right: this is Dail Righe (possibly meaning the King's Field, ie used for a royal camp).
Dalganachan (derelict)
d60 m1
B
Thurso
River
Dail Righe (camping)
Glutt Water
Dail Righe is tonight's recommended camping ground: a perfect place to put your tent up. Needless to say there are no facilities here!
Glutt Lodge
Road barrier
B
Glutt Lodge is occupied by the estate keeper & there is also holiday accommodation (but not B&B). Your reception here will probably be a friendly one: they don't get many passers-by.
A
5
Red Burn
4. The track becomes grassy & fords the burn four times in quick succession. In wet weather skirt left.
blue octagonal hut (unlocked - walkers welcome)
The uncompromisingly steep mountain that appears ahead to the right from the Knockfin Heights is Morven (706m).
Glutt Water
3. Look ahead for this track when it comes in from the north. Climb up to it: it doesn't descend to the stream.
2. The initial pathless section down Glutt Water varies in difficulty underfoot but is generally reasonable. The gradient is gradual, & in places it even feels like the stream flows uphill!
3
2
1
Glutt Water
d59 m1
Knockfin Heights 438m
1. Leave the OS column on a bearing of 120 degrees & keep that direction as well as you can in the peat morass. It is important not to go further south than this or you may end up in the wrong valley. As soon as you meet an obvious stream bed (usually with running water), follow it, keeping the stream on your right, heading east.
4
A

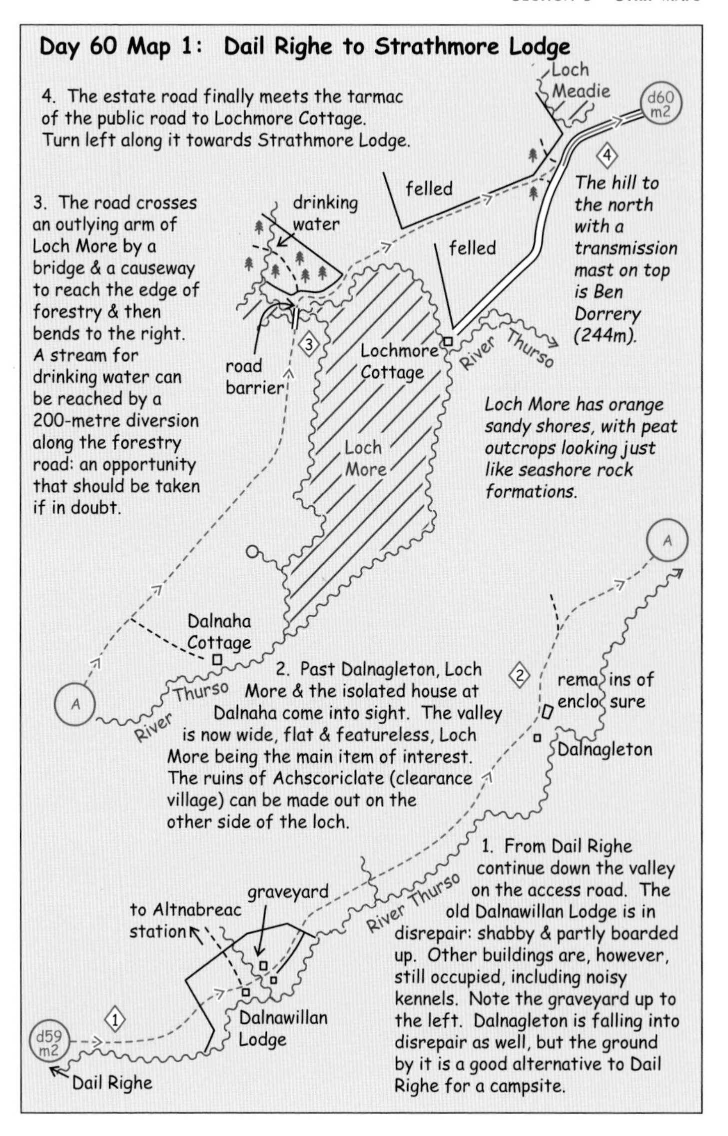
Day 60 Map 1: Dail Righe to Strathmore Lodge
Loch Meadie
d60 m2
4. The estate road finally meets the tarmac of the public road to Lochmore Cottage. Turn left along it towards Strathmore Lodge.
felled
drinking water
felled
The hill to the north with a transmission mast on top is Ben Dorrery (244m).
3. The road crosses an outlying arm of Loch More by a bridge & a causeway to reach the edge of forestry & then bends to the right. A stream for drinking water can be reached by a 200-metre diversion along the forestry road: an opportunity that should be taken if in doubt.
road barrier
Lochmore Cottage
River Thurso
Loch More has orange sandy shores, with peat outcrops looking just like seashore rock formations.
Loch More
A
Dalnaha Cottage
2. Past Dalnagleton, Loch More & the isolated house at Dalnaha come into sight. The valley is now wide, flat & featureless, Loch More being the main item of interest. The ruins of Achscoriclate (clearance village) can be made out on the other side of the loch.
remains of enclosure
A
River Thurso
Dalnagleton
1. From Dail Righe continue down the valley on the access road. The old Dalnawillan Lodge is in disrepair: shabby & partly boarded up. Other buildings are, however, still occupied, including noisy kennels. Note the graveyard up to the left. Dalnagleton is falling into disrepair as well, but the ground by it is a good alternative to Dail Righe for a campsite.
graveyard
to Altnabreac station
River Thurso
Dalnawillan Lodge
d59 m2
Dail Righe

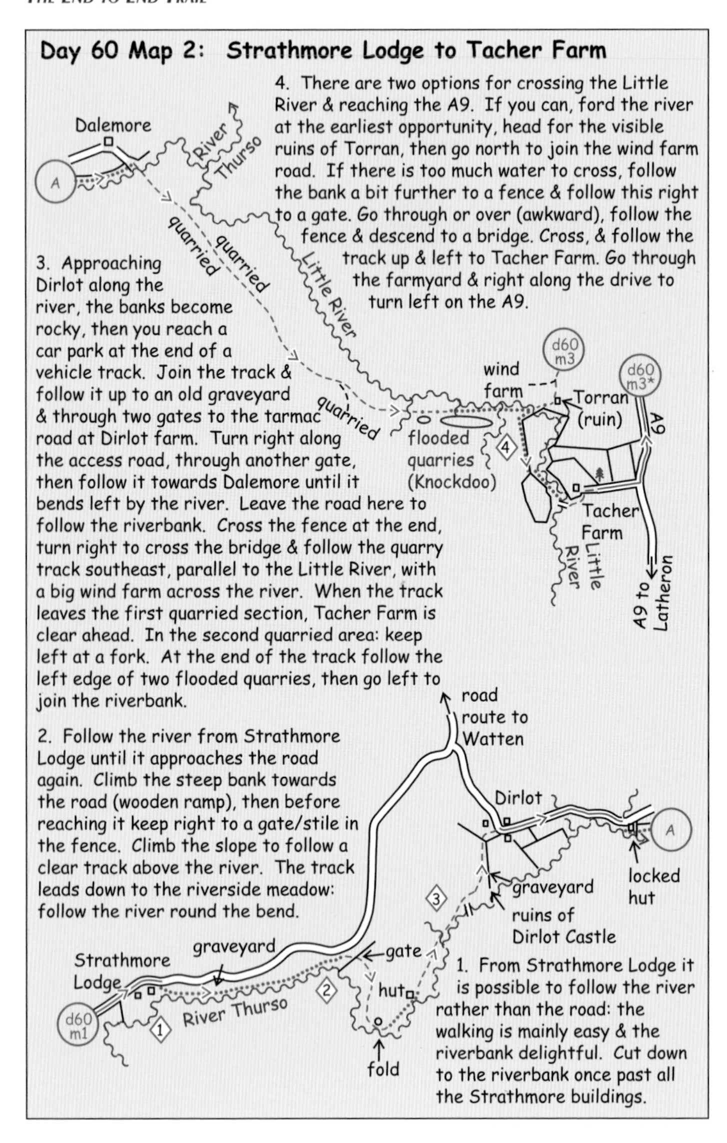
Day 60 Map 2: Strathmore Lodge to Tacher Farm
4. There are two options for crossing the Little River & reaching the A9. If you can, ford the river at the earliest opportunity, head for the visible ruins of Torran, then go north to join the wind farm road. If there is too much water to cross, follow the bank a bit further to a fence & follow this right to a gate. Go through or over (awkward), follow the fence & descend to a bridge. Cross, & follow the track up & left to Tacher Farm. Go through the farmyard & right along the drive to turn left on the A9.
Dalemore
A
River Thurso
quarried
quarried
Little River
3. Approaching Dirlot along the river, the banks become rocky, then you reach a car park at the end of a vehicle track. Join the track & follow it up to an old graveyard & through two gates to the tarmac road at Dirlot farm. Turn right along the access road, through another gate, then follow it towards Dalemore until it bends left by the river. Leave the road here to follow the riverbank. Cross the fence at the end, turn right to cross the bridge & follow the quarry track southeast, parallel to the Little River, with a big wind farm across the river. When the track leaves the first quarried section, Tacher Farm is clear ahead. In the second quarried area: keep left at a fork. At the end of the track follow the left edge of two flooded quarries, then go left to join the riverbank.
quarried
d60 m3
wind farm
d60 m3*
Torran (ruin)
A9
flooded quarries (Knockdoo)
4
Tacher Farm
Little River
A9 to Latheron
road route to Watten
2. Follow the river from Strathmore Lodge until it approaches the road again. Climb the steep bank towards the road (wooden ramp), then before reaching it keep right to a gate/stile in the fence. Climb the slope to follow a clear track above the river. The track leads down to the riverside meadow: follow the river round the bend.
Dirlot
A
locked hut
graveyard
3
ruins of Dirlot Castle
graveyard
Strathmore Lodge
gate
2
hut
d60 m1
1
River Thurso
fold
1. From Strathmore Lodge it is possible to follow the river rather than the road: the walking is mainly easy & the riverbank delightful. Cut down to the riverbank once past all the Strathmore buildings.

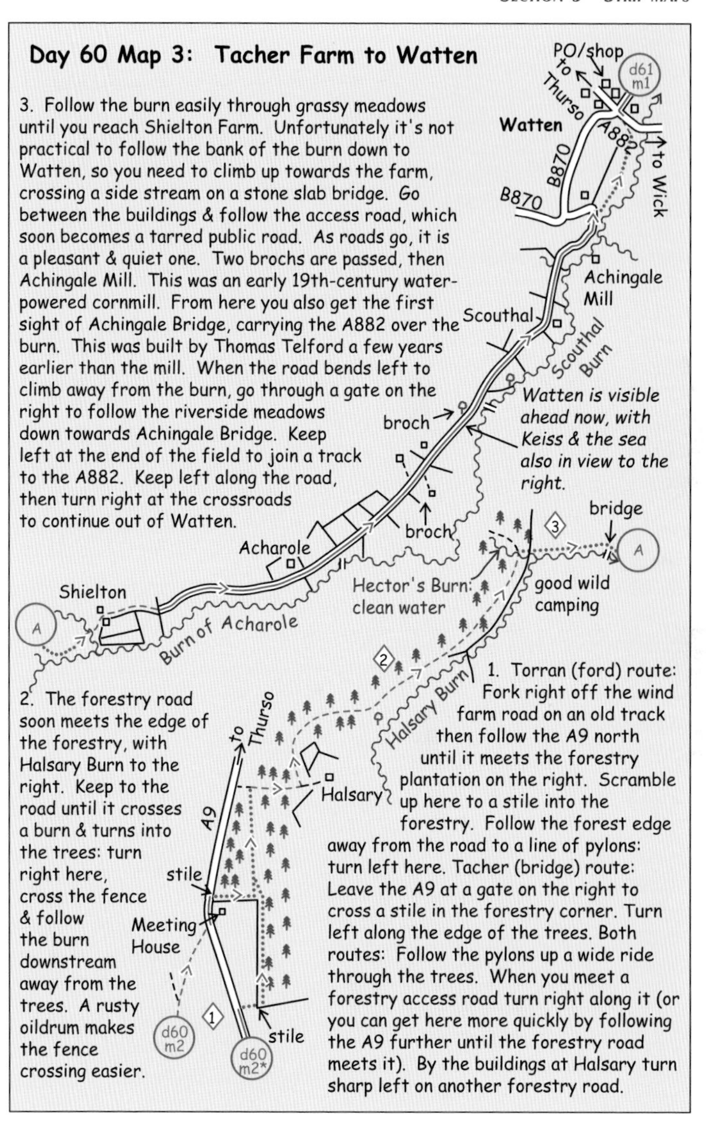

Day 60 Map 3: Tacher Farm to Watten
3. Follow the burn easily through grassy meadows until you reach Shielton Farm. Unfortunately it's not practical to follow the bank of the burn down to Watten, so you need to climb up towards the farm, crossing a side stream on a stone slab bridge. Go between the buildings & follow the access road, which soon becomes a tarred public road. As roads go, it is a pleasant & quiet one. Two brochs are passed, then Achingale Mill. This was an early 19th-century water-powered cornmill. From here you also get the first sight of Achingale Bridge, carrying the A882 over the burn. This was built by Thomas Telford a few years earlier than the mill. When the road bends left to climb away from the burn, go through a gate on the right to follow the riverside meadows down towards Achingale Bridge. Keep left at the end of the field to join a track to the A882. Keep left along the road, then turn right at the crossroads to continue out of Watten.
PO/shop
to Thurso
d61 m1
Watten
A882
to Wick
B870
B870
Achingale Mill
Scouthal
Scouthal Burn
Watten is visible ahead now, with Keiss & the sea also in view to the right.
broch
broch
bridge
3
A
Acharole
Shielton
A
Burn of Acharole
Hector's Burn: clean water
good wild camping
2
Halsary Burn
1. Torran (ford) route: Fork right off the wind farm road on an old track then follow the A9 north until it meets the forestry plantation on the right. Scramble up here to a stile into the forestry. Follow the forest edge away from the road to a line of pylons: turn left here. Tacher (bridge) route: Leave the A9 at a gate on the right to cross a stile in the forestry corner. Turn left along the edge of the trees. Both routes: Follow the pylons up a wide ride through the trees. When you meet a forestry access road turn right along it (or you can get here more quickly by following the A9 further until the forestry road meets it). By the buildings at Halsary turn sharp left on another forestry road.
2. The forestry road soon meets the edge of the forestry, with Halsary Burn to the right. Keep to the road until it crosses a burn & turns into the trees: turn right here, cross the fence & follow the burn downstream away from the trees. A rusty oildrum makes the fence crossing easier.
to Thurso
A9
Halsary
stile
Meeting House
1
stile
d60 m2
d60 m2*

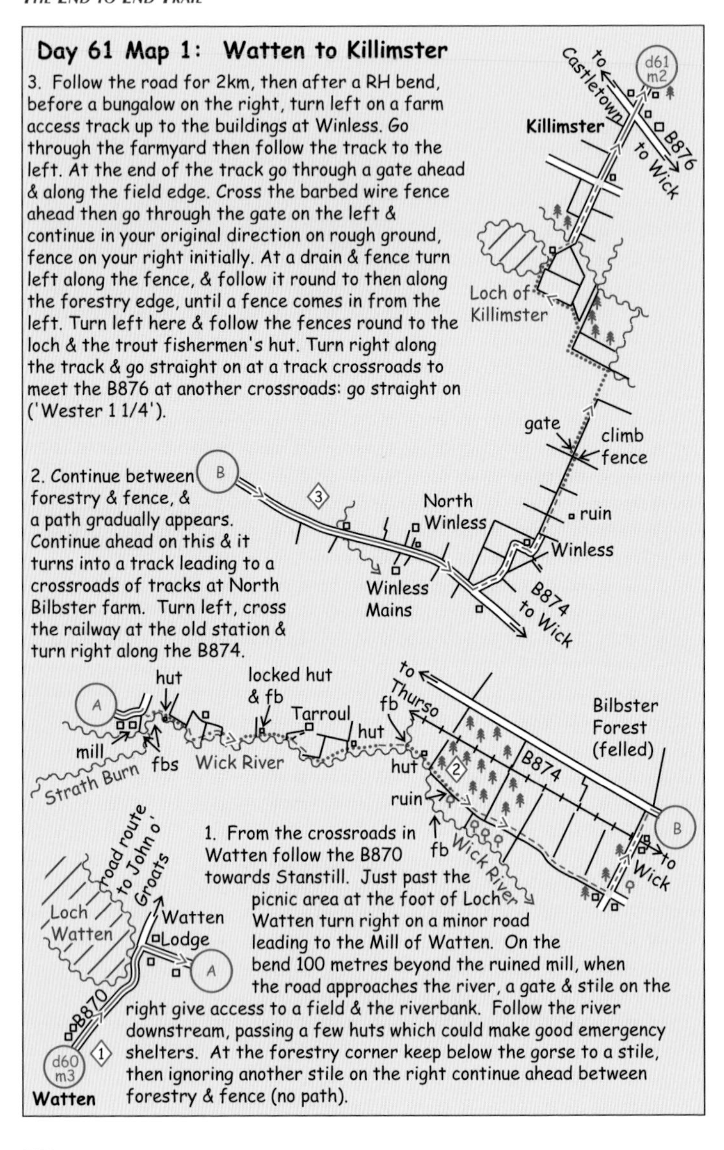
Day 61 Map 1: Watten to Killimster
3. Follow the road for 2km, then after a RH bend, before a bungalow on the right, turn left on a farm access track up to the buildings at Winless. Go through the farmyard then follow the track to the left. At the end of the track go through a gate ahead & along the field edge. Cross the barbed wire fence ahead then go through the gate on the left & continue in your original direction on rough ground, fence on your right initially. At a drain & fence turn left along the fence, & follow it round to then along the forestry edge, until a fence comes in from the left. Turn left here & follow the fences round to the loch & the trout fishermen's hut. Turn right along the track & go straight on at a track crossroads to meet the B876 at another crossroads: go straight on ('Wester 1 1/4').
to Castletown
d61 m2
Killimster
B876 to Wick
Loch of Killimster
gate
climb fence
ruin
North Winless
Winless
Winless Mains
B874 to Wick
2. Continue between forestry & fence, & a path gradually appears. Continue ahead on this & it turns into a track leading to a crossroads of tracks at North Bilbster farm. Turn left, cross the railway at the old station & turn right along the B874.
B
3
hut
locked hut & fb
Tarroul
hut
fb
to Thurso
Bilbster Forest (felled)
A
mill
fbs
Wick River
Strath Burn
hut
2
B874
ruin
fb
Wick River
B
to Wick
road route to John o' Groats
Loch Watten
Watten Lodge
A
B870
1
d60 m3
Watten
1. From the crossroads in Watten follow the B870 towards Stanstill. Just past the picnic area at the foot of Loch Watten turn right on a minor road leading to the Mill of Watten. On the bend 100 metres beyond the ruined mill, when the road approaches the river, a gate & stile on the right give access to a field & the riverbank. Follow the river downstream, passing a few huts which could make good emergency shelters. At the forestry corner keep below the gorse to a stile, then ignoring another stile on the right continue ahead between forestry & fence (no path).

Day 61 Map 2: Killimster to Keiss

2. In the dunes, pick up a track heading northeast behind the main sandhills. Unless the tide is really high, when the track nears the dunes, cross them & climb down onto the beach of Sinclair's Bay. Turn left & walk north along the sand. At the end of the beach, head left to follow a track between a fence & the stony shore. (If the tide is high, stay on the track behind the dunes to a fence, then climb the dunes to join a path along the top, which leads to the same point.) The track passes some houses, then bends left & heads inland. A

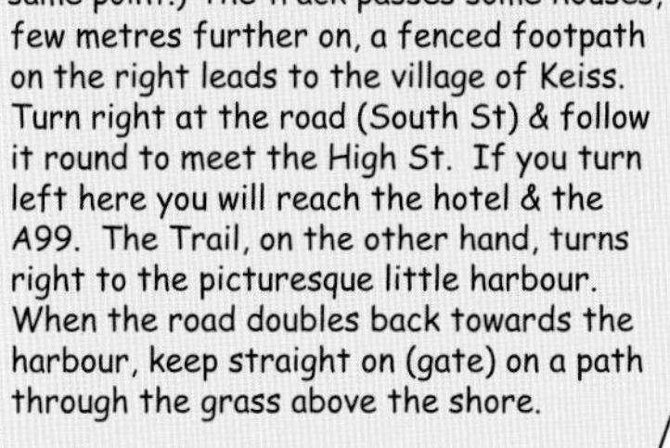

few metres further on, a fenced footpath on the right leads to the village of Keiss. Turn right at the road (South St) & follow it round to meet the High St. If you turn left here you will reach the hotel & the A99. The Trail, on the other hand, turns right to the picturesque little harbour. When the road doubles back towards the harbour, keep straight on (gate) on a path through the grass above the shore.

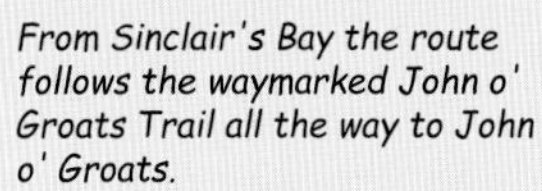

From Sinclair's Bay the route follows the waymarked John o' Groats Trail all the way to John o' Groats.

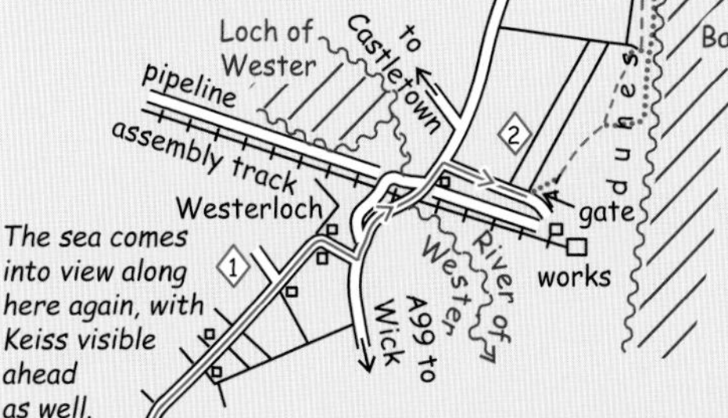

Sinclair's Bay has miles of deserted sandy beach. To the south you can see Noss Head & its lighthouse, Castle Sinclair Girnigoe & Ackergill Tower. To the north is Keiss, with its castles old & new behind the village.

The sea comes into view along here again, with Keiss visible ahead as well.

1. Follow the road until it bends right at a farm to meet the busy A99 Wick to John o' Groats road. As you walk along the minor road, the Subsea 7 Wester assembly line stretches to left & right ahead. This consists of 8km of twin railway tracks on which are assembled undersea pipelines which are then floated out to sea with the help of barges. Turn left on the A99, cross the River of Wester, & continue past a house to the tarmac access road for the works. Turn right here, ignoring the 'no access' sign, & at the first bend go through a gate on the left into the dunes.

Day 61 Map 3: Keiss to Freswick Bay

3. Keep between the cliff edge & the fence until you reach the farm buildings at Freswick. Officially the route keeps right of all buildings to reach the burn. If you are stopped by nettles you will need to cross the wall/fence earlier & keep left of all the farm buildings & the castle to the burn. Ford the burn near the sea to follow the beach (or use the bridge if the water's high then join the beach via a gate). If the tide is right in, you can follow the bottom edge of the rough sandy pasture instead.

2. From the car park continue between sea & fence. At the harbour of Milltown Haven descend steps to the shore then climb steeply up the other side to a ruin. Walk round it on the right & continue along the cliff top. The contorted strata around Bucholly Castle are impressive & the situation of the ruined castle mindboggling.

1. Follow the cliff top to Helberry car park, with manoeuvres in places to avoid barbed wire. From Keiss Castle keep to the seaward side of the fence. On reaching the open ground before Lady's Hole, keep left to get round the geo, then return to the cliff edge (low here) to cross or skirt the barbed wire fence. At the odd little monument of Mervyn Tower pick up a made path leading to the car park.

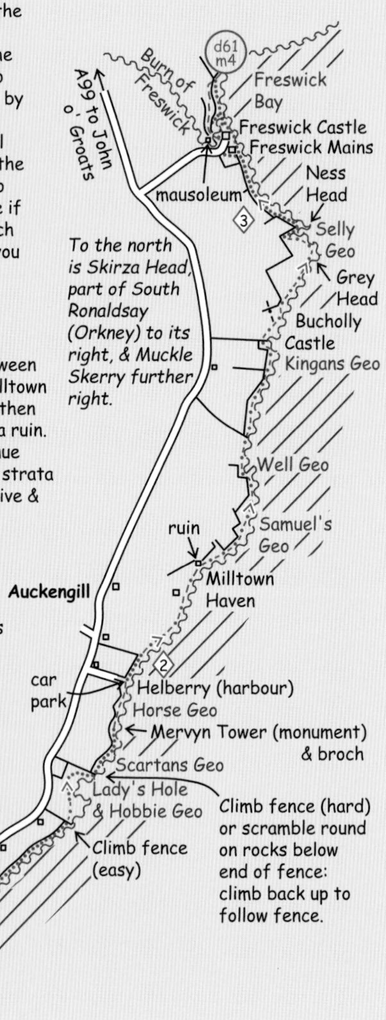

d61 m4
Burn of Freswick
A99 to John o' Groats
Freswick Bay
Freswick Castle
Freswick Mains
mausoleum
Ness Head
3
Selly Geo
Grey Head
To the north is Skirza Head, part of South Ronaldsay (Orkney) to its right, & Muckle Skerry further right.
Bucholly Castle
Kingans Geo
Well Geo
ruin
Samuel's Geo
Milltown Haven
Auckengill
2
car park
Helberry (harbour)
Horse Geo
Mervyn Tower (monument) & broch
Scartans Geo
Lady's Hole & Hobbie Geo
Climb fence (hard) or scramble round on rocks below end of fence: climb back up to follow fence.
Climb fence (easy)
'new' Keiss Castle
gate
A99
gate
Keiss Castle (ruin)
1
d61 m2

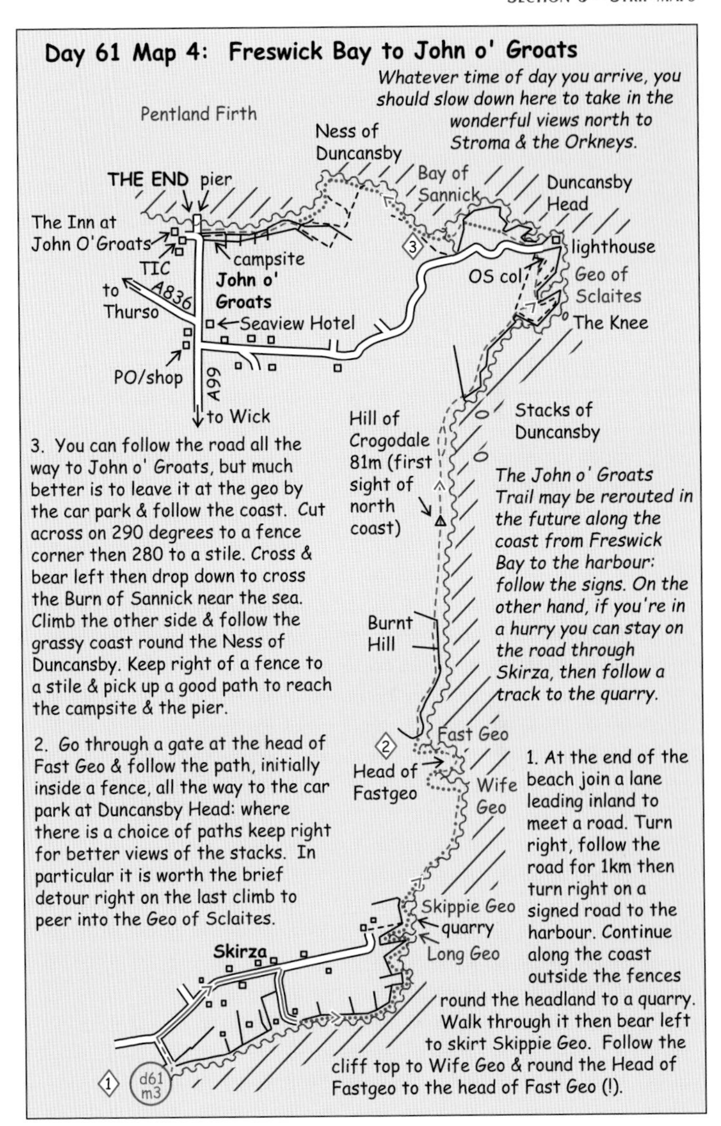
Day 61 Map 4: Freswick Bay to John o' Groats
Whatever time of day you arrive, you should slow down here to take in the wonderful views north to Stroma & the Orkneys.
Pentland Firth
Ness of Duncansby
Bay of Sannick
Duncansby Head
THE END
pier
The Inn at John O'Groats
TIC
campsite
John o' Groats
to Thurso
A836
Seaview Hotel
PO/shop
A99
to Wick
lighthouse
OS col
Geo of Sclaites
The Knee
Stacks of Duncansby
Hill of Crogodale 81m (first sight of north coast)
Burnt Hill
Fast Geo
Head of Fastgeo
Wife Geo
Skippie Geo
quarry
Long Geo
Skirza
d61 m3
3. You can follow the road all the way to John o' Groats, but much better is to leave it at the geo by the car park & follow the coast. Cut across on 290 degrees to a fence corner then 280 to a stile. Cross & bear left then drop down to cross the Burn of Sannick near the sea. Climb the other side & follow the grassy coast round the Ness of Duncansby. Keep right of a fence to a stile & pick up a good path to reach the campsite & the pier.
The John o' Groats Trail may be rerouted in the future along the coast from Freswick Bay to the harbour: follow the signs. On the other hand, if you're in a hurry you can stay on the road through Skirza, then follow a track to the quarry.
2. Go through a gate at the head of Fast Geo & follow the path, initially inside a fence, all the way to the car park at Duncansby Head: where there is a choice of paths keep right for better views of the stacks. In particular it is worth the brief detour right on the last climb to peer into the Geo of Sclaites.
1. At the end of the beach join a lane leading inland to meet a road. Turn right, follow the road for 1km then turn right on a signed road to the harbour. Continue along the coast outside the fences round the headland to a quarry. Walk through it then bear left to skirt Skippie Geo. Follow the cliff top to Wife Geo & round the Head of Fastgeo to the head of Fast Geo (!).

Knockfin Heights (Day 59)

APPENDIX A

Route summary tables

The following tables summarise the daily stages of the two schedules: the two-month main schedule and the three-month alternative schedule. Some key points are as follows.

- Distances are given to the nearest kilometre and nearest mile, measured from 1:25,000 OS maps with mapping software.
- The road walking is an estimate of the proportion of the day's distance that must be walked on tarmac roads that may be shared with motor traffic. It has been calculated by adding up the distances walked on public roads and pavements next to them. Tarmac cycle paths, towpaths and private roads are not included in this. Some of the roads can be avoided on the South West Coast Path by taking to the beaches, provided the tides are out far enough. In any event, virtually all the roads followed are either very quiet lanes in the country, or roads in villages and towns with good pavements. There is very little traffic dodging.
- The ascent per day is given in metres, again measured with mapping software. This is only approximate, particularly when the route follows the coast or takes motorway bridges. Your GPS will give you a different figure (and somebody else's GPS will give you yet another).
- The accommodation and other key facilities listed are usually within a few minutes' walk of the stage end. Exceptions to this are explained in the main text of the book covering that day's route. Where little or no accommodation is shown at a stage end, again your options are explained in the main text. The hotels indicated are usually reasonably inexpensive – again exceptions are noted in the main text of the book.
- Where a pub or pubs are indicated at a stage end, there will be at least one pub that normally serves evening meals. Be aware, however, that some pubs do not serve meals on Sunday or Monday nights.

Main schedule

Day	Stage end	Km	Miles	% on roads	Metres of ascent	B&B/Hotel	Hostel/ Bunkhouse	Bothy	Campsite	Wild camping	Pub	Café/ Restaurant	Grocer	Post office	Outdoor shop	Bank	ATM	Page
	Land's End (& Sennen)					x	x		x		x	x	x	x				
1	Zennor	26	16	5	960	x			x		x							59
2	Gwithian	24	15	17	610	x			x		x	x						61
3	Perranporth	30	19	7	1130	x	x		x		x	x	x	x			x	63
4	Mawgan Porth	28	18	12	910	x			x		x	x						64
5	Wadebridge	28	17	17	680	x			x		x	x	x	x	x	x	x	65
6	Boscastle	32	20	18	1300	x	x				x	x	x	x	x		x	67
7	Bude	26	16	6	1350	x	x		x		x	x	x	x	x	x	x	69
8	Clovelly	38	23	1	2090	x					x	x	x					70
9	Barnstaple	37	23	22	990	x			x		x	x	x	x	x	x	x	72
10	Warren Farm (& Simonsbath)	34	21	31	1090	x			x		x							87
11	Roadwater	29	18	14	660	x					x		x	x				90
12	Bridgwater	36	22	23	930	x					x	x	x	x	x	x	x	93
13	Cheddar	33	20	31	180	x	x		x		x	x	x	x	x	x	x	95
14	Easton-in-Gordano (& Pill)	45	28	19	920	x					x		x	x			x	98
15	Chepstow	29	18	41	370	x	x				x	x	x	x		x	x	100
16	Monmouth	28	17	15	960	x			x		x	x	x	x	x	x	x	103
17	Pandy	26	16	26	610	x			x		x							104
18	Hay-on-Wye	26	16	10	750	x	x		x		x	x	x	x	x	x	x	106
19	Knighton	45	28	21	1450	x			x		x	x	x	x		x	x	107

Day	Stage end	Km	Miles	% on roads	Metres of ascent	B&B/Hotel	Hostel/ Bunkhouse	Bothy	Campsite	Wild camping	Pub	Café/ Restaurant	Grocer	Post office	Outdoor shop	Bank	ATM	Page
20	Craven Arms	23	14	27	690	x					x	x	x	x		x	x	154
21	Ironbridge (& Coalport)	36	23	9	760	x	x				x	x	x	x			x	155
22	Penkridge	40	25	33	410	x			x		x	x	x	x		x	x	159
23	Abbots Bromley	26	16	15	300	x					x	x	x					162
24	Thorpe	34	21	12	640	x			x		x							165
25	Youlgreave	26	16	20	630	x	x		x		x	x	x	x				168
26	Hathersage (& North Lees)	29	18	9	860	x	x		x		x	x	x		x	x	x	171
27	White Gate	39	24	9	1240	x			x									175
28	Hebden Bridge	40	25	14	1300	x	x		x		x	x	x	x	x		x	179
29	Thornton in Craven	36	22	19	1260				x									238
30	Horton in Ribblesdale	40	25	20	1170	x	x		x		x	x			x			239
31	Hawes	22	14	10	540	x	x		x		x	x	x	x	x	x	x	241
32	Keld	20	12	6	740	x	x		x		x	x						242
33	Middleton-in-Teesdale	33	21	13	800	x	x		x		x	x	x	x		x	x	243
34	Dufton	32	20	11	710	x	x		x		x							244
35	Alston	31	19	4	1070	x	x		x		x	x	x	x	x		x	246
36	Greenhead	26	16	4	610	x	x		x		x	x						247
37	Bellingham	35	22	10	950	x	x		x		x	x	x	x			x	248
38	Byrness	24	15	5	550	x	x	x	x		x							250
39	Jedburgh	31	19	18	800	x			x		x	x	x	x		x	x	251
40	Melrose	29	18	21	630	x			x		x	x	x	x		x	x	267

Day	Stage end	Km	Miles	% on roads	Metres of ascent	B&B/Hotel	Hostel/ Bunkhouse	Bothy	Campsite	Wild camping	Pub	Café/ Restaurant	Grocer	Post office	Outdoor shop	Bank	ATM	Page
41	Traquair (& Innerleithen)	29	18	9	990	x			x	x	x	x	x	x		x	x	269
42	West Linton	36	22	33	1060	x					x	x	x	x				271
43	Linlithgow	44	27	9	750	x			x		x	x	x	x		x	x	273
44	Kilsyth	33	20	0	290	x					x	x	x	x		x	x	277
45	Drymen	38	24	15	450	x	x		x	x	x	x	x	x			x	280
46	Inverarnan	46	29	5	1600	x	x		x		x	x						282
47	Bridge of Orchy	30	18	1	770	x	x			x	x							285
48	Kinlochleven	34	21	14	960	x	x		x		x	x	x	x			x	287
49	Fort William	24	15	12	710	x	x		x		x	x	x	x	x	x	x	289
50	Glen Garry (Loch Poulary)	38	23	17	930					x								315
51	Glen Affric	26	16	20	970		x	x		x								319
52	Bendronaig Lodge	34	21	0	900			x		x								321
53	Kinlochewe	33	20	4	1070	x	x		x	x	x	x	x	x				324
54	Inverlael	41	25	8	1510	x	x			x								326
55	Oykel Bridge	30	19	2	890	x				x	x							329
56	Overscaig	38	24	20	880	x				x	x							330
57	Crask	16	10	2	400	x			x	x	x							333
58	Kinbrace	41	25	4	490					x								336
59	River Thurso (Dail Righe)	26	16	1	420					x								338
60	Watten	33	21	21	140	x				x	x		x	x				341
61	John o' Groats	39	24	19	1020	x			x		x	x	x	x				343

Alternative three-month schedule

Day	Stage end	Km	Miles	% on roads	Metres of ascent	B&B/Hotel	Hostel/ Bunkhouse	Bothy	Campsite	Wild camping	Pub	Café/ Restaurant	Grocer	Post office	Outdoor shop	Bank	ATM
	Land's End (& Sennen)					x	x		x		x	x	x	x			
A1	Pendeen	15	9	6	540	x			x		x	x	x	x			
A2	St Ives	20	12	4	730	x	x		x		x	x	x	x	x	x	x
A3	Portreath	27	17	17	640	x	x				x	x	x	x			x
A4	Perranporth	18	11	7	810	x	x		x		x	x	x	x			x
A5	Newquay	19	12	9	630	x	x		x		x	x	x	x	x	x	x
A6	Trevone	25	15	13	730	x					x	x	x				
A7	Port Isaac	23	14	35	450	x					x	x	x				x
A8	Boscastle	21	13	4	1080	x	x				x	x	x	x	x		x
A9	Bude	26	16	6	1350	x	x		x		x	x	x	x	x	x	x
A10	Hartland Quay (& Stoke)	23	14	2	1240	x	x		x		x						
A11	Clovelly	15	9	0	880	x					x	x	x				
A12	Westward Ho!	17	11	25	830	x					x	x	x	x			x
A13	Barnstaple	20	12	19	160	x			x		x	x	x	x	x	x	x
A14	Challacombe	21	13	47	700	x					x	x	x	x			
A15	Warren Farm (& Simonsbath)	14	9	6	390	x			x		x						

Day	Stage end	Km	Miles	% on roads	Metres of ascent	B&B/Hotel	Hostel/ Bunkhouse	Bothy	Campsite	Wild camping	Pub	Café/ Restaurant	Grocer	Post office	Outdoor shop	Bank	ATM
A16	Luxborough	24	15	11	515	x				x	x						
A17	Bicknoller	16	10	24	480						x		x				
A18	Bridgwater	25	16	23	600	x					x	x	x	x	x	x	x
A19	Blackford (& Mark)	21	13	46	90	x			x		x		x	x			
A20	Sandford	27	17	7	650	x					x		x				x
A21	Easton-in-Gordano (& Pill)	29	18	24	360	x					x		x	x			x
A22	Chepstow	29	18	41	370	x	x				x	x	x	x		x	x
A23	Monmouth	28	17	15	960	x			x		x	x	x	x	x	x	x
A24	Pandy	26	16	26	610	x			x		x						
A25	Hay-on-Wye	26	16	10	750	x	x		x		x	x	x	x	x	x	x
A26	Kington	24	15	31	710	x	x		x		x	x	x	x			x
A27	Knighton	21	13	10	750	x			x		x	x	x	x		x	x
A28	Craven Arms	23	14	27	690	x					x	x	x	x		x	x
A29	Much Wenlock	29	18	7	620	x			x		x	x	x	x			x
A30	Kemberton	15	9	27	290	x					x						
A31	Penkridge	32	20	33	260	x			x		x	x	x	x		x	x
A32	Abbots Bromley	26	16	15	300	x					x	x	x				
A33	Thorpe	34	21	12	640	x			x		x						

Day	Stage end	Km	Miles	% on roads	Metres of ascent	B&B/Hotel	Hostel/ Bunkhouse	Bothy	Campsite	Wild camping	Pub	Café/ Restaurant	Grocer	Post office	Outdoor shop	Bank	ATM
A34	Youlgreave	26	16	20	630	x	x		x		x	x	x	x			
A35	Baslow	13	8	15	300	x					x	x	x				
A36	Moscar	19	12	4	630												
A37	Flouch	22	14	3	740	x					x						
A38	Marsden	26	16	18	640	x			x		x	x	x	x			x
A39	Hebden Bridge	24	15	15	870	x	x		x		x	x	x	x	x		x
A40	Cowling (& Ickornshaw)	25	16	13	840	x	x		x		x	x	x				
A41	Malham	28	17	26	750	x	x		x		x	x			x		
A42	Horton in Ribblesdale	23	14	19	860	x	x		x		x	x			x		
A43	Hawes	22	14	10	540	x	x		x		x	x	x	x	x	x	x
A44	Tan Hill	26	16	5	1010	x	x		x		x						
A45	Middleton-in-Teesdale	26	16	16	510	x	x		x		x	x	x	x		x	x
A46	Langdon Beck	13	8	4	300	x	x				x						
A47	Dufton	20	12	16	410	x	x		x		x						
A48	Alston	31	19	4	1070	x	x		x		x	x	x	x	x		x
A49	Greenhead	26	16	4	610	x	x		x		x	x					
A50	Twice Brewed	12	7	2	430	x	x		x		x	x					

Day	Stage end	Km	Miles	% on roads	Metres of ascent	B&B/Hotel	Hostel/ Bunkhouse	Bothy	Campsite	Wild camping	Pub	Café/ Restaurant	Grocer	Post office	Outdoor shop	Bank	ATM
A51	Bellingham	24	15	14	520	x	x		x		x	x	x	x			x
A52	Byrness	24	15	5	550	x	x	x	x		x						
A53	Jedburgh	31	19	18	800	x			x		x	x	x	x		x	x
A54	Melrose	29	18	21	630	x			x		x	x	x	x		x	x
A55	Traquair (& Innerleithen)	29	18	9	990	x			x	x	x	x	x	x		x	x
A56	Peebles	15	9	36	490	x			x		x	x	x	x	x	x	x
A57	West Linton	21	13	30	580	x					x	x	x	x			
A58	Broxburn (& Uphall)	30	19	13	610	x					x	x	x	x		x	x
A59	Falkirk (off-route)	28	18	0	310	x					x	x	x	x	x	x	x
A60	Lennoxtown	31	19	1	210	x					x	x	x	x			x
A61	Drymen	25	16	22	360	x	x		x	x	x	x	x	x			x
A62	Rowardennan	24	15	9	750	x	x			x	x						
A63	Inverarnan	22	14	1	850	x	x		x		x	x					
A64	Tyndrum	19	12	0	590	x	x		x		x	x	x	x	x		x
A65	Kingshouse	30	19	12	690	x	x			x	x						
A66	Kinlochleven	14	9	8	450	x	x		x		x	x	x	x			x
A67	Fort William	24	15	12	710	x	x		x		x	x	x	x	x	x	x
A68	Gairlochy (& Mucomir)	14	9	14	100	x			x								

Day	Stage end	Km	Miles	% on roads	Metres of ascent	B&B/Hotel	Hostel/ Bunkhouse	Bothy	Campsite	Wild camping	Pub	Café/ Restaurant	Grocer	Post office	Outdoor shop	Bank	ATM
A69	Glen Garry (Loch Poulary)	23	15	19	830					x							
A70	Glen Affric	26	16	20	970		x	x		x							
A71	Loch Cruoshie	26	16	0	690			x		x							
A72	Craig	24	15	1	750		x			x							
A73	Kinlochewe	16	10	7	520	x	x		x	x	x	x	x	x			
A74	Loch an Nid	18	11	6	660					x							
A75	Inverlael	23	15	10	850	x	x			x							
A76	Strath Mulzie	17	11	0	740					x							
A77	Oykel Bridge	13	8	5	150	x				x	x						
A78	Glen Cassley	28	17	5	690					x							
A79	Overscaig	11	7	59	190	x				x	x						
A80	Loch Choire	27	17	2	570			x		x							
A81	Kinbrace	30	18	5	320					x							
A82	River Thurso (Dail Righe)	26	16	1	420					x							
A83	A9 (Halsary)	23	14	11	100					x							
A84	Keiss	30	18	40	120	x				x	x						
A85	John o' Groats	21	13	2	950	x			x		x	x	x	x			

APPENDIX B

Bibliography

These are a few of the many books I have read while researching Land's End to John o' Groats. Each book has been included either because it includes valuable information or is thought-provoking, or because it is (in my opinion) a good book. Some books are all three, but be warned that they are not all good literature. Many more people have written End to End books – for a more complete bibliography visit the website www.longwalks.org.uk.

Some of these books are out of print, but may be available from your local library for a small fee if you ask the librarian to track them down for you. Other than that, you'll have to search the second-hand bookshops, or websites such as www.abebooks.co.uk and www.bookfinder.com.

Essential guidebooks

If you want to follow a guidebook all the way from End to End you will need the following – they contain maps and detailed route descriptions that are not included in this guidebook.

The South West Coast Path by Paddy Dillon (Cicerone, 2nd edition, 2016; reprinted 2019)

Walking Offa's Dyke Path by Mike Dunn (Cicerone, 2016)

The Pennine Way by Paddy Dillon (Cicerone, 4th edition, 2017)

The West Highland Way by Terry Marsh (Cicerone, 4th edition, 2016; reprinted 2019)

Recommended End to End books

A Tour Through the Whole Island of Great Britain by Daniel Defoe (1724–26). Penguin Classics published an abridged version in 1986. This isn't really an End to End book, but does purport to document a series of journeys Defoe made, including to Land's End and John o' Groats. It's well worth reading.

A Walk from London to John O'Groat's by Elihu Burritt (Sampson Low, Son & Marston, 1864) and *A Walk from London to Land's End and Back* by Elihu Burritt (Sampson Low, Son & Marston, 1865). Elihu Burritt was appointed US Consul to Birmingham by Abraham Lincoln. In 1863 he walked from London to John o' Groats, and the following year he completed his End to End walk by walking from London to Land's End and back. He tends to concentrate on the grand buildings he sees and their wealthy and/or aristocratic owners, rather than the walking or the scenery – the books were written with an American agriculturalist audience in mind. It is perhaps not too surprising that his writing doesn't chime well with modern walkers, as his motivation was very different. Having said all that, he probably has to be given the credit for coming up with the idea of walking between Land's End and John o' Groats. He did it in two parts only because he couldn't start early enough in 1863. The second book improves a lot once he gets away from 'civilisation'.

From John o' Groat's to Land's End by Robert and John Naylor (Caxton Publishing Co Ltd, 1916). This is a fascinating account of what may well have been the first continuous walk between Land's End and John o' Groats. The Naylor brothers were well-to-do young men from Cheshire who were presumably inspired to attempt the walk by the writings of Elihu Burritt, although they don't actually say so in their account of their walk. Although the book was published in 1916, they actually did the walk in 1871. John Naylor wrote up and published the account from their earlier notes after the death of his brother, 45 years after their expedition! The book is well written, and the Naylors had a modern approach to their walking that is easy to identify with today – they were doing it for a challenge, and to see as much of the country as they could. They refused to take ferries, and walked every step of the way. There is rather a lot of interspersed historical fact, and also some historical myth, which is how the book ends up weighing in at 659 pages, but there is plenty of personal account in it as well.

Cross Country by Theo Lang (Hodder & Stoughton, 1948). Theo Lang was a journalist and novelist who walked a rambling route from Land's End to John o' Groats in 1946, just months after the end of World War II. He set off on 17 March and finished just under five months later, having walked about 1500 of the 2200 miles he travelled. He wrote articles as he went for the *Sunday Chronicle*, and later wrote them up into a book. The account is an entertaining one by a professional writer, and has a similar feeling to John Hillaby's account (see below). If you enjoy that, then this is worth seeking out.

Blaise Hamlet (Day 15)

The Big Walk by A Walker (Prentice-Hall, 1961). This is an account of the race from John o' Groats to Land's End organised and sponsored by Billy Butlin, the holiday camp entrepreneur. It's a hilarious read, and full of mind-boggling examples of what not to do. Billy Butlin conceived the idea of sponsoring a race after the publicity given to Dr Barbara Moore's 22-day walk, presumably as a publicity stunt for his holiday business. The race was on roads all the way, and started from the John O'Groats House Hotel at 5pm on 26 February 1960 – not the ideal time of year for the racers, but nicely timed before the start of the Butlin's holiday season. Of the 715 starters, only 138 finished, and many of the competitors had no idea of what they were embarking on, only competing to win the £1000 prizes for the first man and woman to finish. The anonymous (presumably) author of the book didn't quite finish the race, so isn't included in the list of finishers. He did, however, write a very good account.

Journey Through Britain by John Hillaby (Constable, 1968; widely reprinted). The book that must have inspired a thousand attempts at walking from Land's End to John o' Groats. John Hillaby made the journey in the late 1960s, mainly avoiding walking on roads, and wrote this extremely entertaining book about it. The only official long-distance path at the time was the Pennine Way, which he incorporated into his route (more or less). He also followed parts of what later became the Offa's Dyke Path and the West Highland Way.

Turn Right at Land's End by John Merrill (Oxford Illustrated Press, 1979). John Merrill is probably the most prolific long-distance walker in Britain, and this book is his account

A59 bridge, Leeds and Liverpool Canal, East Marton (Day30)

of the longest walk in Britain – following the coast all the way round. He set off on 3 January 1978, finished on 8 November, and estimated the distance he walked at 6824 miles. Naturally the walk included joining Land's End to John o' Groats, walking 3800 miles between the two. Oh yes, and he also walked Land's End to John o' Groats three months earlier for a warm up. This walk qualifies for a 'don't try this at home' warning, and you wouldn't have thought it would have had many repeats, although a number of accounts have been written of similar walks since. The walk was obviously very hard both mentally and physically, and included a lot of unavoidable road walking and urban and industrial areas. It is well worth reading for his approach to preparation, and his experience of how to cope with very long walks. Where else are you going to get statistically valid estimates of the life expectancy of boots and socks, for instance?

Hamish's Groat's End Walk by Hamish Brown (Victor Gollancz, 1981) (also Paladin paperback). This is Hamish Brown's account of his 1979 walk from John o' Groats to Land's End with his Shetland collie, Storm. The route was an indirect one, taking in mountains in Scotland (to complete his sixth round of Munros), England, Wales and Ireland, and the trip took about five months to complete. He generally kept to the mountains where he could, camping wild a lot, and making up for this by staying in comfortable hotels from time to time (a good way to travel, I think). The book is a very readable account which I found difficult to put down, and I have to recommend it strongly as excellent pre-walk mental preparation. There is also plenty of practical information in the book. It has a very good section on what he took and why, and an extensive bibliography.

Land's End to John o'Groats: A Choice of Footpaths for Walking the Length of Britain by Andrew McCloy (Hodder & Stoughton, 1994) (also Coronet paperback). An excellent book in which the author outlines three different off-road walking routes. This is a guidebook rather than an account of his journeys, and a recommended read for anyone planning to walk off-road from Land's End to John o' Groats. It doesn't give a lot of detail of the routes, so you would still need to do a lot of planning or improvising to follow one of them. The End to End Trail coincides in part with two of the routes.

One Woman's Walk by Shirley Rippin (Shirley Rippin/Logaston Press, 1998). A well-written and relaxed account by an experienced walker. The route includes the Pennine Way and the West Highland Way.

One Pair of Boots by Tony Hobbs (Logaston Press, 2000). An account of the author's walk from Land's End to John o' Groats in 1997, this is well worth reading. He set out to follow one of Andrew McCloy's routes, having done minimal preparation, and buying guidebooks and maps as he went along. The book is full of things such as his account of squeezing pus out of his toes, and a list of every pint of beer consumed on the trip (285 pints of 83 varieties). Therapeutic reading for anyone who tends to overplan their life.

A Walk for Jim by Sally Thomas (published privately, 2001). A moving and readable account of Sally Thomas's walk from Land's End to John o' Groats in aid of leukaemia research – her son had died of leukaemia shortly before her walk. Her route was

Milton of Campsie station, Strathkelvin Railway Path (Day 45)

largely off-road and avoided hilly country, so is worth considering if you don't want to climb many hills.

The Land's End to John o'Groats Walk by Andrew McCloy (Cordee, 2002). This is a more detailed description of one of the three routes (the 'Central Route') outlined in Andrew McCloy's earlier book. It is still not a detailed route description, though, and to follow the route described will require detailed planning with maps for the sections not covered by waymarked routes.

No Fixed Abode by Douglas Legg (Colby Press, 2002). An account of a 5000-mile coastal walk that in many respects bore more resemblance to the journeys of an old-fashioned 'man of the road' than a modern long-distance walk.

Follow the Spring North by Christine Roche (Trafford Publishing, 2004). An account of a backpacking End to End walk, following a route that had been well researched. Worth reading for some of the route suggestions. Although this is an account of a walk, there is enough information about the route to be able to follow it accurately most of the way.

Land's End to John O'Groats: A Thousand Mile Walking Route by Mike Salter (Folly Publications, 2006). This is the only other off-road End to End walking guide I know about still in print. It gives a complete route, shown on sketch maps with some text description, and two routes through Scotland. Worth looking at if you're considering other route options, as it varies from the End to End Trail route for a lot of the way.

Other End to End books referenced in this guide

A Ride from Land's End to John o' Groats by Evelyn Burnaby (Sampson Low, Marston & Co, 1893)

From Land's End to John o' Groat's by GH Allen (Fowler, 1905)

2000 Miles on Foot by EW Fox (Walter Scott Publishing, 1911)

On Old-World Highways by Thos D Murphy (LC Page & Co, Boston, USA, 1914)

From Land's End to John O'Groat's by Jessie Barker Gardner (published privately, USA, 1930)

Land's End to John o' Groats by William Dawson (Cunliffe Brothers, 1934)

From Land's End to John o' Groats by Colin Howard (Blackie, 1939)

The Great Backpacking Adventure by Chris Townsend (Oxford Illustrated Press, 1987)

Recommended general information books

A Journey to the Western Islands of Scotland by Samuel Johnson (1775) and *The Journal of a Tour to the Hebrides* by James Boswell (1786). These two classic accounts of a trip through the Scottish Highlands in 1773 have been republished by Penguin Classics in a single volume. They are both fascinating books, and include a lot of detail that conveys vividly what it must have been like to travel in Scotland in the days of the clearances. Boswell's book also gives enormous insight into the personalities involved, many of them larger than life. The Penguin edition is recommended reading to carry with you for the Scottish part of the walk – good value in words per ounce, relevant, and brilliant writing.

Romany Hints for Hikers by Gipsy Petulengro (Methuen, 1936). This is a well-written and entertaining book of backpacking and camping tips from an early practitioner who knew what he was talking about, and had the right attitude right down the line. I've included some of the tips in this guidebook but the original publication is worth seeking out.

Trail Life by Ray Jardine (AdventureLore Press, USA, 2009). This is an updated and generalised edition of Ray's classic *Pacific Crest Trail Hiker's Handbook*, and is the best book in existence on how to travel light. The importance of Ray Jardine to the current ethic of lightweight hiking can't be overemphasised. Large amounts of the material written in the UK outdoor magazines, and a lot of the products on the market, have been influenced significantly by Ray, either directly or indirectly. Buy this book and you will end up with a lighter rucksack as a result. Don't take everything in it as gospel, though, as things that work in America don't necessarily work over here. Anyone trying to use an umbrella in a typical Pennine rainstorm, or sleep under a tarp in the Highland midge season, is likely to regret it!

Scottish Hill Tracks, edited by DJ Bennet and CD Stone (Scottish Rights of Way and Access Society, 5th edition, 2012). An invaluable publication giving brief descriptions of over 300 routes in the Scottish hills and mountains. It concentrates on routes between places, rather than bagging peaks, which makes it much more useful for our purposes than most other Scottish walking guides. I have followed a number of the paths described in this book – it saved me a lot of research time. If you plan to walk in Scotland again, you should get a copy.

The Scottish Bothy Bible by Geoff Allan (Wild Things Publishing, 2017). This wonderful book is full of photos and details of most of the bothies in Scotland. It tells you what there is at each bothy and how to get there. It almost makes you want to turn your walk into a bothy-bagging trip instead.

The Independent Hostel Guide, Backpackers Press (distributed by Cordee, revised annually). This lists independent bunkhouse accommodation throughout the British Isles.

Good Beer Guide, CAMRA Books (revised annually). This is an annual guide to the best British pubs and best traditional British beer. It is indispensable to a certain class of walker, of which I am most definitely one. CAMRA is the pressure group that saved the tradition of British beer in the 1970s, and is still providing sterling service today.

Other publications referenced in this guide

The Complete Guide to the South West Coast Path, South West Coast Path Association (revised annually)

Walking in Somerset by James Roberts (Cicerone, 1997)

Macmillan Way West, Macmillan Way Association (2001)

The Limestone Link, Yatton Ramblers (revised 2007)

The Cotswold Way by Kev Reynolds (Cicerone, 4th edition, 2016)

The Severn Way by Terry Marsh (Cicerone, 2nd edition, 2019)

The Monarch's Way, Book 2: Stratford-upon-Avon to Charmouth by Trevor Antill (Monarch's Way Association, revised 2016)

The Heart of England Way by Stephen J Cross (Sigma Press, 2nd edition, 2018)

The Wye Valley Walk by the Wye Valley Walk Partnership (Cicerone, 2011; reprinted 2018)

Offa's Dyke Castles Alternative Route, Offa's Dyke Association, revised 1994

Guide to the Maelor Way by Gordon Emery, via Wrexham Borough Council

The South Cheshire Way, Mid-Cheshire Footpath Society

The Wales Coast Path by Paddy Dillon (Cicerone, 2015; reprinted 2016)

The North Cheshire Way, Mid-Cheshire Footpath Society

The Limestone Way, Derbyshire Dales District Council

The Alternative Pennine Way by Denis Brook and Phil Hinchliffe (Cicerone, 1992) (out of print)

The M48 bridge over the Severn Estuary (Day 15)

St Oswald's and St Cuthbert's Way by Rudolf Abraham (Cicerone, 2013)

From the Pennines to the Highlands by Hamish Brown (Lochar, 1992)

John Muir Way by Sandra Bardwell and Jacquetta Megarry (Rucksack Readers, 2014)

Exploring the Edinburgh to Glasgow Canals by Hamish Brown (Mercat Press, 2nd edition, 2006) (out of print)

Not the West Highland Way by Ronald Turnbull (Cicerone, 2010)

The Rob Roy Way by Jacquetta Megarry (Rucksack Readers, 3rd edition, 2012)

Walking The Great Glen Way by Paddy Dillon (Cicerone, 2nd edition, 2016)

John o' Groats Trail by Andy Robinson and Jay Wilson (draft edition, 2018). This is available via the John o' Groats Trail website www.jogt.org.uk, and will be replaced by a Cicerone edition in due course.

The Cape Wrath Trail by David Paterson (Peak Publishing, 1996) (out of print)

The Cape Wrath Trail by Iain Harper (Cicerone, 2013)

APPENDIX C

Other sources of information

Walking associations

Land's End John o' Groats Association
www.lejog.org
To quote their website: 'Anyone who has completed the journey from Land's End to John o' Groats in either direction, by whatever means of transport, is eligible for membership of the Association'.

Long Distance Walkers Association (LDWA)
www.ldwa.org.uk
The aim of the LDWA is 'to further the interests of those who enjoy long-distance walking'. Among other things, they maintain a register of long-distance walking routes, organise long-distance walking events and publish a useful newsletter.

Scottish Rights of Way and Access Society
www.scotways.com

Trail websites

Official National Trails site
www.nationaltrail.co.uk
This website covers all the National Trails in England and Wales, including accommodation information. This includes the South West Coast Path, Offa's Dyke and the Pennine Way.

Scotland's official Great Trails site
www.scotlandsgreattrails.com
This website covers all the Scottish Great Trails (ie the Scottish equivalent of the National Trails in England and Wales), including the West Highland Way. It doesn't include accommodation information.

South West Coast Path Association (SWCPA)
www.southwestcoastpath.org.uk
The SWCPA is a volunteer 'user group' that promotes use and improvements on the South West Coast Path. Membership includes newsletters and the annual handbook.

Offa's Dyke Association (ODA)
https://offasdyke.org.uk
The Offa's Dyke equivalent of the SWCPA, although the ODA came first, having been founded in 1969. Membership includes newsletters and a badge. There is an accommodation guide on the website.

West Highland Way
www.westhighlandway.org
The official West Highland Way website.

Accommodation

Youth Hostels Association (YHA)
www.yha.org.uk
Runs hostels and camping barns in England and Wales.

Hostelling Scotland
www.hostellingscotland.org.uk
Runs hostels in Scotland.

Independent Hostel Guide
https://independenthostels.co.uk
Information about all the independent hostels on this register is provided on the website.

Mountain Bothies Association (MBA)
www.mountainbothies.org.uk
The MBA maintains bothies, most of which are in Scotland. They publish regular newsletters.

Maps and equipment

Stanfords
7 Mercer Walk
Covent Garden
London
WC2H 9FA
tel 0207 836 1321
www.stanfords.co.uk
The Covent Garden shop is the best map shop in the UK, and they also have a shop in Bristol.

Ultralight Outdoor Gear
www.ultralightoutdoorgear.co.uk
If you want to get the lightest equipment around, this is a good place to start.

Other

www.longwalks.org.uk
This is my own website, and among other things it features the latest updates to this book, and further Land's End to John o' Groats information. If you come across anything incorrect or out of date in this guidebook, please email me via www.longwalks.org.uk so that I can put the information onto the website.

- 1956km (1215 miles) • the length of mainland Britain
- follows national trails and hill routes wherever possible
- unspoilt scenery, unique and ever-changing landscapes

This guide describes a 1956km (1215 mile) walking route from Land's End in Cornwall to John o' Groats in Scotland's far north – the two points on mainland Britain that are the furthest apart. The route avoids road walking as much as possible and frequently takes advantage of existing long-distance trails, including the South West Coast Path, Pennine Way and West Highland Way. Since it passes through remote terrain and keeps to the hills where practical, this is a route intended for experienced hill walkers.

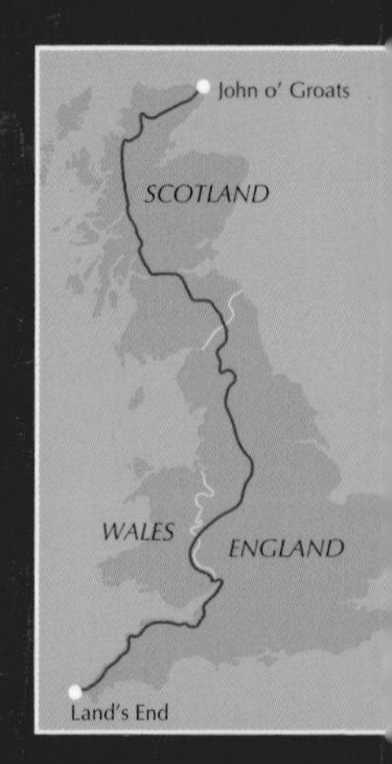

- presented in 61 days, averaging around 32km (20 miles) each day
- includes an alternative three-month schedule
- preparation and safety advice
- information about accommodation and services

CICERONE
www.cicerone.co.uk
WALKING | ENGLAND, SCOTLAND, WALES

US $29.95